CORPVS CHRISTIANORVM

CONCILIORUM OECUMENICORUM GENERALIUMQUE DECRETA

Istituto per le scienze religiose – Bologna – fscire.it

CORPVS CHRISTIANORVM

CONCILIORUM OECUMENICORUM GENERALIUMQUE DECRETA

Edidit
Istituto per le scienze religiose
BOLOGNA

General Editors
GIUSEPPE ALBERIGO †
ALBERTO MELLONI

TURNHOUT
BREPOLS
2023

CONCILIORUM OECUMENICORUM GENERALIUMQUE DECRETA

EDITIO CRITICA

VI/1/2

Synods of the Churches
of and after the Reformation

The Dawn of the Reformation
(16th-17th Centuries)

Part 2

Curantibus
O. Bexell, G. Braghi, I. Dingel, I. Hazlett,
J. Hund, H. P. Jürgens, T. Kirby, A. Mühling,
G. Murdock, M. Ptaszyński

Edidit
A. Melloni

Adlaborante
G. Braghi

TURNHOUT
BREPOLS
2023

CORPVS CHRISTIANORVM

CONCILIORUM OECUMENICORUM GENERALIUMQUE DECRETA

The research and publication of this volume were made possible by the support of Ministero dell'Università e della Ricerca (MUR), Ministero della Cultura (MIC), and Regione Emilia Romagna

D/2023/0095/167
ISBN 978-2-503-54506-6 (2 vols.)
Printed in the EU on acid-free paper

© 2023, Brepols Publishers n.v./s.a., Turnhout, Belgium

All rights reserved. No part of this publication may be reproduced, stored in a retrieval system, or transmitted, in any form or by any means, electronic, mechanical, photocopying, recording, or otherwise, without the prior permission of the publisher.

LIST OF ABBREVIATIONS

BSELK	*Bekenntnisschriften der Evangelisch-Lutherischen Kirche*, hrsg. K. Breuer, I. Dingel, *e.a.*, Göttingen 2014
BSLK	*Bekenntnisschriften der evangelisch-lutherischen Kirche*, hrsg. P. Althaus, H. Lietzmann, *e.a.*, Göttingen ¹³2010
Calv., *Instit.* (1559)	*Ioannis Calvini Institutio Christianae religionis*, 2 vols, hrsg. A. Tholuck, Berlin 1834; 1835
CC SL	*Corpus Christianorum. Series Latina*, Turnhout 1953-
COGD	*Corpus Christianorum. Conciliorum Oecumenicorum Generaliumque Decreta*, Turnhout 2006-
CR	*Corpus reformatorum*, Halle 1834-
CSEL	*Corpus Scriptorum Ecclesiasticorum Latinorum*, Wien 1866-
EKO	*Die Evangelische Kirchenordnungen des 16. Jahrhunderts*, Leipzig – Tübingen 1902-
MWA	*Melanchthons Werke in Auswahl*, Gütersloh 1951
PL	*Patrologiae cursus completus. Series Latina*, vol. 1- 221, ed. J. P. Migne, Paris 1844-1864
PG	*Patrologiae cursus completus. Series Graeca*, vol. 1-161, ed. J. P. Migne, Paris 1847-1886
PSB	*Polski słownik biograficzny*, Kraków 1935-
RefBK	*Reformierte Bekenntnisschriften*, 8 vols, Neukirchen-Vluyn 2002-2016
SC	*Sources Chrétiennes*, Paris 1941-

VI	LIST OF ABBREVIATIONS

VD 16	*Verzeichnis der im deutschen Sprachbereich erschienenen Drucke des 16. Jahrhunderts* (online: bsb-muenchen.de)
WA	*D. Martin Luthers Werke, Kritische Gesammtausgabe* (*Weimarer Ausgabe*), Weimar 1883-2009
	WA = Abteilung Schriften / Werke
	WA DB = Abteilung Deutsche Bibel

CONCILIUM LONDINENSE

1563-1571

edidit
Torrance KIRBY

THE *ARTICLES OF RELIGION* OF THE CHURCH OF ENGLAND, COMMONLY CALLED THE *THIRTY-NINE ARTICLES* 1563-1571

The principal doctrinal formulary of the reformed Church of England achieved full canonical status in 1571, when thirty-nine *Articles of Religion* were formally agreed upon by both Convocation and Parliament and received royal assent. According to the Queen's ratification appended to two editions of the *Articles*, one in Latin published by John Day and one in English by Richard Jugge and John Cawood, 'this Book of Articles before rehearsed, is again approved and allowed to be holden and executed within the Realm by the assent and consent of our Sovereign Lady Elizabeth [...] which Articles were deliberately read, and confirmed again by the subscription of the hands of the Archbishop and Bishops of the Upper House, and by the subscription of the whole Clergy of the Nether House in their Convocation in the year of our Lord God, 1571'. In a statute passed by Elizabeth's third Parliament and granted Royal Assent on 29 May 1571, subscription to the *Articles* was required of all clergy who had been ordained in the reign of Queen Mary. [1] Similar subscription was required of all clergy upon presentation to a benefice and of all candidates for ordination. As the full title proclaims, the *Articles of Religion* were framed with a view to 'avoiding diversities of opinions, and for the stablishing of consent touching true Religion'. [2] As the title also reveals, they had been some time in the making, having been 'agreed' by the clergy at Convocation in 1562 (Old Style), but not fully and constitutionally accepted by Parliament and promulgated by Royal Assent until almost a decade later.

The mid-sixteenth century was a remarkably rich period for the production of Reformed confessions of faith. The *Consensus Tigurinus* appeared in 1549, followed by the *Gallican Confession*, also known as the *Confession de foi de La Rochelle* in 1559, then the *Scotch Confession* (1560), the *Belgic Confession* (1561), and the *Second Helvetic Confession* (1566) in relatively quick succession. The gestation of the *Thirty-Nine Articles* covers this entire period. Indeed, the history of their composition goes back even further. In 1538, the year that Pope Paul III excommunicated King Henry VIII for having claimed the title of

---

(1) 13 Eliz. I *c.* 12, 'An Act to reform certain disorders touching Ministers of the Church', *Statutes of the Realm*, vol. IV/1, p. 310-312.

(2) See *Articles whereupon it was agreed.*

570 CONCILIUM LONDINENSE – 1563-1571

Supreme Head of the Church of England – and at the height of what has been described as the evangelical moment of Henry's reign – the King invited three Lutheran divines to consult with Thomas Cranmer, archbishop of Canterbury, and two other English bishops to draw up a mutually-agreed formula of doctrine. The *Augsburg Confession* provided the formal basis for this confessional discussion. Although never formally ratified or published, a thoroughly Lutheran formulary of *Thirteen Articles* drafted by Thomas Cranmer was the concrete result of this international colloquy. (3)

The *Articles* are closely modelled on the first seventeen articles of Philip Melanchthon's 1536 formulation of the *Augsburg Confession* delivered to two of Henry VIII's ambassadors, Edward Fox (bishop of Hereford) and Nicholas Heath (archibishop of York). Some of Cranmer's *Thirteen Articles* were virtually identical to their counterparts in the *Augsburg Confession*, and this may be said to constitute the high-water mark of Lutheran influence on the doctrine of the Church of England. (4) As matters turned out, the 1538 draft of the *Thirteen Articles* would prove to be the first stage of a lengthy process of composition and substantive revision of what eventually resulted in the Reformed confession of 1571, and thus represents the critical link between the *Thirty-Nine Articles* and the *Augsburg Confession*. (5)

From 1540 until the death of Henry VIII, the pace of the Reformation in England – at least on a public level – was considerably slowed. At the accession of Edward VI in 1547, Cranmer and his colleagues were able to pursue with vigour the work of reformation. First came the *Book of Common Prayer* (1549), followed by its more thoroughly Reformed revision of 1552. While no new articles were formally authorised by Parliament and Convocation during Edward's brief reign, a royal commission, headed by Thomas Cranmer, was charged in November 1551 with drawing up a scheme for the thorough reform of Church law and discipline, formally known as the *Reformatio legum ecclesiasticarum*. (6) At the same time, Cranmer was directed to prepare a more

---

(3) Bray, *Documents*, p. 184-221. This is a very useful edition owing to the setting of phrases used by Cranmer in the *Forty-Two Articles* (1553) in bold type.

(4) See A. Ryrie, 'The Strange Death of Lutheran England', *Journal of Ecclesiastical History* 53/1 (2002), p. 64-92.

(5) This influence of the *Augsburg Confession* can be discerned particularly in Articles I, II, IV, IX, XIV, XVI, XXIII, XXIV, and XXV.

(6) *Reformatio legum ecclesiasticarum ex authoritate primum Regis Henrici. 8. inchoata: deinde per Regem Edouardum 6. prouecta, adauctaq*[ue] *in hunc modum, atq*[ue] *nunc ad pleniorem ipsarum reformationem in lucem aedita*, London 1571. For a critical edition, see Bray, *Tudor Church Reform*. For an historical introduction to the work of the royal commission authorised to reform the canon law of England, see Bray, *Tudor Church Reform*, p. xli-cxvi. See also Kirby, 'Lay Supremacy'.

CONCILIUM LONDINENSE – 1563-1571   571

succinct confessional book of articles to promote uniformity of doctrine, and in May 1552 the Convocation was asked to present them to the Privy Council. They originally numbered forty-five, but after revision were reduced by three and promulgated on 19 June 1553. These *Forty-Two Articles* were published shortly before Edward's death on the following 6 July. (7)

When the *Forty-Two Articles* were issued under royal authority in 1553, they arguably constituted the most thorough and advanced systematic expression of Reformed doctrine at that time. In doctrinal substance, particularly on crucial matters concerning grace and the sacraments, the *Articles* are comparable to both the *Gallican Confession* of 1559 and the *Second Helvetic Confession* of 1566, authored by John Calvin and Heinrich Bullinger respectively. On matters of ecclesiastical polity and discipline, the *Articles* lean more towards Zurich than Geneva. (8) Although never published as a canonically-sanctioned formulary, the *Reformatio legum ecclesiasticarum* accords closely in both doctrine and articulation with a considerable number of the *Forty-Two Articles* produced. Given the strong resemblance between the *Reformatio legum* and the Edwardine *Articles* in both language and theology, it is probable that the two formularies were the joint work of members of one and the same commission of thirty-two members, led principally by Thomas Cranmer, Richard Cox (dean of Westminster and the King's almoner), Thomas Goodricke (bishop of Ely and Lord Chancellor), and Peter Martyr Vermigli (then Regius Professor of Divinity at Oxford). (9) Within just a few weeks of the promulgation of the *Forty-Two Articles* Edward VI died, and these *Articles* were summarily dropped at the accession of Queen Mary. Moreover, it was the fate of the *Reformatio legum ecclesiasticarum* never to receive canonical recognition, although the historian John Foxe, one of the royal commissioners, arranged for its publication in 1571, the same year that saw the Edwardine *Articles* of 1553 (reduced by three in number) achieve full canonical status as the *Thirty-Nine Articles*. (10)

---

(7) The *Forty-Two Articles* were published in May, almost three weeks before royal authorisation. Cfr. *Articles agreed on by the Bishops and other learned men in the Synod at London in the year of our Lord God 1552, for the avoiding of controversy in opinions, and the establishment of a godly concord, in certain matters of Religion. Published by the King's Majesty's commandment, in the Month of May A.D. 1553*, London 1553.

(8) See Kirby, *The Zurich Connection and Tudor Political Theology*, Leiden – Boston 2007.

(9) For the royal proclamation appointing the commission, see Bray, *Tudor Church Reform*, p. 167-168.

(10) See Kirby, 'Lay Supremacy'.

After the accession of Edward's sister Elizabeth in 1558, a revised extract of the *Forty-Two Articles* was reintroduced for debate in Convocation by Archbishop Matthew Parker. ([11]) After some substantive revision, these were subsequently approved by both houses of the clergy, although not yet by Parliament. The Latin text of the *editio princeps* of the Articles – the so-called *Thirty-Eight Articles of Religion* – had been adopted by Convocation (i.e. the provincial Synod of Canterbury) in January 1563 (1562 Old Style, i.e. 'according to the computation of the Churche of Englande') and were issued under royal authority by the Queen's printer, Reginald Wolfe. ([12]) The *Articles* of 1563 were based closely upon the text of the *Forty-Two Articles* of 1553 promulgated at the end of the reign of Edward VI.

In the Library of Corpus Christi College, Cambridge, there is a manuscript copy of the original Edwardine *Forty-Two Articles* presented by Archbishop Matthew Parker to Convocation in 1562, with various additions, deletions, and emendations together with the signatures of the bishops who subscribed to them. ([13]) In the Parker manuscript of the revision of 1563, four articles were added, four were removed, and seventeen others were modified either by amplification or reduction, thus yielding thirty-nine in all. Article II on Christ, Article V on the Holy Ghost, Article X on the freedom of the will, Article XI on justification by faith, Articles XII and XIII on good works, and Article XX on the authority of the Church all include phrases or adaptations of language found in the *Württemberg Confession*. This extended revision by Johannes Brenz of the *Augsburg Confession* was presented in 1552 at the Council of Trent and aimed to show the consistency of the evangelical churches with apostolic doctrine and patristic orthodoxy. ([14]) After the approval of the bishops in Convocation but before being printed, however, Queen Elizabeth struck out Article XXIX ('De manducatione corporis Christi, et impios illud

---

(11) *A declaration of certain principal articles of religion, set out by the order of both archbishops [...] and the rest of the bishops, for the unity of doctrine to be taught,* University of Cambridge, Corpus Christi College Library, MS 106, fol. 421-422. Although the authorship is uncertain, Matthew Parker probably played a leading role in its preparation.

(12) *Articuli, de quibus conuenit inter archiepiscopos, & episcopos vtriusq[ue] prouinciae, & clerum vniuersum in synodo, Londini. an. Dom. 1562 secundum computationem ecclesiae Anglicanae, ad tollendam opinionum dissentionem, & consensum in vera religione firmandum. Aediti authoritate serenissimae Reginae,* Londini 1563.

(13) *Articuli de quibus in synodo Londinensi, A. D. 1562, ad tollendam opinionum dissensionem et consensum in vera religione firmandum inter episcopos convenit,* MS 121.126, The Parker Library, Corpus Christi College, Cambridge.

(14) For the text of the *Württemberg Confession,* see E. Bizer, *Confessio Virtembergica: Das Württembergishe Bekenntnis von 1551,* Stuttgart 1952, p. 139-190.

non manducare'), most probably on the ground that it might offend Lutheran sensibilities on the question of the real presence in the Lord's Supper; however, this was more of a diplomatic and political gambit than a determined theological position. When all likelihood of cooperation with the Lutheran churches had faded in the 1560s, the article concerning the *manducatio impiorum* was restored in the revision of 1571. A short preamble was also added to Article XX ('De ecclesiae auctoritate'). At the time of Parker's re-presentation of the *Articles* to Convocation and Parliament in 1571, Article XXIX was restored: thus, the canonically-approved formulary of thirty-eight articles came to consist of thirty-nine. ([15])

The *Thirty-Nine Articles* opened with a statement in five articles of Trinitarian and Christological orthodoxy based on the authority and teaching of the ancient creeds and the formulae of the first four ecumenical councils of the early Church. There was very little of a polemical nature, with all substantive points agreed upon by the other principal Lutheran, Reformed, and Tridentine formularies. The atmosphere shifted dramatically in a more polemical direction in the following three articles on the authority of Scripture and its sufficiency to salvation. Articles IX through XIX addressed the critical matters of sixteenth-century soteriological debates: original sin, the freedom of the will, grace, faith and justification, works, and predestination. Articles XX to XXV treated ecclesiology, Articles XXVI to XXX the sacraments, Articles XXXI to XXXVI discipline, worship, and ceremonies, and Article XXXVI through the final article addressed the office of civil magistracy and the political duty of Christians.

BIBLIOGRAPHY

Sources (and Their Abbreviations)

Articles whereupon it was agreed by the archbishoppes and bishoppes of both prouinces and the whole cleargie, in the conuocation holden at London in the yere of our Lorde God. 1562 according to the computation of the Churche of Englande, for the auoiding of the diuersities of opinions, and for the stablishyng of consent touching true religion. Put foorth by the Queenes aucthoritie, London 1571 [= *Articles whereupon it was agreed*].

(15) See *Articles whereupon it was agreed*.

Articuli de quibus in Synodo Londinensi Anno Domini, iuxta ecclesiae Angli-canae computationem, MDLXII ad tollendam opinionum dissensionem, et firmandum in vera Religione consensum, inter Archiepiscopos Episcoposque utriusque Prouinciae, nec non etiam uniuersum Clerum convenit, Londini 1563 [= *Articuli de quibus in Synodo Londinensi*].

Documents of the English Reformation, ed. G. Bray, Cambridge 1994 [Bray, *Documents*].

C. Hardwick, *A History of the Articles of Religion to which is Added a Series of Documents, from A.D. 1536 to A.D. 1615; together with Illustrations from Contemporary Sources*, London 1895.

T. Kirby, 'The *Articles of Religion* of the Church of England (1563/1571), Commonly Called the *Thirty-Nine Articles*', in *RefBK*, vol. 2/1 (2009), p. 371-410.

Tudor Church Reform: The Henrician Canons of 1535 and the Reformatio legum ecclesiasticarum, Woodbridge, ed. G. Bray, 2000 [= Bray, *Tudor Church Reform*].

LITERATURE (AND ITS ABBREVIATIONS)

E. J. Bicknell, *A Theological Introduction to the Thirty-Nine Articles of the Church of England*, London 1946.

E. C. S. Gibson, *The Thirty-Nine Articles of the Church of England*, London 1912.

W. H. Griffith Thomas, *The Principles of Theology: An Introduction to the Thirty-Nine Articles*, Grand Rapids (MI) 1979.

H. G. G. Herklots – G. W. H. Lampe – J. I. Packer – J. C. de Satgé, *The Articles of the Church of England*, London 1964.

B. J. Kidd, *The Thirty-Nine Articles: Their History and Explanation*, New York 1901.

T. Kirby, 'Lay Supremacy: Reform of the Canon Law of England from Henry VIII to Elizabeth I (1529-1571)', *Reformation and Renaissance Review* 8/3 (2006), p. 349-370 [= Kirby, 'Lay Supremacy'].

T. Kirby, The Zurich Connection and Tudor Political Theology, Leiden and Boston 2007.

O. O'Donovan, *On the Thirty-Nine Articles: A Conversation with Tudor Christianity*, Exeter 1986.

CONCILIUM LONDINENSE – 1563-1571

Subscription and Assent to the Thirty-Nine Articles: A Report of the Archbishops' Commission on Christian Doctrine, ed. Church of England Doctrine Commission, London 1968.

MONITUM

LATIN TEXT (Editio Latina princeps)

Articuli de quibus in Synodo Londinensi Anno Domini, iuxta ecclesiae Anglicanae computationem, MDLXII ad tollendam opinionum dissensionem, et firmandum in vera Religione consensum, inter Archiepiscopos Episcoposque utriusque Prouinciae, nec non etiam uniuersum Clerum convenit, Londini 1563.

ENGLISH TEXT (Authorised English Articles)

Articles whereupon it was agreed by the archbishoppes and bishoppes of both prouinces and the whole cleargie, in the conuocation holden at London in the yere of our Lorde God. 1562 according to the computation of the Churche of Englande, for the auoiding of the diuersities of opinions, and for the stablishyng of consent touching true religion. Put foorth by the Queenes aucthoritie, London 1571.

CONCILIUM LONDINENSE
1563-1571

ARTICULI DE QUIBUS IN SYNODO LONDINENSI ANNO DOMINI, IUXTA ECCLESIAE ANGLICANAE COMPUTATIONEM, MDLXII AD TOLLENDAM OPINIONUM DISSENSIONEM, ET FIRMANDUM IN VERA RELIGIONE CONSENSUM, INTER ARCHIEPISCOPOS EPISCOPOSQUE UTRIUSQUE PROUINCIAE, NEC NON ETIAM UNIUERSUM CLERUM CONVENIT.

| I DE FIDE IN SACROSANCTAM TRINITATEM

Unus est vivus et verus Deus, aeternus, incorporeus, impartibilis, impassibilis, immensae potentiae, sapienti, ac bonitatis, creator et conservator omnium, tum visibilium tum invisibilium. Et in unitate huius divinae naturae tres sunt Personae eiusdem essentiae, potentiae, ac aeternitatis, Pater, Filius, et Spiritus Sanctus.

---

7 I] Articles I through V treat the substance of the faith contained in the doctrine of God and the Trinity (I), the incarnation (II-IV), and the Holy Ghost (V). Article I is derived almost entirely from the *Confession of Augsburg* (1530), Article 1 'De Deo': 'Ecclesiae magno consensu apud nos docent, decretum Nicaenae synodi de unitate essentiae divinae et de tribus personis verum et sine ulla dubitatione credendum esse, videlicet, quod sit una essentia divina, quae et appellatur et est Deus, aeternus, incorporeus, impartibilis, immensa potentia, sapientia, bonitate, Creator et Conservator omnium rerum, visibilium et invisibilium; et tamen tres sint personae eiusdem essentiae et potentiae, et coaeternae, Pater, Filius et Spiritus Sanctus' 8/ 12 Unus – Sanctus] the first article is derived from Thomas Cranmer's draft of *Thirteen Articles* (1538). The latter formulary was discovered among Cranmer's papers in the nineteenth century and was first published in T. Cranmer, *Works*, ed. J. Cox, Cambridge 1846. This article was transmitted unchanged from the first of the *Forty-Two Articles* of 1553. The same language also appears in *Reformatio legum*, Article 1, 'De summa Trinitate et fide catholica', in Bray, *Tudor Church Reform*, p. 170. The aim of the article is to condemn the ancient Sabellian and Arian heresies which were revived in the sixteenth century by some of the radical reformers such as Michael Servetus and Sebastian Castellio

ARTICLES WHEREUPON IT WAS AGREED BY THE ARCH-
BISHOPPES AND BISHOPPES OF BOTH PROUINCES AND THE
WHOLE CLEARGIE, IN THE CONUOCATION HOLDEN AT LON-
DON IN THE YERE OF OUR LORDE GOD, 1562, ACCORDING TO
THE COMPUTATION OF THE CHURCHE OF ENGLANDE, FOR
THE AUOIDING OF THE DIUERSITIES OF OPINIONS, AND FOR
THE STABLISHYNG OF CONSENT TOUCHING TRUE RELIGION.

| [I] Of fayth in the holie Trinitie

There is but one lyuyng and true God, euerlastyng, without body, partes,
or passions, of infinite power, wysdome, and goodnesse, the maker and
preseruer of al things both visible and inuisible. And in vnitie of this Godhead
there be three persons, of one substaunce, power, and eternitie, the father, the
sonne, and the holy ghost.

4/5 according – Englande] Convocation met in January. According to the or Julian
calendar, 25 March marked the new year. Dates given in the notes are according to the
New Style, and thus the *Articles* are dated 1563

580   CONCILIUM LONDINENSE – 1563-1571

II Verbum Dei, verum hominem esse factum

Filius, qui est Verbum Patris, ab aeterno a Patre genitus, verus et aeternus
Deus, ac Patri consubstantialis in utero beate Virginis ex il|lius substantia A₂ᵛ
naturam humanam assumpsit: ita ut duaenaturae, divina et humana, integre
atque perfecte in unitate personae, fuerint inseparabiliter coniunctae: ex
quibus est unus Christus, verus Deus et verus homo: qui vere passus est, cruci-
fixus, mortuus, et sepultus, ut Patrem nobis reconciliaret, essetque hostia non
tantum pro culpa originis verum etiam pro omnibus actualibus hominum
peccatis.

III De descensu Christi ad inferos

Quemadmodum Christus pro nobis mortuus est, et sepultus, ita est etiam
credendus ad inferos descendisse. Non corpus usque ad resurrectionem in
sepulchro iacuit, Spiritus ab illo emissus, cum spiritibus qui in carcere sive in
inferno detinebantur fuit, illisque praedicavit, quemadmodum testatur Petri
locus.

---

22 III] cfr I Petr. 3, 18-55; 6   **23/24** Quemadmodum – descendisse] cfr Eph. 4, 9
26/27 quemadmodum – locus] cfr I Petr. 3, 18-20

13 II] derived from Article 3 of the *Augsburg Confession* mediated by Cranmer's draft
of the *Thirteen Articles*, Article 2. The Latin text of this article published in 1563 is
identical to the earlier Edwardine version of Article 2 in the *Forty-Two Articles* of 1553.
The language of the article evokes the theological grammar of the *Tome of Leo* and the
decrees of the Council of Chalcedon (451) as well as the *Athanasian Creed*   **14/**
15 ab – consubstantialis] this passage is based on the *Württemberg Confession* (1552),
an extended revision of the *Augsburg Confession* presented in 1552 to the Council of
Trent and in which the author Johannes Brenz aimed to show that the evangelical
churches agreed with apostolic doctrine and patristic orthodoxy. See Article 2, 'De filio
Dei', *Confessio piae doctrinae quae nomine illustrissimi Principis ac Domini Christophori
Ducis Wirtembergensis et Teccensis, ac Comitis Montisbeligardi, per legatos ejus Die
XXIIII mensis Januarij, Anno MDLII Congregationi Tridentini Concilii proposita est*,
Tübingen 1551; H. Heppe, *Die Bekenntniss-Schriften der altprotestantischen Kirche
Deutschlands*, Cassel 1855, p. 491-554. See also *Confessio Virtembergica. Das
württembergische Bekenntnis von 1551*, hrsg. E. Bizer, Stuttgart 1952, p. 139 and 197
22 III] based on the *Augsburg Confession*, Article 3, this article addresses the statement
in the *Apostles' Creed* around which violent controversy swirled at the Reformation

14/15 ab – consubstantialis] *additur anno 1563*   **24/27** Non – locus] *extat in*
Quadraginta Duos Articulos *(1553); omittitur post revisionem (1563)*

[II] Of the worde or sonne of God which was made very man

The Sonne, which is the worde of the Father, begotten from euerlastyng of the Father, the very and eternall GOD, of one substaunce with the Father, toke man's nature | in the wombe of the blessed Virgin, of her substaunce: so that two whole and perfect natures, that is to say, the Godhead and manhood, were ioyned together in one person, neuer to be diuided, whereof is one Christe, very GOD and very man, who truely suffered, was crucified, dead, and buried, to reconcile his father to vs, and to be a sacrifice for all sin of man, both original and actual.

[III] Of the goyng downe of Christe into hell

As Christe dyed for vs, and was buryed: so also it is to be beleued that he went downe into hell. For the body lay in the sepulchre until the resurrection, but his Ghost departing from him, was with the ghosts that were in prison, or in Hell, and did preach to the same, as the place of St. Peter doth testify.

21/22 for – actual] *textus sicut in editionem 1571; olim (1553)* not only for originall gylt, but also for all actuall sinnes of men   **25/27** For – testify] *om. post revisionem 1563*

582 CONCILIUM LONDINENSE – 1563-1571

IV Resurrectio Christi

Christus vere a mortuis resurrexit, suumque corpus cum carne, ossibus,
30 omnibusque ad integritatem hu|manae naturae pertinentibus, recepit, cum   A3r
quibus in coelum ascendit, ibique residet, quoad extremo die ad iudicandos
homines revertatur.

V De Spiritu Sancto

Spiritus sanctus, a Patre et Filio procedens, eiusdem est cum Patre et Filio
35 essentiae, maiestatis, et gloriae, verus ac aeternus Deus.

29/32 Christus – revertatur] cfr I Cor. 15; Matth. 28, 6; Luc. 24, 6; Ioh. 20   **34/**
35 Spiritus – Deus] cfr Gal. 4, 6; Act. 16, 7; Rom. 8, 9; praecipue Ioh. 25, 26

28 IV] composed afresh in 1552-1553, and not dependent on the *Augsburg Confession*,
this article emphasises the full humanity of Christ (Luc. 24, 39, Ioh. 20, 20-27) and his
session in heaven until the day of judgement. See *Reformatio legum*, Article 1, 4, in
Bray, *Tudor Church Reform*, p. 172   **33** V] derived from the *Württemberg Confession*,
Article 3, 'Von dem heiligen Geist', in *Confessio Virtembergica. Das württembergische
Bekenntnis von 1551*, hrsg. E. Bizer, Stuttgart 1952, p. 139 and 198   **34/35** Spiritus –
Deus] this article brings a Trinitarian completeness to the series of the first five articles.
It is notable for its affirmation of the *filioque* clause added to the *Nicene Creed* at the
provincial Synod of Toledo (589). The *Articles* are thus committed to this distinctive
formula of Western Christendom. While the Father is alone the 'fountain' of godhead
which the Son, as begotten, is not, the *filioque* serves to reinforce the co-equality and
consubstantiality of these two persons in relation to the procession of the third. This
implied confirmation of the Son's status as *vere Deus* serves to balance the
Chalcedonian Christological emphasis on the fullness of Christ's humanity in the
previous articles

---

32 revertatur] *ante 1563* reversurus sit   **33/35** V – Deus] *additur anno 1563*

CANTERBURY – 1571

[IV] Of the Resurrection of Christe

Christe dyd truly *aryse* agayne from death, and toke agayne his body, with
flesh, bones, and all thinges apperteyning to the perfection of man's nature,
wherewith he ascended into heauen, and there sitteth, vntyll he returne to
iudge all men at the last day.

[V] Of the holy ghost

The holy ghost, proceedyng from the Father and the Sonne, is of one
substaunce, maiestie, and glorie, with the Father, and the Sonne, very and eternall God.

---

28 Of – Christe] this article can be interpreted as a departure from the quasi-
Eutychian emphasis of Lutheran teaching on Christ's glorified body. This distinctively
Reformed Christology will have important consequences for the sacramental doctrine
expounded in later articles

---

32 all] *additur anno 1571*

584 CONCILIUM LONDINENSE – 1563-1571

VI Divinae scripturae doctrina sufficit ad salutem

Scriptura sacra continet omnia, quae ad salutem sunt necessaria, ita, ut quicquid in ea nec legitur, neque inde probari potest, non sit a quoquam exigendum, ut tanquam articulus fidei credatur, aut ad salutis necessitatem requiri putetur.

Sacrae Scripturae nomine, eos Canonicos libros Veteris et Novi Testamenti intelligimus, de quorum | authoritate in Ecclesia nunquam dubitatum est.

De nominibus et numero librorum sacrae Canonicae Scripturae veteris Testamenti.

Genesis.
Exodus.
Leviticus.
Numeri.
Deuteronomium.
Iosuae.
Iudicum.

---

36 VI] Articles VI through VIII address the rule of faith as contained in the Holy Scriptures and the ancient creeds of the Church. Article VI declares the supreme authority of Scripture as the rule of faith. This Reformed principle challenges the Tridentine 'Decree concerning the Canonical Scriptures' of Pope Paul III of 1546 which 'receives and venerates' ecclesiastical traditions together with the Scriptures, 'whether they relate to faith or to morals, as having been dictated either orally by Christ or by the Holy Ghost, and preserved in the Catholic Church in unbroken succession' (see Sess. IV. 'Decretum primum: recipiuntur libri sacri et traditiones apostolorum', in *COGD* III, p. 15-16). The article's restriction of the sufficiency of Scripture to 'matters necessary to salvation' had important implications for debates in the Elizabethan period over matters of Church government, discipline, and ceremonies where the authority of tradition was permitted to hold sway. See *Reformatio legum*, Article 1, 9-12, in Bray, *Tudor Church Reform*, p. 178-180   **37/40** Scriptura – putetur] this paragraph is based on a similar statement in Article 5 of the *Forty-Two Articles* of 1553   **41/43** Sacrae – est] this clause is derived from the *Württemberg Confession*, Article 27, 'Von der heiligen Schrift', in Bizer, *Württembergische Bekenntnis*, p. 178: '[d]ie heilige Schrift nennen wir die ordenlichen, bestätigten Bücher des Alten und Neuen Testaments, an deren Glaubwirdigkeit in der Kirchen nie kein Zweifel gewesent ist'. The catalogue of canonical books of the Old and New Testaments and of the apocrypha was not included in the Edwardine formulary of 1553, but was added by Matthew Parker in the revision of 1563

38/39 non – exigendum] *ante 1563* licet interdum a fidelibus, ut pium et conducibile ad ordinem et decorum admittatur, attamen a quoquam non exigendum   **41/ 88** Sacrae – Canonicis] *additur anno 1563*

CANTERBURY – 1571

| [VI] Of the sufficiency of the Holy Scriptures for saluation 5

Holy Scripture conteyneth all thinges necessarie to saluation: so that whatsoeuer is not read therein, nor may be proued therby, is not to be required of anye man, that it shoulde be beleued as an article of the fayth, or be thought requisite or necessarie to saluation.

In the name of Holy Scripture, we do vnderstand those Canonicall bookes of the olde and newe Testament, of whose aucthoritie was neuer any doubt in the Churche.

Of the names and number of the Canonical Books.

Genesis.
Exodus.
Leuiticus.
Numerie.
Deuteronomium.
Iosue.
Iudges.
Ruth.
The 1 boke of Samuel.

---

39 not¹] *ante revisionem 1563* neither   **39/40** is² – beleued] *ante revisionem 1563* although it be sometime received of the faithful, as godly and profitable for an order and comeliness: yet no man ought to be constrained to believe it   **40/41** or – thought] *ante revisionem 1563* or repute it   **41** or – to] *ante revisionem 1563* to the necessity of

586 CONCILIUM LONDINENSE – 1563-1571

Ruth.

Prior liber Samuelis.

Secundus liber Samuelis.

Prior liber Regum.

Secundus liber Regum.

Prior liber Paralipomenon.

Secundus liber Paralipomenon.

Primus liber Esdrae.

Secundus liber Esdrae.

Liber Hester.

Liber Iob.

Psalmi.

Proverbia.

Ecclesiastes vel Concionator.

Cantica Solomonis.

IV Prophetae maiores.

XII Prophetae minore.

Alios autem libros (ut ait Hieronymus) legit quidem Ecclesia ad exempla vitæ et formandos mores; illos tamen ad dogmata confirmanda | non adhibet: A4r ut sunt

Tertius liber Esdrae.

Quartus liber Esdrae.

Liber Tobiae.

Liber Iudith.

Reliquum libri Hester.

Liber Sapientiae.

Liber Iesu filii Sirach.

Baruch Propheta.

---

77 Reliquum libri Hester] *additur anno 1571*   **80** Baruch Propheta] *additur anno 1571*

CANTERBURY – 1571   587

55   The 2 boke of Samuel.
      The 1 booke of Kinges.
      The 2 booke of Kinges.
      The 1 booke of Chroni.
      The 2 booke of Chroni.
60   The 1 booke of Esdras.
      The 2 booke of Esdras.
      The booke of Hester.
      The booke of Job.
      The Psalmes.
65   The Prouerbes.
      Ecclesia, or the Preacher.
      Cantica, or songes of Sa.
      4 Prophetes the greater.
      12 Prophetes the lesse.

70 | And the other bookes, (as Hierome saith) the Churche doth reade for   6
      example of lyfe and instruction of manners; but yet doth it not apply them to
      establishe any doctrene. Such are these followyng:
      The third boke of Esdras.
      The fourth boke of Esdras.
75   The booke of Tobias.
      The booke of Iudith.
      The reste of the booke of Hester.
      The booke of Wisdome.
      Iesus the sonne of Sirach.
80   Baruch the prophet.

70/72 And – followyng] the formulation of Article VI approximates the teaching of
the *French Confession* of 1559, allowing that the Church may read and take instruction
from these books so far as they agree with canonical Scripture, 'but they are far from
having such power and efficacy that we may from their testimony confirm any point of
faith of the Christian religion; and much less may they be used to detract from the
authority of the other, that is, the sacred books' (Article VI; cfr *COGD* VI.1.1, p. 549).
The *Westminster Confession* (1647), on the other hand, excludes apocryphal books
altogether from the canon. See Article I, 3 (Westminster Confession, ed. T. Kirby, in
COGD VI.2, forthcoming). See also Hieronymus, *Praefatio in Libros Salomonis Juxta
LXX Interpretes* (*PL* 29), Paris 1846, col. 403

77 The reste of the booke of Hester] *additur anno 1571*   **80** Baruch the prophet]
additur anno 1571

588 CONCILIUM LONDINENSE – 1563-1571

Canticum trium puerorum.
Historia Susannae.
De Bel et Dracone.
Oratio Manassis.
85   Prior liber Machabaeorum.
Secundus liber Machabaeorum.
    Novi Testamenti omnes libros (ut vulgo recepti sunt) recipimus, et habe-
mus pro Canonicis.

VII De Veteri Testamento

90   Testamentum Vetus Novo contrarium non est, quandoquidem tam in
Veteri quam in Novo per Christum, qui unicus est Mediator Dei et hominum,
Deus et Homo, aeterna vita humano generi est proposita. Quare male
sentiunt, qui veteres tantum in promissiones temporarias sperasse confingunt.
Quanquam Lex a Deo data per Mosen, quoad ceremonias et ritus, Chri|stia- A4v
95 nos non astringat, neque civilia eius praecepta in aliqua republica necessario
recipi debeant: nihilominus tamen ab obendientia mandatorum quae moralia
vocantur nullus quantumvis Christianus est solutus.

91/92 Christum – proposita] cfr Ioh. 8, 56; Hebr. 10, 1; 11, 6

89 VII] Article VII is a revised combination of two separate articles from the
Edwardine formulary of 1553: Article 6 (the first two sentences) and Article 19 (the
final sentence from 'Quanquam' through to the end). The original wording of the
former part in the *Forty-two Articles* is as follows: 'Testamentum Vetus, quasi Novo
contrarium sit, non est repudiandum, sed retinendum, quando quidem tam in veteri
quam novo per Christum qui unicus est Mediator Dei et hominum, Deus et homo,
æterna vita humano generi est proposita. Quare non sunt audienda, qui veteres tantum
in promissiones temporarias sperasse confingunt'

81 Canticum – puerorum] *additur anno 1571*   **82** Historia Susannae] *additur anno
1571*   **83** De Bel et Dracone] *additur anno 1571*   **84** Oratio Manassis] *additur anno
1571*

CANTERBURY – 1571

589

The Song of the 3 Children.
The storie of Susanna.
Of Bel and the Dragon.
The prayer of Manasses.
85   The 1 boke of Machab.
The 2 Booke of Machab.
All the bookes of the newe Testament, as they are commonly receaued, we do receaue, and accompt them for Canonicall.

[VII] Of the Olde Testament

90   The olde Testament is not contrary to the newe, for both in the olde and newe Testament euerlastyng lyfe is offered to mankynde by Christe, who is the onlye mediatour betweene God and man. Wherefore they are not to be hearde whiche faigne that the olde fathers dyd looke only for transitorie promises. Although the lawe geuen | from God by Moses, as touchyng 7 95 ceremonies and rites, do not bynde Christian men, nor the ciuile preceptes thereof, ought of necessitie to be receaued in any common wealth: yet notwithstandyng, no Christian man whatsoeuer, is free from the obedience of the commaundementes, which are called morall.

94/98 Although – morall] cfr Rom. 8, 1-2; Act. 15, 1; 28, 29

90/98 The – morall] the first part of the article is directed against Marcionite tendencies among some of the radical Anabaptist and antinomian reformers and affirms Heinrich Bullinger's position concerning the unity of the Covenant. The latter part anathematises the opposite extreme of an extreme legalism. The distinction drawn between the ceremonial and moral commandments of the Old Testament reiterates Calvin's position on Christian liberty articulated in Calv., *Instit.* (1559), 3. 19 (vol. 2, p. 73 sqq.)

81 The Song of the 3 Children] *additur anno 1571* **82** The storie of Susanna] *additur anno 1571* **83** Of Bel and the Dragon] *additur anno 1571* **84** The prayer of Manasses] *additur anno 1571*

590 CONCILIUM LONDINENSE – 1563-1571

VIII Symbola tria

Symbola tria, Nicaenum, Athanasii, et quod vulgo Apostolorum appella-
100 tur omnino recipienda sunt et credenda; Scripturarum testimoniis probari
possunt.

100/101 Scripturarum – possunt] cfr Act. 4, 29-31; I Thess. 2, 13; II Cor. 2, 17

98 VIII] this article was composed in 1553 to affirm the Church of England's
commitment to patristic catholicity. This catholicity as embodied in the ancient credal
formulae is implicit in much of the Trinitarian and Christological doctrine contained
in both Lutheran and Reformed confessions. Cfr *Reformatio legum*, Article 1, 5 ('De
tribus symbolis') and 1, 13 ('Symbola fidei utilia sunt ad interpretandam Scripturam'),
in Bray, *Tudor Church Reform*, p. 172 and 180. As quoted in the note to the first article
above, the *Augsburg Confession* affirms the decree of the Nicene Council on the Trinity.
The *Second Helvetic Confession*, Chapter 3, explicitly affirms: '[b]reviter recipimus
Symbolum Apostolorum, quod veram nobis fidem tradit' **99/100** Symbola – sunt]
appears as Article 7 in 1553. Also affirmed by the *French Confession* of 1559, Article 5 (see
p. 548, 39-49). See also Article 9 of the *Confessio Belgica*, asserting the catholic
character of Reformed doctrine. All three creeds are prescribed for regular liturgical
use in the *Book of Common Prayer* (1559). The *Prayer Book* refers to the *Athanasian
Creed* as 'commonly so-called' and is usually designated by its opening words
'Quicunque vult' **100/101** Scripturarum – possunt] in keeping with the claim
concerning the sufficiency of Scripture to salvation in Article VI, the three creeds must
be referred to Scripture for acceptance

---

100 et credenda] *additur anno 1563*

[VIII] Of the three Credes

The *three Credes*, Nicene Crede, *Athanasian Crede*, and that whiche is commonlye called the Apostles' Crede, ought *throughlye* to be receaued and beleued: for they may be proued by moste certayne warrauntes of holye scripture.

592   CONCILIUM LONDINENSE – 1563-1571

IX Peccatum originale

Peccatum originis non est ut fabulantur Pelagiani et hodie Anabaptistae repetunt, in imitatione Adami situm, sed est vitium et depravatio naturae
105 eiuslibet hominis ex Adamo naturaliter propagati, qua fit ut ab originali iusti- tia quam longissime distet, ad malum sua na|tura propendeat, et caro semper A5r adversus spiritum concupiscat; unde in unoquoque nascentium iram Dei atque damnationem meretur. Manet etiam in renatis haec naturae depravatio, qua fit ut affectus carnis, Graece φρόνημα σαρκὸς (quod alii sapientiam, alii
110 sensum, alii affectum, alii studium carnis interpretantur, legi Dei non sub- iiciatur. Et quanquam renatis et credentibus, nulla propter Christum est con-

---

109/110 qua – subiiciatur] cfr Rom. 8, 1   **111/113** Et – Apostolus] cfr Rom. 6, 12; Gal. 5, 16-24

102 IX] the series of Articles IX through XIX address the elements of the doctrine of salvation. Article IX begins the series by defining the human condition with a firmly Augustinian emphasis on original sin, while Article X defines its effects upon the will. There follows a definition of justification (XI) and works (XII-XIV). The impossibility of works of supererogation is reinforced by the teaching that Christ alone is sinless (XV) and that men sin after baptism (XVI). Article XVII treats predestination and election; the series is drawn to completion by the affirmation of salvation 'tantum in nomine Christi', by Christ alone. Article IX is derived from the second of the *Thirteen Articles* which in turn is based on Article 2 of the *Augsburg Confession*. Concern at the renewal of Pelagianism is a theme also taken up in the *Reformatio legum*, Article 2, 7, in Bray, *Tudor Church Reform*, p. 192: '[i]n labe peccati ex ortu nostro contracta, quam vitium originis appellamus, primum quidem Pelagianorum, deinde etiam Anabaptistarum nobis vitandus et submovendus est error [...]'   **103** Peccatum originis] the phrase 'peccatum originis' is not scriptural, but derived from the soteriology of Augustine   **105** naturaliter propagati] original sin is not an imitative unrighteousness, but rather a passive and inherited lack of the original *justitia* – or birth sin. The fault is universal in extent (Gen. 6, 12) and in effect privative (loss of *iustitia*), positive (inclination towards evil), and punitive (warfare of flesh and spirit, sin and ultimately death as the penalty, as in Rom. 5, 12-21; I Cor. 15, 22)   **108** naturae depravatio] cfr Trent, Sess. V. 'Decretum super peccato originali' (*COGD* III, p. 18, 241-248) where original sin is defined as follows: Si quis non confitetur primum hominem Adam cum mandatum Dei in paradiso fuisset transgressus statim sanctitatem et iustitiam in qua constitutus fuerat amisisse incurrisse que per offensam praevaricationis huiusmodi iram et indignationem Dei atque ideo mortem quam antea illi comminatus fuerat Deus et cum morte captivitatem sub eius potestate qui mortis deinde habuit imperium hoc est diaboli totum que Adam per illam praevaricationis offensam secundum corpus et animam in deterius commutatum fuisse: a[nathema] s[it].

107/108 nascentium – depravatio] *additur anno 1563*   **110** interpretantur] *ante 1563* vocant

CANTERBURY – 1571

[IX] OF ORIGINALL OR BIRTH SINNE

105   Originall sinne standeth not in the following of Adam (as the Pelagians do vaynely talke) which also the Anabaptists do nowadays renew but it is the fault and corruption of the nature of euery man, that naturally is engendered of the ofspring of Adam, whereby man is very farre gone from originall ryghteousness, (which he had at his creation) and is of his owne nature enclined to
110 euyill, so that the fleshe lusteth alwayes contrary to the spirite; and therefore in euery person borne into this worlde, it deserueth Gods wrath and | damnation. And this infection of nature doth remayne, yea in them that are regenerated, whereby the luste of the fleshe called in Greke φρόνημα σαρκὸς which some do expounde the wisdome, some sensualitie, some the affection, some
115 the desyre of the fleshe, is not subiect to the lawe of God. And although there

---

106 which – renew] The phrase contains words from Article VIII of the Edwardine formulary of 1553 dropped in the revision of 1563   **108** originall] *ante 1563* his former **109** enclined] *ante 1563* given   **110** lusteth] *ante 1563* desireth   **112** regenerated] *ante 1563* baptized

594 CONCILIUM LONDINENSE – 1563-1571

demnatio, peccati tamen in sese rationem habere concupiscentiam fatetur Apostolus.

X De Libero Arbitrio

115 Ea est hominis post lapsum Adae conditio, ut sese, naturalibus suis viribus et bonis operibus, ad fidem et invocationem Dei convertere ac praeparare non possit. Quare abs|que gratia Dei, quae per Christum est, nos prae- A5v veniente ut velimus, et cooperante dum volumus, ad pietatis opera facienda, quae Deo grata sint et accepta, nihil valemus.

XI De hominis Iustificatione

120

Justificatio ex sola fide Jesu Christi, eo sensu quo in Homelia de justificatione explicatur, est certissima et saluberrima Christianorum doctrina. Tantum propter meritum Domini ac Servatoris nostri Jesu Christi, per fidem, non propter opera et merita nostra, iusti coram Deo reputamur. Quare sola fide

---

115/119 Ea – valemus] cfr Rom. 7, 14; Gal. 5, 16-17 **117/118** gratia – volumus] cfr Ps. 59, 10; Phil. 2, 13 **124** sola fide] cfr Rom. 3, 28; 4, 5

114 X] nothing is stated affirmatively concerning the freedom of the will in this article **115/117** ut – possit] cfr *Württemberg Confession*, Article 4, 'Von der Sünde'. Owing to the *depravatio naturae* (see Article IX above) the human condition is considered to be utterly corrupt **120** XI] by drawing a clear distinction between justification and sanctification, the article adheres to the stance taken by other Reformed confessions, and corrects the Tridentine 'Decree on Justification', Sess. VI. cap. 7 (*COGD* III, p. 27-28), where justification is defined as both the remission of sins and 'the sanctification and renewal of the inner man' **122/124** Tantum – reputamur] this sentence is based on the *Württemberg Confession*, Article 5, 'Von der Rechtfertigung'

115/117 Ea – possit] *additur anno 1563; olim* Article IX *formularii Regis Eduardi (1553)* **121/122** Justificatio – doctrina] *omittitur post revisionem 1563*

CANTERBURY – 1571

is no condemnation for them that beleue and are baptized: yet the Apostle
doth confesse that concupiscence and luste hath of it selfe the nature of synne.

[X] Of free wyll

The condition of man after the fall of Adam is suche, that he can not
turne and prepare hym selfe by his owne naturall strength and good workes, to
fayth and calling vpon God: Wherefore we haue no power to do good workes
pleasaunt and acceptable to God, without the grace of God by Christe
preuentyng us, that we may haue a good wyll, and workyng with vs, when we
haue that good wyll.

[XI] Of the iustification of man

We are accompted righteous before God, only for the merite of our Lord
and sauiour Jesus Christe, by faith, and not for our owne | workes or deseruyn-
ges. Wherefore, that we are iustified by fayth onely, is a most wholesome doc-

---

121/124 we – wyll] the language of 'prevenient' and 'cooperating' grace derives from
Augustine. The former inclines the will to good (Ioh. 6, 44) while the latter assists in
the action (I Cor. 15, 10). See Augustinus, *Ad Valentinum et cum Illo Monachos
Adrumetinos Epistolae Duae* 1 (*PL* 44), Paris 1865, col. 876. In the *Book of Common
Prayer* (1559), a collect appointed to follow the offertory in the 'Order for the
Administration of the Lord's Supper' reads as follows: '[p]revent us, O Lord, in all our
doings with thy most gracious favour, and further us with thy continual help; that in all
our works, begun, continued, and ended in thee, we may glorify thy holy Name, and
finally by thy mercy obtain everlasting life; through Jesus Christ our Lord. *Amen*'
122 the grace of God] an article titled 'De Gratia' was inserted in the formulary of 1553
between 'De libero arbitrio' and 'De hominis iustificatione'. The article was deleted in
the revision of 1563. The text is as follows: 'Gratia Christi, seu Spiritus Sanctus, qui per
eundem datur, cor lapidem aufert, et dat cor carneum. Atque licet ex nolentibus quæ
recta sunt volentes faciat, et ex volentibus prava, nolentes reddat, voluntati nihilominus
violentiam nullam infert. Et nemo hac de causa, cum peccaverit, seipsum excusare
potest, quasi nolens aut coactus peccaverit, ut eam ob causam accusari non mereatur
aut damnari'. In English: 'The Grace of Christ, or the holy Ghost by him given doth
take away the stony heart, and giveth an heart of flesh. And although, those that have
no will to good things, he maketh them to will, and those that would evil thinges, he
maketh them not to will the same: Yet nevertheless he enforceth not the will. And
therefore no man when he sinneth can excuse himself, as not worthy to be blamed or
condemned, by alleging that he sinned unwillingly, or by compulsion'

119/121 The – Wherefore] *additur anno 1563; olim* Article IX *formularii Regis
Eduardi (1553)*

596 CONCILIUM LONDINENSE – 1563-1571

125 nos iustificari, doctrina est saluberrima, ac consolationis plenissima; ut in Homilia de Iustificatione hominis fusius explicatur.

XII De bonis operibus

Bona opera, quae sunt fructus fidei et iustificatos sequuntur, quanquam peccata nostra expiare et divini iudicii severitatem ferre non possunt, | Deo A6r
130 tamen grata sunt et accepta in Christo, atque ex vera et viva fide necessario profluunt, ut plane ex illis aeque fides viva cognosci possit atque arbor ex fructu iudicari.

XIII Opera ante iustificationem

Opera quae fiunt ante gratiam Christi et Spiritus eius afflatum, eum ex
135 fide Iesu Christi non prodeant, minime Deo grata sunt, neque gratiam (ut multi vocant) de congruo merentur: imo cum non sint facta ut Deus illa fieri voluit et praecepit, peccati rationem habere non dubitamus.

XIV Opera supererogationis

Opera quae supererogationis appellant non possunt sine arrogantia et
140 impietate praedicari. Nam illis declarant homines non tantum se | Deo redde- A6v

---

128/130 Bona – Christo] cfr Eph. 2, 10   131/132 ut – iudicari] cfr Matth. 7, 16-20; Iac. 2, 17   134/135 Opera – sunt] cfr Rom. 8, 7-8; Ioh. 15, 5   135/136 neque – merentur] cfr Rom. 4, 1-4; 9, 11-13; Tit. 3, 5   138 XIV] cfr Luc. 17, 10   139 Opera – appellant] cfr Luc. 10, 35 (Vulgata)

125 doctrina – plenissima] cfr Article XVII, where predestination is described as 'dulcis, suavis, et ineffabilis consolationis plenas est'   127 XII] this article, composed in 1563, constitutes a corollary to the doctrine of justification by faith alone. Faith works through love (Gal. 5, 6). Compare *Württemberg Confession*, Article 7, 'Von den guten Werken'   135/136 neque – merentur] there can be no natural human merit apart from that imputed by Christ alone   138 XIV] Article 13 of 1553, unchanged in the revision of 1563, constitutes a corollary of the preceding article. According to dogma authorised by Clement VI in 1343, the works of the saints constituted a spiritual treasure which the Pope was able to draw upon and to apply to the benefit of souls in purgatory. There can be neither measurable excess nor need of merit when Christ's merit is infinite

CANTERBURY – 1571 597

trine, and very full of comfort, as more largely is expressed in the Homilie of
iustification.

[XII] OF GOOD WORKES

Albeit that good workes which are the fruites of fayth, and folowe after
iustification, can not put away our sinnes, and endure the seueritie of Gods
iudgement: yet are they pleasing and acceptable to God in Christe, and do
spring out necessarily of a true and liuely fayth, in so muche that by them, a
lyuely fayth may be as euidently knowen, as a tree discerned by the fruit.

[XIII] OF WORKES BEFORE IUSTIFICATION

Workes done before the grace of Christe, and the inspiration of his
spirite, are not pleasaunt to God forasmuche as they spring not of fayth in Jesu
Christ, neither do they make men meete to receaue grace, or (as the schole
aucthours saye) deserue grace of congruitie: but because they are not done as
GOD hath wylled and commaunded them to be done, we doubt not but they
haue the nature of synne.

| [XIV] OF WORKES OF SUPEREROGATION   10

Voluntarie workes besydes, ouer and aboue Gods commaundementes,
which they call workes of supererogation, can not be taught without arrogan-

---

129/130 the Homilie of iustification] this homily appeared under the title 'A Sermon
of the Salvation of Mankind' in the *First Book of Homilies*, first authorised by
Convocation in 1542, but not published until after the accession of Edward VI in 1547.
The *Homilies* were revoked by Queen Mary and restored by Elizabeth. See Article
XXXV below   **137** XIII] a second corollary to the article on justification composed
in 1553, and retained without alteration in 1563. There is a discrepancy between the title
and the text, where the latter identifies 'works done before the grace of Christ'. The text
agrees with the title in an earlier draft of the Edwardine *Articles* signed by six royal
chaplains in 1552, but the text (although curiously not the title of the article) was later
emended by Cranmer to read as it now stands. The clear implication is that the grace of
God may in fact precede justification. The effect of this change is to delimit even more
radically the realm of possibility in the performance of good works without
'prevenient' grace (see Article X). Cfr Article VII, 'Von den guten Werken', in Bizer,
Württembergische Bekenntnis, p. 144

141 but because] *post revisionem 1563* yea rather for that *(iam in formulario Regis
Eduardi 1553)*

598   CONCILIUM LONDINENSE – 1563-1571

re quae tenentur, sed plus in eius gratiam facere quam deberent: eum aperte
Christus dicat: Cum feceritis omnia quaecunque praecepta sunt vobis, dicte,
servi inutiles sumus.

XV Nemo praeter Christum est sine peccato

145   Christus in nostrae naturae veritate per omnia similis factus est nobis,
excepto peccato, a quo prorsus est immunis, tum in carne tum in spiritu. Venit
ut agnus absque macula esset, qui mundi peccata per immolationem sui semel
factam tolleret: et peccatum, ut inquit Iohannes, in eo non erat. Sed nos
reliqui, etiam baptizati et in Christo regenerati, in multis tamen offendimus
150 omnes: et, si dixerimus quia peccatum non habemus, nos ipsos seducimus, et
veritas in nobis non est.

| XVI De lapsis post baptismum   A7r

Non omne peccatum mortale post Baptismum voluntarie perpetratum,
est peccatum in Spiritum Sanctum, et irremissibile. Proinde lapsis a Baptismo
155 in peccata locus penetentiae non est negandus. Post acceptum Spiritum Sanc-

---

145/151 Christus – est] cfr Ioh. 1, 14; 1, 29; I Petr. 1, 19; I Ioh. 2, 2; 3, 5; 1, 8   **152** XVI]
cfr Matth. 12, 31-32; Marc. 3, 28-29; Luc. 12, 10; Hebr. 6, 4-6   **154/155** Proinde –
negandus] cfr I Cor. 5, 1-5; II Cor. 2, 5-11   **155/157** Post – resipiscere] cfr Ioh. 1, 8

144 XV] the article's emphasis on 'solus Christus' reinforces the rejection of
supererogatory merit in Article XIV. See *Reformatio legum*, Article 2, 9, in Bray, *Tudor
Church Reform*, p. 194   **145/146** Christus – peccato] cfr Article IX. 'Human nature'
is to be distinguished from 'corrupt human nature'   **152** XVI] composed in 1553 in
response to the view that the truly regenerate cannot fall into sin and that sin cannot be
forgiven through repentance after baptism. This shows some influence by Article 16 of
the *Augsburg Confession*. Exception was taken to this article in particular by the
Puritans John Field and Thomas Wilcox in *An Admonition to the Parliament* (1572) on
the ground of its inconsistency with the irresistibility of grace. See also *Reformatio
legum*, Article 2, 8, in Bray, *Tudor Church Reform*, p. 192-195. In the revision of 1563,
Archbishop Matthew Parker insisted on the excision of Article 16 from the 1553
formulary. The article titled 'Blasphemia in Spiritum Sanctum' aimed to define deadly
sin positively, while the present article is formulated negatively   **155/157** Post –
resipiscere] although baptism sin need not 'reign in us' on account of baptism (Rom.
6, 14), this does not mean that there is no longer danger of sinning (II Petr. 1, 10;
Matth. 5, 13). The formulation of the doctrine of perseverance aims at resolving these
differences

CANTERBURY – 1571

cie and iniquity. For by them men do declare that they do not onely render vnto God as muche as they are bounde to do, but that they do more for his sake than of bounden duetie is required: Whereas Christe sayth playnly, When ye have done al that are commaunded to you, say, We *be* vnprofitable seruantes.

[XV] OF CHRISTE ALONE WITHOUT SINNE

Christe in the trueth of oure nature, was made lyke vnto vs in al thinges (sinne only except) from which he was clearley voyde, both in his fleshe, and in his spirite. He came to be the lambe without spot, who by *the* sacrifice of hym self once made, shoulde take away the sinnes of the worlde: and sinne, (as S. John sayeth) was not in hym. But al we the rest, (although baptized, and borne agayne in Christ) yet offende in many thinges, and if we say we haue no sinne, we deceaue our selues, and the trueth is not in vs.

| [XVI] OF SINNE AFTER BAPTISME

Not euery deadly sinne willingly committed after baptisme, is sinne agaynst the holy ghost, and vnpardonable. Wherefore the place for penitents is not to be denyed to such as fall into sinne after baptisme. After we have receaued the holy ghost, we may depart from grace geuen, and fall into sinne,

---

147 iniquity] *ante 1571* impietie **152** Of – sinne] *ab anno 1571. In formulario anni 1553 titulus erat* No man is without sin, but Christ alone **162** the^2 – penitents] *ante 1571* the graunt of repentaunce

600 CONCILIUM LONDINENSE – 1563-1571

tum possumus a gratia data recedere atque peccare, denuoque per gratiam Dei resurgere ac resipiscere. Ideoque illi damnandi sunt qui se quamdiu hic vivant, amplius non posse peccare affirmant, aut vere resipiscentibus veniae locum denegant.

160 XVII DE PRAEDESTINATIONE ET ELECTIONE

Praedestinatio ad vitam est aeternum Dei propositum, quo, ante iacta mundi fundamenta, suo consilio, nobis quidem occulto, constan|ter decrevit A7v eos, quos in Christo elegit ex hominum genere, a maledicto et exitio liberare, atque ut vasa in honorem efficta per Christum ad aeternam salutem adducere.
165 Unde qui tam praeclaro Dei beneficio sunt donati, illi, Spiritu eius opportuno tempore operante, secundum propositum eius vocantur; iustificatur gratis; adoptantur in filios Dei; unigeniti eius Iesu Christi imagini efficiuntur conformes; in bonis operibus sancti ambulant; et demum ex Dei misericordia pertingunt ad sempiternam felicitatem.
170 Quemadmodum Praedestinationis et Electionis nostrae in Christo pia consideratio dulcis, suavis, et ineffabilis consolationis plena est vere | piis et his A8r qui sentiunt in se vim Spiritus Christi, facta carnis et membra quae adhuc sunt super terram mortificantem, animumque ad coelestia et superna rapientem, tum quia fidem nostram de aeterna salute consequenda per Christum pluri-
175 mum stabilit atque confirmat, tum quia amorem nostrum in Deum vehemen-

---

157 Ideoque – vivant] cfr I Ioh. 3, 6   **163/164** quos – adducere] cfr Eph. 1, 3-11   **165/169** Unde – felicitatem] cfr Rom. 8, 28-30

---

160 XVII] this longest article of the formulary was composed in 1553 (also Article 17). The *Reformatio legum* testifies to widespread disputes concerning predestination in the early 1550s. Such polemics became even more pronounced during the reign of Elizabeth. See *Reformatio legum*, Article 2, 22, in Bray, *Tudor Church Reform*, p. 210-213 **163/164** quos – adducere] the article avoids mention of a positive decree of reprobation in a manner reminiscent of Heinrich Bullinger's formulation of the doctrine of predestination, with emphasis on the secrecy ('occultu') of the decree. The positive statement of the doctrine is thoroughly scriptural (Matth. 12, 14; Rom. 9, 21-22. Compare Peter Martyr Vermigli, who spoke of election as predestination, and not reprobation (although he also recognized reprobation), on the grounds that 'the Scriptures speak this way for the most part'. P. M. Vermigli, 'Locus on Predestination' 9, in F. A. James (ed.), *Predestination and Justification: Two Theological* loci (*Sixteenth Century Essays and Studies* 68), Kirksville (MO) 2003, p. 16 **163** in Christo] the revision of 1563 refined the definition of election as 'in Christo' **165/169** Unde – felicitatem] a list of the seven stages in the progress from election to glory **170/179** Quemadmodum – securitatem] the phenomenal and experiential aspects of election became increasingly important in the latter half of the sixteenth century

CANTERBURY – 1571

601

165 and by the grace of God (we may) aryse agayne, and amend our lyues. And therefore, they are to be condemned, whiche say they can no more sinne as long as they lyue here, or denie the place for penitents of forgeuenesse to such as truely repent and amend their lives.

[XVII] OF PREDESTINATION AND ELECTION

170   Predestination to lyfe, is the euerlastyng purpose of God, whereby (before the foundations of the world were layd) he hath constantly decreed by his councell secrete to vs, to deliuer from curse and damnation, those whom he hath chosen *in Christe* out of rnankynd, and to bryng them *by Christe* to euerlastyng saluation, as vessels made to honour. Wherefore they which be indued 175 with so excellent a benefite of God, be called accordyng to Gods purpose by his spirite workyng in due season: they through grace obey the callyng: they be iustified freely: they be made sonnes of God by adoption: they be made lyke | the image of his onelye begotten sonne Jesus Christe: they walke 12 religiously in good workes, and at length by Gods mercy, they attaine to euer-180 lastyng felicitie.

    As the godly consyderation of predestination, and our election in Christe, is full of sweete, pleasaunt, and vnspeakeable comfort to godly persons, and such as feele in themselues the working of the spirite of Christe, mortifying the workes of the fleshe, and their earthlye members, and drawing vp their 185 mynde to hygh and heauenly thinges, as well because it doth greatly establyshe and confirme their fayth of eternal saluation to be enjoyed through Christe, as

---

167 for penitents] *om. post revisionem 1571*   **168** and amend their lives] *om. post revisionem 1571*   **172** councell] *ante 1571* own judgment   **173/174** in – saluation] *ante 1571* ...saluation by Christ   **174/175** Wherefore – God] *ante 1571* Whereupon such as have   **175** be called] *ante 1571* given unto them

602   CONCILIUM LONDINENSE – 1563-1571

ter accendit: ita hominibus, curiosis carnalibus et Spiritu Christi destitutis, ob oculos perpetuo versari Praedestinationis Dei sententiam perniciosissimum est praecipitium, unde illos diabolus protrudit vel in desperationem vel in aeque pernitiosam impurissimae vitae securitatem.

180   Deinde licet praedestinationis decreta sunt nobis ignota promissiones tamen divinas sic amplecti oportet, ut nobis in sacris literis generaliter proposites sunt; et Dei voluntas in nostris actio|nibus ea sequenda est quam in verbo   A8v Dei habemus deserte revelatam.

XVIII Tantum in nomine Christi speranda est aeterna salus

185   Sunt et illi anathematizandi qui dicere audent unumquemque in lege aut secta quam profitetur esse servandum, modo iuxta illam et lumen naturae accurate vixerit: eum sacrae literae tantum Iesu Christi nomen praedicent in quo salvos fieri homines oporteat.

XIX De Ecclesia

190   Ecclesia Christi visibilis est coetus fidelium, in quo verbum Dei purum praedicatur et sacramenta, quoad ea quae necessario exiguntur, iuxta Christi institutum recte administrantur. Sicut erravit Ecclesia Hierosolymitana,

---

180/183 Deinde – revelatam] cfr Ioh. 3, 16; I Tim. 2, 3-4

180/183 Deinde – revelatam] the emphasis is on rejecting stoical fatalism, and on embrace of the promise of salvation   **184** XVIII] composed in 1553 and unrevised since. The article condemns the hyper-rationalist tendency manifest among such radical reformers as Michael Servetus, Lelio and Fausto Sozzini and the Polish Brethren, and Bernardino Ochino   **189** XIX] Articles XIX through XXXI deal with matters ecclesiological: the Church, ministry, and sacraments. Omitted from the Edwardine formulary is Article XIX, 'Omnes obligantur ad moralia legis praecepta servanda'. Article XIX (originally XX of the *Forty-Two Articles*) was composed in 1553 and propounds a definition of the visible Church distinguished by two 'notae'   **190** Ecclesia] 'ecclesia' in the classical Greek sense is a representative assembly called out or elected from the citizenry. In the Septuagint and Vulgate, the same word designates 'Kahal', the congregation of Israel (Iud. 20, 2; Ioel 2, 16; Act. 7, 38)

---

180 licet – ignota] *omittitur anno 1563*   **181** tamen] *omittitur anno 1563*

CANTERBURY – 1571   603

because it doth feruently kindle their loue towardes God. So, for curious and
carnal persons, lacking the spirite of Christe, to haue continually before their
eyes the sentence of Gods predestination, is a most daungerous downefall,
190   whereby the deuyll doth thrust them either into desperation, or into rechelesnesse of most vncleane liuing, no lesse perilous then desperation.

Furthermore, although the decrees of predestination are unknown to us,
yet we must receaue Gods promises in such wyse, as they be generally set
foorth to vs in holy scripture: and in our doynges, that wyl of God is to be
195   folowed, which we haue expreslye declared vnto vs in the worde of God.

| [XVIII] Of obtaynyng eternall saluation, only by the name of   13
Christe

They also are to be had accursed and abhorred that presume to say, that
euery man shal be saued by the lawe or sect which he professeth, so that he be
200   diligent to frame his life accordyng to that lawe, and the light of nature. For
holy scripture doth set out vnto vs only the name of Jesus Christe, whereby
men must be saved.

[XIX] Of the Church

The visible Church of Christe, is a congregation of faythfull men in the
205   which the pure worde of God is preached, and the Sacramentes be duely ministred, accordyng to Christes ordinaunce in all those thynges that of necessitie

---

206 accordyng – ordinaunce] Matth. 28, 19-20; II Tim. 4, 2

205 duely ministred] see Article XXV below. A possible third mark of the visible
Church is suggested by the phrase 'duly administered'. The question of this third mark
embodied in 'disciplina ecclesiastica' became the focus of attacks on the Elizabethan
settlement by Walter Travers, Thomas Cartwright, and others in the course of the so-
called Admonition Controversy of the 1570s. This controversy between Archbishop
John Whitgift and promoters of the Genevan model of reform in England was in
many respects a replay of the dispute on the continent between Thomas Erastus and
Theodore Beza

190 doth] *ante revisionem 1563* may   **192/193** although – yet] *om. post revisionem
1563*   **198** and abhorred] *om. post revisionem 1571*

604 CONCILIUM LONDINENSE – 1563-1571

Alexandrina, et Antioche|na: ita et erravit Ecclesia Romana, non solum quoad B1r
agenda et caeremoniarum ritus, verum in his etiam quae credenda sunt.

195   XX De Ecclesiae auctoritate

Habet Ecclesia ritus statuendi ius et in fidei controversiis auctoritatem;
quamvis Ecclesiae non licet quicquam instituere quod verbo Dei scripto adver-
setur, neque unum Scripturae locum sic exponere potest, ut alteri contradicat.
Quare licet Ecclesia sit divinorum librorum testis et conservatrix; attamen, ut
200 adversus eos nihil decernere, ita praeter illos nihil credendum de necessitate
salutis debet obtrudere.

199/201 Quare – obtrudere] cfr Rom. 3, 2

196/197 Habet – quamvis] this article is from the *Forty-Two Articles* of 1553 with the
addition of this first clause from the *Württemberg Confession*, Article XXIX, 'Von der
Kirchen' added in 1563 and 1571 to the Latin and English versions respectively. See
especially clauses vi, vii, and vii in Bizer, *Württembergische Bekenntnis*, p. 182 and
198-199. This clause was not ratified until 1571. It is absent from the Latin manuscript of
the *Articles* signed by the bishops on 29 January 1563; nor is it in the English edition
printed by Jugge and Cawood in 1563 referred to by the Statute of 1571 authorising the
Articles (13 Eliz. c. 12). The clause is included in an early Latin draft of the *Thirty-Nine
Articles* preserved among the Elizabethan *State Papers*, and is thought to have been
added by royal prerogative. The article defends the Church's authority against
Anabaptists who denied it altogether, against disciplinarian Puritans who sought to
minimise it in matters of government and ceremony, and against Rome that
exaggerated it in the definition of doctrine. 'Ius' and 'auctoritas' belong to the Church
as a 'corpus politicum', and thus Scripture cannot be taken as the sole source of
authority in matters of doctrine and practice

CANTERBURY – 1571

are requisite to the same. As the Church of Hierusalem, Alexandria, and Anti-oche haue erred: so also the Church of Rome hath erred, not only in their liuing and maner of ceremonies, but also in matters of their fayth.

[XX] OF THE AUCTHORITIE OF THE CHURCH

The Church hath power to decree Rites or Ceremonies, and aucthoritie in controuersies of fayth: And yet it is not lawfull for the Church to ordayne any thyng that is contrarie to Gods worde written, neyther may it so expounde one place of | scripture, that it be repugnaunt to another. Wherefore, although the Churche be a witnesse and a keper of holy writ: yet, as it ought not to decree any thing agaynst the same, so besides the same, ought it not to enforce any thing to be beleued for necessitie of saluation.

207/208 the² – erred¹] these churches compromised their orthodoxy during the Arian controversy of the fourth century   208/209 also – fayth] under Pope Zosimus (417) Rome endorsed Pelagius and under Honorius (634) supported Monotheletism. The chief point is that the visible Church, as a human politic society, of its very nature cannot be infallible   214/217 Wherefore – saluation] Scripture is nonetheless supreme and may not be contradicted by positive ecclesiastical ordinance. The article is ambiguous concerning the locus of such power, whether it be with universal visible Church or with particular national churches. See Article XXXIV below

---

209 their] *omittitur post revisionem 1571*

606 CONCILIUM LONDINENSE – 1563-1571

XXI De auctoritate conciliorum generalium

Generalia Concilia sine iussu et voluntate principum congregari non | B<small>IV</small> possunt. Et ubi convenerint, quia ex hominibus constant, qui non omnes
205 Spiritu et verbo Dei reguntur, et errare possunt, et interdum errarunt, etiam in his quae ad normam pietatis pertinent. Ideoque quae ab illis constituuntur, ut ad salutem necessaria, neque robur habent neque auctoritatem nisi ostendi possint e sacris literis esse desumpta.

XXII De purgatorio

210 Scholasticorum doctrina Romanensium de purgatorio, de indulgentiis, de veneratione tum imaginum tum reliquiarum, nec non de invocatione sanctorum, res est futilis, inaniter conflicta, et nullis Scripturarum testimoniis innititur; imo verbo Dei perniciose contradicit.

---

202 XXI] originally Article 22 of the Edwardine formulary, this article provides a corollary to the preceding treatment of the authority of the visible Church. On the authority of the ancient councils of the Church, see *Reformatio legum*, Article 1, 14, in Bray, *Tudor Church Reform*, p. 180-182   **206/208** Ideoque – desumpta] this reaffirms the full sufficiency of Scripture in matters of faith and salvation. See Article VI above **210** doctrina – de²] see *Reformatio legum*, Article 2, 10, in Bray, *Tudor Church Reform*, p. 194-197   de indulgentiis] pardons were dispensed out of the so-called treasury of merits built up through works of supererogation as means of shortening the pains of purgatory. See Article XIV above. The Council of Trent (Sess. XXV. 'Decretum III de indulgentiis', in *COGD* III, p. 175-176, 5559-5571) abolished some of the excesses of the doctrine of indulgences. The ecclesiological force of the present article is to reinforce the clear distinction between the external/visible and mystical/invisible aspects of the Church   **213** imo – contradicit] Christ alone is affirmed to be the mediator of salvation in the sphere of the external as well as the mystical means of grace. This ecclesiological Christocentrism complements the soteriology of Articles XI-XVIII

---

210 Romanensium] *post revisionem 1563* Scholasticorum   **213** perniciose] *omittitur anno 1563*

[XXI] OF THE AUCTHORITIE OF GENERALL COUNSELLES

Generall Counsels may not he gathered together without the commaundement and wyll of princes. And when they be gathered together (forasmuche
as they be an assemblie of men, whereof all be not gouerned with the spirite
and word of God) they may erre, and sometyme haue erred not only in worldly matters, but also euen in thinges parteynyng vnto God. Wherfore, thinges
ordayned by them as necessary to saluation, haue neyther strength nor
aucthoritie, vnlesse it may it declared that they be taken out of holy Scripture.

[XXII] OF PURGATORIE

The Romishe doctrine of School-authors concernyng purgatorie,
pardons, worshipping and adoration, as well of images, as of reliques, and also
inuocation of Saintes, is a fonde thing, vainly inuented, and grounded vpon
no warrantie of Scripture, but rather repugnaunt to the worde of God.

219/220 Generall – princes] a familiar sixteenth-century reassertion of the
Constantinian model. Indeed all seven ecumenical councils of the ancient Church
were summoned by emperors. In the Act of Supremacy of 1534 (26 Hen. VIII, c. 1),
Henry VIII's title 'Head of the Church' is predicated on the claim made previously in
the Act in Restraint of Appeals (1533) that the Realm of England is an 'empire'
governed by one Supreme Head, namely the king himself, and that under his rule the
Church was wholly self-sufficient 'without the intermeddling of any exterior person or
persons', chief among them the 'Bishop of Rome' as he was now officially designated
(24 Hen. VIII, c. 12). This Act of Supremacy was repealed by Queen Mary and
reenacted by Elizabeth's first Parliament, with the alteration of style of headship to
'Supreme Governor'. The original draft of 1553 included the following clause: 'Kings
and pious magistrates can without waiting for the decision or gathering together of
General Councils, in their own state according to the word of God, decide about
matters of religion'. This claim was substantively revised in the version of 1563 printed
here. See also Article XXXVII below   **227** purgatorie] an intermediate condition
between death and judgement is attested by Scripture (Ioh. 11, 11-13; I Thess. 4, 13-16) as
one of sleep. The so-called 'Romish' doctrine of a purgatorial fire before the Last
Judgement is evident in the theology of Augustine (*De civitate Dei: Libri XI-XXII*
21, 13-16, ed. D. Dombart – A. Kalb (*CC SL* 48), Turnhout 1955, p. 778-783), but was
not authoritatively formulated until the Council of Florence in 1439 and subsequently
reaffirmed at the final session of the Council of Trent in the same year of the
promulgation of the *Articles* by Convocation (1563)

222/223 not – also] *omittitur post revisionem 1571*   **227** Romishe] *omittitur post
revisionem 1571*   of School-authors] *additur post revisionem 1571*

608 CONCILIUM LONDINENSE – 1563-1571

| XXIII Nemo in Ecclesia ministret nisi vocatus

B2r

215   Non licet cuiquam sumere sibi munus publice praedicandi aut administrandi sacramenta in ecclesia, nisi prius fuerit ad haec obeunda legitime vocatus et missus. Atque illos legitime vocatos et missos existimare debemus, qui per homines, quibus potestas vocandi ministros atque mittendi in vineam Domini publice concessa est in ecclesia, co-optati fuerint et asciti in hoc opus.

220   XXIV Agendum est in Ecclesia lingua quae sit populo nota

Lingua populo non intellecta publicas in Ecclesia preces peragere aut sacramenta administrare, verbo Dei et primitivae Ecclesiae consuetudine plane repugnat.

215/217 Non – missus] cfr Matth. 3, 16   **217/219** Atque – opus] cfr Act. 6, 3-6; 14, 23; II Tim. 1, 6   **221/223** Lingua – repugnat] cfr I Cor. 14, 9-26

215/217 Non – missus] the article continues the definition of the external visible Church with the affirmation of the necessity of an external and visible vocation to ministry. Christ himself waits for the call which comes at his baptism

221/223 Lingua – repugnat] *ante 1563* Decentissimum est et Verbo Dei maxime congruit, ut nihil in Ecclesia publice legatur aut recitetur lingua populo ignota, idque Paulus fieri vetuit, nisi adesset qui interpretaretur

| [XXIII] Of Ministryng in the congregation

It is not lawful for any man to take vpon hym the office of publique preachyng, or ministring the Sacramentes in the congregation, before he be lawfully called and sent to execute the same. And those we ought to iudge lawfully called and sent, whiche be chosen and called to this worke by men who haue publique aucthoritie geuen vnto them in the congregation, to call and sende ministers into the Lordes vineyarde.

[XXIV] Of speakyng in the congregation in such a tongue as the people understandeth

It is a thing playnely repugnaunt to the worde of God, and the custome of the primitiue Churche, to haue publique prayer in the Churche, or to minister the Sacramentes in a tongue not vnderstanded of the people.

---

231 XXIII] the first statement of this article is derived from Article XIV of the *Augsburg Confession* as mediated by the tenth of the *Thirteen Articles* of 1538. *Augsburg* reads as follows: 'De ordine ecclesiastico docent, quod nemo debeat in ecclesia publice docere aut sacramenta administrare, nisi rite vocatus'. The 1538 formulary ascribes this public power of ordination 'to whom it belonged [...] by the Word of God and the laws and customs of each country'. This clause was dropped in 1553 and was not revived thereafter **234/237** And – vineyarde] on the distinction between *co-optati* and *asciti*, the community in the Acts of the Apostles are described as 'electing' the seven deacons, but the Apostles nonetheless 'appointed' them to their office **238** XXIV] cfr *Augsburg Confession*, Article XXIV. Latin came to be used in public worship throughout the western Church by virtue of being the language of the Roman Empire. The use of Latin in public worship was continued after the Reformation owing to its being the common language of educated people. The *Book of Common Prayer* (1559) was translated into Latin and published in 1560 principally for use in the universities of Oxford and Cambridge under the title *Liber precum publicarum*. In some notable instances the *Liber* follows the more conservative order of the first Edwardine *Prayer Book* of 1549. The *Ordo Administrandi Coenam Domini sive Sacram Communionem* continues to be celebrated in the University Church, Oxford at beginning of each new term

| XXV De Sacramentis

225 Sacramenta per verbum Dei a Christo instituta non tantum sunt notae professionis Christianorum, sed certa quaedam potius testimonia et efficacia signa gratiae atque bonae in nos voluntatis Dei, per quae invisibiliter ipse in nobis operatur, nostramque fidem in se, non solum excitat verum etiam confirmat.

230 Duo a Christo Domino nostro in Evangelio instituta sunt Sacramenta, scilicet, Baptismus et Coena Domini.

Quinque illa vulgo nominata Sacramenta, scilicet, Confirmatio, Poenitentia, Ordo, Matrimonium, et Extrema Unctio, pro Sacramentis Evangelicis habenda non sunt, ut quae partim a prava Apostolorum imitatione profluxe|runt, partim vitae status sunt in Scripturis quidem probati, sed Sacramentorum eandem cum Baptismo et Coena Domini rationem non habentes, ut quae signum aliquod visibile seu ceremoniam a Deo institutam non habeant.

Sacramenta non in hoc instituta sunt a Christo ut spectarentur aut circumferrentur sed ut rite illis uteremur. Et in his duntaxat qui digne percipiunt, salutarem habent effectum : qui vero indigne perci piunt, damnationem, ut inquit Paulus, sibi ipsis acquirunt.

230/231 Duo – Domini] cfr Matth. 28, 19; I Cor. 11, 24-25   **239/241** Et – acquirunt] cfr I Cor. 11, 29

---

224 XXV] Article XXV defines the nature, number, and use of the dominical sacraments. The first paragraph is based largely on Article 9 of the *Thirteen Articles* (1538), which in turn repeats the language of Article 13 of the *Augsburg Confession* (1530). The second and third paragraphs were composed in 1563. See *Reformatio legum*, Article 2, 17, in Bray, *Tudor Church Reform*, p. 202   **225** per verbum Dei] this brief alteration of the text (see Apparatus 3) is yet another instance of the Christocentrism implicit in the revision of the *Articles* in 1563   **230/231** Duo – Domini] this new clause added in 1563 (see Apparatus 3) affirms the substance of Article 35 of the *French Confession*   **232/237** Quinque – habeant] Peter Lombard was the first to have fixed the number of the sacraments at seven (IV Sent., d. 23) and this was officially adopted at Trent, Sess. VII. can. 1 ('De sacramentis in genere', in *COGD* III, p. 40). The other five 'commonly-called sacraments', although not of dominical origin, continue nonetheless to be represented in the offices of the *Book of Common Prayer*. As the laying on of hands, confirmation is of apostolic origin (Act. 8, 14-17); penance is replaced by the form of a general confession in the liturgy; matrimony, in the language of the form of its 'Solemnisation' in the *Prayer Book*, 'was adorned and beautified by His presence and first miracle that he wrought in Cana of Galilee' (Ioh. 2, 1-11); orders also were of apostolic institution (Act. 6, 6); extreme unction was dropped from the *Prayer Book* and was replaced by an 'Order for the Visitation of the Sick'

---

225 per verbum Dei] *additur anno 1563*   **230/231** Duo – Domini] *additur anno 1563*

CANTERBURY – 1571

[XXV] Of the Sacramentes

Sacramentes ordayned of Christe, be not onely badges or tokens of Christian mens profession: but rather they be certaine sure witnesses and effectuall
signes of grace and Gods good wyll towardes vs, by the which he doth worke
inuisiblie | in vs, and doth not only quicken, but also strengthen and confirme   16
our fayth in hym.

There are two Sacramentes ordayned of Christe our Lorde in the Gospell,
that is to say, Baptisme, and the Supper of the Lorde.

Those fyue, commonly called Sacramentes, that is to say, Confirmation,
Penaunce, Orders, Matrimonie, and extreme Vnction, are not to be compted,
for Sacramentes of the gospel, being such, as haue growen partly of the corrupt
folowing of the Apostles, partly are states of life alowed in the scriptures: but
yet haue not lyke nature of Sacramentes with Baptisme and the Lordes Supper,
for that they haue not any visible signe or ceremonie ordayned of God.

The Sacramentes were not ordayned of Christ to be gased vpon, or to be
caryed about; but that we shoulde duely use them. And in such only, as wor-
thyly receaue the same, they haue a wholesome effect or operation: But they
that receaue them vnworthyly, purchase to them selues damnation, as S. Paul
sayth.

244/248 Sacramentes – hym] the first section repudiates Anabaptist and Zwinglian
memorialism. The phrase defining sacraments as 'efficacia signa gratiae' is a significant
revision of the 1553 text. This represents a classically-Reformed affirmation of the
instrumental realism characteristic of Peter Martyr Vermigli's sacramental theology as
set forth in his *Tractatio de sacramento Eucharistiae,* London 1549, and agrees with
Article XXXVIII of the *French Confession*   **257/258** The – them] this final statement
emphasises the Reformed insistence on faithful 'reception' or 'spiritual feeding' as
essential to the true definition of a sacrament. The necessary corollary of this position is
to reject adoration as idolatry. See Calv., *Instit.* (1559), 4. 17. 35 (vol. 2, p. 430-431)

612 CONCILIUM LONDINENSE – 1563-1571

XXVI Ministrorum malitia non tollit efficaciam institutionum divinarum

Quamvis in Ecclesia visibili bonis mali semper sunt admixti, atque inter-
245 dum ministerio verbi et | sacramentorum administrationi praesint; tamen B3v
cum non suo sed Christi nomine agant, eiusque mandato et auctoritate minis-
trent, illorum ministerio uti licet cum in verbo Dei audiendo tum in sacramentis percipiendis. Neque per illorum malitiam effectus institutorum Christi
tollitur aut gratia donorum Dei minuitur quoad eos qui fide et rite sibi oblata
250 percipiunt, quae propter institutionem Christi et promissionem efficacia sunt,
licet per malos administrentur.

Ad Ecclesiae tamen disciplinam pertinet, ut in eos ministros inquiratur,
accusenturque ab his qui eorum flagitia noverint; atque tandem, iusto convicti
iudicio, deponantur.

255 | XXVII De Baptismo B4r

Baptismus non est tantum professionis signum ac discriminis nota qua
Christiani a non Christianis discernantur, sed etiam est signum regenerationis,
per quod, tanquam per instrumentum, recte baptismum suscipientes Ecclesiae
inseruntur; promissiones de remissione peccatorum atque adoptione nostra in
260 filios Dei per Spiritum Sanctum visibiliter obsignantur; fides confirmatur, et vi

---

252/254 Ad – deponantur] cfr I Tim. 5, 19-20 **256/259** Baptismus – inseruntur] cfr Rom. 11, 17

255 XXVII] composed by English reformers in 1553 and unchanged with the exception of a more emphatic affirmation of infant baptism in the concluding statement in the revision of 1563. Cfr *Reformatio Legum*, Article 2, 18, in Bray, *Tudor Church Reform*, p. 200 **256/259** Baptismus – inseruntur] As in Article XXV, 'signum' is to interpreted as an effectual instrument whereby a real engrafting into the body of Christ (*insitio in Christum*) is effected. The sign effects the regeneration (Tit. 3, 5). Cfr Calv., *Instit.* (1559), 3. 2. 24 (vol. 1, p. 369-370) and 4. 16 (vol. 2, p. 379 sqq.). Augustine speaks of circumcision as a 'signum regenerationis' in Augustinus, *De civitate Dei: Libri XI-XXII* 16, 27, ed. D. Dombart – A. Kalb (*CC SL* 48), Turnhout 1955, p. 532, 28-29

252 eos] *ante 1563* in malos

CANTERBURY – 1571

[XXVI] Of the unworthynesse of the ministers, which hinder not the effect of the Sacramentes

Although in the visible Churche the euyl be euer myngled with the good, and sometime the euyll haue cheefe aucthoritie in the ministra|tion of the worde and Sacramentes: yet forasmuch as they do not the same in their own name but in Christes, and do minister by his commission and aucthoritie, we may vse their ministrie, both in hearing the word of God, and in the receauing of the Sacramentes. Neither is yᵉ effect of Christes ordinaunce taken away by their wickednesse, nor the grace of Gods gyftes diminished from such as by fayth and ryghtly do receaue the Sacramentes ministered vnto them, which be effectuall, because of Christes institution and promise, although they be ministred by euyll men.

Neuerthelesse, it apperteyneth to the discipline of the Churche, that enquirie be made of *euyl ministres*, and that they be accused by those that haue knowledge of their offences: and finally, beyng founde gyltie by iust iudgement, be deposed.

[XXVII] Of Baptisme

Baptisme is not onely a signe of profession, and marke of difference, whereby Christian men are discerned from other that be not christened: but is also a signe of regeneration or newe byrth, whereby as by an instrument, they that receaue baptisme rightly, are grafted into the Church: the promises of the forgeuenesse of sinne, and of our adoption to be the sonnes of God, by the

---

262 XXVI] unchanged since 1553 and substantially derived from Article VIII of the *Augsburg Confession* as mediated by Article V of the *Thirteen Articles*. The article builds on the distinction drawn between the visible and invisible Church and condemns the revived Donatist heresy, according to which the holiness of the minister was essential to the valid preaching of the Word or administration of the sacraments (Matth. 23, 3). The Church is a 'mixed' body (Matth. 13, 24-30 and 47-50; Ioh. 15, 2). Cfr also *Second Helvetic Confession*, Chapter 18

---

267 in – his] *ante revisionem 1571* do minister by Christ's   **269** Christes] *ante revisionem 1571* God's   **275** euyl ministres] *ante revisionem 1571* such

614   CONCILIUM LONDINENSE – 1563-1571

divinae invocationis gratia augetur. Baptismus parvulorum omnino in Ecclesia retinendus est, ut qui cum Christi institutione optime congruat.

XXVIII De coena Domini

Coena Domini non est tantum signum mutuae benevolentiae Christianorum inter sese, verum potius est sa|cramentum nostrae per mortem Christi redemptionis. Atque ideo rite digne et cum fide sumentibus, panis quem frangimus est communicatio corporis Christi: similiter poculum benedictionis est communicatio sanguinis Christi.

Panis et vini transubstantiatio in Eucharistia ex sacris literis probari non potest, sed apertis Scripturae verbis adversatur, sacramenti naturam evertit, et multarum superstitionum dedit occasionem.

Corpus Christi datur, accipitur, et manducatur in Coena, tantum coelestis et spirituali ratione. Medium autem quo corpus Christi accipitur et manducatur in Coena, fides est.

---

264 Coena Domini] cfr I Cor. 11, 20   **272/273** Corpus – ratione] cfr I Cor. 11, 27-28; Ioh. 6, 48-63

261/262 Baptismus – congruat] cfr the similar affirmation of infant baptism in Article 35 of the *French Confession* of 1559 (see p. 560). According to the first Article of the *Schleitheim Confession* (see p. 79, 58/67), infant baptism was the 'chief abomination of the papacy'. Remarkably the Council of Trent treated adult baptism as dogmatically normative in Sess. VI. cap. 5 & 6 (1547) (see *COGD* III, p. 26), although infant baptism was endorsed in liturgical practice in Sess. VII, can. 13 ('Canones de sacramento baptismi', in *COGD* III, p. 42). Both Anabaptists and the bishops at Trent opposed the key Reformed teaching on passive, forensic justification where the prevenient grace of regeneration precedes repentance and conversion and which order is so effectively signified by the baptism of infants. While infant baptism cannot be proved directly from Scripture, the principle is nonetheless established by the authority of Scripture and is internally coherent with the first principles of Reformed soteriology **263** XXVIII] this revised formulation of 1563 affirms a real partaking of Christ's body and blood in the faithful receiver. This is the so-called instrumental realism of Peter Martyr Vermigli and John Calvin. See Vermigli's *Tractatio de sacramento Eucharistiae* and the formulation of this position in Article 37 of the *French Confession* and Calv., *Instit.* (1559), 4. 17. 19 seq. (vol. 2, p. 413 sqq.). The article as it appeared in the 1553 formulary (then Article 29) explicitly denied 'real and bodily presence of Christ's flesh and blood in the sacrament of the Lord's supper'. There was a substantial change in the revision of 1563 and this denial of real presence was eliminated

CANTERBURY – 1571

holy ghost, are visibly signed and sealed: fayth is confyrmed: and grace
285 increased by vertue of pray|er vnto God.

The baptisme of young children, is in any wyse to be retayned in the
Churche, as most agreable with the institution of Christe.

[XXVIII] Of the Lordes Supper

The Supper of the Lord, is not only a signe of the loue that Christians
290 ought to haue among them selues one to another: but rather it is a Sacrament
of our redemption by Christes death. Insomuch that to suche as ryghtlie, wor-
thyly, and with fayth receaue the same the bread whiche we breake is a part-
takyng of the body of Christe, and likewyse the cuppe of blessing, is a communion of the blood of Christe.

295 Transubstantiation (or the chaunge of the substaunce of bread and wine)
in the Supper of the Lorde, can not be proued by holye writ, but is repugnaunt
to the playne wordes of scripture, ouerthroweth the nature of a Sacrament,
and hath geuen occasion to many superstitions.

The body of Christe is geuen, taken, and eaten in the Supper only after an
300 heauenly and spirituall maner: And the meane whereby the body of Christe is
receaued and eaten in the Supper, is fayth.

299/300 The – maner] the body of Christ is given, received, and eaten in the Supper
in a spiritual manner. Here 'coelestis' and 'spirituali' denote the contrary of 'carnal'
eating rather than of 'bodily' eating, i.e. there is a spiritual discernment on the part of
the communicant. The presence is thus real, but not sensible

---

293 communion] *ante revisionem 1571* partakyng

CONCILIUM LONDINENSE – 1563-1571

275 Sacramentum Eucharistiae ex institutione Christi non servabatur, circumferebatur, elevabatur, nec adorabatur.

XXIX De manducatione corporis Christi, et impios illud non manducare

Impii et viva fide destituti, licet carnaliter et visibiliter (ut Augustinus
280 loquitur) corporis et sanguinis Christi sacramentum dentibus premant, nullo tamen modo Christi participes efficiuntur; sed potius tantae rei sacramentum seu symbolum ad iudicium sibi manducant et bibunt.

| XXX De Utraque Specie

B5r

Calix Domini laicis non est denegandus, utraque enim pars Dominici
285 sacramenti, ex Christi institutione et praecepto, omnibus Christianis ex aequo administrari debet.

---

285 ex¹ – praecepto] cfr I Cor. 11, 24-28; 10, 16

277 XXIX] this article was composed in 1563 and appears in the Parker manuscript of the *Articles* signed by the bishops, but was omitted from those published by Reginald Wolfe in 1563, hence the usual designation of this edition as the *Thirty-Eight Articles*. Article XXIX was approved with the final revision passed by Convocation and Parliament in 1571, and has ever since been included among the *Thirty-Nine Articles*. The article constitutes a corollary of the doctrine of real presence set out in Article XXVIII, i.e. that the body and blood of Christ is eaten 'coelestis et spirituali ratione' and not 'carnaliter et visibiliter'. See the treatment of 'impanation' in *Reformatio legum*, Article 2, 19, in Bray, *Tudor Church Reform*, p. 204-207   **279/280** ut Augustinus loquitur] Augustinus, *In Iohannis evangelium tractatus CXXIV* 26, 12, ed. R. Willems (*CC SL* 36), Turnhout 1954, p. 266, 20-22   **281/282** sed – bibunt] Thomas Aquinas, *Summa Theologiae* IIIa, q. 80, art. 3 (ed. De Rubeis, Billuart et aliorum notis selectis ornata, cum textu ex recensione leonina, Taurini – Roma 1948, vol. 4, p. 542-543), holds that the wicked receive both the 'signum' and the 'res', but not the 'virtus sacramenti'. The term 'sacramentum' as employed here, however, cannot refer to the 'res' as construed by Article XXVIII, i.e. as something received by the medium of faith. It must therefore be the mere 'signum', which is consumed to their condemnation. The body of Christ is offered ('datur'), but not received ('accipitur'), and therefore there is properly no sacrament for the impious. Cfr *Confessio Belgica*, Article 35   **285/286** omnibus – debet] see *Augsburg Confession*, Article 22: 'Laicis datur utraque species Sacramenti in Cœna Domini, quia hic mos habet mandatum Domini (Matth. 26, 27): Bibite ex hoc omnes'

CANTERBURY – 1571

The Sacrament of the Lordes Supper was not by Christes ordinaunce reserued, caryed about, lyfted vp, or worshipped.

| [XXIX] Of the wicked which do not eate the body of Christe
in the vse of the Lordes Supper

The wicked, and suche as be voyde of a liuelye fayth, although they do carnally and visibly presse with their teeth (as Saint Augustine sayth) the Sacrament of the body and blood of Christ: yet in no wyse are the partakers of Christe, but rather to their condemnation do eate and drinke the signe or Sacrament of so great a thing.

[XXX] Of both kindes

The cuppe of the Lorde is not to be denyed to the laye people. For both the partes of the Lordes Sacrament, by Christes ordinaunce and commaunde-ment, ought to be ministred to all Christian men alike.

302/303 The – worshipped] given that reception is intrinsic to the reality of presence, certain traditional medieval uses of the sacrament were no longer acceptable. Reservation, procession, elevation, and adoration of the host exemplify an externalising, localising, and sensible objectification of the presence in a manner separable from the sense of presence involved in the spiritual lifting of the heart *coram Deo* (Eph. 2, 6) in a spiritual eating. Cfr Article XXXVI of the *French Confession* (*COGD* VI.1.1, p. 560-561)   **311** XXX] composed by Archbishop Matthew Parker in 1563. The aim is to restore participation in both species of the sacrament. The denial of the cup to the laity had been customary in the Western Church since early in the twelfth century, though the practice had been condemned as late as 1118 by Pope Paschal II

302/303 The – worshipped] *additur anno 1563*   **303** reserued] *ante revisionem 1571* to be kept

XXXI De unica Christi oblatione in cruce perfecta

Oblatio Christi, semel facta, perfecta est redemptio, propitiatio, et satisfactio pro omnibus peccatis totius mundi, tam originalibus quam actualibus; neque praeter illam unicam est ulla alia pro peccatis expiatio. Unde missarum sacrificia, quibus vulgo dicebatur sacerdotem offerre Christum in remissionem poenæ aut culpae pro vivis defunctis, blasphema figmenta sunt et pernitiosae imposturae.

| XXXII De conjugio sacerdotum

Episcopis, Prebyteris et Diaconis nullo mandato divino praeceptum est, ut aut coelibatum voveant aut a matrimonio absteneant. Licet igitur etiam illis, ut caeteris omnibus Christianis, ubi hoc ad pietatem magis facere iudicaverint, pro suo arbitratu matrimonium contrahere.

---

287 XXXI] this article dates from 1553, and is the last in the series relating to Church, ministry, and sacraments (Articles XIX-XXXI). It rejects the doctrine of the sacrifice of the Mass, defined by the Council of Trent in 1562 (Sess. XXII. can. 1 'Canones de sanctissimo misse sacrificio', in *COGD* III, p. 102) and asserts the uniqueness and perfect sufficiency of the sacrifice of the Cross   **290/293** Unde – imposturae] the final statement condemns the sacramental apparatus attached to the doctrine of works of supererogation and a treasury of merit (Article XIV), as well as of purgatory (Article XX)   **294** XXXII] appeared in the *Forty-Two Articles* under the title 'Caelibatus ex verbo Dei praecipitur nemini'; see also *Reformatio legum*, Article 2, 21, in Bray, *Tudor Church Reform*, p. 208. The addition to the second clause (see Apparatus 3) positively asserts the propriety of the marriage of the clergy rather than simply denying the validity of celibacy. Cfr *Augsburg Confession*, Article 23, 'De coniugio sacerdotum'

---

295 nullo – est] *ante revisionem 1563* non est mandatum   **296** ut – absteneant] *ante revisionem 1563* neque iure divino coguntur matrimonio abstinere   **296/298** aut² – contrahere] *additur post revisionem 1563*

CANTERBURY – 1571

315 [XXXI] Of the one oblation of Christe finished vppon the
Crosse

The offering of Christ once made, is *the* perfect redemption, propiciation,
and satisfaction for all the sinnes of the whole worlde, both originall and actuall, and there is none other satisfaction for sinne, but that alone. Wherefore
320 the sacrifices of Masses, in the which it was commonly said that the Priestes
did offer Christe | for the quicke and the dead, to haue remission of payne or 20
gylt, were blasphemous fables, and daungerous deceits.

[XXXII] Of the marriage of Priestes

Byshops, Priestes, and Deacons, are not commaunded *by Gods lawe*
325 eyther to vowe the estate of single lyfe or to abstayne from mariage neither by
God's law are they compelled to abstain from matrimony. Therefore it is
lawfull also for them, as for all other Christian men, to mary at ther owne
discretion, as they shall iudge the same to serue better to godlynesse.

317/318 The – worlde] this article echoes the language of Thomas Cranmer's prayer
of consecration in the 'Order for the Administration of the Lord's Supper' in the *Book
of Common Prayer* (1552): 'God our heavenly father whiche of thy tender mercye,
diddest give thine onely Sonne Jesus Christ, to suffer death upon the Crosse for our
redemption, who made ther (by his one oblation of himself once offered) a ful, perfect
and sufficient sacrifice, oblation, and satisfaction for the synnes of the whole
worlde [...]' **318/319** both – alone] the uniqueness and perfection of Christ's
oblation is made clear in Hebr. 7, 26-27; 9, 11-14; 10, 10-14 and ties the articles on the
sacrament back to the soteriological articles on justification (Article XI), of Christ
alone without sin (Article XV), and of salvation only by the name of Christ (Article
XVIII)

---

325 or – from] *ante revisionem 1571* without   **325/326** neither – matrimony]
omittitur post revisionem 1571 **327** also] *additur post revisionem 1571*

XXXIII Excommunicati vitati sunt

300 Qui per publicam Ecclesiae denunciationem rite ab unitate Ecclesiae praecisus est et excommunicatus, is ab universa fidelium multitudine, donec per poenitentiam publice reconciliatus fuerit arbitrio iudicis competentis, habendus est tanquam ethnicus et publicanus.

XXXIV Traditiones ecclesiasticae

305 | Traditiones atque caeremonias easdem non omnino necessarium est esse ubique, aut prorsus consimiles; nam et variae semper fuerunt et mutari possunt, pro regionum temporum et morum diversitate, modo nihil contra verbum Dei instituatur. B6r

---

299 XXXIII] cfr I Esdr. 10, 8; Luc. 6, 22; Ioh. 9, 22; 16, 2; 12, 42; Rom. 16, 17; II Thess. 3, 14; Tit. 3, 10; II Ioh. 10 **303** habendus – publicanus] cfr Matth. 18, 17

299 XXXIII] composed in 1553 and unchanged in the revisions of 1563 and 1571. The Church, like any self-governing society, reserves the right to exercise discipline and to expel members who are disloyal to its principles **304** XXXIV] the first statement is derived from the *Thirteen Articles* of 1538, and both it and the second statement constitute Article 33 of the 1553 formulary. The third statement is based on a 1559 draft by Matthew Parker. The substance of the article is tied closely to that of Article XX, 'De ecclesiae auctoritate'

CANTERBURY – 1571

[XXXIII] Of excommunicate persons, howe they are to be auoided

That person whiche by open denuntiation of the Churche, is rightly cut of from the vnitie of the Churche, and excommunicated, ought to be taken of the whole multitude of the faythfull as an Heathen and Publicane, vntill he be openly reconciled by penaunce, and receaued into the Churche by a iudge that hath aucthoritie thereto.

[XXXIV] Of the Traditions of the Churche

It is not necessarie that traditions and ceremonies be in al places one, or vtterly like, for at all | times they haue ben diuerse, and may be chaunged accordyng to the diuersitie of countreys, times, and mens maners, so that nothing be ordeyned against Gods worde.

---

334 iudge] the judge is bishop or Ordinary. In the *Canons* of 1604, notorious crimes and scandals are to be referred to the ecclesiastical courts. The practice of the Church of England was to continue the distinction of the apostolic Church between 'greater' and 'lesser' excommunication, the former a complete exclusion from the divine society, the latter a deprivation of participation in worship and the sacraments. See *Reformatio legum*, Article 19, 11 ('Excommunicatio quomodo sit exercenda') and Article 32 ('De excommunicatione') in Bray, *Tudor Church Reform*, p. 342 and 462-475. Statutory approval by Parliament of the *Articles of Religion* in 1571 followeed upon the excommunication of Queen Elizabeth by Pope Pius V in the bull *Regnans in excelsis* (1570) **337/340** It – worde] the affirmation of the diversity of traditions, customs, and ceremonies may be taken as a response both to the Council of Trent's assertion of a universal uniformity and to the anarchic insistence of some radical Protestants on the exercise of private judgement in such matters

622 CONCILIUM LONDINENSE – 1563-1571

Traditiones et caeremonias ecclesiasticas quae cum verbo Dei non
310 pugnant et sunt autoritate publica institutae atque probatae, quisquis privato
consilio volens et data opera publice violaverat, is ut qui peccat in publicum
ordinem Ecclesiae, quique laedit autoritatem magistratus, et qui infirmorum
fratrum conscientias vulnerat, publice, ut caeteri timeant, arguendus est.

Quaelibet Ecclesia particularis si|ve nationalis autoritatem habet insti- B6v
315 tuendi mutandi aut abrogandi caeremonias aut ritus ecclesiasticos, humana
tantum autoritate institutos, modo omnia ad aedificationem fiant.

XXXV HOMILIAE

Tomus secundus Homiliarum, quarum singulos titulos huic Articulo
subiunximus, continet piam et salutarem doctrinam et his temporibus necessa-
320 rium, non minus quam prior tomus Homiliarum, quae editae sunt tempore
Edwardi Sexti: itaque eas in Ecclesiis per ministros diligenter et clare, ut a
populo intelligi possint, recitandas esse iudicamus.

314/316 Quaelibet – fiant] cfr Rom. 14, 19; I Cor. 14, 26

314/316 Quaelibet – fiant] the sovereignty of national churches can be interpreted as
the ecclesiological means of ensuring peace, order, and good government in the
regulation of things in themselves indifferent ('adiaphora') and therefore subject to
human authority in the visible, external realm ('forum politicum') as distinct from the
realm of the spiritual life ('forum conscientiae'). See Calv., *Instit.* (1559), 3. 19. 15 (vol. 2,
p. 82-83). The power to 'ordain, change, or abolish' rites and ceremonies belongs finally
to the magistrate, whose duty it is to ensure the stability of the Church as a human,
political society, with the condition that 'all things be done to edifying' **317** XXXV]
from the formulary of 1553 re-composed in 1563. The corresponding Article (33) of 1553
ran: 'The Homilies of late given, and set out by the king's authority, be godly and
wholesome, containing doctrine to be received of all men: and therefore are to be read
to the people diligently, distinctly, and plainly'. The *Homilies* were sermons composed
by prominent divines and were intended to counter 'such errors as were then by
ignorant preachers sparkled among the people'. The majority of those in the *Second
Book of Homilies* are attributed to John Jewel, Edmund Grindal, Matthew Parker, and
James Pilkington. See *The seconde tome of homelyes of such matters as were promised and
intituled in the former part of homelyes, set out by the aucthoritie of the Quenes Maiestie:
and to be read in euery paryshe churche agreablye*, London 1563 **320/321** editae –
Sexti] the *First Book of Homilies* (1547), consisting of twelve sermons, was largely the
work of Thomas Cranmer, although some are attributed to Hugh Latimer and Thomas
Becon

CANTERBURY – 1571 623

Whosoeuer through his priuate iudgement, wyllyngly and purposely doth openly breake the traditions and ceremonies of the Church, which be not repugnaunt to the worde of God, and be ordayned and approued by common aucthoritie, ought to be rebuked openly (that other may feare to do the lyke), as he that offendeth agaynst the Common order of the Churche and hurteth the aucthoritie of the Magistrate, and woundeth the consciences of the weake brethren.

Euery particuler or nationall Churche, hath aucthoritie to ordaine, chaunge, and abolishe ceremonies or rites of the Churche ordeyned onlye by mans aucthoritie, so that all thinges be done to edifiyng.

[XXXV] OF HOMILIES

The seconde booke of Homilies, the seuerall titles whereof we haue ioyned vnder this article, doth conteyne a godly and wholesome doctrine, and necessarie for these tymes, as doth the former booke of Homilies, which were set foorth in the time of Edwarde the sixt: and therefore we iudge them to be read in Churches by the Ministers diligently, and distinctly, that they may be vnderstanded by the people.

341/347 Whosoeuer – brethren] the article is supported here by the preface to the *Book of Common Prayer* (1549): 'And although the keping or omytting of a ceremonie (in itselfe considered) is but a small thyng: Yet the wilfull and contemptuous transgression, and breakyng of a common ordre, and disciplyne, is no small offence before God. Let all thynges bee done among you (sayeth Sainte Paule) in a semely and due ordre. The appoyntemente of the whiche ordre pertayneth not to pryvate menne: Therfore no manne ought to take in hande nor presume to appoynte or alter any publyke or common ordre in Christes Churche, excepte he be lawfully called and autorized thereunto. And whereas in this our tyme, the myndes of menne bee so diverse, that some thynke it a greate matter of conscience to departe from a peece of the leaste of theyr Ceremonies (they bee so addicted to their olde customes), and agayne on the other syde, some bee so newe fangle that they woulde innovate all thyng, and so doe despyse the olde that nothyng canne lyke them, but that is newe: It was thought expediente not so muche to have respecte howe to please and satisfie eyther of these partyes, as howe to please God, and profitte them bothe' **355/357** and – people] a number of the clergy were opposed to the doctrine propounded by the *Homilies*, and so read them unintelligibly. Abolition of the *Homilies* was one of the demands made by Puritan critics of the Elizabethan settlement, Thomas Wilcox and John Field, in *An Admonition to the Parliament* (1572)

624 CONCILIUM LONDINENSE – 1563-1571

Catalogus Homiliarum

1. De recto Ecclesiae usu
325   2. Adversus idolatariae pericula
3. De reparandis ac purgandis Ecclesii
| 4. De bonis operibus; de ieiunio   B7r
5. In gulae atque ebrietatis vitia
6. In nimis sumptuosos vestium apparatus
330   7. De oratione sive precatione
8. De loco et tempore orationi destinatis
9. De publicis precibus ac sacramentis, idiomate vulgari omnibusque noto, habendis
10. De sacrosancta verbi divini auctoritate
335   11. De eleemosyna
12. De Christi nativitate
13. De Dominica passione
14. De resurrectione Christi
15. De digna corporis et sanguinis dominici in coena Domini participatione
340
16. De donis Spiritus Sancti
17. In diebus, qui vulgo Rogationum | dicti sunt, concio   B7v
18. De matrimonii statu
19. De otio seu socordia
345   20. De poenitentia

XXXVI De episcoporum et ministrorum consecratione

Libellus de Consecratione Archiepiscoporum et Episcoporum et de ordinatione Presbyterorum et Diaconorum, editus nuper temporibus Edwardi

---

346 XXXVI] cfr Act. 20, 17-28; Tit. 1, 5-7

323 Catalogus Homiliarum] the order of homilies 19 and 20 was reversed in 1571 when the homily against rebellion was also added in response to the Northern Rebellion of 1569   **346** XXXVI] composed in 1563 to replace a more vaguely formulated article in the Edwardine formulary. As does Article XXXII, it affirms the threefold ministry of bishops, presbyters, and deacons. Bishop and presbyter are convertible terms in the Scripture (see Apparatus 1). Some objectors to this article insisted on parity of ministers in the name of realising a scriptural polity and discipline, as for example in *An Admonition to the Parliament* (1572). See *Reformatio legum*, Article 20, in Bray, *Tudor Church Reform*, p. 346-369

CANTERBURY – 1571

| *Of the names of the Homilies*
1. Of the right vse of the Churche.
2. Agaynst perill of Idolatrie.
3. Of repayring and keping cleane of Churches.
4. Of good workes, first of fastyng.
5. Agaynst gluttony and drunkennesse.
6. Agaynst excesse of apparell.
7. Of prayer.
8. Of the place and time of prayer.
9. That common prayer and Sacramentes ought to be ministred in a knowen tongue.
10. Of the reuerente estimation of Gods worde.
11. Of almes doing.
12. Of the Natiuitie of Christe.
13. Of the passion of Christe.
14. Of the resurrection of Christe.
15. Of the worthie receauing of the Sacrament of the body and blood of Christe.
16. Of the gyftes of the holy ghost.
17. For the Rogation dayes.
18. Of the state of Matrimonie.
19. Of repentaunce.
20. Agaynst Idlenesse.
21. Agaynst rebellion.

[XXXVI] Of consecration of Bishops and ministers

The booke of Consecration of *Archbishops, and* Byshops, and orderyng of Priestes and Deacons, *lately set foorth in the time of* | *Edwarde the sixt, and*

384/385 set – Parliament] the Edwardine *Ordinal* – as it is called – was first published in 1550 under statutory sanction of 3 and 4 Edw. VI c. 12, and in a revised form in 1552 sanctioned by the Second Act of Uniformity, 5 and 6 Edw. VI c. 1

626 CONCILIUM LONDINENSE – 1563-1571

Sexti et auctoritate Parliamenti illis ipsis temporibus confirmatus, omnia ad
350 eiusmodi consecrationem et ordinationem necessaria continet; et nihil habet
quod ex se sit aut supersitiosum aut impium.

Itaque quicunque iuxta ritus illius libri consecrati aut ordinati sunt, ab
anno secundo praedicti Regis Edwardi usque ad hoc tempus aut in posterum
iuxta eosdem ritus consecrabuntur aut ordinabuntur, rite, atque ordine, atque
355 legitime | statuimus esse et fore consecratos et ordinatos.   B8r

XXXVII De civilibus magistratibus

Regia Maiestas in hoc Angliae regno ac caeteris eius dominiis summam
habet potestatem, ad quam omnium statuum huius regni, sive illi ecclesiastici
sive civiles, in omnibus causis suprema gubernatio pertinet, et nulli externae
360 iurisdictioni est subiecta, necesse debet.

Cum Regiae Maiestati summam gubernationem tribuimus, quibus titulis
intelligimus animos quorundam calumniatorum offendi, non damus regibus
nostris aut verbi Dei aut sacramentorum administrationem, quod etiam
Iniunctiones ab Elizabetha Regina nostra nuper editae apertissime testantur:
365 sed eam tantum prae|rogativam quam in Sacris Scripturis a Deo ipso omnibus   B8v
piis principibus videmus semper fuisse attributam, hoc est, ut omnes status
atque ordines fidei suae a Deo commissos, sive illi ecclesiastici sint sive civiles,
in officio contineant, et contumaces ac delinquentes gladio civili coerceant.

---

356 XXXVII] composed in 1553 and rewritten in 1563. The first sentence of the
Edwardine formulary stated that 'the King of England is Supreme Head in earth, next
under Christ, of the Church of England and Ireland'. The language of headship is
replaced in 1563 with the affirmation of 'highest power of dominion' ('dominiis
summam potestatem') and 'supreme governance' ('suprema gubernatio'). When
Parliament restored to the crown its 'ancient jurisdiction over the estate ecclesiastical
and spiritual' in the Act of Supremacy of 1559 (1 Eliz. c. 1), the Queen was styled as 'the
only Supreme Governor of this realm [...] as well in all ecclesiastical things or causes as
temporal'. See also *Reformatio legum*, Article 2, 21, in Bray, *Tudor Church Reform*,
p. 208-210   **363** sacramentorum administrationem] the article distinguishes here
between the *potestas ordinis* and the *potestas iurisdictionis*

CANTERBURY – 1571

385 *confirmed at the same tyme by aucthoritie of Parliament*, doth conteyne all thinges necessarie to suche consecration and orderyng: neyther hath it any thing, that of it selfe is superstitious *or* vngodly.

And therefore, whosoeuer are consecrate or ordered accordyng *to the rites of that booke, sence the seconds yere of the aforenamed king Edwarde, vnto this*
390 *time or hereafter shal be consecrated or ordered accordyng to the same rites*, we decree all such to be ryghtly, orderly, and lawfully consecrated and ordered.

[XXXVII] Of the ciuill Magistrates

The Queenes Maiestie hath the cheefe power in this Realme of Englande, and other her dominions, vnto whom the cheefe gouernment of all estates of
395 this Realme, whether they be Ecclesiasticall or Ciuile, in all causes doth apparteine, and is not, nor ought to be subiect to any forraigne iurisdiction.

Where we attribute to the Queenes Maiestie the cheefe gouernment, by whiche titles we vnderstande the mindes of some slanderous folkes to be offended: we geue not to our princes the ministring either of God's word, or
400 of Sacraments, the which thing the injunctions also lately set forth by Elizabeth our Queene, doth most plainlie testifie: But that only prerogatiue whiche we see to haue ben geuen alwayes to all godly Princes | in holy Scriptures by 24 God him selfe, that is, that they should rule all estates and degrees committed to their charge by God, whether they be Ecclesiasticall or Temporall, and
405 restraine with the ciuill sworde the stubberne and euyll doers.

386/387 neyther – vngodly] the article vindicates the rites of ordination against the Roman objection of deficiency of form as well as against the Puritan charge of superstitious excess. The essence of ordination consists in 'publique prayer with the imposition of hands' (Act. 6, 6) as stated in the preface to the *Ordinal*   **388/391** And – ordered] this second statement affirms the statutory legality of the *Ordinal* as having been attached to the *Book of Common Prayer* restored by Act of Parliament in 1559 (1 Eliz. c. 2). The legality of the *Ordinal* was confirmed again in 1565 by 'An Act declaring the making and consecration of the Archbishops and Bishops of this realm to be good, lawful, and perfect' (8 Eliz. c. 1)   **400/401** the' – testifie] see the *Iniunctions geuen by the Queenes Maiestie, Anno Domini 1559*, London [1564]. Drawn up by William Cecil and members of the privy council, these detailed regulations of ecclesiastical practice were issued in June 1559 under the authority of the royal prerogative to be administered by visitors within each diocese   **401/403** But – selfe] the scriptural exemplars of the royal supremacy are the kings of ancient Israel: David, Solomon, Josiah, and Hezekiah. That the Old Testament should be taken as authoritative in matters of ecclesiastical polity shows the strong influence of the Huldrych Zwingli, Heinrich Bullinger and the *schola tigurina* on the institutions of the Church of England

628 CONCILIUM LONDINENSE – 1563-1571

Romanus Pontifex nullam habet iurisdictionem in hoc regno Angliae. Magistratus civilis est a Deo ordinatus atque probatus, quamobrem illi, non solum propter iram sed etiam propter conscientiam, oboediendum est.

Leges regni possunt Christianos propter capitalia et gravia crimina morte punire.

Christianis licet ex mandato Magistratus arma portare et iusta bella administrare.

XXXVIII Christianorum bona non sunt communia

Facultates et bona Christianorum | non sunt communia quoad ius et Cɪr possessionem, ut quidam Anabaptistae falso iactant; debet tamen quisque de his quae possidet, pro facultatum ratione, pauperibus eleemosynas benigne distribuere.

XXXIX Licet Christianis iurare

Quemadmodum iuramentum vanum et temerarium a Domino nostro Iesu Christo et ab Apostolo eius Iacobo Christianis hominibus interdictum esse fatemur, ita Christianorum religionem minime prohibere censemus quin, iubente magistratu in causa fidei et caritatis iurare liceat, modo id fiat iuxta Prophetae doctrinam in iustitia, in iudicio, et veritate.

---

374 Christianis – administrare] cfr Rom. 13. 1; I Petr. 2, 13-17 **376** XXXVIII] cfr Marc. 10, 17-22; Act. 2, 42-47; 4, 32-35; Eph. 4, 28 **381** XXXIX] cfr Ier. 4, 2 **383** Iacobo] cfr Iac. 5, 12

---

369 Romanus – Angliae] the article reaffirms the Henrician 'Act Extinguishing the Authority of the Bishop of Rome', passed by Parliament in 1536 (28 Henry VIII c. 10) **374** Christianis – administrare] in these final clauses, the coercive power of the prince is affirmed against antinomian objections. Cfr Article 40 of the *French Confession* **376** XXXVIII] composed for the *Forty-Two Articles* in 1553 and unchanged since, it condemns Anabaptists and other radical reformers. The article holds to the view that Christians are not bound to a community of possession but rather to a degree of community of use **381** XXXIX] since attestation by oath is allowed in Scripture, Christians may help in the administration of the law by testifying in civil courts. This completes the series of articles concerning the exercise of civil power as one of the external means of grace

---

370/371 Magistratus – est] *omittitur post revisionem 1563* **383** ab] *omittitur post revisionem 1563*

CANTERBURY – 1571

The bishop of Rome hath no iurisdiction in this Realme of Englande. The Civil Magistrate is ordained and allowed of God; wherefore we must obey him, not only for fear of punishment but also for conscience sake.

The lawes of the Realme may punishe Christian men with death, for heynous and greeuous offences.

It is lawfull for Christian men, at the commaundement of the Magistrate, to weare weapons, and serue in the warres.

[XXXVIII] OF CHRISTIAN MENS GOODES, WHICH ARE NOT COMMON

The ryches and goodes of Christians are not common, as touching the ryght, title, and possession of the same, as certayne Anabaptistes do falsely boast. Notwithstandyng euery man ought of suche thinges as he possesseth, liberally to geue almes to the poore, accordyng to his habilitie.

[XXXIX] OF A CHRISTIAN MANS OTHE

As we confesse that vayne and rashe swearing is forbidden Christian men by our Lord Jesus Christe, and James his Apostle: So | we iudge that Christian religion doth not prohibite, but that a man may sweare when the Magistrate requireth, in a cause of faith and charitie, so it be done accordyng *to the prophetes* teaching, in iustice, iudgement, and trueth.

406/408 The[2] – sake] the statement refers to the classic Reformed teaching on the authority of the magistrate derived from Rom. 13. Cfr Article XXXIX of the *French Confession* (*COGD* VI.1.1, p. 562) and Article XXXVI of the *Belgic Confession* **418** XXXIX] another article against the political teachings of the Anabaptists dating from 1553 and unchanged since. Some Christians refused the administration of oaths, frequently on the strength of Matth. 5, 33-37 and Iac. 5, 12 among other passages. Yet the use of oaths on solemn occasions is affirmed elsewhere in Scripture (Hebr. 6, 17) and even employed by Paul (II Cor. 1, 23). When Christ was put on oath by the high priest regarding his messiahship, he answered with a simple affirmation (Matth. 26, 62-64). Cfr *Reformatio legum*, Article 39, in Bray, *Tudor Church Reform*, p. 548-555

406/408 The[2] – sake] *omittitur post revisionem 1571*

630 CONCILIUM LONDINENSE – 1563-1571

| Hos Articulos fidei Christianae, continentes in uniuersum nouemde Civ
cimpaginas in autographo, quod asseruatur apud Reuerendissimum in Christo
patrem, Dominum Matthaeum Centuariensem Archiepiscopum, totius
390 Angliae Primatem & Metropolitanum, Archiepiscopi & Episcopi utriusque
Prouinciae regni Angliae, in sacra prouinciali Synodo legitimè congregati,
unanimi assensu recipiunt & profitentur, & ut ueros atque Orthodoxos,
manuum suarum subscriptionibus approbant, uicesimo nono die mensis
Ianuarij: Anno Domini, secundum computationem ecclesiae Anglicanae,
395 millesimo quingentesimo sexagesimo secundo: uniuersusque Clerus Inferioris
domus, eosdem etiam unanimiter & recepit & professus est, ut ex manuum
suarum subscriptionibus patet, quas obtulit & deposuit apud eundem Reuerendissimum, quinto die Februarij, Anno praedicto. Quibus omnibus articulis,
Serenesima princeps Elizabeth, Dei gratia Angliae, Franciae, & Hiberniae
400 Regina, fidei Defensor, &c. per seipsam diligenter prius lectis & examinatis,
Regium suum assensum praebuit.

393/395 uicesimo – secundo] i.e. 19 January 1562 (Old Style)

This Booke of Articles before rehearsed, is agayne approued, and allowed
to be holden and executed within the Realme, by the ascent and consent of
our Soueraigne Ladye Elizabeth, by the grace of GOD, of Englande, Fraunce,
and Irelande Queene, defender of the fayth, &c. Which Articles were deliberately read, and confirmed agayne by the subscription of the handes of the
Archbyshop and Byshoppes of the vpper house, and by the subscription of the
whole Cleargie in the neather house in their Conuocation, in the yere of our
Lorde GOD, 1571.

CONCILIUM ANTVERPIANUM

1564

ediderunt
Gianmarco BRAGHI – Graeme MURDOCK

THE SYNOD OF 'LA VIGNE'
ANTWERP, 1564*

INTRODUCTION

In the summer of 1559 Philip II left the Netherlands for Spain. Philip's choice of governor, his half-sister Margaret of Parma, faced inter-related political and religious challenges not the least of which was growing support for the Reformed faith. In the autumn of 1561 copies surfaced of a *Belgic Confession* compiled by the minister of the Reformed congregation at Tournai (Doornik), Guido de Brès. This confession largely followed the *Gallican Confession* which had been agreed by a Synod held at Paris in 1559. (¹) The *Belgic Confession* came to the attention of the authorities when a copy was reported to have been nailed to the doors of the Roman Catholic church in Tournai. Then, on the evening of 1 November 1561, a copy of the *Belgic Confession* was thrown over the walls of the castle in Tournai. These gestures of protest signalled the growing confidence of supporters of the Reformed cause. (²) During the early 1560s a number of clandestine synods were held by representatives from emerging Reformed congregations in the southern region of the Habsburg Netherlands. A 1563 Synod decided that clergy and lay officials should subscribe to the *Belgic Confession* to promote doctrinal unity among congregations in the Netherlands. Further synods held in 1564 and 1565 agreed on a range of organisational and practical matters. These synods included a meeting held on 1 May 1564 at 'La Vigne', code for Antwerp. (³)

The Reformed Church in the Netherlands was not the result of a direct Genevan mission effort either before or after Calvin's death in May 1564. Only one minister was sent from Geneva following a request from Antwerp during the late 1550s. However, other ministers who worked in congregations in the Netherlands had been trained at either Lausanne or Geneva. Churches 'under the Cross' in the Netherlands maintained very close links with – and received support from – a number of Reformed refugee communities and

---

(*) Introduction by Graeme Murdock; critical edition by Gianmarco Braghi.
(1) See *Gallican Confession* in this volume, ed. Irene Dingel, p. 531-563.
(2) Gootjes, *The Belgic Confession*, p. 62-67 and 112-114.
(3) Kist, 'De Synoden der Nederlandsche Hervormde Kerken onder het Kruis'.

exile churches in Frankfurt, Wesel, Emden, London, and Sandwich. (4) There were also strong connections between the churches of the southern Netherlands and the Reformed Church in France as the resolutions agreed at the May 1564 Synod confirm. The Antwerp Synod borrowed and adapted articles from the French Church's *Discipline ecclésiastique* which had been agreed at the 1559 Paris Synod as well as other resolutions which had been adopted by early French synods. The first set of articles agreed at Antwerp in 1564 about the organisation of churches and their consistories bears a very close similarity to articles in the French *Discipline*. There was greater innovation at the Antwerp Synod with regard to regulations around the work of deacons (articles 12-21) and in articles about the treatment of different cases of moral discipline and a range of other practical issues (articles 32-48). (5)

The Church structures agreed at the Antwerp Synod outlined the authority of congregational consistories and provincial synods. This de-centralised form of Church organisation was believed to be of Biblical warrant and was also well-suited to the context of an underground religious movement threatened by state persecution. The Synod's resolutions present an aspiration to organisational stability that proved difficult to realise. The late 1550s had witnessed a spike in prosecutions, banishments, and executions of ministers and members of Reformed congregations. There was a rapid turnover of ministers during these years as preachers moved between congregations in the Netherlands and exile communities as necessity required. Churches sent representatives to attend synods which met in secret out of fear of the reaction of the authorities. Decisions were likely reached without the luxury of lengthy debate around a prepared draft text, which also helps to explain the close similarities with existing articles of the French Church. Antwerp was the obvious location for these early synods. Antwerp acted as a hub for the spread of Reformed ideas in Brabant, Flanders, Hainault, and Artois, and the city also became a place of refuge for those persecuted elsewhere in the region. There were organised Dutch- and French- speaking congregations in Antwerp from the mid-1550s served by ministers including Gaspar van der Heyden, Adriaan van Haemstede, and Herman Moded. There were at least hundreds of com-

---

(4) Backhouse, *The Flemish and Walloon Communities of Sandwich*; Pettegree, *Emden and the Dutch Revolt*; Id., *Foreign Protestant Communities*; Id., 'The Exile Churches'; Spohnholz, *The Convent of Wesel*. See Wesel/Emden in this volume, ed. Henning Juergens, p. 657-733.

(5) Knetsch, 'Church Ordinances and Regulations'. Knetsch provided a table to show the influence of different French sources on the Antwerp text (p. 205).

mitted members of these Reformed congregations in the city and many others who sympathised with the movement and attended some meetings. ([6])

The resolutions of the May 1564 Synod held in Antwerp reflect primarily on matters relating to the organisation of the Church and everyday life of congregations. The Synod's decisions offer little comment on the contradictions of organising an illegal religious movement that claimed to respect the authority of civil magistrates. However, the Synod did recognise the danger of interfering with the appropriate functions of magistrates in cases regarding marriage. Likewise, Church members were required to cooperate with any inquiries made by their consistory but without – the Synod claimed – thereby seeking in any way to diminish the authority of civil magistrates. In adopting advice regarding appropriate modesty in clothing – similar to measures adopted by the French national Synod in 1562 – the synod also noted that the Church should not issue regulations in areas that were properly the concern of magistrates (Article 45).

The central themes of the Synod's decisions include a determination to establish appropriate and clear structures of authority in the Church. The Synod stressed the mutual accountability of synods, ministers, and congregational consistories. Each congregation was to have a consistory made up of its minister or ministers along with lay elders and deacons. ([7]) There was to be no formal hierarchy between consistories, between ministers, or between elders and deacons in any consistory. The accountability of consistories was to be aided by requiring a careful written record to be kept of their decisions. These records were to be given over to the provincial Synod. Ministers were also accountable to their consistories. They could not leave their congregations without prior agreement and could be removed from office if deemed unsatisfactory. Ministers were also accountable to each other and could not publish books without the prior agreement of two or three other ministers. Elders were appointed to the task of visiting Church members in their districts and they were charged to look out for any problems that should be reported to the consistory. Deacons were to deal with the needs of the poor and to visit the sick. Elders and deacons were accountable to their congregational consistories for how they performed their functions.

---

(6) Marnef, *Antwerp in the Age of Reformation*, p. 61-87; Id., 'The Changing Face of Calvinism'.

(7) The Synod explicitly required that there be only one consistory in each congregation. This seems to be a concern for any overlap in authority rather than any issue at this stage about divisions between linguistic communities. See Knetsch, 'The National Synod of Dordrecht'.

The Synod also provided guidelines about the practice of moral discipline, about issues relating to marriage, and about the management of poor relief. The Synod showed great concern to prevent any scandals that might disrupt congregations or impact upon the reputation of the Church. Elders were to look out for any scandals in the lives of Church members and report back to the consistory. Elders were to proceed through stages of disciplinary action against accused Church members, first issuing private warnings and admonishing individuals. Consistories could then require Church members to appear before them to repent of their sins, or appear before the whole congregation to acknowledge their faults. Consistories could suspend unrepentant and persistent offenders from participation in the sacraments or finally excommunicate people from membership of the Church. (8) The faithful were instructed to avoid any scandals in arranging marriages. The Church's focus was on maintaining the stability of marriages and the Synod advised reconciliation in response to any suspicion of infidelity. Deacons were instructed to examine the faith of the poor to determine those who qualified for assistance from the Church. If those in receipt of relief were later found to be begging in the city then all assistance from the Church would cease. Deacons might provide some assistance along with religious instruction to others in the city who were in great distress but who could not provide clear evidence of their faith. (9)

These articles agreed at the Antwerp Synod reveal something of the outlook and character of the clandestine Reformed Church in the Netherlands at this stage in its early development. The Synod's decisions speak clearly of a desire to support and mould the lives of the faithful in their congregations. Church members were clearly demarcated from those outside the flock who lived without belief in God or in ignorance of the Gospel. The Synod extended some sympathy to those who lived without access to the Bible and who were not therefore aware of their own immorality. For example, the Synod allowed those who co-habited ahead of formal marriage 'during the period of their ignorance' (Article 30) to seek repentance only before the consistory rather than in full view of the entire congregation. The greater spiritual and moral burden on Church members to respond to the truth of the Gospel meant that those who persisted in false opinions or in immoral conduct should be excommunicated. The Synod spoke about the need to be watchful

(8) On these practices of suspension and excommunication see *Dire l'interdit: The Vocabulary of Censure and Exclusion in the Early Modern Reformed Tradition*, ed. R. A. Mentzer – F. Moreil – P. Chareyre, Leiden 2010.

(9) On the issue of poor relief see Parker, *The Reformation of Community*; Fehler, *Poor Relief and Protestantism*.

against those declared to be 'schismatics' and about 'Anabaptists or other heretics' (Article 43). Anabaptists were significant rivals for the Reformed Church in the Netherlands during this period but the Synod advised against entering into any debates with them. The Synod also rejected any connection with 'paganism' through the choice of inappropriate names at baptism (Article 24).

The Synod warned above all about the risks of infection from the idolatry and superstitions of the Roman Church. The Synod was watchful about the need to subject any former priests or monks who wished to become Reformed ministers to long and detailed investigation about their doctrine and about their lives (Article 7). Printers, artists, and all the faithful were warned that they could not permit their work to support the 'superstitions of the Roman church' (Article 30). Church members would face the discipline of the Church if they participated in Catholic rituals and 'polluted themselves with idolatry' (Article 39). The Reformed Church through its own funeral ceremonies had to ensure that it avoided all 'superstitious' practices (Article 40). Deacons could try to seek assistance for poor and needy members in their districts through alms houses but only if they could avoid the risk of pollution from idolatry and superstition (Article 21). Ministers could not conduct the marriages of those who were 'pure Papists' until the couple renounced the 'Mass and all other superstitions' (Article 25). The faithful were surrounded by those who lived 'under of the tyranny of Antichrist' (Article 40). They should live as far as possible in isolation from the Catholic Church and protect themselves within the shelter of their congregations under the guidance and with the support of their minister, elders, and deacons. The responsibility fell to ministers and consistories to provide for the spiritual and practical needs of Church members and to defend the integrity and reputation of their congregations.

Even as this Synod at Antwerp and other early synods set about the task of organising the Reformed Church within the Habsburg Netherlands, there were obvious and growing tensions between Reformed attitudes and aspirations and the repressive measures employed by the Habsburg authorities in their efforts to curtail the spread of heresy. Ministers, lay officials, and Church members remained under threat. A few months after the Synod was held in Antwerp a Reformed minister called Christoffel Fabritius was burned as a heretic. However, in a sign of growing support for the Reformed cause this execution was met with a public disturbance and the city authorities were forced to retreat under a hail of stones. ([10]) Tensions culminated in 1566 as

---

(10) Marnef, *Antwerp in the Age of Reformation*, p. 87.

CONCILIUM ANTVERPIANUM – 1564

substantial public support for the Reformed cause was demonstrated in large open-air services (or 'hedge-preaching') over the summer. Then, on 20 August 1566 a Reformed crowd attacked what they regarded as a source of superstition and polluting idolatry in the images and statues of the cathedral of Our Lady in Antwerp. As outbreaks of iconoclasm spread across the Netherlands, the Reformed cause in the southern Netherlands achieved a temporary triumph in its 'wonder-year'. (11)

Note on the Edition

For a brief overview of manuscript copies of synods 'under the Cross', Nicolaas Christiaan Kist's analysis remains fundamental as no modern scholar provides much discussion on this matter. (12) Robert McCune Kingdon checked Kist's critical edition against several variant manuscript copies of the proceedings of Antwerp 1564 held in the Archief van der Waalsche Kerk, Rotterdam, and reported that variant wordings of copies of these early Synod results were 'practically all trivial'. (13) Émile Bourlier, in the preface to his critical edition of these early proceedings, tried to put these variants – which he considered not always trivial – in the context of manuscript transmission and circulation. (14)

We used Cornelis Hooijer's transcription of the discipline agreed upon at Antwerp as a source text (see Bibliography and Monitum) and we indicated variants as found in other transcriptions and critical editions (see Conspectus Siglorum).

(11) Crew, *Calvinist Preaching and Iconoclasm.*

(12) Kist, 'De Synoden der Nederlandsche Hervormde Kerken onder het Kruis', p. 3-13.

(13) R. M. Kingdon, *Geneva and the Consolidation of the French Protestant Movement, 1564-1572: A Contribution to the History of Congregationalism, Presbyterianism and Calvinist Resistance Theory* (*Travaux d'Humanisme et Renaissance* 92), Genève 1967, p. 125, note 2.

(14) *Livre synodal,* p. 3-15.

CONCILIUM ANTVERPIANUM – 1564

BIBLIOGRAPHY

Sources (and Their Abbreviations)

Acta van de Nederlandsche synoden der zestiende eeuw, uitg. F. L. Rutgers, Utrecht 1889.

'Die Discipline ecclésiastique von 1559', in *RefBK*, vol. 2/1 (2009), p. 57-83 [= 'Discipline ecclésiastique'].

Livre synodal contenant les articles résolus dans les Synodes des Eglises wallonnes des Pays-Bas, éd. É. Bourlier, 2 vols, La Haye 1896-1904 [= *Livre synodal*].

Oude kerkordeningen der nederlandsche hervormde gemeenten (1563-1568), uitg. C. Hooijer, Zalt-Bommel 1865, p. 14-19 [= Hooijer, *Oude Kerkordeningen*].

'De Synoden der Nederlandsche Hervormde Kerken onder het Kruis, gedurende de jaren 1563-1577 gehouden in Braband, Vlaanderen enz.', uitg. N. C. Kist, in *Nederlandsch Archief voor Kerkelijke Geschiedenis* 9/20 (1849), p. 141-150 [= Kist, 'De Synoden der Nederlandsche Hervormde Kerken onder het Kruis'].

Tous les synodes nationaux des églises réformées de France..., éd. J. Aymon, 2 vols, La Haye 1710 [= Aymon, *Tous les synodes nationaux*].

Literature (and Its Abbreviations)

M. Backhouse, *The Flemish and Walloon Communities of Sandwich during the Reign of Elizabeth I, 1501-1603*, Brussel 1995 [= Backhouse, *The Flemish and Walloon Communities of Sandwich*].

G. Braghi, 'Between Paris and Geneva: Some Remarks on the Approval of the Gallican Confession (May 1559)', *Journal of Early Modern Christianity* 5 (2018), p. 197-219.

P. M. Crew, *Calvinist Preaching and Iconoclasm in the Netherlands, 1544-1569*, Cambridge 1978 [= Crew, *Calvinist Preaching and Iconoclasm*].

Dire l'interdit: The Vocabulary of Censure and Exclusion in the Early Modern Reformed Tradition, ed. R. A. Mentzer – F. Moreil – P. Chareyre, Leiden 2010.

T. Fehler, *Poor Relief and Protestantism. The Evolution of Social Welfare in Sixteenth-Century Emden*, Aldershot 1999 [= Fehler, *Poor Relief and Protestantism*].

N. H. Gootjes, *The Belgic Confession: Its History and Sources*, Grand Rapids (MI) 2007 [= Gootjes, *The Belgic Confession*].

Judging Faith, Punishing Sin: Inquisitions and Consistories in the Early Modern World, ed. C. H. Parker – G. Starr-Lebeau, Cambridge 2017.

F. R. J. Knetsch, 'Church Ordinances and Regulations of the Dutch Synods «Under the Cross» (1563-1566) compared with the French (1559-1563)', in J. Kirk (ed.), *Humanism and Reform: The Church in Europe, England, and Scotland, 1400-1643* (*Studies in Church History – Subsidia* 8), Oxford 1991, p. 187-203 [= Knetsch, 'Church Ordinances and Regulations'].

—, 'The National Synod of Dordrecht, 1578, and the Position of the Walloon Churches', in *The Low Countries Yearbook 1980 – Acta Historiae Neerlandicae XIII*, p. 40-50 [= Knetsch, 'The National Synod of Dordrecht'].

L'organisation et l'action des églises réformées de France (1557-1563). Synodes provinciaux et autres documents, éd. P. Benedict – N. Fornerod (*Travaux d'Humanisme et Renaissance* 504 / *Archives des Églises Réformées de France* 3), Genève 2012 [= *L'organisation et l'action des églises réformées*].

G. Marnef, *Antwerp in the Age of Reformation*: *Underground Protestantism in a Commercial Metropolis, 1550-1577*, Baltimore 1996 [= Marnef, *Antwerp in the Age of Reformation*].

—, 'The Changing Face of Calvinism in Antwerp, 1550-1585', in A. Pettegree – A. Duke – G. Lewis (eds), *Calvinism in Europe, 1540-1620*, Cambridge 1994, p. 143-158 [= Marnef, 'The Changing Face of Calvinism'].

G. Moreau, 'Les synodes des églises wallonnes des Pays-Bas en 1563', *Nederlands Archief voor Kerkgeschiedenis* 47 (1965), p. 1-11.

C. H. Parker, *The Reformation of Community: Social Welfare and Calvinist Charity in Holland, 1572-1620*, Cambridge 1998 [= Parker, *The Reformation of Community*].

A. Pettegree, *Emden and the Dutch Revolt*: *Exile and the Development of Reformed Protestantism*, Oxford 1992 [= Pettegree, *Emden and the Dutch Revolt*].

—, 'The Exile Churches and the Churches «Under the Cross»: Antwerp and Emden during the Dutch Revolt', *Journal of Ecclesiastical History* 38 (1987), p. 187-209 [= Pettegree, 'The Exile Churches'].

—, *Foreign Protestant Communities in Sixteenth-Century London*, Oxford 1986 [= Pettegree, *Foreign Protestant Communities*].

A. Spicer, '«*Le quatriesme ordre*»: The Diaconate in the French-Walloon Churches of London and Sandwich, c. 1568-1573', *Proceedings of the Huguenot Society of Great Britain and Ireland* 29 (2008), p. 1-13.

J. Spohnholz, *The Convent of Wesel. The Event that Never Was and the Invention of Tradition*, Cambridge 2017 [= Spohnholz, *The Convent of Wesel*].

G. S. Sunshine, *Reforming French Protestantism: The Development of Huguenot Ecclesiastical Institutions, 1557-1572*, Kirksville (MO) 2003 [= Sunshine, *Reforming French Protestantism*].

Monitum

Oude kerkordeningen der nederlandsche hervormde gemeenten (1563-1568), uitg. C. Hooijer, Zalt-Bommel 1865, p. 14-19.

CONCILIUM ANTVERPIANUM
1564

CONSPECTUS SIGLORUM

K   N. C. Kist (uitg.), 'De Synoden der Nederlandsche Hervormde Kerken onder het Kruis, gedurende de jaren 1563-1577 gehouden in Braband, Vlaanderen enz.', in *Nederlandsch Archief voor Kerkelijke Geschiedenis* 9/20 (1849), p. 141-150

N   É. Bourlier (éd.), *Livre synodal contenant les articles résolus dans les Synodes des Eglises wallonnes des Pays-Bas*, 2 vols, La Haye 1896-1904, vol. 1 (1896), p. 6-10

| DU SYNODE TENU A LA VIGNE, LE 1R DE MAY 1564.

1. En chaque Eglise ny faut avoir qu'un Consistoire, composé de Ministres, Diacres et Anciens exerceans fidelement leur charges, lesquels pourront appeler pour conseil telles gens que bon leur semblera quand l'affaire le requerra.

2. Nulle Eglise ne pourra pretendre primauté ni domination l'une sur l'autre, ni semblablement les Ministres les uns sur les autres, et notamment ceux qui sont d'une mesme Eglise, ni semblablement les Diacres et Anciens.

| 3. Les Ministres presideront par ordre en leur consistoire et conseil, afin que personne ne pretende superiorité sur son compagnon.

4. En chaque Synode sera esleu d'un commun accord un president pour recueillir les voix et declarer le plus grand nombre : prononcer la conclusion : faire que chacun parle par ordre et sans confusion : imposer silence à ceux qui sont trop aspres et contentieux : s'ils ne veulent obéir les faire sortir : adviser à la censure qui appartiendra : faire les remonstrances et les responses à ceux qui demandent conseil. On envoyera lettres durant le Synode selon l'advis d'iceluy et sera luy-mesmes sujet aux censures.

---

2 1] the same problem arose in France, where the habit of gathering two parallel consistories – the *consistoire de la police* for Church government *stricto sensu* and political affairs and the *consistoire de la censure* for the implementation of ecclesiastical discipline – was discouraged. See *L'organisation et l'action des églises réformées*, p. xxxii and lviii-lxiv; Sunshine, *Reforming French Protestantism*, p. 129-130   6 2] cfr 'Discipline ecclésiastique', p. 74 (Article 1). For discussion about the influence of French Reformed synods over the Dutch synods 'under the Cross', see Knetsch, 'Church Ordinances and Regulations'

2 chaque] chacune *N*   ny] ne *N*   quun] plus d'un *N*   3 exerceans] exercans *K N* leur] leurs *N*   6 ni] ne *N*   7 ni] ne *N*   9 consistoire et conseil] Consistoire et Conseil *N*   11/17 En – censures] En chacun Synode sera esleu d'un commun accord un president pour recueillir les voix et declarer le plus grand nombre, prononcer la conclusion, faire que chacun parle par ordre et sans confusion, imposer silence à ceux qui sont trop aspres et contentieux : s'ils ne veulent obeir les faire sortir, adviser à la censure qui appartiendra, faire les remonstrances et les responses à ceux qui demandent conseil, ou envoyeront lettres durant le Synode, suivant l'advis d'icelui, et sera lui-mesmes subiect aux censures *N*

648 CONCILIUM ANTVERPIANUM – 1564

5. Le ministre d'une Eglise ne pourra prescher en une autre sans le consentement du ministre d'icelle, et en son absence le Consistoire luy en pourra donner authorité, et si le troupeau estoit dispersé par persequution ou autres troubles, il taschera de r'assembler les Diacres et Anciens, ce que ne pouvant faire pourra prescher pour reünir le troupeau.

6. Nul pasteur ne pourra laisser son troupeau sans le congé de son Consistoire, ou sans avoir approbation des Eglises voisines de la cause de son partement. Toutefois sera bon d'admonester en ce cas les Eglises de subvenir aux choses necessaires de leur pasteur, qui, si le secours necessaire ne leur estoit donné apres la semonce faite, en ce cas leur sera loisible de s'allier à une autre Eglise.

7. Les nouveaux introduits en l'Eglise notamment les moines et prestres, ne pourront estre esleus au ministere sans longue et diligente inquisition et approbation tant de leur vie que de leur doctrine.

8. D'autant qu'il n'est licite ni expedient d'aller ouir les prescheurs Papistiques, ou autres qui se sont introduits sans legitime vocation es lieux, où il y a Ministere de la parole de Dieu dressé, pource doivent les vrays Pasteurs empescher ceux de leur troupeau d'y aller tant qu'il leur est possible.

9. Les ministres qui enseignent mauvaise doctrine, si apres avoir esté suffisamment admonestez ne desistent: item ceux qui n'obeiront aux Saintes

---

18 5] cfr 'Articles arrestés au Synode Provincial tenu à Teurs, le 26 d'Avril l'an 1563', in Hooijer, *Oude kerkordeningen*, p. 9: '23. Que nulle eschange de ministre ne soit faite sinon en temps de persequution ou necessité extreme, quand la personne du ministre seroit recherchée par les ennemis de la verité; ou que sa personne seroit dommageable au troupeau, et ce par le consentement mutuel des deux Eglises à qui la chose touchera; ou pour quelque autre raison de grand poids, de quoy le Synode pourra juger, les Eglises par commun consentement et accord pourront changer de ministre'. Cfr also 'Discipline ecclésiastique', p. 76 (Article 9) and 77 (Article 14) **23** 6] cfr 'Discipline ecclésiastique', p. 76 (Article 9) and 77 (Article 13) **34** Ministere – dressé] in the French Reformed tradition, an *église dressée* had an operational consistory, while an *église plantée* did not. See P. Wilcox, '«*Eglises plantées*» and «*Eglises dressées*» in the Historiography of Early French Protestantism', *Journal of Ecclesiastical History* 44 (1993), p. 689-695

---

18 ministre] Ministre *K N*   une] *a.c.* un   **19** ministre] Ministre *K N*   luy] lui *N*
20 persequution ou] persecutions et *N*   **21** taschera] tachera *N*   rassembler]
rassembler *N*   **22** reünir] reunir *N*   **23** pasteur] Pasteur *K N*   **24/25** partement.
Toutefois] partement, toutesfois *N*   **26** leur pasteur] leurs Pasteurs *N*   pasteur]
Pasteur *K*   **27** de s'allier à] s'allier en *N*   **30/31** et approbation] *deest N*   **32** Papistiques] papistiques *N*   **34** pource] pour ce *N*   vrays] vrais *N*   **35** est] sera *N*
36 ministres] Ministres *N*   **37** n'obeiront] n'obeissent *N*   Saintes] *a.c.* Stes; sainctes
N

CONCILIUM ANTVERPIANUM – 1564

admonitions puisées de la parole de Dieu, qui leur seront faites par le Consistoire; et ceux qui seront de vie scandaleuse, meritant punition du magistrat ou
40 excommunication: et ceux qui seront | totalement insuffisans et malpropres, 16 que leur ministere ne sera point à edification, seront depozez, exceptes ceux qui par viellesse ou maladies, ou autres tels inconveniens, seront rendus incapables d'administrer leurs charges: auquel cas l'honneur leur demeurera, et seront entretenus de leurs Eglises, lesquelles cependant seront pourveües d'un
45 autre qui fera leur charge.

10. Les Ministres ou autres de l'Eglise, ne pourront faire imprimer livres quelconques, ou autrement les publier, sans le communiquer à deux ou trois Ministres de la parole de Dieu non suspects.

11. L'office des Anciens sera d'assembler le peuple, r'apporter les scandales
50 au Consistoire, et autres choses semblables selon qu'un chacun advisera, et ce selon les circonstances, qu'ils visitent pour le moins tous les mois leurs quartiers, pour voir s'il n'y a nuls troubles ou bien povreté et mesnages. S'ils ne le font qu'ils soyent vivement repris du Consistoire.

12. Quant à l'office des Diacres, leur charge est de recueillir et distribuer
55 les deniers des povres, des prisonniers et des malades, les visiter, aller par les maisons les catechiser, et en cas qu'ils seront trouvez propres et capables, s'ils promettent de se dedier et consacrer entierement au service de Dieu et au ministere, alors pourront estre esleus par le Ministre et le Consistoire, pour catechiser en public selon la forme receüe en l'Eglise et ce pour estre plus
60 amplement esprouvez, sans qu'ils puissent administrer les Sacremens.

13. Les Diacres avant qu'assister les povres, les examineront de leurs foy, et ceux qui seront trouvez instruicts, avec leur famille, seront enregistrez et leur distribueront l'aumosne selon la faculté de l'Eglise.

14. S'ils ne sont instruicts qu'a demi et qu'il soyent pressez de grande
65 povreté, ils aviseront de les assister, mais non point si largement qui s'ils estoyent bien instruicts, et leur assigneront temps pour estre enseignez trois ou 4 mois, afin qu'ils soyent incitez par ce moyen à bien apprendre.

---

38 seront faictes] sont faictes *N*   **39** meritant] meritans *N*   magistrat] Magistrat *N*
41 depozez] deposez *K N*   exceptes] exceptez *K*; excepté *N*   **43** leurs charges] leur charges *K*; leur charge *N*   **46** ou] et *N*   **47** ou'] ni *N*   le] les *N*   **49** rapporter] rapporter *N*   **52** et] de *N*   **53** repris] reprins *N*   **55** les visiter] et les visiter *N*
58 le Ministre et le Consistoire] le Ministre et Consistoire *N*   **60** Sacremens] sacremens *N*   **61** leurs] leur *N*   **62** instruicts] instruits *N*   **64** qu'a demi] à demy *N*
67 4] quatre *N*

650 CONCILIUM ANTVERPIANUM – 1564

15. S'ils sont du tout ignorans avec leur faute, on leur baillera terme de 4 ou 5 mois, et que lors on leur promette assistance, n'est que la presente necessité les esmeuve à leur donner quelque chose.

16. Les autres pour descharger leur bourse aviseront de mettre au mestier les enfans de leurs povres, et les donner à gens fideles. Si | les maistres demandent quelques deniers pour leur apprentissage, et que la bourse n'y puisse subvenir, on advisera au lieu de l'argent de prolonger le temps de leur apprentissage.

17. Item ils adviseront sur les filles des povres fideles, afin de les colloquer es maisons des fideles, et quelles soyent instruictes à conduire un mesnage en la crainte de Dieu.

18. Les Diacres adviseront que nul de leurs povres qui sont enregistrez n'aillent mendier par la ville, sur peine d'estre privez de toute assistance.

19. Quant aux malades les Diacres les visiteront tant pour leur departir consolation spirituelle que corporelle.

20. Quant aux povres estrangers, qu'ils soyent examinez de leur foy, et par ce moyen on descouvrira s'ils sont vagabonds et affronteurs.

21. Que les Diacres taschent par tous moyens que les povres de leur charge soyent assistez des aumosnes communes des hospitaux, s'il se peut faire sans que Dieu soit offensé, cest à dire, sans se polluer en idolatrie et superstition.

22. Tant que faire se pourra, faut qu'en chacune Eglise soit dressée proposition selon la commodité des lieux et des personnes.

23. Quand quelque enfant sera presenté au Baptesme le père ou le parain le tiendra.

24. Touchant les noms qui sont imposez aux enfans, les ministres rejetteront tous ceux qui resteront du viel paganisme et n'imposeront aux enfans des noms attribuez à Dieu en l'Escriture Sainte ni pareillement les noms d'offices, comme Baptiste, Ange, Apostre, en adverteront et admonesteront les peres et parains de prendre des noms approuvez en l'Escriture Sainte autant qu'il sera possible.

---

68 baillera] donnera *N*   **68/69** 4 ou 5 mois] quatre ou cinq mois *N*   **69** presente] pressante *N*   **71** aviseront] adviseront *N*   **73** quelques] quelque *N*   **79** Les Diacres adviseront] Que les Diacres advisent *N*   nul] nuls *N*   **80** mendier] mandier *N*   **84** on descouvrira] on les descouvrira *N*   vagabonds] vagabonde *K*; vagabons *N*   **90** Baptesme] baptesme *N*   **92** ministres] Ministres *N*   rejetteront] reietteront *N*   **93** viel paganisme] viel paganisme ou payennerie *N*   des] les *N*   **94** en l'Escriture Sainte] es sainctes escritures *N*   Sainte] *a.c.* Ste   ni] ne *N*   d'offices] d'office *N*   **95** en] ou *N*   **96** l'Escriture Sainte] l'escriture saincte *N*   Sainte] *a.c.* Ste

CONCILIUM ANTVERPIANUM – 1564

25. Les ministres n'espouseront ceux qui sont purement papistes s'ils ne font protestation notamment de renoncer à la Messe et à toutes autres super-stitions, mesmes ores que le mari fut fidele et la femme infidele, cela ne sera receu sans protestation, afin de ne profaner l'acte et mesme la priere qui se fait.

26. On ne celebrera nuls mariages de personnes estrangeres au lieu où le mariage se fera, sans attestation de l'Eglise de laquelle ils sont partis.

27. Touchant les consanguinitez ou affinitez, les fideles ne pourront contracter mariage dont pourroit advenir scandale, dont l'Eglise cognoistra.

28. Les fideles qui auront leurs parties convaincues de paillardise seront admonestez de se reunir avec elles. S'ils ne le veuillent faire on leur declarera la liberté qu'ils ont par la parole de Dieu: mais les Eglises ne dissoudront point les mariages afin de n'entreprendre par dessus l'authorité des magistrats.

29. Les Eglises ne pourront marier les parties dissoutes, sinon avec l'obser-vation qui s'ensuit: Quant à la partie offensée et qui n'aura point failli, elle sera tenüe de poursuivre en jugement devant le magistrat la partie qui aura offensé, jusqu'à ce que par sentence definitive elle soit deüement convaincue, laquelle sentence la partie offensée fera apparoir au Consistoire donnant congé et permission de se marier: | lequel Consistoire apres avoir appelé les dites 18 parties, procedera à la permission. Et pour le regard de la partie qui a offensé, elle ne pourra estre receüe à se marier, devant que la partie offensée le soit, sinon qu'icelle, apres longtemps passé, declare ne se vouloir marier, alors l'Eglise pourra proceder au mariage de la partie qui aura offensé, apres avoir fait penitence publique, telle que le Consistoire jugera; et ce jusques à ce que les Eglises ayent plus grande liberté. Le semblable sera observé, en cas qu'il advint qu'apres les promesses de mariage faites et avant l'accomplissement du

---

98 25] only pastors were allowed to conduct marriages, and this had to be done before the assembly of the faithful, as had been decreed in Tournai in 1563. Cfr 'L'arrest du Synode du lieu de la Palme', in Hooijer, *Oude kerkordeningen*, p. 10 (Articles 4-5). It is interesting to note how several articles of this Church order focus on issues connected to marriage (Articles 25-31)

---

98 ministres] Ministres *N*   **99** Messe] messe *N*   autres] *deest N*   **100** mari] mary *N*   **102** nuls mariages] nul mariage *N*   **102/103** le mariage] le dit mariage *N*   **103** sont] seront *N*   **104** ou] et *N*   **105** dont pourroit advenir scandale] dont grand scandale en pourroit advenir *N*   **106** convaincues] conveincues *K*; convainques *N*   **107** elles] elle *N*   **109** magistrats] Magistrats *N*   **111** failli] faillie *N*   **112** jugement] iugement *N*   magistrat] Magistrat *N*   **113** jusqu'à] iusques à *N*   definitive] deffinitive *N*   convaincue] convainque *N*   **114** laquelle] de laquelle *N*   **114/116** la – permission] la partie fera apparoir au Consistoire, [qui] apres avoir appelé lesdites parties procedera à ladite permission *N*   **119** la] ladite *N*   **120** jusques] iusques *N*   **122** advint] advient *N*   faites] faictes *N*

CONCILIUM ANTVERPIANUM – 1564

dit mariage l'une des parties se trouve avoir paillardé, et que cela eust esté ignoré à l'autre partie promise.

125 30. Ceux qui auront habité ensemble avant qu'estre legitimement et solemnellement mariez, demandans à se marier, feront penitence publique ou devant le Consistoire selon la discretion d'iceluy et puis sera procedé au mariage, toutes les solemnitez requises observées, exceptez ceux qui auront habité ensemble pendant le temps de leur ignorance, ou bien qu'il n'y avoit
130 d'ordre d'Eglise dressé aux lieux de leur demeurances, lesquels seront seulement appelez au Consistoire afin que là leur mariage sera ratifié. Mais si quelques jeunes gens ont paillardé ensemble et desirent s'allier par mariage, moyennant le consentement de leurs parens et leurs fautes preallablement cognues avec promesses de se renger, ils seront receus au mariage, toutefois le
135 Consistoire jugera des circonstances.

31. Le mariage contracté par celuy qui aura laissé sa femme à cause de ladrerie, est nul et pourtant un tel ne doit estre receu à la Cene sans separation de sa seconde femme et aussi reparation du scandale publicq.

32. Que les consistoires soyent advertis de recueillir soigneusement les
140 memoires notables de leurs Eglises, et les envoyer au Synode Provincial.

33. Touchant les interests des argents a esté arresté que l'on se comporte en tout et par tout selon les edits du Roy, et qu'un chacun sur ce fait, ait esgard à la charité.

34. Ceux qui auront esté excommuniez viendront au Consistoire deman-
145 der d'estre reconciliez à l'Eglise, laquelle jugera lors de leur repentance, et s'ils

---

139 32] in France, an analogous historiographical endeavour helped shape Theodore Beza's *Histoire ecclésiastique*. Cfr M. Carbonnier-Burkard, 'L'*Histoire ecclésiastique des églises réformées*... : la construction bézienne d'un «corps d'histoire»', in I. Backus (éd.), *Théodore de Bèze (1519-1605). Actes du colloque de Genève (Septembre 2005) publiés par l'Institut d'histoire de la Réformation* (*Travaux d'Humanisme et Renaissance* 424), Genève 2007, p. 145-161; M. Greengrass, '«J'ay finalement essayé de réduire toutes ces pieces en un corps»: Historical Coherence and the Histoire Ecclésiastique des Eglises réformées de France (1580)', in P.-O. Léchot – H. Daussy – P. Benedict (eds), *L'identité huguenote. Faire mémoire et écrire l'histoire (XVIe-XXIe siècles)* (*Publications de l'Association suisse pour l'Histoire du refuge huguenot* 9), Genève 2014, p. 66-86

---

123 trouve] trouvera *N*　**126** solemnellement] solennellement *N*　**127** d'iceluy] d'icelui *N*　**128** solennitez] solennitez *N*　requises observées] requises et observees *N*　**129** ny] *a.c.* n'i　**130** d'ordre] ordre *K*　d'Eglise] de l'Eglise *N*　**132** jeunes] ieunes *N*　**133** preallablement] prealablement *N*　**134** cognues] recognues *N*　promesses] promesse *N*　renger] ranger *N*　toutefois] touteffois *N*　**135** jugera] iugera *N*　**137** un tel] *deest N*　doit] peut *N*　**138** publicq] public *N*　**140** memoires] *litteris cursivis excusus*; *in K quoque*　**141** les] des *N*　**145** jugera] iugera *N*

CONCILIUM ANTVERPIANUM – 1564

653

ont esté declarez excommuniez publiquement, ils feront penitence publique; s'ils n'ont point esté declarez publiquement, ils le feront seulement devant le consistoire.

35. Celuy qui est declaré heretique ou scismatique en une Eglise, sera aussi declaré tel aux autres; afin qu'on s'en donne garde.

36. Ceux qui auront fait abnegation ou persequution ne seront plus admis en l'Eglise, sinon en faisant penitence publique devant le peuple.

37 Quant aux ivrognes, pour la premiere fois, ils seront repris bien aigrement et rigoureusement; à la seconde fois ils recognoistront leur faute publiquement; à la troisieme fois seront suspendus de la Cene. S'ils persistent, seront du tout excommuniez.

38. Quant à ceux qui font mestier de se desborder en quelque vice notable, pour la premiere fois, on les ira reprendre pour les r'amener à bon chemin. S'ils persistent seront suspendus selon l'exigence du cas, de quoy le Consistoire jugera avec discretion.

| 39. Ceux qui oyent la parole n'estans point rangez, et se pollüent es idolatries ou commettent quelque autre faute, la premiere fois seront admonestez vivement; la seconde fois on le menacera de la privation de la parole; la troisieme on les suspendra tant qu'on y voye amendement.

40. On ne fera prieres ni predications à l'enterrement des morts, pour obvier à toutes superstitions. Quant aux convois que l'on peut faire es païs qui sont sous la tyrannie de l'Antichrist, ils se peuvent garder selon le contenu en l'Article 8 du Synode, tenu à la Vigne, à la St. Jean 1563.

41. Les imprimeurs, libraires, peintres et en general tous fideles, notamment ceux qui ont charge en l'Eglise sont admonestez de ne faire aucune chose de leur art ou estat qui despende des superstitions de l'Eglise Romaine, ou y

---

165 40] cfr 'Du Synode tenu à la Vigne à la St. Jean 1563', in Hooijer, *Oude kerkordeningen*, p. 14: '8. Quand il sera question de conduire quelque mort en terre il sera licite de s'y trouver, moyennant qu'il n'y ait nulles idolatries ni superstitions'

146 declarez] declarés *N*   **147** point] *deest N*   declarez] declarés *N*   le¹] la *N*
148 consistoire] Consistoire *N*   **149** Celuy] Celui *N*   scismatique] schysmatique *N*
151 ou persequution] en persecution *N*   **152** en faisant] qu'en faisant *N*
153 ivrognes] ivrongnes *K*; yvrognes *N*   **158** ira] pourra *N*   ramener] ramener *N*   à
bon chemin] au droict chemin *N*   **159** quoy] quoi *N*   **160** jugera] iugera *N*   **161** es]
aux *N*   **164** amendement] amandement *N*   **165** predications] predication *N*
167 tyrannie] tirannie *N*   **168** à la St. Jean 1563] à la Sᵗ Jean l'an 1563 *N*
169 imprimeurs] Imprimeurs *N*   libraires] Libraires *N*   peintres] Peintres *N*
notamment] notammant *N*   **170** ont] auront *N*   sont] seront *N*   **171** despende]
depende *N*

654 CONCILIUM ANTVERPIANUM – 1564

favorise et quant aux faits particuliers et à la correction qui sera necessaire, ce sera au Consistoire d'en juger.

42. Les fideles pourront estre adjurez par le Consistoire de dire verité de 175 ce qui leur sera demandé, d'autant que cela ne derogue rien à l'authorité du Magistrat.

43. Que les fideles ayent à fuir autant qu'en eux est toutes disputes et paroles pour le fait de la religion avec les Anabaptistes, ou autres heretiques : mais pour remedier à leur insuffisance ou simplicité, ils advertiront le Consis- 180 toire ou quelcun d'iceluy pour y donner ordre.

44. Nul ne peut amener personne es compagnies, si non du consentement pour le moins du Ministre ou de l'Ancien.

45. Les fideles seront admonestez tant hommes que femmes, d'avoir la modestie recommandée singulierement es habits, pour retrancher leur exces et 185 superfluitez qui se commettent ordinairement. Toutefois les Eglises ne feront ordonnances sur choses appartenantes au Magistrat, ains feront diligemment observer les ordonnances du Roy, et ne pourront lesdites Eglises excommunier, seulement pour quelque facon d'habits, laquelle seroit ordinaire et accoustu-mée en ce païs.

190   46. Les articles icy contenus selon la discipline Ecclesiastique, ne sont tellement arrestez entre nous, que si l'utilité de l'Eglise le requerroit ils ne puissent estre changez : mais ce ne sera en la puissance d'un particulier sans l'advis et consentement d'un Synode.

---

183 45] on this theme see among others G. Murdock, 'Dress, Nudity, and Calvinist Culture in Sixteenth-Century France', in C. Richardson (ed.), *Clothing Culture, 1350-1650*, Aldershot 2004, p. 125-138; G. Murdock, 'Dressed to Repress? Protestant Clergy Dress and the Regulation of Morality in Early Modern Europe', *Fashion Theory: The Journal of Dress, Body and Culture* 4 (2000), p. 179-199   **190** 46] cfr 'Discipline ecclésiastique', p. 82 (Article 40)

172 faits] faicts *N*   **173** juger] iuger *N*   **174** adjurez] adiurez *N*   **175** qui] qu'il *N* **178** religion] Religion *N*   **180** d'iceluy] d'icelui *N*   **181** Nul] Que nul *N*   es compagnies] aux Compagnies *N*   si non du consentement] si ce n'est du consentement *N*   **184** leur] tous *N*   **185** superfluitez] superfluités *N*   Toutefois] Touteffois *N*   **188** facon] façon *N*   d'habits] d'habit *N*   laquelle seroit] laquelle ne seroit *N*   **190** icy] ici *N*   **191** arrestez] arrestés *N*

CONCILIUM ANTVERPIANUM – 1564

47. Quant il sera question de faire d'un Diacre, un Ancien, l'élection en estant faite au Consistoire, il suffira d'en admonester le peuple avec remonstrance de sa suffisance et capacité audit office.

48. Il est licite et non point necessaire de faire les annonces au temple des papistes.

---

194 47] Article 47 seems to imply that the eldership was seen as a ministry wielding more authority and which brought more burdens than those required of deacons. In Nîmes, for example, the situation was reversed: see P. Chareyre, '«La fleur de tous les anciens» ou le ministère des diacres à Nîmes, XVIe-XVIIe siècles', in D. Poton – R. Mentzer (eds), *Agir pour l'église. Ministères et charges ecclésiastiques dans les églises réformées (XVIe-XIXe siècles)*, Paris 2013, p. 91-110

---

194 Quant] Quand *N*   **197** non] *deest N*   au temple] aux temples *N*

CONVENTUS VESALIENSIS ET SYNODUS EMBDANA

1568-1571

edidit
Henning P. JÜRGENS

THE CONVENT OF WESEL AND THE SYNOD OF EMDEN
1568-1571

INTRODUCTION

The assemblies of Wesel (1568) and Emden (1571) were synods in exile. Those in attendance belonged to the communities of Flemish and Walloon refugees who had settled in the neighbouring areas of the Netherlands. The resolutions laid out at Wesel and Emden became reference points both for these communities as well as for the future church in the Netherlands.

The anti-Reformation policy of the Habsburg authorities of the Spanish Netherlands triggered a constant flow of Protestant migrants since the 1540s. These tended to gather in the bordering areas of the Lower Rhine, the Palatinate, East Frisia, and England, establishing Reformed refugee communities. The ecclesiological ideas of the refugees found a first formulation in the *Forma ac ratio*, the church order of the congregation of London (1550-1553) by Johannes à Lasco and Marten Micron. ([1]) The temporary expulsion of Protestant refugees from England during the reign of Mary I (1553-1558) put an end to these initial attempts to organise. Most of the expellees were welcomed in East Frisia, Wesel, Cologne, Frankfurt, in the Palatinate, but also in Geneva, i.e. in the territories where other Dutch refugees had already settled. Once established, these émigrés exercised some degree of influence on the local congregations.

After a period of relative calm and the so-called 'miracle year' (*wonderjaar*) of 1566 in the Netherlands – which saw an explosive upswing in the Reformation movement – the number of migrants *religionis causa* increased considerably under the governorship of the duke of Alba and the beginning of the Dutch Revolt in 1568. ([2]) The resolutions of the Convent of Wesel and of the Synod of Emden laid the foundations for the independent organisation of these refugee communities, as well as of clandestine communities 'under the

---

([1]) A critical edition of the *Forma ac ratio* (1555) can be found in Kuyper, *Joannis a Lasco opera*, vol. 2, p. 1-274. On the forms and relevance of the church order of London, see Becker, *Gemeindeordnung und Kirchenzucht*.

([2]) van Schelven, *De nederduitsche vluchtelingenkerken der XVIe eeuw in Engeland en Duitschland*, p. 36, estimates the number of migrants at around 500,000.

660 CONVENTUS VESALIENSIS ET SYNODUS EMBDANA – 1568-1571

Cross' (3) that had remained in the Netherlands. This form of organisation was implemented in the hope of setting up a national church at the end of the Revolt. At the same time, it was necessary to preserve the theological unity of the churches, settle disputes, and strengthen ties with the Protestant movements of other countries.

THE CONVENT OF WESEL

The Convent of Wesel probably took place at Wesel (Lower Rhine) late in autumn 1568. The protocol of the meeting that has survived is dated: 'Actum Wesaliae 3° Novembris anni 1568'. The town of Wesel had provided shelter for Walloon émigrés as early as 1545. Following the expulsion of the English refugees in 1554, Wesel had temporarily taken in further groups of French- and English-speaking migrants. After the beginning of the governorship of the duke of Alba in 1567, several thousands of Flemish refugees came to the city, most of whom remained until 1577.

Nonetheless, the exact date and venue of the assembly remain unclear. In the absence of other sources confirming that the Convent did take place, the minutes are the only evidence of the meeting. It might have been held in the chapel of the former Augustinian convent of the town, but we have no sources to prove this was the case, and the building was destroyed during the Second World War. Due to these and other problematic issues, the Dutch researcher Jan Pieter van Dooren called into question the location of the Convent of Wesel, along with its 1568 dating. (4) Later scholarship, however, has reverted to the assumption that the assembly met in Wesel, although without the addition of any new evidence to support this conclusion. The most recent contribution to this debate, by historian Jesse Spohnholz, completely denies that the event took place and describes the reception of the Convent in later centuries as an 'invention of tradition'. (5)

---

(3) See the edition of the proceedings of the Convent of Wesel below, Chapter I, Article 3: '[...] postea quam Dominus Euangelii praedicationi ianuam in Belgio aperuerit' (see p. 676).

(4) van Dooren, 'Der Weseler Konvent'. Recently, this hypothesis has also been taken up by Pettegree, *Emden and the Dutch Revolt*, p. 136 and following; p. 177.

(5) In favour of the existence of the Convent of Wesel, although with a later date, see Boersma, *Vluchtig voorbeeld*, p. 197-206. On recent arguments on the accuracy of the dating, see Kipp, *Landstädtische Reformation*, p. 411-417. See Spohnholz, *The Convent of Wesel*, passim. In his earlier work, *The Tactics of Toleration* the author endorses the established hypothesis on the location of the assembly, but without explaining the reasons why: see *ibid.*, p. 73 and note 24.

The minutes offer no information on the duration of the negotiations: they do, however, register 63 signatories, among whom there were preachers and other members of the refugee communities in the Netherlands who had settled in the Lower Rhine, East Frisia, and England. Among others, we can find the names of Petrus Dathenus, preacher from the refugee congregation of Frankenthal, who is listed as president (*praeses*) of the gathering; Hermann Moded, preacher from the Norwich community, who is cited as *assessor*; and Cornelius Walraven, listed as *scriba*. The most prominent signatory, however, is the Dutch politician, scholar, and poet Philips van Marnix, lord of Saint-Aldegonde. Most of the signatories were preachers, but there were also politicians, jurists, and other elders from several communities. We have no indication that there were German participants, nor do the documents state that any representatives from the congregation of Wesel attended. Apparently, some of the signatures were only added after the meeting took place by persons who had not taken part in it. Other signatures were made on behalf of already-departed participants.

The resolutions of the Convent can be described as a set of recommendations aimed at the establishment of a consistorial-synodal church and congregational order. Taking up the models of the Genevan church order of John Calvin and the order of the London Refugee Church of Johannes à Lasco and Marten Micron as blueprints, efforts were made to develop an orderly and appropriate church system. The French Reformed *Discipline ecclésiastique* of 1559 was also taken into consideration.

The preserved original protocol consists of 26 pages and – after the naturalised counting of the first editions – 123 articles which are summarised in the original with headings in eight chapters. These are devoted to the classical-synodal order of the Church, the ministries of the congregation, the catechism, the sacraments, marriage issues, and ecclesiastical discipline in a not entirely systematic structure. For the first time in a Reformed church order, the Convent of Wesel established the institute of *classes* as an authority between the congregations and the provincial synods. This resulted in a four-stage construction of the church system. (6) The Convent's minutes are an in-depth assessment of the functioning of the congregation and of ecclesiastical discipline with a view to reinforcing the cohesion of refugee congregations and the congregations 'under the Cross'. At the same time, the proceedings

---

(6) Regarding the issue as to whether French congregations were divided into classes before Wesel, see Nijenhuis, 'The Synod of Emden, 1571', p. 120.

provide answers to controversial questions regarding fundamental issues raised by the congregations of Norwich and London. (7)

Due to its particular status, the Convent of Wesel is not to be understood as a Synod but rather as an assembly of a 'private character [...] to which, however, given its participants, should be attributed a high level of authority on specific issues'. (8) The proceedings of the Convent are characterised by wordings that appear tentative and hypothetical. The articles borrow freely from the *Forma ac ratio*, the church order of the refugee community of London, the Genevan *Ordonnances ecclésiastiques*, and the French *Confession de foi*, as well as from the ecclesiastical ordinances of the Palatinate. (9) The proceedings are full of formulas such as: it will be 'useful', 'meaningful', 'not absurd' or 'practical' to make certain arrangements. The title itself defines the regulations of the Convent as 'partim necessarios, partim utiles'.

Despite the situation of the refugee congregations and the congregations under persecution at that time, the articles include positive evaluations of the role of secular authorities in ecclesiastical matters. Provisional regulations are foreseen only for the time necessary to establish a godly – i.e. Reformed – rule in the Netherlands. The true intention of these provisions can be seen, for example, in the articles dealing with the assignment of pastors to parishes, the deacons, or matrimonial law, which again provide for the involvement of the authorities after a change in the political situation. (10)

THE SYNOD OF EMDEN

The Synod of Emden stands at the beginning of the series of synods of the Dutch Reformed Church. Even though this gathering did not define itself as a 'General Synod', its decisions later became church ordinances endowed with such legal efficacy (11) as to continue into our modern times. (12)

---

(7) See Goeters, 'Der Weseler Konvent', p. 104-108.

(8) Frost, 'Der Konvent von Wesel', p. 83 and following.

(9) Frost, 'Der Konvent von Wesel', p. 94.

(10) See the edition of the Convent of Wesel offered below: Chapter VII, Article 4; Chapter II, Article 3; Chapter V, Article 11; Chapter VIII, Article 22.

(11) See *Kerkorde van de Christelijke Gereformeerde Kerken in Nederland*. The *Gereformeerde Kerk in Nederland* (The Congregation of the Reformed Churches in the Netherlands) reunited under a new confederation in 2014, the *Protestantse Kerk in Nederland*.

(12) Nijenhuis, 'The Synod of Emden, 1571', p. 124: '[i]n the consciousness of the Netherland Reformed, the history of their synods begins with that of Emden. Although this assembly did not yet correspond to the norms for a general synod laid

The Synod was preceded by an invitation letter, sent from Heidelberg and dated 30 June 1571. It was signed by the Dutch preachers Petrus Dathenus, Johannes Taffin, and Petrus Colonius, and was addressed to several refugee congregations in Germany and the clandestine congregations in the Netherlands. The only surviving copy of the letter is the one addressed to the French-speaking community of Emden. ([13]) The document was more a general letter than a clear invitation as it was a reflection on the holding of a Synod. It contained a comprehensive theological argumentation and proposed a meeting before the winter on October 1 in Cologne. ([14]) The decision to hold a Synod was taken on the occasion of an assembly held in Bedburg-Reifferscheidt on 3-4 July 1571, where Philips van Marnix ([15]) was among the participants. Marnix, a confidant and counsellor of William of Orange, sent a letter from Bedburg to the Refugee Church of London, listing the issues to be examined in the context of the Synod. These included the unification of the Dutch congregations, the alignment with the Reformed congregations of France, and potentially an agreement with those churches in the Netherlands that abided by the *Confessio Augustana*. William of Orange harboured a political interest in this endeavour, hoping for an alliance with the Protestant princes of the Holy Roman Empire.

Two noble emissaries, Geerd van Kuilenburg and Willem van Zuylen van Nyeveldt, were sent from Bedburg to Wesel and Emden to investigate the possibility of holding a Synod in both towns and then to announce the place and time of the Synod to the congregations in England, the Netherlands, and Germany. Emden was chosen over Frankenthal and Siegen as it was easier to reach for the representatives from the English refugee churches. Furthermore, given that the Synod would take place at the same time as an important autumn market, it could take place without drawing much attention. Since the 1540s, Emden had become one of the most important destinations for Dutch religious émigrés. Due to this migratory flow, it had doubled its population. ([16]) The core of the refugee community from London also eventually

---

down by the convention at Wesel, from the beginning the content of its decisions possessed the strength of law in the Netherlands'.

(13) A facsimile of the letter is found in Evangelische-reformierte Kirche in Nordwestdeutschland (ed.), *Emder Synode 1571-1971. Beiträge zur Geschichte und zum 400jährigen Jubiläum*, Neukirchen-Vluyn 1973, illustrations 11-14, p. 54-55.

(14) On the letter, Weerda, 'Eine Einladung zur Emder Synode', p. 68-75. There is also a reproduction of the Latin text (p. 72-75). Weerda had found the writing in the archives of the French congregation in Emden.

(15) See Lomberg, 'Ursachen, Vorgeschichte, Verlauf und Auswirkungen', p. 21-23.

(16) On the significance of Emden, Pettegree, *Emden and the Dutch Revolt*, passim; Nauta, 'Emden toevluchtsoord van ballingen'.

settled in Emden following their expulsion from England in 1554. A separate, French-speaking congregation was established for the Walloon refugees who fled from persecution in England; however, most refugees spoke Dutch and were integrated with the local congregation in Emden, whose members spoke Low German. Separate institutions were founded for the so-called 'foreign poor' (17) in the context of the congregation's poor relief structures. After 1566, the number of refugees began to rise once again.

However, the support for the Synod by the local congregation of Emden and initially even by refugee groups from the Northern provinces was rather restrained. (18) Only three representatives from the French congregation and none from the Emden consistory are registered as participants. In the minutes of the Emden consistory the Synod finds practically no mention. This lacklustre response might be the reason why the Synod was postponed to October, as preparations had not been completed by the time the emissaries from the Palatinate had arrived. (19)

The Synod took place from 4 to 13 October 1571. It was held in the *Stadthalle* in Große Faldernstraße, the municipal arsenal that served as the meeting place for the French-speaking refugee congregation. The building was destroyed during the Second World War. Only 29 delegates took part, less than half of the signatories of the *Articles* of Wesel. The English refugee churches were not represented. Although the invitation of 24 July 1571 had arrived in London after some delays at the beginning of September, the representatives of the English congregations were forbidden from participating by the English government. The following representatives attended the Synod: Flemish and Walloon pastors from the Lower Rhine and the Palatinate, pastors from Holland who lived in Emden, and a handful pastors and deacons from certain congregations 'under the Cross'. (20) Seven among the participants had already signed the resolutions of the Convent of Wesel. The role of Synod's *praeses* was carried out by Caspar Heyden, a pastor from Frankenthal. Johannes Polyander, a pastor serving in the Walloon community of Emden, compiled the minutes as *scriba*. Johannes Taffin, the preacher of the Walloon congregation of Heidelberg, took part in the Synod as *assessor*. Taffin was the

---

(17) See Fehler, *Poor Relief and Protestantism*.

(18) Weerda, 'Eine Einladung zur Emder Synode', p. 72; For background, Pettegree, *Emden and the Dutch Revolt*, p. 178-183.

(19) *Die Kirchenratsprotokolle der Reformierten Gemeinde Emden*, vol. 1; van Meer, *De Synode te Emden*, p. 137-141; Woltjer, 'De politieke betekenis van de Emdense synode', p. 46-49.

(20) A complete list of the participants as well as their biographies can be found in van Dooren, 'Teilnehmerliste der Emder Synode von 1571'.

only one of three signatories of the invitation to attend the Synod. Dathenus and Colonius had been prohibited from attending by the civil authorities of the Palatinate. Marnix was also presumably not in attendance. ([21])

Very little is known about the negotiations and discussions that occurred during these ten days. The resolutions were recorded in the Synod's proceedings and signed by the participants. Decisions were divided into 53 'Generalia' articles, 25 'Particularia' articles, and 26 articles on the synodal-classical church ordinances. The 53 general articles were undersigned on 12 October and the remaining were signed the following day. Two of the framing 'Generalia' articles are particularly characteristic of the tenor of the resolutions. Article 1 establishes that there should be no primacy or control and no rule of one congregation over another, of a preacher, elder or deacon over another, and that any appearance thereof shall be avoided. This clear anti-hierarchical opening corresponds with a rejection of independentist approaches at the end, when it is said that the preceding articles have been drawn up 'mutuo consensu'. The articles could be subject to modifications and amendments, but not by authority of a single congregation ('privata ecclesia'). The form of the resolutions had to be respected unless a synod (or multiple synods) agreed to update them.

Regarding the necessity of a shared doctrinal statement, the Synod adhered both to the *Confessio Belgica* and the *Confessio Gallicana*. In doing so, it expressed its agreement with the French Reformed Church in faith and doctrine. In order not to leave this relationship based on unilateralism, two pastors were instructed to give notice of this decision at the following national Synod of the Reformed Churches of France and report its answer at the following planned meeting. ([22]) The signing of the *Confessio Belgica* was also expected of the pastors who did not attend the Synod of Emden, as well as of all newly-appointed pastors. This underlying confessional orientation was also displayed in the articles on catechisms, where the use of the *Genevan Catechism* was recommended for the French-speaking congregations; on the other hand, the *Heidelberg Catechism* was selected for German- and Dutch-speaking congregations. Nonetheless, local churches were free to adopt other catechisms as long as they adhered to the Word of God.

---

(21) van Dooren, 'Teilnehmerliste der Emder Synode von 1571', p. 36. Van Dooren holds that the participation of the three was 'quite improbable'. Confirmation is also found in the text of articles 48, 49, and 50, where Marnix is directed to draft a history of the Church of the Netherlands.

(22) Johannes Taffinus and – in his absence – Petrus Dathenus were entrusted with this responsibility. The recognition of the *Confessio Belgica* by the French Reformed churches was officialised on the occasion of the national Synod of Figeac (1579).

In this context, it is interesting to note that William of Orange's clearly-expressed support for an openness towards the *Confessio Augustana* did not find fertile ground in the Synod's participants. (23) This refusal led to unpleasant political consequences for William. On the other hand, the Emden resolutions are relatively broad in ceremonial and other matters. In order to defuse disputes, various liturgical practices were exempted as *adiaphora*. (24) The 25 'Particularia' articles are further proof of an effort to bring balance. These articles answer to requests expressed by individual congregations. Some questions of a fundamental nature, such as how to achieve a correct translation of the Bible into Dutch, were postponed to a later Synod.

On the occasion of the first Synod of the Provinces of Holland and Zeeland, held 15-28 June 1574 in Dordrecht, the minutes of the Synod of Emden – often referred to during synodal works – were read out loud to the delegates. (25) As had occurred in Emden, Gaspar Heydanus assumed the role of *praeses*. Thus, the resolutions of the Synod of Emden entered conclusively into the statutes of the Dutch Reformed Churches. Moreover, at the national Synod of 1578 (also held in Dordrecht), the Emden resolutions were once again approved. Article 102 – the last of the general articles in the proceedings – includes the verbatim translation into Dutch of the first article of Emden. (26)

Given these considerations, it is difficult to frame the relationship between the Convent of Wesel and the Synod of Emden. The articles of Wesel were not mentioned in Emden, nor were they mentioned in later synods. Dutch scholars have examined the relationship between these two assemblies in great depth. Beginning with the research of Doede Nauta, (27) the idea that there is no objective opposition between Wesel and Emden was established. (28) The current consensus is that the Synod of Emden followed up on the elaborations and perspectives that had emerged at Wesel without any

---

(23) See de Jong, 'Die Emder Generalsynode', p. 20.

(24) See Hovius, *Notities betreffende de Synode te Emden*, p. 29-31. The fact that certain issues (not merely of a ceremonial nature) were defined as *adiaphora* shows that the Synod of Emden did not consider church discipline from a mainly juridical point of view, but rather from a pastoral one.

(25) Rutgers, *Acta van de Nederlandsche Synoden der zestiende eeuw*, p. 134 and passim until p. 220.

(26) Rutgers, *Acta van de Nederlandsche Synoden der zestiende eeuw*, p. 261.

(27) See Nauta, 'Wezel (1568) en Emden (1571)', reprinted in Nauta, *Opera minora. Kerkhistorische verhandelingen over Calvijn en de geschiedenis van de kerk in Nederland*, Kampen 1961, p. 30-56, with an in-depth examination of less recent studies. See also Dankbaar, 'Von Wesel (1568) bis Dordrecht (1618/1619)', p. 74 for a similar stance.

(28) Unlike other Dutch scholars, Goeters, 'Der Weseler Konvent', p. 90 and following, downplays Wesel's relevance.

specific, official reference to it. ([29]) In the forty years following the commemoration of the four-hundredth anniversary of the two assemblies, the two assemblies have received relatively scarce scholarly attention.

NOTES ON THE EDITIONS

The text of the (or one) original Latin protocol of the Convent of Wesel is located in the Synodaal Archief of the Nederlands Hervormde Kerk Den Haag, in the *fonds* 1401 of the Oud Synodaal Archief. This archive is now held in the Het Utrechts Archief, Utrecht. In 1889, Rutgers edited the text for the first time. Goeters published on the occasion of the four-hundredth anniversary in 1968 an edition with a photographic reproduction of the original and a normalised version (the nouns' upper and lower cases as well as *u/v* and *i/j* spelling and punctuation). The text presented here reproduces the original. The sections' numbering follows the one used in both former editions, which has established itself as a convention, even if it is not in the original protocol.

As per the Synod of Emden, the original Latin protocol of 1571 has disappeared without trace since the seventeenth century, but various copies have survived. Again, previous editions by Rutgers (1889) and Goeters (1971) are available. In contrast to the former edition, the latter differs in the spelling of some place names, normalises all nouns except for the proper names to lower case, reproduces *u* and *v* according to their phonetic value, and sets the punctuation marks according to German rules. Goeters used a large number of sources for his edition and ultimately edited a hybrid text based primarily on the slightly more recent manuscripts held in Arnhem, Amsterdam, and Utrecht. Thus, the text offered here follows the edition by Goeters and tacitly reproduces the emendations made, none of which resulted in significant changes of the text.

The text of this introduction was written in 2012 and revised in October 2018. All literature published after that date, especially on the occasion of the 450th anniversary of the Synod of Emden in October 2021, has not been included.

---

(29) Frost, 'Der Konvent von Wesel', p. 98-99.

BIBLIOGRAPHY

SOURCES (AND THEIR ABBREVIATIONS)

Acta van de Nederlandsche Synoden der zestiende eeuw (*Werken der Marnix-Vereeniging* II/3), uitg. F. L. Rutgers, Utrecht 1889 [= Rutgers, *Acta van de Nederlandsche Synoden der zestiende eeuw*].

Die Akten der Synode der Niederländischen Kirchen zu Emden. Vom 4.–13. Oktober 1571. Im lateinischen Grundtext mitsamt der alten niederländischen, französischen und deutschen Übersetzung, hrsg. J. F. G. Goeters (*Beiträge zur Geschichte und Lehre der reformierten Kirche* 34), Neukirchen-Vluyn 1971 [= Goeters, *Die Akten der Synode zu Emden 1571*].

Die Beschlüsse des Weseler Konvents von 1568, hrsg. J. F. G. Goeters (*Schriftenreihe des Vereins für Rheinische Kirchengeschichte* 30), Düsseldorf 1968 [= Goeters, *Die Beschlüsse des Weseler Konvents von 1568*].

Die evangelischen Kirchenordnungen des XVI. Jahrhunderts, hrsg. E. Sehling et al., 24 vols, Leipzig – Tübingen 1902-2017. [= *EKO*].

Joannis a Lasco opera tam edita quam inedita duobus voluminibus comprehensa, ed. A. Kuyper, 2 vols, Amsterdam 1866 [= Kuyper, *Joannis a Lasco opera*].

Kerkorde van de Christelijke Gereformeerde Kerken in Nederland. Vastgesteld en gewijzigd door de synoden van Emden (1571), Dordrecht (1574), Dordrecht (1578), Middelburg (1581), 's-Gravenhage (1586), Dordrecht (1619), Amsterdam (1840) en Utrecht (1947), met enige synodale besluiten, het laatst gewijzigd en aangevuld door de synode van Haarlem-Noord (1998), uitg. Deputaten voor de uitgave van de Kerkorde van de Christelijke Gereformeerde Kerken in Nederland, Amsterdam 1999 [= *Kerkorde van de Christelijke Gereformeerde Kerken in Nederland*].

Die Kirchenratsprotokolle der Reformierten Gemeinde Emden, 1557-1620, hrsg. H. Schilling – K.-D. Schreiber (*Städteforschung* C3, 1/2), Köln 1989-1992 [= *Die Kirchenratsprotokolle der Reformierten Gemeinde Emden*].

LITERATURE (AND ITS ABBREVIATIONS)

J. Becker, *Gemeindeordnung und Kirchenzucht. Johannes a Lascos Kirchenordnung für London (1555) und die reformierte Konfessionsbildung* (*Studies in Medieval and Reformation Traditions* 122), Leiden 2007 [= Becker, *Gemeindeordnung und Kirchenzucht*].

CONVENTUS VESALIENSIS ET SYNODUS EMBDANA – 1568-1571   669

O. Boersma, *Vluchtig voorbeeld. De nederlandse, franse en italiaanse vluchtelingenkerken in Londen, 1568-1585*, Diss. Theol., Kampen 1994 [= Boersma, *Vluchtig voorbeeld*].

W. F. Dankbaar, 'Von Wesel (1568) bis Dordrecht (1618/1619)', in *Weseler Konvent 1568-1968. Eine Jubiläumsschrift (Schriftenreihe des Vereins für Rheinische Kirchengeschichte* 29), Düsseldorf 1968, p. 73-87 [= Dankbaar, 'Von Wesel (1568) bis Dordrecht (1618/1619)'].

J. P. van Dooren, 'Der Weseler Konvent von 1568. Neuere Forschungsergebnisse', *Monatshefte für Evangelische Kirchengeschichte des Rheinlands* 31 (1982), p. 41-55 [= van Dooren, 'Der Weseler Konvent'].

—, 'Teilnehmerliste der Emder Synode von 1571', in Evangelische-reformierte Kirche in Nordwestdeutschland (ed.), *Emder Synode 1571-1971. Beiträge zur Geschichte und zum 400jährigen Jubiläum*, Neukirchen-Vluyn 1973, p. 36-44 [= 'Teilnehmerliste der Emder Synode von 1571'].

—, 'Voorbereiding en deelnemers', in D. Nauta (ed.), *De Synode van Emden, oktober 1571. Een bundel opstellen ter gelegenheid van de vierhonderdjarige herdenking*, Kampen 1971, p. 75-87 [= van Dooren, 'Voorbereiding en deelnemers'].

T. G. Fehler, *Poor Relief and Protestantism. The Evolution of Social Welfare in Sixteenth-Century Emden (St Andrews Studies in Reformation History* XX), Aldershot 1999 [= Fehler, *Poor Relief and Protestantism*].

H. Frost, 'Der Konvent von Wesel im Jahre 1568 und sein Einfluß auf das Entstehen eines deutschen evangelischen Kirchenverfassungsrechts', in M. Baldus (ed.), *Ausgewählte Schriften zum Staats- und Kirchenrecht (Ius ecclesiasticum* 65), Tübingen 2001, p. 63-115 [= Frost, 'Der Konvent von Wesel'].

—, 'Gedanken über das reformierte Kirchenverfassungsrecht am Niederrhein zwischen Emden (1571) und Duisburg (1610)', in M. Baldus (ed.), *Ausgewählte Schriften zum Staats- und Kirchenrecht (Ius ecclesiasticum* 65), Tübingen 2001, p. 116-173.

J. F. G. Goeters, 'Der Weseler Konvent niederländischer Flüchtlinge vom 3. November 1568', in *Weseler Konvent 1568-1968. Eine Jubiläumsschrift (Schriftenreihe des Vereins für Rheinische Kirchengeschichte* 29), Düsseldorf 1968, p. 88-114 [= Goeters, 'Der Weseler Konvent'].

—, 'Die Emder Synode von 1971', in Evangelische-reformierte Kirche in Nordwestdeutschland (ed.), *Emder Synode 1571-1971. Beiträge zur Geschichte und zum 400jährigen Jubiläum*, Neukirchen-Vluyn 1973, p. 183-202.

670   CONVENTUS VESALIENSIS ET SYNODUS EMBDANA – 1568-1571

—, *Studien zur niederrheinischen Reformationsgeschichte (Schriftenreihe des Vereins für Rheinische Kirchengeschichte* 153), Köln 2002.

H. von Hoffmann, *Das Kirchenverfassungsrecht der Niederländischen Reformierten Kirche bis zum Beginne der Dordrechter Nationalsynode von 1618/1619*, Leipzig 1902.

J. Hovius, *Notities betreffende de Synode te Emden, 1571, en haar artikelen (Apeldoornse Studies* 4), Kampen 1972 [= Hovius, *Notities betreffende de Synode te Emden*].

J. de Jong, *De voorbereiding en constitueering van het kerkverband der Nederlandsche Gereformeerde Kerken in de zestiende eeuw. Historische studiën over het Convent te Wezel (1568) en de Synode te Emden (1571), eerste gedeelte*, Groningen 1911.

O. J. de Jong, 'Die Emder Generalsynode vor dem Hintergrund der westeuropäischen Reformationsgeschichte', *Jahrbuch der Gesellschaft für niedersächsische Kirchengeschichte* 68 (1970), p. 9-24 [= de Jong, 'Die Emder Generalsynode'].

H. Kipp, *«Trachtet zuerst nach dem Reich Gottes». Landstädtische Reformation und Rats-Konfessionalisierung in Wesel (1520-1600) (Schriften der Heresbach-Stiftung Kalkar* 12), Bielefeld 2004 [= Kipp, *Landstädtische Reformation*].

J. Lindeboom, 'Het voorloopig Karakter der Synode te Emden', *Nederlandsch Archief voor Kerkgeschiedenis* 35 (1946-1947), p. 1-14.

E. Lomberg, 'Ursachen, Vorgeschichte, Verlauf und Auswirkungen der Emder Synode von 1571', in Evangelische-reformierte Kirche in Nordwestdeutschland (ed.), *Emder Synode 1571-1971. Beiträge zur Geschichte und zum 400jährigen Jubiläum*, Neukirchen-Vluyn 1973, p. 7-35 [= Lomberg, 'Ursachen, Vorgeschichte, Verlauf und Auswirkungen'].

B. van Meer, *De Synode te Emden, 1571*. Dissertation University of Amsterdam 1892, 's-Gravenhage 1892 [= van Meer, *De Synode te Emden*].

D. Nauta, 'Emden toevluchtsoord van ballingen', in D. Nauta et al. (ed.), *De Synode van Emden, oktober 1571. Een bundel opstellen ter gelegenheid van de vierhonderdjarige herdenking*, Kampen 1971, p. 7-21 [= Nauta, 'Emden toevluchtsoord van ballingen'].

—, 'Der Konvent von Wesel in seinem Verhältnis zu Genf', in *Weseler Konvent 1568-1968. Eine Jubiläumsschrift (Schriftenreihe des Vereins für Rheinische Kirchengeschichte* 29), Düsseldorf 1968, p. 60-72.

—, 'Wezel (1568) en Emden (1571)', in *Nederlandsch Archief voor Kerkgeschiedenis NF* 36 (1948), p. 220-246 [= Nauta, 'Wezel (1568) en Emden (1571)'].

W. H. Neuser, 'Die Aufnahme der Flüchtlinge aus England in Wesel (1553) und ihre Ausweisung trotz der Vermittlung Calvins und Melanchthons (1556/1557)', in *Weseler Konvent 1568-1968. Eine Jubiläumsschrift* (*Schriftenreihe des Vereins für Rheinische Kirchengeschichte* 29), Düsseldorf 1968, p. 28-49.

W. Nijenhuis, 'The Synod of Emden, 1571', in W. Nijenhuis (ed.), *Ecclesia reformata. Studies on the Reformation* (*Kerkhistorische bijdragen* 16), 2 vols, Leiden 1994, vol. 2, p. 101-124 [= Nijenhuis, 'The Synod of Emden, 1571'].

A. Pettegree, *Emden and the Dutch Revolt. Exile and the Development of Reformed Protestantism*, Oxford 1992 [= Pettegree, *Emden and the Dutch Revolt*].

J. Plomp, 'De kerkorde van Emden', in D. Nauta et al. (ed.), *De Synode van Emden, oktober 1571. Een bundel opstellen ter gelegenheid van de vierhonderdjarige herdenking*, Kampen 1971, p. 88-120.

A. A. van Schelven, *De nederduitsche vluchtelingenkerken der XVIe eeuw in Engeland en Duitschland. In hunne beteekenis voor de Reformatie in de Nederlanden*, 's-Gravenhage 1909 [= van Schelven, *De nederduitsche vluchtelingenkerken der XVIe eeuw in Engeland en Duitschland*].

H. Schilling, 'Die niederländischen Exulanten des 16. Jahrhunderts. Ein Beitrag zum Typus der frühneuzeitlichen Konfessionsmigration', *Geschichte in Wissenschaft und Unterricht* 43 (1992), p. 67-78.

W. van 't Spijker, 'Stromingen onder de reformatorisch gezinden te Emden', in D. Nauta et al. (ed.), *De Synode van Emden, oktober 1571. Een bundel opstellen ter gelegenheid van de vierhonderdjarige herdenking*, Kampen 1971, p. 50-74.

J. A. Spohnholz, *The Convent of Wesel. The Event that Never was and the Invention of Tradition*, Cambridge 2018 [= Spohnholz, *The Convent of Wesel*].

—, *The Tactics of Toleration. A Refugee Community in the Age of Religious Wars*, Newark 2011 [= Spohnholz, *The Tactics of Toleration*].

—, 'Olympias and Chrysostom. The Debate over Wesel's Reformed Deaconess, 1568-1609', *Archiv für Reformationsgeschichte* 98 (2007), p. 84-106 [= Spohnholz, 'Olympias and Chrysostom'].

672 CONVENTUS VESALIENSIS ET SYNODUS EMBDANA – 1568-1571

A. Sprengler-Ruppenthal, *Mysterium und Riten. Nach der Londoner Kirchenordnung der Niederländer (ca. 1550 bis 1566)*, Köln 1967.

J. R. Weerda, 'Eine Einladung zur Emder Synode', in A. Sprengler-Ruppenthal (ed.), *Nach Gottes Wort reformierte Kirche. Beiträge zu ihrer Geschichte und ihrem Recht*, München 1964, p. 68-75 [= Weerda, 'Eine Einladung zur Emder Synode'].

A. Wolters, *Reformationsgeschichte der Stadt Wesel, bis zur Befestigung ihres reformirten Bekenntnisses durch die Weseler Synode*, Bonn 1868 [= Wolters, *Reformationsgeschichte der Stadt Wesel*].

J. J. Woltjer, 'De politieke betekenis van de Emdense synode', in D. Nauta et al. (ed.), *De Synode van Emden, oktober 1571. Een bundel opstellen ter gelegenheid van de vierhonderdjarige herdenking*, Kampen 1971, p. 22-49 [= Woltjer, 'De politieke betekenis van de Emdense synode'].

MONITUM

CONVENTUS VESALIENSIS

Oud Synodaal Archief, *fonds* 1401, Synodaal Archief, Nederlands Hervormde Kerk Den Haag, Het Utrechts Archief, Utrecht, fol. 1-26.

SYNODUS EMBDANA

Die Akten der Synode der Niederländischen Kirchen zu Emden. Vom 4.–13. Oktober 1571. Im lateinischen Grundtext mitsamt der alten niederländischen, französischen und deutschen Übersetzung, ed. J. F. G. Goeters (*Beiträge zur Geschichte und Lehre der reformierten Kirche* 34), Neukirchen-Vluyn 1971, p. 14-88.

CONVENTUS VESALIENSIS
1568

| CERTA QUAEDAM CAPITA SEU ARTICULI QUOS IN MINISTERIO ECCLESIAE BELGICAE MINISTRI EIUSDEM ECCLESIAE PARTIM NECESSARIOS PARTIM VTILES ESSE IUDICARUNT.

Praecipit apostolus Paulus vt in ecclesia Dei omnia fiant ordine et decenter: quò non modò vnanimis ecclesiae in doctrina, verum etiam in ipso ordine et politica ministerii gubernatione constet ac habeatur consensus. Vt autem earum rerum consimilis ratio in omnibus Belgicis ecclesiis seruari possit, visum fuit haec subsequentia capita, de quibus apud optimè reformatas ecclesias consultatum est, ordine proponere, quò ad salutarem ecclesiae fructum à Belgii ministris vnanimi consensus et obsignentur et obseruentur.

[Cap. I.]
De Collegiis ac prouinciarum Classibus.

I.

Quandoquidem et ad constituendas ritè ecclesias inprimis erit necessarium summam ac praecipuam adhiberi curam vt pii, docti et in Scripturarum cognitione praestantes viri qui verbum Dei rectè norint secare ecclesiis praeficiantur ministri ac pastores, ei rei linguarum disciplinarumque cognitionem, ac explicandarum Scripturarum assiduas exercitationes (quas propositiones siue prophetias vocant) maximè conducere nemo ambigit. Et illis porro constitutis ad vnum omnium consensum tum in doctrina, tum in ceremoniarum ac disciplinae ratione, quoad eius fieri potest, ineundum retinendumque, omnino expediet frequentes vicinarum ecclesiarum conuentus institui, ad quos de singulis rebus referatur.

---

17 qui – secare] cfr II Tim. 2, 15

5 Praecipit – Paulus] *in marg.* I. Cor. 14,40

676 CONVENTUS VESALIENSIS – 1568

25 2.

Ideo putamus quidem ante omnia laborandum vt et Collegia disciplina-
rum instituantur, in quibus doceantur tres linguae, ac imprimis theologiae
syncera professio diligensque exercitatio vigeat. Et simul Belgiae singulae
prouinciae in certas ac ratas classes seu paroecias distribuantur: quò cuique
30 ecclesiae constare possit, cum quibus grauiora quaeque negocia quae ad publicam vtilitatem spectare videbuntur ei sint conferenda consultandaque.

3.

Sed quia hoc tempore de istiusmodi rebus necdum quicquam decerni
potest, antequam ipse vsus rerumque experientia docuerit quae loca quibusque
35 rebus futura sint maximè accommoda, Propterea existimamus postea quam
Dominus Euangelii praedicationi ianuam in Belgio aperuerit, tum primo quoque tempore omnibus ecclesiis ecclesiarumque Ministris omni studio fore
enitendum vt ad cogendam Synodum prouincialem totius Belgii nummi in
commune conferantur: quò possit legitima Synodo statui quid in iis aliisque
40 rebus omnibus ad communem ecclesiarum constitutionem ordinisque quàm
pulcherrimi obseruationem sequendum erit.

| 4.   2

Ad eam putamus esse referendum de Collegiorum institutione, Doctorum honorariis, munere, authoritate, Scholarum exercitiis, Theologicis profes-
45 sionibus, propositionum prophetiarumque obseruationibus, coeterisque
omnibus ad eam rem pertinentibus.

5.

Ac item de prouinciarum rata et aequabili per classes seu paroecias dis-
tributione, de singularum classium sigillatim atque omnium vniuersim ratis
50 conuentibus, eorundemque ordine, ratione, authoritate, censura:

---

25 2.] the establishment of a division in *classes* is explicitly mentioned here for the first
time in Reformed constitutional law. It is however questionable whether such classical
synods were held in an unofficial capacity before Wesel took place. See Frost, 'Der
Konvent von Wesel', p. 94-95. The partition of the Dutch communities *sub cruce* and
other refugee communities into *classes* took place at the Synod of Emden (Articles
10-12) **42/57** 4. – consentaneum] cfr Synod of Emden, Articles 7-9

CONVENTUS VESALIENSIS – 1568

6.

ac deinceps de causis matrimoniorum, de rationibus diuortiorum, ac denique de omnibus omnino rebus, quae ad omnes ecclesias et commune ministerium generatim spectant. Nam quae omnes pariter attingunt, ea vel
55 hoc tempore vel posthac per vnam aliquam aut alteram statui ecclesiam non adhibito coeterarum ecclesiarum, ad quas peraequè spectant calculo, neque authoritati Scripturae nec aequitati legum est consentaneum.

7.

Sin autem eiusmodi Synodus vel rerum vel temporum difficultate iniri
60 omnino non poterit, tum censemus, ex praecipuis quibusque prouinciarum ecclesiis praestantissimos aliquot viros fore deligendos, qui tum distribuendarum Classium tum Collegii instituendi, coeterorumque difficilium negociorum explicandorum, ac totius denique ecclesiae constituendae rationem quam optimam, primum quidem pro se singuli aut, si videbitur bini, aut terni quique
65 perscribant: deinde vero in commune conferant, et certam aliquam ex omnibus formulam concipiant, quae singularum atque omnium ecclesiarum calculo vel approbetur, vel si quid erit correctione dignum, communi consensus corrigatur, ac in meliorem formam reducatur.

8.

70 Interea autem temporis quandoquidem patefacta Dei beneficio Euangelii ianua cunctationi locus non erit, et tamen ordo aliquis ac decor in commune debebit obseruari quo tanquam vinculo ecclesiarum communis consensus retineatur, videtur aliqua esse ineunda ac certis capitibus consignanda ratio; quam pro se quisque in ea cui praefectus erit, ecclesia tantisper sequatur, donec
75 coacta Synodo rectius aliquid atque perfectius constitutum fuerit.

9.

Haec autem visa est nobis quàm proximè accedere tum ad Apostolorum doctrinam constitutionemque, tum ad vetustioris puriorisque ecclesiae exemplar inculpatum: vt primum quidem in iis omnibus rerum circumstantiis,
80 quae, cum | natura sint adiaphorae, neque in Apostolorum doctrina exemplo- 3 que certum habent fundamentum, nec denique necessariam aliquam atque ineuitabilem rationem, tum ad declinandam conscientiarum tyrannidem, tum ad omnes dissentionum ansas praecidendas, nulla praescripta formula ecclesiarum libertas constringatur; sed liceat id cuique sequi quod res et vsus

678   CONVENTUS VESALIENSIS – 1568

85 quemque docuerit esse conuenientissimum. Atque id quidem donec Synodo prouinciali certi quippiam in huiusmodi rebus sancitum fuerit.

10.

Eiusmodi videntur esse, in baptismi quidem administratione semel aut bis aut ter tingendi baptizati discrimen, Idque num vel ante concionem vel post
90 fiat, Ascitisue certis testibus an commissa parentibus ac toti ecclesiae baptizatorum cura. In coenae vero celebratione num mensae accumbatur, an stando eundoue panis calixque porrigantur. An lectio Scripturarum an psalmorum cantus dum coena fit instituatur, et si quae alia sunt eiusmodi (de quorum libero vsu populum rudiorem diligenter, si ita res postulat, instituent) quae nisi
95 certis et grauissimis de causis, iisque totius prouinciae consensu approbatis, à cuiusque ecclesiae arbitrio remoueri minime debent.

11.

Quae vero alterius sunt generis vt vel in Dei verbo vel in Apostolorum vsu atque exemplo, vel in ecclesiarum perpetua, eaque grauibus ac necessariis
100 rationibus subnixa consuetudine fundata sunt, in iis non temerè a communi ecclesiarum consensu ac inueterato vsu recedatur. Ea autem propemodum omnia sequentibus hisque capitibus quàm potuimus et absolutissimè et compendiosissimè complexi sumus. Cum enim quatuor potissimum ministerii ordines in ecclesia authoribus Apostolis proponantur, Ministrorum nimirum,
105 Doctorum, Seniorum, et Diaconorum, ad quos et verbi diuini sincerè administrandi et honestatis ac morum cura pertineat: quibus deinde adiicitur Sacramentorum ac disciplinae ecclesiasticae consideratio, quae coniuncta verbo Dei legitima sunt ecclesiae testimonia, Sanè iis ritè constitutis nihil esse amplius putamus quod in ecclesiae constitutione possit magnopere desiderari.

103/105 Cum – Diaconorum] cfr 'Ordonnances ecclésiastiques, Genf 1541/1561', hrsg. P. Opitz, in *RefBK*, vol. 1/2 (2006), p. 229-278, here p. 246

106 morum] *eadem manu sup. l. abscr.* pauperorumque]

| [Cap. II.]
De Ministris et Doctoribus.

1.

Ac primum vt ad verbi Dei ministerium ecclesiaeque qualemcunque ordinem, sine legitima vocatione, electione, ratihabitione iustoque examine, et ordine legitimo nemo admittatur est prorsus necessarium.

2.

Vocatio autem electioque legitima censeri nullo iure potest, nisi in qua et vocati ambitus, et plebis impotentes ac temerariae inclinationes, et Seniorum praefectorumque ambitiosum imperium, quoad eius fieri potest, excludantur.

3.

Quod vt fieri rectè possit, optandum sanè fuerit, vt pius magistratus maturo Seniorum iudicio ac prudenti delectui mutuam praebere velit operam. Ea enim ratione tutò possit plebis omne arbitrium in eorum coniuncta authoritate acquiescere. Quod cum sperari vix posse videatur, non putamus meliorem institui rationem posse, quam vt ecclesiae communis calculus ad Seniorum accedat authoritatem, Idque in vnaquaque ecclesia tantisper obseruetur, donec distributis classibus, Synodus censuerit, plurium ecclesiarum ministros ac Seniores ad vnius electionem explorationemque debere convenire. Id enim si fiat, non magnopere videntur plebis suffragia debere desiderari, cum Seniorum impotentiam (si quae fortasse, quod Deus auertat, irrepsisset) frenare possit plurium ecclesiarum authoritas.

4.

Interea autem dum id confici nondum potest, ne iusto amplius imperium ac licentia Senioribus in plebem concedatur, censemus maturo eorum delectu probatos exploratosque duplo plures (si omnino haberi possint) esse plebi nominatim consignandos, ex quibus deinde per singulorum suffragia media pars electa in ministerii functionem adhibeatur.

5.

Quibus tamen locis plebs ad electionem minus erit idonea, vel propter fidelium infrequentiam vel propter hominum doctorum expertorumque

680 CONVENTUS VESALIENSIS – 1568

inopiam, vel propter contraria partium studia: vel denique propterea quod nulli ante hac Ministri, nullaque ecclesiae constitutio iis locis fuerit, non putamus nisi accedente alterius, eiusque praecipuae alicuius, et si fieri potest, vicinae ecclesiae authoritate ac iudicio in ministerium ascisci quemquam posse.

145 | 6. 5

Interea censemus, exemplo Apostolorum instituendum esse ieiunio precibusque solennibus diem: quò plebis iudicio ac suffragiis, simul et Seniorum delectui atque explorationi, Spiritus sancti aspiret auxilium.

7.

150 Examen iustum partim doctrinam spectat, partim mores.

8.

In doctrina quatuor obseruari erit vtile, primum vt requiratur testimonium siue ecclesiae siue Scholae aut etiam Ciuitatis in qua ante hac vixit: vt certò constare possit an cuipiam haeresi addictus fuerit, an exoticis et curiosis
155 quaestionibus speculationibusque otiosis plus aequo se oblectarit, an hereticorum libros studiosius quam par est legerit, hominumque fanaticorum et suis somniis indulgentium consuetudine multa vsus fuerit. Deinde quaeratur, ecquid per omnia consentiat cum ea doctrina quae in ecclesia publice retinetur secundum ea quae Confessione fidei primum Galliarum Regi per ecclesiarum
160 illius regni ministros oblata, deinde etiam in vernaculam linguam conuersa Hispaniarum regi, coeterisque inferioris Germaniae magistratibus inscripta exhibitaque fuit, denique etiam Catechesi continentur. Tertio interrogetur de primariis quibusque religionis Capitibus. Ac postremo proponantur ei vt minimum bis terue aliquot Scripturae loca coram Ministris si adfuerint ac Pro-
165 phetis seu Doctoribus; vel (sin minus aderint) coram Senioribus in prophetiae morem explicanda.

9.

In morum exploratione, testimonio eorum apud quos vixerit est acquiescendum.

159/160 Confessione – oblata] cfr *Gallican Confession*, ed. I. Dingel (p. 547-563, 1/404)   **160/161** deinde – regi] cfr 'Confessio Belgica von 1561', hrsg. E. Busch, in *RefBK*, vol. 2/1 (2009), p. 319-370

CONVENTUS VESALIENSIS – 1568

10.

Haec autem omnia (si ita à Synodo statutum fuerit) posthac in Classis seu paroeciae conuentu Classibus distributis erunt peragenda. Ante id tempus vero non possunt nisi in cuiusque ecclesiae Consistorio confici. Tamen quibuscunque erit commodum, ii quos cupiunt sibi asciscere Ministros, in exteras ecclesias reformatas primum mittent: vt earum incorrupto iudicio, et non suspectae examinationi, tutius possint incumbere.

11.

Iam ita exploratos populique suffragiis comprobatos Ministros, censemus vel solis solennibus precibus, vel manuum etiam impositione (quam liberam relinquimus) coram tota ecclesia, more Apostolorum, esse confirmandos. Ea confirmatio fiet vel ab eiusdem ecclesiae (si quis est) vel a vicinae ecclesiae (si nemo in illa superest) Ministro cuius authoritas in electione examinationeque fuerit interposita.

| 12.

Nec tamen antequam illi ipsi, à quo manus imponendae sint, coram vniversa ecclesia sanctè sese obstrinxerit Dei dumtaxat gloriae propagandae, eiusque verbo syncerè administrando, ecclesiaeque aedificandae daturum operam: neque ad suas priuatas cupiditates Spiritus sancti oracula esse detorturum, neque à veritate, vel gratia vel pretio, vel metu ne tantillum declinaturum, ac simul religiosè obseruaturum receptas ecclesiae constitutiones, quaecunque ad ordinem et tranquillitatem ecclesiarum spectant, ac denique officio pro virili functurum in exhortando, increpando, consolandoque, ac docendo, vbicunque opus fuerit omni gratia ac personarum respectu procul excluso.

178/180 Iam – confirmandos] cfr Act. 8, 17; II Tim. 1, 6

190 ac – constitutiones] the most important examples are John Calvin's *Institutio*, the Genevan *Ordonnances ecclésiastiques*, as well as Johannes à Lasco's *Forma ac ratio*, in Kuyper, *Joannis a Lasco opera*, vol. 2, p. 1-263. See also the 'Pfälzer Kirchenordnung 1563', in *EKO*, vol. 14 (1969), p. 333-408 **190/193** quaecunque – excluso] see the oath taken by newly-appointed pastors in Geneva in 'Ordonnances', hrsg. Opitz, in *RefBK*, vol. 1/2 (2006), p. 249-250

682 CONVENTUS VESALIENSIS – 1568

13.

195 Ministrorum enim, quos et Pastores et Episcopos, nonnumquam etiam Seniores seu presbyteros vocat Scriptura, munus potissimum versari in verbo Dei annunciando, ac ritè secando, et ad doctrinam, exhortationem, consolationem, increpationemque, prout res fert, tum publicè tum priuatim accommodando, atque in administrandis Sacramentis ac disciplina obseruanda, est 200 extra controuersiam.

14.

Ministris adiuncti sunt Doctores ac Prophetae, quorum vnum quidem est docendi munus, sed diuersa functionis ratio.

15.

205 De Doctoribus hoc quidem tempore nihildum potest statui, donec ipsa res ac tempus quid e re ecclesiarum sit, eos qui Synodo aderunt plenius edocuerit.

16.

Prophetas vocamus hoc loco eos, qui in coetu ecclesiae propositum Scrip-210 turae locum ordine exponunt, prout est à Paulo institutum: eosque à Ministris distinguimus, quod his propriè, ac potissimum explicandi Scripturas docendique munus, illis multa praeterea alia, vt ante declarauimus, sunt imposita.

17.

Quare iudicamus in omnibus ecclesiis, siue nascentibus, siue vegetis, vbi 215 qua ratione fieri poterit, prophetiae ordinem ex Pauli instituto esse obseruan-

---

195/196 Ministrorum – Scriptura] cfr Act. 14, 22; I Tim. 4, 14   **202** Ministris – Prophetae] cfr Act. 13, 1   **209/210** Prophetas – institutum] cfr I Cor. 12, 28; Eph. 4, 11   **215** prophetiae – instituto] cfr I Cor. 14, 3-5

196/200 munus – controuersiam] cfr 'Ordonnances', hrsg. Opitz, in *RefBK*, vol. 1/2 (2006), p. 246-247; *Forma ac ratio*, p. 51-52. The word 'bishop' is found in the latter but not in the former   **214/227** Quare – censemus] Articles 17 and 18 explicitly refer to the praxis of the London refugee community, in turn derived from the *Prophezei* of Zurich. See *Forma ac ratio*, p. 106-112. Not surprisingly, given the recent dispute in the London community, the practice of free questioning is rejected

CONVENTUS VESALIENSIS – 1568   683

dum eoque instituendum Collegium prophetarum: qui quidem constituto
aliquo die, singulis septimanis; vel certè binis | quibusque, vel à concione vel 7
quouis commodissimo tempore coram ecclesia conueniant, vbi ad omnium
aedificationem librum aliquem Scripturarum, rato ordine vicissim explicent.
220 Vbi autem is, cuius erunt partes, suas vices expleuerit, licebit et iis, qui sub-
selliis eum insequuntur, si quid visum erit, adiicere, quod ad aedificationem
pertineat, Ac tum demum concepta precatione ab eo cuius sunt praecipuae
partes, coetum claudere.

18.

225   Illam autem nuper exortam prophetandi formam, quae quaestionibus
constat et responsionibus, vt et à Pauli instituto alienam, et simultatum con-
tentionumque persaepe occasionem omnino deuitandam, censemus.

19.

    In hoc Prophetarum Collegium coaptabuntur non modo Ministri sed
230 etiam Doctores ac ex Senioribus et Diaconis atque adeo ex ipsa plebe, si qui
erunt qui cupient donum prophetiae à Domino acceptum in ecclesiae communem vtilitatem conferre: Ita tamen vt prius habitis identidem propositionibus,
Ministrorum ac coeterorum Prophetarum iudicio sese probarint, et simul in
vniuersae ecclesiae conspectu, vel saltem apud eos, penes quos est ius explorandi-
235 di, promiserint Scripturam minimè detorsuros: sed ad Dei gloriam et ecclesiae
aedificationem quam syncerissimè explicaturos, et ecclesiae censuram, quae in
Classium conuentu futura sit non grauatè subituros.

20.

    Prophetis autem et Doctoribus in Consistorio seu Senatu ecclesiastico,
240 locus erit, quoties de doctrina vel ceremoniis aliqua inciderit controuersia:
cum spirituum ac doctrinarum probatio ad eos vel maximè pertineat.

21.

    Ad eosdem etiam, vel certè vbi eorum non erit potestas, ad Ministrum vel
ad Seniores censemus esse referenda dubia singulorum in ecclesia fidelium, si
245 quae occurrent. Et si ii nequeant satisfacere, scripto comprehendantur, atque

---

231 donum – acceptum] cfr I Cor. 14, 1   **241** spirituum – probatio] cfr I Cor. 12, 10

684 CONVENTUS VESALIENSIS – 1568

ad Ministrum vel si ne ille quidem satisfacere poterit, ad Classis conuentum deferantur. Plebis autem aures variis quaestionibus exagitandas turbandasque, neque publicè neque priuatim censemus.

| 22.

8

250 Porro in ratione tum concionandi tum prophetandi nihil potest cuiquam peculiare praescribi, nisi vt quisque pro dono Spiritus sancti accepto, conetur Scripturam quam planissimè explicare, et ad auditorum captum stylo quàm accommodatissimo. Fugiat autem omnem odiosam ac putidam affectationem, in quam multi multa ociosè speculando, extra propositum Scripturae scopum
255 diuagando, variis et acutis allegoriis ludendo: ethnicis testibus ac persaepe etiam profanis fabulosisque historiis ad ostentationem producendis, patrum testimoniis studiosius, quàm par est, conquirendis laudandisque, obscuritate, vel sententiarum vel verborum, affectanda, vel alia denique quapiam arte ad inanem ostentationem potius quam ad aedificationem comparata, non rarò
260 incidunt.

23.

Referat verò omnia ad illa duo praecipua Euangelii capita, fidem nimirum et poenitentiam: In illa Christi cognitionem, in hac veram vitae mortificationem viuificationemque tanquam vnicum sibi scopum proponat. Et conetur
265 quàm poterit maximè omnes humani cordis sinus atque abdita inuolucra, tum in falsis opinionibus atque haeresibus, tum in prauis moribus redarguendis, explicare. Neque crassa tantum scelera et manifesta flagitia insectetur, sed occultam etiam animorum hypocrisin conetur excutere, et impietatis, superbiae, ac ingratitudinis seminarium, vel in optimis quibusque delitescens, in
270 lucem trahere, et, quàm poterit aptissimè extirpare.

24.

Cauebit etiam ne nimis prolixis concionibus auditoris et memoriam oneret, et zelum obtundat fastidioque stomachum afficiat, et quidem maximè iis diebus quibus est ad operas manuarias plebi concedendum quibusque prophe
275 tiae locus est dandus. Quare studebit ad vnius horae spatium orationem temperare.

---

251 nisi – accepto] cfr II Petr. 1, 2 seq.

258 arte ad] *eadem manu sup. l. abscr.* simili

CONVENTUS VESALIENSIS – 1568   685

| 25.

Haec tamen omnia in cuiusque arbitrio, et Spiritus sancti mensura ita relinquimus, vt sciant interea et Pastores et Prophetae, lenem ac modestam censuram in Classium conuentu, vltro ac libenter super hisce rebus sibi esse admittendam.

26.

Sicubi autem in maioribus oppidis atque ecclesiis frequentioribus erit commodum, omnino suademus priuatas propositiones haberi, quibus se intra domesticos parietes exerceant ii, de quibus bona spes est, posse aliquando ecclesiae Dei inseruire, publicaque munia capescere: Idque praeside ac moderatore vno aliquo ex Ministris vel certè Prophetis ac Doctoribus.

27.

Vnus vt minimum in hebdomade dies, pro cuiusque ecclesiae commodo, solennibus precationibus consecrabitur, quo vel ante vel post concionem peccatorem publica atque solennis confessio ac submissa deprecatio pro populo habeatur: quam quisque Minister vel dictante Spiritu, vel si volet formula ecclesiae Geneuensis alteriusue cuiuspiam sibi proposita concipiet.

28.

Quae autem sub finem concionis prophetiaeque ordinariae fient preces, eae vel a Ministro, vel Propheta, quàm aptissimè ad argumentum, in concione propositum, accommodabuntur, et si fieri potest, praecipua quaeque in concione explicata capita hic attingentur: vt ea ratione res ipsa in auditorum animis altius haerere possit, et simul quis sit Scripturarum in precando vsus, a rudibus intelligi.

29.

Tantisper dum in concionem conueniunt, ne inanibus confabulationibus et animi distrahantur, | et verbi Dei ministerium afficiatur contumelia, non erit inutile primum quidem à Seniorum vel Diaconorum quopiam, vel quouis

---

292/293 formula – Geneuensis] i.e. the *Forme de prières et chantz ecclesiastiques*, in *CR*, vol. 34 (1867), p. 181-184

686 CONVENTUS VESALIENSIS – 1568

305 denique alio ad hanc rem constituto, vnum aut alterum ex Scriptura caput ad
populum legi, ac deinde pro more, Psalmos decantari.

30.

Meminerint tamen lectores sui haud esse muneris Scripturam explicare:
Quare ab omni interpretatione abstineant: ne et falcem in alienam messem
310 immittant, et intempestiuis explicationibus, ordinarium ecclesiae ritum inter-
turbent.

31.

In cantu ecclesiastico retinebuntur per omnes Belgii ecclesias psalmi à
Petro Datheno conuersi: ne varietate versionum quicquam minus concinnum
315 minusque ad aedificationem pertinens, interueniat.

32.

In quibus ecclesiis erunt Scholae quibus sit Musices peritus aliquis
Scholarcha, is in psalmodia pueris praeibit, ac pueros coetera deinceps turba
insequetur. Vbi verò vel non erunt Scholae vel propter musices imperitiam
320 Scholarchis praeire non erit integrum, ibi erit vtile vnum vt minimum aliquem
Cantorem adhiberi, qui populi cantum moderetur, et in psalmodia praeeat, et
quidem maximè, si est musices ignarus verbi minister.

33.

Nec erit alienum, in ecclesiis habere tabellas suspensas, quibus breuiter et
325 dilucidè perscripta sit psalmorum decantandorum ratio, et vulgaris canendi
ars compendiosè explicata: ne plebis canentis disphonia, vel scandalum infidelibus, vel ridendi argumentum praebeat.

309/310 ne – immittant] cfr Marc. 4, 29

313/314 In – conuersi] Petrus Dathenus completed in 1566 a Dutch translation of the
Genevan *Psalter*. See P. Dathenus, *De Psalmen Davids, ende ander Lofsanghen, wt den
francoyschen Dichte In Nederlandschen ouerghesett, Doer Petrvm Dathenvm. Metgaeders
den Christelicken Catechismo, Ceremonien ende Ghebeden*, Heydelbergh 1566. This
translation was adopted by the Convent under Dathenus' chairmanship, and his
edition became the official basis for liturgical psalm-singing in the Netherlands until
1773

CONVENTUS VESALIENSIS – 1568

34.

His adiungentur aliae tabellae, quibus significabitur qui quoque die psalmi cantabuntur: vt possint, si qui volent, ante meditari quod erit canendum:
nisi fortè ab initio, deinceps ordine continuo psalmos omnes canere | videbitur
commodius. Quo enim ordine psalmi decantentur, in cuiusque ecclesiae arbitrio stare debere existimamus.

[Cap. III.]
De Catechismo.

I.

Ministerii ac prophetiae muneri non abs re coniungimus catechisandi
consuetudinem, quam ab Apostolis eorumque discipulis acceptam, in omnibus ecclesiis obseruandam esse planè censemus.

2.

Catechismi autem formulam, in ecclesiis quidem Gallicanis, Geneuen-
sem, in Teutonicis vero Heydelbergensem, potissimum sequendam ducimus:
Quam tamen vsque ad futuram Synodum liberam relinquimus.

3.

Tempus Catechisandi, quibusque ecclesiis pro loci ac rerum opportunitate sit liberum. Ratio hactenus vsitata retineatur: omnisque adhibeatur
diligentia, vt pueri quibus per aetatem licet Catechismi verba, non ad numerum syllabarum tantum discant recitare, sed etiam rem ipsam intelligere, eamque non modo memoriae, sed intimis etiam praecordiis mandare. Quare non
verba modo recitata, sed ipsam etiam rei substantiam à Catechista planè ac
dilucidè expositam, interrogabuntur. Eritque ante omnia opus in explicando
Catechismo sermone vti quam familiarissimo, et vel ad puerorum captum

---

328 34.] the consecutive singing of all psalms was common in Geneva. However, this
practice was not adopted everywhere in Reformed Europe. See R. Weeda, 'Die
Rezeption des Genfer Psalters im 16. Jahrhundert', in P. E. Bernoulli et al. (ed.), *Der
Genfer Psalter. Eine Entdeckungsreise*, Zürich 2001, p. 43-56 **340** 2.] i.e. the *Genevan
Catechism* and the *Heidelberg Catechism*. See 'Genfer Katechismus von 1542', hrsg.
E. Saxer, in *RefBK*, vol. 1/2 (2006), p. 279-362; 'Heidelberger Katechismus von 1563',
hrsg. W. H. Neuser, in *RefBK*, vol. 2/2 (2009), p. 167-211

688 CONVENTUS VESALIENSIS – 1568

accomodato: ac serio etiam commonefacere Catechumenorum parentes et
Ludimagistros, vt eos domi et in Scholis diligenter instituant, et quae in eccle-
355 sia proposita sunt, assuescant etiam sua sponte ruminare, et Scripturarum
appositis testimoniis corroborare.

4.

Imprimis autem ad modestiam in Templis et conuentibus obseruandam
eos instruant. Sanè quicunque haberi se membra ecclesiae volunt, ii liberos
360 suos, quam primum aetas patietur, catechisandos offerant: vt ab ineunte aetate
in vera religione ac pietate possint institui. Qui recusabunt, ecclesiae censurae
procul dubio subiacebunt.

|[Cap. IV.]
De Senioribus.

12

365 I.

Sequitur ordo Seniorum siue Presbyterorum qui a Paulo κυβερνήσεων i. e.
gubernatorum vel τῶν προϊσταμένων i. e. eorum qui praesunt, nomine cen-
sentur: eoque Senatum ecclesiasticum siue Consistorium vna cum Ministris
constituunt.

370 2.

Quare est extra omnem controuersiam, eorum munus in hoc versari, vt
singuli suis paroeciis sedulò inuigilent, et domatim sibi commissos semel ad
minimum in hebdomade et quoties pro singularum ecclesiarum ratione ex vsu
erit inuisant, maximè autem sub tempus coenae celebrandae, deque eorum
375 vitae ac morum integritate pietatisque exercitiis, fideli familiae institutione, ac
pro familia mane ac vesperi concipiendis precationibus, et de eius generis simi-
libus diligenter inquirant: placidè et tamen seriò moneant, et pro rei vsu ac
opportunitate vel ad constantiam hortentur, vel ad patientiam confirment, vel
ad serium Dei timorem incident: quique vel consolatione vel increpatione
380 indigebunt consolentur atque increpent, et sicubi opus fuerit ad eos referant,
qui secum fraternis correctionibus praeerunt: quibuscum vnà correctionem
pro ratione delicti instituant. Meminerint etiam omnes ac singulos in sua
paroecia hortari, vt liberos suos ad Catechismum mittant.

---

366 a Paulo] *in marg.* I. Cor. 12, 28. Rom. 12, 8

CONVENTUS VESALIENSIS – 1568

3.

Ad eam rem exequendam necesse erit primo quoque tempore singulas ecclesias in certas paroecias pro multitudine et commodo fidelium ea loca incolentium dispertire: singulis paroeciis singulos praeficere Seniores, qui singulis septimanis die constituto in commune Consistorium referant, ecquid omnia in suis paroeciis rectè gerantur et ex sententia. Et sese ita gerant, vt meminerint sibi non modo coram ecclesia, sed coram ipso Deo animarum sibi commissarum reddendam fore rationem.

4.

In partitione autem paroeciarum non tam consanguinitatis affinitatis aut mutuae consuetudinis, quàm habitationis ac vicinitatis rationem haberi et Senioribus commodum et eorum functioni est accommodatum.

5.

Seniorum eligendorum confirmandorumque eadem quae Ministrorum est ratio: nisi quod in examine non magna habetur ratio eorum quae propriè ad ministerium verbi pertinent, neque in confirmatione exterorum Ministrorum praesentia opus sit.

6.

Summopere autem erit enitendum vt adsint ea quae Paulus requirit: Vita nimirum inculpata, religio syncera, pietas eximia, pru|dentia spiritualis, ad quam rerum etiam ciuilium nonnullam cognitionem accedere erit apprime vtile. Sed sint ante omnia ab omni ambitione gloriaeque cupiditate, adeoque ab omni ambitus suspicione quàm remotissimi.

7.

Electi spondebunt in Ministri manus coram coeteris Senioribus vel etiam si commodum fuerit coram tota ecclesia sese pro suo officio impugnaturos omnem idololatriam, blasphemiam, haereses, luxum, coeteraque omnia, quae cum Dei gloria ecclesiaeque reformatione manifestè pugnant: moniturosque diligenter ac fideliter eos qui curae suae commissi erunt, pro quauis rerum occasione et oportunitate. Et si quae digna videbuntur ad Consistorium rela-

---

401 6.] cfr I Tim. 3, 2-4

690   CONVENTUS VESALIENSIS – 1568

turos; suoque officio functuros quàm fidelissimè: nulla vel gratia vel pretio
415 inductos iri, sed solius ecclesiae nominisque diuini habituros rationem. Neque
vllum imperium dominandique licentiam vsurpaturos, siue erga Ministros siue
erga ecclesiam, neque vllas nouas leges pro suo arbitrio introducturos, sed
staturos constitutionibus ecclesiasticis ac Synodalibus. Et si quid noui exortum
fuerit quod accuratiore disquisitione indigeat, ad Classis seu prouincialis pa-
420 roeciae conuentum relaturos: vt ibi quod ex re ecclesiarum erit communibus
suffragiis statuatur. Ac tum demum praeeuntibus solennibus precibus (nam
hic quoque manuum impositionem liberam relinquimus) in Ministerii functionem admittentur.

8.

425   Sciant autem seniores munus suum etiam ad aegros inuisendos consolan-
dosque pertinere. Quanquam et Diaconis pro sua vocatione ea cura incumbit,
vt aegros non modò rebus ad victum necessariis refocillent, sed etiam reficiant
consolatione. Quare necessum erit a Senioribus aegrorum ac praesertim
inopum nomina Diaconis consignari, quò possint illi suo officio rectius fungi.

430 9.

     Leges autem condere vel imperium exercere siue erga Ministros Collegas-
que siue erga ecclesiam: Ac vel Consistorium seu Senatum ecclesiasticum pro
suo arbitratu cogere, Ministris ignorantibus vel absentibus, sciant a suo munere esse quàm alienissimum.

435 10.

     Quod si autem Ministris absentibus erit cogendum Consistorium, debe-
bunt certè Seniores et occasionem indicti Senatus, et quid in eo gestum sit
fideliter illis aperire.

| 11.

              14

440   Si etiam erit aliquo Minister ablegandus non debebit illud a Senioribus
nisi conuocato altero ministro vel certè doctoribus ac prophetis decerni: eo
quod illo absente in hos vel inscios vel inuitos non debeat ecclesiae solicitudo
cadere.

---

421 precibus] *eadem manu sup. l. abscr.*

CONVENTUS VESALIENSIS – 1568

12.

445 Quoties autem communi consensu vel verbi Minister vel alius quis publicum munus gerens aliquo ablegatus fuerit, alioue quopiam munere, quod sit ex vsu ecclesiae, oneratus, debet hoc ipsum libenter et non grauatè in se recipere ac promptissima voluntate exequi; cogitans in Domini nostri Jesu Christi negocio se minimè esse sui iuris. Alioqui si fratrum vel Classis vel Consistorii 450 iudicio stare renuerit, forma disciplinae ecclesiasticae cum eo agendum erit.

13.

Quemadmodum verò multis de causis non vtile tantum sed necessarium prorsus esse censemus, vt peculiari quodam libro acta Consistorii omnia per vnum quempiam ex Seniorum numero ad hoc deputatum diligenter annoten-455 tur, Ita etiam Diaconos recepta dispensataque omnia sedulo adscribere Consistorioque singulis mensibus vel, quoties alioqui videbitur, rationes reddere verbo Domini omnino consentaneum est.

[CAP. V.]
DE DIACONIS.

460 ### I.

Diaconorum officium in eo esse, vt mensae inseruiant i. e. pauperum inopiis succurrant, et collectis eleemosynis necessaria administrent, Scriptura teste certissimum est.

2.

465 Eorum electionem confirmationemque non alio ritu debere fieri quam qui in Senioribus est supra declaratus consentaneum est, nisi quod in examine maxima habebitur ratio fidelitatis atque industriae, et potissimum cauebitur auaritiae nota. Per omnia autem obseruabitur ratio a Paulo praescripta I. Timot. 3.

---

460 I.] cfr Act. 6, 1-6   **468** Per – I. Timot. 3.] cfr I Tim. 3, 8-13

692   CONVENTUS VESALIENSIS – 1568

470

3.

Debent etiam diligenter commonefacere eos quibus per facultates licet vt ecclesiae inopiae et necessitati pauperum subueniant.

4.

Eorum numerum in singulis ecclesiis non posse hoc tempore praescribi, cum circunstantiarum sit habenda maxime ratio, existimamus.

| 5.

Atqui in maioribus praesertim Ciuitatibus Diaconorum duo genera institui non erit alienum, quorum alii eleemosynis colligendis distribuendisque operam dabunt, et simul pauperibus bona legata si quae fuerit ea curae habebunt, vt ritè ab haeredibus erogentur, et legatariis fideliter distribuantur.

6.

Alii potissimum aegrorum, sauciorum captiuorumque curam gerent: quos erit necesse praeter fidelitatem atque industriam etiam dono consolationis et verbi cognitione non vulgari esse praeditos; Et sedulo a Senioribus inquirere num qui sint in paroeciis aegri atque infirmi, qui consolatione sustentationeue indigeant.

7.

Quicunque lecto aegri decubuerint ii suam valetudinem per Diaconos siue Seniores Ministro verbi indicent: vt si opus fuerit vel accedat ipse, aegrumque verbo Dei consoletur, vel eam prouinciam Senioribus vel Diaconis mandet, vbi ei per alia publica et maioris momenti negocia minus erit integrum.

8.

Aduenarum etiam ac peregrinorum rationem haberi iubet charitatis ratio.

---

482 Alii – gerent] cfr Matth. 25, 36   **493** 8.] cfr III Ioh. 5

CONVENTUS VESALIENSIS – 1568

9.

Quare Diaconorum erit diligenter de Senioribus aliisque ecclesiae membris exquirere, num qui fideles aduenae seu peregrini in ea loca venerint: vt eis hospitalitatis beneficium et reliqua fidelis ac Christiana opera praestari possit. Et si sint inopes etiam necessaria subministrentur. Eorum autem curam ad prius Diaconorum genus pertinere est extra dubium.

10.

Quibus locis erit oportunum existimamus etiam mulieres spectata fide ac probitate et aetate prouectas ad hoc munus Apostolorum exemplo rectè ascisci posse.

11.

Prouidebunt etiam Diaconi an ecclesiae viduis pupillisue alicunde vis vel iniuria sit illata: Et si quid resciuerint, referent ad Consistorium: quò statim certi aliquot deligantur qui pro rei qualitate curent à magistratu ius reddi.

12.

Iam porro necessarium erit, praeter hos Diaconos alios etiam viros bonos ac spectatae fidei ac probitatis magno delectu conquiri qui colligant Ministrorum stipendia, coeteraque quae ad vsum ministerii erunt necessaria.

| 13.

In quibus numeramus etiam ea quae ad congregandas Synodos, ad ablegandos vbi erit necesse vel Ministros vel quosuis alios ad necessaria ecclesiae negocia, et simul quaecunque ad templorum siue basilicarum structuram pertinebunt.

---

501 10.] see for example the deaconness Phoebe in Rom. 16, 1. Female diaconate is a special feature of the *Articles of Wesel*. It was never implemented in Geneva, London, or in France, and later Dutch Reformed sources do not mention it. In Wesel, this office was only temporarily established. See J. Spohnholz, 'Olympias and Chrysostom'

694   CONVENTUS VESALIENSIS – 1568

14.

Quanquam in maioribus Ciuitatibus, vbi omnino poterit, haec munia
520 etiam distingui satius esse ducimus: ac Ministrorum curam a coeterarum
rerum solicitudine disiungi. Verum haec in Synodo commodissimè decerni
poterunt, Cui etiam Scholarum curam constitutionemque relinquimus.

15.

De constituendo porro Argentario aliquo siue Quaestore, de reddendis
525 Consistorio tum accepti tum expensi rationibus, deque iis quae ad hanc rem
pertinebunt debet à singulis ecclesiis pro cuiusque ratione et modo posthac
statui, vel certè a Synodo in genere aliquid decerni.

16.

Senioribus autem ecclesiae facultatum qualescunque tandem sint, aut
530 vndecunque obuenerint erogationem administrationemque ab eorum munere
ducimus esse penitus alienam.

17.

Praeter eas quae quotidie accidunt difficultates, ipsa etiam res clamat
Seniores et Diaconos qui in vocatione sua aliquandiu fidi extiterunt, non nisi
535 magno rei domesticae dispendio hoc ipsum facere: proinde vtile censemus vt
quotannis noua eorum fiat electio: ita vt exacto anno vel sex mensibus (prout
res et oportunitas postulabunt) dimidia pars ab officio relaxetur, atque alii in
eorum locum deligantur qui cum reliquis adhuc remanentibus ecclesiae praeficiantur. Ita tamen vt liberum sit Consistorio Seniores et Diaconos maximè
540 idoneos et promptae voluntatis rogare et precari, vt dimidium vel integrum
subsequentem annum (prout Consistorio videbitur) ecclesiae in sua vocatione
inseruiant.

18.

Publica persona vt Minister seu Pastor, Doctor, Senior, Ludimagister, aut
545 Diaconus etcet. ecclesiam cui inseruit minimè deseret sine legitima causae
cognitione, et interposito totius Classis seu paroeciae (postquam in paroecias

---

532 17.] see 'Discipline ecclésiastique von 1559', hrsg. P. Opitz – N. Fornerod, in
RefBK, vol. 2/1 (2009), p. 57-83, here p. 79 (Article 21)

CONVENTUS VESALIENSIS – 1568

diuisae erunt prouinciae) iudicio. Neque vicissim ecclesiis erit liberum suum vel Ministrum vel Doctorem Senioremue etcet. destituere, nisi paroeciae classisue prouincialis consensus intercesserit.

19.

Nec tamen Classium conuentibus quicquam iuris hac in re concedendum putamus in vllam ecclesiam, eiusue Ministros, nisi illa vltro consentiente: ne suo iure et authoritate inuita priuetur ecclesia.

|[Cap. VI.]
De Sacramentis.

Ac primum de Baptismo.

1.

Sacramenta quia sunt cum verbi administratione indiuiduo nexu copulata ad Ministrorum officium pertinere nemo ambigit. Quare non censemus, ab alio quam à verbi Ministro Baptismum ritè conferri posse.

2.

Administretur autem Baptismus forma vsitata, et in ecclesiasticis constitutionibus expressa. Et quidem non alibi neque alias quam in ecclesiae conuentu sub concione et catechismo. Nisi fortasse initio nascentis ecclesiae infirmorum quorundam rationem haberi erit necesse, et in eorum gratiam ad euitandum scandalum pueros valetudine afflictos domi baptizare. Quod ipsum tamen non conceditur, nisi praesentibus vt minimum quatuor vel quinque fidelibus. Et quidem tantisper donec Synodi decreto aliter cautum fuerit.

3.

Testium autem particularium (quos Compatres vulgus vocat) vsum et tingendi formam libera relinqui debere iam ante diximus.

562/563 Administretur – expressa] see *Forma ac ratio*, p. 105-114; 'Pfälzer Kirchenordnung 1563', *EKO*, vol. 14 (1969), p. 338-341

696 CONVENTUS VESALIENSIS – 1568

4.

Atqui parentes et testes qui ad Baptismum pueros adferent iis verbis quae in forma baptismi expressa sunt interrogabuntur.

575

5.

Nomina infantium parentum ac Testium publicis tabulis consignari tum ecclesiae tum reipublicae maxime conducere in confesso est. Quibus etiam seorsim eorum nomina adscribi poterunt, qui post editam in ecclesia confessionem in Christo moriuntur.

580

De Coena Domini.

6.

Coenae celebrandae tempus ad populum referri ante quartumdecimum diem putamus esse perutile: tum vt singular ecclesiarum membra sese maturè praeparare, tum vt Seniores in obeundis paroeciis officio suo ritè fungi possint.

585

7.

Nemo autem ad coenam dominicam admittatur, nisi qui fidei confessionem ante ediderit et se disciplinae ecclesiasticae subiecerit.

8.

Qui ad coenam admitti cupient, octiduo ante praestitutum coenae diem
590 nomina apud Ministrum edent, et mox Seniorum vni aut pluribus pro ratione paroeciae | ac numero personarum negocium à Consistorio dabitur, vt sedulò 18 ac diligenter de eorum anteacta vita inquirant, et ad Consistorii cognitionem quod acceperint referant: vt si quid obstet quo minus recipi debeant maturè intercedatur, Sin minus, ad fidei examinationem procedatur.

---

572 4.] see *Forma ac ratio*, p. 135 seq.; 'Pfälzer Kirchenordnung 1563', *EKO* , vol. 14 (1969), p. 340.   **576/577** Nomina – est] a baptismal register was kept in the London refugee community. See *Forma ac ratio*, p. 106

CONVENTUS VESALIENSIS – 1568

595 9.

Eam autem propter multas causas publicè fieri debere haud necesse ac ne vtile quidem iudicamus: sed priuatim coram ministro et doctoribus ac prophetis, vel si minus eorum potestas fuerit, coram aliquot Senioribus et Ministro instituatur secundum ea quae in constitutionibus ecclesiasticis 600 proponuntur.

10.

Pueros autem qui ex catechumenis excesserunt non erit alienum coram vniuersa ecclesia examinari, secundum breuioris catechismi formam, cui etiam adiungentur maioris catechismi summa capita: idque octiduo ante constitu- 605 tum coenae diem.

11.

Qui autem erunt ritè examinati, siue pueri sint, siue adulti, ii sistent sese ecclesiae pridie eius diei quo celebranda est coena, et propositis fidei ac religio- nis primariis capitibus, eorum assensio postulabitur; et simul subiicient sese 610 ecclesiasticae disciplinae, eorumque nomina publicis tabulis adscribentur: atque tum demum ad plebem referentur, vt si nihil causae obstet possint postridie ad mensam dominicam admitti.

12.

Panis fractionem, quia est a Christo manifestè instituta, et ab Apostolis 615 totaque vetustiori ecclesia non sine grauissimus causis obseruata, necessariam esse omnino censemus.

---

614 Panis – instituta] cfr Matth. 26, 26; Marc. 14, 22; Luc. 22, 19; 24, 30   et ab Apostolis] cfr Act. 2, 46

601 10.] likely a reference to the catechism of the London refugee community: *Compendium Doctrinae de vera unicaque Dei et Christi ecclesia, eiusque fide et confessione pura: in qua peregrinorum ecclesia Londini instituta est* [...], Londini 1551, critical edition by A. Mühling, 'Nederländer Bekenntnis, London 1550/1551', in *RefBK*, vol. 1/3 (2007), p. 59-77. In London, the Dutch translation by Marten Mircron was probably used for children. See *Een kort begrijp der leeringhe van de warachtighe ende eenighe Gemeynte Gods ende Christi, ende van haer ghelooue ende oprechtige belydinghe*, Emden 1565, critical edition in Kuyper, *Joannis a Lasco opera*, vol. 2, p. 285-339. See also Wolters, *Reformationsgeschichte der Stadt Wesel*, p. 399 seq.; 422 seq.

698 CONVENTUS VESALIENSIS – 1568

13.

Verba coenae quae in Constitutionibus ecclesiasticis proponuntur, quia sunt et cum institutione, et cum manifesto Christi praecepto, et denique cum 620 Pauli declaratione quam maximè consentanea, putamus planè esse retinenda.

14.

Communem verò panem non peculiarem aliquem aut azymum aut aliud quid superstitionis resipientem putamus in omnibus ecclesiis esse vsurpandum.

625

15.

Sedendo verò an stando Coenam celebrari, et dum ea celebratur, vel Scripturam legi vel psalmos decantari indiscriminatim posse existimamus.

16.

Tempus autem celebrandae Coenae vnum aliquod | omnibus ecclesiis 19 630 praescribi nondum potest, donec in Synodo quid ex communi vsu ecclesiarum sit dispectum fuerit.

17.

Prouidendum autem est, ne tempore celebrandae Coenae conciones in eas horas extrahantur quae coenae conficiendae dari debent: vt habeatur 635 populi ac praesertim mulierum praegnantium coeterorumque valetudine affectorum ratio.

---

619 cum manifesto Christi praecepto] cfr Marc. 14, 22; 26, 26; Luc. 22, 19; 24, 30
619/620 cum Pauli declaratione] cfr I Cor. 11, 23-26

625 15.] cfr the regulations of the London refugee community, allowing only sitting celebration, in *Forma ac ratio*, p. 115 seq., as well as the Pfälzer Kirchenordnung, providing no clear instructions on sitting or standing, and leaving open the question about reading or singing

[CAP. VII.]
DE MATRIMONIO.

I.

Matrimonio copulandorum nomina ternis diebus dominicis pro suggesto ad populum edi, et vsus rerum et experientia quotidiana debere, testatur.

2.

Antea vero quam haec nominum editio fiat, sistent se vnà cum parentibus aut Curatoribus Ministro et duobus suae Classis Senioribus: vt de iis quae necessaria esse existimabuntur possint interrogari. Quo facto eorum nomina tabulis publicis consignabuntur.

3.

Quouis die indiscriminatim Matrimonia celebrari possunt, modo eodem die concio ad populum habeatur. Exceptis tantum ieiunio sacratis diebus quibus est potissimum precationi et luctui incumbendum.

4.

Coetera, quae ad Matrimoniorum rationem et considerationem Diuortiorum spectare possunt putamus in Synodo esse sigillatim discutienda.

[CAP. VIII.]
DE DISCIPLINA.

I.

Omnino vigilandum est ne vlla nascens ecclesia neglecta disciplina ecclesiastica instituatur. Quam enim illa sit et salutaris et necessaria ipsa Christi domini, et Apostolorum tum institutio tum doctrina, atque etiam apostolicae totiusque vetustioris ecclesiae vsus, et ipsa denique quotidiana rerum experientia luculenter docet.

658/659 Quam – domini] cfr Matth. 18, 15-18

700 CONVENTUS VESALIENSIS – 1568

2.

Ac proinde neminem ad verbi ministerium admitti debere aequum est, nisi qui hanc disciplinae rationem tueri retinereque paratus fuerit.

3.

Disciplinam censemus constare tum censura doctrinae | siue religionis ac morum tum correctione legitima, tum etiam excommunicatione, in qua potissimum versatur potestas clauium à Domino ecclesiae data.

4.

Religionis ac morum censuram quod ad singula ecclesiae membra attinet debere ad Senatum ecclesiasticum, Seniorum inquam conuentum adhibitis Ministris Doctoribus ac Prophetis, si qui fuerint, spectare, est extra controuersiam.

5.

Ad quos enim cuiusque rei cognitio pertinet eosdem à iudicio et censura excludi praeter omne ius et fas esse omnes vident. Quare propriè quidem doctrinae censura ad Ministros et Doctores, morum vero ad Seniores videtur pertinere. Sed debent procul dubio vtrobique mutuas praestare operas.

6.

Iam cui censura relinquitur apud eum correctionis arbitrium stare, est procul dubio rationi et aequitati consentaneum. Quare ad Consistorii iudicium hanc causam pertinere putamus esse quam conuenientissimum.

7.

Proinde si quis aliena dogmata et haereses clam palamue sparserit, eius nomen à Senioribus ad Consistorium referatur: eò vocatus moneatur, et si se ecclesiae iudicio submiserit, in gratiam recipiatur: Sin autem iterum ac tertiò monitus animum pertinaciter obfirmarit, à fidelium communione arceatur.

---

668 potestas – data] cfr Matth. 16, 19

CONVENTUS VESALIENSIS – 1568

8.

Eodemque modo si quis ecclesiae ordinem conuentumque superbe fastidierit ac identidem monitus minimè resipuerit, huic ecclesiae communio interdicatur.

9.

In morum autem censura correctioneque Christi institutio per omnia obseruetur, vt in criminibus occultis, et à publico scandalo remotis nemo ad ecclesiae iudicium trahatur nisi obstinato animo saepius repetitas monitiones fastidiosè reiecerit. Delatus autem ad Consistorium seriò moneatur: et nisi resipuerit tanquam putre membrum abscindatur.

10.

In publicis autem et cum aperto scandalo coniunctis criminibus Consistorii Senatusue ecclesiastici authoritas primo quoque tempore interponatur, monendo primum et placidè in gratiam recipiendo si paruerit: Sin minus excommunicatione feriendo. | In atrocibus porro flagitiis ac sceleribus, etiam si monitioni obtemperauerint, tamen à communione in certum aliquod tempus suspendantur, donec resipiscentiae specimen ac testimonium luculentum praebuerint.

11.

Liceat autem si quis se hac via, vel alia quauis ratione iniuria affectum putet, à Consistorii sententia ad Classium (postquàm erunt institutae) iudicium appellare, et rursus à Classium decisione Synodi auxilium implorare. Et sane eiusmodi tergiuersatio ac recusatio agnoscendae culpae peruicatiae nota non carebit.

12.

Atqui in Ministris ac Senioribus paulo aliam obseruari rationem aequum est: ne facile pateant calumniis. Nisi forte (quod auertat Deus) publico aliquo scelere ac flagitio sese contaminarint. Tum enim quàm primum non expectato Classis iudicio cum ignominia et dedecore ab officio mouendos esse nemo dubitat.

---

692 9.] cfr Matth. 18, 16 seq.

702 CONVENTUS VESALIENSIS – 1568

13.

Sin autem crimine aliquo occulto tenebuntur referatur ad conuentum
720 Classis censura: in quo singulorum Ministrorum Seniorumque diligens exploratio habeatur et quomodo se quisque in officio gesserit, iis egredi iussis, sump-
toque à coeteris iureiurando neminem proditurum quid aut à quo quicquam
dictum sit, diligenter inquiratur. Et si monitione videbitur indigere, reuocatus
in conuentum moneatur, sin reprehensione castigationeque reprehendatur, et
725 pro criminis magnitudine vel leuitate castigetur.

14.

Porro crimina quae in Ministris tolerari nequaquàm debent ea fere sunt
istiusmodi. Haeresis. Schisma. Manifestus ordinis ecclesiastici contemptus.
Blasphemia manifesta et animaduersione ciuili digna. Simonia. Inhonestus
730 ambitus ad alterius locum inuadendum. Desertio sui muneris suaeque ecclesiae sine legitimo consensu ac vocatione. Crimen falsi. Periurium. Scortatio.
Furtum. Ebriositas. Vis armata omnisque vis correctione ciuili digna. Foenus
illicitum. Alea coeterique ludi inhonesti ac legibus interdicti. Manifesta affectatio tyrannidis in ecclesiam et Collegas. Coeteraque alia eiusmodi quae vel
735 inurunt infamiam, vel separationem ab ecclesia in aliis merentur.

15.

Alterius vero generis crimina sunt quae tolerantur quidem, sed tamen
reprehensioni ac censurae sunt obnoxia. Qualia sunt Inanis quaestionum
inutilium curiositas. | Aliena et affectata Scripturas pertractandi ratio quae 22
740 scandalum pariat auditoribus: qualis est eorum, qui vel suis speculationibus
plus aequo indulgent, vel allegoriis intempestiuis ludunt, vel denique aliena vel
a scopo vel a dignitate Scripturarum ad ostentationem ingerunt. Noui quippiam et quod sit prorsus inusitatum in ecclesiam pro libidine inuehere. In
studiis et Scripturarum lectione manifestè negligentem esse. In vitiis castigan-
745 dis plus aequo remissum se praebere et adulationi quam proximum esse. In
coeteris denique rebus quae officii sui sint nimis esse lentum ac socordem.
Scurrilitas seu facetiae indecorae. Mendacium. Detractio siue maledicentia.
Sermones impuri. Verba contumeliosa. Temeritas. Dolus malus. Manifesta
auaritia. Ambitio et inanis gloriae cupiditas. Praeceps ac immoderata iracun-

---

726 14.] cfr 'Ordonnances', hrsg. Opitz, in *RefBK*, vol. 1/2 (2006), p. 251   **736** 15.]
cfr 'Ordonnances', hrsg. Opitz, in *RefBK*, vol. 1/2 (2006), p. 251-252

CONVENTUS VESALIENSIS – 1568

750 dia. Dissidium in familia. Odia et rixae. Obiurgationes plus aequo acres ac immoderatae. Omnis immoderatus luxus in habitu mensa coeterisque rebus, qui verbi Diuini Ministrum dedeceat. Occulta affectatio imperandi ac tyrannidem in ecclesiam vel Collegas exercendi.

16.

755 In prioris generis criminibus qui conuictus erit, ab officio in consessu Classis remouebitur.

17.

In coeteris verò fraterna admonitio ac lenis castigatio adhibebitur, ab iis qui in classis conuentum erunt vocati. Quam si iterum ac tertio repetitam 760 respuerit, referatur ad Classium comitia siue ad Synodi iudicium, atque ibi quod erit e re et commodo ecclesiae constituatur.

18.

In leuioribus porro vitiis quae ne iudicio quidem consessus digna videbuntur, seruetur ea quae est in coeteris omnibus à Christo praescripta ratio.

765 ### 19.

Vt autem hic ordo censurae commodius obseruetur, putamus fore vtile vt in binos vel vt minimum in ternos menses Classis cuiusque conuentus habeatur in quibus de huiusmodi rebus diligens fiat exploratio. Totius autem prouinciae Classes semestri interuallo conuenire non foret inutile. Ac in 770 singulos denique annos totius Belgii prouincialem Synodum institui. Sed de iis quia nihil constitui potest, in arbitrio Synodi censemus esse relinquenda.

| 20.

Videtur etiam fore vtile, ne hi singularum Classium conuentus ad censuram instituti vno semper loco habeantur: sed potius vt persaepe loca varien-775 tur: Tum vt ecclesiarum alterius in alteram dominatio impediatur, tum verò vel maximè vt singularum ecclesiarum explorationi eo diligentius qui conueniunt possint inuigilare, et qualis cuiusque sit ordo tum in verbi doctrina, tum

---

762 18.] cfr Matth. 18, 15-18

704 CONVENTUS VESALIENSIS – 1568

in ceremoniarum et disciplinae ratione, et denique an Seniores ac Ministri suo
officio probè ac sedulo fungantur sigillatim exquirere.

780

21.

Postremo si quid singulare in ecclesia aliqua sit quod ad ordinem et
rectam ecclesiae constitutionem pertineat, liberum erit vnicuique ecclesiae id
sequi quod maximè ad aedificationem erit accommodum: Habita semper
circumstantiarum diligenti ratione vt ipsum ecclesiae corpus in vnitate spiritus
785 ac vinculo pacis continuo cursu retineatur.

22.

In his autem capitibus constituendis quae pro ecclesiarum Belgicarum
incolumitate, et vniformi atque aequabili constitutione hactenus perscripta
sunt, publicè, et coram Deo ac hominibus testatum volunt esse qui his colli-
790 gendis operam dederunt Ministri, nullo aliarum ecclesiarum praeiudicio id a
se factum esse, sed tantum habuisse rationem temporis, locorum, personarum
ac coeterarum circumstantiarum pro quibus quid ecclesiis Belgicis conducat
vel non conducat summa cura ac diligentia (implorato prius diuino auxilio)
exquisiuerunt. Et ita rem temperarunt vt si contingat Dominum nostrum
795 Jesum Christum vberiorem gratiae suae fructum Belgiae posthac aliquando
concedere, tam quod ad magistratus piam reformationem attinet, quàm quod
ad ecclesiae prouentum spectat, haec ipsa capita latius extendere, et pro re ac
tempore vel augere vel minuere vel quae videbuntur immutare liceat.
Actum Wesaliae 3° Nouembris anni 1568.

800 Petrus Dathenus subscripsit.
Hermanus Moded.
Cornelius Walrauen.
Herm. Moded nomine Jacobi Michaelis.
Johannes Lippius.
805 Godefridus Pistorius.
Guilielmus Zulenus Nijueldius.
Petrus de Rycke.

783/785 Habita – retineatur] cfr Eph. 4, 3

799 Actum – 1568] on the signatories listed below, see Goeters, 'Der Weseler
Konvent', p. 92-96; Sponholz, *The Convent of Wesel*, p. 66-93

803 Herm.] *intellege* Hermannus   nomine] *a.c.* no^ie

CONVENTUS VESALIENSIS – 1568

Joannes Asperensis.
Joannes nomine Hermanni Millenii.
810 | Ita est Joannes Masius.
Joannes Wicodurstadius.
Hermannus Vander Meere.
Gerardus Larenius.
Joannes Woudanus.
815 Cornelius de Vos.
Gerardus Culenborganus.
Gerhardus Venradius.
Adrianus Vossius.
Jacobus Richoboscus.
820 Ego Johannes Lippius subsequentium nomine signo ad hoc requisitus:
Gasparus Coelaes.
Philippus Raesuelt.
Hermannus Rahemius.
Cornelius Egidii.
825 Petrus Dathenus Joannis Ostendorpii nomine subscripsit.
Leonardus Panhusius.
Albertus Goudrianus.
Christianus Sinapius Venlo.
Ludouicus Sanarii Eecloniensis.
830 Georgius Octauius Syluanus.
Joannes Cubus.
Henricus Michael.
Johannes Pedonius.
Franciscus Franckennus.
835 Philippus Marnixius.
Hubertus Busseurs.
Cornelius Poppius.
Simeon van Habosch.
Joannes Houe Bergensis.
840 Jacobus Pontifortius alias Sterckenbrugge.
Jacobus Laubegeois.
Christophorus Becanus.
Cornelius Rhetius subscripsit.
Gaspar van Bygaerden Bruxellensis.

---

809 nomine] *a.c.* no^{ie} **820** nomine] *a.c.* no^{ie} **825** Joannis] *a.c.* Jo^{is} nomine] *a.c.*
no^{ie} **833** Johannes Pedonius] *lectio dubia* **843** subscripsit] *supplevi*; *a.c.* ss.

706   CONVENTUS VESALIENSIS – 1568

845 | Dese naervolghende persoonen, de lecture der ouerghezette copie hen 25
ghedaen zynde hebben ooc onderteeckent

Reynier de Pestere.

Gooris vanden Bogaerde.

Lieven de Somere.

850   Jan van Winghene vuer mij seluen ende Mathijs vander Loo.

Pieter van Hoorebeke.

Crystoffels wut Waes.

Jacobus Miggrodius.

Cornelius Sperinxius.

855   Abraham Roussau.

Jan Morell.

Joos Faes.

Pieter Bauters.

Corneles Francken.

860   Joannes Castercomius.

Nomine Anthonii Algoet, ministri ecclesiae belgicae, et nomine Caroli Ricjwart, eiusdem ecclesiae Ministri apud Noruicenses, Hermannus Moded, requisitus, subscripsit.

| Joannes Cubus nomine Laurentii Bruninck, alias Bruxellensis, et Chris- 26
865 tophori Lantsochtii Brugensis.

---

845 der ouerghezette copie] it can be deduced that several copies of the *Articles* were prepared, and that not all the signatories were present in Wesel. There are no other surviving copies of the *Articles*. This copy appears to have been brought to England after the Convent and to have returned to the Netherlands only in the seventeenth century. See Goeters, 'Der Weseler Konvent', p. 95

---

861 Nomine] *a.c.* No^ie   ecclesiae] *a.c.* eccl^ae   nomine] *a.c.* no^ie   **862** ecclesiae] *a.c.* eccl^ae   Hermannus] *supplevi*; *a.c.* Herm.   **864** nomine] *a.c.* no^ie

SYNODUS EMBDANA
1571

|ACTA SYNODI ECCLESIARUM BELGICARUM, QUAE SUB CRUCE SUNT ET PER GERMANIAM ET PHRISIAM ORIENTALEM DISPERSAE, HABITAE EMBDAE 4. DIE OCTOBRIS ANNO 1571.

1.

Nulla ecclesia in alias, nullus minister in ministros, nullus senior in seniores, diaconus in diaconos primatum seu dominationem obtinebit, sed potius ab omni et suspitione et occasione cavebit.

2.

Ad testandum in doctrina inter ecclesias Belgicas consensum, visum est fratribus confessioni ecclesiarum Belgicarum subscribere, et ad testandum harum ecclesiarum cum ecclesiis regni Galliae consensum et coniunctionem confessioni fidei ecclesiarum illius regni similiter subscribere, certa fiducia earum ecclesiarum ministros confessioni fidei ecclesiarum Belgicarum vicissim ad mutuum testandum consensum subscripturos.

3.

Delecti sunt Petrus Dathenus et Joannes Taffinus, qui id ad proximam synodum Galliae ministris significent responsumque proximo fratrum conventui referant.

---

6 Nulla – alias] see 'Die Discipline ecclésiastique von 1559', hrsg. P. Opitz – N. Fornerod, in *RefBK*, vol. 2/1 (2009), p. 57-83. Article 1 (p. 74) rejects any 'principauté ou domination' of one congregation over others. See also the Gallican Confession (ed. I. Dingel), Article 30 (p. 558, 290/294)   **10/11** Ad – subscribere] see 'Confessio Belgica von 1561', ed. E. Busch, in *RefBK*, vol. 2/1 (2009). p. 319-370   **12/13** cum – subscribere] cfr Gallican Confession, ed. I. Dingel (p. 547-563, 1/404)   **17** Petrus Dathenus] on the names of the signatories, see below. Dathenus is not listed among the signatories. Although he was one of the authors of the invitation letter to the Synod of Emden, composed in Heidelberg, he was ultimately forbidden to participate in the Synod by the Palatine government   **17/19** qui – referant] the *Confessio Belgica* was recognised by the national Synod of the French Reformed Churches held in Figeac (1579). See Hovius, *Notities betreffende de Synode te Emden*, p. 26

SYNODUS EMBDANA – 1571

| 4.

Admonebuntur quoque ministri Belgici, qui ab hoc coetu absunt, ut in eandem subscriptionem consentiant. Idem et ab aliis omnibus praestabitur, qui in posterum ad ministerium verbi vocabuntur, antequam ministerium exercere incipiant.

5.

Catechismi formulam in ecclesiis quidem Gallicanis Genevensem, in Teutonicis vero Heydelbergensem sequendam duxerunt fratres, sic tamen, ut, si quae ecclesiae alia catechismi formula verbo Dei consentanea utantur, necessitate illius mutandae non astringantur.

6.

In singulis ecclesiis consessus erunt seu consistoria ministrorum, seniorum et diaconorum, quae singulis ut minimum hebdomadibus habebuntur, loco et tempore, quae singulis ecclesiis commodissima videbuntur.

7.

Praeter hos consessus erunt classici tertio vel sexto quoque mense vicinarum aliquot ecclesiarum conventus | pro earum commoditate et necessitate.

8.

Singulis praeterea annis habebuntur conventus omnium, quae per Germaniam et Phrisiam orientalem dispersae sunt ecclesiarum inter se, Anglicanarum inter se et earum, quae sub cruce sunt, inter se.

---

26 Catechismi – Genevensem] see 'Genfer Katechismus von 1542', hrsg. E. Saxer, in *RefBK*, vol. 1/2 (2006), p. 279-362   **26/27** in² – fratres] see 'Heidelberger Katechismus von 1563', hrsg. W. H. Neuser, in *RefBK*, vol. 2/2 (2009), p. 167-211   **27/ 29** sic – astringantur] for example, the Church of Emden, which included Flemish-speaking refugees, adopted a Low German *Small Catechism* in 1554 and adhered to it. See 'Der Kleine Emder Katechismus', hrsg. A. Rauhaus, in *RefBK*, vol. 1/3 (2007), p. 295-328

SYNODUS EMBDANA – 1571

9.

Secundo denique quoque anno conventus omnium simul ecclesiarum Belgicarum habebitur.

Classes ecclesiarum Belgicarum per Germaniam et Phrisiam orientalem dispersarum.

10.

Classicum conventum constituent utraque ecclesia Francofordensis, Schonoviensis, Gallica Heydelbergensis, Franckendalensis et S. Lambertana. Alium utraque Coloniensis, utraque Aquisgranensis, Traiectensis, Limburgensis, Novesiensis et, quae in Juliacensi sunt ditione. Alium Wesaliensis, Embricensis, Gochensis, Resensis, Gennepensis et, si quae aliae sunt in Clivensi ditione. Alium Embdana cum peregrinis ministris et senioribus Brabantiae, Hollandiae et Phrisiae occiduae.

| Classes ecclesiarum sub cruce.

11.

Classicum conventum constituent ecclesia utraque Antwerpiana, Buscoducensis, Bredana, Bruxellensis et, si quae aliae sunt in Brabantia. Alium

---

42/43 Secundo – habebitur] the first provincial Synod of Holland and Zealand was held 15-28 June 1574, while the first national Synod of the Netherlands was held 3-18 June 1578. Both were held in Dordrecht. See Rutgers, *Acta van de Nederlandsche Synoden der zestiende eeuw*, p. 42-119

47 Francofordensis] *intellege* Frankfurt am Main   **48** Schonoviensis] *intellege* Schönau im Odenwald, near Heidelberg   Gallica Heydelbergensis] *intellege* Heidelberg   Franckendalensis] *intellege* Frankenthal   S. Lambertana] *intellege* Lambrecht   **49** Coloniensis] *intellege* Köln   Aquisgranensis] *intellege* Aachen   Traiectensis] *intellege* Maastricht   Limburgensis] *intellege* Limbourg   **50** Novesiensis] *intellege* Namur   Juliacensi] *intellege* the county of Jülich   Wesaliensis] *intellege* Wesel   Embricensis] *intellege* Emmerich   **51** Gochensis] *intellege* Goch   Resensis] *intellege* Rees   Gennepensis] *intellege* Gennep   **51/52** in Clivensi ditione] *intellege* the county of Kleve   **52** Embdana] *intellege* Emden   Brabantiae] *intellege* the province of Brabant   **53** Phrisiae] *intellege* the province of Friesland   **56** Antwerpiana] *intellege* Antwerp   Buscoducensis] *intellege* 's-Hertogenbosch   **57** Bredana] *intellege* Breda   Bruxellensis] *intellege* Brussels

SYNODUS EMBDANA – 1571

Gandavensis, Marterensis, Roncensis, Aldernadensis, Verwicensis, Cominensis et ceterae, quae in utraque Flandria sunt. Alium Tornacensis, Insulensis, Atre-
60 batensis, Duacensis, Armenteriensis, Valencinensis et ceterae idiomatis Gallici. Alium Amsterdamensis, Delphensis et ceterae Hollandicae, Transisulanae et Phrisiae occiduae.

12.

Admonebuntur, qui in Anglia sunt, ut suas ecclesias per classes distri-
65 buant.

13.

Ministri eligentur a consistorio cum iudicio conventus classici aut duorum triumve ministrorum vicinorum. Electi autem sistentur coram ecclesia, ut vel tacitis suffragiis comprobentur vel, si quid sit, cur in electionem minus
70 consentire velit ecclesia, intra dies plus minus quindecim | obiiciatur. Si quae tamen ecclesiae consuetudinem electionis popularis, quae apud eas est, mutandam non esse censerunt, ferentur, donec aliter synodo generali sit constitutum.

14.

Eadem ratio in electione seniorum et diaconorum observabitur, nisi quod
75 classici conventus aut vicinorum ministrorum non erit expetendum iudicium.

15.

Singulis annis dimidia pars tum seniorum, tum diaconorum mutabitur, ascitis in eorum locum aliis, qui itidem biennium inserviant, relicta tamen

---

77/78 Singulis – inserviant] see 'Discipline', hrsg. Opitz – Fornerod, in *RefBK*, vol. 2/1 (2009), p. 79; *Conventus Vesaliensis*, Chapter V, Article 17

---

58 Gandavensis] *intellege* Gent   Marterensis] *locus incertus, forsitan* Mortier Roncensis] *intellege* Ronse   Aldernadensis] *intellege* Oudenaarde   Verwicensis] *intellege* Wervik   Cominensis] *intellege* Comines (France) *et* Comines-Warneton (Belgium)   **59** Tornacensis] *intellege* Tournai   Insulensis] *intellege* Lille Atrebatensis] *intellege* Arras   **60** Duacensis] *intellege* Douai   Armenteriensis] *intellege* Armentières   Valencinensis] *intellege* Valenciennes   **61** Delphensis] *intellege* Delft   Transisulanae] *intellege* the province of Overijssel   **64** qui in Anglia sunt] *intellege* the Dutch refugee churches in London, Norwich, Glastonbury, and Sandwich

SYNODUS EMBDANA – 1571

ecclesiis praesertim sub cruce constitutis vel longioris vel brevioris temporis
80 libertate, pro earum commoditate et necessitate.

16.

Examinabuntur ministri ab iis, a quibus eliguntur. Si probetur eorum
doctrina et vita, confirmabuntur cum solemnibus precibus et impositione
manuum, absque superstitione tamen et necessitate.

85 | 17.

Nulli ministro in aliena ecclesia concionari absque illius ecclesiae ministri
et consistorii, aut ministro absente absque consistorii consensu licebit.

18.

Qui se in ministerium iis locis insinuant, ubi ministerium iam constitu-
90 tum est, ut abstineant, a consistorio admonebuntur. Si nihilominus pertinaciter prosequantur, convocatis statim tribus quatuorve aut etiam pluribus, si fieri
potest, ministris vicinis ex classe, cuius est illa ecclesia, schismaticus ibidem
declarabitur. Quod vero ad auditores attinet, si contemptis pertinaciter admonitionibus audire schismaticum illum iam declaratum pergent, consistorium
95 ex praescripto disciplinae ecclesiasticae aget.

DE ADIAPHORIS IN BAPTISMO.

19.

Unica vel trina tinctio pro adiaphora censetur, proinde ecclesiis liberum
usum apud ipsas receptum relinquimus, donec aliter in proxima synodo gene-
100 rali statuatur.

---

96 De adiaphoris in baptismo] the issues of simple or triple immersion and of
godparents had led to a heated argument in the London refugee community. In Wesel,
both issues were treated as *adiaphora*. See the *Conventus Vesaliensis*, Chapter I, Article
10

---

98 tinctio] immersio *scr. J. van Foreest in apographo suo*; *uide app. ed. Rutgers, Acta van
de Nederlandsche Synoden der zestiende eeuw, p. 64*

714 SYNODUS EMBDANA – 1571

| 20.

Testes adhibere vel non adhibere ad baptismum rem adiaphoram arbitramur, proinde usus receptus in ecclesiis servabitur pro sua cuiusque libertate, donec aliter in synodo generali statuatur.

IN COENA.

21.

In ecclesiis, quarum instituendarum nobis libertas datur, pane communi seu cibario utendum eumque fragendum esse in sacrae coenae administratione censemus. Eundo autem stando vel sedendo sacrae coenae communicare indifferens iudicamus, idcirco ratione utentur ecclesiae, quae ipsis commodissima videbitur.

Cantare psalmos aut sacras literas legere, dum sacra coena administratur, liberum ecclesiis relinquitur, quemadmodum et verbis Christi vel Pauli uti in exhibendo pane et vino, qua in re cavebitur, ne verborum pronunciatio in consecrationis speciem vel opinionem tandem trahatur.

| DE MATRIMONIO.

22.

Nemo, qui sub parentum potestate est aut eorum, qui parentum locum obtinent, sine eorum consensu matrimonium contrahere debet; et fides matrimonii sine eorum consensu data nullius est momenti. Siqui tamen ita se iniquos hac in re praestarent ac difficiles, ut consentire nullo modo vellent (quod interdum religionis odio et aliis de causis accidit), an tam sancti instituti impediendi iusta sit causa, consistorii erit iudicare.

---

113 verbis Christi] cfr Matth. 26, 26-28; Marc. 14, 22-24; Luc. 22, 19 seq.   vel Pauli] cfr I Cor. 11, 23-26

105 In coena] see *Conventus Vesaliensis*, Chapter I, Article 10

SYNODUS EMBDANA – 1571

23.

Sponsalia legitime contracta, ne utriusque quidem partis consensu dissolvi poterunt, quin et operae pretium erit, iis contrahendis interesse vel ministrum vel seniorem ecclesiae, ut, antequam reciproca fiat promissio, intelligatur, an puram religionem amplectatur uterque, an consentiant parentes et, si alterutra aut utraque pars ante matrimonio iuncta fuerit, an de morte priorum coniugum legitimo testimonio constet.

| 24.

Matrimonio copulandorum nomina ternis diebus dominicis aut alioqui per tres vices iustis intervallis pro concione edentur.

DE DISCIPLINA ECCLESIASTICA.

25.

Ecclesiasticam disciplinam in singulis ecclesiis observandam esse censemus. Ministrorum itaque partes erunt non solum publice docere, hortari, arguere, sed et privatim unumquemque officii sui admonere, qua in re et seniores operam suam impendere oportet.

26.

Sive autem quis in doctrinae puritate erraverit, sive in morum sanctitate peccaverit, si id occultum est et a scandalo publico remotum, observabitur regula, quam diserte praescribit Christus Matth. 18.

27.

Peccata igitur occulta, quorum peccatorem privatim vel ab uno vel duobus tribusve testibus adhibitis admonitum poenituerit, non sunt ad consistorium deferenda. Occulta tamen vel reipublicae vel ecclesiae gravem per-

---

140 26.] cfr Matth. 18, 15-18

125/126 Sponsalia – poterunt] the Convent of Wesel postponed the decision as to whether divorce was admitted. See *Conventus Vesaliensis*, Chapter VII, Article 4
131 24.] see *Conventus Vesaliensis*, Chapter VII, Article 1

niciem adferentia, ut sunt proditiones vel animarum seductiones, ministro significabuntur, ut ex eius consilio, quid ea in re agendum sit, dispiciatur.

| 28.

Siquis in occultis duas tresve admonitiones non audierit aut publicum peccatum perpetraverit, ad consistorium deferetur.

29.

Peccatorum autem natura sua publicorum aut propter contemptum admonitionum ecclesiae publicatorum, publica fiet reconciliatio, non ex unius aut alterius, sed totius consistorii arbitrio eoque modo et forma, quae ad aedificationem cuiuslibet ecclesiae commodissima iudicabitur.

30.

Qui pertinaciter consistorii admonitiones reiecerit, a coenae communione suspendetur, quod si ita suspensus post iteratas admonitiones nullum poenitentiae signum dederit, hic erit ad excommunicationem progressus.

31.

Publice e suggestu peccatorem obstinatum admonebit minister, peccatum exponet, officia in eo reprehendendo, a coena suspendendo posteaque diligenter exhortando praestita declarabit; ecclesiam, ut pro hoc peccatore inpoenitente sedulo oret, monebit, antequam ad ultimum ex|communicationis remedium descendere ecclesia cogatur. Eiusmodi tres fient admonitiones. In prima non nominabitur peccator, ut aliquo modo ei parcatur. In secunda nomen edetur. In tertia ecclesiae significabitur, nisi resipiscat, excommunicandum esse, ut, si pertinax fuerit, tacitis ecclesiae suffragiis excommunicetur. Intervalla admonitionum in consistorii arbitrio erunt. Si ne his quidem officiis ad resipiscentiam possit adduci, promulgabitur coram ecclesia eiusmodi pertinacis peccatoris a corpore ecclesiae excommunicatio et abscissio. Usum et finem excommunicationis fuse exponet minister admonebitque fideles, ne familiarem et non necessariam cum excommunicato consuetudinem habeant, sed eius consortium vitent, hoc praecipue consilio, ut pudore suffusus excommunicatus de resipiscentia serio cogitet.

SYNODUS EMBDANA – 1571

32.

Qui gravia, ecclesiis probrosa et magistratus auctoritate plectenda | pecca-
ta perpetraverint, etiamsi verbis poenitentiam testentur, a coenae tamen communione suspendentur; quot autem vicibus, in arbitrio consistorii erit.

33.

Si ministri, seniores et diaconi peccatum publicum, ecclesiae probrosum
vel auctoritate magistratus plectendum perpetraverint, seniores quidem et
diaconi statim auctoritate consistorii munere abdicabuntur, ministri autem
suspendentur a functione. An vero abdicandi sint ministerio, classici conventus erit iudicare, cuius sententiae, si non acquieverint, ad synodum provincialem provocabunt.

34.

An vero ministri, seniores et diaconi iam abdicati, postquam poenitentia
ecclesiae satisfecerint, si denuo eligantur, admitti debeant, quod ad seniores et
diaconos attinet, consistorii, quod vero ad ministros spectat vel pertinet, classici conventus erit iudicare.

| 35.

Ministri Belgio oriundi, qui exteris ecclesiis operam addixerunt, si ab
ecclesiis Belgicis revocentur, dabunt operam, ut vocationi obtemperent, constituto ecclesiis suis legitimo tempore, quo sibi de aliis ministris prospiciant.
Quod si exterae illae ecclesiae illos dimittere nolint, ad alias non suspectas erit
provocatio. Admonebuntur autem ii, qui nondum operam suam cuiquam
addixerunt, ut libertatem obtemperandi vocationi retineant.

36.

Admonebuntur etiam membra ecclesiarum, quae ministri alicuius opera
libertatis tempore usae sunt, ut de alimentis ei, si egeat, prospiciant.

37.

Qui ex hac dispersione in aliqua civitate collecti sunt, studiosos aliquot
alent, quos sibi devinctos habeant, quorum opera, si qui aluerunt, carere

718 SYNODUS EMBDANA – 1571

possint, et patiantur, ut alia quaepiam ecclesia plene sibi addictos habeat, sumptus factos repetere poterunt, secus ve|ro, si ad tempus tantum concedant. 40

38.

210   Conscriptus est catalogus ministrorum nunc ministerio destitutorum et aliorum ad verbi ministerium aptorum. Delecti sunt singuli singularum classium ministri, qui hic sunt, qui classis suae ministros huius synodi nomine hortentur, ut diligenter inquirant, num quae sint in suis classibus ecclesiae ministris destitutae, eas hortentur, ut ministrum vocent, aliquos ex catalogo 215 proponant, ut mutuo consilio aliquis vocetur.

39.

Delecti sunt Embdae Dominicus Julius, Cornelius Rhetius, Joannes Arnoldi, Wesaliae Joannes Lippius, Petrus Rickius, Michael Jordanis, ut ecclesiae Belgico-germanicae ministris destitutae sciant ad hos viros scribendum, ut 220 ministros in iis aut vicinis locis degentes indicent.

40.

Si tanta egestate laboret ulla ecclesia, ut ministrum, quem vocat, alere | 42 non possit, classis dispiciet an primo plures ecclesiae vicinae coniungi poterunt. Praeterea ministri ecclesiarum dispersarum admonebuntur, ut ecclesiae 225 membra hortentur ad opem ferendam. Praesertim autem eos monebunt, qui ex ea erunt provincia, in qua est illa ecclesia, ipsi quoque ministri hac in parte aliis exemplo erunt.

41.

Ministri classis iis locis, in quibus ministerium verbi constitui non poterit, 230 lectores, seniores et diaconos constituent, ut sic colligantur ecclesiae.

42.

Ministri et seniores classium, quae sunt sub cruce, in omnibus civitatibus et pagis classium suarum et vicinis diligenter inquirent eos, qui propensi sunt

---

216 39.] only Lippius and Arnoldi can be found among the signatories of the decisions of the Synod of Emden. Peter Rickius (also known as de Rycke) and Cornelius Rhetius were among the signatories of the proceedings of the Convent of Wesel

ad puram religionem, ut eos ad officium hortentur. Itaque ecclesias aut saltem
ecclesiarum initia colligere studebunt, quod, ut melius executioni mandetur,
partientur classes hae inter se civitates et pagos vicinos, ne quid negligatur.
Eandem curam gerent ecclesiae dispersae civitatum et aliorum locorum vicinorum, praesertim a classibus procul dissitorum. Fideles dispersi illos classium
sub cruce ministros hac in re iuvabunt, indicando circumspecte nomina
eorum, quos cognoverint ad | religionem esse propensos in iis locis, unde eiecti 44
vel digressi sunt.

43.

Utilissimum est eam esse ecclesiarum coniunctionem, ut mutuis inter se
literis crebro significent, quae ad ecclesiarum in genere vel aliquarum privatim
conservationem et incrementum pertinere videbuntur, et nominatim haereti-
cos, schismaticos, mercenarios, cursores et alios eius generis homines exitiosos
designent, ut ecclesiae sibi ab illis caveant.

44.

Ut gravibus ecclesiarum oneribus occurratur, quae indies augentur eorum
levitate, qui nimis facile sedes | mutant, et aliorum, qui praetextu paupertatis 46
et religionis eleemosynas domesticis fidei necessarias et debitas praeripiunt,
consultum esse iudicavimus, ut in singulis ecclesiis publicetur eos, qui inde
migrabunt, non esse in posterum ut domesticos fidei iuvandos in aliis ecclesiis,
nisi testimonium ante actae in ecclesia, unde proficiscuntur, vitae et doctrinae
habeant.

45.

Dabunt autem operam ministri, ut, quicunque testimonium postulabunt,
eos, qua de causa migrare velint, interrogent negentque praecise testimonium,
si non satis iustam profectionis esse causam deprehenderint, cavebuntque
ministri et diaconi, ne proclives et faciles sint in exonerandis ecclesiis suis pauperibus, quibus alias nulla necessitate gravent. Quibus testimonium dandum
esse censebunt, in eo nomina et cognomina eorum, unde oriundi sint, quod sit
eorum opificium, quae causa migrationis, quamdiu in ea ecclesia egerint, quomodo se gesserint, quo tempore inde proficiscantur, quo se recipere statuerint
et alia eiusmodi ascribent.

| 46.

Dabitur autem profecturis, quantum usque ad proximam eeclesiam, qua transituri sunt, satis esse videbitur; quantum vero id sit, in testimonii literis annotabitur. Idem praestabunt aliae, per quas transibunt ecclesiae pro sua quaeque facultate, ut exhibito testimonio, si legitimum sit, ceteraque probentur, tantum largiantur, quantum opus esse ad proximam usque eeclesiam iudicabunt, idque testimonii literis adscribent et, quo die inde discedant, notabunt. Ita se et aliae gerent eeclesiae, donec ad designatum pertigerint locum, ubi testimonium exhibitum lacerabitur.

47.

Qui post mensem proximum Novembris sine ullo testimonio aut aliquo, sed non ad hanc normam conscripto ab ecclesiis migrabunt, non habebuntur pro fidei domesticis, quibus maxime benefaciendum esse docet Paulus. Si qui tamen ex ecclesiis, quae sunt sub cruce, vel iis locis, | ubi nullum est ministerium constitutum, venerint, examinari eos operae pretium est, an sciant precari et possint rationem fidei reddere, qua de causa migrarint, et de aliis eiusmodi. Diaconorum autem erit prudentiae, quatenus istiusmodi sint iuvandi, dispicere.

48.

Rogabitur Sant Aldegundius huius synodi nomine, ut rerum in Belgio gestarum abhinc aliquot annos conscribat historiam ac praecipue earum, quae ad instaurationem ecclesiarum, persecutiones earum, idolorum deiectionem et restitutionem, martyrum constantiam, horrenda Dei in persecutores iudicia, mutationes politiarum etc. pertinent.

49.

Dabunt autem operam singularum ecclesiarum ministri et alii omnes, qui opera sua hoc institutum iuvare poterunt, ut, quae eo spectabunt, diligenter

---

278 quibus – Paulus] cfr Gal. 6, 10; I Tim. 5, 8

285 Sant Aldegundius] i.e. Philips van Marnix, Lord of Saint-Aldegonde (1540-1598), a collaborator of Wilhelm of Orange **286** conscribat historiam] eventually, Marnix failed to write this history of the Dutch Reformed churches, notwithstanding the fact that this request was reiterated by the national Synod of Dordrecht (1578)

SYNODUS EMBDANA – 1571

sciscitentur et inquirant et alicui ex his, qui ad hoc electi sunt, consignata mittant, quae postea ad Sant Aldegundium fideliter perferenda curent.

| 50.

Delecti sunt Embdae Christophorus Becanus et Cornelius Rhetius, Wesaliae Petrus Rickius et Carolus Niellius, Coloniae Adrianus Koningsloe et Joannes de Roy, Aquisgrani Joannes Christiani et Joannes Hueckelom, Francofurti Dominus de Balieu et Sebastianus Matte, Heydelbergae Petrus Dathenus et Joannes Taffinus, Franckendalii Caspar Heydanus et Petrus Anthonius, Schonoviae Franciscus Junius, S. Lamberti Nicolaus Schoubroeck.

51.

Nemo librum a se aut alio compositum, in quo de religione agatur, imprimendum vel alioqui evulgandum curabit aut patietur, nisi a ministris classis aut publicis theologiae professoribus nostrae confessionis examinatum et probatum.

52.

In ecclesiis frequentioribus operae pretium erit propositiones privatas haberi, quibus ii concionando exerceantur, de quibus spes bona est posse aliquando ecclesiae inservire; atque ad ordinem servandum praesidebit actioni minister aliquis.

| Conclusio.

53.

Articuli hi ad legitimum ecclesiae ordinem spectantes ita mutuo consensu sunt constituti, ut, si utilitas ecclesiarum aliud postulet, mutari, augeri et minui possint ac debeant. Non erit tamen alicuius privatae ecclesiae id facere, sed dabunt omnes operam, ut illos observent, donec a synodo aliter constituatur.

---

295 50.] the list of municipalities mentioned here coincides with the list of the addressees of the invitation letter sent from Heidelberg on 30 June 1571. See van Dooren, 'Voorbereiding en deelnemers', and Weerda, 'Eine Einladung zur Emder Synode' **302** 51.] a clear role model for the censorship of theological books is found in 'Discipline', hrsg. Opitz – Fornerod, in *RefBK*, vol. 2/1 (2009), p. 80 (Article 26)

Embdae, 12. die Octobris anno 1571, a quarto die usque ad duodecimum

Casparus Heydanus, praeses, manu propria subscripsit

320 Joannes Polyander, scriba.

FACTA PARTICULARIA SEU QUAESTIONES PARTICULARES.

I.

Audita expostulatione et petitione utriusque ecclesiae Embdanae, pro-miserunt fratres synodi se cum primum reversi domum erunt curaturos, ut 325 significetur ecclesiis suarum classium, ecclesiae Embdanae diaconos iis, qui legitimum ecclesiarum, unde proficiscuntur, vitae fideliter et pie anteactae testimonium exhibebunt, ut domesticis fidei opem laturos aliarum ecclesia-rum, per quas transeunt, exemplo, sed quae in multos dies aut menses aliquot, ut interdum fit, con|sistentibus, dum ventum secundum expectant, quo in 56 330 Angliam traiiciant, opus essent, in posterum suppeditare non posse, ne quis vana fiducia confisus sedes leviter mutet.

2.

Primae Coloniensium quaestioni an omnia scripturis sacris sint confir-manda responderunt fratres, quae conscientiae sunt, verbo Dei probanda; 335 quae vero ad ordinem spectant aut indifferentia sunt, ad eam necessitatem non esse redigenda.

3.

Ad alteram quaestionem de bibliorum correcta translatione Flandrica quod attinet, eam ad synodum generalem reiiciendam censuerunt fratres.

---

323 utriusque ecclesiae Embdanae] two communities are mentioned here: in fact, in addition to the local congregation, which the Flemish-speaking Dutch Reformed believers joined, there also was a French-speaking community of Walloon exiles. They set up two independent systems of poor relief, which also took care of fellow Reformed believers travelling to England via Emden **332** 2.] this article explains the relatively small number of Biblical references in the decisions

SYNODUS EMBDANA – 1571

340

4.

Tertiae quaestioni et quartae responsum est in articulis 51., 'Nemo librum', et 52., 'In ecclesiis'.

5.

Quintae quaestioni de actis synodi Rupellensis in Galliis, ut satis fiat, D. Petro Datheno et Joanni Taffino mandarunt fratres.

| 6.

Sextae quaestioni respondet articulus 38. de vocatione ministrorum 'Conscriptus est catalogus'.

7.

Ad septimam sic responsum est, quod testes adhibere et audire in consistorio licet, iis autem deficientibus iuramentum in re gravi exigere seu deferre, non tamen imperando, quod solius est magistratus, sed monendo et hortando, et quamvis liceret forma solenni et apud magistratum consueta uti, expedit tamen abstinere propositaque serio Dei in periuros vindicta, ut veritatem quis agnoscat, obtestari. Consultissimum autem est, quam rarissime et testes adhibere et iuramentum exigere.

8.

Ad Coloniensium quaestionem de marito, quem uxor sequi non vult, responsum est, proclamationes auctoritate magistratus esse necessarias; proinde ad eam civitatem se recipere poterit maritus, ubi magistratus operam et auctoritatem suam interponere velit.

---

343 5.] at the seventh national Synod of the French Reformed Churches, held in La Rochelle in 1571, a revised version of the *Confessio Gallicana* was adopted (see p. 547-563, 1/404)

724 SYNODUS EMBDANA – 1571

9.

Ad decimam fratrum Coloniensium quaestionem, an liceat papistae alicuius infantem baptizare, qui testatur baptismi formam in ecclesiis | refor- 60 matis receptam sibi puriorem videri quam eam, quae in papatu usurpatur. Qui sibi satisfieri cupiunt, exemplar sumant articuli a fratribus Genevensibus ea de re conscripti.

10.

Ad undecimam Coloniensium quaestionem, an possent susceptores admitti, qui etiamsi religionem puram amplectantur, sese tamen ecclesiae nolint adiungere, sic responsum est: Quia visum est fratribus susceptorum in baptismo usum liberum relinquere, quibus in ecclesiis adhibebuntur, ut testes dumtaxat sint baptismi collati, ii, de quibus agitur, admittentur; sed ubi adhibentur sic, ut curam quoque instituendi infantis suscipiant, eos ecclesiae membra esse oportet.

11.

Quaesierunt Aquisgranenses et Colonienses fratres, an impie vivens frater post multas admonitiones frustra adhibitas excommunicandus sit an vero ad tempus differenda excommunicatio, quando ecclesiae dissipationem minatur, responsum est: Qui excommunicandus alioqui secundum Dei verbum est, excommunicabitur, quamvis ecclesiae dissipationem minitetur. Quia tamen tempora ad|monitionum publice faciendarum et excommunicationis pronun- 62 ciandae in iudicio et arbitrio consistoriorum relicta sunt, ad monitionum et excommunicationis tempora differri poterunt sic, ut et conservationis ecclesiae ratio habeatur et excommunicatio necessaria non negligatur.

12.

Ad propositionem fratrum Antwerpiensium de iis ministris, qui otiosi et alio vocati parere recusant, sic responsum est: Ministri, qui ministerio destituuntur et ab aliqua vocantur ecclesia et obtemperare recusant, an urgendi sint, iudicabit classicus conventus.

---

362 9.] this text, which is not included in the *Correspondance de Théodore de Bèze*, seems to have been written in 1570 for the Norwich community. It is reproduced in Dutch translation in Rutgers, *Acta van de Nederlandsche Synoden der zestiende eeuw*, p. 93 seq. See also Goeters, 'Die Emder Synode von 1971', p. 198

SYNODUS EMBDANA – 1571

13.

Ad eorundem propositionem, an liceat mulieri fideli et infideli marito coniunctae, illo invito infantem suum ecclesiae baptizandum offerre, responsum est: Licere quidem et debere; sed, quia forsitan non semper expediret, pro ecclesiarum conditione operae pretium erit, ut ea in difficultate consistorii consilium requiratur, cuius prudentiae erit, nec timidioribus frena laxare nec rigore nimio conscientias gravare.

| 14.

Quaerentibus ecclesiis, an fratribus liceat exercere mercaturam cum aliorum principum monetis, easdem fundere vel, ut fundantur et in peiores redigantur, curare aut occasionem praebere, responsum est: Pecuniam colligere, ut in deteriorem fundatur, et alioqui cudere vel cudi curare, unde aliquid reipublicae detrimenti adferatur, etiam dissimulante id eius loci magistratu, iustitiae et charitati contrarium esse et iis, qui puram religionem profitentur, indignum.

15.

Propositioni fratrum Gandavensium et Antwerpiensium responsum est: Pro gravitate peccati et offendiculi magnitudine, frequenti lapsus iteratione et ratione locorum aliarumque circumstantiarum dispiciet et maturo consilio iudicabit consistorium, an quis arcendus sit non solum a coena, sed etiam a coetu in ecclesiis sub cruce; si quid amplius requiritur, ad classicum conventum referetur.

16.

Rogavit frater Gandavensis, an haec peccata publica censenda sint, an vero occulta, nempe in secreto indulgentias accipere, matrimonium | inter papistas contrahere, infantem a sacrifico curare baptizari, inter privatos parietes coram consule vel aliquo ex magistratu Christum abnegare, per sanctos iurare. Haec quaestio, quia varie disputabatur, in alium coetum est reiecta.

17.

Aquisgranensium quaestionem de iuvene et ancilla reiiciunt fratres ad diligens omnium circumstantiarum totius negotii examen, a consistorio faciendum et postea classico coetui referendum.

726   SYNODUS EMBDANA – 1571

18.

Antwerpiensis ecclesiae Gallicae quaestioni, quid agendum sit mulieri alleganti maritum in bello mortuum abhinc quatuor quinqueve annos, mor-
425 tem tamen certo testimonio probare nequeunti, responsum est: Utendum esse proclamationem auctoritate magistratus remedio, quod, si obtinere non possit, petet a magistratu, ut quantum temporis sit ei expectandum, statuat; si neutrum obtinere queat, consuletur ei, ut in eam civitatem se recipiat, ubi magistratus operam et auctoritatem suam interponere velit.

430   ### 19.

Alteri eiusdem ecclesiae quaestioni, de viduis mulieribus mense uno | aut   68 altero a mariti obitu nubere volentibus, responsum est: Consistorium nec posse nec debere definire tempus, cum Paulus viduis permittat nubere sine temporis definitione, tamen honestatem postulare, ne ad secundas transeunt
435 nuptias ante menses quatuor quinqueve et, si gravidae essent, menses circiter duos a partu.

20.

Tertiae eiusdem ecclesiae quaestioni de eo, qui suspensus a coena ob grave peccatum, uxorem ducere vult in ecclesia, non agnito prius publice peccato,
440 responsum est: Censuris ecclesiasticis agendum esse in eum; si resipiscat, admittendum; sin minus, admonendam mulierem, ne contrahat matrimonium cum viro, gravi aut publico peccato contaminato, ecclesiae contemptore et a coena suspenso et excommunicato.

21.

445 Quaesitum est, quoto gradu affinitatis et consanguinitatis prohibitum sit matrimonium, responsum est: Consultissimum esse, praesertim ubi magistra-

---

433/434 cum – definitione] cfr I Tim. 5, 14; I Cor. 7, 9

444 21.] canon law forbade marriages between spouses with certain degrees of consanguinity. Failure to observe these prohibitions could result in punishment by civil magistrates in Catholic areas. Looser regulations were promulgated in several Protestant states. Unlike in the proceedings of the Convent of Wesel, where secular authorities are mentioned at various stages (Chapter VII, Article 4; Chapter II, Article 3; Chapter V, Article 11; Chapter VIII, Article 22), the decrees of the Synod of Emden make no other reference to the civil magistrates' participation

SYNODUS EMBDANA – 1571

tus est infidelis, loci leges et consuetudines observare, quandoquidem id sine Dei offensa fieri potest, | ne matrimonium contra eas contractum a magistratu 70 declaretur nullum liberique illegitimi, haereditas alia deferatur vel devolvatur 450 aliaque eiusmodi mala contingant.

22.

Quaestioni de ministro uxorem habente haereticam, ab Aquisgranensibus propositae, responsum est: Quoniam iam in ministerio est constitutus, diligens a consistorio fiet inquisitio, quantum studium et operam adhibuerit 455 tum sancta conversatione, tum assiduis e verbo Dei admonitionibus, ut uxorem Christo lucrifaceret. Quod si negligentior in hoc officio fuisse et esse deprehenditur, iudicio et auctoritate consistorii cum classe a ministerio suspendetur; et si consistorium remissius se gerat, aliquorum fratrum ecclesiae iudicio, tum illi a consistorii vel negligentia vel sententia ad classem provocare 460 poterunt.

23.

Convocabitur synodus generalis ad proximum ver, si modo declarent | 72 Anglicae ecclesiae se aliquos ad eam ablegare velle et posse, etiamsi non omnes in hoc consentirent; sin minus, reiicietur synodus generalis in alterum ver anni 465 73.

24.

Delecta est classis Palatinatus ad convocandam synodum generalem.

25.

Delectae sunt hae in singulis classibus ecclesiae, ad quas scribendum erit, 470 Embdana, Wesaliensis, Coloniensis, Heydelbergensis, Antwerpiensis, Gandavensis, Tornacensis et Alckmariensis in Hollandia.

Embdae, 13. Octobris 1571

Gasparus Heydanus, praeses
Joannes Polyander, scriba.

---

461 23.] the first national Synod of the Dutch churches did not take place until 1578

DE CLASSICIS CONVENTIBUS.

1.

In classicis conventibus ministrorum unus concionem in ecclesia habebit, de ea ceteri collegae una collecti iudicabunt et, si quid corrigendum sit, indicabunt. Idem ceteri suo | quisque ordine praestabunt in proximis classicis conventibus.

2.

Postea praeses communibus collegarum suffragiis electus post conceptas preces singulos rogabit, num habeantur consessus consistoriales in eorum ecclesiis, an disciplina ecclesiastica vigeat, an certamen habeant cum haereticis, an dubitationis quid habeant in aliquo doctrinae capite, an pauperum et scholarum cura geratur, an ad gubernationem ecclesiae egeant collegarum consilio et opera et pleraque huius generis alia.

3.

Si quid in aliqua classis ecclesia acciderit, quod in illius consistorio componi non possit, in conventu classico discutietur et iudicabitur, a quo ad provincialem erit appellatio.

4.

Ceterum in conventibus classicis, quae ad classis illius ecclesias pertinebunt, tractabuntur.

5.

His peractis proponet praeses unam aut alteram quaestionem de capitibus in religione controversis inter nos, papistas et alios, qua ratione se mutuo erudiant et ad studia excitent.

| 6.

In eo conventu classico, qui proxime provincialem praecedit, deligentur, qui ad provincialem classis illius nomine ablegentur.

SYNODUS EMBDANA – 1571

7.

Mittentur autem ex singulis classibus duo ministri cum totidem senioribus aut diaconis aut saltem unus cum seniore uno vel diacono.

8.

Antequam capita conscribantur in synodo provinciali proponenda, consultum est, ut legantur accurate praecedentium synodorum acta et constitutiones, ne in synodis provincialibus ac praecipue generalibus, quae ante tractata
et definita communi consensu fuerunt, denuo proponantur, nisi nova dubitan-
di de eo, quod decisum fuerit, causa subsit.

9.

Postremo locus et tempus proximi conventus designabitur gratiaeque
Deo agentur, quas concipiet praeses.

DE PROVINCIALIBUS SYNODIS.

I.

Qui ad provincialem conventum mittentur, literas dimissionis et capita
proponenda scriptis consignata afferent, neque alia conscribentur, quam quae
in consistoriis et conven|tibus classicis definiri non potuerunt vel ad ecclesias
omnes illius provinciae pertinebunt, ne conventus provincialis quaestionibus
non necessariis protrahatur.

2.

Cum convenerint, loci minister aut, si nullus sit, is, qui superiori conventui praefuit, preces concipiet ad praesidis, assessoris, scribae electionem.

3.

Praeses electus preces habebit ad totam actionem accommodatas. Postea
nomina eorum, qui aderunt, conscribi, absentium notari, ut absentiae causam
reddant, curabit. Literas dimissionis seu testimoniales postulabit, ut legantur

---

502 7.] see Opitz – Fornerod, 'Discipline', Article 3

730   SYNODUS EMBDANA – 1571

instructiones seu mandata singulorum scriptis consignata, quorum singula ordine proponet, totius coetus iudicium exquiret, suffragia colliget, quae
530 maioris et sanioris partis erit sententia, exponet, eam scriba excipiet, exceptam diserte leget, ut omnium calculis probetur.

| 4.   80

Quae ad doctrinam primum, deinde quae ad disciplinam ecclesiasticam pertinebunt, et legentur et scriptis distincte consignabuntur, deinde facta
535 particularia.

5.

Officium praesidis est iubere, ut unusquisque ordine suo loquatur, silentium acrioribus et contentiosis imperare, nisi taceant, ut egrediantur ex coetu praecipere, ut ex fratrum iudicio censura digna reprehendantur.

540   6.

Praesidis officium cum actione finitur, liberum autem erit proximo conventui provinciali vel eundem vel alium eligere.

7.

Seniores aut diaconi, qui ad conventus hos mittentur, suffragium habebunt in omnibus sessionibus una cum suarum ecclesiarum ministris. Ex senioribus autem loci, in quo convenerint, duorum dumtaxat sententiae suffragii vim obtinebunt, quantumvis ceteris quoque senioribus interesse et sententiam dicere liceat.

8.

550 Omnes sessiones inchoabit praeses a precibus, claudet autem gratiarum actione.

9.

Articuli omnes constituti scriptisque consignati denuo legentur, ut ab omnibus et probentur et subscribantur. Unusquisque autem eorum exemplar
555 referet, a praeside et scriba | subscriptum, ut in consistoriis singularum eccle- 82 siarum legantur.

SYNODUS EMBDANA – 1571

10.

Totius conventus provincialis consensu eligetur ecclesia, cui cum aliorum classis suae ministrorum iudicio constituendi locum et tempus proximi conventus provincialis et ius et cura delegabitur.

11.

Ad hanc ecclesiam, quaecunque in aliis occurrent difficiliora, quaeve in consistoriis et classicis conventibus definiri non potuerunt, aut quae graviora ad universam provinciam pertinebunt, diligenter et mature mittentur.

12.

Haec ecclesia locum et tempus provincialis conventus proximi constitutum ceteris ecclesiis trimestre ante significabit exemplarque eadem opera illorum omnium capitum seu articulorum, qui ad eam missi fuerint, transmittet, de quibus mature unaquaeque ecclesia cogitet iudiciumque suum in conventu classico proferat, ut, qui illius classis nomine ablegabuntur, iam praemeditata et ab omnibus illius classis ecclesiis discussa proferant.

13.

Ne tamen ecclesia, cui cura designandi loci et temporis ad convo|candam proximam synodum provincialem mandata est, scribendis ad singulas omnium illius provinciae classium ecclesias literis plus aequo gravetur, in unaquaque classe eligetur ecclesia, ad quam scribet, ut illa, quae acceperit, cum suae classis ministris communicet.

14.

Communibus uniuscuiusque classis sumptibus intererunt synodo, qui ad eam ablegabuntur.

15.

Absolutis synodi negotiis celebrabitur sacra coena inter ministros et seniores, qui ad synodum convenerunt, et ecclesiam loci, in quo collecta est, si loci ratio id feret.

732 SYNODUS EMBDANA – 1571

585 16.

Ecclesiae, in qua synodus habetur, cura incumbet, ut ad proximam synodum acta seu constitutiones illius synodi vel afferat vel mittat.

DE GENERALIBUS SYNODIS.

Eadem in synodis generalibus servabuntur, quibus intererunt non a classi-
590 bus, sed provinciis delegati ministri et seniores cum literis testimonialibus et mandatis ad doctrinam, disciplinam et facta particularia spectantibus, quae in conventibus provinciali|bus definiri non potuerunt aut ad omnes ecclesias 86 spectant.

| Interfuerunt huic coetui atque subsignaverunt hi ministri   88

595   Jasparus Heydanus, minister Franckendalensis ecclesiae
      Joannes Taffinus, Heydelbergensis ecclesiae Gallicae minister
      Polyander, Embdanae ecclesiae Gallicae minister
      Hermannus Modet
      Carolus Niellius, Wesaliensis ecclesiae Gallicae minister
600   Sybertus Loo, Coloniensis ecclesiae minister
      Joannes Hueckelom, Aquisgranensis ecclesiae minister
      Joannes Lippius, minister Wesaliensis
      Henricus Holtenus, ecclesiae Embricensis minister
      Joannes Woudanus, Antwerpiensis ecclesiae minister
605   Valerius Pauli Tophusanus, Gandavensis minister
      Franciscus Pauli, in Flandria minister
      Joannes Arnoldi, Amsterdamensis ecclesiae minister
      Petrus Gabriel, Amsterdamensis ecclesiae minister
      Gysbertus Zythopaeus, Schaganae ecclesiae minister
610   Andreas Cornelii, Brielensis minister
      Clemens Martini, Hornanus minister
      Andreas Theodoricus Castricomius, Frisiae occiduae minister
      Cornelius Joannis, Twiscanus minister
      Cornelius Christiani, futurus minister

---

594 Interfuerunt – ministri] on the participants' identification, see van Dooren, 'Teilnehmerliste der Emder Synode'; 'Voorbereiding', p. 81-87   **595** Jasparus Heydanus] Gaspar van Heyden was listed as moderator of the Synod **598** Hermannus Modet] Moded, Lippius, Woudanus, Michaelis, Bigardus, Becanus, and Meranus were among the signatories of the decisions of the Convent of Wesel

SYNODUS EMBDANA – 1571

615 Henricus Michaelis, futurus minister
Jasparus Bigardus, futurus minister
Joannes Cocus, in Flandria minister   ⎫
                                        ⎬ quondam
Joannes Ilstanus, in Frisia minister   ⎭

620   *Seniores*

Carolus de Noude   ⎫
                            ⎬ seniores ecclesiae Embdanae Gallicae
Christophorus Becanus   ⎭
Joannes de Roy, Coloniensis
625 Hermannus Meranus, Wesaliensis
Gabriel, Antwerpianus

CONCILIUM SANDOMIRIENSE

1570

edidit
Maciej PTASZYŃSKI

THE SYNOD, *CONCORD*, AND *CONFESSION* OF SANDOMIERZ 1570[*]

The *Concord of Sandomierz* was an agreement among Polish Calvinists, Lutherans, and Bohemian Brothers upon intercommunion and several organisational regulations. At the Synod, the delegates also agreed upon a confession of faith, which was merely a translation into Polish of Heinrich Bullinger's *Second Helvetic Confession*.

The choice of Sandomierz as the venue of the Synod was not incidental. Dialogue between these three confessions in Poland was prompted by the political conjuncture as well as by the theological offensive of the Roman Catholic Church, which had led to a wave of reconversions. The spread of Anti-trinitarianism also played a part in the decision to summon this Synod. In political terms, the state of affairs had dramatically changed after the Union of Lublin (1569), replacing Sigismund II Augustus Jagiellon's personal union of the Kingdom of Poland and the Grand Duchy of Lithuania with a formal union. During the proceedings at Lublin, important matters regarding faith still had to be settled. [1] Sigismund II, in a speech delivered on 12 August, revealed his anxieties about 'the diversity of religions and the different understandings of the holy Christian religion'. [2] Just four days earlier, he had allowed the construction of a Protestant cemetery in Cracow. [3] As Jan Pirożyński argued, 'no one should think [Sigismund II] was going to convert

---

[*] The final stage of preparation of this introduction and of the critical edition offered below was supported by project DEC-2018/203I/B/HS3/00351 of the National Science Centre in Poland (*Narodowe Centrum Nauki*).

[1] *Volumina legum*, pod red. J. Ohryzko , 8 vols, Petersburg 1859-1860, vol. 2 (1859), p. 101.

[2] *Dnevnik ljublinskago sejma 1569 g.*, pod red. M. O. Kojalovič, Sankt-Peterburg 1869, p. 634-635: '[n]iepomału mnie to troszcze iż to przyszło za panowanie mego – ta różność wiar i różne rozumienie około wiary świętej chrześcijańskiej, bo to czuję, iż to na mnie należy, aby jeśli inny rząd aby był w Rzeczypospolitej, tedy owszem, wiara święta chrześcijańska w kościele jednostajnym chrześcijańskim aby była'.

[3] Printed in *Kronika zboru ewangelickiego krakowskiego przez X. Wojciecha Węgierskiego*, pod red. M. Pawelec, Kraków 2007, p. 64-65.

738   CONCILIUM SANDOMIRIENSE – 1570

anyone with cruelty or severity'. (4) His words could indeed be perceived as a spark of hope by Protestants seeking to legalise their confessions, provided that they could accept to be reunited in a single Church. However, the King was a fifty-year-old man without a direct heir to the throne, and his third wife, Catherine of Austria, had left Poland in 1566. On the one hand, Protestants hoped that the King could be persuaded to divorce; on the other hand, they feared that his successor might resort to persecution. (5)

Synodal works were held from 9 to 14 April 1570. (6) Following the tradition, the divine service and the election of moderators preceded the opening of the Synod. Four moderators were chosen: two secular (the *palatinus* of Sandomierz Piotr Zborowski and the leading nobleman Stanisław Iwan Karmiński) and two clerical (Reformed pastors Paweł Gilowski and Andrzej Prażmowski). This choice reveals the crucial role played by the nobility and the Reformed clergy of Lesser Poland in the Synod of Sandomierz. The high nobility of Lesser Poland was represented, among others, by the *palatinus* and *capitaneus* of Cracow Stanisław Myszkowski, the *capitaneus* of Oświęcim Zygmunt Myszkowski, and the *castellanus* of Lublin Stanisław Słupecki; (7) probably, the *castellanus* of Biecz Stanisław Szafraniec also participated in the Synod. (8) Local political leaders such as Leonard Strasz (9) and Mikołaj Dłuski (10) were also in Sandomierz. Other regions and other confessions did not share the enthusiasm of Lesser Poland. The Reformed Church of the Grand

(4) J. Pirożyński, *Sejm 1570 r.*, Kraków 1972, p. 9-10. See Theodore Beza to Krzysztof Trecy, 18 June 1570, in H. Meylan – A. Dufour et al. (eds), *Correspondance de Théodore de Bèze*, 42 vols to date, Genève 1960–, vol. 11 (1983), p. 189-192, here 189: '[r]egiae Majestatis consilium de compescendis sectis valde probo, modo ne tam sit irritum quam edictum illud quo jampridem illarum authores e regno suo extruserat. Est tamen, fateor, illud metuendum de quo scribis, nimirum ne boni quoque cum malis involvantur'.

(5) Krzysztof Trecy to Heinrich Bullinger, 19 January 1570, in *Der Briefwechsel der Schweizer mit den Polen*, p. 312-317, here 315: '[q]uid igitur iam futurum sit, in manu dei est, et speramus meliora et metuimus deteriora'; Pirożyński, *Sejm 1570 r.*, p. 19-22.

(6) The best summaries can be found in Jabłoński, *Historia*, p. 37-59; Halecki, *Zgoda sandomierska*, p. 199-259; Bidlo, *Jednota bratrská v prvním vzhnanství*, vol. 2, p. 151; Jordt Jørgensen, *Ökumenische Bestrebungen*, p. 263-265; Pirożyński, *Sejm 1570 r.*, p. 30-32; Bartel, 'Zgoda Sandomierska', p. 3-30, here 9-12.

(7) H. Kowalska, 'Słupecki Stanisław', in *PSB*, vol. 39 (1999-2000), p. 115-118.

(8) I. Kaniewska, 'Szafraniec Stanisław', in *PSB*, vol. 46 (2009-2010), p. 471-479; H. Kowalska, 'Stanisław Szafraniec z Pieskowej Skały', *Odrodzenie i Reformacja w Polsce* 3 (1958), p. 99-130.

(9) I. Kaniewska, 'Strasz Leonard', in *PSB*, vol. 44 (2006-2007), p. 206-208.

(10) This is not mentioned in H. Barycz, 'Dłuski Mikołaj', in *PSB*, vol. 5 (1939-1946), p. 195-197; see Halecki, *Zgoda sandomierska*, p. 203.

CONCILIUM SANDOMIRIENSE – 1570

Duchy of Lithuania failed to send any delegates to the Synod; the Lutheran Church of Greater Poland sent only two pastors, Erazm and Mikołaj Gliczner, and Stanisław Bniński, the *iudex* of Poznań; the Bohemian Brethren sent only a deacon, Simeon Teofil Turnowski, who later had a distinguished career in the Brethren, but in 1570 was a young and inexperienced man. At any rate, the high number of participants represented a great success for this intra-Protestant initiative, although the information found in some Roman Catholic sources – according to which thousands of noblemen attended the Synod – is certainly exaggerated. ([11])

On 10 April (the second day of synodal works), the churches' delegations presented their letters, which were discussed by the assembly. In the first speech, Erazm Gliczner, spokesman of the Lutherans, evoked the authority of Martin Luther, declared his commitment to the *Augsburg Confession*, and criticised the Brethren. The latter's orator, Andrzej Prażmowski (Jędrzej Prasmovius), defended the reputation of the Brethren and their confession from Gliczner's criticisms. ([12]) In his apologetical speech, he glorified over 150 years of history of the Brethren, going back to the times of Jan Hus and proven by the blood of the martyrs. ([13]) After hearing the speeches of the other delegations, the assembly questioned some members of the anti-trinitarian community and eventually expelled them from the Synod. Their decision to show up at the Synod of Sandomierz might be a sign of the growing tendency of the *ecclesia minor* (as the anti-trinitarians defined themselves) to seek to rejoin other Protestant churches. ([14]) Magisterial Protestants, however, were persuaded that their clear refutation of the 'Arians' (as they called anti-trinitarians) was a *condicio sine qua non* of the success of the Synod. Simeon Teofil Turnowski, an unofficial representative of the Brethren, wrote that after a public examination of the anti-trinitarians the real confessional debate was held during a private colloquium of the clergy on 11 April. ([15])

The expulsion of the 'Arians' opened on 10 April the third session of the proceedings, focusing on the debate over the *Concord* and the text of a confession of faith. During the discussions, Reformed pastors and secular patrons strongly supported the idea of a 'common and Polish confession'. On the

---

(11) We refer here to a letter of Jan Dymitriusz Solikowski to Marin Kromer, quoted in J. Łukaszewicz, *Dzieje Kościoła helweckiego w Małopolsce*, Poznań 1853, p. 249, note 2: 'celebrant suum conventiculum haeretici Sandomirae; feruntur ad aliquot millia confluxisse'.

(12) M. Sipayłło, 'Presmovius Andrzej', in *PSB*, vol. 28 (1984-1985), p. 350-351.

(13) Cfr Jabłoński, *Historia*, § 28, p. 42-44.

(14) Halecki, *Zgoda sandomierska*, p. 221-222.

(15) 'Odłożeni na privatum colloquium cum ministris'.

following day, the confession was read and discussed. On 12 April, when Turnowski agreed to the new confession, 'in Gliczneris cernere erat vultus subinde mutabiles'. As Lutherans realized that the agreement between the Reformed believers of Lesser Poland and the Brethren of Greater Poland had been reached, they appeared to be willing to accept the confession.

Krzysztof Trecy and Jean Thenaud were asked to prepare the first draft of the *Concord*. (16) A new phase of discussions began: debates over key theological question took the place of the previous hair-splitting about the translation. A bitter controversy, however, emerged over the Eucharist and the presence of Christ. On the one hand, Turnowski objected to the use of the term 'substantialiter' and proposed the word 'vere' instead; on the other hand, Lutherans demanded the acceptance of the formula from the *Confessio Saxonica*, a revised version of the *Confessio Augustana*, as they maintained that this confession had been accepted by Theodore Beza during the Colloquy of Worms in 1557. (17) However, they failed to remember – or pretended not to remember – that Beza's endorsement of the *Augustana* specifically excluded the article concerning the Eucharist; (18) on top of that, this *ex auctoritate* argument could not be accepted by the representatives of the Brethren (in Turnowski's words: 'ne illius [Beza's] quidem auctoritas apud me tanti est, ut aliter faciam, quam iam dixi'). Further discussions were focused on the possibility to admit

---

(16) Jan Birn incorrectly assumed that they were obliged to prepare 'a Confession'. Cfr. J. Birn, 'Francuz wśród kalwinów małopolskich. Jan Thenaud', *Reformacja w Polsce* 4 (1926), p. 41-44, here 44: '[n]owe wyznanie wiary mają znów ułożyć Trecy wraz z Thénaudem'. Theodor Wotschke neglected Tretius' activity, although he admitted that 'the Union of Sendomir [...] was for the most part his work'. Cfr. T. Wotschke, 'Christoph Thretius. Ein Beitrag zur Geschichte des Kampfes der reformierten Kirche gegen den Antitrinitarismus in Polen', *Altpreussische Monatsschrift* 44 (1907), p. 1-41 and 151-210, here 205.

(17) *Scriptum legatorum Gallicorum ad Theologos in colloquio Vuormatiensi congregatos*, in *CR*, vol. 9 (1842), p. 332-334. It was signed by Guillaume Farel, Johannes Budaeus, Gaspard Carmel, Theodore Beza. See E. K. Sturm, *Der junge Zacharias Ursin. Sein Weg vom Philippismus zum Calvinismus (1534-1562)*, Neukirchen-Vluyn 1972, p. 87-99. This aspect of the colloquy is not mentioned in B. Slenczka, *Das Wormser Schisma der Augsburger Konfessionsverwandten von 1557. Protestantische Konfessionspolitik und Theologie im Zusammenhang des zweiten Wormser Religionsgesprächs*, Tübingen 2010, p. 484.

(18) *Scriptum legatorum Gallicorum*, p. 333: '[e]t cum legerimus vestram confessionem, quae Augustae exhibita est, Anno 1530, prorsus (in omnibus articulis) illam congruere cun nostris Ecclesiis iudicamus, et eam amplectimur, excepto tament uno articulo, videlicet de Coena Domini, in quo controversiae haerent, de quibus colloquia cum vestris semper expetivimus, et speramus, dirimi eas posse, si eruditorum et piorum explicatio audiatur'.

CONCILIUM SANDOMIRIENSE – 1570

Roman Catholics to partake in the Eucharist and on infant baptism. Finally, on 13 April, the *Concord* was accepted and ratified by the representatives of the three confessions and reconfirmed during the closing celebration on the following day.

Above all, the *Concord of Sandomierz* represented a mutual acknowledgement of the three confessions in all regions of the new Polish-Lithuanian Commonwealth. The first article declared that in the *Confessio Helvetica Posterior*, the *Confessio Augustana* and the *Confessio Bohemica* there were no differences with regard to God, the Holy Trinity, the incarnation of Christ, justification, and 'aliis primariis capitibus fidei Christianae'. ([19]) However, in the text of the *Concord* there was no explicit reference to the *Confessio Helvetica Posterior*: the *Concord* referred to it as 'our confession' ('confessio nostra'), which was a clear and obvious manipulation. During the proceedings, on 10 April, Stanisław Myszkowski championed 'our, Polish' ('naszą, wszechpolską') confession. In very similar terms, Krzysztof Trecy had pleaded the previous day for 'our Polish, and not Czech, Saxon, or Helvetic confession' ('Chcemy mieć konfesyją nie czeską, saską, helwecką etc., ale polską własną'). On the one side, this was a hint at an old idea of a national Synod that could quench confessional quarrels; on the other hand, this phrase was formulated this way to get rid of any Lutheran resistance to the agreement. ([20]) Both Myszkowski and Trecy knew well, however, that this confession was merely a translation into Polish of Bullinger's work. In January 1570, Trecy had informed Bullinger that he had been ordered to prepare a translation of the *Second Helvetic Confession*, which the Protestant nobility of Poland intended to offer to the King. ([21]) This translation had probably been already printed before the Syn-

---

(19) See Völker, 'Unionsgedanken', p. 510; Jørgensen, *Ökumenische Bestrebungen*, p. 267.

(20) Halecki, *Zgoda sandomierska*, p. 229.

(21) Krzysztof Trecy to Heinrich Bullinger, 21 January 1570, in *Der Briefwechsel der Schweizer mit den Polen*, p. 312-317, here 314: '[m]ihi vero demandata est a generali omnium provinciarum synodo cura transferendi in linguam polonicam confessionem vestram, quam universi status evangelici regi pro suo confessione offerre in proximis comitiis volunt. Nec dubitant palatini nostri approbaturum regem, quam posthac ad vos etiam lingua polonica transmittam [...]. Interea nos quoque synodos cogimus ac cum longa deliberatione ad actus comitiorum futuros nos praeparamus ac praesertim hac translatione confessionis vestrae, quae a proceribus regni et ecclesiis omnibus nostris offeretur pro universo corpore doctrinae sonantis et docentis in ecclesiis nostris'. See also Wotschke, *Christoph Thretius*, p. 183.

742 CONCILIUM SANDOMIRIENSE – 1570

od took place, although it was not circulated. (22) This improper use of the *Second Helvetic Confession* had consequences in the long run: for example, in his history of the Polish Reformation, Andrzej Węgierski called the *Confession of Sandomierz* the 'Confessio tertia Helvetica'. (23)

The *Concord*'s second article concerned the Eucharist, which was defined in harmony with Reformed tradition and with the tradition of the Bohemian Brethren (1535 and 1561 confessions), but also with a consistent openness to Lutheran sensibility. (24) The authors of the *Concord* declared their agreement on 'the meaning of words'. It is important to underline here the difference between the manuscript version of the *Concord* and its later printed editions. While the handwritten minutes enigmatically feature the wording 'in sententia verborum', printed editions feature 'in sententia verborum Domini Nostri Iesu Christi'. (25) There is no doubt that the proper meaning of the phrase was fully grasped in the printed and official version. (26) The expression 'in sententia verborum' refers to the Words of Institution of Christ. In their definition of the Eucharist, the authors of the *Concord* referred to Irenaeus of Lyon and his *Adversus Haereses* (27). The *Confession* stated that this phrase meant that

(22) Stanisław Grzepski to Marcin Kromer, 22 May 1570, quoted in H. Barycz, 'Dwa nieznane listy Stanisława Grzepskiego', *Kwartalnik Historii Nauki i Techniki* 10 (1965), p. 96: 'Confessionem Polonicam haeretici priusquam Sendomiriam abirent excudendam curaverunt. Sed non est publicata, quoad ex Sendomiria redirent. Nam ego cum Antonio doctore in gratiam Leopoliensis laborabamus multum, ut exemplar nancisceremur, cum adhuc illi essent in conventiculo illo, sed obtinere non potuimus'. See also Pirożyński, *Sejm 1570 r.*, p. 29.

(23) A. Węgierski, *Slavonia reformata*, pod red. J. Tazbir, Warszawa 1973, p. 88; Jørgensen, *Ökumenische Bestrebungen*, p. 252.

(24) Völker, 'Unionsgedanken', p. 516-518.

(25) *Consensus in fide et religione Christiana*, s.l. 1586, p. x (Polish) and 11 (Latin); *Consensus in fide et religione Christiane*, Haidelbergae [*sic*] 1605, p. 11. See also Jabłoński, *Historia*, p. 190.

(26) This has been overlooked by D. Petkunas, 'The Consensus of Sandomierz: An Early Attempt to Create a Unified Protestant Church in Sixteenth-Century Poland and Lithuania', *Concordia Theological Quarterly* 73 (2009), p. 318-346, here 329-330.

(27) *Opus Eruditissimum Divi Irenaei Episcopi Lugdunensis*, apud inclytam Basileam 1560, IV, 34, p. 238: '[q]uemadmodum enim qui est a terra panis percipiens vocationem dei, iam non communis panis est, sed Eucharistia, ex duabus rebus constans, terrena et coelesti'. In the modern edition Iren., *Adver. Haeres.*, Patrologia Graeca, vol. 7, IV, 18, p. 1028-1029. On the reception of Irenaeus, see I. Backus, 'Irenaeus, Calvin and Calvinist Orthodoxy: The Patristic Manual of Abraham Scultetus (1598)', *Reformation and Renaissance Review* 1 (1999), p. 41-53; E. P. Meijering, 'Bemerkungen zum Nachleben des Irenäus im Streit der Konfessionen', *Vigiliae Christianae* 53 (1999), p. 74-99; J. van Oort, 'John Calvin and the Church Fathers' in I. Backus (ed.), *The Reception of the Church Fathers in the West*, 2 vols, Boston 2001, vol. 1, p. 661-700; Petkunas, 'The

the Eucharist was not merely a symbol, but a very specific kind of representation, which is for believers the same thing as what it stands for. This interpretation of the Eucharist was clearly not Lutheran, and could be found both in the *Second Helvetic Confession* and in the Bohemian Brethren's confessions. (28) The Lutheran tenet of the 'substantial presence of Christ' in the Eucharist was explained according to the Reformed tradition. The adjective 'substantial' was transformed into an adverb ('vere'). The sacrament was offered to the believers according to its nature. (29) This explanation, typical of the Reformed tradition, was nonetheless juxtaposed to an article from the *Confessio Saxonica*, defining baptism and the Eucharist as 'testimonies and tokens of grace'; during the administration of these sacraments, ('in usu'), Christ was present 'really and substantially' ('vere et substantialiter'). (30)

In spite of the dispute of 13 April, which made emerge growing discrepancies, the article as was approved was, on the whole, consistent. The version accepted by the Brethren and the Reformed representatives emphasised the sacramental nature of the presence, which Turnowski formulated in the discussion as 'secundum sacramentorum naturam'. The goal of this formulation was to avoid any ambiguity on the 'real presence of the body of Christ'

Consensus of Sandomierz', p. 329. See also K.-H. zur Mühlen, *Reformatorische Prägungen. Studien zur Theologie Martin Luthers und zur Reformationszeit*, hrsg. A. Lexutt – V. Ortmann, Göttingen 2011, p. 15-21.

(28) *Confessio Helvetica Posterior*, Article 21: '[f]ideles accipiunt quod datur a ministro domini, et edunt panem domini ac bibunt de poculo domini; intus interim opera Christi per spiritum sanctum percipiunt etiam carnem et sanguinem domini [...]. Et qui foris vera fide sacramentum percipit, idem ille non signum duntaxat percipit, sed re ipsa quoque, ut diximus fruitur'. Cfr. the commentary to this passage in E. Koch, *Die Theologie der Confessio Helvetica Posterior*, Neukirchen-Vluyn 1968, p. 293-313. On the Brethren's interpretation see J. Bidlo, 'O konfessi bratrske z r. 1573', in *Festschrift zu J. Golls 60. Geburtstag*, s.l. 1906, p. 246-278. On this Reformed understanding of the Eucharist see W. Janse, 'Calvin's Eucharistic Theology: Three Dogma-Historical Observations', in H. J. Selderhuis (ed.), *Calvinus sacrarum literarum interpres*, Göttingen 2008, p. 37-69; *Calvin Handbuch*, hrsg. H. J. Selderhuis, Tübingen 2008, p. 346.

(29) Pelikan, 'The Consensus of Sandomierz', p. 834.

(30) *Repetitio Confessionis Augustanae* [Confessio Saxonica], in *CR*, vol. 28 (1860), p. 327-468, here 415-418: '[e]t Baptismus et Coena Domini sunt pignora et testimonia gratiae, ut antea dictum est, quae de promissione et tota redemtione nos commonefaciunt, et ostendunt, beneficia Evangelii ad singulos pertinere, qui his ritibus utuntur etc. Item. Nec admittuntur ulli ad communionem, nisi prius a Pastore aut Collegis ejus auditi sint, et absoluti. In hac exploratione interrogantur et erudiuntur rudiores de tota doctrina et deinde absolutio promulgatur. Docentur etiam homines Sacramenta esse actiones divinitus institutas, et extra usum institutum, res ipsas non habere rationem Sacramenti: sed in usu instituto in hac communione vere et substantialiter adesse Christum et vere exhiberi sumentibus Corpus et Sanguinem Christi'.

('corporaliter'). This formulation was similar to the one found in the *Confessio Saxonica*, which included a 'moderate' interpretation of the mystery of the presence of Christ, typical of Philip Melanchthon's theology. ([31]) This formulation was allegedly proposed by Gliczner (a Philippist) as a good ground for compromise. ([32]) Gliczner would certainly have wanted the word 'body' to feature in the *Concord*, along with the concepts of 'communicatio idiomatum' and 'manducatio idignorum'; ([33]) however, this did not prevent his acceptance of the *Concord*.

Some theological and liturgical issues were purposely avoided in the text of the *Concord*. It stated that each confession should preserve its specificities in liturgical matters as in the *Augustana* and in the *Saxonica*, which was a clear hint at the category of *adiaphora*. Regardless of these differences, though, the different confessions should cooperate on an administrative and organisational level; believers could attend sermons delivered by ministers of other confessions ('auditione verbi frequentando') as well as the Eucharist; the three confessions should hold general synods together. Participants also expressed the wish to publish a common 'compendium corporis doctrinae' (the *corpora doctrinae* are a literary genre typical of Protestant confessions; Melanchthon put together a popular anthology himself, the *Corpus Doctrinae Misnicum*) ([34]) and to print all the confessions of faith together in order to show their orthodoxy and uniformity. Finally, the authors of the *Concord of Sandomierz* promised to work for peace and unity among the churches, and they silenced all opponents of the *Confession* and the *Concord*.

If compared to the crucially-important *Concord*, the *Confession of Sandomierz* was not particularly significant. ([35]) The Synod formally recognised it as a shared creed, but its status in Poland remained secondary to the confes-

---

(31) G. Wartenberg, 'Die *Confessio Saxonica* als Bekenntnis evangelischer Reichsstände', in C. Roll (hrsg.), *Recht und Reich im Zeitalter der Reformation. Festschrift für Horst Rabe*, Frankfurt a. M. 1996, p. 275-294.

(32) Wotschke, 'Erasmus Gliczner', p. 1-73; Völker, 'Unionsgedanken', p. 519-521; Müller, 'Der Consensus Sendomirensis'.

(33) Wotschke, 'Erasmus Gliczner', p. 28-29.

(34) L. Ullrich, 'Corpus (od. Corpora) Doctrinae', in *Lexikon für Theologie und Kirche. Dritte Auflage*, 11 vols, Freiburg i. B. 1993-2001, vol. 2 (1994), p. 1319-1320; a different meaning of *doctrina* in: C. Strohm, 'Der Begriff "Doctrina" in der reformierten Tradition des 16. Jahrhunderts', in C. Moser – P. Opitz (hrsg.), *Bewegung und Beharrung. Aspekte der reformierte Protestantismus, 1520-1650*, Leiden 2009, p. 413-432.

(35) U. Augustyniak, 'Wstęp historyczny', in K. Długosz-Kurczabowa (pod red.), *Konfesja Sandomierska*, Warszawa 1995, p. 26; Müller, 'Der Consensus Sendomirensis', p. 398-399.

CONCILIUM SANDOMIRIENSE – 1570

sions of faith of the single churches (except for Reformed churches). It had been rapidly attracting interest among the Polish and Lithuanian Reformed congregations since Bullinger sent it to Poland in 1567, recommending it as it was acknowledged 'in France, England, Scotland, and other nations'. (36) It was quickly adopted by the Reformed churches of Lesser Poland and preserved its official status throughout the seventeenth and eighteenth centuries. (37) Krzysztof Trecy, while translating its text, modified it in several aspects. He added an original preface in Polish and an appendix with the *Confessio Saxonica*'s article on the Eucharist as well as Theodore Beza's considerations. The preface addressed the King in person and had a slight apologetical character as it refuted any accusations of rebellion and political dissent, stating that liturgical differences did not jeopardise the 'unity of the faith' ('jedność wiary'). It also stated that the King's formal acceptance of the *Confession of Sandomierz* would grant him political success. According to Jerzy Lehmann, the preface affirmed the monarch's right to suppress any form of confessional dissent. (38) This translation in Polish showed traces of Melanchthonian tendencies, as well as some remnants of the Catholic tradition; nevertheless, generally speaking, it was quite faithful to the original version. (39) Despite his overall insignificant modifications, Trecy did not hesitate to send his translation to the original author of the *Second Helvetic Confession*. (40)

(36) Heinrich Bullinger to Jan Kiszka, 15 June 1567, in *Der Briefwechsel der Schweizer mit den Polen*, p. 285-286: '[n]on ita multos ante menses scripsi tibi, princeps illustrissime, simul etiam misi exemplum confessionis fidei et doctrinae ecclesiarum Helveticarum impressum typis et colligatum ac spero Magn. Tuam ea recepisse omnia'.

(37) *Akta Synodów Różnowierczych*, vol. 3 (1983), p. x and 192. J. Lehmann, *Konfesja sandomierska na tle innych wyznań*, Warszawa 1937, p. 104.

(38) Lehmann, *Konfesja sandomierska*, p. 138; a short summary can be found in Bartel, 'Zgoda Sandomierska', p. 12.

(39) For example in Chapter 5, on the merits of the saints, the translation rendered the phrase 'laetantur meriti, sui nos esse conservos' as 'weselą się z nas jako s spolnych towarzyszow zasług swoich'. The Latin phrase means, with 'sui', the merits of Christ, while the Polish phrase refers to the merits of the saints. Długosz-Kurczabowa, *Konfesja Sandomierska*, p. 52; Lehmann, *Konfesja sandomierska*, p. 161. Other deviations from the original can be found in Długosz-Kurczabowa, *Konfesja Sandomierska*, p. 83 (on the *Corpus Christi*) and 194-195 (on the Eucharist).

(40) Krzysztof Trecy to Heinrich Bullinger, 1 September 1571, in *Der Briefwechsel der Schweizer mit den Polen*, p. 342-343: '[...] cuius exemplar superiore anno ad te misi'. Krzysztof Trecy to Johann Wolf, 1 September 1571, *ibid.*, p. 345-346, here 346: '[c]eterum quod tibi consensus noster placeat, deum opt. max. celebramus eumque piis precibus continenter adhibitis invocare non cessabimus, ut is diu in sui nominis gloriam duret'. See also *ibid.*, p. 326; H. Gmiterek, *Bracia Czescy a Kalwiniści w Rzeczypospolitej. Połowa XVI – połowa XVII w.*, Lublin 1987, p. 72.

746 CONCILIUM SANDOMIRIENSE – 1570

The acceptance of the *Concord* on 13/14 April 1570 opened up a long process of formal ratification within the Lutheran Church and the Bohemian Brethren. On 18 May 1570, representatives of both confessions met in Poznań to thoroughly discuss the *Concord*. (41) Once again, the articles on the Eucharist stirred a bitter controversy as Erazm Gliczner demanded that some amendments were made to the text. (42) Other disputes involved the issue of liturgical vestments, still worn in the Lutheran Church but withdrawn in the other two. (43) On 20 May the representatives of the Brethren and of the Lutheran Church signed a version of the *Concord* with some amendments ('consignationes'). (44) This theological agreement, however, did not quell debates over the *Concord*. In October, a Lutheran Synod gathered in Poznań accused the Reformed Church of Cracow of not respecting its rules. (45) Jan Łasicki warned Bullinger that the Lutherans were considering forsaking the agreement. (46)

From a strictly political point of view, the *Concord* was equally unfruitful. In Sandomierz, the three confessions decided to take up their debate again at the Diet of Warsaw (16 April 1570). Oskar Halecki and Jan Pirożyński hypothesise that Protestants prepared a document which was supposed to be

(41) Smend, *Die Synoden*, p. 65-70. Jabłoński, *Historia*, p. 6-65; Halecki, *Zgoda sandomierska*, p. 303-305; Völker, 'Unionsgedanken', p. 511-512.

(42) Smend, *Die Synoden*, p. 67: '[n]os vitaturos Explicationes, verba et terminos alienos a Doctoribus Augustanae Confessionis'.

(43) Smend, *Die Synoden*, p. 67: '[...] quod censeamus reiciendas Casulas et ornatus, quae Ceremoniae Saxonicis sunt usitatae et permissae'.

(44) Smend, *Die Synoden*, p. 69-73; Jordt Jørgensen, *Ökumenische Bestrebungen*, p. 274-276.

(45) Smend, *Die Synoden*, p. 74-76: '[ż]adne, mówi, Zgromadzenie z swoją Confessią śię wynośić nie miało, ale wszyscy społem się zjechawszy, mieliśmy spisać Corpus Doctrinae. Ale Bracia Cracovienses wynoszą się z swoją (od nas nie przyjętą, bo w niej wiele błędów) Confessią et jam fere pro Corpore Doctrinae obtrudunt, tak jakby była universalis Confessio wszystkich Kościołów Polskich, y waszych y naszych: A ku temu się nie mają, aby stosowali insze Corpus Doctrinae. Denique Testimonia od Niemieckich Akademiey u siebie mają, a do nas ich nie przysyłają, acz y w tym mieli nam dać znać, gdy tam słali'.

(46) Jan Łasicki to Heinrich Bullinger, 11 December 1570, in *Der Briefwechsel der Schweizer mit den Polen*, p. 335-336: '[...] ego superioribus diebus excurreram in maiorem Poloniam, ubi cum essem, intellexi Lutheranos Posnanienses nostris Cracoviensibus nonnihil subiratos esse, ita ut de rumpenda illa nuper inita concordia cogitarunt'.

CONCILIUM SANDOMIRIENSE – 1570   747

accepted by the Diet. (⁴⁷) The Sejm consultations, which began on 3 May, were dominated by the issue of the King's marriage and the succession to the throne. (⁴⁸) However on 13 May, as soon as confessional issues were brought up, the debate fired up. (⁴⁹) Under the nobility's pressure, the King declared that nobody should be accused *pro haeresi* and confirmed his statement on 24 May. It is unclear whether the King accepted the *Confession* or not. According to Jan Łasicki's dispatch to Johann Wolf, written immediately after the Diet, the King had declared his intention to formally approve it, but Łasicki was ultimately unaware of any royal sanction. (⁵⁰) Krzysztof Trecy claimed that the *Confession of Sandomierz* was 'shown' ('exhibita') to the King, (⁵¹) which

(47) *De modo concordiae inter statum spiritualem et saecularem*, in T. Wierzbowski (pod red.), *Uchańsciana, czyli zbiór dokumentów wyjaśniających życie i działalność Jakóba Uchańskiego*, 5 vols, Warszawa 1884-1895, vol. 2 (1884), p. 256-259; Pirożyński, *Sejm 1570 r.*, p. 33-34; Halecki, *Zgoda sandomierska*, p. 262 and 291-294.

(48) *Diariusze sejmów koronnych 1548,1553 i 1570*, pod red. J. Szujski, Kraków 1872, p. 113-132; Wierzbowski, *Uchańsciana*, vol. 4 (1892), p. 261-263.

(49) See Pirożyński, *Sejm 1570 r.*, p. 41-64; Jakub Uchański to Stanislaus Hosius, 6 May 1570, in Wierzbowski, *Uchańsciana*, vol. 3 (1890), p. 241: '[t]errarum nuntii circa salutationem Sacrae Mtis Regiae ab Ipsa petierunt, ut iuxta regni statuta statum ecclesiasticum cum saeculari conciliaret, tam in iis, quae ad laudem Dei spectant, quam quae ad reditus'; Walenty Rosarius to Marcin Kromer, 10 June 1570, Bibliteka Czartoryskich (Kraków), MS 1611, fol. 255: '[c]omitia satis habemus turbulenta, oppugnantur reditus ecclesiae et regis, neque id tacite tantum sed palam etiam'.

(50) Jan Łasicki to Johann Wolf, 12 September 1570, in *Der Briefwechsel der Schweizer mit den Polen*, p. 332: '[r]es in praeteritis comitiis Warssaviensibus ita de religione gesta est, ut paene bellum civile ortum fuerit. Attamen rex visus et favere ecclesiae Cracoviensi, pollicitus ei privata quadam lege libertatem, quin et compendium illius libelli Polonici, quod vobis a me acceptum Thretius misit, approbaturum se dixit. Quod an fecerit ignoro, nam episcopos reverebatur'. See also Heinrich Bullinger to Theodore Beza, 19 July 1570, in *Correspondance de Théodore de Bèze*, vol. 11 (1983), p. 211-214, here 214: '[s]cribit Thretius Polonos coepisse magna celebrare comitia mense Maio, et in his nostrae religionis Regi offerre in suam linguam conversam nostram Confessionem aeditam anno 1566, sperareque Regem non damnaturum eam, qui alioqui omnes cogitet proscribere sectas. Expectamus ergo quid factum sit'.

(51) Krzysztof Trecy to Theodore Beza, 13 June 1570, in *Correspondance de Théodore de Bèze*, vol. 11 (1983), p. 163-167, here 164: '[e]xhibita est ergo Regi, cum praefatione ad suam majestatem scripta, Ecclesiarum Helveticarum et vestrarum confessio a me translata; inscriptione tantum immutata, velut vocant, titulo, propterea quod nomine omnium Polonicarum et Lituanicarum Ecclesiarum offertur. Ea igitur confessio, ita Polonica facta, in Sendomiriensi nostra Synodo unamini nostrarum Ecclesiarum consensu fuerat prius recepta, quamvis id etiam factum est post longas et graves disceptationes'. See also Krzysztof Trecy to Jan Rokita, 1 August 1571, in *Akta Synodów Różnowierczych*, vol. 3 (1983), p. 1-3, here 2: '[Confessio nostra] nuper Regi et senatui oblata'.

748 CONCILIUM SANDOMIRIENSE – 1570

enraged the bishops. (52) A few months later, Trecy declared that the King had received both the *Concord* and the *Confession*; however, there was 'no response' from him. (53) It is presumable that the *Confession* was offered to the King in private during the Diet or shortly after the proceedings, but it is unlikely that it was formally accepted and ratified. (54)

When on 7 July 1572 the King died, the nobility had to elect his successor. In an attempt to secure peace in a multi-confessional state, the nobility signed in January 1573 the Confederation of Warsaw, which guaranteed the noblemen the right to profess their own Christian confession regardless of the confession of the King. (55) Despite several scholarly attempts to draw similarities between the *Concord of Sandomierz* and the Confederation of Warsaw, connections between these two documents are ultimately unproven. On the contrary, they seemed to pursue opposite goals: whereas the *Concord* was a theological agreement concerning mutual recognition of the confessions involved, intercommunion, and the edition of a common *corpus doctrinae*, the Confederation was a legal act trying to resolve Polish religious issues through the same principle put forward in the Peace of Augsburg, i.e. *cuius regio, eius et religio*.

Debates over the *Concord of Sandomierz* did not cease after the promulgation of the Confederation. The *Concord* was discussed at the synods held in Cracow (1571, 1573, 1576, 1578), Warsaw (1578), Piotrków (1578), Poznań (1582), and Włodzisław (1583). (56) Polish Protestant churches eventually confirmed the *Concord* at the general Synod of in Toruń (1595), known as the

---

(52) Krzysztof Trecy to Theodore Beza, 8 October 1570, in *Correspondance de Théodore de Bèze*, vol. 11 (1983), p. 275-282, here 277.

(53) Krzysztof Trecy to Theodore Beza, 10 March 1571, in *Der Briefwechsel der Schweizer mit den Polen*, p. 336-338, also in *Correspondance de Théodore de Bèze*, vol. 12 (1986), p. 57-59: '[c]aeterum proceres nostri doctrinae confessionem et consensum illum regi obtulerunt, sed sine ullo responso res ad proxima comitia dilata est, in quibus de pacificatione inter status praecipue agetur'.

(54) Pirożyński, *Sejm 1570 r.*, p. 42-44; Halecki, *Zgoda sandomierska*, p. 336.

(55) M. Korolko, *Klejnot swobodnego sumienia*, Warszawa 1974; M. G. Müller, '"Nicht für die Religion selbst ist die Conföderation inter dissidentes eingerichtet...". Bekenntnispolitik und Respublica-Verständnis in Polen-Litauern', in L. Schorn-Schütte (hrsg.), *Aspekte der politischen Kommunikation im Europa des 16. und 17. Jahrhunderts*, München 2004, p. 311-328.

(56) Smend, *Die Synoden*, p. 76,83-85,86-96; *Akta Synodów Różnowierczych*, vol. 3 (1983), p. 5, 18-20, 31, 38, 40, 76-82. The decisions of these synods were published together with the *Concord* in 1586 and were reprinted in 1587 (with a translation into Polish), 1592, 1596, and 1628. See *Consensus sive concordia in fide et religione Christiana*, s.l. 1586; Völker, 'Unionsgedanken', p. 514-515.

CONCILIUM SANDOMIRIENSE – 1570

largest Polish Protestant assembly in the sixteenth century. (57) All pastors serving in Poland and Lithuania were supposed to hold a copy of the *Confession* and read it. Moreover, Paul Gericke, Lutheran pastor from Poznań and a zealous opponent of the *Concord*, was removed from office. (58) Gericke's *affaire* stands as testimony to the issues connected to the *Concord*'s reception in Poland. On 23 August 1595, at the Synod of Toruń, Gericke declared that he 'was ordained according to the Augsburg Confession, and [...] will stick to it; the Concord [...] is a shapeless mixture and a Samaritan union'. (59) Radical Lutherans repeatedly criticised the *Concord*. Erazm Gliczner, as the superintendent of the Lutheran Church of Greater Poland, had to deal with pastors such as Jakob Beinhard, Johann Enoch, and Paul Gericke, who lampooned the *Concord* and brought forward the *Augustana* in radical disagreement with the *Confession of Sandomierz*. After 1595, the Church in Pleszewo (Pleschen) became the centre of Lutheran orthodoxy. In May 1578, the independent Lutheran churches of Vilnius decided to break with the Union. (60) Gliczner himself abandoned his former support for the *Concord*, and from 1578 onwards he championed the *Augustana*. Although the Synod of Toruń required him to use the formulary included in the *Concord* during pastoral ordinations, he never did so. (61) The Lutheran churches of Royal Prussia refused to sign the *Concord* in Sandomierz in 1570, and pastors such as Benedictus Morgenstern or Simon Musäus preached openly against it. In Royal Prussia, however, those members of local councils who sympathised with Philippism or the Reformed Chruch did support the *Concord*. (62)

---

(57) Smend, *Die Synoden*, p. 107; *Akta Synodów Różnowierczych*, vol. 3 (1983), p. 601-602; Sławiński, *Toruński synod generalny 1595 roku*, p. 241-242,294.

(58) H. Kleinwächter, 'Paulus Gericke, Deutscher Prediger Augsburgischer Konfession in Posen', *Zeitschrift der historischen Gesellschaft für Provinz Posen* 25 (1910), p. 219-244.

(59) *Akta Synodów Różnowierczych*, vol. 3 (1983), p. 137: '[o]rdinatus sum et promotus in confessione Augustana, illam solam teneo, Consensus autem praecipit omnes tres amplecti in constitutione Vladislaviensi, quaecum sit incondita mixtura et Samaritana unio, ego eam non possum probare'.

(60) Bickerich, 'Zur Geschichte der Auflösung', p. 355, 369.

(61) As at the Synod of Poznań in 1582, in Smend, *Die Synoden*, p. 88: '[o]wa obaczyliśmy to, że Erasmus aliud heri, aliud hodie et postridie loquitur. A consensus Sendomirsky że mu jest tak wdzięczny jako powroz na szyi, który sam tam zawiązał, że go zbyć nie może'. See also Bickerich, 'Zur Geschichte der Auflösung', p. 356-358, 370; Sławiński, *Toruński synod generalny 1595 roku*, p. 66-67, 82.

(62) M. G. Müller, *Zweite Reformation und städtische Autonomie im Königlichen Preußen: Danzig, Elbing und Thorn in der Epoche der Konfessionalisierung (1557-1660)*, Berlin 1997, p. 76-77, 88, 92, 96-97, 103, 107.

Relations between churches were strained by small everyday quarrels. When Reformed preacher Paweł Gilowski published an edition of a catechism (1579) and a postil (1584) with the word 'Christian' in the title, Lutheran churches perceived this as an insult. In his polemical treatises against the Jesuits, Reformed leader Andreas Volanus defended the symbolic interpretation of the Eucharist. (63) The Bohemian Brethren was openly attacked by Morgenstern and Gericke. At the Synod of Brodnica (29 June 1597), the Brethren voiced its resentment towards its Lutheran critics. The Lutheran congregations of Pleszewo, Gnin and Poznań reintroduced Catholic vestments and images in church buildings. Enoch, though removed from his office in Poznań, served as pastor in Łagiewniki. Some pastors of the Brethren such as Stefan Petrasius, Maciej from Grodzisko, and Stanisław Scribonius, who were removed from office for disciplinary reasons, found refuge in the Lutheran churches. (64) The process leading to the withdrawal of the *Concord* was complex, and confessionalisation in Europe (especially in the Holy Roman Empire) played a part in it. Although Polish Lutherans and Calvinists refused to subscribe to the *Formula of Concord* (1578) and the *Harmony of Confessions* (1583), they were strongly exposed to the pressure of all confessional fronts. (65) Gliczner's death (1603) was a symbolic moment, slowly leading to the disbanding of the union between Lutheran and Reformed churches; on the eve of the Thirty Years' War, this was inevitable.

Nevertheless, the *Concord* was used as the basis for the coalition of Calvinists and the Brethren in Poland. Between 1615 and 1627, the Reformed churches of Greater Poland joined the ecclesiastical organisation of the Brethren, as confirmed in Ostroróg in 1627. (66) The church of the Bohemian Brethren joined the Reformed provinces, although differences in theology, liturgy and church discipline were still profound. In 1632-1633, the Reformed churches launched a project for a new translation of the Bible, as well as for a

---

(63) K. Daugirdas, *Andreas Volanus und die Reformation im Grossfürstentum Litauen*, Mainz 2008.

(64) Bickerich, 'Zur Geschichte der Auflösung', p. 376-381; *Akta Synodów Różnowierczych*, vol. 4 (1997), p. 125-128.

(65) Their removal is found in *Akta Synodów Różnowierczych*, vol. 3 (1983), p. 29-31, 79-80; Smend, *Die Synoden*, p. 83.

(66) The proceedings of the synod in Ostroróg (10-14 December 1627) can be found in *Akta Synodów Różnowierczych*, vol. 4 (1997), p. 310-312, here 310. A. Węgierski, *Slavonia reformata*, p. 120; J. Dworzaczkowa, *Bracia czescy w Wielkopolsce w XVI i XVII wieku*, Poznań 1997, p. 103. H. Gmiterek, *Bracia czescy a kalwini w Rzeczypospolitej. Połowa XVI-połowa XVII wieku*, Lublin 1987, p. 146.

CONCILIUM SANDOMIRIENSE – 1570

new agenda to unify liturgy. ([67]) At the Synod of Włodawa (1634), the churches of Lithuania, Greater Poland, and Lesser Poland decided to amalgamate certain aspects of their ecclesiastical discipline, while allowing a significant degree of local independence in liturgical matters. ([68]) The partnership between the Brethren and the Reformed Church, firmly grounded in the *Concord of Sandomierz*, was so robust and durable that Polish historiography usually does not make any clear distinctions between the two confessions.

The *Concord* remained an important subject in theological debates after the end of the Thirty Years' War. It was often quoted by David Pareus, John Dury, Batholomaeus Bythner, Samuel Hartlib, John Amos Comenius, and Hugo Grotius. The Enlightenment brought about a significant revival of the *Concord of Sandomierz*, and it was used, among others, by Daniel Ernst Jablonski and Gottfried Leibniz.

BIBLIOGRAPHY

SOURCES (AND THEIR ABBREVIATIONS)

A) ITER SENDOMIRIENSIS

Original manuscript in Národní muzeum (Praha), Fragm. 1 E b 1/3, fol. 1r-38v (*Iter*); fol. 39r-44r (*Consensus*). According to Maria Sipayłło, the handwriting of this manuscript is Simeon Theophil Turnowski's.

G. W. T. Fischer, *Versuch einer Geschichte der Reformation in Polen*, Grätz 1855, p. 257-286.

J. Łukaszewicz, *O kościele braci czeskich w dawnej Wielkiejpolsce*, Poznań 1935, p. 74-105.

---

(67) H. Gmiterek, 'Prowincje czy konfesje? Przyczynek do sprawy ujednolicenia obrządu w zborach kalwińskich i braci czeskich w XVII wieku', *Odrodzenie i Reformacja w Polsce* 29 (1984), p. 145-153; Gmiterek, 'Problemy unifikacji liturgii'; Z. Nowak, 'Andrzej Hünefeld jako nakładca i drukarz Biblii Gdańskiej z 1632 roku', *Libri Gedanenses* 1 (1967), p. 35-55; S. Tworek, 'Starania o ujednolicenie obrządku kalwińskiego w Polsce w XVII wieku', *Odrodzenie i Reformacja w Polsce* 16 (1971), p. 117-139.

(68) Tworek, *Starania*, p. 129: '[w]arunek dobrowolności powinien być w pełni przestrzegany. Tak zwane "drugorzędne sprawy" pozostawione prowincjom wskazywały na niemożliwość usunięcia różnic. Sprawę obrzędów towarzyszących "wieczerzy pańskiej" pozostawiono do rozstrzygnięcia poszczególnym prowincjom'.

752 CONCILIUM SANDOMIRIENSE – 1570

—, *Dzieje kościołów wyznania helweckiego w dawnej Małej Polsce*, Poznań 1853, p. 249-251.

M. Sipayłło (pod red.), *Akta Synodów Różnowierczych w Polsce*, 4 vols, Warszawa 1966-1997, vol. 2 (1972), p. 272-301 [= *Akta Synodów Różnowierczych*].

B) CONSENSUS SENDOMIRIENSIS

O. Bartel, 'Zgoda Sandomierska na tle dążeń ekumenicznych protestantów polskich i litewskich w XVI-XVIII wieku (w 400-lecie jej powstania)', *Rocznik Teologiczny* 12 (1970), p. 13-15 [= Bartel, 'Zgoda Sandomierska'].

Collectio Confessionum in Ecclesiis Reformatio Publicatarum, ed. H. A. Niemeyer, Lipsiae 1840, p. 553-561.

Consensus sive concordia in fide et religione Christiana, s.l. 1586.

Consensus, oder Christliche Vereinigung in Religions und Glaubens Sachen, [Amberg] 1605.

D. E. Jabłoński, *Historia Consensus Sendomiriensis, inter Evangelicos Regni Poloniae, et M.D. Lithuaniae in Synodo Generali Evangelicorum utriusque partis, Sendomiriae An. MDLXX. Die 14. Aprilis*, Berolini 1731, p. 185-195 [= Jabłoński, *Historia*].

H. P. Jürgens – K. Daugirdas, 'Konsens von Sandomierz – Consensus Sendomiriensis, 1570', in *RefBK*, vol. 3/1 (2012), p. 1-20.

J. Łukaszewicz, *O kościołach Braci czeskich w dawnej Wielkiejpolsce*, Poznań 1935.

Ostmitteleuropas Bekenntnisschriften der evangelischen Kirche A. und H.B. des Reformationszeitalters, hrsg. P. Barton, vol. 3/1, Budapest 1987, p. 273-279.

D. Pareus, *Irenicum sive De Unione Et Synodo Evangelicorum Concilianda Liber Votivus*, Francoforti – Heidelbergae 1614, p. 120-125.

J. Pelikan, 'The Consensus of Sandomierz: A Chapter from the Polish Reformation', *Concordia Theological Monthly* 18 (1947), p. 826-830; repr. in: D. Petkunas, 'The Consensus of Sandomierz: An Early Attempt to Create a Unified Protestant Church in Sixteenth-Century Poland and Lithuania', *Concordia Theological Quarterly* 73 (2009), p. 344-346 [= Pelikan, 'The Consensus of Sandomierz'].

M. Sipayłło, *Akta Synodów Różnowierczych w Polsce*, 4 vols, Warszawa 1966-1997, vol. 2 (1972), p. 272-295 (*Iter*), 295-298 (*Consensus*).

G. Smend, *Die Synoden der Kirche Augsburgischer Konfession in Großpolen im 16., 17. und 18. Jahrhundert*, Posen 1930, p. 61-64 [= Smend, *Die Synoden*].

CONCILIUM SANDOMIRIENSE – 1570

S. Strimesius, *Consensus Sendomiriensis, ab Evangelicis, Augustanae, Bohemicae et Helveticae, Confessionis Sociis olim initus*, Francofurti Adviadrum 1704, p. 1-18.

c) *CONFESSIO*

K. Długosz-Kurczabowa (pod red.), *Konfesja Sandomierska*, Warszawa 1995 [= Długosz-Kurczabowa, *Konfesja Sandomierska*].

LITERATURE (AND ITS ABBREVIATIONS)

O. Bartel, 'Zgoda Sandomierska na tle dążeń ekumenicznych protestantów polskich i litewskich w XVI-XVIII wieku (w 400-lecie jej powstania)', *Rocznik Teologiczny* 12 (1970), p. 3-30; repr. in German as O. Bartel, 'Der Consensus Sendomiriensis vom Jahre 1570 im Lichte der ökumenischen Bestrebungen in Polen und Litauen im 16., 17. und 18. Jahrhundert', *Luther-Jahrbuch* 40 (1973), p. 107-128.

F. Bickerich, 'Zur Geschichte der Auflösung des Sendomirer Vergleichs', *Zeitschrift für Kirchengeschichte* 49 (1930), NF XII, p. 350-381 [= Bickerich, 'Zur Geschichte der Auflösung'].

J. Bidlo, *Jednota bratrská v prvním vzhnanství*, 4 vols, Praha 1909, vol. 3, p. 154, 166-173, 184-185 [= Bidlo, *Jednota bratrská v prvním vzhnanství*].

Der Briefwechsel der Schweizer mit den Polen , hrsg. T. Wotschke (*Archiv für Reformationsgeschichte*, Ergänzungsband 3), Leipzig 1908 [= *Der Briefwechsel der Schweizer mit den Polen*].

J. Dworzaczkowa, *Bracia czescy w Wielkopolsce w XVI i XVII wieku*, Poznań 1997, p. 39-41.

H. Gmiterek, 'Problemy unifikacji liturgii braci czeskich i kalwinów w Rzeczypospolitej XVI-XVII wieku', *Annales Universitatis Mariae Curie-Skłodowska*, Sec. F, XL (1985), p. 93-115 [= Gmiterek, 'Problemy unifikacji liturgii'].

—, 'Obóz różnowierczy w Polsce wobec idei colloquium charitativum za Władysława IV', *Annales Universitatis Mariae Curie-Skłodowska*, Sec. F, XXXV/XXXVI (1980-1981), p. 69-88.

—, 'Szymon Teofil Turnowski w obronie zgody sandomierskiej', *Annales Universitatis Mariae Curie-Skłodowska*, Sec. F, XXXI (1976), p. 13-39.

O. Halecki, *Zgoda sandomierska 1570 r.*, Warszawa 1915 [= Halecki, *Zgoda sandomierska*].

754 CONCILIUM SANDOMIRIENSE – 1570

K. E. Jordt Jørgensen, *Ökumenische Bestrebungen unter den polnischen Protestanten bis zum Jahre 1645*, København 1942 [= Jordt Jørgensen, *Ökumenische Bestrebungen*].

J. Lehmann, *Konfesja sandomierska na tle innych wyznań*, Warszawa 1937.

I. Lukšaitė, *Reformacija Lietuvos Didžiojoje Kunigaikštystėje ir Mažojoje Lietuvoje. XVI a. trečias dešimtmetis – XVII a. pirmas dešimtmetis*, Wilno 1999, p. 334-336.

J. Małłek, 'Sandomir, Consensus von', in *Theologische Realenzyklopädie*, 36 vols, Berlin – New York 1976-2004, vol. 30 (1999), p. 29-31.

M. G. Müller, 'Der Consensus Sendomirensis – Geschichte eines Scheiterns? Zur Diskussion über Protestantismus und protestantische Konfessionalisierung in Polen-Litauen im 16. Jahrhundert', in K. Lambrecht – J. Bahlcke – H.-C. Maner (hrsg.), *Konfessionelle Pluralität als Herausforderung. Koexistenz und Konflikt in Spätmittelalter und Früher Neuzeit*, Leipzig 2006, p. 397-408 [= Müller, 'Der Consensus Sendomirensis'].

D. Petkunas, 'Consensus of Sendomir: A Unique Ecumenical Document in Sixteenth-Century Polish-Lithuanian Protestant Christianity', *Tiltai/Bridges* 9 (2005), p. 181-200.

Polski słownik biograficzny, pod red. W. Konopczyński et al., 52 vols to date, Kraków 1935– [= *PSB*].

K. Völker, 'Die Unionsgedanken Consensus Sendomiriensis', *Zeitschrift für Osteuropäische Geschichte NF* 3 (1933), p. 508-525 [= Völker, 'Unionsgedanken'].

W. Sławiński, *Toruński synod generalny 1595 roku. Z dziejów polskiego protestantyzmu w drugiej połowie XVI wieku*, Warszawa 2002 [= Sławiński, *Toruński synod generalny 1595 roku*].

J. Tazbir, 'Die Religionsgespräche in Polen', in G. Müller (hrsg.), *Die Religionsgespräche der Reformationszeit*, Gütersloh 1980, p. 127-144.

W. Urban, 'Consensus Sendomiriensis', in H. J. Hillerbrand (ed.), *Oxford Encyclopedia of the Reformation*, 4 vols, New York 1996, vol. 1, p. 413-414.

T. Wotschke, 'Erasmus Gliczner', *Aus Posens kirchlicher Vergangenheit* 6 (1917/1918), p. 1-73 [= Wotschke, 'Erasmus Gliczner'].

—, 'Christoph Thretius. Ein Beitrag zur Geschichte des Kampfes der reformierten Kirche gegen den Antitrinitarismus in Polen', *Altpreussische Monatsschrift* 44 (1907), p. 1-41, 151-210 [= Wotschke, 'Christoph Thretius'].

P. Wrzecionko, 'Die Religionsgespräche in Polen unter dem Aspekt ihrer Unionsbestrebungen', in G. Müller (hrsg.), *Die Religionsgespräche der Reformationszeit*, Gütersloh 1980, p. 145-152.

Monitum

Národní muzeum (Praha), Fragm. 1 E b 1/3, fol. 1r-38v (*Iter*); fol. 39r-44r (*Consensus*).

CONCILIUM SANDOMIRIENSE
1570

CONSPECTUS SIGLORUM

Ja D. E. Jabloński, *Historia Consensus Sendomiriensis, inter Evangelicos Regni Poloniae, et M.D. Lithuaniae in Synodo Generalis Evangelicorum utriusque partis, Sendomiriae An. MDLXX. Die 14. Aprilis*, Berolini 1731, p. 185-195

| ITER SENDOMIRIENSE

| Anno a Natali Salvatoris dulcissimi 1570 Martii die 28 (quae erat dies
Martis feria 3 Paschatos) missus a fratribus, praecipue fratre Georgio Israele et
fratre Ioanne Laurentio, feliciter iter ingressus etc.

Aprilis die 4, quae erat Martis, veni Piotrków et ibi forte in hospitio inve-
ni Nicolaum et Erasmum Gliczneros Sendomiriam quoque euntes, missos a
domino palatino Posnaniensi etc. Cum illis nec amice nec hostiliter, sed
tamen familiariter actum abs me est; miram benevolentiam in omnibus mihi
declararunt.

5 Aprilis. Postridie harum una perreximus etc.

6 Aprilis. Ad meridiem venimus in villam Bliżyna, gdzie nas na pokarmie
dogonił jego miłościwy pan Leonardus Strasz, który też do Sędomirza jechał
etc. Na noc wespół przyjechaliśmy ku Bodzęcinu. Tamże poczęli między sobą

---

3 Georgio Israele] Georg Israel (Jerzy Izrael, 1505-1588), first superintendent of the
Bohemian Brethren in Poland, minister in Kwidzyń, Poznań, and Koźminek
4 Ioanne Laurentio] Jan Laurentius (Jan Lorenc, 1520-1587), senior of the Bohemian
Brethren in Poland   feliciter iter ingressus] Simon Theophil Turnowski, representative
of the Bohemian Brethren, set off for Sandomierz on 28 March, probably from
Ostroróg. See Halecki, *Zgoda sandomierska*, p. 208   **6** Nicolaum et Erasmum
Gliczneros] Erasmus Gliczner (Erazm Gliczner, 1535-1603), since 1566 superintendent
of the Lutheran Church of Greater Poland. Until 1562, he hesitated between Calvinism
and Lutheranism. He served as pastor in Toruń, and Grodzisk. Nicolaus Gliczner
(Mikołaj Gliczner), Erasmus' brother, was a Lutheran pastor in Brodnica and Poznań
7 palatino Posnaniensi] *palatinus posnaniensis* (*wojewoda poznański*) Łukasz Górka
(1533-1573), voyvode (*palatinus*) of Poznań since 1565. He first sympathised with
the Bohemian Brethren, but after 1566 he joined the Lutherans. W. Dworzaczek,
'Górka Łukasz', in *PSB*, vol. 8 (1959-1960), p. 412-414; *Urzędnicy wielkopolscy XVI-
XVIII wieku. Spisy*, pod red. A. Bieniaszewski, Wrocław 1987, p. 144-145   **11** Bliżyna]
Bliżyn, a village in the Świętokrzyskie voivodeship, in south-central Poland
12 Leonardus Strasz] Leonard Strasz was from Lesser Poland, and between 1563 and
1577 he was *magnus procurator arcis cracoviensis* (*burgrabia krakowski*). See *Urzędnicy
województwa krakowskiego XVI-XVIII wieku. Spisy*, pod red. S. Cynarski –
A. Falniowska-Grabowska – A. Gąsiorowski, Kórnik 1990, p. 177   **13** Bodzęcinu]
now Bodzentyn, a city in the Świętokrzyskie voivodeship, in south-central Poland

---

3 fratre] *a.c.* fr.   **4** fratre] *a.c.* fr.   Laurentio] *a.c.* L.   **7** domino] *a.c.* d.   **10** Aprilis]
supplevi   **11** Aprilis] *supplevi*   **12** jego miłościwy pan] *a.c.* j. m. p.

760 CONCILIUM SANDOMIRIENSE – 1570

rozmawiać ewangelicy z panem Straszem a ministrem jego Gregoryjem Żar-
15 nowickim, | praecipue o klękaniu przy używaniu Wieczerze Pańskiej, Erasmo 2v
acriter defendente non aperte adorationem, sed caeremoniam illam klękania
etc. Na tym się spokoili, aby każdy na swym sensu dobrze rozumiawszy został,
a drugim dla różnej ceremoniji nie gardził. Jam tu nie tylko milczał, ale ako-
modując się cyrkumstancyjam mało słuchał, subinde odchodzc etc. Przysze-
20 dłem zaś ku temu, gdzie x. Gregorius odpowiedał x. Erazmowi na kwestyją,
jeśli się bracia z nimi, tj. krakowskimi albo helweckimi, zgadzaj. Tam x. Grzegorz tak mówil: Poniewadż bracia Valdenses mają Confessionem contrariam
Konfesyji helweckij, a my się helweckij dzierżymy, łacno obaczać, iż się nie
zgadzamy. Z czego x. Erasmus z bratem pociechę swą na obliczu pokazali. | 3r
25 Ego, etiam ira commotus, tum licet eam volverem, non potui prodire sermone,
quia ad cenam vucati sumus. Distuli igitur.

7 Aprilis. Nazajutrz tedy, niżeśmy wyjechali, odwiedszy na stronc x. Gre-
goryja rzekłem do niego: Księże miły Grzegorzu, odpuśćcie, że króciuchno
dotknę tej rozmowy, którąście wczora pod wieczór z księżą etc. mieli, gdziem
30 między inszymi mowami zasłechł odpowiedź, którąście dali x. Erazmowi o
zgodzie waszj z bracią i o Konfesyji brackij a helweckij. A tak wm. teraz
prosząc pytam, jeśliście to rozmyślnie a dowodnie, czyli tak obiter etc., powiedzieli, iż, pry, Konfesyja waldeńska est contraria Confissioni Helveticae (bo
bych to rad pewnie wiedział i rationes tego slyszał, gdyż jednak ja a tym
35 inaczyj pewnie rozumiem), a w czym?

| Tam x. Grzegorz, zapłonąwszy się, barzo się jął omawiać, oświadszając się 3v
w tym, iż o braciej i Konfesyji ich z swymi towarzyszmi wybornie rozumie etc,
ale co powiedział de contrarietate sententiae circa Sacramentum, abs se dictum
esse. Tamżeśmy się słowy obracali, aźśmy ku temu przyszli, że zeznać musiał
40 Confessionem fratrum Confessioni Helveticae non esse contrariam, immo
vero re ipsa in omnibus cum ea convenire, in verbis saltem quibusdam circa
rem sacramentariam contrarietatem videri, re ipsa non esse etc. Tamżem, go
prosił, iżeby to constanter wszędzie wyznawał et in nullius hominis gratiam
aut odium veritatem dissimulet.

---

14 ewangelicy] i.e. Nicolaus and Erasmus Gliczner   Gregoryjem Żarnowickim]
Gregor Żarnowiecki (Grzegorz of Żarnowiec, c. 1528-1601), a Reformed pastor in
Włoszczowa, and author of a very popular postil   **16** klękania] kneeling. The first
debate of the Synod started before the proceedings and was over differences in the
celebration of the Eucharist. Lutherans defended kneeling as part of the ceremony
23/24 nie zgadzamy] this was the obvious rebuttal of the *Concord of Koźminek* (1555),
where the Reformed Church accepted the *Confession* of the Brethren

---

14 panem] *a.c.* p.   Żarnowickim] *a.c.* Żarnowicki   **27** Aprilis] *supplevi*   **28** Księże]
a.c. K.

CONCILIUM SANDOMIRIENSE – 1570

45 Gdyśmy wyjechali, w drodze pan Strasz przez sługę zawołał mię | do 4r
siebie do rydwana. Tamżem podle niego jadąc, z nim i Gregoryjem ministrem
jego rozmawiał. Naprzód prosił mię z sobą, iżebych opuściwszy Erazma etc. z
nim naprzód jechał. Consensi. Potem poczęliśny de flexione genuum przy
Wieczerzy Pańskiej. Multa utrinque modeste dicta, tandem ego hac protuli:
50 Dwie przyczyny mi się widzą być, dla których ta ceremonija klękania przy
używaniu Wieczerzy Pańskij nie ma być temere mutowana. Naprzód iż ta
akcyja nie jest niejaka publiczna, świecka, ale osobliwa, w której się dzieje
gorącym sercem rozmyślanie śmierci Pańskij i pożytków jij, iż się człowiek
pobożny przy tym ma z wielką ochotą modlić Bogu a onego chwalić etc., a
55 modlitwy godzi się czynić klękając, a snadź i na twarz padając etc. | Druga 4v
przyczyna, iż ponieważ to jest wyborny porządek w kościele, żeby nie sami
ludzie rękoma sobie brali a służyli, ale od ministrów służących w usta brali
propter multas causas etc. Sposób tedy tam temu chce, aby klęczącym służono
było, bo stojącym albo siedzącym to tak sposobnie dziać się nie może etc.
60 Na tym pan Strasz z ministrem swym ochotnie przystali. A wszakże, pry, i
nasze rationes niech u bogobojnych ludzi mają miejsce: iż my dlatego nie
klękamy, aby bałwochwalcy nie mniemali, że przed chlebem klękamy etc.,
gdyż jednak przed Panem sercem swym tamże klękamy.
Owa quia haec sunt accidentalia, nas dzielić nie będą. Gdzie też exempla
65 sunt adducta utrinque, iż u nich pan jeden klęczał, | gdzie ony stali, a u nas pan 5r
Jirzy Latalski stojał, gdzieśmy my klęczeli. Zatem de ubiquitate contra
Erasmum aliqua utrinque prolata etc.
Na obiad wstąpiliśmy w Opatowie do panów Konieckich na zamek, gdzie
in colloquio convivali hoc notavi, że facta mentione ministrów poznańskich
70 pana wojewodzinych pan Koniecki jeden (qui ad tritheismum vergere videba-
tur) powiedział: I to, pry, tych ministrów nabożeństwo musi być nijakie,
cygańskie, iż takiego człowieka bezbożnego, nie pokutujacego etc. w zborze
swym cierpią etc.

---

63 klękamy] Strasz and Grzegorz of Żarnowiec refuted the rite of kneeling **66** Jirzy
Latalski] a son of Janusz Latalski **68** Opatowie] Opatów, a city in the Świętokrzyskie
voivodeship. However, it is unclear which castle the source refers to **70** pana
wojewodzinych] i.e. Łukasz Górka (1533-1573) Koniecki] it is unclear which member
of the Koniecki family is implied here

45 pan] *a.c.* p. **60** pan] *a.c.* p. **65** pan²] *a.c.* p. **70** pan] *a.c.* p.

762 CONCILIUM SANDOMIRIENSE – 1570

Na noc przyjechaliśmy do pana Jakubowskiego do Słaboszyc, gdzieśmy
75 zastali pana wojewodę krakowskiego, do ktorego mię wwiódł pan Strasz. Tam
mię benevole przywitawszy jegomość pytał, | od kogom przyjechał. Powie- 5v
działem, iż przednie od bracij z Ostroroga z listy do synodu, w czym mojej
posługi i ich miłościwi panowie z Wielgij Polski użyli, iż przez mię list swój do
synodu posłali. Pytał, do kogo mam listy, jedzie li kto z Wielkiej Polski etc. Na
80 wszystkom mu odpowiedział. Osobliwie subinde pytał o br. waldeńskich,
czemu nie jadą, okazując to, że by je tu był naraczyj widział etc. Jam wymawiał
etc.

8 Aprilis po ranu zawołał mię zaś jego miłościwy pan wojewoda do siebie,
pytał, co w Wielkij Polszcze slyszeć nowego o wojnie niemieckij. Powiedzia-
85 łem, potem o listach, które mam. Upomniał, iżem bych ich nic dawał, aż się
synod zgromadzi etc., omnia benignissime. | Tegoż dnia, 8 Aprilis w sobotę, 6r
przyjechaliśmy do Sędomirza.

Szukałem x. Jędrzeja, z Krakowa który ledweż był przyjechał. Tam
naszedszy go z Trecyjem, salutowałem decenter od bracij a oddałem listy etc.
90 Potem zarazem, niżem się widział z x. Sarnickim, jęli ze mną mówić plurimis

---

74 Jakubowskiego] probably Andrzej Jakubowski († 1575), a Calvinist, and the father
of Jan Walenty Jakubowski (1552-1582). See W. Budka, 'Jakubkowski Jan Walenty h.
Topór', in *PSB*, vol. 10 (1962-1964), p. 385   Słaboszyc] i.e. Słaboszowice, a village close
to Sandomierz, belonging to Andrzej Jakubowski. See *Polska XVI wieku pod względem
geograficzno-statystycznym*, pod red. A. Pawiński, 13 vols, Warszawa 1883-1915, vol. 10
(1894), p. 771   **75** wojewodę krakowskiego] i.e. Stanisław Myszkowski (1520-1580).
H. Kowalska, 'Myszkowski Stanisław', in *PSB*, vol. 22 (1977), p. 394-395; Halecki,
Zgoda sandomierska, p. 200-201   **75/76** Tam – przyjechał] this proves that
Turnowski was not officially representing the Brethren   **84** co – niemieckij]
Myszkowski asked Turnowski about the Northern Seven Years' War (1563-1570)
88 Szukałem – przyjechał] probably the Reformed pastor Andrzej Prażmowski
(† 1592). In Sandomierz, he represented the Bohemian Brethren. See M. Sipayłło,
'Prasmovius Andrzej', in *PSB*, vol. 28 (1984-1985), p. 350-351   **89** Trecyjem] Krzysztof
Trecy (c. 1530-1591), one of the Calvinist leading characters in Poland. He kept closely
in contact with the leaders of the Swiss Reformation. See Wotschke, 'Christoph
Thretius', p. 1-41 and 151-210; J. Czubek, 'Krzysztof Trecy. Przywódca kalwinów
małopolskich', *Reformacja w Polsce* 1 (1921), p. 35-42   **90** Sarnickim] the Reformed
pastor Stanisław Sarnicki (1532-1597) preached and campaigned against the Union in
Koźminek (1555), but in Sandomir he opposed Bullinger's confession and supported
the Brethren. Probably Sarnicki represented those who in the Reformed Church
wished to join the Brethren. See H. Kowalska – J. Sikorski, 'Sarnicki Stanisław', in *PSB*,
vol. 35 (1994), p. 214-223; J. Bidlo, *Jednota bratrská v prvním vzhnanství*, 4 vols, Praha
1900-1932, vol. 2 (1903), p. 144-145; cfr Halecki, *Zgoda sandomierska*, p. 208

---

74 pana] *a.c.* p.   **75** pana] *a.c.* p.   pan] *a.c.* p.   **78** ich miłościwi] *a.c.* i. m.
81 naraczyj] *a.c.* naraczy   **83** jego miłościwy pan] *a.c.* j. m. p.

CONCILIUM SANDOMIRIENSE – 1570   763

verbis. Owa summa tego, iż na tym stanęli, mając po swej stronie pany wojewody etc., aby Confessio Tigurinorum Królowi podana była, którą już po
polsku wydrukowali, gdzie triumphantes suas probationes proferebant magno
studio id ipsum urgentes ad cetera, quae in consilium offerebantur, plane
95 suadi. Interea tamen uterque mirum amorem Unitatis fratrum profitebatur et
eius rei praefatio etc. | satis firmum et evidens praebebat testimonium.   6v

Interea ego urgebam fratrum sententiam, ut potius Confessio nostra, jam
Regi oblata, iterum cum Apologia offeratur etc., sed surdi erant pro gaudio ob
scriptam et impressam a se Confessionem Helveticam. Hanc sententiam ceu
100 optimam et fratribus etiam commodissimam durissime triumphabundi urgebant et ceteros sibi adversantes accusabant: Sunt, inquit, hinc quidam ministri gloriam suam, non Dei, quaerentes, qui huic nostro conatui obsistunt
volumque impedire oblationem Regi et publicationem huius Confessionis
Helveticae. Inter hos est praecipuus Sarnicius, qui, inquit, urget approbatio-
105 nem Confessionis fratrum, potius fratrum, quam huius nostrae idque facit
studio suae laudis, quia non abs | eo, sed a nobis cum fratre Brzozovio Confes-   7r
sio haec scripta est etc. Multis acerrime accusabant Sarnicium uterque etc.

Tak żeśmy tymi rozmowami dokończyli tego dnia, z ktorych się okazało,
iż fr. Andreas cum Trecio acz bracim życzą; wszakże Konfesyją tę swą wolą
110 publikować niż bracką, a x. Sarnickiego, który się im w tym sprzeciwia, za
nieprzyjaciela mają, Erasmum cum fratre prosto niecnotą niezgodliwą mianu-
ją. Interim też oznajmił mi x. Jędrzej consilium synodi, iż już to Konfesyja
helwecka od wszystkich z ich strony z pany jest aprobowana i z prefacyją (o
czym ich ledwo czterej wiedzą) impressa. A jeśliby się który temu zamknieniu
115 ich sprzeciwiali z ministrów, iż je chce synod i panowie jako niezgodne odrzucić, ekskomunikować etc.

| Nazajutrz, w niedzielę 9 Aprilis, oddałem we zborze listy etc. x. Sarnic-   7v
kiemu i tamem się z nim trochę rozmówił, gdzie mię prosił, abych się z nim

---

92 Confessio Tigurinorum] the *Confessio Helvetica Posterior* had already been
translated by Krzysztof Trecy and printed   **97/98** Interea – offeratur] the *Confession*
of the Brethren was offered to the King in 1564   **107** Multis – uterque] the
accusations had already been formulated by Trecy in his letter to Heinrich Bullinger, 21
January 1570, in *Der Briefwechsel der Schweizer mit den Polen*, p. 407   **112/**
114 Jędrzej – impressa] the translation and edition of the *Confessio* was kept secret.
Halecki, *Zgoda sandomierska*, p. 210-211   **114/116** A – ekskomunikować] the
supporters of the *Second Helvetic Confession* planned to demand its implementation
under threat of the excommunication. Halecki, *Zgoda sandomierska*, p. 211

760 CONCILIUM SANDOMIRIENSE – 1570

hned po zborze widział. Kazał x. Sylvius na Ewangeliją Joannis 10. Po kazaniu
120 wezwał mię do siebie x. Sarnicki z Sylwijuszem. Tamże naprzód przeczytał
Sylwijuszowi listy od bracij, potem nie tylko z żalem, ale i ze łzami powiedał o
x. Jędrzejowi, iż z Trecyjuszem przeciwią się im a tej to poradzie brackiej,
chcąc obtrudere Confessionem Helveticam pro fraterna etc. Zatem prosił,
mam li sobie co poruczonego od bracij o tych rzeczach albo jak rozumim ex
125 colloquiis sentencyjam eorum, iżebych przełożył.
Odpowiedziałem, iż mu tego | pomagam barzo żalować, co tu o x. Jędrze-   8r
jowi powiedacie, jakoby on, zgadzając się z bracią pozwirzchnym zjednoce-
niem a sposobem, że re ipsa im i sentencyji ich się sprzeciwia. A summą iż z
tego nawiętszą przyczynę żałości mam, że wasze miłości, którzy ze strony bracij
130 jesteście, a o których to bracia rozumieli, iż im życząc sententiam eorum tuebi-
mini, teraz o to sami się nie zgadzacie et odia tristia inter vos alitis. Co się
lepak dotycze pytania waszych miłości, jać nic nie mam sobie od bracij zlece-
nego a annotowanego, nulla enim mihi instructio data est, tylkom z listy
poslan. Wszakże com z bracij zrozumial o tej sentencyji, exponam.
135 Widząc to bracia, iż Confessio ich non est adeo splendida, a ta Tigurina
iż jest auctior et illustrior etc., wszakże ani inszej przyjmować, ani swej popra-
wować na ten czas nie chcą, sed hanc etiam suam a nobis Regi offerre non
cupiunt, a to dla tych przyczyn: Jedno, iż confessiones inter ceteris causis
dlatego | też praecipue wydawany bywają, ut hostibus satisfieret, bo aedificatio   8v
140 ecclesiae plus consistet bez tego in concionibus sacris etc. A otoż bracia, exer-
citati cum hostibus, i w wydawaniu konfesyj baczą to, iż tą Konfesyją, która
jest succincta, dosyć czyniono być może hostibus, i nie amplifikuja jej ani
obszyrniejszyj żadnyj nie przyjmują na tej miesce, aby nieprzyjaciele malevoli
mnij zacz szarpać mieli etc.

---

119 Sylvius] Jakub Sylvius was a Reformed pastor serving in Chrzcięcice and one of the
vice-superintendents of the Church. S. Tworek, 'Z zagadnień organizacji zborów
kalwińskich w Małopolsce z XVI-XVII w.', *Rocznik Lubelski* 8 (1965), p. 63-75;
J. Wijaczka, 'Protestantyzm w regionie świętokrzyskim w XVI-XVII wieku (ze
szczególnym uwzględnieniem dawnego powiatu radomskiego)', in J. Kłaczkow (pod
red.), *Ewangelicy w Radomiu i regionie (XVI-XX w.)*, Radom 2007, p. 11-32   **140/
144** A – mieli] Turnowski voiced the negative stance of the Brethren towards the new
confession. The Brethren was unwilling to accept the *Confessio Helvetica* and equally
unwilling to change its own confession. According to the Brethren, the new confession
would not support the union of the Prostestant churches, but would be used only in
confessional polemics and debates. On the contrary, they supported the idea of a
confessional union founded on the ground of common teaching and forms of piety

129 wasze miłości] *a.c.* w. m.   **132** waszych miłości] *a.c.* w. m.

CONCILIUM SANDOMIRIENSE – 1570

145 Druga przyczyna zda mi się być, iż ta Konfesyja, jakkoli jest succincta, wszakże jest już, praeclare privilegiata testimoniis i Helvetiorum, i Saxonum, czego żadna konfesyja nie ma, a tak wedle nij nasnadnij zgoda tych wszech być może.

Trzecia, iż już ta Confessio tu w Polszcze, a nie insza z ewangeliskich, plac 150 sławny odzierżała, gdyż jest Królowi podana, a przed nieprzyjaciółmi obroniona nowowydaną apologiją albo Odpowiedzią Niemojewskiego. | Za którą 9r była li by insza podana, nie mogłoby to być bez ubliżenia tej to i bez rozmaitego zgorszenia etc. (Multa copiosius in hanc sententiam dixi). Ale za tym wedle tego, czegom już wprzód namienił około niezgody waszych miłości z x. 155 Jędrzejem, proszę, iżebyście się sami jako narychlij między sobą zgodzili, bo alias in synodo turpis confusio etc., nostris adversariis confessionistis consolatio et ad turbandum occasio et mode ipsis forsan antichristianis gaudium sequitur. Proszę tedy jako napilniej, iżebyście się natychmiast zeszli z x. Jędrzejem i Trecyjuszem i pogodzili przed tą sprawą, która iam a prandiis od synodu 160 będzie zaczęta.

To oni obadwaj wszystko wdzięcznie przyjąwszy obiecali, iż się hned z nimi chcą rozmówić, a potem iż im oznajmią, co sprawią. Odchodząc od nich potrafiłem się z Trecyjem, a namieniwszy o tym, ile się zdała potrzeba, | 9v prosiłem, ut pie ageret illa, quae ad gloriam Dei spectant, plus veritatern quam 165 praeiudicia qualiacumque spectans etc. Za tym byłem przez pana Strasza a podstolego pana wojewody wezwan do stołu pana wojewody krakowskiego, gdzie mira reverentia et nimio honore byłem częstowan po to czasy. Tam ministri, qui aderant, honorificentissime fratrum mentionem faciebant, zwlaszcza quidam Valentinus, minister z Rusi, iż, pry, maxima est auctoritas 170 vestrorum inter nos omnes. Panie Boże daj, ut ea scientia et felicitate possemus eodem secare ecciesiam Domini ac vestri fratres. (Z tego colloquium Sarnicii cum Andrea nic nie było).

Po obiedzie hora 19 zeszlimy sic et acta synodica zaczęte.

Primum praefatus pana wojewoda krakowski, potem sędomirski. Tamże 175 to zrządzono, | którzy mają być directores colloquii, na imię: pan wojewoda 10r

---

146 praeclare – Saxonum] the Brethren's *Confession* was accepted by John Calvin and Martin Luther   **151** apologiją – Niemojewskiego] i.e. J. Niemojewski, *Odpowiedź na książki księdza Benedykta Herbesta*, Cracow 1569. Jakub Niemojewski (c. 1532-1584), a Reformed nobleman and an active parliamentarian; he authored various polemical tracts against the Jesuits, Benedykt Herbest and Jakub Wujek   **166** wojewody krakowskiego] i.e. Stanisław Myszkowski   **169** minister – Rusi] probably Walenty z Brzozowa   **175/176** wojewoda sedomirski] Piotr Zborowski (c. 1530-1580)

154 waszych miłości] *a.c.* w. m.   **165** pana] *a.c.* p.   **166** pana[1]] *a.c.* p.   pana[2]] *a.c.* p.   **174** pana] *a.c.* p.   **175** pan] *a.c.* p.

766 CONCILIUM SANDOMIRIENSE – 1570

sedomirski z panem Iwanem, x. Paweł Gilowski z x. Jędrzejem; item, praecipui collocutores wedle dystryktów: krakowskiego, chęcińskiego, poznańskiego, oświęcimskiego, ruskiego, lubelskiego, piotrkowskiego, kujawskiego etc., po 3, po 4, po 5 etc., i godzina, i miejsce zgromadzenia naznaczone.

180 Po rozejściu z tego zgromadzenia mówiłem wiele z Trecyjem, praecipue urgens to, iż lepij, aby była Konfesyja bracka tu przyjęta, niżeli nowa ta helwecka. Toczyliśmy się około tego na trzy godziny tumultuarie. Owa ego urgebam rationes coram Sarnicio propositas addens nonnulla et ad illius obiecta respondens, gdzie jednak te jego były rationes: Chcemy mieć kon-
185 fesyją nie czeską, saską, helwecką etc., ale polską własną. O zgodzie z bracią a podpisami Konfesyji ich | w tych stronach mało co wimy a mało kto wi. X. 10v Sarnicki tego nigdy na synodzie po ty czasy nie spomniał, ino immo proclivis erat na Kofesyją augszpurską, nadto uczynił zjednoczenie cum Helvetiis. Confessio bracka, acz ma testimonia praeclara, wszakże illi ipsi viri in eam animad-
190 verterunt et nunc etiam illi papistae et Lutherani repugnant. Tu w tym kraju ministrowie nie wiedzą o inszyj konfesyji, jedno tyj helweckij, tyj się dzierżą, i z pany, a pochwalił ją br. Maciej Czerwonka i wy chwalicie. A jest necessarium perfectissimum. Myśmy będąc we Francyji etc. z nij się prawego nabożeństwa nauczyli etc. Denique z tymi się nam złączyć przystoi, którzy nas nie opuszcza-
195 ją, ale ochotnie ratują przeciw nieprzyjaciołom tryteitom etc. consiliis scriptis, gdzieśmy my od braci ani od żadnego inszego takiej pomocy dożądać a dożdać nie mogli a nie mieli.

A jam mu przydał, iż to potissima ratio est, że już Konfesyją tę wydruko-wali a nieradzi by, aby praca ich, per se optima, in cassum iret. | Ad omnia ista 11r
200 et talia plurima facillime et feliciter respondi, to wszakże minując, iż im bracia ku pomocy przeciw nieprzyjaciolom statecznic nie bywali.

---

176 Iwanem] Stanisław Iwan Karmiński (vel Karniński, c. 1510-1603). See H. Kowalska, 'Karniński Stanisław Iwan', in *PSB*, vol. 12 (1966-1967), p. 70-72 **180 /**
185 Po – własną] Trecy's argument that the translation of the *Confessio Helvetica* would be 'our Polish confession' and not 'Bohemian, Saxon or Helvetic' seems very odd. Halecki, *Zgoda sandomierska*, p. 215 **185/190** O – repugnant] Benedykt Herbest criticised the *Confessio Bohemorum*. See B. Herbest, *Chrześcijańska porządna odpowiedź na tę Confessią, ktora pod tytułem barciej zakonu Chrystusowego niedawno jest wydana*, Kraków 1567 **193** Myśmy – Francyji] Trecy visited France in 1561 and participated in the Colloquy of Poissy

176 panem] *a.c.* p.

CONCILIUM SANDOMIRIENSE – 1570   767

Owaśmy się tak rozmawiali, iż testimonio auditorum Trecius mi winien
zostawał, gdyż też więcyj się puszcza za swym zdaniem a czyimkoli, niźli za
brackim, o ktorych to pisali oni doktorowie helweccy do Polaków, aby ich,
205 jako to doświadczonych w nabożeństwie, radzi się radzili, dokładali a słuchali
etc.
Za tym dlugim colloquium wezwali mię panowie ministrowie od stołu
pana wojewodzinego do siebie na wieczerzą. Tam byli praecipui: x. Paweł
Gilowski, x. Jędrzej, Trecius, doktor Różanka etc., Petrus z Dębnice, Jędrzej z
210 Lisowa etc. Facta iterum collatio eadem de re me acriter defendente sententiam fratrum, ibi praeter scriptas iam rationrs haereticorum prolata est, a
Tricesio: | Gdybyśmy my, chcąc zgodę postanowić, Saxonicis obtrudowali   11v
waszę Konfesjyą, i oni, i inszych wiele zarazem by się odwrócili przeciwiąc się
Konfesyji waszyj etc.
215   X. Gilowski zaszedł na mię tym argumentem, iż Kalwin, Luter i inszy,
pochwaliwszy Konfesyją bracką, przecie swe własne wolno wydawali, a tak i
my to tu w Małyj Polszcze czynić możemy. Na com mu odpowiedział, iż jest
dissimilitudo in exemplis, bo tu w Polszcze bracia sami już Królowi Konfesyją
podali etc. Za tym dołożył graviter tej racyji, iż jest tego ich consilium barzo
220 wielka przyczyna z strony Króla, którego, jako głowy, tym (wiedząc już przyczyny) leczą, a tak consulunt sanitati omnium in hoc Regno ecclesiarum et
occurrunt enim imminenti gravissimo periculo, czego by inaczyj dowieść nie
mogli. Także doktor Rożanka multa... inquit: Fratres, hanc Confessionem nos
subscribemus.
225 | Także x. Jędrzej Prasnicius przydał, iż tego doświadczyli a pilnym rozmy-   12r
słem doszli, te ecclesia multo felice potent aedificari edita hac Confessione, in
quam plurimi in orbe Christiano consenserunt. A gdyby w tym baczył

202/205 Owaśmy – słuchali] as in a letter of the Swiss reformers to the Reformed
churches of Lesser Poland found in A. Gindely, *Quellen zur Geschichte der böhmischen
Brüder vornehmlich ihren Zusammenhand mit Deutschland betreffend*, Wien 1859,
p. 215-218   208 wojewodzinego] i.e. Stanisław Myszkowski   209 Trecius] i.e.
Krzysztof Trecy   Różanka] Stanisław Różanka (c. 1520-1572), a Reformed medical
doctor and humanist from Cracow. See H. Barycz, 'Rożanka (Rosarius) Stanisław', in
PSB, vol. 32 (1989-1991), p. 431-433   Petrus z Dębnice] Piotr Tarnowski, a Reformed
pastor serving in Dębnica   209/210 Jędrzej z Lisowa] Andrzej z Przesnysza (Andrzej
Prażmowski or Prasmovius, † 1592), a Reformed pastor from Radziejów acting as
superintendent in Kujawy. See M. Sipayłło, 'Prasmovius, Andrzej', in *PSB*, vol. 28
(1984-1985), p. 350-351   212 Tricesio] i.e. Krzysztof Trecy   212/214 Gdybyśmy –
waszyj] Trecy expanded on his argument and claimed that the Lutherans would not
accept any confession of faith of other Churches, except for the new 'Polish' *Confession*

207 panowie] *a.c. p.*   208 pana] *a.c. p.*   223 multa] *lectio dubia*

768 CONCILIUM SANDOMIRIENSE – 1570

namniejszą szkodę bracij, te by k temu przyzwolić nie chciał, by mu do gardła odpirać było.

230 K temu i inszy się ozywali, it pro fratribus carissimis tamquam pro aris et focis pugnabunt et eorum militate ac honori in primis studebunt. A wydaniem tej Konfesyji w prefacyji, iż Confessionem nostram plus ornabunt et honorificentius commendabunt, quam si illi simpliciter ci immediate subscriberent etc.

235 Za tym ja, bacząc, quod nihil proficio, quamvis satisfaciens omnibus illorum argumentis, quin immo magis ac magis triumphant amorem et merita sua in fratres praedicantes, jużem tam przestał z nimi ea de re contendere et intentus eram na ty sprawy, jak pájdą a dojdą.

| Die 10 Aprilis. Zgromadziliśmy się hora II aż do 20.   12v

240 I. Naprzód kazał x. Valentinus z Brzozowa na słowa epistoły ad Ephesos.

II. Potem poselstwa a legationes były sprawowany:

1. Poznańscy Saxonici: Jesteśmy posłani od Jego miłościwego pana wojewody poznańskiego, pana gnizieńskiego, brzeskiego, Rokossowskiego a zboru poznańskiego, od których naprzód wasze miłości uniżenie salutujemy. Potem

245 oznajmujemy, it nam kazali przywieść na pamięć waszym miłościom, jakośmy my z dawna przez Marcina Lutra wywiedzieni z błędów, przywiedzeni ku prawdziwej nauce o usprawiedliwieniu, Wieczerzy Pańskij, bonis operibus, zatem iż z tego zasmuceni byli, że turbowano było przez niektórą społu bracią, którzy się wdawali w dworne kwestyje de Cena Domini, de ubiquitate etc., z

250 czego schismata i kacerstwa poszły, pocieszeni tedy zaś z tego, | iż się wasze 13r miłości o zgodzie starając synod-ście tu złożyli. Na który zbór wybrał pana wojewodę a pana gnizieńskiego, którzy, tu nie mogąc być, nas posłali z panem Bnińskim. Gdzie tu oto gotowi jesteśmy ku społecznej zgodzie, a wasze miłości prosiemy, iżebyście nam oznajmili przyczynę, dla którejście nas tu wezwali.

---

232 prefacyji] i.e. the preface to the *Confession*: Długosz-Kurczabowa, *Konfesja Sandomierska*, p. 3-22   240 Valentinus – Brzozowa] a Calvinist minister in Dobrków 242 Poznańscy Saxonici] i.e. Erasm and Nicolaus Gliczner   242/243 wojewody poznańskiego] Łukasz Górka (1533-1573)   243 pana gnizieńskiego] Jan z Tomic (Tomicki, † 1575), since 1564 *castellanus* (*kasztelan*) of Gniezno   brzeskiego] *castellanus* of Brześć   Rokossowskiego] Jakub Rokossowski († 1580), since 1569 *castellanus* of Śrem (*kasztelan śremski*) and *supremus thesaurarius* (*podskarbi wielki koronny*) since 1580

240 ad Ephesos] *a.c.* Ephes.   242 Jego miłościwego pana] *a.c.* J. m. p.   243 pana gnizieńskiego] *sic*   pana] *a.c.* p.   244 wasze miłości] *a.c.* w. m.   245 waszym miłościom] *a.c.* w. m.   250/251 wasze miłości] *a.c.* w. m.   251 pana] *a.c.* p. 252 pana] *a.c.* p.   panem] *a.c.* p.   253 wasze miłości] *a.c.* w. m.

CONCILIUM SANDOMIRIENSE – 1570

255   2. Druga legacyja braterska (które tam obiecnie waldeńskimi wszyscy przezywali). Tam x. Jędrzej Prasmovius powstawszy salutował od bracij a niebytność ich wymówił i na mię, z nich jednego tu oblicznego, pokazał. Zatem multis verbis praefatus honorificentissime de fratribus, którzy już przez półtora sta lat nie piórkiem a książkami tylko, ale własną krwią od Husa etc.
260 Konfesyji swej podpirali etc. Konfesyją też firmiter zaleciwszy, pisania ich podał. Tam naprzód pan wojewoda sędomirski | czytał sam synodowi list od 13v panów bracij. Drugi list od ministrów bracij czytał notarius synodi x. Sokołowski. Potem odpowiedział pan wojewoda sędomirski, iż bracią w omówkach ich łaskawie przyjmują, a czasu swego na ich pisanie odpowiedzą etc.
265   3. Legatio od pana wojewody ruskiego;

4. od starosty bełskiego;

5. od pana chełmskiego;

6. z radomskiego kraju;

7. z radziejowskiego kraju (prosili porząd o ministry);

270   8. od pana Jirzego Latalskiego;

9. Marcina Czuryło, egregie commendans Confessionem fratrum;

10. od zboru krakowskiego;

11. x. Walenty z Brzozowa od pana radomskiego;

12. Jakub Sylvius;

275   13. Strasz;

14. x. Paweł Gilowski;

---

255 legacyja braterska] according to Turnowski, the delegation of the Brethren was the second to speak; Jabłoński claimed they were the third, and Jazłowiecki was the second. Jabłoński, *Historia*, p. 39-41; Halecki, *Zgoda sandomierska*, p. 219   **262** ministrów – Sokołowski] Mikołaj Sokołowski, a Reformed pastor serving in Książ, Kotuszów, and Kurozwęki   **265** wojewody ruskiego] Jerzy Jazłowiecki (c. 1510-1575), a Reformed believer. See R. Żelewski, 'Jazłowiecki Jerzy', in *PSB*, vol. 11 (1964-1965), p. 121-123   **266** starosty bełskiego] Stanisław Zamojski (1519-1572), a Reformed believer. See *Urzędnicy województwa bełskiego i ziemi chełmskiej XIV-XVIII wieku. Spisy*, pod red. H. Gmiterek – R. Szczygieł – A. Gąsiorowski, Kórnik 1992, p. 63, no. 321   **267** pana chełmskiego] Jan Orzechowski († 1569 or 1572), or perhaps his son Paweł, who however was not *castellanus* of Chełm. See S. Tworek, 'Orzechowski Paweł', in *PSB*, vol. 24 (1979), p. 283-284; Gmiterek – Szczygieł – Gąsiorowski, *Urzędnicy województwa bełskiego*, p. 153, no. 1102-1103   **270** Jirzego Latalskiego] Jerzy Latalski (1541-1602), son of Janusz Latalski († 1557), married to Dorota Kobylańska, lord of Dębnica in Greater Poland   **271** Marcina Czuryło] Marcin Czuryło, *capitaneus* (*starosta*) in Niepołomice, married to Anna Jazłowiecka. See A. Dembińska, 'Czuryło Marcin', in *PSB*, vol. 4 (1938), p. 374   **273** pana radomskiego] i.e. Jan Tarło († 1587)

---

261 pan] *a.c.* p.   **263** pan] *a.c.* p.   **265** pana] *a.c.* p.   **267** pana] *a.c.* p.   **270** pana] *a.c.* p.   **273** pana] *a.c.* p.

770 CONCILIUM SANDOMIRIENSE – 1570

15. x. Stanisław od starosty nowomiestskiego;
16. z piotrkowskiego kraju etc.

| III. Zatem examen porząd, jeśli niemasz których w smysłu pokażonych a 14r
280 przewrotnych. Gdzie się deklarowali x. Alexander, x. Melcher, dwaj ministrowie z Rusi, x. Clemens z Gorlic etc. Odłożeni na privatum colloquium cum
ministris.

IV. X. Gilowski z poruczenia oznajmił przyczyny synodu:
1. abyśmy o sobie wiedzieli po onym rozerwaniu przez haereses: którzy,
285 gdzie, jak, wiedzmy; 2. zgodzili się, tak jako już my niektórzy z sobą i z kościoły helweckimi etc. A na tym stanęło, aby to Konfesyja była wydrukowana po
polsku, tak ją obwarowawszy, aby nie było ubliżenia tym, którzy swe osobne
sposoby w nabożeństwie mają, wszakże z nami trwają na jednym fundamencie
prawdziwym wiary krześcijańskiej, jako są bracia waldeńscy a bracia konfesyji
290 augszpurskij. Tę umieniliśmy | podać Królowi, na nij się zgodziwszy, a w prefa- 14v
cyji obwarowawszy etc. A tak to prefacyja i potem Konfesyja ku rozsądku
będzie podana. Legit praefationem Trecius.

V. Vota na prefacyją.

Z dystryktu krakowskiego x. Sarnicki: 1. Przydać mentionem tego tu
295 naszego zgromadzenia, a w nim na tę Konfesyją zjednoczenia. 2. W Daniji
ledwo jest nauka zgodna tej Konfesyji. 3. Lucos vertendum gaje, nie: lasy. X.

---

296 3 – lasy] cfr II Par. 34, 4

277 Stanisław] unknown   starosty nowomiestskiego] Andrzej Gnojeński
(c. 1500-1572), since 1542-1544 he was *capitaneus* (*starosta*) in Nowe Miasto Korczyn,
and since 1548-1549 *wójt* in Żarnowiec. Since 1551-1552 he converted to Calvinism.
W. Urban, 'Gojeński (Gnoiński) Andrzej', in *PSB*, vol. 8 (1959-1560), p. 17
280 Alexander] Aleksander Vitrelinus († c. 1586), pastor in Bytom, then in Pińczów.
After 1570 he became an Anti-Trinitarian. Cfr Halecki, *Zgoda sandomierska*,
p. 221-222; H. Barycz, *Śląsk w polskiej kulturze umysłowej*, Katowice 1979, p. 50
Melcher] unknown minister   **281** Clemens – Gorlic] Lutheran pastor in Gorlice
294/295 1 – zjednoczenia] Długosz-Kurczabowa, *Konfesja Sandomierska*, p. 10:
'iżebyśmy to s strony swej pokazali otośmy tę Konfessyją albo to społeczne wyznanie
Kościołów świętych, na prawdziwem Słowie Pańskim fundowanych, ktorechmy już
zgodnemi a jednostajnemi myślami przyjęli, a mocnie przy nich stanęli' **295/296** 2 –
Konfesyji] Długosz-Kurczabowa, *Konfesja Sandomierska*, p. 1 **296** 3 – lasy] Długosz-
Kurczabowa, *Konfesja Sandomierska*, p. 8: 'A jako zasię tym Pan błogosławić raczył,
ktorzy wymysły ludzkie kazili, niszczyli, ony węże miedziane łamali, one lasy, ony
ołtarze wymyślone'

CONCILIUM SANDOMIRIENSE – 1570   771

Jędrzej haec omnia refutavit. Pan Przełęcki approbavit. Pan Mikołaj Dłuski prudenter fatus approbavit praefationem etc. Dr Rożanka, Trecius approbarunt.

300 Z dystryktu chęcińskiego Sylvius publicandam censuit: Bom, pry, o to tylko się bał, abyśmy chcąc budować, | drugiego nie obalali, ale widzę, że się to 15r dobrze obwarowało. X. Łęski. X. Marcin Kalisz: Addatur ratio, cur haec submittitur ceteris confessionibus, quas etiam approbavimus, Valdensis, Augustanae etc. Pan Szafraniec, pan biecki, Oleśnicki.

305 Z dystryktu poznańskiego x. Mikołaj: Wotować nie zda mi się: 1. iż nam jeszcze przyczyna wezwania nie oznajmiona; 2. pan Bniński nie przyjechał. Wszakże każecie li, dicam aliquid ex privata persona. (Każemy). Dobrze jest czynić wyznanie wiary, ale wiele konfesyj mieć źle. Są dwie w Rzeszy przednie, saska a wirtemberska, ale nalepij przyjąć obecnie auszpurską, która już jest 310 szyroce przyjęta, wielkimi świadectwy potwierdzona, a przy nij się zgoda zachowuje. Gdzie też tu czynicie zmiankę Konfesyji waldeńskij (acz jest insza inszych waldensów okrom tej prawdziwsza), | którą wy tu sobie jako za funda- 15v ment niejaki macie a ważycie, wiedzieć raczcie, iż ci bracia waldeńscy mają wiele konfesyj, w czym nam są podejźrzeni, k temu, iż są niestateczni w swej

---

297 Pan Przełęcki] Marcin Przyłęcki († 1583), the *burgrabia krakowski*, and a Reformed believer. I. Kaniewska, 'Przyłęcki Marian (Marcjan)', in *PSB*, vol. 29 (1986), p. 197-199   Pan² – Dłuski] Mikołaj Dłuski (c. 1540-1584), an important Calvinist nobleman and a parliamentarian. See H. Barycz, 'Dłuski Mikołaj', in *PSB*, vol. 5 (1939-1946), p. 195-197   **302** X Łęski] Piotr Łęski (Łącki), pastor in Międzyrzecze and Spytkowice   X² – Kalisz] Marcin z Kalisza (Calissianus), pastor in Secemin and Chmielnik   Addatur ratio] cfr Długosz-Kurczabowa, *Konfesja Sandomierska*, p. 11-12 **304** Pan Szafraniec pan biecki] Stanisław Szafraniec (1530/1531-1598), *castellanus* (*kasztelan*) of Biecz and Sandomierz, one of the most prominent leaders of the Calvinist nobility. See I. Kaniewska, 'Szafraniec Stanisław', in *PSB*, vol. 46 (2009-2010), p. 471-479   Oleśnicki] probably Mikołaj Oleśnicki († 1586), son of Mikołaj Oleśnicki († 1566-1567)   **305** x Mikołaj] i.e. Mikołaj Gliczner   **306** pan Bniński] Stanisław Bniński († after 1574), *iudex terrestris* (*sędzia ziemski*) in Poznań, one of the most prominent supporters of Lutheranism in Greater Poland. His arrival in Sandomierz was delayed due to his talks with Albrecht Friedrich from the Duchy of Prussa. In Sandomierz, he supported the Gliczner brothers, and represented the Górka family. K. Lepszy, 'Bniński Stanisław h. Łodzia', in *PSB*, vol. 2 (1936), p. 148 **309** saska – wirtemberska] i.e. the *Confessio Augustana*, prepared by Philip Melanchthon for the Diet of Augsburg (1530). After the Diet, Melanchthon prepared different versions of his confession, including the famous *Confessio Augustana Variata* (1540). In May 1551 he wrote the *Confessio Saxonica* to be read at the Council of Trent. The *Konfesja wirtemberska* was a confession of faith written in 1551 by Johann Brenz for the same purpose

---

297 Pan¹] *a.c.* P.   Pan²] *a.c.* P.   **304** Pan] *a.c.* P.   pan] *supplevi*   **306** pan] *a.c.* p.

772   CONCILIUM SANDOMIRIENSE – 1570

315 wierze, co jaśnie nuper pokazali na synodzie w Poznaniu, drugdzie się z nami zgadzając, drugdzie zaś odpirając, drugdzie raz pozwalając, raz zaś w tymże nazad się cofając. O czym jeśliście wasze miłości wszyscy nie wiedzieli, wiedzieć już raczcie. A tak gdyż my z nimi o tej Konfesyji in controversia jesteśmy, jej pozwolić nie możemy. A jednak i żadnej inszej nie przyjmujemy, ale
320 przy augszpurskiej, jak nam to zlecono, constanter się ozywamy, a przy nij do roźlania krwie stoimy.

Erasmus etc.: Znać z list tych waldensów a jednak i z procesu waszego, iż wy | jeszcze konfesyji własnyj żadnyj nie macie. A tak i zeszło by się teraz o 16r tym mówić, jaka by confessio miała być od was przyjęta, na którą byśmy się
325 zobopólnie zgodzili. Ku zjedoceniu-śmy gotowi, ale trzeba wielkiego rozsądku. A proszę panów, abyście się o to przecię starali. Wiele konfesyj, ale nalepsza augspurska, z Pisem św. zebrana, na miescu zacnym podana, świadectwy potwierdzona, przyjęta i względem czasu etc. A dobrze by, aby tu to jedna była u nas w Polszcze.
330 Tum-em się dał znać, żem chcę mówić.

Odpowiedział pan wojewoda krakowski:

Abom ja słabo mówił, albo mię źle już tu jeden zrozumiał (okazawszy Erazma), przypisując mi to, na com nie myślił, a co by źle od niemyj twarzy słyszeć etc., iżebyśmy my konfesyji żadnyj nie mieli, czego Boże uchowaj, bać
335 by to było atheorum. Ale iż jako wy się szczycicie auspurską, bracia | waldeń- 16v scy swą własną, tak też my naprzednij helwecką. Lecz poznawszy takowe rozdzielenie być złe, abyśmy nie mówili: Ego sum Cephae, ego Apollinis, na tośmy się tu zjechali, abyśmy się wszyscy na jedną sine tali cognomine zgodzili, która by była naszą, wszechpolską, w której byśmy się samą prawdą Krystuso-
340 wą szczycili. Ale widzimy, iż wy ku temu się nie macie. O Lutrze wim, którego wy sobie za oraculum bierzecie etc., a onże dał testimonium bracij waldeńskij, a iście nieleda testimonium, gdzie nie tylko je z sobą porównał, ale w nauce prawdziwej porównawszy, w rządu kościelnym a dyscyplinie św. nad siebie a kościoły swoje wystawił a wyświadczył. Ale wy nie wim czego jeszcze nad to
345 szukacie, przyganiając | tej ich Konfesyji, wdawając się w niepotrzebnę dyspu- 17r tacyje, nie przestawając na prostej a szczyrej Konfesyji ich, z której się nie dają słuszne przyczyny ku różnicam. A snadnie to rozumim o bracij, iż pokój miłu-

---

337 Ego – Apollinis] cfr I Cor. I, 12

315 synodzie – Poznaniu] i.e. a Synod held on 14 February 1570. Its proceedings can be found in *Akta Synodów Różnowierczych*, vol. 2 (1972), p. 227-249   **322** Erasmus] i.e. Gliczner **336** helwecką] i.e. the *Second Helvetic Confession*

317 wasze miłości] *a.c.* w. m.   **331** pan] *a.c.* p.

CONCILIUM SANDOMIRIENSE – 1570

ją; a fundament nauki prawdziwyj trzymając, w te takowe repliki nieradzi się wdawają, a chwalę im to, mądrze czynią etc.

350 Ja zatem, chcąc mówić, miescam nie miał.

Z dystryktu oświęcimskiego x. Gilowski defendit fratres, iż konfesyj różnych nie mają, chociażby było wiele egzemplarzów różnych czasów etc. drukowanych etc. X. Adam. Pan Stanisław oświęcimski.

Pan Gierołtowski: Ja rozumim, pry, iż ta Konfesyja musi być odmieniona 355 dla panów sasi, którzy pełne garści krwie okazują przy swej Konfesyji, a to oświadczają, | iż ku naszyj Konfesyji od saskiej żadną miarą przystać nie chcą. 17v Trudno z tymi zgody szukać etc.

Tu pan wojewoda sędomirski z panem Iwanem nomine synodi dali mi miesce ku mówieniu. Powstawszy tedy, in hone modum fere verbum a verbo 360 locutus sum:

Jaśnie wielmożni miłościwi panowie, uczciwi ojcowie i bracia łaskawie mili, kilka przyczyn jest, które mię do tego przywodziły, iżbych w tym to zacnym waszych miłości zgromadzeniu spokojem siedział a milczał, których przyczyn potrzeba mi namienić.

365 1. Jako naprzód, iż ja nie jestem tu legatem niejakim cum plenipotentia vel mandatis, abych czynił a sprawował i mówił, co by mi się widziało, gdyż i wiek mój ku temu mię niedostatecznego być okazuje, ale tylko jestem tu posłan od bracij naszyj, ich miłościwych panów, którzy przy bracij stoją, z listy do | syno- 18r du, iżbych ony waszym miłościom oddał.

370 2. Przy tym upominał mię ku milczeniu wzgląd tenuitatis ingenii mei, iż ledwo co godnego przed waszymi miłościami mówić będę mógł.

3. Nadto i respectus tego, co to od waszych miłości gravi iudicio a za wielkim uważaniem jest potanowiono a zarządzono ku przywiedzieniu w zgodę świętą kościoła Bożego a budowaniu onego, iż co bych kolwiek mówił, ledwo 375 by już jakie miesce a powagę w tej mierze mieć mogło. Quin potius, iż jestem

---

353 X Adam] unknown minister   Pan Stanisław oświęcimski] according to Halecki it was Stanisław Oświęcimski, whereas according to Sipayłło it was the *capitaneus* (*starosta*) of Oświęcim, Zygmunt Myszkowski. Sipayłło argued that the author had mistaken Zygmunt Myszkowski for his brother Stanisław. Cfr Halecki, *Zgoda sandomierska*, p. 230 and *Akta Synodów Różnowierczych*, vol. 2 (1972), p. 282, note 3
354 Pan Gierołtowski] Jan or Jakub Gierołtowski (Gierałtowski), *burggrabius capitanei* of Cracow   355 panów sasi] i.e. the Lutherans

353 Pan] *a.c.* P.   354 Pan] *a.c.* P.   358 pan] *a.c.* p.   panem] *a.c.* p.   361 Jaśnie wielmożni] *a.c.* J. w.   363 waszych miłości] *a.c.* w. m.   368 ich miłościwych] *a.c.* i. m.
369 waszym miłościom] *a.c.* w. m.   371 waszymi miłościami] *a.c.* w. m.
372 waszych miłości] *a.c.* w. m.

774 CONCILIUM SANDOMIRIENSE – 1570

powinien, ut gratularer ecclesiae et gratias agam Deo i tym, którzy staraniem i pracą swą tę pomoc ku zgodzie kościoła Bożego sposobili.

Teć, rzekę, przyczyny wiodły mię ku temu, abych spokojem siedząc milczał.

380 Wszakże na drugę stronę pobudzon jestem ku temu, iżebych tu przed waszymi miłościami mówił, a to za przyczyną tego, co tu od panów bracij konfesyji | saskij przeciw Jednocie bracij naszych i Konfesyji naszyj dosyć vehe- 18v menter mówiono jest. Ja tedy, będąc wiernym synem Jednoty tej brackiej, ku temu się oddawszy z młości mojej, żebych nałaskawszemu Zbawicielowi swe-

385 mu tu służył, te rzeczy sobiem słyszał, a tak iż w czym docirali panowie bracia sascy na ojce moje miłe, to się też mojej skóry dotykało. Umieniłem ich miłości to, jako ex privata persona odpowiedź dać, ale iż już jego miłościwy pan wojewoda krakowski w rzeczach przedniejszych wybornie odpowiedzieł a bracij łaskawie obronić raczył, ja tego, co podlejszego jest, dołożę. A waszym

390 miłością proszę, iżebyście mię łaskawym uchem słyszeli, co by mi się niedostało w mowie mojij, to iżbyście mądrością i łaską swą nadstawić raczyli.

| Ta propozycyja jest podana od synodu ku rozsądku a wotowaniu, jeśli 19r praefatio Konfesyji przeczytana approbanda est. Wszakże za przyczynami od niej daleko się odniosło, tak iż już nie na jednę rzecz wotować a mówić potrze-

395 ba. Iżbych tedy votum swoje naprzód około prefacyji powiedział, zda mi się to być rzecz potrzebna, co już bracia spominali (x. Sarnicki), aby się w prefacyji namieniło apertius miesca tegoż, w którym się ugoda na tę Konfesyją dzieje. Gdyż et ipso locus w tej mierze habet aliquam vim argumenti, ile jacy teraz ludzie są a jakie rzeczy baczyć zwykli, co waszym miłościom rozum szerzyj

400 okazać może.

Drugie, zda mi się też to rzecz być potrzebna, którą już (x. Martinus Kalisz) jeden z bracij spominał, aby były jaśniej przyczyny dołożone, dla których wżdy ta Konfesyja się wydawa nad | ony, ktore w tejże prefacyji się 19v uchwalają. Zatem niech i o tym wspomnię, z przyczyny słów x. Mikołajowych,

405 gdzie powiedział o Konfesyji naszyj, mianując ją waldeńską, acz, pry, inna lepsza, nie tych waldensów, Konfesja wydana. Z tych tedy słów namienić tego chcę, iż nas w tej prefacyji niewłaśnie zowiecie waldeńskimi, a Konfesyją naszę waldeńską. Bo inszy byli waldensowie mając powód swój z Francyji, a inszy my z Czech. Rad bych to tedy z strony swej widział, iżebyście nas nie zwali

410 tym przezwiskiem, a w tej prefacyji onym nie opisowali, ale abo simpliciter bracią, jako się zowiemy, albo więc bracią czeskimi, jeślibyście dyferencyj

---

381 waszymi miłościami] *a.c.* w. m.   **386** ich miłości] *a.c.* i. m.   **387** jego miłościwy pan] *a.c.* j. m. p.   **389/390** waszym miłością] *a.c.* w. m.   **399** waszym miłościom] *a.c.* w. m.

CONCILIUM SANDOMIRIENSE – 1570

patrzyć chcieli. | Godzi mi się też odpowiedzieć panom bracij saskim na to, co 20r
tu powiedzieli, iż bracia naszy mają wiele Konfesyj a z tego iż są podejrzeni. Tu
tedy ja powiadam, iż bracia mieli a mają Konfesyją tylko jedną. A aczkolwiek
415 bywały egzemplarze różne (wszakże niesprzeciwne), z przyczyn tych, iż bracia
z ciemności antykrystowych wychodząc zawżdy gotowi a chutliwi bywali ku
uczeniu się a nabywaniu więtszego światła od mężów tych, które Pan Bóg po
różnych stronach w kościele swym wzbudzał, a iż też z różnych przyczyn
ludziom różnym Konfesyję podawali, w tych te, w inszych insze rzeczy, jak
420 gdzie przyczyna była, opisując, a wszakoż jednak (abych się długo nie bawił)
jedurnyż egzemplarz mają raz wydrukowany | w Polszcze, który Król Jego 20v
Miłość podali a ku któremu jednemu się w tym Królestwie ozywają.

Na ostatek i tego dotknę, co tu panowie bracia sascy mówili a dowodzili,
iżby Konfesyja saska na miescu tej od synodu podanej przyjęta od wszech-
425 zgodnie była. Na to tedy mówię, iż gdybyśmy o tym rozsądek mieli czynić,
snadnie by się to firmis rationibus okazało, żeć by w tej mierze przedniejszy
plac Konfesyja nasza miała, która już sama w Królestwie tym jest przednie
rozsławiona, ufundowana, Królowi Jego Miłości padana i przed nieprzyjacioły
obroniona. Ale iż o tym jest rozsądek własny wszystkiego synodu, więcej
430 mówić nie chcę.

| Mogło by się tu więcej słusznie a dowodnie odpowiedzić bracij saskim 21r
na to, gdzie o bracij naszych dosyć nieprzystojnie mówili. Ale czasowi i inszym
rzeczam folgując, niechaj teraz tak zadosyć będzie.

Tę oracyją panowie i bracia wszyscy za łaską Bożą benigne a wdzięcznie
435 słyszeli. In Gliczneris cernere erat vultus subinde mutabiles. Owa ira perciti,
skorom mówić przestał, głowami trzęsąc, to i owo szemrali. Gdzie ich miłościwi panowie, a przednie jego miłościwy pan wojewoda krakowski suscepit
partes meas meque et orationem istam defendit et omnia comprobavit seque
libenter ista audivisse dixit, cum alia cetera, tum id, quod alii fuerint Valdenses
440 praeter nos.

Cui rei Erasmus | repugnabat et conversus ad me dixit: Własne jest to 21v
wasze przezwisko, wy jestście ci waldensowie, czego ja dowiodę. Tamżem mu
rzekł: A ja w tym waszym miłościom simpliciter na odpór wstępuję et firmis
argumentis probabo secundum veritatem historiae non esse nos Valdenses et
445 improprie ita cognominari.

W tymże szemraniu x. Mikołaj repetował, iż my wiemy, że bracia teraz
mają różne Konfesyje, bo nam je w Poznaniu okazowali (a Erasmus dołożył, iż

421/422 Król Jego Miłość] *a.c.* K. J. M.   **428** Królowi – Miłości] *a.c.* K. J. M.
436 ich miłościwi] *a.c.* i. m.   **437** jego – pan] *a.c.* j. m. p.   **443** waszym miłościom]
a.c. w. m.

776 CONCILIUM SANDOMIRIENSE – 1570

ich mają pięć). W tym panowie i bracia okazowali, iż im tę jedną oto posłali, a tej iż oni się dzierżąc świadectwo ji dają etc.

450 | Zatem porząd z dystryktów wotowali, bracij ochotnie defendując, aż 22r przyszło na nijakiego pana lubelskiego, po wojewodziech tam nazacniejszego. Ten maxima cum vehemeintia invectus est in Saxonicos, tamquam turbatores iniquissimos eius boni, cuius causa synodus convocata est, którzy za razem okazali upór swój, krwią się chcąc przy samej swej Konfesyji popisować etc.

455 Zatem iżby było lepij, za razem aby ich tu nie było, aby nie eksplorowali spraw naszych. A co się tycze Konfesyji braci waldeńskich, która oni tu poganieli, jać ją baczę być szczyrą, od ludzi spokojnych z Pisem św. prościuchno spisaną, gdzie oni dobrzy Iudzie w pokoju, ledwy ostatka i pod dębinką tą nie dopisowali. | Ale Confessio ta augszpurska pisana jest w inakszych przyczynach, 22v

460 gdzie byli zgromadzeni ludzie vertiginosi, drudzy i papistae, a więcej się tam akomodowano ludziom niż samej prawdzie, chcąc papieżniki przyłączyć ewangelikom. A tak pewnie, żebych wolał bracką przyjąć, niż tę, i rad się pod nię podpisuję etc. Haec militari oratione vehementer exposuit, aż się Glicznerowie znoili.

465 Sub finem pan Zborowski napominal sasów ku zgodzie a inakszym postępkom:

Wszak wy, powieda, kto do was przyjdzie, i nieznajomy, a wyzna, iż jest na fundamencie wiary krześcijańskiej a z grzechów | pokutuje, takiemu służy- 23r cie z Stołu Pańskicgo a przypuszczacic go do siebie zgodnie. I czemuż nas ku

470 mniejszym rzeczam, zgodne z wami in fundamento, przypuszczać nie chcecie, gdyż my was e contra radzi przyjmujemy a znosić chcemy? Proszę, rozmyślajcie się pilnie a miejcie się do zgody statecznie, bo my, którzy jesteśmy consiliarii królewscy, wiemy, co się dzieje a jak gravissimae causae sunt tego, iżbyśmy się w ten sposób tu w Polszcze złączyli. Co gdyby wam z drugimi wiadomo

475 było, iście byście się inaczyj czuli a do zgody kwapili!

In eandem sententiam locutus pan Iwan | a upominał, iżby się z myślami 23v spokojnymi rozeszli, gdzie die sequenti w łasce społecznej będą już same Konfesyją rozbirać. Aczkoli de praefatione przez ten dzień nihil certe conclusum, i nie może być, aż się w Konfesyji rozbiraniu wszyscy na czym pewnym zgodzą.

480 Jutro hora 11 redeant.

Postquam egressi sumus, mira alacritate exceptus eram a dominis et fratribus ministris, concurrebant undique, salutabant, gratulabantur, extollebant, animabant, de fratribus multa quaerebant et praeclare testabantur.

---

451 pana lubelskiego] the *castellanus* (*kasztelan*) of Lublin Stanisław Słupecki († 1575). See H. Kowalska, 'Słupecki Stanisław z Konar', in *PSB*, vol. 39 (1999-2000), p. 115-118

458 pod dębinką] *intellege* under threat **465** pan] *a.c.* p. **476** pan] *a.c.* p.

CONCILIUM SANDOMIRIENSE – 1570

| 11 Aprilis, die Martis. Kazał x. Sylvius na słowa: Ecce quam pulchra et 24r
485 decora es, amica mea etc., terribilis ut castrorum acies.

1. Legacyja z Litwy a nowina, iż się tam niedawno zbory saskie z helweckimi w Wilnie 2 Martii do re sacramentaria zgodziły, której ugody formuła
czytana.

2. X. Matusz z Krelowa, Saxonicus, głuchy, wotował o wczorajszyj propo-
490 zycyji, profitując się być konfesyji augustańskij, a one wychwalał. A iż, pry, brat
jeden powiedział, że ona nie jest tu w Polszcze tak podana Królowi, jako bracka, a ja powiadam, iż augustańska jest podana wszemu światu. A by się ją w
Polszcze dzierżeli, nie byłoby tyle sekt etc. Tu mu mowa przerwana od panów,
iż go źle sprawiono etc.

495 | 3. Konfesyja jest czytana. 24v
I artykuł. Zgodzili się wszyscy, tylko x. Mikołaj powiedział, iż się im zgoła
odpowiadać nie godzi, ale przeczytawsz sobie powoli, iż porząd na wszystko
odpowiadać będą. Na to nic mu nie rzeczono.

Artykuł II, III, IV. Tu pan lubelski censuit, aby sic co inszego traktowało
500 etc., gdyż ten panowie bracia saskiej konfesyji powiedzieli, iż chcą cos osobne-
go sobie zgromadzać a odpowiedać. Mogliby tedy teraz odejść a tam osobno
sobie mninować etc. Także pan Miękicki acriter invectus in Saxonicos. Sed
perrectum est etc.

Na obiad prosił nas z Trecyjem pan Miękicki z panem Fredrusem, gdzie-
505 śmy naprzód mówili contra subtilitates arianicas, z przyczyny artykułu piąte-
go. | Potem erat acris inquisitio de voce Valdenses, bo panowie sunt periti 25r
historiarum. Wszakże ta sententia plac obdzierżała, gdziem powiedział: 1. Bracia byli zwani od ludzi zacnych tym przezwiskiem i sami temuż przezwisku nie
odmawiali, jako i teraz z większyj części nie odmawiają. 2. Wszakże secundum
510 veritatem historiae improprie sic vocantur, cum nec propagati sint a Valdensi-
bus, nec doctrinam ab eis acceperint. Sed hoc novum illis accidit ratione loci,

---

484/485 Ecce – acies] cfr Cant. 4, 1; 6, 4 et 9; 7, 6

486 1] the *Consensus of Vilnius*. See Halecki, *Zgoda sandomierska*, p. 234-235 **489** X
Matusz z Krelowa] Mateusz from Raków, pastor in Kryłów **496** I artykuł] see
Długosz-Kurczabowa, *Konfesja Sandomierska*, p. 29-35 **499** Artykuł II III IV] see
Długosz-Kurczabowa, *Konfesja Sandomierska*, p. 35-48 **504** pan Miękicki] i.e.
Krzysztof Miękcicki panem Fredrusem] i.e. Jerzy Fredro, since 1578 *wojski* of Sambor
505 artykułu piątego] see Długosz-Kurczabowa, *Konfesja Sandomierska*, p. 48-53: 'O
chwale, czci i modlitwie ktora się czyni Bogu przez jedynego Pośrzednika Krystusa
Pana'

---

499 pan] *a.c.* p. **502** mninować] *intellege* rozważac, 'consider' pan] *a.c.* p.
504 pan] *a.c.* p. panem] *a.c.* p.

778 CONCILIUM SANDOMIRIENSE – 1570

iż też Valdenses annis circiter 100 ante originem fratrum pulsi ex Galliis in Bohemia morabantur. Drugie też, ratione doctrinae, to się także papieżowi przeciwiali etc. Erat tamen semper aliquod discrimen in doctrina, ob quod
515 fratres faciebant differentiam inter suas et Valdensium ecclesias seque improprie Valdenses dictos scribebant etc. Et quod ad meam personam attinet, żadnemu się nie ozwę, kto mię waldeńczykiem zawoła etc.

| A prandiis. Była akcyja z x. Aleksandrem. Wybran był a synodo Trecius 25v et Ioannes Thenaudus, iżby mu pokazali, że Pater, Filius et Spiritus S. auctoritate Scripturae unus Deus dicitur. Forte przydało się, żem ja między nimi
520 dwiema siedział. Gdy tedy słabo rzecz prowadzili, szyroce się rozwodząc, iż nie było znać, jakie jest ich argumentum, o co im x. Aleksander przymawiał, szeptałem Trecyjowi argument z dialektyki sporządzony. Zatem się wyrwał gość Lithuanus pomagając Aleksandrowi. Tamżem, instinctu Trecii a pana Iwana,
525 rozkazano mi od synodu, iżebych, gość przeciw gościowi, powstał. Ja tedy z chucią gościowi naprzód na jego | obiectionem odpowiedział, potem subsu- 26r mując słowa Trecyjowe długie, wiodłem przeciw Aleksandrowi argument prosty etc. Zatem synod nie chciał mię puścić, ale przymusił do tego, żem z obranymi dysputatory aż do końca przeciw Aleksandrowi in arena trwał.
530   Na wieczerzą wzięli mię patroni Aleksandrowi, pan Ossowski, Jakubowski etc. Tam w rozmowie pokazowałem, że jaśnie w Piśmie stoją ty słowa: Bóg Ojciec, Bóg Syn, Bóg Duch św. jest jeden prawdziwy Bóg. Te, rzkę, słowa są w Piśmie, acz nie po gromadzie, ale na rożnych miescach etc. Czemu się panowie niepomału ruszyć dali. Zatem rozkazano mi od dyrektorów synodu, iżebych tę
535 akcyją z x. Aleksandrem spisał, com uczynił a im podał etc.

| Die 12 Aprilis. Kazał x. Jędrzej. 26v
Legationes niektóre. Saxonici też etc. O wybraniu rozmówców etc. Czytana Konfesyja. Kazano wotować na Konfesyją, doczytawszy ją. Na co pan wojewoda krakowski: Nie zda mi się rzecz potrzebna czas trawić wotowaniem,

---

518/520 Była – dicitur] i.e. Aleksander Vitrelin. On this controversy, *Akta Synodów Różnowierczych*, vol. 2 (1972), p. 298-301 **519** Ioannes Thenaudus] Jean Thenaud was born in Bourges (France). He studied in Geneva, and in 1555 became Mikołaj and Wojciech Dłuski's preceptor. In 1558 he moved to Poland, where he taught at the Academy of Pińczów and collaborated to the first Protestant translation of the Bible in Polish (the *Biblia brzeska*). See J. Birn, 'Francuz wśród kalwinów małopolskich. Jan Thenaud', *Reformacja w Polsce* 4 (1926), p. 41-44; S. Tworek, *Działalność oświatowo kulturalna kalwinizmu małopolskiego*, Lublin 1970 **530** pan Ossowski] unknown Jakubowski] Andrzej Jakubowski, since 1557 *capitaneus* (*starosta*) of Leżajsk. In 1563 he was appointed secretary to the King of Poland, and from 1577 he served as tax collector in Sandomierz

524 pana] *a.c.* p. **530** pan] *a.c.* p. **538** pan] *a.c.* p.

CONCILIUM SANDOMIRIENSE – 1570

540 bowiem my się wszyscy zgodzimy na tym, iż prawdziwa jest, gdyż się ji dawno
dzierżymy, a wotowaniem ji nam zalecać nie trzeba. Ale gdyż ta jest naprzed-
niejsza przyczyna zjachania naszego, abyśmy się złączyli z bracią konfesyji
waldeńskij, jako zowią, a saskiej, oni niechaj wotują o tej Konfesyji, zgadza li
się z Pismy św., a chcą li z nami przy niej stać, abyśmy ją communi nomine nie
545 za helwecką, ale własną swoją polską wszyscy wydali.

| To takowe wotowanie placuit fieri in loco, privato delectis certis personis   27r
etc. Wybrani tedy są pauci, bo pan wojewoda powiedział, że musi być respectus person przy stronach: z braci saskich jedno dwaj ministrowie a pan Bniński; z braci waldensów, jako zowią, acz byli pilnie wokowani, nie widząc tu,
550 jeno jednego oto posła, a drugi x. Jędrzej na miejscu ich. A tak odeszli do pana
wojewodzinyj gospody ku tej sprawie:

Z augustańskich ministrowie: x. Mikołaj, x. Erasmus Glicznerowie, patronus pan Bniński, sędzia poznański.

Z bracij ministrowie: x. Jędrzej Prasnicius, Simeon Bogomił. Patronus
555 nullus nobis affuit, sed tamen Dominus adstitit nobis.

| Z helweckich ministrowie: x. Jakub Sylvius, x. Paweł Gilowski; patroni: 27v
jego miłościwy pan Stanisław Myszkowski, wojewoda krakowski; jego miłościwy pan Piotr Zborowski, wojewoda sędomirski; doktor Stanisław Rożanka.
Potem też pan Dłuski.
560 Tam naprzód nam kazali wotować o tej Konfesyji.

Poradziwszy się ze sobą, x. Jędrzej rzekł, iżbyśmy radzi pierwyj słyszeli
odpowiedź waszych miłości na list bracki, gdzie oni żądają, aby Konfesyja ich
była od waszych miłości przyjęta.

Odpowiedział pan wojewoda krakowski, żeśmy się nie dlatego tu zjechali,
565 abyśmy czyją konfesyję przyjmowali a mówili: Ego sum Cephae vel Apollinis
etc., ale abyśmy jedną prawdziwą Konfesyję mutuo consensu in vinculum concordiae wydali, która by ani bracka, ani saska, ani helwecka, ale nasza własna,
polska, krześcijańska była. To z niejakim zatrwożeniem mówił.

| Zatem x. Jędrzej wotował, iż tę Konfesyją za prawdziwą a tak swoję wła-   28r
570 sną przyjmujemy. Tam panowie pytali mnie na votum. Jam odpowiedział, iż
ich miłości wiedzą, że nie ja jestem plenipotens, ale x. Jędrzej, na tego votum
że ja mam przestawać. Nihilominus wszyscy urgebant i x. Jędrzej prosił, at
ipsemet sententiam meam aperirem. Tamżem rzekł:

---

565 Ego – Apollinis] cfr I Cor. 1, 12

547 pan] *a.c.* p.   **548** pan] *a.c.* p.   **550** pana] *a.c.* p.   **553** pan] *a.c.* p.   **557** jego
miłościwy pan Stanisław Myszkowski] *a.c.* j. m. p. S. M.   **557/558** jego miłościwy pan
Piotr Zborowski] *a.c.* j. m. p. P. Z.   **559** pan] *a.c.* p.   **562** waszych miłości] *a.c.* w. m.
563 waszych miłości] *a.c.* w. m.   **564** pan] *a.c.* p.   **571** ich miłości] *a.c.* i. m.

780 CONCILIUM SANDOMIRIENSE – 1570

Miłościwi panowie a bracia łaskawi, aczkolwiek bracia wielkie a znamie-
575 nite przyczyny tego mają, dla których radzi by to widzieli, aby Konfesyja, od
nich Jego Królowskiej Miłości podana, była od waszych miłości wszech przyjęta, z których przyczyn niektóre tu wasze miłości, w pisaniu swym oznajmili,
a insze też osobliwe samem ad nich słyszał, wszakoż jednak iż zawżdy bracia
nawięcej się o to starali a tego pragnęli, iżby kościół Boży szczęśiliwie był
580 budowan a pomnażan, tak rozumim, iż gdy to od waszych miłości skutecznie | 28v
poznają, że więtsze a zacniejsze przyczyny tego wasze miłości, (z którychem
ich już niemało od waszych miłości namienionych słyszał) macie, iżby insza
konfesyja od wszech spólnie ku zgodzie a pomnożeniu kościoła Bożego publi-
kowana była, żeć też przeciw temu nie będę. A ja, iżem Konfesyję tę Tiguri-
585 nam dawno pierwyj przedtem czytał, a to poznał, że jest prawdziwa a nasza
własna, z naszej nieco szyrzej a jaśniej eadem methodo spisana, onej nie przy-
ganiam, ale za prawdziwą a własną przyjmuję.
To z wielką pociechą usłyszeli, a zwłaszcza pan wojewoda krakowski, aż
mu łzy z oczu od radości znacznie poszły. Testabantur multis verbis laetitiam.
590 Zatem ja, rozmyśliwszy się na rzecz potrzebną, powstałem i hnedże mi mówić
kazali:
| Miłociwi panowie, wasze miłości raczcie wiedzieć, iżem tę Konfesyją 29r
waszych miłości za własną też naszę w ten sposób wyświadczył, iżby bracia onę
za swoją przyjąwszy swojej pierwszej odrzucić nie byli powinni, ale owszem,
595 iżby przy niej jako pierwyj trwali.
Tamże hned pan wojewoda krakowski: I owszem, bracij przy ich własnej
zostawujemy, Boże uchowaj, abyśmy mieli po bracij tego żądać, żeby przy swej
pierwszej konfesyji trwać nie mieli.
Tego, rzekę, między inszymi przyczynami dlategom dołożył, iżby bracia,
600 trwając przy własnyj konfesyji sub hac generaliori, trwali a zostawali przy
obrzędach, w zborze swym zwyczajnych, a zwłaszcza przy dyscyplinie etc.
K temu się ozwali wszyscy, a zwłaszcza pan wojewoda sędomirski: I
owszem, a o tym radzić dalij będziem, aby i między nami rząd kościelny i dys-
cyplina lepsze postanowienie wzięła etc.
605 | Już zatem omnium oculi coniecti erant in Saxonicos, qui antea durissime 29v
resistebant etc. Atque ita inter summum gaudium ci metum mire erant dd.
palatini solliciti ac nolentes, ne triste Saxonicorum responsum hanc laetitiam

---

574 Miłościwi] *a.c.* Mościwi   576 Jego Królowskiej Miłości] *a.c.* J. K. M.   waszych
miłości] *a.c.* w. m.   577 wasze miłości] *a.c.* w. m.   580 waszych miłości] *a.c.* w. m.
581 wasze miłości] *a.c.* w. m.   582 waszych miłości] *a.c.* w. m.   588 pan] *a.c.* p.
592 Miłociwi] *a.c.* Mościwi   wasze miłości] *a.c.* w. m.   593 waszych miłości] *a.c.* w.
m.   596 pan] *a.c.* p.   602 pan] *a.c.* p.

CONCILIUM SANDOMIRIENSE – 1570

781

turbaret, diligentissime eos praemonuerunt et ad talem responsionem, qualem optabant, sedulo paraverunt.

610 Naprzód pan wojewoda krakowski upominał, aby naprzedniejszy wzgląd mieli na chwałę Boża a pomnożenie kościoła i zachowanie onego etc., Konfesyją augszpurską iżby sobie nie przeszkadzali, gdyż iście jest w wiela rzeczach imperfecta. Wiem, kto ją, za jakimi przyczynami pisał, jakie o niej rozumienie ludzi godnych, a i w nij wiele jeszcze papieskiego etc.

615 Longiorem orationem habuit palatinus sendomiriensis: Wiem ci to, iż wy jesteście posłowie Boży, którzy nas macie rządzić w rzeczach | zbawiennych. Ale też to wiem, iż nas Pan Bóg dał wam za patrony a 30r obrońce przed nieprzyjacioły i jest to nasza własna powinność, dla chwały Bożyj zastawować się za was etc. A tak proszę, iżebyście w tym należytą baczność na wszystko mieć chcieli. Nie iżeby ty już tylko o to się starał, żeby w kościele dobrze powiedał słowo Boże, a w inszych rzeczach na mię baczności żadnej nie miał, a tak się rządził, żeby mnie w sprawowaniu wezwania mego drogę zakładał, a potem i ze mną nie wiem gdzie się ostał. A iście człowiekem ci też, tak czyńcie, jako byście i mnie nie zgorszyli, gdybych waszą niebaczność i niewdzięczność poznał. Bo wy nie wicie, co się dzieje, jaką my pracę ustawicznie o was mamy przeciw czujnym nieprzyjaciołom. Waszy panowie z Wielkiej Polski nic nam jednak nie | pomagają, na sejmiech nie bywaj. My 30v sami ku chwale Bożej za was czujemy. Niechajże wżdy wasza będzie na nas w tym jaka baczność. Tak czyńcie, abyście też nas już tymi brzemiony nie przełomili. My wiemy, iż co czynimy, za słusznym uważeniem a wielkimi przyczynami się dzieje od nas ku pożytku kościoła Bożego. A zgodzim li się tak, wielka nadzieja jest (co niech od was daleko nie wychodzi) i o Panie naszym, że naszą religiją przyjmie. Jaka radość wszystkim dobrym, jaki smętek nieprzyjaciołom z zgody naszej pójdzie, którym prawie omnia consilia turbabimus! Pamiętajcie, prze miły Bóg, ocz nam idzie, a miejcie się uprzejmie ku zgodzie a miłości zobopólnej, którą nam Pan nad wszystko rozkazał etc.

| Tak mówił z osobliwym afektem, łzy w sobie z zaczerwienieniem oczu 31r dzierżąc, które potem, rzewno się wylawszy, oracyji jego koniec uczyniły. Tam też wojewoda krakowski dobrze mu płakać pomógł.

640 Już tu nie wiem de sequentibus actibus jednak jak pisać, bo czasem aniśmy sami wszyscy wiedzieli, co się dzieje, owa iż mira celeritate gravissimis impedimentis cedentibus zgoda się do nas kwapiła. A wszyscyśmy to z chwaleniem Boga wyznawać musieli, iż Dominus ipse in medio nostri, qui nobis nescio quid pueriliter mollientibus mirabiliter opus suum perfecit.

---

610 pan] *a.c.* p.

782 CONCILIUM SANDOMIRIENSE – 1570

645   Po tym naszym radosnym złączeniu a oracyjach rzewnych panów wojewodów Glicznerowie inakszego ducha pokazować poczęli, jakoż sobą trwożąc, a nie wiedząc, co czynić. Oracyją tedy swą ku | naszemu consilium stosowali. ₃₁ᵥ Obaczywszy, żeśmy my się z krakowskimi złączyli tak, iż przy swej konfesyji i dyscyplinie etc. zostawamy, i oni w tym się ożywając, iż w swej wierze zostawać
650 chcą, a wszakże na słowa pana wojewody krakowskiego saskiej konfesyji zaletać już nie chcąc ani też helweckij przyjąć! (bo rzekł Erasmus, iż na helwecką kompozycyją nigdy nie zezwoli). A zatem tu ukazował jij niedostatki, naprzód Pisma źle przywiedzione per malam periphrasin etc., gdzie drugichśmy mu pozwalali, drugich nic. Ja dostałem egzemplarza greckiego, a z niegom praw-
655 dziwej sentencyji dowodził. Potem jął dowodzić błędów w nij, powiadając, iż w nij są. Dziwnie jakoś od tego przestał. Zatem poczęli o tym radzić, iżby była insza właśnie polska spisana od wszech społu etc., a w tym jakoś niebacznie zrazu do tego się przyznali, iż się już z nami złączają. Tam to spisanie nowej konfesyji ochotnie im pozwolono od panów wojewodów, aby się hned na
660 Świątki do Warszawy zjechali, gdyż panowie patroni po gromadzie będą li, ale w tym jakaś | wątpliwość zostawiona, będzie li tego gdy trzeba etc.   ₃₂ᵣ
    Interea przyszła tu conclusio, abyśmy teraz na dowód tej zgody spisali taki reces, jaki w Wilnie jest złożon, w którym by był consensus de re sacramentaria etc.
665   Tam pan wojewoda sędomirski zjednał x. Jędrzeja z Erazmem ad suscriptam consensionem.
    Quis laetitiam eam describere possit, quae tamen praecipue conspicua erat in palatinis. Hanc egressi in omnes propagavimus.
    Tam mię pan wojewoda sędomirski krakowskiemu a Iwanowi gwałtem na
670 swój obiad wziął et coram d. Bniński nimis laudibus extollebat. Locutum de disciplina.
    | A prandiis. Nowina to dobra opowiedziana publice; na czym rzecz ₃₂ᵥ stanęła. Potem był examen person, ku tej zgodzie należących, gdzie wojewodowie protestowali, iż in fundamento błądzących bronić nic chcą. Tam Alexan-
675 der tritheismi semicondemnatus. Inszy mnodzy suspecti redibant ad ecclesiam poenitentiam agentcs et confessionem edentes, inter quos redibant quidam ministri circiter 7 a Stancari dogmate, a wyznali, iż człowiek Krystus Jezus jest pośrzednikiem naszym u Ojca, tak iż człowieczeństwo jego ku godności a dostateczności pośrzednictwa skutek swój bierze a ma od bóstwa jego.

659/660 na Świątki] i.e. 14 May

650 pana] *a.c.* p.   **652/656** A – przestał] *scriba interpolavit aut corr.*   **665** pan] *a.c.* p. **669** pan] *a.c.* p.

CONCILIUM SANDOMIRIENSE – 1570 783

680 Po rozejściu ex synodo zeszliśmy się ku spisaniu recesu, którego formulam już | spisali byli Trecius cum Thenaudo. Zeszli się: pan Iwan, x. Sarnicki, x. 33r Jędrzej, Glicznerowie, Simeon Bogomił. Tamśmy i tytuł, i nieco w tekstu sprawili. Interea o tym wspominano, iż się podpisować pod to mamy. Przy sprawowaniu tekstu egi cum compositoribus, Trecio et Thenaudo, de particula, qua 685 asserebant in Coena Domini corporis substantialem praesentiam dixique me nullo modo subscripturum in hanc particulam, utpote quia non sit recepta a fratribus. Sufficere, si dicamus veram. Effeci id (postea post discessum Gliczne-rorum), quod in descriptione vox illa ita, ut volui, mutata est. Constituimus etiam, ut fiat mentio caeremoniarum, quia libertati Christianae permittentur. 690 Interim (me cum Thenaudo de illa substantiali praesentia susurrante) subiece-runt | Gliczneri, in quod reliqui statim consenserunt, ut ponatur in recessu de 33v communione mutua in sacramentis. (Quod, cum post sero rescivissem, effeci, ut poneretur particula generalis cuiusque ecclesiae ritibus et discipline etc.).

Denique Gliczneri exigebant, ut integer articulus ille Saxonicus de Cena 695 Domini recessui addatur. In quod x. Jędrzei i jednak wszyscy drudzy natych-miast zezwolili, me nequaquam consentiente, sed repugnante, modestius quidem Gliczneris praesentibus, acrius vero illis absentibus. A gdyśmy to jako napilnij rozkładali, conclusum est ab omnibus tego nie pozwalać re reiecta in dd. palatinos, upomniawszy a promowawszy o tym.

700 | Die 13 Aprilis Iovis. Naprzód szedłem do tych, co reces pisali, w którym- 34r śmy kila rzeczy poprawili, deleto etiam epitheto, quod fratribus addebatur: venerandi etc.

Dokoła gdyśmy się zeszli, praefatus est x. Sylvius gratulans de optimis concordiae principiis etc. Zatem czytan reces albo formula concordiae. Po 705 przeczytaniu Erasmus postulował, aby im był dan reces ku przejrzeniu, bo baczą, iż jest nieco od wczorajszego odmieniony etc. Podan im tedy jest reces i wyszli z nim, z panem Bnińskim.

Tam gdy in commune mówiono, co li w nim poprawiać chcą, ja powie-działem: Jedno, iż rozumiem, że będą chcieć włożyć pro vera substantialem 710 praesentiam corporis Christi in Cena. Drugie, że chcą, aby cały | artykuł ten 34v Confiessionis Saxonicae de Cena Domini był przy recesie wpisan. A prosiłem, aby tego synod nie pozwalał, causis quibusdam monstratis. To oboje radzi wszyscy przyjęli, a rozbirając postanowili secundum votum meum. Tam zawo-łał mię do siebie x. Jędrzej, cum de istis a me propositis sententiae ferrentur, a 715 powiedział, iż pewnie wie, że tak jest, jakom przed synodem powiedział, iż chcą położyć to słowo substantialem. Cóż tedy, pry, chcemy czynić? Ku temu przyczynił się i Trecius, gdzie oba to afirmowali, iż możemy admitować illam

---

681 pan] *a.c.* p. **707** panem] *a.c.* p.

784 CONCILIUM SANDOMIRIENSE – 1570

particulam, bo jij i Beza używa, a i w tym już przyjętym saskim artykule przyjęliśmy istam phrasim.

720 Ja na to odpowiedział, iż się tego żadnym obyczajem nię będę ważył, abych się podpisał pod sposób mówienia | od bracij nigdy nie przyjęty, ale jako 35r niesłuszny, wzgardzony, a iżbych też miał przypuścić do pacyfikacyji słowo to, które esset causa disputationum, discordiae et turbandae pacis, quam constituimus. Co się tycze Bezy, ne illius quidem auctoritas apud me tanti est, ut 725 aliter faciam, quam iam dixi. Ale rad bych widział locum, in quo istam particulam posuit, i rozumim to, że ją położył w inszym sposobie, niźliby tu stała, i pewnie, jako człowiek baczny, circumscripsit suis terminis etc. W tym artykule saskim, przyjętym od nas, gdyż jest to particula, popatrzmy, jakim sposobem tam stoi etc.

730 Tamże naleźliśmy, iż asserit substantialem praesentiam Christi in Cena, non autem substantialem praesentiam corporis Christi. | Inferowałem tedy 35v hnedże z tego, abyśmy nie chcieli więcyj koncedować, niżeśmy tu w tym artykule przyjęli. A w tym też iż się nam trzeba teraz opatrzyć a deklarować ingenue, jak to rozumiemy, ne in alium sensum quis detorqueat. Wybornie się tedy 735 temu zabieżało addita particula secundum sacramentorum naturam. Konkludowaliśmy tedy, a te konkluzyją synodowi oznajmili, iżbyśmy defendowali veram praesentiam corporis Christi, sin vero urgerent nos auctoritate articuli recepti, concedemus substantialem praesentiam Christi, id est, praesentiam corporis Christi, servata maioris declamationis loco particula secundum natu- 740 ram sacramentorum, id est, sacramentaliter.

Interea, gdy jeszcze Saxonici z recesem nie przyszli, były sprawy około porządku kościołow, rozdawanie ministrów do parafij etc., rozdzielenie dystryktów.

| Agitata quaestio o służbie papieżników Ciałem Bożym ludziom podda- 36r 745 nym panów bracij. Konkludowali tego im nie dopuszczać. Jeśli im lekarstwa dać nie możemy, wżdy ich truć nie dopuszczajmy etc. Item, o krczeniu dziatek, gdzie też tak konkludowano, ut ecclesia aliquatenus ministerio gladii regatur. Ego tacui.

Interim redeunt Saxonici cum recessu, a proponowali te dwie rzeczy:
750 1. Że chcą słowa niektóre potrzebne dołożyć.
2. Aby był cały artykuł z Konfesyji saskij do recesu przypisan etc.

Na co utrinque barzo tęgo bito. Tandem vix vix auctoritate palatinorum temu odeprzono et petitio ista illis denegata est.

CONCILIUM SANDOMIRIENSE – 1570   785

W tym wszedł x. Stanisław Marcyjan, legatus z Litwy, oddał listy od
755 Andrzeja księcia Wiszniowieckiego etc. imieniem zboru dziawołtowskiego.
(Póty legacyji).

Fuit magna concertatio cum Saxonicis de | substantiali praesentia corpo-   36v
ris Christi omnibus isti phrasi reclamantibus. Gdzie też pan Miękicki powiedział do sasów: Panowie bracia, nie dziwujcie się, iż się tak przeciwko wam
760 zastawiamy, bo abyście wiedzieli, iż nam tu o to idzie jako powiedział Rej do
biskupa krakowskiego: Jeśli mam wierzyć, że tu jest cały Krystus, boję się,
abych się golenią jego nie udawił.

Owa na tym stanęło, aby było wymazano słowo corporis, a położono substantialem praesentiam Christi. Voluit etiam habere Erasmus veram, quod illi
765 voluerunt concedere me concedente, przy czym protestatio facta: jeśliby nas w
tej partykule substantialem kto chciał nad rozumienie nasze wykładać, mamy
już przełożone w tymże procesie słowa, którymi się deklarujemy: secundum
naturam sacramentorum. Ty słowa nie są Saxonicis okazane, wszakże pozwoli-
li na to, gdyż słowa są in recessu. Ta protestatio nasza wpisana | jest in acta   37r
770 synodica, i to, że jij Saxonici pozwolili, bo nam tego potrzeba.

Potem za postulacyją Erazmową wymazany słowa per occasionem.

Si opus fuerit, scilicet nos conventuros ad conscribendam generalem
Confessionem, et fere conclusum (aut potius concessum Saxonicis), abyśmy
się teraz wszyscy zjachali po Świątkach do Warszawy, gdyż tam panowie patro-
775 ni nas wszech będą etc.

Zatem Marcyjan deklarował wiarę swą, iż non sentit cum tritheitis,
których pełno w Litwie, a iż przyjęty są w zborze ich wileńskim modus loquendi: Hi tres sunt unum et: Hi tres sunt unus.

Przy tym auditores Aleksandrowi prosili o radę a pomoc i baczenie etc.
780 Consultationes ecclesiasticae około tych tam zborów, ministrów szkół.
Panowie wojewodowie pozwolili się dawać każdy rok na szkołę 100 fl., a senio-
res mają w plebanijach tego doglądać, co by było z prowentów | nad słuszne   37v
wychowanie ministrów, to iżby zgromadzano było na podpomaganie uboż-
szych ministrów a fundowanie szkół, a zwłaszcza unius praecipue, quam in

---

778 Hiⁱ – unus] cfr I Ioh. 5, 8-9

754 x Stanisław Marcyjan] pastor Stanisław Marcjan, from Dziewałtów, in the Grand
Duchy of Lithuania. See I. Lukšaitė, *Reformacija Lietuvos Didžiojoje Kunigaikštystėje ir
Mažojoje Lietuvoje. XVI a. trečias dešimtmetis – XVII a. pirmas dešimtmetis*, Vilnius
1999, p. 220, 243-244, 335, 368   **755** Andrzeja księcia Wiszniowieckiego] Andrzej
Wiśniowiecki († 1584), owner of Dziewałtów, since 1568 *kasztelan* in Wołyń, from 1572
kasztelan in Bracław, and from 1576 *wojewoda* of Wołyń

758 pan] *a.c.* p.   **761** że] *a.c.* ż   **781** Panowie] *a.c.* P.

786 CONCILIUM SANDOMIRIENSE – 1570

785 certo loco constituent. Talia tractata et ordinata sunt in synodo me absente, bom odszedł ku przepisaniu akcyji albo dysputacyji habitae cum Alexandro, bo ją synod obiecał dać audytorom jego, a mnie rozkazano ją im wypisać. W tym przyniesiony 4 egzemplarze recesu sprawionego, pod które się podpisowali. Tam iżem był absens, posłali mię szukać, iżbych się też podpisał.

790 Ja, bojąc się tego uczynić, gdyż mi ta moc od bracie nie była dana, przyszedłszy wymawiałem się z tego, iż się już plenipotens bracki podpisał, a ja iżem tylko poseł z listy. Urgebant nihilominus omnes, a pan wojewoda | sędomirski 38r mowił: Nie za posła z listy, ale za legata brackiego te cognoscimus et functus es recte officio legati i inaczyj być nie może, wszyscy to requirimus a te, abyś się 795 podpisał.

Potem jeszcze niektóre negocyja zborów sprawowane były.

Die 14 Aprilis, Veneris. Zgromadzenie było, gratulatio ecclesiae, dzięki a chwały Bogu i modlitwy. Tam też działy się protestationes, iż przy tym recesie stąd a według onego wszyscy postępować będziemy. Tam też protestował 800 Erasmus, iż z bracią chcą amicitiam, caritatem et pacem colere, et finem imponunt disputationi cum illis inceptae Posnaniae. A na potwierdzenie tego, iż chce, aby się społecznie zgromadzili w Poznaniu z bracią, a w | zobopólnej 38v łasce ku zgodzie świętyj się przyjęli.

Na to mu x. Jędrzej odpowiedział, że bracia, którzy zawtżdy szukają 805 dobra kościoła Bożego a chwały Bożej, pokój ten radzi przyjmują a z nimi się zgromadzą etc.

Zatem cum gaudio magno manus mutuo porrectae etc., et gratiis Deo actis ad suos quisque cum laeto nuntio perreximus.

Confirma hoc Deus, quod operatus es in nobis.

810 Cum Sarnicio, Trecio et Gilovio ad comitia Regni cum palatinis illustrissimis multa contuli quaerens, quod omnino conclusum sit de Confessione ista Helvetica et hortatus sum Trecium ac Gilovium, ne quod praeter consensum agere praesumant etc. Sperabo tamen.

| FORMULA RECESSUS 39r

815 Consensus mutuus in religionis Christianae capitibus inter ecclesias Maioris et Minoris Poloniae, Russiae, Lithuaniae, Samogitiae, quae iuxta confessionem Augustanam, fratrum Valdensium (ut vocant) et Helveticam aliquo

---

809 Ps. 67 (68), 29

792 pan] *a.c.* p. **794** abyś] *a.c.* aby **809** in] *supplevi* **810** illustrissimis] *a.c.* ilmis

CONCILIUM SANDOMIRIENSE – 1570

modo a se dissentire videbantur, factus in synodo Sendomiriensi anno 1570 14 Aprilis.

820 Posteaquam diu multumque cum sectariis, tritheitis, Ebionitis, anabaptistis conflictatum esset, tandem divino favore ex tot tantisque certaminibus et deplorandis contentionibus emersimus, visum est iisdem ecclesiis Polonicis reformatis et orthodoxis, quae in quibusdam capitibus et formulis doctrinae hostibus veritatis et evangelii minime consentire videbantur, pacis et concordiae studio | synodum convocare ac consensionem mutuam testari. Quare 39v habita collatione amica et Christiana sic iunctis compositisque animis consenserunt in haec capita:

Primum. Quemadmodum et nos, qui in praesenti synodo Confessionem nostram edidimus, et fratres, nunquam credidimus eos, qui Augustanam con-
830 fessionem amplectuntur, aliter quam pie et orthodoxe sensisse de Deo et Sacra Trinitate atque incarnatione Filii Dei et iustificatione aliisque praecipuis capitibus fidei nostrae, ita etiam ii, qui Augustanam confessionem professi sunt, candide et sincere se vicissim tam de nostrarum ecclesiarum, quam de fratrum, quos Valdenses vocant, confessione de Deo et Sacra Triade, incarnatione Filii
835 Dei, iustificatione et aliis primariis capitibus fidei Christianae nihil agnoscere, quod sit absonum ab orthodoxa veritate et puro verbo Dei. Ibique sancte invicem polliciti sumus unanimiter secundum regulam verbi Dei defensuros | 40r consensum hunc mutuum in vera et pura Christi religione contra pontificios, contra sectarios, contra denique omnes hostes evangelii et veritatis.

840 Deinde vero quantum ad infelix illud dissidium de Cena Domini attinet, convenimus in sententia verborum, ut illa orthodoxe intellecta sunt a patribus ac imprimis Irenaeo, qui duabus rebus, scilicet terrena et coelesti, mysterium hoc constare dixit. Neque elementa signave illa nuda et vacua esse asserimus, sed simul re ipsa credentibus exhibere et praestare fide, quod significant. Deni-
845 que, ut expressius clariusque loquamur, convenimus, ut credamus et confiteamur substantialem praesentiam Christi non significari dumtaxat, sed vere in Cena vescentibus representari, distribui et exhiberi symbolis adiectis ipsi rei minims nudis, secundum sacramentorum naturam. Ne vero diversitas formu-

---

841/843 ut – dixit] cfr Irenaeus Lugdunensis, *Adversus haereses* 4, 18, 5, éd. A. Rousseau – B. Hemmerdinger – L. Doutreleau – C. Mercier (*SC*, 100.2), Paris 1965, p. 612, 120 (= *PG* 7/1, col. 1029)

826 consenserunt] consensimus *Ja* **833/834** quam – vocant] quam de Fratrum Bohemicorum (quos quidam rerum ignari Waldenses vocant) *Ja* **846/848** vere – naturam] vere in Coena eo vescentibus repraesentari, distribui & exhiberi CORPUS ET SANGUINEM DOMINI, symbolis adjectis ipsi rei *Ja*

788 CONCILIUM SANDOMIRIENSE – 1570

larum loquendi contentionem aliquam pariat, placuit praeter articulum, | qui 40v
850 est insertus nostrae Confessioni, mutuo consensu ascribere articulum Confessiones Saxonicarum ecclesiarum de Cena Domini ad Tridentinum Concilium a.D. 1551 missae, quem etiam pium agnoscimus et recipimus. Cuius Confessionis haec sunt verba: Et baptismus et Cena Domini sunt pignora etc. etc., usque ad finem articuli huius verba integra.

855 Huius autem sancti mutuique consensus vinculum fore arbitrati sumus convenimusque, ut quemadmodum illi nos nostrasque ecclesias et Confessionem nostram, in hac synodo publicatam, et fratrum orthodoxas esse testantur, sic etiam eorum ecclesias eodem Christiano amore prosequamur et orthodoxas fateamur. Extremumque valedicamus et altum silentium imponamus
860 omnibus rixis, distractionibus, dissidiis, quibus evangelii cursus non sine | 41r maxima multorum piorum offensione impeditus est et unde adversariis nostris non levis calumniandi et verae Christianae religioni nostrae contradicendi occasio sit subministrata. Quin potius, paci et tranquillitati publicae studere, caritatem mutuam exercere et operas mutuas ad aedificationem ecclesiae pro
865 fraterna coniunctione nostra praestare debemus.

Ad haec recipimus mutuo consensu omni studio nostris fratribus omnibus persuasuros atque eos invitaturos ad hunc Christianum et unanimem consensum amplectendum et obsignandum, praecipue auditione verbi frequentando tam huius, quam alterius cuiusque confessionis coetus et sacra-
870 mentorum usu, observato tamen recto ordine et gradu tam disciplinae, quam consuetudinis uniuscuiusque ecclesiae.

Ritus autem et caeremonias liberos uniuscuiusque ecclesiae hac concordia et coniunctione relinquimus. Non enim multum | refert, qui ritus observentur, 41v modo sarta tecta et incorrupta existat ipsa doctrina et fundamentum fidei ac
875 salutis nostrae. Quemadmodum et ipsa Confessio Augustana et Saxonica de ea re docent et in hac Confessione nostra, in praesenti synodo Sendomiriensi publicata, id ipsum expressimus. Quamobrem consilia officiave caritatis mutua inter nos conferre et in posterum de conservatione et incremento omnium totius Regni, Lithuaniae, Samogitiae piarum orthodoxarum et reformatarum
880 ecclesiarum, tamquam de uno corpore, consulere polliciti sumus ac recepimus.

Et siquando synodos generales celebrabunt, nobis quoque significent et ad nostras etiam generales vocati non gravatim veniant, si opus fuerit.

849/852 placuit – recipimus] *in Ja extat textum articuli Confessionis Saxonicae* **859** valedicamus] vale dicamus *Ja* **863** Quin potius] Quinpotius *Ja* **867/868** et – obsignandum] et unanimem Consensum amplectandum, colendum, & conseruandum, illumque alendum & obsignandum *Ja*

CONCILIUM SANDOMIRIENSE – 1570

789

Atque ut colophonem huic consensui et mutuae concordiae imponamus ad hanc fraternam societatem, conservandam | tuendamque, non incom- 42r
885 modum fore putamus in locum certum convenire, ubi una ex mutuis Confessionibus compendium corporis doctrinae, improbitate hostium veritatis ad id adacti, eliceremus et in publicum edeamus, ut invidorum hominum ora obturarentur, cum maximo omnium piorum solacio, sub titulo omnium ecclesiarum Polonicarum reformatarum et Lithuanicarum et Samogiticarum nostrae
890 Confessioni consentientium.

Datis igitur iunctisque dextris sancte promisimus et recepimus invicem omnes fidem et pacem colere, fovere et indies ad aedificationem regni Dei magis magisque amplificare velle omnesque occasiones distractionis ecclesiarum evitaturos. Denique se immemores et oblitos sui ipsius, ut veros Dei
895 ministros decet, solius Jesu Christi Salvatoris nostri gloriam promoturos et evangelii illius veritatem propagaturos tum dictis tum factis | recepimus. 42v

Quod ut felix ratum firmumque sit in perpetuum, oramus ardentibus votis Deum Patrem, totius consolationis et pacis auctorem et fontem uberrimum, qui nos ex densis papatus tenebris nostrasque ecclesias eripuit donavit-
900 que puro verbi sui et sacrosancto veritatis lumine hancque nostram sanctam pacem, consensionem, coniunctionem et unionem benedicere ad sui nominis gloriam et ecclesiae aedificationem velit. Amen. Amen.

Stanisław Myszkowski, palatinus Cracoviensis, personaliter consensus. Piotr Zborowski, palatinus Sendomiriensis, personaliter consensit mpp. Stani-
905 slaw Bniński, starszy kościoła, imieniem jmp. Łukasza z Górki, wojewody poznańskiego, Jana | z Tomic, kasztelana gnieźnieńskiego i wszystkich zborów 43r Augustanae confessionis. Stanislaus Chrząstovius, nuncius md. palatini terrarum Russiae etc. nomine eiusdem ac aliorum confratrum subscripsit. Sigismundus Myszkowski personaliter consentiens manu propria subscripsit.
910 Prokop Broniewski, chorąży kaliski, ręką własną.

---

903 Stanisław Myszkowski] Stanisław Myszkowski. Cfr H. Kowalska, 'Myszkowski Stanisław', in *PSB*, vol. 22 (1977), p. 394-395; Halecki, *Zgoda sandomierska*, p. 200-201 **904/905** Stanislaw Bniński] († after 1574) **905** Łukasza z Górki] Łukasz z Górki (*Górka*), *palatinus* since June 1565 († 23 January 1573) **906** Jana z Tomic] Jan z Tomic (*Tomicki*, † 1575), since 1564 *kasztelan* of Gniezno **907** Stanislaus Chrząstovius] i.e. Stanisław Chrząstowski, a Reformed pastor serving in Jazłowiec **908/909** Sigismundus Myszkowski] Zygmunt Myszkowski, *capitaneus* (*starosta*) of Oświęcim **910** Prokop Broniewski] the nobleman Prokop Broniewski, a member of the Brethren. See K. Chodynicki, 'Broniewski Prokop', in *PSB*, vol. 2 (1936), p. 464-465

---

896 evangelii – veritatem] Evangelii ipsius veritatem *Ja* **909** personaliter – subscripsit] personaliter consensi & subscripsi *Ja*

790 CONCILIUM SANDOMIRIENSE – 1570

Erasmus Gliczner, ecclesiarum in Maiori Polonia confessionis Augustanae superintendens, suo et aliorum fratrum nomine manu propria etc. Nicolaus Glicznerus, senior districtus Posnaniensis, nomine fratrum Maioris Poloniae manu propria. Matthaeus a Rakow, minister Criloviensis, missus a nobilitate Belzensi manu propria. Andreas Prasmovius, minister coetus Cracoviensis, nomine fratrum, ut vocant, Valdensium, facultate sibi commissa propria manu scripsi. Simeon Bogomil diaconus, Unitatis fratrum legatus, manu propria. Stanislaus Sarnicius, senior ecclesiarum districtus Cracoviensis, suo et aliorum fratrum nomine. | Iacobus Sylvius, senior districtus Chęcinensis, suo et aliorum fratrum nomine. Stanisław Karniński Iwan ręką własną, rector colloquii in synodo a fratribus electus, subscribit.

Daniel Chrobiewski, Stanislaus Rożanka medicos, consultes Cracovienses et Christophorus Trecius, ecclesiae urbanae Cracoviensis seniores et ad praesentem synodum nuntii, suo et fratrum nomine subscripserunt.

Stanislaus Marcianus, minister ecclesiae Dievoltensis, ex Lithuania, ducis de Wiśniowiec etc. legatus. Paulus Gilovius, senior districtus Zathoriensis et Oświecimensis, suo et omnium fratrum nomine. Valentinus, senior, nomine ecclesiarum Podgoriensium in Dobrków, subscribit. Andreas a Kruszwica, minister in Lisowo, nomine suo et coetus | Radzieioviensis subscribit. Petrus Tarnovius, minister in Dębnica, suo et md. Georgii Latalski nomine subscribit.

---

914 Matthaeus a Rakow] Mateusz a Raków, pastor in Kryłów **915** Andreas Prasmovius] i.e. Andrzej Prażmowski († 1592) **917** Simeon Bogomil diaconus] i.e. Szymon Bogumił Turnowski **918** Stanislaus Sarnicius] i.e. Stanisław Sarnicki **919** Iacobus Sylvius] i.e. Jakub Sylwiusz **922** Daniel Chrobiewski] († 1598), elder of the Calvinist Church in Kraków Stanislaus Rożanka] (c. 1520-1572) **925** Stanislaus Marcianus] i.e. Stanisław Macyjan (Marcjan), pastor from Dziewałtów, in the Grand Duchy of Lithuania **926** Paulus Gilovius] i.e. Paweł Gilowski **927** Valentinus] a Calvinist minister in Dobrków **928** Andreas a Kruszwica] i.e. Andrzej z Kruszwicy, Calvinist pastor in Lisowo **929/930** Petrus Tarnovius] i.e. Piotr Tarnowski, Calvinist pastor in Dębnica **930** Georgii Latalski] i.e. Jerzy Latalski

---

912 etc.] Magnifici Domini Lucae de Gorka Palatini Posnaniensis, & Domini Johannis Tomiczki Castellani Gnesnensis, atque omnium Confessionis Augustanae Ecclesiarum nomine, Stanislaus Bninski, Senior Ecclesiae consensi & subscripsi *Ja* **914** a¹] *supplevi* **915/917** Andreas – scripsi] Prasmovius, Minister coetus Radziejoviensis, nomine fratrum Confessionis Bohemicae, facultate sibi commissa, M.P. *Ja* **917/918** Simeon – propria] Simeon Theophilus alias Bogomil Turnovius, Diaconus in Communitate Fratrum Bohemicae Confessionis, & ad praesentem Synodum legatus M.P. *Ja* **927** Valentinus] Valentinus Brzovius *Ja* **928** a] *supplevi*

CONCILIUM SANDOMIRIENSE – 1570

Georgius Israel, Joannes Lorencius, seniores ecclesiarum fratrum, nomine omnium ministrorum manu propria eidem consensui subscripserunt ex coetu fratrum Bohemorum Posnaniae 19 Maii.

---

932 Georgius Israel] i.e. Jerzy Izrael   Joannes Lorencius] i.e. Jan Wawrzyniec

933/934 eidem – Maii] Eidem Consensui subscripserunt personaliter ex coetu Fratrum Bohemicae Confessionis, in Synodo Posnaniensi 20. Maji *Ja*

CONCILIUM SAXONICUM

1577

ediderunt
Irene DINGEL – Johannes HUND

THE *EPITOME* OF THE *FORMULA OF CONCORD*
1577

The *Epitome* is the first part of the *Formula of Concord*. As a brief and concise presentation of the *Formula*'s twelve articles, it forms a summary of the much longer and identically constructed *Solida Declaratio*, the detailed exposition of the articles. The authors of the *Formula of Concord* did not want their work to be understood as a new confession, but as an explanation and clarification of the *Confessio Augustana* of 1530, intending it as the final settlement of the earlier disputes. The text of the *Formula* was finalised in 1577 and was first published on 25 June 1580 – on the fiftieth anniversary of the *Augustana* – as the final piece of the *Book of Concord*. It was made binding in many, but not all, Lutheran territories of the Holy Roman Empire. Not only does this text represent a substantial piece of legal significance; it also embodies an echo of the theological controversies of the previous decades.

As the Schmalkaldic War ended in 1547, Emperor Charles V took the initiative to take hold of the religious divisions in the Empire. The *Augsburg Interim* (1548) ordered Protestants to revert to the old faith both in teaching and liturgical matters – although it made concessions on clerical marriage and on communion under both kinds – while waiting for the decisions of the Council of Trent. Philip Melanchthon as well as other members of the University of Wittenberg worked out a particular formula for electoral Saxony which preserved the main points of evangelical theology, but retained Roman Catholic liturgy as *adiaphora*. This discredited Melanchthon among Luther's strict adherents, who gathered around Matthias Flacius Illyricus; this division engendered a number of intra-Protestant disputes, involving clashes between Gnesio-Lutherans and Philippists, as well as several quarrels not directly connected to theology.

In the so-called Adiaphoristic Controversy of 1548, Flacius Illyricus affirmed that 'nihil est adiaphoron in casu confessionis et scandali'. The Majoristic Controversy of 1552 saw a bitter dispute between Wittenberg professor Georg Major and Nicolaus von Amsdorf, a former friend and colleague of Major's. In harmony with the *Leipzig Interim*, Major defended the necessity of good works for salvation, while Amsdorf championed the Lutheran view of justification by faith without human works. He brusquely answered to Major that good works were even harmful to salvation. This led to the second Antinomian Controversy, which was centred upon the so-called 'third use of the law'. Against the positions held by Anton Otho and Andreas Poach, Flacius Illyricus and his like-minded colleagues emphasised the pedagogical function of divine law for God's reborn children. During the Synergistic Controversy of 1555, Leipzig theologian Johann Pfeffinger defended the thesis that the Word of God, the Holy Spirit, but also human will – which accepts divine grace – work together for the conversion of man. Pfeffinger wanted to preserve moral responsibility for Christians; however, Flacius Illyricus and Amsdorf maintained that Pfeffinger was limiting God's justifying action. The 1560 controversy on original sin between Flacius Illyricus and Viktorin Strigel, professor of theology, was closely connected to the Synergistic Controversy. Flacius Illyricus emphasised the depth of mankind's sinful corruption and the human inability to do good, implying that original sin was inherent to human nature; Strigel contradicted him and described original sin as merely accidental, i.e. with no effect on the essential determination of man. In this regard, Flacius Illyricus' radical views engendered opposition even amongst his own Gnesio-Lutheran circle.

There were other controversies not directly connected to the *Interim*. The first was the so-called Osiandrian Controversy, when Andreas Osiander defended his doctrine of justification – which was inclined towards spiritualism and saw justification as the result of the fact that man was inhabited by the essential justice of Christ's divinity – against both Philippists and Gnesio-Lutherans. The latter two also opposed Francesco Stancaro, who argued (against Osiander) that Jesus accomplished his work of redemption only through his human nature. The Strasbourg controversy of 1561 over predestination between Johannes Marbach and Girolamo Zanchi – representing the Lutheran view on election and a fully-fledged Reformed concept of election and reprobation respectively – only had an indirect impact. This controversy was mediated through Jakob Andreae. On the other hand, the controversies over the Lord's Supper had more lasting effects. They re-emerged with the 'Second Lord's Supper Controversy' between John Calvin and Joachim Westphal. A treatise by physician Joachim Curaeus, published posthumously in 1574, revealed that a Reformed understanding of the Lord's Supper had spread among Melanchthon's followers in electoral Saxony, and that it had affected their teaching on the two natures of Christ. These 'crypto-Calvinists' were arrested and forced to recant their teachings under the *Torgau Confession* or face expulsion.

These intra-Protestant controversies and the failure of the Colloquy of Worms (1557) prompted the princes of the Empire to resume the project of Christoph, duke of Württemberg, to create a supra-territorial union of Protestant churches. A diet of princes took place in Frankfurt in 1558. Its formula of agreement was not accepted by Duke John Frederick II of Saxony and by the free cities of northern Germany. Flacius Illyricus produced the *Weimar Book of Confutation* at the behest of the prince in 1559. The Diet of Naumburg, which took place in 1561, had just as little success. The princes agreed to sign once again the *Confessio Augustana*, but also accepted Melanchthon's amended version of 1540, which altered the article on the Lord's Supper, as a legitimate interpretation. Frederick III, Elector Palatine of the Rhine – who was sympathetic to Calvinism – was behind this decision. However, Ernestine Saxony withdrew its approval, and John Frederick II left the meeting in protest. Princely ambitions towards unity proved ineffective.

Meanwhile, the Lutheran territories of the Empire began to establish their own norms of doctrine. The Leipzig printer Ernst Vögelin published in 1560 his *Corpus doctrinae Philippicum*, a collection of writings that included, alongside the ancient Christian creeds, exclusively works by Melanchthon. This publication was introduced as a confessional basis in several territories. Other than Vögelin's *Corpus*, various other *corpora doctrinae* were put together. The Lutheran-oriented *Corpus* of Brunswick-Luneburg (1576) and the *Corpus Julium* of Brunswick-Wolfenbüttel were forerunners of the *Book of Concord* of 1580. In the face of this theological and confessional fragmentation, the *Formula of Concord* was a last attempt by Lutheran theologians to achieve comprehensive unity. Duke Julius of Brunswick-Wolfenbüttel as well as William, landgrave of Hesse, and Christoph, duke of Württemberg – and after 1568 his son and successor Ludwig – were the champions of Church unity. After the fall of the 'crypto-Calvinists', Prince-Elector August of Saxony joined this group, while the landgrave of Hesse – a Philippist – soon abandoned the project. Their circles of theologians were decisive for the writing of the *Formula*. Jakob Andreae, provost and chancellor of the University of Tübingen, represented Württemberg and electoral Saxony. Martin Chemnitz, superintendent of Brunswick, acted for Brunswick-Wolfenbüttel, and theologian Nikolaus Selnecker spoke for electoral Saxony alongside Jakob Andreae. David Chytraeus, a professor based at Rostock, was also consulted on account of his considerable reputation. Andreas Musculus and Christoph Corner, both professors in Frankfurt (Oder), represented electoral Brandenburg.

It was Andreae who started this project of concord in 1568 with his *Fünf Artikel*, which he used as basis for the *Sechs christliche Predigten von den Spaltungen* (written in 1573); but he had to amend several articles the following year as these sermons had not been accepted as a formula of unity. As happened for the *Swabian Concord*, these articles were accepted by the Tübingen theologians and the consistory of Stuttgart. However, in Lower Saxony, where the *Swabian Concord* was sent with a request for approval, the template was changed into the *Swabian-Saxon Concord*. Meanwhile, Duke Ludwig of Württemberg, Margrave Charles of Baden, and George Ernest, count of Henneberg, entrusted their theologians with the writing of an expertise to the question in order to determine a possible basis for concord. As a result, the *Maulbronn Formula* evolved under the decisive influence of Lucas Osiander. The six 'Theologians of Concord' combined this *Formula* with the *Swabian-Saxon Concord* to produce the *Torgau Book* at a convent in Torgau in 1576. This was sent to all imperial Estates with the request for a statement. A general Synod was postponed in order not to jeopardise the arduous work of unity in process. At the same time, Andreae created a *Kurzen summarischen Auszug*, an epitome of the voluminous *Torgau Book*.

The following year, Andreae, Chemnitz, Selnecker, Chytraeus, Musculus and Cornerus met again in the monastery of Bergen (near Magdeburg), seeking to revise the *Torgau Book* based on the feedback they had received, especially from Pomerania, Hesse, and electoral Palatinate. The revision of the Torgau Book in its final form – also known as the *Bergen Book* or the *Solida Declaratio* – was the final stage in the development of the *Formula of Concord*. With the *Epitome*, written by Andreae, and the *Solida Declaratio*, created collaboratively in the monastery of Bergen, the *Formula of Concord* was finalised in 1577. This was followed by an intense campaign to rally support for the work of unity. About two thirds of the Protestant Estates of the Empire, including the three secular electors, accepted the *Formula of Concord*.

Note on the Edition

The German text presented below is based on the first Dresden edition of the *Book of Concord* of 1580. (1) The Latin text follows the first official translation by Nicolaus Selnecker, printed in Leipzig in 1584. (2) The spelling of the sources is largely preserved. Doubling and nasal lines are silently resolved, as are Latin abbreviations. The & sign is written out. The punctuation of the

---

(1) *Concordia.* | | היה | | Christliche / | | Widerholete / einmütige Bekentnüs | | nachbenanter Churfürsten / Fürsten vnd Stende | | Augspurgischer Confession / vnd derselben zu ende | | des Buchs vnderschriebener Theologen | | Lere vnd glaubens. [...] | | Dreßden [: Gimel Bergen d.Ä. und Matthes Stöckel d.Ä.] M.D.LXXX (VD 16 ZV 20351).

(2) Concordia. | | PIA ET VNANIMI | | CONSENSV REPETITA | | Confessio Fidei & doctrinae | | ELECTORVM, PRINCIPVM, | | ET ORDINVM IMPERII, | | At[que] eorundem Theologorum, qui | | Augustanam Confessionem am- | | plectuntur. [...] | | LIPSIAE [: Georg Deffner], | | ANNO M.D.LXXXIIII. | | Cum gratia & priuilegio Elect. Sax. (VD 16 K 2006).

German text is adapted to modern orthography. The case-sensitivity was preserved. Only two majuscules at the beginning of a word were normalized. Capitalisation and the use of lower-case letters after punctuation follows modern orthography, as does the construction of compounds as separate words or as a single word. (3)

BIBLIOGRAPHY

SOURCES (AND THEIR ABBREVIATIONS)

Concordia. | | יהוה | | Christliche / | | Widerholete / einmütige Bekentnüs | | nachbenanter Churfürsten / Fürsten vnd Stende | | Augspurgischer Confession / vnd derselben zu ende | | des Buchs vnderschriebener Theologen | | Lere vnd glaubens. [...] | | Dreßden [: Gimel Bergen d.Ä. und Matthes Stöckel d.Ä.] M.D.LXXX (VD 16 ZV 20351).

Concordia. | | PIA ET VNANIMI | | CONSENSV REPETITA | | Confessio Fidei & doctrinae | | ELECTORVM, PRINCIPVM, | | ET ORDINVM IMPERII, | | At[que] eorundem Theologorum, qui | | Augustanam Confessionem am- | | plectuntur. [...] | | LIPSIAE [: Georg Deffner], | | ANNO M.D.LXXXIIII. | | Cum gratia & priuilegio Elect. Sax. (VD 16 K 2006).

LITERATURE (AND ITS ABBREVIATIONS)

J. Baur, 'Christologie und Subjektivität. Geschichtlicher Ort und dogmatischer Rang der Christologie der Konkordienformel', in Id. (hrsg.), *Einsicht und Glaube. Aufsätze*, Göttingen 1978, p. 189-205.

—, *Wahrheit der Väter – Hilfe für morgen. 400 Jahre Konkordienformel*, Stuttgart 1977.

Bekenntnis und Einheit der Kirche. Studien zum Konkordienbuch, hrsg. M. Brecht – R. Schwarz, Stuttgart 1980.

---

(3) Johannes Hund, translator of this introduction and editor of the *Epitome*, would like to thank the Mainz *Bekenntnisschriften der Evangelisch-Lutherischen Kirche* (*BSELK*) project, and in particular Marion Bechtold-Mayer for generously offering advice and texts and for her cooperation in the critical edition. He would also like to thank Andrew Hansen for stylistic suggestions.

Bekenntnis zur Wahrheit. Aufsätze über die Konkordienformel, hrsg. J. Schöne, Erlangen 1978.

H. C. Brandy, 'Jakob Andreaes *Fünf Artikel* von 1568/69', *Zeitschrift für Kirchengeschichte* 98 (1987), p. 338-351.

I. Dingel, 'The Culture of Conflict in the Controversies Leading to the *Formula of Concord* (1548-1580)', in R. Kolb (ed.), *Lutheran Ecclesiastical Culture, 1550-1675*, Leiden 2008, p. 15-64.

—, 'Bekenntnis und Geschichte. Funktion und Entwicklung des reformatorischen Bekenntnisses im 16. Jahrhundert', in J. Loehr (hrsg.), *Dona Melanchthoniana. Festgabe für Heinz Scheible zum 70. Geburtstag*, Stuttgart – Bad Cannstatt 2001, p. 61-81.

—, 'Flacius als Schüler Luthers und Melanchthons', in G. Graf (hrsg.), *Vestigia Pietatis. Studien zur Geschichte der Frömmigkeit in Thüringen und Sachsen. Ernst Koch gewidmet*, Leipzig 2000, p. 77-93.

—, 'Melanchthon und die Normierung des Bekenntnisses', in G. Frank, *Der Theologe Melanchthon*, Stuttgart 2000, p. 195-211.

—, 'Die Torgauer Artikel (1574) als Vermittlungsversuch zwischen der Theologie Luthers und der Melanchthons', in H.-G. Nieden – M. Nieden (hrsg.), *Praxis Pietatis. Beiträge zu Theologie und Frömmigkeit in der Frühen Neuzeit. Fs. Wolfgang Sommer zum 60. Geburtstag*, Stuttgart 1999, p. 119-134.

—, *Concordia controversa. Die öffentlichen Diskussionen um das lutherische Konkordienwerk am Ende des 16. Jahrhunderts (Quellen und Forschungen zur Reformationsgeschichte 63)*, Gütersloh 1996.

—, 'Ablehnung und Aneignung. Die Bewertung der Autorität Martin Luthers in den Auseinandersetzungen um die Konkordienformel', *Zeitschrift für Kirchengeschichte* 105 (1994), p. 35-57.

J. C. Ebel, 'Die Herkunft des Konzeptes der Konkordienformel. Die Funktion der fünf Verfasser neben Andreae beim Zustandekommen der Formel', *Zeitschrift für Kirchengeschichte* 91 (1980), p. 237-282.

—, 'Jacob Andreae (1528-1590) als Verfasser der Konkordienformel', *Zeitschrift für Kirchengeschichte* 89 (1978), p. 78-119.

D. Gehrt, *Ernestinische Konfessionspolitik. Bekenntnisbildung, Herrschaftskonsolidierung und dynastische Identitätsstiftung vom Augsburger Interim 1548 bis zur Konkordienformel 1577 (Arbeiten zur Kirchen- und Theologiegeschichte 34)*, Leipzig 2011.

—, 'Strategien zur Konsensbildung im innerlutherischen Streit um die Willensfreiheit. Edition der Declaratio Victorini und der ernestinischen Visitationsinstruction von 1562', *Zeitschrift für Thüringische Geschichte* 63 (2009), p. 143-190.

B. Hägglund, 'Die Rezeption Luthers in der Konkordienformel', in H. Foerster (hrsg.), *Luther und die Bekenntnisschriften (Veröffentlichungen der Luther-Akademie Ratzeburg 2)*, Erlangen 1981, p. 107-120.

H.-P. Hasse, *Zensur theologischer Bücher in Kursachsen im konfessionellen Zeitalter. Studien zur kursächsischen Literatur- und Religionspolitik in den Jahren 1569 bis 1575 (Arbeiten zur Kirchen- und Theologiegeschichte 5)*, Leipzig 2000.

J. Hund, 'Autorität und Identität. Die Bedeutung Luthers in den nachinterimistischen Streitkreisen im Bereich der Wittenberger Reformation', in S. Michel – C. Speer (hrsg.), *Georg Rörer (1492-1557). Der Chronist der Wittenberger Reformation (Leucorea-Studien zur Geschichte der Reformation und der Lutherischen Orthodoxie* 15), Leipzig 2012, p. 287-311.

—, 'Kryptocalvinismus oder Kryptophilippismus? Die Wittenberger Abendmahlslehre und Christologie in den Jahren 1567-1574', in I. Dingel – A. Kohnle (hrsg.), *Philipp Melanchthon. Lehrer Deutschlands, Reformator Europas (Leucorea-Studien zur Geschichte der Reformation und der Lutherischen Orthodoxie* 13), Leipzig 2011, p. 271-288.

—, *Das Wort ward Fleisch. Eine systematisch-theologische Untersuchung zur Debatte um die Wittenberger Christologie und Abendmahlslehre in den Jahren 1567 bis 1574 (Forschungen zur systematischen und ökumenischen Theologie* 114), Göttingen 2006.

J. Hund – H. P. Jürgens, 'Pamphlets in the Theological Debates of the Later Sixteenth Century: The Mainz Editorial Project *Controversia et Confessio*', in M. Walsby – G. Kemp (eds), The Book *Triumphant. Print in Transition in the Sixteenth and Seventeenth Centuries (Library of the Written Word* 15), Leiden 2011, p. 158-177.

Das Interim 1548/1550. Herrschaftskrise und Glaubenskonflikt, hrsg. L. Schorn-Schütte (*Schriften des Vereins für Reformationsgeschichte* 203), Gütersloh 2005.

T. Kaufmann, 'Das Bekenntnis im Luthertum des konfessionellen Zeitalters', *Zeitschrift für Theologie und Kirche* 105 (2008), p. 281-314.

—, *Das Ende der Reformation. Magdeburgs 'Herrgotts Kanzlei' (1548-1551/1552) (Beiträge zur historischen Theologie* 123), Tübingen 2003.

W. Klän, 'Der "vierte Mann". Auf den Spuren von Nikolaus Selneckers (1530-1592). Beitrag zu Entstehung und Verbreitung der Konkordienformel', *Lutherische Theologie und Kirche* 17 (1993), p. 145-174.

E. Koch, 'Auseinandersetzungen um die Autorität von Philipp Melanchthon und Martin Luther in Kursachsen im Vorfeld der Konkordienformel von 1577', *Lutherjahrbuch* 59 (1992), p. 128-159.

—, 'Der kursächsische Philippismus und seine Krise in den 1560er und 1570er Jahren', in H. Schilling (hrsg.), *Die reformierte Konfessionalisierung in Deutschland – Das Problem der 'Zweiten Reformation'. Wissenschaftliches Symposion des Vereins für Reformationsgeschichte*, Gütersloh 1985, p. 60-77.

—, *Aufbruch und Weg. Studien zur lutherischen Bekenntnisbildung im 16. Jahrhundert (Aufsätze und Vorträge zur Theologie und Religionswissenschaft* 79), Berlin 1983.

R. Kolb, *Die Konkordienformel. Eine Einführung in ihre Geschichte und Theologie (Oberurseler Hefte* 8), Göttingen 2011.

—, 'The Flacian Rejection of the *Concordia*. Prophetic Style and Action in the German Late Reformation', *Archiv für Reformationsgeschichte* 73 (1982), p. 196-217.

—, *Andreae and the* Formula of Concord. *Six Sermons on the Way of Lutheran Unity*, St Louis 1977.

H. Kropatschek, *Das Problem theologischer Anthropologie auf dem Weimarer Gespräch von 1560 zwischen Matthias Flacius Illyricus und Viktorin Strigel*, Diss. theol. Göttingen 1943 (masch.).

Die lutherische Konfessionalisierung in Deutschland. Wissenschaftliches Symposion des Vereins für Reformationsgeschichte 1988, hrsg. H.-C. Rublack (*Schriften des Vereins für Reformationsgeschichte* 197), Gütersloh 1992.

I. Mager, *Die Konkordienformel im Fürstentum Braunschweig-Wolfenbüttel. Entstehungsbeitrag, Rezeption, Geltung (Studien zur Kirchengeschichte Niedersachsens* 33), Göttingen 1993.

—, 'Jacob Andreaes lateinische Unionsartikel von 1568', *Zeitschrift für Kirchengeschichte* 98 (1987), p. 70-86.

T. Mahlmann, *Das neue Dogma der lutherischen Christologie. Problem und Geschichte seiner Begründung*, Gütersloh 1969.

Politik und Bekenntnis. Die Reaktionen auf das Interim von 1548, hrsg. I. Dingel – G. Wartenberg (*Leucorea-Studien zur Geschichte der Reformation und der Lutherischen Orthodoxie* 8), Leipzig 2006.

M. Richter, *Gesetz und Heil. Eine Untersuchung zur Vorgeschichte und zum Verlauf des sogenannten Zweiten Antinomistischen Streits, (Forschungen zur Kirchen- und Dogmengeschichte* 67), Göttingen 1996.

CONCILIUM SAXONICUM – 1577

—, 'Andreas Poach und sein Anteil am 2. Antinomistischen Streit', *Archiv für Reformationsgeschichte* 85 (1994), p. 119-137.

G. Seebass, *Das reformatorische Werk des Anreas Osiander* (*Einzelarbeiten aus der Kirchengeschichte Bayerns* 44), Nürnberg 1967.

B. Slenczka, *Das Wormser Schisma der Augsburger Konfessionsverwandten von 1557. Protestantische Konfessionspolitik und Theologie im Zusammenhang des zweiten Wormser Religionsgesprächs* (*Beiträge zur historischen Theologie* 155), Tübingen 2010.

M. Stupperich, *Osiander in Preußen. 1549-1552* (*Arbeiten zur Kirchengeschichte* 44), Berlin 1973.

Widerspruch, Dialog und Einigung. Studien zur Konkordienformel der Lutherischen Reformation, hrsg. W. Lohff – L. W. Spitz, Stuttgart 1977.

MONITUM

GERMAN EDITION

Concordia. | | יהוה | | Christliche / | | Widerholete / einmütige Bekentnüs | | nachbenanter Churfürsten / Fürsten vnd Stende | | Augspurgischer Confession / vnd derselben zu ende | | des Buchs vnderschriebener Theologen | | Lere vnd glaubens. [...] | | Dreßden [: Gimel Bergen d.Ä. und Matthes Stöckel d.Ä.] M.D.LXXX (VD 16 ZV 20351).

LATIN EDITION

Concordia. | | PIA ET VNANIMI | | CONSENSV REPETITA | | Confessio Fidei & doctrinae | | ELECTORVM, PRINCIPVM, | | ET ORDINVM IMPERII, | | At[que] eorundem Theologorum, qui | | Augustanam Confessionem am- | | plectuntur. [...] | | LIPSIAE [: Georg Deffner], | | ANNO M.D.LXXXIIII. | | Cum gratia & priuilegio Elect. Sax. (VD 16 K 2006).

CONCILIUM SAXONICUM
1577

806 CONCILIUM SAXONICUM – 1577

SUMMARISCHER BEGRIFF DER STREITIGEN ARTICKEL ZWISCHEN DEN THEOLOGEN AUGSPURGISCHER CONFESSION IN NACHVOLGENDER WIDERHOLUNG NACH ANLEITUNG GOTTES WORTS CHRISTLICH ERKLERET UND VERGLICHEN. MIT CHURF. G. ZU SACHSEN BEFREIHUNG. DRESSDEN. 1579.

VON DEM SUMMARISCHEN BEGRIFF, REGEL UND RICHTSCHNUR, NACH WELCHER ALLE LEER GEURTHEILET UND DIE EINGEFALLENE IRRUNGEN CHRISTLICH ENTSCHEIDEN UND ERKLERET WERDEN SOLLEN

229r

Wir gleuben, leren und bekennen, das die einige Regel und Richtschnur, nach welcher zugleich alle Leren und Lerer gerichtet und geurteilet werden sollen, seind allein die Prophetischen und Apostolischen Schrifften, altes und neues Testaments, wie geschrieben stehet: 'Dein Wort ist meines fusses Leuchte und ein Liecht auff meinem wege', Psal. 119. Und S. Paulus: 'Wenn ein Engel vom Himel keme und predigte anders, der sol verflucht sein', Galat. 1. Andere schrifften aber der alten oder neuen Lerer, wie sie namen haben, sollen der heiligen Schrifft nicht gleich gehalten, sondern alle zumal mit einander derselben unterworffen und anders oder weiter nicht angenommen werden, dann als zeugen, welcher gestalt nach der Apostel zeit und an welchen örten solche Lere der Propheten und Apostel erhalten worden.

1.

Und nachdem gleich nach der Apostel zeit auch noch bey irem leben falsche Lerer und Ketzer eingerissen und wider dieselbige in der ersten Kirchen Symbola, das ist kurtze runde Bekentnissen, gestellet, welche vor den einhelligen, allgemeinen, christlichen glauben und bekentnus der rechtgleubigen und warhafftigen Kirchen gehalten, als nemlich das Symbolum Apostolicum, Symbolum Nicaenum und Symbolum Athanasii, bekennen wir uns zu denselben und verwerffen hiermit alle Ketzereien und Leere, so denselben zuwider in die Kirche Gottes eingefürt worden sind.

2.

13/14 Ps. 119 (Vulgata 118), 105   **14/15** Gal. 1, 8

EPITOME

ARTICULORUM, DE QUIBUS CONTROVERSIAE ORTAE SUNT INTER THEOLOGOS AUGUSTANAE CONFESSIONIS. QUI IN REPETITIONE SEQUENTI SECUNDUM VERBI DEI PRAESCRIP-TUM PIE DECLARATI SUNT ET CONCILIATI.

| DE COMPENDIARIA REGULA ATQUE NORMA, AD QUAM OMNIA DOGMATA EXIGENDA ET QUAE INCIDERUNT CERTAMINA PIE DECLARANDA ET COMPONENDA SUNT.

I. Credimus, confitemur et docemus unicam regulam et normam, secundum quam omnia dogmata omnesque doctores aestimari et iudicari oporteat, nullam omnino aliam esse quam Prophetica et Apostolica scripta cum Veteris, tum Novi Testamenti, sicut scriptum est: *Lucerna pedibus meis verbum tuum et lumen semitis meis.* Et Divus Paulus inquit: *Etiamsi Angelus de coelo aliud praedicet Evangelium, anathema sit.* Reliqua vero sive Patrum sive Neotericorum scripta, quocunque veniant nomine sacris literis nequaquam sunt aequiparanda, sed universa illis ita subiicienda sunt, ut alia ratione non recipiantur, nisi testium loco: qui doceant, quod etiam post Apostolorum tempora et in quibus partibus orbis doctrina illa Prophetarum et Apostolorum sincerior conservata sit.

Psal. 119
Galat. 1.

II. Et quia statim post Apostolorum tempora, imo etiam cum adhuc superstites essent, falsi doctores et haeretici exorti sunt, contra quos in primitiva Ecclesia Symbola sunt composita, id est, breves et categoricae confessiones, quae unanimem Catholicae Christianae fidei Consensum et Confessionem Orthodoxorum et verae Ecclesiae complectebantur (ut sunt Symbolum Apostolicum, Nicenumet Athanasianum): profitemur publice nos illa amplecti et reiicimus omnes haereses omniaque dogmata, quae contra illorum sententiam unquam in Ecclesiam Dei sunt invecta.

808 CONCILIUM SAXONICUM – 1577

So viel aber die trennung in glaubenssachen belanget, zu unsern zeiten 3.
eingefallen, halten wir vor den einhelligen Consens und erklerung unsers
Christlichen glaubens und bekentnis besonders wider des Bapsthumbs und
dessen falschen Gottesdienst, Abgötterey, Aberglauben und andere Secten als
dieser zeit unserm Symbolo, die erste | ungeenderte Augspurgische Con- 229v
feßion, Keiser Carolo V. zu Augspurg Anno 30. etc. in der grossen Reichsver-
samlung ubergeben, sampt derselben Apologi und Artickeln zu Schmalkalden
Anno 37. gestellet und von den vornemsten Theologen domals unterschrieben
worden.

Und weil solche sachen auch den gemeinen Leyen und derselben Seelen
seligkeit betreffen, bekennen wir uns auch zu dem kleinen und grossen Catechismo Doctor Luthers, wie solche beide Catechismi in den Tomis Lutheri
verfasset, als zu der Leyen Bibel, darin alles begriffen, was in heiliger Schrifft
weitleufftig gehandelt und einem Christen Menschen zu seiner seligkeit zu
wissen von nöten ist.

Nach dieser anleitung, wie oben vermeldet, sollen alle leren angestellet
und was derselben zuwider, als unsers glaubens einhelliger erklerung entgegen,
verworffen und verdammet werden. Solcher gestalt wird der unterschied
zwischen der heiligen Schrifft, altes und neuen Testaments, und allen andern
Schrifften erhalten und bleibt allein die heilige Schrifft der einige Richter,
Regel und Richtschnur, nach welcher als dem einigen Probirstein sollen und
müssen alle Leren erkant und geurteilet werden, ob sie gut oder bös, recht
oder unrecht sein.

Die andere Symbola aber und angezogene Schrifften sind nicht Richter
wie die heilige Schrifft, sondern allein zeugnis und erklerung des glaubens, wie
jederzeit die heilige Schrifft in streitigen Artickeln in der Kirchen Gottes von
den damals lebenden verstanden und ausgeleget und derselben widerwertige
Leer verworffen und verdammet worden.

I. VON DER ERBSÜNDE 230r

Status Controversiae

Die Hauptfrage in dieser Zwispalt

Ob die Erbsünde sey eigentlich und one allen unterschied des Menschen
verderbte natur, substantz und wesen oder ja das fürnemste und beste teil
seines wesens als die vernünfftige Seele selbst in irem höchsten grad und kreff-

EPITOME – 1577

| Quod vero ad schismata in negociis fidei attinet, quae in nostra tempora III. | 556
inciderunt, iudicamus unanimem consensum et declarationem Christianae
30 nostrae fidei et Confessionis, inprimis contra Papatum et huius falsos ac idola-
tricos cultus et superstitiones et alias sectas, esse nostri temporis Symbolum,
Augustanam illam primam et non mutatam Confessionem, quae Imperatori
Carolo V. Augustae Anno 30. in magnis imperii Comitiis exhibita est, similiter
et Apologiam et Articulos Smalcaldicos Anno 37. conscriptos et praecipuorum
35 Theologorum illius temporis subscriptione comprobatos.

Et quia haec Religionis causa etiam ad Laicos, quos vocant, spectat
eorumque perpetua salus agitur, profitemur publice, nos etiam amplecti
Minorem et Maiorem D. Lutheri Cathechismos, ut ii Tomis Lutheri sunt
inserti, quod eos quasi Laicorum Biblia esse censeamus, in quibus omnia illa
40 breviter comprehenduntur, quae in sacra scriptura fusius tractantur et quorum
cognitio homini Christiano ad aeternam salutem est necessaria.

Ad has rationes paulo ante monstratas omnis doctrina in Religionis negocio conformanda est et, si quid iis contrarium esse deprehenditur, id
reiiciendum atque damnandum est, quippe quod cum unanimi fidei nostrae
45 declaratione pugnet. Hoc modo luculentum discrimen inter sacras veteris et
novi Testamenti literas et omnia aliorum scripta retinetur et sola sacra scriptura Iudex, norma et regula agnoscitur, ad quam ceu ad Lydium lapidem omnia
dogmata exigenda sunt et iudicanda, an pia, an impia, an vera, an vero falsa
sint.

50 Caetera autem Symbola et alia scripta, quorum paulo ante mentionem
fecimus, non obtinent autoritatem Iudicis; haec enim dignitas solis sacris
literis debetur: sed duntaxat pro Religione nostra testimonium dicunt eamque
explicant ac ostendunt, quomodo singulis temporibus sacrae literae in articulis
controversis in Ecclesia Dei a doctoribus, | qui tum vixerunt, intellectae et 557
55 explicatae fuerintet quibus rationibus dogmata cum sacra scriptura pugnantia
reiecta et condemnata sint.

I. DE PECCATO ORIGINIS

Status controversiae.

An peccatum Originale sit proprie et absque omni discrimine ipsa homi-
60 nis corrupti natura, substantia et essentia aut certe principalis et praestantissi-
ma pars ipsius substantiae, utpote ipsa rationalis anima in summo suo gradu et

810 CONCILIUM SAXONICUM – 1577

ten? Oder ob zwischen des Menschen substantz, natur, wesen, Leib, Seele
auch nach dem Fall und der Erbsünde ein unterschied sey, also das ein anders
65 die natur und ein anders die Erbsünde sey, welche in der verderbten natur
steckt und die natur verderbet?

Affirmativa

Reine leer, glaub und bekentnis vermöge vorgesetzter Richtschnur und sum-
marischer erklerung

70   Wir gleuben, leren und bekennen, das ein unterschied sey zwischen der 1.
Natur des Menschen, nicht allein wie er anfangs von Gott rein und heilig one
sünde erschaffen, sondern auch wie wir sie itzunder nach dem fall haben, nemlich zwischen der natur, so auch nach dem fall noch ein Creatur Gottes ist und
bleibet, und der Erbsünde, und das solcher unterschied so gros als der unter-
75 schied zwischen Gottes und des Teuffels werck sey.

Wir gleuben, leren und bekennen auch, das uber solchem unterschied 2. | 2.
mit höchstem fleis zuhalten, weil diese Lere, das zwischen unser verderbten
menschennatur und der Erbsünde kein unterscheid sein solte, wider die
Hauptartickel unsers Christlichen glaubens von der Erschaffung, Erlösung,
80 Heiligung und Aufferstehung unsers fleisches streitet und neben denselben
nicht bestehen kan.

Dann nicht allein Adams und Eva Leib und Seel vor dem fall, sondern Deu
auch unser Leib und Seel nach dem fall, unangesehen das sie verderbet, Gott Isai.
geschaffen, welche auch Gott noch vor sein werck erkennet, wie geschrieben 64.
Actc
85 stehet, Iob 10: 'Deine hende haben mich gearbeitet und gemacht alles was ich Iob
umb und umb bin.' Psal.
139.
Es hat auch der Son Gottes in einigkeit seiner Person solche menschliche Eccl
natur doch one sünde und also nicht ein frembd, sondern unser fleisch an sich
genommen und nach demselben unser warhafftiger Bruder worden. Heb. 2:
90 'Nach dem die kinder fleisch und blut haben, ist ers gleichermas teilhafftig
worden.' Item: 'Er nimpt nirgend die Engel an sich, sondern den samen Abraham nimmet er an sich, daher muss er allerdings seinen Brüdern', ausgenom-
men die sünde, 'gleich werden'. Also hat es auch Christus erlöset als sein
werck, heiliget es als sein werck, erwecket es von den todten und zieret es herr-

---

85/86 Iob 10, 8; Deut. 32, 9; Is. 45, 9-12; 54, 5; 64, 7 seq.; Act. 17, 24-28; Ps. 100
(Vulgata 99), 3; 139 (138), 13-16; Eccle. 12, 1 **90/91** Hebr. 2, 14 **91/93** Hebr. 2, 16f

EPITOME – 1577

in summis ipsius viribus considerata. An vero inter hominis Substantiam, naturam, essentiam, corpus et animam, etiam post lapsum humani generis, et inter Originale peccatum aliquod sit discrimen, ita ut aliud sit ipsa natura et aliud ipsum peccatum Originis, quod in Natura corrupta haeret et Naturam etiam depravat.

Affirmativa.

Sincera doctrina, fides et Confessio
cum superiore Norma et compendiosa declaratione consentiens.

Credimus, docemus et confitemur, quod sit aliquod discrimen inter ipsam hominis naturam, non | tantum quemadmodum initio a Deo purus et sanctus et absque peccato homo conditus est, verum etiam qualem iam post lapsum naturam illam habemus; discrimen, inquam, inter ipsam Naturam, quae etiam post lapsum est, permanetque Dei creatura, et inter peccatum Originis, et quod tanta sit illa Naturae et peccati Originalis differentia, quanta est inter opus Dei et inter opus Diaboli. — I. — 558

Credimus, docemus et confitemur, quod summo studio hoc discrimen sit conservandum propterea, quod illud dogma, nullum videlicet inter Naturam hominis corrupti et inter peccatum Originis esse discrimen, cum praecipuis fidei nostrae articulis (de creatione, de redemtione, de sanctificatione et resurrectione carnis nostrae) pugnet neque salvis hisce articulis stare possit. — II.

Deus enim non modo Adami et Hevae corpus et animam ante lapsum, verum etiam corpora et animas nostras post lapsum creavit, etsi haec iam sunt corrupta. Et sane hodie Dominus animas et corpora nostra creaturas et opus suum esse agnoscit, sicut scriptum est: *Manus tuae fecerunt me et plasmaverunt me totum in circuitu.*

Deut. 32.
Isa. 45. 54.
64.
Actor. 17.
Iob. 10.
Ps. 100. 139.
Eccles. 12.

Et Filius Dei unione personali illam humanam naturam, sed sine peccato, assumsitet non alienam, sed nostram carnem sibi adiungens arctissime copulavit eiusque assumtae carnis ratione vere frater noster factus est, ut scriptura testatur Hebr. 2: *Posteaquam pueri commercium habent cum carne et sanguine et ipse similiter particeps factus est eorundem.* Item: *Non Angelos assumit, sed semen Abrahae assumit, unde et debuit per omnia fratribus assimilari, excepto peccato.* Eandem humanam nostram Naturam (opus videlicet suum) Christus redemit, eandem (quae ipsius opus est) sanctificat, eandem a mortuis resusci-

95　lich als sein werck. Aber die Erbsünde hat er nicht erschaffen, nicht angenommen, nicht erlöset, nicht geheiliget, wird sie auch nicht erwecken an den auserwelten, weder zieren noch selig machen, sondern in der aufferstehung gar vertilget sein wird.

Daraus der unterschied zwischen der verderbten natur und der verder-
100　bung, so in der natur stecket, und die natur dadurch verderbet worden, leichtlich zuerkennen.

Wir gleuben, leren und bekennen aber hinwiderumb, das die Erbsünde 　3.
nicht sey eine schlechte, sondern so tieffe verderbung menschlicher Natur, das nichts gesundes oder unverderbet an Leib und Seel des Menschen, seinen
105　innerlichen und eusserlichen Krefften geblieben, sondern wie die Kirche singet: 'Durch Adams fall ist gantz verderbt menschlich natur und wesen', welcher schade unaussprechlich, nicht mit der vernunfft, sondern allein aus Gottes wort erkennet werden mag, und das die natur und solche verderbung der natur niemand voneinander scheiden könne denn allein | Gott, welches 　231r
110　durch den todt in der aufferstehung gentzlich geschehen, da unser natur, die wir itzt tragen, one die Erbsünde und von derselben abgesondert und abgescheiden aufferstehen und ewig leben wird, wie geschrieben stehet Iob. 19.: 'Ich werde mit dieser meiner haut umbgeben werden und werde in meinem fleisch Gott sehen. Denselben werde ich mir sehen und meine augen werden
115　in schauen.'

Negativa

Verwerffung der falschen Gegenlere

Demnach verwerffen und verdammen wir, wann geleret wird, das die 　1.
Erbsünde allein ein Reatus oder schuld von wegen frembder verwirckung one
120　einige unserer natur verderbung sey.

Item, das die bösen lüste nicht sünde, sondern angeschaffene, wesentliche 　2.
eigenschafften der natur seien, oder als were der obgemelte mangel oder schade nicht warhafftig sünde, darumb der Mensch, ausserhalb Christo, ein Kind des zorns sein solte.

113/115 Iob 19, 26f

106 cfr the choral 'Durch Adams Fall ist ganz verderbt menschlich Natur und Wesen' by Lazarus Spengler (1524): *Evangelisches Kirchengesangbuch* 243, not in *Evangelisches Gesangbuch*

EPITOME – 1577

95 tat et ingenti gloria (opus videlicet suum) ornat. Peccatum autem Originale non creavit, non assumsit, non redemit, non sanctificat, non resuscitabit in electis, neque unquam gloria coelesti ornabit aut salvabit, sed in beata illa resurrectione plane abolitum erit.

| Ex his, quae a nobis allata sunt, discrimen inter corruptam Naturam et 559
100 inter corruptionem, quae naturae infixa est et per quam Natura est corrupta, facile agnosci potest.

Vicissim autem credimus, docemus atque confitemur, peccatum originis III. non esse leve, sed tam profundam humanae Naturae corruptionem, quae nihil sanum, nihil incorruptum in corpore et anima hominis atque adeo in
105 interioribus et exterioribus viribus eius reliquit. Sicut Ecclesia canit: *Lapsus Adae vi pessima Humana tota massa, natura et ipsa essentia corrupta, luce cassa* etc. Hoc quantum sit malum, verbis revera est inexplicabile neque humanae rationis acumine indagari, sed duntaxat per verbum Dei revelatum agnosci potest. Et sane affirmamus, quod hanc naturae corruptionem ab ipsa Natura
110 nemo, nisi solus Deus separare queat, id quod per mortem in beata illa Resurrectione plene fiet. Ibi enim ea ipsa Natura nostra, quam nunc circumferimus, absque peccato Originis et ab eodem omnino separata et remota resurget et aeterna felicitate fruetur. Sic enim scriptum est: *Pelle mea circumdabor et in* Iob. 19. *carne mea videbo Deum, quem ego visurus sum mihiet oculi mei eum conspecturi*
115 *sunt.*

Negativa.

Reiectio falsorum dogmatum,
quae commemoratae sanae doctrinae repugnant.

Reiicimus ergo et damnamus dogma illud, quo asseritur, peccatum Origi- I.
120 nale tantummodo reatum et debitum esse ex alieno delicto absque ulla naturae nostrae corruptione in nos derivatum.

Item, concupiscentias pravas non esse peccatum, sed concreatas Naturae II. conditiones et proprietates quasdam Essentiales, aut, defectus illos et malum ingens a nobis paulo ante commemoratum non esse peccatum, propter quod
125 homo Christo non insertus sit filius irae.

814 CONCILIUM SAXONICUM – 1577

125 Desgleichen verwerffen wir auch den Pelagianischen irthumb, da vorge- 3.
geben wird, das die natur des Menschen auch nach dem fall unverderbet und
sonderlich in geistlichen sachen gantz gut und rein in iren naturalibus, das ist
in iren natürlichen krefften, geblieben sey.

Item, das die Erbsünde nur von aussen, ein schlechter, ringschetziger, 4.
130 eingesprengter fleck oder anfligende mackel sey, darunter die natur ire gute
krefften auch in geistlichen sachen behalten habe.

Item, das die Erbsünde sey nur ein eusserlich hindernis der guten, geistli- 5.
chen krefften und nicht eine beraubung oder mangel derselben, als wann ein
Magnet mit Knobloch safft bestrichen wird, dadurch seine natürliche krafft
135 nicht weggenommen, sondern allein gehindert wird; oder das dieselbige
mackel wie ein fleck vom angesicht oder farbe von der wandt leichtlich abge-
wischet werden köndte.

Item, das im Menschen nicht gar verderbet sey Menschlich natur und 6. | 2
wesen, sondern der Mensch habe noch etwas guts an im auch in geistlichen
140 sachen, als nemlich frömkeit, geschicklichkeit, düchtigkeit oder vermögen in
geistlichen sachen etwas anzufahen, zu wircken oder mitzuwircken.

Dargegen verwerffen wir auch die falsche lere der Manicheer, wann gele- 7.
ret wird, das die Erbsünde als etwas wesentlichs und selbststendigs durch den
Sathan in die natur eingegossen und mit derselben vermenget, wie Gifft und
145 Wein gemenget werden.

Item, das nicht der natürlich Mensch, sonden etwas anders und frembdes 8.
im Menschen sündige, deswegen nicht die natur, sondern allein die Erbsünde
in der natur angeklaget werde.

Wir verwerffen und verdammen auch als ein Manicheischen irrthumb, 9.
150 wenn geleret wird, das die Erbsünde sey eigentlich und one allen unterscheid
des verderbten menschen substantz, natur und wesen selbst, also das kein
unterscheid zwischen der verderbten natur nach dem fall an ir selbst und der
Erbsünde solte auch nicht gedacht noch mit gedancken voneinander unterschieden werden können.

---

125 Pelagianischen] Pelagius had been practicing in Rome since around 400 AD. He
openly opposed Augustine by supporting the idea of free will and mankind's choice of
being good or evil, thereby dismissing the concept of original sin. This resulted in the
so-called 'Pelagian Argument' **133/135** als – wird] popular legend, for the first time
refuted by William Gilbert in the year 1600   **142** Manicheer] Manichaeism is a
gnostic religion of the fourth century, that traces back to the Persian Mani. It is based
on a dualistic world view, that separates the empire of light from the empire of darkness
and contrasts the father of the light with the king of darkness together with their
powers and activities

EPITOME – 1577

| Reiicimus etiam Pelagianam haeresin, qua asseritur, hominis naturam III. | 560
post lapsum incorruptam esse et quidem in spiritualibus rebus totam bonam
et puram in viribus suis naturalibus mansisse.

Item, peccatum Originis externum levem et nullius prope momenti esse IIII.
130 naevum aut aspersam quandam maculam, sub qua nihilomnius natura bonas
suas vires etiam in rebus spiritualibus retinuerit.

Item, peccatum Originale tantum esse externum impedimentum bona- V.
rum spiritualium virium et non esse despoliationem et defectum earundem,
sicuti, cum Magnes allii succo illinitur, vis eius naturalis attrahendi ferrum non
135 tollitur, sed tantum impeditur; aut sicut macula de facie aut color de pariete
abstergi facile potest.

Item, hominis Naturam et essentiam non prorsus esse corruptam, sed VI.
aliquid boni adhuc in homine reliquum, etiam in rebus spiritualibus, videlicet
bonitatem, capacitatem, aptitudinem, facultatem, industriam aut vires, quibus
140 in rebus spiritualibus inchoare aliquid boni, operari aut cooperari valeat.

Contra autem reiicimus etiam falsum dogma Manichaeorum, cum do- VII.
cetur peccatum Originis tanquam quiddam essentiale atque substantiale a
Satana in Naturam esse infusum et cum eadem permixtum, quemadmodum
venenum et vinum miscentur.

145 Item, non ipsum animalem hominem, sed aliquid aliud et peregrinum VIII.
quiddam, quod sit in homine, peccare, ideoque non ipsam Naturam, sed
tantummodo peccatum Originale in natura existens accusari.

Reiicimus etiam atque damnamus ut Manichaeum errorem, quando doce- IX.
tur, originale peccatum proprie et quidem nullo posito discrimine esse ipsam
150 hominis corrupti Substantiam, naturam et Essentiam, ita ut inter Naturam
corruptam post lapsum per se ipsam consideratam et inter peccatum Originis
nulla prorsus sit differentia neque | ulla distinctio cogitari aut saltem peccatum 561
illud a Natura cogitatione discerni possit.

CONCILIUM SAXONICUM – 1577

155   Es wird aber solche Erbsünde von Luthero Natursünde, Personsünde, 10.
wesentliche sünde genennet, nicht das die natur, person oder das wesen des
Menschen selbst one allen unterscheid die Erbsünde sey, sondern das mit
solchen worten der unterscheid zwischen der Erbsünde, so in der menschlichen Natur stecket, und den andern sünden, so man wirckliche Sünde nennet,
160 angezeiget würde.

    Denn die Erbsünde ist nicht eine sünde, die man thut, sondern sie stecket 11.
in der natur, substantz und wesen des Menschen; also: wenn gleich kein böser
gedanck nimmer im hertzen des verderbten menschen auffstiege, kein unnütz
wort geredet noch böse that geschehe, so ist doch die natur verderbet durch
165 die Erbsünde, die uns im sundlichen samen angeboren wird und ein brunquell
ist aller anderer wircklichen sünden, als böser gedancken, wort und wercke,
wie geschrieben stehet: 'Aus dem hertzen komen arge gedancken.' Item: 'Das Mat
tichten des menschlichen hertzens ist bös von jugent auff.' Gen

    So ist auch wol zu mercken der ungleiche verstandt des wortes Natur, 12.
170 dadurch die Manicheer iren irrthum bedecken und viel ein | feltiger Leute irre 232r
machen. Dann zu zeiten heisset es des Menschen wesen, als wann gesagt wird:
Gott hat die Menschliche natur geschaffen. Zu zeiten aber heisset es die art
und unart eines dings, die in der natur oder wesen stecket, als wenn gesagt
wird: der Schlangen natur ist stechen, und des Menschen natur und art ist
175 sündigen und sünde; da das wort Natur nicht die substantz des Menschen,
sondern etwas heisset, das in der natur oder substantz stecket.

    Was aber die Lateinische wort Substantia und Accidens belanget, weil es 13.
nicht heiliger Schrifft wort sind, darzu dem gemeinen Man unbekant, sollen
dieselbigen in den Predigten vor dem gemeinen, unverstendigem Volck nicht
180 gebraucht, sondern des einfeltigen volcks darmit verschonet werden. Aber in
der Schule bey den Gelerten, weil sie wol bekant und one allen missverstandt

---

167 Matth. 15, 19   **167/168** Gen. 6, 5; 8, 21

155/156 Erbsünde – genennet] cfr M. Luther, 'Kirchenpostille (1522). Evangelium am
Neujahrstag, Luc. 2, 21', in *WA* 10/I/1 (1910), p. 504-519; cfr also 'Festpostille (1527).
Evangelium am Tage Mariä Empfengnis, Luc. 11, 27 seq.', in *WA* 17/2 (1927), p. 280-289
and 'Predigt über Gen. 22, 18 (1526)', in *WA* 20 (1898), p. 336-348   **177** Was –
Accidens] during the argument over original sin, Matthias Flacius Illyricus defined
original sin as 'substantial', i.e. the nature of man. His opponent Victorin Strigel denied
the possibility that original sin could have any effect on the essential determination of
man, and therefore called it 'accidental'

D. Lutherus quidem Originis illud malum peccatum Naturae, personale, essentiale vocat, sed non eam ob causam, quasi Natura, persona aut essentia hominis absque omni discrimine sit ipsum peccatum Originis, sed ideo ad hunc modum loquitur, ut huiusmodi phrasibus discrimen inter peccatum Originale, quod humanae naturae infixum est, et inter alia peccata, quae actualia vocantur, melius intelligi possit.

Peccatum enim Originis non est quoddam delictum, quod actu perpetratur, sed intime inhaeret infixum ipsi naturae, substantiae et Essentiae hominis. Et quidem, si maxime nulla unquam prava cogitatio in corde hominis corrupti exoriretur, si nullum verbum ociosum proferretur, si nullum malum opus aut facinus designaretur: tamen Natura nihilominus corrupta est per Originale peccatum, quod nobis ratione corrupti seminis agnatum est, quod ipsum etiam scaturigo est omnium aliorum actualium peccatorum, ut sunt pravae cogitationes, prava colloquia, prave et scelerate facta. Sic enim scriptum legimus: *Ex corde oriuntur cogitationes malae.* Et alibi: *Omne sigmentum cordis tantummodo malum est a pueritia.*

Est etiam diligenter observanda varia significatio vocabuli 'Naturae', cuius aequivocatione Manichaei abutentes errorem suum occultant multosque simplices homines in errorem inducunt. Quandoque enim 'Natura' ipsam hominis substantiam significat, ut cum dicimus: Deus humanam Naturam creavit. Interdum vero per vocabulum 'Naturae' intelligitur ingenium, conditio, defectus aut vitium alicuius rei, in ipsa natura insitum et inhaerens, ut cum dicimus: Serpentis natura est icere, hominis natura est peccare et peccatum. Et in hac posteriore significatione vocabulum 'Natura' non ipsam hominis substantiam, sed aliquid, quod in natura aut substantia fixum inhaeret, denotat.

| Quod vero ad Latina vocabula Substantiae et Accidentis attinet, cum ea non sint scripturae sacrae vocabula, praeterea etiam a plebe non intelligantur, abstinendum est ab illis in publicis sacris concionibus, ubi indocta plebs docetur, et hac in re simplicium et rudiorum merito habenda est ratio. In scholis

gebraucht, dadurch das wesen eines jeden dings und was im zufelliger weise anhanget, eigentlich unterschieden werden, solche wort auch billich in der Disputation von der Erbsünde behalten.

Dann der unterscheid zwischen Gottes und des Teuffels werck auff das deutlichste dardurch angezeigt, weil der Teuffel kein substantz schaffen, sondern allein zufelliger weise, aus Gottes verhengnis, die von Gott erschaffene substantz verderben kan.

II. Vom freien Willen

Status Controversiae

Die Hauptfrage in dieser Zwispalt

Nachdem des Menschen willen in vier ungleichen stenden gefunden, Nemlich: 1. Vor dem Fall. 2. Nach dem Fall. 3. Nach der Widergeburt. 4. Nach der aufferstehung des fleisches. Ist die Hauptfrage allein von dem willen und vermögen des Menschen im andern | stande, was derselbige nach dem fall unser ersten Eltern vor seiner widergeburt aus im selbst in geistlichen sachen vor kreffte habe, und ob er vermöge, aus seinen eigenen krefften, zuvorn und ehe er durch den Geist Gottes widergeborn, sich zur gnade Gottes schicken und bereiten und die durch den heiligen Geist im wort und heiligen Sacramenten angebotene gnade annemen oder nicht?

Affirmativa

Reine Lere vermöge Gottes worts von diesem Artickel

Hiervon ist unser lere, glaub und bekentnis, das des Menschen verstand und vernunfft in geistlichen sachen blind, nichts verstehe aus seinen eigenen krefften, wie geschrieben stehet: 'Der natürliche Mensch vernimmet nichts vom Geist Gottes; es ist im eine thorheit, und kan es nicht begreiffen', wann er wird von geistlichen sachen gefraget.

Desgleichen gleuben, leren und bekennen wir, das des Menschen unwidergeborner wille nicht allein von Gott abgewendet, sondern auch ein

---

205/206 I Cor. 2, 14

182 zufelliger] without any effects on the essential state

EPITOME – 1577

autem et apud homines doctos (quibus horum vocabulorum significatio nota
185 est et qui iisdem recte atque citra abusum uti possunt proprie discernentes
essentiam alicuius rei ab eo, quod aliunde ei accidit et per accidens inhaeret) in
disputatione de peccato Originis retinenda sunt.

Nam hisce vocabulis discrimen inter opus Dei et inter opus Diaboli quam
maxime perspicue explicari potest. Diabolus enim substantiam nullam creare,
190 sed tantummodo per accidens, permittente Domino, substantiam a Deo crea-
tam depravare potest.

II. De libero arbitrio.

Status controversiae.

Cum hominis voluntas quadruplicem habeat considerationem, primo
195 ante lapsum, secundo post lapsum, tertio post regenerationem, quarto post
resurrectionem carnis, nunc quaestio praecipua est tantum de voluntate et
viribus hominis in secundo statu, quasnam vires post lapsum primorum parentum nostrorum ante regenerationem ex seipso habeat in rebus spiritualibus: an
propriis viribus, antequam per spiritum Dei fuerit regeneratus, possit sese ad
200 gratiam Dei applicare et praepararet num gratiam divinam (quae illi per
Spiritum sanctum in verbo et Sacramentis divinitus institutis offertur) accipe-
re et apprehendere possit nec ne.

Affirmativa.

563

Sincera doctrina de hoc articulo cum immota Regula verbi divini congruens.

205 De hoc negocio haec est fides, doctrina et confessio nostra:,quod videlicet I.
hominis intellectus et ratio in rebus spiritualibus prorsus sint coeca, nihilque
propriis viribus intelligere possint. Sicut scriptum est: *Animalis homo non*   I. Cor. 2.
percipit ea, quae sunt spiritus; stulticia illi est et non potest intelligere, quia de
spiritualibus examinatur.
210 Credimus, docemus et confitemur etiam, voluntatem hominis nondum II.
renatam non tantum a Deo esse aversam, verum etiam inimicam Deo factam,

820 CONCILIUM SAXONICUM – 1577

feind Gottes worden, das er nur lust und willen hat zum bösen und was
Gott zuwider ist, wie geschrieben stehet: 'Das dichten des Menschen hertzen   Gene
ist bös von jugend auff.' Item: 'Fleischlich gesinnet sein ist eine feindschaft   Rom.
wider Gott, sintemal es dem Gesetz nicht unterthan ist, denn es vermag es
auch nicht.' Ja, so wenig ein todter leib sich selbst lebendig machen kan zum
leiblichen irdischen leben, so wenig mag der Mensch, so durch die sünde geistlich todt ist, sich selbst zum Geistlichen leben aufrichten, wie geschrieben
stehet: 'Da wir todt waren in Sünden hat er uns sampt Christo lebendig   Ephe
gemacht', darumb wir auch aus uns selbst 'als aus uns nicht tüchtig seind,
etwas guts zu gedencken, sondern das wir tüchtig sind, das ist von Gott',
2. Corinth. 3.

Die bekerung aber wircket Gott, der heilige Geist, nicht one mittel, son-   3.
dern gebraucht darzu die predigt und das gehör Gottes worts, | wie geschrie-   233r
ben stehet: 'Das Evangelium ist eine krafft Gottes selig zu machen.' Item: 'Der   Rom.
Glaube kommet aus dem gehör Gottes worts. Und ist Gottes wille, das man   Rom.
Psalm
sein wort hören und nicht die Ohren verstopffen solle.' Bey solchem wort ist
der heilige Geist gegenwertig und thut auff die hertzen, das sie wie die Lydia in
der Apostel Geschichte 16. Capitulo darauff mercken und also bekeret werden
allein durch die gnad und krafft des heiligen Geistes, dessen werck allein ist die
bekerung des Menschen, dann one seine gnade ist unser 'wollen und lauffen',   Rom.
unser 'pflanzen, seen und begiessen' alles nichts, wann er nicht 'das gedeyen   1. Cor
darzu verleihet', wie Christus saget: 'One mich vermüget ir nichtes.' Mit
welchen kurtzen worten er dem freien willen seine kreffte abspricht und alles
der Gnaden Gottes zuschreibet, 'damit sich nicht jemands vor Gott rhümen
möchte', 1. Corinth. 9.

Negativa

Widerwertige falsche Lehre

Demnach verwerffen und verdammen wir alle nachfolgende irthumb als
der Richtschnur Gottes worts zu wider:

211/212 Gen. 8, 21   **212/214** Rom. 8, 7   **217/218** Eph. 2, 5   **218/219** II Cor. 3, 5
223 Rom. 1, 16   **223/224** Rom. 10, 17   **224/225** Ps. 95, 7f   **227** Apostel –
Capitulo] Act. 16, 14   **229** Rom. 9, 16   **230/231** I Cor. 3, 7   **231** Ioh. 15, 5   **233/**
234 I Cor. 9, 16; 1, 29; Ier. 9, 23

EPITOME – 1577

ita ut tantummodo ea velit et cupiat iisque delectetur, quae mala sunt, et voluntati divinae repugnant. Scriptum est enim: *Sensus et cogitatio humani cordis in malum prona sunt ab adolescantia sua.* Item : *Affectus carnis inimicitia* est adversus Deum, neque enim legi subiicitur ac ne potest id quidem.* Itaque credimus, quantum abest, ut corpus mortuum seipsum vivificare atque sibiipsi corporalem vitam restituere possit, tantum abesse, ut homo, qui ratione peccati spiritualiter mortuus est, seipsum in vitam spiritualem revocandi ullam facultatem habeat, sicut scriptum est: *Cum essemus mortui in peccatis, convivificavit nos cum Christo* etc. Itaque etiam ex nobismet ipsis, *tanquam ex nobis,* *non sumus idonei, ut aliquid boni cogitemus; quod vero idonei sumus, idipsum a Deo est.*

Conversionem autem hominis operatur Spiritus sanctus non sine mediis, sed ad eam efficiendam uti solet praedicatione et auscultatione verbi Dei, sicut scriptum est: *Evangelion est potentia Dei ad salutem omni credenti.* Et: *Fides est ex auditu verbi Dei.* Et sane vult Dominus, ut ipsius Verbum audiatur neque ad illius praedicationem aures obdurentur. Huic verbo adest praesens Spiritus san|ctus et corda hominum aperit, ut sicut Lydia in Actis Apostolicis diligenter attendant et ita convertantur sola gratia et virtute Spiritus sancti, cuius unius et solius opus est hominis conversio. Si enim Spiritus sancti gratia absit, nostrum *velle et currere,* nostrum *plantare, seminare et rigare* prosus frustranea sunt, si videlicet *ille incrementum non largiatur,* sicut Christus inquit: *Sine me nihil potestis facere.* Et his quidem paucis verbis Christus libero arbitrio omnes vires derogat, omniaque gratiae divinae adscribit, *ne quis coram Deo habeat, de quo glorietur.*

Marginalia:
- Genes. 8.
- Rom. 8.
- Ephes. 2.
- 2. Cor. 3.
- III.
- Rom. 1. | Rom. 10. Psal. 95.
- 564 | Actor. 16.
- Rom. 9. | 1. Cor. 3.
- Iohan. 15.
- 1. Cor. 1.
- Ierem. 9.

Negativa.

Reiectio contrariae et falsae doctrinae.

Repudiamus igitur et damnamus omnes, quos iam recitabimus, errores cum verbi divini regula non congruentes.

822 CONCILIUM SAXONICUM – 1577

Den schwarm der Philosophen, so man Stoicos genennet hat, wie auch 1.
240 die Manicheer, die geleret haben, das alles, was geschehe, müsse also geschehen und könne nichts anders geschehen, und das der Mensch alles aus zwang thue, was er auch in eusserlichen dingen handele und zu bösen wercken und thaten, als unzucht, raub, mord, diebstal und dergleichen gezwungen werde.

Wir verwerffen auch der groben Pelagianer irthumb, die geleret haben, 2.
245 das der Mensch aus eigenen krefften, one die gnade des heiligen Geistes sich selbst zu Gott bekeren, dem Evangelio glauben, dem Gesetz Gottes mit hertzen gehorsamen und also vergebung der sünden und ewiges leben verdienen könne.

Wir verwerffen auch der Halbpelagianer irthumb, welche leren, das der 3.
250 mensch aus eigenen krefften den anfang seiner bekerung machen, aber one die gnad des heiligen Geistes nicht volbringen möge.

Item, da geleret wirdt, obwol der Mensch mit seinem freien Willen vor 4.|2
seiner widergeburt zu schwach, den anfang zu machen und sich selbst aus eigenen krefften zu Gott zu bekeren und Gottes Gesetz von hertzen gehorsam zu
255 sein, jedoch wann der heilige Geist mit der Predigt des worts den anfang gemacht und seine gnade darinne angeboten, das alsdann der wille des Menschen aus seinen eigenen natürlichen krefften etlichermassen etwas, wiewol wenig und schwächlich, darzu thun, helfen und mitwircken, sich selbst zur gnade schicken, bereiten, dieselbige ergreiffen, annemen und dem Evangelio
260 gleuben könne.

Item, das der Mensch, nachdem er widergeboren, das Gesetz Gottes 5.
volkommen halten und gentzlichen erfüllen könne und das solche erfüllung unser gerechtigkeit vor Gott sey, mit welcher wir das ewige Leben verdienen.

Item, Wir verwerffen und verdammen auch den irthumb der Enthusias- 6. Ent
265 ten, welche dichten, das Gott one mittel, one gehör Gottes worts, auch one asten
gebrauch der heiligen Sacramenten die Menschen zu sich ziehe, erleuchte, Predi
gerecht und selig mache. tes wc

Item, das Gott in der bekerung und widergeburt des alten Adams himli
substantz und wesen und sonderlich die vernünfftige Seele gantz vertilge und erleuc
des G
warte
7.

---

239 Stoicos] Zeno founded the school of Stoa in the fourth century BC. In the sixteenth century the main teaching of the Stoics was the so-called absolute necessity **249** Halbpelagianer] in contrast to Pelagianism, the Semipelagianism of the fifth century taught that, although human will was weakened through the fall, a predisposition to good still remains in mankind. Divine grace then steps in and helps mankind, so that human will and divine grace complement each other **264** Enthusiasten] the *Formula of Concord* defines as Enthusiasts those who desire and expect enlightenment by the Holy Spirit for themselves outside the sermon of the Word of God

EPITOME – 1577 823

240 Primo delirum philosophorum Stoicorum dogma quemadmodum et I.
Manichaeorum furorem, qui docuerunt, omnia, quae eveniant, necessario fieri
et aliter fieri prorsus non posse, et hominem omnia coactum facere, etiam ea,
quae in rebus externis agat, eumque ad designanda mala opera et scelera (qualia sunt libidines vagae, rapinae, caedes, furta et similia) cogi.

245 Repudiamus etiam crassum illum Pelagianorum errorem, qui asserere non II.
dubitarunt, quod homo propriis viribus sine gratia Spiritus sancti sese ad
Deum convertere, evangelio credere, legi divinae ex animo parere et hac ratione peccatorum remissionem ac vitam aeternam ipse promereri valeat.

Praeter hos errores reiicimus et Semipelagianorum falsum dogma, qui III.
250 docent, hominem propriis viribus inchoa|re posse suam conversionem, absol- 565
vere autem sine Spiritus sancti gratia non posse.

Item, cum docetur, licet homo non renatus ratione liberi Arbitrii ante sui IIII.
regenerationem infirmior quidem sit, quam ut conversionis suae initium facere
atque propriis viribus sese ad Deum convertere et legi Dei toto corde parere
255 valeat: tamen, si Spiritus sanctus praedicatione verbi initium fecerit suamque
gratiam in verbo homini obtulerit, tum hominis voluntatem propriis et naturalibus suis viribus quodammodo aliquid, licet id modiculum, infirmum et
languidum admodum sit, conversionem adiuvare atque cooperari et seipsam
ad gratiam applicare, praeparare, eam apprehendere, amplecti et Evangelio
260 credere posse.

Item, hominem post regenerationem legem Dei perfecte observare atque V.
implere posse eamque impletionem esse nostram coram Deo iusticiam, qua
vitam aeternam promereamur.

Reiicimus etiam damnamusque Enthusiastarum, qui fingunt, Deum VI. Enthu-
265 immediate absque verbi Dei auditu et sine Sacramentorum usu homines ad se siastae
trahere, illuminare, iustificare et salvare. vocantur,
qui neglecta
praedication
e verbi
Item, Deum in conversione et regeneratione hominis Substantiam et divini
Essentiam veteris Adami et praecipue animam rationalem penitus abolere coelestes
revelationes
Spiritus
expectant.
VII.

824   CONCILIUM SAXONICUM – 1577

270 ein neues wesen der Seele aus nichts in der bekerung und widergeburt erschaffe.

Item, wann diese reden one erklerung gebraucht, daß des Menschen wille   8.
vor, in und nach der bekerung dem heiligen Geist widerstrebe, und das der
heilige Geist gegeben werde denen, so ime vorsetzlich und beharrlich wider-
275 streben, dann Gott in der bekerung aus den unwilligen willige machet und in
den willigen wonet, wie Augustinus redet.

Was dann die reden der alten und neuen Kirchenlerer belanget, als da
gesagt wird: 'Deus trahit, sed volentem trahit', das ist: 'Gott zeucht, zeucht
aber, die da wöllen'; Item: 'Hominis voluntas in conversione non est ociosa,
280 sed agit aliquid', Das ist: 'Des Menschen wille ist nicht müssig in der bekerung, sondern wircket auch etwas'. Weil solche reden zu bestetigung des
natürlichen, freien Willens in der bekerung des Menschen wider die Lere von
der Gnade Gottes eingeführet, halten wir, das sie der form der gesunden Lere
nicht ehnlich und demnach, wann von der bekerung zu Gott geredet wird,
285 billich zu meiden seien.

Dagegen aber wirdt recht geredet, das Gott in der bekerung durch das   234r
ziehen des heiligen Geistes aus widerspenstigen, unwilligen willige menschen
mache, und das nach solcher bekerung in teglicher ubung der Bus des menschen widergeborner wille nicht müssig gehe, sondern in allem wircken des
290 heiligen Geistes, die er durch uns thut, auch mitwircke.

Item, das Doctor Luther geschrieben, das des menschen wille in seiner   9.
bekerung sich halte 'pure paßive', das ist, das er gantz und gar nichts thue, das
solches zuverstehen sey 'respectu divinae gratiae in accendendis novis motibus', das ist, wann der Geist Gottes durch das gehörte wort oder durch den
295 brauch der heiligen Sacramenten des menschen willen angreifft und wircket
die neue geburt und bekerung. Dann so der heilige Geist solches gewircket
und ausgerichtet und des menschen wille allein durch sein Göttliche krafft
und wirckung geendert und erneuert, als dann ist der neue wille des menschen

---

272/276 wann – redet] cfr Augustinus, *Contra duas epistulas Pelagianorum* I 19, 37,
hrsg. C. F. Vrba – J. Zycha (*CSEL* 60), Wien – Leipzig 1913, p. 454, 10-21 (= *PL* 44,
col. 568)   **280/281** the text refers to a controversial statement by Melanchthon in his
Loci theologici (1535). In his statement, he references a sermon attributed to Basil the
Great († 379) about penance and one of John Chrysostom († 407). Cfr
P. Melanchthon, 'Loci praecipui theologici (1559)', in *CR* 21 (1854), col. 658 = *MWA*
2/1 (1952), p. 244, 1-11; Ps. Basilius (i.e. Eusebius Emesenus), *Homilia de paenitentia* 4
(*PG* 31), Paris 1857, col. 1482; Iohannes Chrysostomus, *Homiliae XXV in quaedam loca
Novi Testamenti. De mutatione nominum IV* (*PG* 51), Paris 1862, col. 143   **291** das¹ –
geschrieben] M. Luther, 'De servo arbitrio (1525)', in *WA* 18 (1908), p. 697, 28;
'Resolutiones Lutherianae super propositionibus suis Lipsiae disputatis (1519)', in *WA* 2
(1884), p. 421, 7

EPITOME – 1577

novamque animae essentiam ex nihilo in illa conversione et regeneratione
270 creare.

Item, cum hi sermones citra declarationem usurpantur, quod videlicet VIII.
hominis voluntas ante conversionem, in ipsa conversione et post conversionem Spiritui sancto repugnet; et quod Spiritus sanctus iis detur, qui ex proposito et pertinaciter ipsi resistunt. Nam Deus in conversione ex nolentibus
275 volentes facit et in volentibus habitat, ut Augustinus loqui solet.

Quod vero ad dicta quaedam tum Patrum tum Neotericorum quorundam doctorum attinet: Deus trahit, sed volentem trahit; et: hominis voluntas in conversione non est ociosa, sed agit aliquid: iudicamus haec formae sanorum | verborum non esse analoga. Afferuntur enim haec dicta ad confir- 566
280 mandam falsam opinionem de viribus humani arbitrii in hominis conversione contra doctrinam, quae soli gratiae divinae id opus attribuit. Ideoque ab eiusmodi sermonibus, quando de conversione hominis ad Deum agitur, abstinendum censemus.

Contra autem recte docetur, quod Dominus in conversione per Spiritus
285 sancti tractionem (id est motum et operationem) ex hominibus repugnantibus et nolentibus volentes homines faciat, et quod post conversionem in quotidianis poenitentiae exercitiis hominis renati voluntas non sit ociosa, sed omnibus Spiritus sancti operibus, quae ille per nos efficit, etiam cooperetur.

Item, quod D. Lutherus scripsit, hominis voluntatem in conversione pure
290 passive se habere, id recte et dextre est accipiendum, videlicet respectu divinae gratiae in accendendis novis motibus, hoc est de eo intelligi oportet, quando Spiritus Dei per verbum auditum aut per usum Sacramentorum hominis voluntatem aggredituret conversionem atque regenerationem in homine operatur. Postquam enim Spiritus sanctus hoc ipsum iam operatus est atque effe-
295 cit hominisque voluntatem sola sua divina virtute et operatione immutavit

ein Instrument und Werckzeug Gottes, des heiligen Geistes, das er nicht allein
die gnade annimmt, sondern auch in folgenden wercken des heiligen Geistes
mitwircket.

Das also vor der bekerung des menschen nur zwo wirckliche ursachen
sich finden: nemlich der heilige Geist und das wort Gottes als das Instrument
des heiligen Geistes, dadurch er die bekerung wircket, welches der mensch
hören sol, aber denselbigen nicht aus eignen krefften, sondern allein durch die
gnade und wirckung Gottes des heiligen Geistes glauben geben und annemen
kan.

III. Von der gerechtigkeit des Glaubens vor Gott

Status Controversiae

Hauptfrage in dieser Zwispalt

Weil einhellig vermüge Gottes Worts und nach inhalt der Augspurgischen Confeßion in unsern Kirchen bekant, das wir arme sünder allein durch
den glauben an Christum vor Gott gerecht und selig werden und also Christus
allein unser gerechtigkeit sey, welcher warhafftiger Gott und mensch ist, weil
in im die Göttliche und menschliche natur mit einander persönlich vereiniget,
Jeremiae 23., 1. Corinth. 1., 2. Corinth. 5., ist eine frage entstanden, nach
welcher natur Christus unser gerechtigkeit seye. Und also zwene widerwertige
irthumb in etlichen Kirchen eingefallen.

Dann der eine teil hat gehalten, das Christus allein nach der Gottheit
unser gerechtigkeit sey, wenn er durch den glauben in uns wonet, gegen
welcher durch den glauben einwonender Gottheit aller menschen sünde wie
ein tropff wasser gegen dem grossen Meer geachtet sey. Dargegen haben andere gehalten, Christus sey unser gerechtigkeit vor Gott allein nach der menschlichen natur.

Affirmativa

Reine lere der Christlichen Kirchen wider beide jetzgesetzte irthumb

Wider beide jetzterzelte irthumb gleuben, leren und bekennen wir einhel-
liglich, das Christus unser gerechtigkeit weder nach der Göttlichen natur

---

311/316 Weil – 5.] Ier. 23, 6; I Cor. 1, 30; II Cor. 5, 21   **322** ein – Meer] Eccli. 18, 8

EPITOME – 1577

atque renovavit: tunc revera hominis nova illa voluntas instrumentum est et organon Dei Spiritus sancti, ut ea non modo gratiam apprehendat, verum etiam in operibus sequentibus Spiritui sancto cooperetur.

Relinquuntur igitur ante conversionem hominis duae tantum efficientes causae (ad conversionem efficaces), nimirum Spiritus sanctus et verbum Dei, quod est instrumentum Spiritus sancti, quo conversionem hominis efficit. Hoc verbum homo certe audire debet, sed tamen, ut illud ipsum vera fide amplectatur, id nequaquam suis viribus propriis, sed sola gratia et operatione Dei Spiritus sancti obtinere potest.

III. DE IUSTICIA FIDEI CORAM DEO.

Status controversiae.

Unanimi consensu (ad normam verbi divini et sententiam Augustanae Confessionis) in Ecclesiis nostris docetur, nos peccatores longe miserrimos sola in Christum fide coram Deo iustificari et salvari, ita ut Christus solus nostra sit iusticia. Hic autem Iesus Christus salvator noster et iusticia nostra verus Deus est et verus homo: etenim divina et humana naturae in ipso sunt personaliter unitae. Quaesitum igitur fuit: secundum quam naturam Christus nostra sit iusticia? Et hac occasione duo errores et quidem inter se pugnantes Ecclesias quasdam perturbarunt.

Ierem. 23.
1. Cor. 1.
2. Cor. 5.

Una enim pars sensit, Christum tantummodo secundum divinam naturam esse nostram iusticiam, si videlicet ille per fidem in nobis habitet; etenim omnia hominum peccata, collata nimirum cum illa per fidem inhabitante divinitate, esse instar unius guttulae aquae cum magno mari comparatae. Contra hanc opinionem alii quidam asseruerunt Christum esse nostram coram Deo iusticiam duntaxat secundum humanam naturam.

Affirmativa.

Sincera doctrina piarum Ecclesiarum
utrique commemorato errori opposita.

Ad refellendum utrunque errorem credimus, docemus et confitemur una- I. nimiter, quod Christus vere sit no|stra iusticia, sed tamen neque secundum

828 CONCILIUM SAXONICUM – 1577

allein noch | auch nach der menschlichen natur allein, sondern der gantze 235r
330 Christus nach beiden naturen, allein in seinem gehorsam, sey, den er als Gott
und mensch dem Vater bis in todt geleistet und uns damit vergebung der sünden und das ewige leben verdienet habe, wie geschrieben stehet: 'Gleich wie
durch eines menschen ungehorsam viel sünder worden, Also durch eines menschen gehorsam werden viel gerecht', Rom. 5.

335   Demnach gleuben, leren und bekennen wir, das unsere gerechtigkeit vor 2.
Gott sey, das uns Gott die sünde vergibet aus lauter gnaden one alle unsere
vorgehende, gegenwertige oder nachfolgende werck, verdienst oder wirdigkeit, schencket und rechnet uns zu die gerechtigkeit des gehorsams Christi,
umb welcher gerechtigkeit willen wir bey Gott zu gnaden angenommen und
340 für gerecht gehalten werden.

Wir gleuben, leren und bekennen, das allein der glaube das mittel und 3.
der werckzeug sey, damit wir Christum und also in Christo solche 'gerechtigkeit, die vor Gott gilt' ergreiffen, umb welches willen uns solcher 'glaube zur
gerechtigkeit zugerechnet wird', Rom. 4.

345   Wir gleuben, leren und bekennen, das dieser glaub nicht sey eine blosse 4.
erkentnis der Historien von Christo, sondern eine solche gabe Gottes,
dadurch wir Christum, unsern Erlöser, im wort des Evangelii recht erkennen
und auff in vertrauen, das wir allein umb seines gehorsams willen aus gnaden
vergebung der Sünden haben, vor from und gerecht von Gott dem Vater
350 gehalten und ewig selig werden.

Wir gleuben, leren und bekennen, das nach art heiliger Schrifft das wort 5.
'Rechtfertigen' in diesem Artickel heisse 'absolviren', das ist, von sünden ledig
sprechen: 'Wer den Gottlosen recht spricht und den gerechten verdammet, Prov.
der ist vor dem Herrn ein greuel.' Item: 'Wer will die auserwelten Gottes Rom
355 beschuldigen? Gott ist hie, der da gerecht machet.'

Und da an desselben stat die wort 'Regeneratio' und 'Vivificatio', das ist,
'lebendigmachung' und 'widergeburt' gebraucht, wie in der Apologia
geschicht, das es auch in gleichem verstand geschehe, dadurch sonst die
erneuerung des menschen verstanden und von der rechtfertigung des glaubens
360 unterscheiden wird.

Wir gleuben, leren und bekennen auch unangesehen, das den | rechtgleu- 6. | 2
bigen und warhafftig widergebornen auch noch viel schwachheit und gebre-
chen anhanget bis in die gruben, do sie doch der ursach halben weder an irer

---

332/334 Rom. 5, 19   **343/344** Rom. 3, 21; 4, 5   **353/354** Prou. 17, 15   **354/
355** Rom. 8, 33

357 Apologia] cfr *Apologia Confessionis Augustanae*, Article 4, in *BSLK*, p. 174, 37-40;
p. 175, 37-39; p. 184, 9-11; p. 192, 33-36; p. 220, 27-29

EPITOME – 1577

solam divinam naturam neque secundum solam humanam naturam, sed totus
Christus secundum utranque naturam in sola videlicet obedientia sua, quam
patri ad mortem usque absolutissimam Deus et homo praestitit, eaque nobis
peccatorum omnium remissionem et vitam aeternam promeruit. Sicut scriptum est: *Sicut per inobedientiam unius hominis peccatores constituti sunt multi,
ita et per unius obedientiam iusti constituentur multi*, Rom. 5.

Credimus igitur, docemus et confitemur, hoc ipsum nostram esse coram II.
Deo iusticiam, quod Dominus nobis peccata remittit ex mera gratia absque
ullo respectu praecedentium, praesentium aut consequentium nostrorum operum, dignitatis aut meriti. Ille enim donat atque imputat nobis iusticiam obe-
dientiae Christi, propter eam iusticiam a Deo in gratiam recipimur et iusti
reputamur.

Credimus etiam, docemus et confitemur, solam fidem esse illud medium III.
et instrumentum, quo Christum salvatorem et ita in Christo *iusticiam illam,
quae coram iudicio Dei consistere potest*, apprehendimus; propter Christum
enim *fides illa nobis ad iusticiam imputatur*, Rom. 4.

Credimus praeterea, docemus et confitemur, fidem illam iustificantem IIII.
non esse nudam notitiam historiae de Christo, sed ingens atque tale Dei
donum, quo Christum Redemtorem nostrum in verbo Evangelii recte agnoscimus ipsique confidimus, quod videlicet propter solam ipsius obedientiam ex
gratia remissionem peccatorum habeamus, sancti et iusti coram Deo Patre
reputemur et aeternam salutem consequamur.

Credimus, docemus et confitemur, vocabulum 'iustificare' phrasi scriptu- V.
rae sacrae in hoc articulo idem significare quod absolvere a peccatis, ut ex dicto
Salomonis intelligi potest: *Qui iustificat impium et qui condemnat iustum,* Prover. 17.
abomnabilis est uterque apud Deum. Item: *Quis accusabit electos Dei? Deus est,* Rom. 8.
qui iustificat.

| Et, si quando pro vocabulo iustificationis vocabula regenerationis et vivi- 569
ficationis usurpantur (quod in Apologia Augustanae Confessionis factum est),
sunt ea in illa superiore significatione accipienda. Nam alias eae voces de
hominis renovatione intelligendae sunt, quae a fidei iustificatione recte discer-
nitur.

Credimus, docemus et confitemur etiam, etsi vere in Christum credentes VI.
et renati multis infirmitatibus et naevis usque ad mortem sunt obnoxii, non

830 CONCILIUM SAXONICUM – 1577

gerechtigkeit, so inen durch den glauben zugerechnet, noch an irer Seelen
365 seligkeit zweiffeln, sondern vor gewis halten sollen, das sie umb Christus
willen vermöge der verheissung und wort des heiligen Evangelii einen gnedigen Gott haben.

Wir gleuben, leren und bekennen, das zu erhaltung reiner lere von der 7.
gerechtigkeit des glaubens für Gott uber den 'particulis exclusivis', das ist,
370 uber nachfolgende wort des heiligen Apostels Pauli, dadurch der verdienst
Christi von unsern wercken gentzlich abgesondert und Christo die ehre allein
gegeben mit besonderm vleis zu halten sey, da der heilige Apostel Paulus
schreibet: 'Aus gnaden, one verdienst', 'one Gesetz, one werck', 'nicht aus den
wercken', welche wort alle zugleich so viel heissen als: 'allein durch den glau-
375 ben' an Christum werden wir gerecht und selig.

Wir gleuben, leren und bekennen, das obwol vorgehende reu und nach- 8.
folgende gute werck nicht in den Artickeln der rechtfertigung vor Gott gehö-
ren, Jedoch sol nicht ein solcher glaub gedichtet werden, der bey und neben
einem bösen vorsatz zu sündigen und wider das gewissen zuhandeln, sein und
380 bleiben köndte, sondern nachdem der mensch durch den glauben gerechtfertiget worden, alsdann ist ein warhafftiger, lebendiger 'glaube durch die liebe
thetig', Gal. 5., also das die gute werck dem gerechtmachenden glauben alzeit
folgen und bey demselben, do er rechtschaffen und lebendig, gewislich erfun-
den werden, wie er dann nimmer allein ist, sondern alzeit liebe und hoffnung
385 bey sich hat.

Antithesis oder Negativa

Gegenlere verworffen

Demnach verwerffen und verdammen wir alle nachfolgende irthumb.

Das Christus unser gerechtigkeit sey allein nach der Göttlichen natur. 1.

390 Das Christus unser gerechtigkeit sey allein nach der menschlichen natur. 2. |
Das in den Sprüchen der Propheten und Aposteln, da von der gerechtig- 3.
keit des glaubens geredet wird, die wort 'Rechtfertigen' und 'gerechtfertiget
werden' nicht sollen heissen 'von sünden ledig sprechen' oder 'gesprochen
werden' und 'vergebung der sünde erlangen', sondern von wegen der durch

---

373 Rom. 3, 24   Rom. 3, 21.28   **373/374** Rom. 11, 6   **374** allein – glauben] Rom.
3, 28   **381/382** Gal. 5, 6

EPITOME – 1577

360 tamen illis vel de iusticia, quae per fidem ipsis imputatur, vel de aeterna salute esse dubitandum, quin potius firmiter illis statuendum esse, quod propter Christum iuxta promissionem et immotum verbum Evangelii Deum sibi placatum habeant.

Credimus, docemus et confitemur, quod ad conservandam puram doc- VII.
365 trinam de iusticia fidei coram Deo necessarium sit, ut particulae exclusivae (quibus Apostolus Paulus Christi meritum ab operibus nostris prorsus separat solique Christo eam gloriam tribuit), quam diligentissime retineantur, ut, cum Paulus scribit, ex gratia, gratis, sine meritis absque lege, sine operibus, non ex operibus. Quae omnia hoc ipsum dicunt: Sola fide in Christum iustificamur et
370 salvamur.

Credimus, docemus et confitemur, etsi antecedens contritio et subse- VIII.
quens nova obedientia ad articulum iustificationis coram Deo non pertinent, non tamen talem fidem iustificantem esse fingendam, quae una cum malo proposito peccandi videlicet et contra conscientiam agendi esse et stare possit,
375 sed postquam homo per fidem est iustificatus, tum veram illam et vivam *fidem* Galat. 5.
esse per charitatem efficacem et bona opera semper fidem iustificantem sequi et una cum ea, si modo vera et viva fides est, certissime deprehendi. Fides enim vera nunquam sola est, quin charitatem et spem semper secum habeat.

Antithesis seu negativa. 570

380 <center>Reiectio contrariae et falsae doctrinae.</center>

Repudiamus ergo et damnamus omnia falsa dogmata, quae iam recitabi-mus:

Christum esse iusticiam nostram solummodo secundum divinam natu- I.
ram.
385 Christum esse iusticiam nostram tantummodo iuxta humanam naturam. II.

In dictis Propheticis et Apostolicis, ubi de iustificatione fidei agitur, voca- III.
bula 'iusticare' et 'iustificari' non idem esse ac a peccatis absolvere et absolvi et remissionem peccatorum consequi, sed nos per charitatem a Spiritu sancto

832 CONCILIUM SAXONICUM – 1577

395 den heiligen Geist eingegossene liebe, tugend und daraus folgender werck mit der that vor Gott gerecht gemacht werden.

Das der glaube nicht allein ansehe den gehorsam Christi, sondern seine 4. Göttliche natur, wie dieselbige in uns wonet und wircket, und durch solche einwonung unser sünde bedecket werden.

400 Das der glaub ein solch vertrauen auff den gehorsam Christi sey, welcher 5. in einem menschen sein und bleiben könne, der gleich keine warhafftige busse habe, do auch keine liebe folge, sondern wider sein gewissen in sünden verharret.

Das nicht Gott selbst, sondern allein die gaben Gottes in den gleubigen 6. 405 wonen.

Das der glaube darumb selig mache, weil die erneuerung, so in der liebe 7. gegen Gott und dem nehesten stehe, in uns durch den glauben angefangen werde.

Das der glaub den vorzug habe in der rechtfertigung, gleichwol gehöre 8. 410 auch die erneuerung und die liebe zu unser gerechtigkeit vor Gott, dergestalt, das sie wol nicht die vornemste ursach unserer gerechtigkeit, aber gleichwol unser gerechtigkeit vor Gott one solche liebe und erneuerung nicht gantz oder volkommen sey.

Das die gleubigen vor Gott gerechtfertiget werden und selig sein zugleich 9. 415 durch die zugerechnete gerechtigkeit Christi und durch den angefangenen neuen gehorsam oder zum teil durch die zurechnung der gerechtigkeit Christi, zum teil aber durch den angefangenen neuen gehorsam.

Das uns die verheissung der gnaden zugeeignet werde durch den glauben 10. im hertzen und durch die bekentnis, so mit dem munde geschicht, und durch 420 andere tugend.

Das der glaube nicht rechtfertige one die gute werck, also das die guten 11. | 2 werck notwendig zur gerechtigkeit erfordert, one derselben gegenwertigkeit der mensch nicht gerechtfertiget werden könne.

IIII. Von guten Wercken

425 Status Controversiae

Die Hauptfrage im streit von den guten Wercken

Uber der Lere von guten Wercken seind zweierley spaltungen in etlichen Kirchen entstanden:

Erstlich Haben sich etzliche Theologen uber nachfolgenden reden 1. 430 getrennet, da der eine teil geschrieben, gute Werck sind nötig zur seligkeit. Es

EPITOME – 1577   833

infusam, per virtutes et per opera, quae a charitate promanant, reipsa coram
Deo iustos fieri.

Fidem non respicere in solam Christi obedientiam, sed in divinam eius IIII.
naturam, quatenus videlicet ea in nobis habitet atque efficax sit, ut per eam
inhabitationem peccata nostra tegantur.

Fidem esse talem fiduciam in obedientiam Christi, quae possit in eo etiam V.
homine permanere et consistere, qui vera poenitentia careat et ubi charitas
non sequatur, sed qui contra conscientiam in peccatis perseveret.

Non ipsum Deum, sed tantum dona Dei in credentibus habitare.   VI.

Fidem ideo salutem nobis conferre, quod novitas illa, quae in dilectione VII.
erga Deum et proximum consistit, per fidem in nobis incoetur.

Fidem in iustificationis negocio primas quidem partes tenere, sed tamen VIII.
etiam renovationem et charitatem ad iusticiam nostram coram Deo pertinere,
ita ut renovatio et | charitas quidem non sint principalis causa nostrae iusti- 571
ciae, sed tamen iusticiam nostram coram Deo (si absint renovatio et charitas)
non esse integram et perfectam.

Credentes in Christum coram Deo iustos esse et salvos simul per imputa- IX.
tam Christi iusticiam et per inchoatam novam obedientiam, vel partim
quidem per imputationem iusticiae Christi, partim vero per inchoatam novam
obedientiam.

Promissionem gratiae nobis applicari per fidem in corde et praeterea X.
etiam per confessionem, quae ore fit, et per alias virtutes.

Fidem non iustificare sine bonis operibus, itaque bona opera necessario XI.
ad iusticiam requiri et absque eorum praesentia hominem iustificari non posse.

IIII. De bonis operibus.

Status controversiae.

In doctrina de bonis operibus duae controversiae in quibusdam Ecclesiis
ortae sunt.

Primum schisma inter Theologos quosdam factum est, cum alii assererent, I.
bona opera necessaria esse ad salutem; impossibile esse salvari sine bonis ope-

834 CONCILIUM SAXONICUM – 1577

ist unmüglich, one gute Werck selig zu werden. Item, es ist niemals jemand one gute werck selig worden. Der andere aber dagegen geschrieben: Gute Werck sind schedlich zur seligkeit.

Darnach Hat sich auch zwischen etzlichen Theologen uber den beiden 2.
435 worten 'Nötig' und 'Frey' eine trennung erhaben, da der eine teil gestritten, man sol das wort 'Nötig' nicht brauchen von dem neuen gehorsam, der nicht aus not und zwang, sondern aus freywilligem Geist herfliesse. Der ander teil Hat uber dem wort 'Nötig' gehalten, weil solcher gehorsam nicht in unser wilkühr stehe, sondern die widergebornen menschen schuldig sein, solchen
440 gehorsam zu leisten.

Aus welcher Disputation uber den worten nachmals ein streit von der sach an ir selbst sich zugetragen, Das der eine teil gestritten, Man solte gantz und gar unter den Christen das Gesetz nicht treiben, | sondern allein aus dem 237r
heiligen Evangelio die leute zu guten Wercken vermanen, Der ander hat es
445 widersprochen.

Affimativa

Reine Lere der Christlichen Kirchen von diesem streit

Zu gründtlicher erklerung und hinlegung dieser Zwispalt ist unser Lere, glauben und bekentnis:
450 Das gute Werck dem warhafftigen glauben, wann derselbige nicht ein 1.
todter, sondern ein lebendiger glaube ist, gewislich und ungezweiffelt folgen als früchte eines guten Baums.

Wir gleuben, leren und bekennen auch, das die gute Werck, gleich sowol 2.
wann von der seligkeit gefraget wird, als im Articfel der Rechtfertigung vor
455 Gott, gentzlichen ausgeschlossen werden sollen, wie der Apostel mit klaren worten bezeuget, do er also geschrieben: 'nach welcher weise auch David sagt, das die seligkeit sey allein des menschen, welchen Gott zurechnet die gerechtigkeit, one zuthun der wercke, do er spricht: Selig sind die, welchen ire ungerechtigkeit nicht zugerechnet wird', Rom. 4. Und abermals: 'Aus gnaden seit
460 ir selig worden. Gottes gabe ist es nicht aus den wercken auff das sich nicht jemands rhüme', Eph. 2.

Wir gleuben, leren und bekennen auch, das alle menschen, sonderlich 3.
aber, die durch den heiligen Geist widergeboren und erneuert, schuldig sein, gute Werck zu thun.

456/459 Rom. 4, 6 **459/461** Eph. 2, 8

EPITOME – 1577

ribus; et, neminem unquam sine bonis operibus salvatum esse. Alii vero doce-
420 rent: Bona opera ad salutem esse perniciosa.

Alterum schisma inter Theologos nonnullos super vocabulis 'necessa- II.
rium'et 'liberum' ortum est. Altera enim pars contendit, vocabulum 'necessarium' non esse usurpandum de nova obedientia; eam enim non a necessitate
quadam et coactione, sed a spontaneo spiritu promanare. | Altera vero pars 572
425 vocabulum 'necessarium' prorsus retinendum censuit, propterea quod illa obedientia non in nostro arbitrio posita et libera sit, sed homines renatos illud
obsequium debere praestare.
Et dum de commemoratis illis vocabulis disputatum est, tandem etiam de
reipsa fuit disceptatum. Alii enim contenderunt, legem apud Christianos pror-
430 sus non esse docendam, sed tantummodo doctrina Evangelii homines ad bona
opera invitandos esse. Alii hanc opinionem impugnarunt.

Affirmativa

Sincera Ecclesiae doctrina de hac controversia.

Ut hae controversiae solide et dextre explicentur atque decidantur, haec
435 nostra fides, doctrina et confessio est:
Quod bona opera veram fidem (si modo ea non sit mortua, sed viva fides) I.
certissime atque indubitato sequantur tanquam fructus bonae arboris.

Credimus etiam, docemus et confitemur, quod bona opera penitus exclu- II.
denda sint, non tantum cum de iustificatione fidei agitur, sed etiam cum de
440 salute nostra aeterna disputatur, sicut Apostolus perspicuis verbis testatur, cum
ait: *Sicut et David dicit beatitudinem hominis, cui Deus accepto fert iusticiam* Rom. 4.
sine operibus. Beati, quorum remissae sunt iniquitates, et quorum tecta sunt
peccata. Beatus vir, cui non imputavit Dominus peccatum etc. Et alibi: *Gratia,* Ephes. 2.
inquit, estis salvati per fidem et hoc non ex vobis; Dei enim donum est, non ex
445 *operibus, ne quis glorietur.*

Credimus, docemus et confitemur, omnes quidem homines, praecipue III.
vero eos, qui per Spiritum sanctum regenerati sunt et renovati, ad bona opera
facienda debitores esse.

836 CONCILIUM SAXONICUM – 1577

465 In welchem verstandt die wort 'Nötig', 'sollen' und 'müssen' recht und 4.
Christlich auch von den widergebornen gebraucht werden und keinesweges
dem vorbilde gesunder wort und reden zu wider sein.

Doch sol durch ermelt wort 'Neceßitas', 'necessarium', 'Not' und 'not- 5.
wendig', wann von den widergebornen geredet, nicht ein zwang, sondern
470 allein der schuldige gehorsam verstanden werden, welchen die rechtgleubigen, Rom
so viel sie widergeborn, nicht aus zwang | oder treiben des Gesetzes, sondern 237v
aus freiwilligem geiste leisten, 'weil sie nicht mehr unter dem Gesetze, sondern
unter der gnade sein'.

Demnach gleuben, leren und bekennen wir auch, wann gesagt wird, Die 6.
475 widergebornen thun gute werck aus einem freien Geist, das solches nicht
verstanden werden sol, als ob es in des widergebornen menschen wilkühr
stehe, gutes zu thun oder zu lassen, wann er wölle, und gleichwol den glauben
behalten müge, wann er in sünden vorsetzlich verharret.

Welches doch anderst nicht verstanden werden sol, dann wie es der Herr 7.
480 Christus und seine Apostel selbst erkleret, nemlich Von dem freigemachten
Geist, das er solches nicht thue aus furcht der straff wie ein Knecht, sondern
aus lieb der gerechtigkeit wie die Kinder, Rom. 8.

Wiewol diese freiwilligkeit in den auserwelten kindern Gottes nicht 8.
volkommen, sondern mit grosser schwacheit beladen sind, wie S. Paulus uber
485 sich selbst klaget, Rom. 7., Gal. 5.

Welche schwacheit doch der Herr seinen auserwelten nicht zurechnet, 9.
umb des Herrn Christi willen, wie geschrieben stehet: 'Es ist nun nichts
verdamlichs in denen, so in Christo Jesu sind', Rom. 8.

Wir gleuben, leren und bekennen auch, das den glauben und die seligkeit 10.
490 in uns nicht die werck, sondern allein der Geist Gottes durch den glauben
erhalte, des gegenwertigkeit und inwonung die guten werck zeugen sein.

Negativa

Falsche Gegenlere

Demnach verwerffen und verdammen wir diese weise zu reden, wann 1.
495 geleret und geschrieben wirdt, das gute werck nötig sein zur seligkeit. Item, das
niemand jemals one gute werck sey selig worden. Item, das es unmüglich sey,
one gute werck selig werden.

472/473 Rom. 6, 14   **480/482** Von – Kinder] Rom. 8, 14   **483/484** Wiewol –
sind] Rom. 7, 14-25; Gal. 5, 17   **487/488** Rom. 8, 1

EPITOME – 1577   837

| Et in hac sententia vocabula illa 'necessarium', 'debere', 'oportere' recte   IIII. | 573
usurpantur etiam de renatis hominibus et cum forma sanorum verborum non
pugnant.

    Sed tamen per vocabula 'necessitas', 'necessarium', quando videlicet de   V.
renatis est sermo, non intelligenda est coactio, sed tantum debita illa obedientia, quam vere credentes, quatenus renati sunt, non ex coactione aut compulsu   Rom. 7. 8.
legis, sed libero et spontaneo spiritu praestant: *quandoquidem non amplius sub*
lege sunt, sed sub gratia.

    Credimus igitur, docemus et confitemur, cum dicitur, renatos bene opera-   VI.
ri libero et spontaneo spiritu, id non ita accipiendum esse, quod in hominis
renati arbitrio relictum sit, bene aut male agere, quando ipsi visum fuerit, ut
nihilominus tamen fidem retineat, etiamsi in peccatis ex proposito perseveret.

    Hoc tamen non aliter quam de spiritu hominis iam liberato intelligen-   VII.
dum est, sicut hanc rem ipse Christus eiusque Apostoli declarant, quod videlicet spiritus hominis liberatus bene operetur, non formidine poenae ut servus,
sed iusticiae amore, qualem obedientiam filii praestare solent.

    Hanc vero libertatem spiritus in electis Dei filiis non perfectam, sed mul-   VIII.
tiplici infirmitate adhuc gravatam agnoscimus, quemadmodum D. Paulus   Rom. 7.
super ea re de sua ipsius persona conqueritur.   Galat. 5.

    Illam tamen infirmitatem Dominus electis suis non imputat, idque prop-   IX.
ter mediatorem Christum. Sic enim scriptum est: *Nihil iam damnationis est*   Rom. 8.
his, qui in Christo Iesu sunt.

    Credimus praeterea, docemus et confitemur, fidem et salutem in nobis   X.
conservari aut retineri non per opera, sed tantum per spiritum Dei et per
fidem (qua scilicet salus custoditur) bona autem opera testimonia esse, quod
Spiritus sanctus praesens sit atque in nobis habitet.

Negativa.   574

Falsa doctrina, superiori repugnans.

    Reiicimus igitur et damnamus subsequentes phrases, cum docetur, bona   I.
opera necessaria esse ad salutem; neminem unquam sine bonis operibus salvatum; impossibile esse, sine bonis operibus salvari.

CONCILIUM SAXONICUM – 1577

Wir verwerffen und verdammen diese blosse rede als ergerlich und 2.|2 Christlicher zucht nachteilig, wann geredet wird, gute werck sind schedlich
500 zur seligkeit. Dann besonder zu diesen letzten zeiten nicht weniger von nöten, die leute zu Christlicher zucht und guten wercken zu vermanen und zu erinnern, wie nötig es sey, das sie zu anzeigung ires glaubens und danckbarkeit bey Gott sich in guten wercken uben, als das die werck in den Artickel der Rechtfertigung nicht eingemenget werden, weil durch ein Epicurischen wahn vom
505 glauben die menschen sowol als durch das Papistisch und Phariseisch vertrauen auff eigene werck und verdienst verdammet werden können.

Wir verwerffen und verdammen auch, wann geleret wird, das der glaub 3. und einwonung des heiligen Geistes nicht durch mutwillige sünde verloren werden, sondern das die heiligen und auserwelten den heiligen Geist behalten,
510 wann sie gleich in Ehebruch und andere sünde fallen und darinnen verharren.

V. Vom Gesetz und Evangelio

Status Controversiae

Die Hauptfrage in dieser Zwispalt

Ob die Predigt des heiligen Evangelii eigentlich sey nicht allein ein
515 gnadenpredigt, die vergebung der sünden verkündiget, sondern auch eine bus und straffpredigt, welche den unglauben straffet, der im Gesetz nicht gestraffet, sondern allein durch das Evangelium gestraffet werde.

Affirmativa   238v

Reine lere Gottes Worts

520 Wir gleuben, leren und bekennen, das der unterscheid des Gesetzes und 1. Evangelii als ein besonder herrlich liecht mit grossem vleis in der Kirchen zu erhalten, dadurch das wort Gottes (nach der vermanung S. Pauli) recht geteilet wird.

---

522 nach – Pauli] cfr II Cor. 3, 7-9

---

504 Epicurischen wahn] an understanding of faith that evades the responsibility for one's own actions before God (in reference to the philosophy of Epicurus).

EPITOME – 1577

Repudiamus et damnamus nudam hanc offendiculi plenam et Christianae disciplinae perniciosam phrasin: Bona opera noxia esse ad salutem. His enim postremis temporibus non minus necessarium est, ut homines ad recte et pie vivendi rationem bonaque opera invitentur atque moneantur, quam necessarium sit, ut ad declarandam fidem atque gratitudinem suam erga Deum in bonis operibus sese exerceant: quam necessarium est cavere, ne bona opera negocio iustificationis admisceantur. Non minus enim homines Epicurea persuasione de fide, quam Pharisaica et Papistica fiducia in propria opera et merita damnationem incurrere possunt.

Praeterea reprobamus atque damnamus dogma illud, quod fides in Christum non amittatur et Spiritus sanctus nihilominus in homine habitet, etiamsi sciens volensque peccet, et quod sancti atque electi Spiritum sanctum retineant, tametsi in adulterium aut in alia scelera prolabantur et in iis perseverent.

V. De lege et Evangelio.

Status contoversiae.

Quaesitum fuit, an Evangelium proprie sit tantummodo concio de gratia Dei, quae remissionem peccatorum nobis annunciet, an vero etiam sit concio poenitentiae arguens peccatum incredulitatis, quippe quae non per legem, sed per Evangelion duntaxat arguatur.

Affirmativa.

Sincera doctrina cum norma verbi Dei congruens.

Credimus, docemus et confitemur discrimen Legis et Evangelii ut clarissimum quoddam lumen singulari diligentia in Ecclesia Dei retinendum esse, ut verbum Dei iuxta admonitionem D. Pauli recte secari queat.

840 CONCILIUM SAXONICUM – 1577

Wir gleuben, leren und bekennen, daß das Gesetz eigentlich sey eine 2.
525 Göttliche lere, welche leret, was recht und Gott gefellig und straffet alles, was
sünde und Gottes willen zuwider ist.

Darumb dann alles, was sünde straffet, ist und gehöret zur Predigt des 3.
Gesetzes.

Das Evangelium aber sey eigentlich eine solche lere, die da leret, was der 4.
530 mensch gleuben sol, der das Gesetz nicht gehalten und durch dasselbige
verdampt, nemlich das Christus alle sünde gebüsset und bezalet und ime one
allen seinen verdienst erlanget und erworben habe vergebung der sünden,
'gerechtigkeit, die vor Gott gilt', und das ewige leben.

Nachdem aber das wort 'Evangelium' nicht in einerley verstandt in heili- 5.
535 ger Schrifft gebraucht, daher dann diese Zwispalt ursprünglich entstanden, so
gleuben, leren und bekennen wir, wann durch das wort 'Evangelium' verstanden wirdt die gantze lere Christi, die er in seinem Lerampt, wie auch seine
Aposteln, gefüret (in welchem verstande es dann Marci 1. Actor. 20.
gebraucht), das recht geredet und geschrieben, das Evangelium sey eine
540 Predigt von der Busse und vergebung der sünden.

Wann aber das Gesetz und Evangelium wie auch Moses selbst ein Gesetz- 6.
lerer und Christus als ein Prediger des Evangeliums gegeneinander gehalten,
gleuben, leren und bekennen wir, daß das Evangelium nicht eine busse oder
straffpredigt, sondern eigentlich anders nichts dann eine trostpredigt und
545 fröliche botschafft sey, die nicht straffet noch schrecket, sondern wider das
schrecken des | Gesetzes die gewissen tröstet, allein auff den verdienst Christi 239r
weiset und mit der lieblichen Predig von der gnad und hulde Gottes, durch
Christus verdienst erlanget, wider auffrichtet.

Was dann die offenbarung der sünde belanget, weil die decke Moses allen 7.
550 menschen vor den augen henget, so lange sie die blosse Predigt des Gesetzes
und nichts von Christo hören und also ire sünde aus dem Gesetz nicht recht
lernen erkennen, sondern entweder vermessene heuchler werden, wie die Pha-
riseer, oder verzweiffeln wie Judas, so nimmet Christus das Gesetz in seine
hende und leget dasselbige geistlich aus, Matth. 5. Rom. 7. Und also wird
555 'Gottes zorn vom Himmel herab geoffenbaret' uber alle sünder wie gros
derselbe sey, dadurch sie in das Gesetz gewiesen werden und als dann aus demselben erst recht lernen ire sünde erkennen, welches erkentnis Mose nimmermehr aus inen hette erzwingen können. Demnach: obwol die Predigt vom

---

533 Rom. 1, 17   **538** Marci – Actor. 20] Marc. 1, 15; Act. 20, 24   **549/550** Was –
henget] II Cor. 3, 13-15   **554** Matth. – Rom. 7] Matth. 5, 17-48; Rom. 7, 7.14
555 Rom. 1, 18

EPITOME – 1577   841

505   Credimus, docemus et confitemur, legem esse proprie doctrinam divini- II.
tus revelatam, quae doceat, quid iustum Deoque gratum sit, quae etiam,
quicqid peccatum est, et voluntati divinae adversatur, redarguat.

    Quare, quicquid extat in sacris literis, quod peccata arguit, id revera ad III.
Legis concionem pertinet.

510   Evangelion vero proprie doctrinam esse censemus, quae doceat, quid IIII.
homo credere debeat, qui Legi Dei non satisfecit et idcirco per eandem dam-
natur, videlicet | quod illum credere oporteat Iesum Christum omnia peccata 576
expiasse atque pro iis satisfecisse et remissionem peccatorum, iusticiam coram
Deo consistentem et vitam aeternam, nullo interveniente peccatoris illius
515 merito, impetrasse.

    Cum autem vocabulum 'Evangelii' non semper in una eademque signi- V.
ficatione in sacra scriptura usurpetur, unde et dissensio illa primum orta est,
credimus, docemus et confitemur, si vocabulum 'Evangelii' de tota Christi
doctrina accipiatur, quam ipse in ministerio suo (quemadmodum et eius Apos-
520 toli) professus est (in qua significatione Marci 1. et Actor. 20. vox illa
usurpatur) recte dici et doceri Evangelium esse concionem de poenitentia et
remissione peccatorum.

    Quando vero Lex et Evangelion, sicut et ipse Moises ut doctor legis et VI.
Christus ut doctor Evangelii inter se conferuntur, credimus, docemus et confi-
525 temur, quod Evangelion non sit concio poenitentiae, arguens peccata, sed
quod proprie nihil aliud sit, quam laetissimum quoddam nuncium et concio
plena consolationis, non arguens aut terrens, quandoquidem conscientias contra terrores Legis solatur, easque in meritum solius Christi respicere iubet et
dulcissima praedicatione de gratia et favore Dei per meritum Christi impetra-
530 to rursus erigit.

    Quod vero ad revelationem peccati attinet, sic sese res habent. Velum VII.
illud Moisis omnium hominum oculis est obductum quamdiu solam Legis
concionem, nihil autem de Christo audiunt. Itaque peccata sua ex Lege non
vere agnoscunt, sed aut hypocritae fiunt, qui iusticiae propriae opinione
535 turgent, quales olim erant Pharisaei; aut in peccatis suis desperant, quod Iudas
proditor ille fecit. Eam ob causam Christus sumsit sibi legem explicandam Matth. 5.
spiritualiter et hoc modo *ira Dei de coelo revelatur* super omnes peccatores, ut Rom. 7.
vera legis sententia intellecta animadvertatur, quanta sit illa ira. Et sic demum
peccatores ad legem remissi, vere et recte peccata sua agnoscunt. Talem vero
540 pec|catorum agnitionem solus Moises nunquam ex ipsis extorquere potuisset. 577

    Etsi igitur concio illa de passione et morte Christi, filii Dei, severitatis et
terroris plena est, quae iram Dei adversus peccata ostendit, unde demum

842 CONCILIUM SAXONICUM – 1577

leiden und sterben Christi des Sons Gottes eine ernstliche und schreckliche
560 Predigt und anzeigen Gottes zorns ist, dadurch die leute erst recht in das
Gesetz gefüret, nachdem inen die decke Moses hinweg gethan, das sie erst
recht erkennen, wie grosse ding Gott im Gesetz von uns erfordert, deren wir
keines halten können und demnach alle unsere gerechtigkeit in Christo
suchen sollen.

565   Doch solang dies alles (nemlich Christus leiden und sterben) Gottes zorn   8.
prediget und den menschen schrecket, so ist es noch nicht des Evangelii
eigentliche Predigt, sondern Moses und des Gesetzes predigt und demnach
ein fremde werck Christi, dadurch er kömpt zu seinem eigenen Ampt, das ist:
gnade predigen, trösten und lebendig machen, welches eigentlich die predigt
570 des Evangelii ist.

Negativa

Gegenlere, so verworffen

Demnach verwerffen wir und halten es vor unrecht und schedlich, wann
geleret wird, daß das Evangelium eigentlich eine bus oder eine straffpredigt
575 und nicht allein eine gnadenpredigt sey, dadurch das Evangelium wi|derumb   239v
zu einer Gesetzlere gemacht, der verdienst Christi und heilige Schrifft
verdunckelt, die Christen des rechten trosts beraubet und dem Bapsthumb die
thür widerumb auffgethan wird.

VI. Vom dritten brauch des Gesetzes

Status Controversiae

580

Die Hauptfrage von diesem streit

Nachdem das Gesetz den menschen umb dreierley ursach willen gegeben:
Erstlich, das dadurch eusserliche zucht wider die wilden, ungehorsamen erhalten. Zum andern, das die menschen dardurch zu erkentnis irer sünden gefüret.
585 Zum dritten, nachdem sie widergeboren und gleichwol das fleisch inen anhanget, das sie, umb desselben willen, eine gewisse regel hetten, nach welcher sie ir
gantzes leben anstellen und regieren sollen, hat sich eine zwispalt zwischen
etzlichen wenigen Theologen uber dem dritten brauch des Gesetzes zugetragen, ob nemlich auch bey den widergebornen Christen solches zu treiben sey
590 oder nicht? Der eine teil hat Ja, der andere Nein gesagt.

EPITOME – 1577

homines ad legem Dei propius adducuntur, postquam velum illud Moisis
ablatum est, ut tandem exacte agnoscant, quanta videlicet Dominus in lege sua
a nobis exigat, quorum nihil nos praestare possumus, ita ut universam nostram
iusticiam in solo Christo quaerere oporteat.

Tamen quamdiu nobis Christi passio et mors iram Dei ob oculos ponunt VIII.
et hominem perterrefaciunt, tamdiu non sunt proprie concio Evangelii, sed
Legis et Moisis doctrina, et sunt alienum opus Christi, per quod accedit ad
proprium suum officium, quod est, praedicare de gratia Dei, consolari et vivificare. Haec propria sunt praedicationis Evangelicae.

Negativa.

Contraria et falsa doctrina, quae reiicitur.

Reiicimus igitur ut falsum et perniciosum dogma, cum asseritur, quod
Evangelion proprie sit concio poenitentiae, arguens, accusans et damnans
peccata, quodque non sit tantummodo concio de gratia Dei. Hac enim ratione
Evangelion rursum in legem transformatur, meritum Christi et sacrae literae
obscurantur, piis mentibus vera et solida consolatio eripitur et Pontificiis erro-
ribus et superstitionibus fores aperiuntur.

VI. De tertio usu legis. 578

Status controversiae.

Cum constet, legem Dei propter tres causas hominibus datam esse:
Primo, ut externa quaedam disciplina conservetur et feri atque intractrabiles
homines quasi repagulis quibusdam coerceantur, secundo, ut per legem homines ad agnitionem suorum peccatorum adducantur, tertio, ut homines iam
renati, quibus tamen omnibus multum adhuc carnis adhaeret, eam ipsam ob
causam certam aliquam regulam habeant, ad quam totam suam vitam formare
possint et debeant etc., orta est inter paucos quosdam Theologos controversia
super tertio usu Legis, videlicet an Lex etiam renatis inculcanda et eius obser-

844   CONCILIUM SAXONICUM – 1577

Affirmativa

Die rechte Christliche lere von diesem streit

Wir gleuben, leren und bekennen, obwol die rechtgleubige und warhaffti- 1.
ge zu Gott bekerte menschen vom fluch und zwang des Gesetzes durch Chris-
595 tum gefreiet und ledig gemacht, das sie doch der ursach nicht one | Gesetz 2401
sein, sondern darumb von dem Son Gottes erlöset worden, das sie sich in demselben tag und nacht uben sollen, Psalm. 119. Wie dann unser ersten Eltern Gene
auch vor dem fall nicht one Gesetz gelebet, welchen das Gesetz Gottes auch in 3.
das hertz geschrieben, da sie zum Ebenbild Gottes erschaffen worden.

600   Wir glauben, leren und bekennen, das die Predig des Gesetzes nicht allein 2.
bey den ungleubigen und unbusfertigen, sondern auch bey den rechtgleubigen, warhafftig bekerten, widergebornen und durch den Glauben gerechtfer-
tigten mit fleis zu treiben sey.

Dann ob sie wol widergeboren und in dem Geist ires gemüts verneuert, so 3.
605 ist doch solche widergeburt und erneuerung in dieser Welt nicht volkomen,
sondern nur angefangen, und stehen die gleubigen mit dem Geist ires gemüts Galat
in einem stetigen kampff wider das fleisch, das ist, wider die vorderbte natur Rom.
und art, so uns biss in Todt anhanget, umb welches alten Adams willen, so im
verstande, willen und allen krefften des menschen noch stecket, damit sie Rom.
610 nicht aus menschlicher andacht eigenwillige und erwelete Gottesdienst vorne-
men, ist von nöten, das inen das Gesetz des Herrn immer vorleuchte, desgleichen, das auch der alte Adam nicht sein eigen willen gebrauche, sondern wider
sein willen nicht allein durch vermanung und drauung des Gesetzes, sondern
auch mit den straffen und plagen gezwungen, das er dem Geist folge und sich
615 gefangen gebe, 1. Corinth. 9., Rom. 6., Galat. 6., Psal. 119., Heb. 13.

Was dann den unterscheid der wercken des Gesetzes und der früchten des 4.
Geistes belanget, glauben, leren und bekennen wir, das die werck, so nach dem
Gesetz geschehen, so lange werck des Gesetzes sein und genennet werden, so
lange sie allein durch treiben der straffen und drauung Gottes zorns aus den
620 menschen erzwungen werden.

593/597 Wir – Psalm. 119] Ps. 119, 1   **597/599** Wie – worden] Gen. 2, 16f; 3, 1-3.11
606/608 und – anhanget] Gal. 5, 17; Rom. 7, 21-23   **611** Gesetz – vorleuchte] Rom.
12, 1f   **615** 1. Corinth. 9 – Heb. 13.] I Cor. 9, 27; Rom. 6, 12f; Gal. 6, 12-14; Ps. 119
(Vulgata 118); Hebr. 13, 21

EPITOME – 1577

570 vatio apud eos urgenda sit an non. Alii urgendam legem censuerunt, alii negarunt.

Affirmativa.

Sincera et pia doctrina de hac controversia.

Credimus, docemus et confitemur, etsi vere in Christum credentes et
575 sincere ad Deum conversi a maledictione et coactione legis per Christum liberati sunt, quod ii tamen propterea non sint absque lege, quippe quos filius Dei
eam ob causam redemit, ut legem Dei diu noctuque meditentur atque in eius
observatione sese assidue ex|erceant. Etenim ne primi quidem nostri parentes
etiam ante lapsum prorsus sine lege vixerunt, quae certe cordibus ipsorum tum
580 inscripta erat, quia Dominus eos ad imaginem suam creaverat.

I.

Psal. 1. 119.

579 | Genes.
2. 3.

Credimus, docemus et confitemur concionem legis non modo apud eos,
qui fidem in Christum non habent et poenitentiam nondum agunt, sed etiam
apud eos, qui vere in Christum credunt, vere ad Deum conversi et renati et per
fidem iustificati sunt, sedulo urgendam esse.

II.

585 Etsi enim renati et spiritu mentis suae renovati sunt, tamen regeneratio
illa et renovatio in hac vita non est omnibus numeris absoluta, sed duntaxat
inchoata. Et credentes illi spiritu mentis suae perpetuo luctantur cum carne,
hoc est cum corrupta natura, quae in nobis ad mortem usque haeret. Et propter veterem Adamum, qui adhuc in hominis intellectu, voluntate et in omni-
590 bus viribus eius infixus resident, opus est, ut homini Lex Dei semper praeluceat,
ne quid privatae devotionis affectu in negocio Religionis confingat et cultus
divinos verbo Dei non institutos eligat. Item, ne vetus Adam pro suo ingenio
agat, sed potius contra suam voluntatem, non modo admonitionibus et minis
Legis, verum etiam poenis et plagis coerceatur, ut spiritui obsequatur seque
595 ipsi captivum tradat.

III.

Galat. 5
Rom. 7.

Rom. 12

1. Cor. 9
Rom. 6.
Galat. 6.
Psal. 119.
Heb. 13.

Iam quod ad discrimen operum legis et fructuum spiritus attinet, credimus, docemus et confitemur, quod opera illa, quae secundum praescriptum
legis fiunt, eatenus opera legis sint et appellentur, quatenus ea solummodo
urgendo et minis poenarum atque irae divinae ab homine extorquentur.

IIII.

846 CONCILIUM SAXONICUM – 1577

Früchte aber des Geistes seind die werck, welche der Geist Gottes, so in 5.
den gleubigen wohnet, wircket durch die widergebornen und von den gleubigen geschehen, soviel sie widergeboren sind, als wann sie von keinem gebot,
drauen oder belohnung wüsten, dergestalt dann die Kinder Gottes im Gesetz
625 leben und nach dem Gesetz Gottes wandeln, welches S. Paulus in sein Epis-
teln das Gesetz Christi und das Gesetz des gemüts nennet.[1]

Also ist und bleibet das Gesetz beides, bey den busfertigen und unbus- 6.|2
fertigen, bey widergebornen und nicht wiedergebornen Menschen, ein einiges
Gesetz, nemlich der unwandelbare wille Gottes; und ist der unterscheid, so
630 viel den gehorsam belanget, allein an dem menschen, do einer, so noch nicht
widergeboren, dem Gesetz aus zwang und unwillig (wie auch die widergebornen nach dem fleisch) thut, was von im erfordert, der gleubig aber one zwang
mit willigem Geist, soviel er neu geboren, thut, das keine drauunge des Gesetzes aus im nimmermehr erzwingen können.

635   Negativa

Falsche gegenlere

Demnach verwerffen wir als ein schedlichen, christlicher zucht und warhafftiger Gottseligkeit widerwertige Lere und Irthumb, wann geleret wird, daß
das Gesetz obgemelter weise und maß nicht bey den Christen und rechtgleu-
640 bigen, sondern allein bey den ungleubigen, unchristen und unbusfertigen
getrieben werden sol.

VII. Vom heiligen Abendmal Christi

Wiewol die Zwinglische Lerer nicht unter die Augspurgische
Confeßionsverwandte Theologen zu rechnen, als von denen sie sich gleich
645 domals, als solche Confeßion ubergeben worden, abgesondert: Jedoch weil sie
sich mit eindringen und iren Irthumb unter derselben Christlichen Confeßion namen auszubringen unterstehen, haben wir von dieser zwispalt auch not-
dürfftigen bericht thun wollen.

---

626 Gesetz[1] – gemüts] Rom. 7, 23; 8, 2

EPITOME – 1577

Fructus vero spiritus sunt opera illa, quae Spiritus Dei in credentibus V.
habitans per homines renatos operatur, et quae a credentibus fiunt, quatenus
renati sunt, ita quidem sponte ac libere, quasi nullum praeceptum unquam
accepissent, nullas minas audivissent nullamque remunerationem expectarent.
Et hoc modo filii Dei in lege vivunt et | secundum normam legis divinae vitam 580
suam instituunt; hanc vivendi rationem D. Paulus vocare solet in suis epistolis Rom. 7. 8.
legem Christi et legem mentis.

Ad hunc modum una eademque lex est manetque immota videlicet Dei VI.
voluntas sive poenitentibus sive impoenitentibus renatis aut non renatis
proponatur. Discrimen autem, quoad obedientiam, duntaxat in hominibus
est, quorum alii non renati legi obedientiam qualemcunque a lege requisitam
praestant, sed coacti et inviti id faciunt (sicut etiam renati faciunt, quatenus
adhuc carnales sunt); credentes vero in Christum, quatenus renati sunt, absque
coactione, libero et spontaneo spiritu talem obedientiam praestant, qualem
alias nullae quantumvis severissimae legis comminationes extorquere possent.

Negativa.

Falsae doctrinae reiectio.

Repudiamus itaque ut perniciosum et falsum dogma, quod Christianae
disciplinae et verae pietati adversatur, cum docetur, quod Lex Dei (eo modo,
quo supra dictum est) non sit piis et vere credentibus, sed tantum impiis,
infidelibus et non agentibus poenitentiam proponenda atque apud hos solo sit
urgenda.

VII. De coena Domini.

Etsi Cingliani doctores non in eorum Theologorum numero, qui Augustanam Confessionem agnoscunt et profitentur, habendi sunt, quippe qui tum,
cum illa Confessio exhibere|tur, ab eis secessionem fecerunt, tamen, cum nunc 581
sese in eorum coetum callide ingerant erroremque suum sub praetextu piae
illius confessionis, quam latissime spargere conentur, etiam de hac controversia
Ecclesiam Dei erudiendam iudicavimus.

Status Controversiae

650   Der Hauptstreit zwischen unser und der Sacramentirer Lere
in diesem Artickel

Ob in dem heiligen Abendmal der warhafftige Leib und Blut unsers Herrn Jhesu Christi warhafftig und wesentlich gegenwertig sey, mit Brot und Wein ausgeteilet und mit dem munde empfangen werde von allen denen, so 655 sich dieses Sacraments gebrauchen, sie sein wirdig oder unwirdig, from oder unfrom, gleubig oder ungleubig, den gleubigen zum trost und leben, den ungleubigen zum Gericht. Die Sacramentirer sagen Nein, wir sagen Ja.

Zu erklerung dieses streits ist anfenglich zu mercken, das zweyerley Sacramentirer seien: Etzliche sein grobe Sacramentirer, welche mit deutschen, 660 klaren worten vorgeben, wie sie im hertzen halten, das im heiligen Abendmal mehr nicht denn Brot und Wein gegenwertig sey, ausgeteilet und mit dem munde empfangen werde. Etzliche aber seind verschlagene und die aller schedlichste Sacramentirer, die zum teil mit unsern worten gantz scheinbar reden und vorgeben, sie gleuben auch eine warhafftige gegenwertigkeit des 665 warhafftigen, wesentlichen, lebendigen Leibs und Bluts Christi im heiligen Abendmal, doch solches geschehe geistlich durch den Glauben; Welche doch unter diesen scheinbaren worten eben die erste grobe meinung behalten, das nemlich nichts denn Brot und Wein im heiligen Abendmal gegenwertig sey und mit dem munde empfangen werde. Dann Geistlich heisset inen anders 670 nichts dann den Geist Christi oder die krafft des abwesenden Leibes Christi und sein verdienst, welcher gegenwertig sey. Der Leib Christi aber sey auff keinerley weise noch wege gegenwertig, sondern allein daroben im öbersten Himel, zu dem wir mit den gedancken unsers Glaubens in Himel uns erheben und doselbsten, aber gar nicht bey Brot und Wein des Abendmals, solchen 675 seinen Leib und Blut suchen sollen.

---

650 Der – Sacramentirer] Luther and his successors used the term 'Sakramentierer' for those who denied the real presence of Christ's body in the Lord's supper.

Status controversiae, quae est inter nos et Sacramentarios in hoc articulo.

Quaeritur, an in sacra Coena verum corpus et verus sanguis Domini nostri Iesu Christi vere et substantialiter sint praesentia atque cum pane et vino distribuantur et ore sumantur ab omnibus illis, qui hoc Sacramento utuntur, sive digni sint sive indigni, boni aut mali, fideles aut infideles, ita tamen, ut fideles e coena Domini consolationem et vitam percipiant, infideles autem eam ad iudicium sumant. Cingliani hanc praesentiam et dispensationem corporis et sanguinis Christi in sacra coena negant, nos vero eandem asseveramus.

Ad solidam huius controversiae explicationem primum sciendum est, duo esse Sacramentariorum genera. Quidam enim sunt Sacramentarii crassi admodum; hi perspicuis et claris verbis id aperte profitentur, quod corde sentiunt, quod videlicet in coena Domini nihil amplius quam panis et vinum sint praesentia ibique distribuantur et ore percipiantur. Alii autem sunt versuti et callidi et quidem omnium nocentissimi Sacramentarii; hi de negocio coenae Dominicae loquentes ex parte nostris verbis splendide admodum utuntur et prae se ferunt, quod et ipsi veram praesentiam veri, substantialis atque vivi corporis et sanguinis Christi in sacra Coena credant, eam tamen praesentiam et manducationem dicunt esse spiritualem, quae fiat fide. Et hi posteriores Sacramentarii sub his splendidis verbis eandem | crassam, quam priores habent, opinionem occultant et retinent, quod videlicet praeter panem et vinum nihil amplius in Coena Domini sit praesens et ore sumatur. Vocabulum enim 'spiritualiter' nihil aliud ipsis significat, quam spiritum Christi seu virtutem absentis corporis Christi eiusque meritum, quod praesens sit; ipsum vero Christi corpus nullo prorsus modo esse praesens, sed tantummodo id sursum in supremo coelo contineri sentiunt et affirmant oportere nos cogitationibus fidei sursum assurgere inque coelum ascendere et ibidem (nulla autem ratione cum pane et vino sacrae Coenae) illud corpus et sanguinem Christi quaerendum esse.

Affirmativa.

241v

Bekentnus reiner Leere vom heiligen Abendmal wider die Sacramentirer.

Wir gleuben, leren und bekennen, das im heiligen Abendmal der Leib 1. und Blut Christi warhafftig und wesentlich gegenwertig sey, mit Brot und
680 Wein warhafftig ausgeteilet und empfangen werde.

Wir gleuben, leren und bekennen, das die wort des Testaments Christi 2. nicht anders zu verstehen sein, dann wie sie nach dem buchstaben lauten, also das nicht das Brot den abwesenden Leib und der Wein das abwesende Blut Christi bedeute, sondern das es warhafftig umb Sacramentlicher einigkeit
685 willen der Leib und Blut Christi sey.

Was dann die Consecration belanget, gleuben, leren und bekennen wir, 3. das solche gegenwertigkeit des Leibs und Bluts Christi im heiligen Abendmal nicht schaffe einiges Menschen werck oder sprechen des dieners, sondern das solche einig und allein der Allmechtigen krafft unsers Herrn Jhesu Christi
690 zugeschrieben werden sol.

Darneben aber gleuben, leren und halten wir auch einhellig, das im 4. gebrauch des heiligen Abendmals die wort der einsatzung Christi keinesweges zu unterlassen, sondern offentlich gesprochen werden sollen, wie geschrieben stehet: 'Der gesegnete Kelch, den wir segnen' etc. 1. Corinth. 11. Welches
695 segnen durch das sprechen der wort Christi geschicht.

Die gründe aber, darauff wir in diesem handel stehen wider die Sacramen- 5. tirer, seind wie D. Luther solche in seinem grossen bekentnis gesetzt hat: 'Der erste ist dieser Artickel unsers Christlichen Glaubens: Jhesus Christus ist warhafftiger, wesentlicher, natürlicher, völliger Gott und Mensch in einer Person,
700 unzertrant und ungeteilet. | Der ander: Das Gottes rechte hand allenthalben 242r ist', zu welcher Christus nach seiner menschlichen natur mit der that und warheit gesetzet gegenwertig regiert, in seinen henden und unter seinen füssen hat alles, was im Himel und auff Erden ist, dahin sonst kein Mensch noch Engel, sondern allein Mariae Son gesetzet ist, doher er auch solches vermagk.
705 'Der dritte, Das Gottes wort nicht falsch ist oder lüge. Der vierdte, Das Gott mancherley weise hat und weis, etwa an einem orte zu sein und nicht allein die einige, welche die Philosophi Localem oder raumlich nennen.'

---

694 Der – 1. Corinth. 11.] I Cor. 10, 16; 11, 23-25

705/707 M. Luther, 'Vom Abendmahl Christi. Bekenntnis (1528)', in *WA* 26 (1909), p. 326, 32-p. 327, 20

EPITOME – 1577

Affirmativa.

Confessio sincerae doctrinae de Coena Domini contra Sacramentarios.

Credimus, docemus et confitemur, quod in Coena Domini corpus et I.
sanguis Christi vere et substantialiter sint praesentia et quod una cum pane et
vino vere distribuantur atque sumantur.

Credimus, docemus et confitemur verba Testamenti Christi non aliter II.
accipienda esse quam sicut verba ipsa ad literam sonant, ita ne panis absens
Christi corpus et vinum absentem Christi sanguinem significent, sed ut propter sacramentalem unionem panis et vinum vere sint corpus et sanguis Christi.

Iam quod ad Consecrationem attinet, credimus, docemus et confitemur, III.
quod nullum opus humanum neque ulla ministri Ecclesiae pronunciatio praesentiae corporis et sanguinis Christi in Coena causa sit, sed quod hoc soli
omnipotenti virtuti Domini nostri Iesu Christi sit tribuendum.

Interim tamen unanimi consensu credimus, docemus et confitemur, in IIII.
usu Coenae Dominicae verba institutionis Christi nequaquam omittenda, sed
publice recitanda esse, | sicut scriptum est: *Calix benedictionis, cui benedicimus,* 583
nonne communicatio sanguinis Christi est? etc. Illa autem benedictio fit, per
recitationem verborum Christi.

Fundamenta autem, quibus in hoc negocio conta Sacramentarios nitimur, V.
haec sunt, quae etiam D. Lutherus in maiore sua de Coena Domini confessione posuit: *Primum fundamentum est articulus fidei nostrae Christianae, vide-*
licet: Iesus Christus est verus, essentialis, naturalis, perfectus Deus et homo in
unitate personae, inseparabilis et indivisus. Secundum: quod Dextera Dei ubique
est, ad eam autem Christus ratione humanitatis suae vere et reipsa collocatus est,
ideoque praesens gubernat, in manu sua et sub pedibus suis, ut scriptura loquitur,
habet omnia, quae in coelo sunt et in terra. Ad eam Dei dexteram nullus alius
homo ac ne Angelus quidem, sed solus Mariae filius collocatus est, unde et ea,
quae diximus, praestare potest. Tertium: quod verbum Dei non est falsum aut
mendax. Quartum: quod Deus varios modos novit et in sua potestate habet,
quibus alicubi esse potest, neque ad unicum illum alligatus est, quem Philosophi
localem aut circumscriptum appellare solent.

852 CONCILIUM SAXONICUM – 1577

Wir gleuben, leren und bekennen, das der Leib und Blut Christi nicht 6.
allein geistlich durch den Glauben, sondern auch mündlich, doch nicht auff
710 Capernaitische, sondern ubernatürliche, himlische weise umb der Sacrament-
lichen vereinigung willen mit dem Brot und Wein empfangen werde, wie
solches die wort Christi klerlich ausweisen, do Christus heisset nemen, essen
und trincken, wie dann von den Aposteln geschehen, dann geschrieben stehet:
'Und sie truncken alle daraus'. Marc. 14. Desgleichen S. Paulus sagt: 'Das Brot,
715 das wir brechen, ist ein gemeinschafft des Leibes Christi', das ist: Wer dis Brot
isset, der isset den Leib Christi, welches auch einhellig die vornembste alte
Kirchenlerer, Chrisostomus, Cyprianus, Leo I., Gregorius, Ambrosius, Augustinus bezeugen.

Wir gleuben, leren und bekennen, das nicht allein die rechtgleubigen und 7.
720 wirdigen, sondern auch die unwirdigen und ungleubigen empfahen den wahr-
hafftigen Leib und Blut Christi, doch nicht zum leben und trost, sondern zum
Gericht und verdamnüs, wann sie sich nicht bekeren und busse thun. Dann ob 1 Cor.
sie wol Christum als ein Seligmacher von sich stosten, so müssen sie in doch
auch wider iren willen als einen strengen Richter zulassen, welcher so gegen-
725 wertig das Gericht auch in den unbussfertigen gesten ubet und erzeiget, als
gegenwertig er leben und trost in den hertzen der Rechtgleubigen und wirdigen geste wircket.

Wir gleuben, leren und bekennen auch, das nur einerley unwirdige geste 8.
seind, nemlich die nicht gleuben, von welchen geschrieben stehet: 'Wer aber Johan
730 nicht gleubet, der ist schon gerichtet.' Welches Gericht durch unwirdigen
brauch des heiligen Sacraments geheuffet, grösser und schwerer wird,
1. Corinth. 11.

Wir gleuben, leren und bekennen, das kein Rechtgleubiger, so lang er 9.|2.
den lebendigen Glauben behelt, wie schwach er auch sein möchte, das heilige
735 Abendmal zum Gericht empfahe, welches sonderlich den schwachgleubigen
doch bußfertigen Christen zum trost und sterckung ires schwachen glaubens
eingesetzet worden.

Wir gleuben, leren und bekennen, das alle wirdigkeit der Tischgeste 10.
dieser Himlischer malzeit sey und stehe allein in dem allerheiligsten gehorsam
740 und volkomenen verdienst Christi, welchen wir uns durch warhafftigen Glauben zueignen und des durch das Sacrament versichert werden und gar nicht in
unsern tügenden, innerlichen und eusserlichen bereitungen.

---

714 Marc. 14, 24   **714/715** I Cor. 10, 16   **719/722** nicht – thun] I Cor. 11, 23-29
729/730 Ioh. 3, 18

EPITOME – 1577

Credimus, docemus et confitemur corpus et sanguinem Christi non VI.
tantum spiritualiter per fidem, sed etiam ore, non tamen Capernaitice, sed
supernaturali et coelesti modo, ratione Sacramentalis unionis, cum pane et
vino sumi. Hoc enim verba Christi perspicue testantur, quibus praecipit acci-
pere, edere, bibere: idque ab Apostolis factum esse scriptura commemorat
dicens: *Et biberunt ex eo omnes.* Et Paulus inquit: *Panis, quem frangimus, est* Marc. 14. | I.
communicatio corporis Christi, hoc est: qui hunc panem edit, corpus Christi Cor. 10.
edit. Idem magno consensu praecipui ex antiquissimis Ecclesiae doctoribus,
Chrysostomus, Cyprianus, Leo primus, Gregorius, Ambrosius, Augustinus
testantur.

| Credimus, docemus et confitemur, quod non tantum vere in Christum VII. | 584
credentes et qui digne ad coenam Domini accedunt, verum etiam indigni et
infideles verum corpus et sanguinem Christi sumant, ita tamen, ut nec consolationem nec vitam inde percipiant, sed potius, ut illis sumptio ea ad iudicium
et damnationem cedat, si non convertantur et poenitentiam agant. Etsi enim
Christum ut Salvatorem a se repellunt, tamen eundem, licet maxime inviti, ut
severum iudicem admittere coguntur. Is vero non minus praesens iudicium
suum in convivis illis impoenitentibus exercet, quam praesens consolationem
et vitam in cordibus vere credentium et dignorum convivarum operatur.

Credimus, docemus et confitemur, unum tantum genus esse indignorum VIII.
convivarum: ii sunt soli illi, qui non credunt. De his scriptum est: *Qui non* Iohan. 3.
credit, iam iudicatus est. Et hoc iudicium indigno sacrae Coenae usu cumulatur 1. Cor. 11
et aggravatur.

Credimus, docemus et confitemur, quod nullus vere credentium, quam- IX.
diu vivam fidem retinet, sacram Domini coenam ad iudicium sumat, quan-
tacunque fidei imbecilitate laboret. Coena enim Domini inprimis propter
infirmos in fide, poenitentes tamen, instituta est, ut ex ea veram consolationem et imbecillis fidei suae confirmationem percipiant.

Credimus, docemus et confitemur totam dignitatem convivarum coelestis X.
huius Coenae in sola sacratissima obedientia et absolutissimo Christi merito
consistere. Illud autem nobis vera fide applicamus et de applicatione huius
meriti per Sacramentum certi reddimur atque in animis nostris confirmamur.
Nequaquam autem dignitas illa ex virtutibus nostris aut ex internis vel externis
nostris praeparationibus pendet.

Negativa

Widerwertige verdampte Lere der Sacramentirer

Dargegen verwerffen und verdammen wir einhellig alle nachfolgende irrige Artickel, so der jetzt gesetzten Lere, einfeltigem Glauben und bekentnüs vom Abendmal Christi entgegen und zuwider sein.

Die Bäpstische Transsubstantiation, do im Bapsthumb geleret wird, das Brot und Wein im heiligen Abendmal ir Substantz und natürlich wesen verlieren und also zu nicht werden, das es in den Leib Christi vorwandelt werde und allein die eusserliche gestalt bleibe. 1.

Die Bäpstische Opffermess für die Sünde der lebendigen und todten. 2.

Das den Leyen nur eine gestalt des Sacraments gegeben und wider die offenbare wort des Testaments Christi der Kelch inen vohrgehalten und seines Bluts beraubet werden. 3.

Wann geleret wird, das die wort des Testaments Christi nicht einfeltig verstanden oder geglaubet werden sollen, wie sie lauten, | sondern das es dunckele reden sein, deren verstand man erst an andern orten suchen müsse. 4. 243r

Das der Leib Christi im heiligen Abendmal nicht mündlich mit dem Brot, sondern allein Brot und Wein mit dem munde, der Leib Christi aber allein geistlich durch den Glauben empfangen werde. 5.

Das Brot und Wein im heiligen Abendmal nicht mehr dann kennzeichen sein, dadurch die Christen einander erkennen. 6.

Das Brot und Wein allein bedeutungen, gleichnüssen und anbildungen des weit abwesenden Leibs und Bluts Christi seien. 7.

Das Brot und Wein nicht mehr dann denckzeichen, siegel und pfandt sein, durch welche wir versichert, wann sich der Glaub uber sich in Himel schwinge, das er doselbsten so warhafftig des Leibs und Bluts Christi teilhafftig werde, so warhafftig wir im Abendmal Brot und Wein essen und trincken. 8.

Das die versicherung und bekrefftigung unsers Glaubens im heiligen Abendmal geschehe allein durch die eusserlichen Zeichen Brots und Weins und nicht durch den warhafftigen, kegenwertigen Leib und Blut Christi. 9.

Das im heiligen Abendmal allein die krafft, wirckung und verdienst des abwesenden Leibs und Bluts Christi ausgeteilet werde. 10.

Das der Leib Christi also im Himel beschlossen, das er auff keinerley weise zumal und zu einer zeit an vielen oder allen orten gegenwertig sein könne auff Erden, da sein heiliges Abendmal gehalten wird. 11.

EPITOME – 1577   855

Negativa.

Contrariae et damnatae Sacramentariorum doctrinae reiectio.

725   Reiicimus atque damnamus unanimi consensu omnes erroneos, quos iam recitabimus, articulos, ut qui commemoratae piae doctrinae, simplicitati fidei et sincerae confessioni de Coena Domini repugnant.

Papisticam Transsubstantiationem, cum videlicet in Papatu docetur I. panem et vinum in sacra Coena substantiam atque naturalem suam essentiam 730 amittere et ita annihilari atque elementa illa ita in Christi corpus transmutari, ut praeter externas species nihil de iis reliquum maneat.

Papisticum Missae sacrificium, quod pro peccatis vivorum et mortuorum II. offertur.

Sacrilegium, quo Laicis una tantum pars sacramenti datur, cum nimirum III. 735 contra expressa verba Testamenti Christi calice illis interdicitur atque ita sanguine Christi spoliantur.

Dogma, quo docetur, quod verba Testamenti Iesu Christi non simpliciter IIII. intelligenda et fide amplectenda sint, uti sonant; ea enim obscura esse ideoque verum eorum sensum ex aliis scripturae locis petendum esse.

740   Corpus Christi in sacra Coena non ore una cum pane sumi, sed tantum V. panem et vinum ore accipi, corpus vero Christi spiritualiter duntaxat, fide nimirum, sumi.

Panem et vinum in Coena Domini tantummodo symbola seu tesseras VI. esse, quibus Christiani mutuo sese agnoscant.

745   Panem et vinum tantum esse figuras, similitudines et typos corporis et VII. sanguinis Christi longissimo intervallo a nobis absentis.

Panem et vinum tantummodo signa memoriae conservandae gratia, instituta esse, quae sigillorum et pignorum rationem habeant, quibus nobis confirmetur, quod fides, | cum in coelum illa ascendit et evehitur, ibi tam vere 586 750 corporis et sanguinis Christi particeps fiat, quam vere nos in sacra coena panem manducamus et vinum bibimus.

Fidem nostram de salute certam reddi et confirmari in coena Domini non IX. nisi signis illis externis, pane et vino, nequaquam autem vere praesentibus vero corpore et sanguine Christi.

755   In sacra coena duntaxat virtutem, operationem et meritum absentis X. corporis et sanguinis Christi dispensari.

Christi corpus ita coelo inclusum esse, ut nullo prorsus modo simul XI. eodem tempore pluribus aut omnibus locis in terris praesens esse possit, ubi coena Domini celebratur.

856 CONCILIUM SAXONICUM – 1577

Das Christus die wesentliche gegenwertigkeit seines Leibes und Bluts im 12.
heiligen Abendmal nicht habe vorheissen noch leisten können, weil die Natur
780 und eigenschafft seiner angenommenen menschlichen Natur solches nicht
leiden noch zugeben könne.

Das Gott nach aller seiner Allmechtigkeit (welches erschrecklich zu 13.
hören) nicht vormöge zuverschaffen, das sein Leib auff eine zeit mehr dann an
einem ort wesentlich gegenwertig sey.

785 Das nicht die Allmechtige wort des Testaments Christi, sondern der 14. |
Glaube die gegenwertigkeit des Leibs und Bluts Christi im heiligen Abendmal
schaffe und mache.

Das die Gleubigen den Leib Christi nicht bey dem Brot und Wein des 15.
heiligen Abendmals suchen, sondern ire augen von dem Brot in Himel erhe-
790 ben und doselbst den Leib Christi suchen sollen.

Das die ungleubige unbußfertige Christen im heiligen Abendmal nicht 16.
den warhafftigen Leib und Blut Christi, sondern allein Brot und Wein empfangen.

Das die wirdigkeit der geste bey dieser Himlischen malzeit nicht allein im 17.
795 warhafftigen Glauben an Christum, sondern auch auff der menschen eusserlichen bereitung stehe.

Das auch die Rechtgleubigen, so einen warhafftigen, lebendigen, reinen 18.
Glauben an Christum haben und behalten, dis Sacrament zum Gericht empfangen künnen, darumb das sie im eusserlichen wandel noch unvolkomen
800 sind.

Das die eusserliche sichtbarn Element Brots und Weins im heiligen Sacra- 19.
ment sollen angebetet werden.

Desgleichen befehlen wir auch dem rechten Gericht Gottes alle fürwitzi- 20.
ge, spöttische, lesterlichen Fragen (so zucht halben nicht zu erzelen) und
805 reden, so auff grobe, fleischliche, Capernaitische und abscheuliche weise von
den ubernatürlichen Himlischen geheimnussen dieses Sacraments gantz
lesterlich und mit grossem ergernüs durch die Sacramentirer vorgebracht werden.

Wie wir dann hiermit das Capernaitische essen des Leibes Christi, als 21.
810 wann man sein fleisch mit Zeenen zureisse und wie andere speise verdauet,
welches die Sacramentirer wider das zeugnus ires gewissens uber all unser
vielfaltig bezeugen, uns mutwillig auffdringen und dergestalt unsere Lehr bey
iren Zuhörern verhasset machen, gentzlich verdammen und dargegen halten
und gleuben vermüge der einfeltigen wort des Testaments Christi, ein warhaff-
815 tig doch ubernatürlich Essen des Leibs Christi wie auch Trincken seines Bluts,
welches menschliche sinne unnd vernunfft nicht | begreiffen, sondern unsern 244r
verstand 'in den gehorsam Christi', wie in allen andern Artickeln des Glau-

EPITOME – 1577

760 Christum, substantialem corporis et sanguinis sui praesentiam neque XII. promittere neque exhibere potuisse, quando quidem id proprietas humanae ipsius naturae assumptae nequaquam ferre aut admittere possit.

Deum ne quidem universa sua omnipotentia (horrendum dictu et auditu) XIII. efficere posse, ut corpus Christi uno eodemque tempore in pluribus quam uno 765 tantum loco substantialiter praesens sit.

Non omnipotens illud verbum Testamenti Christi, sed fidem praesentiae XIIII. corporis et sanguinis Christi in sacra Coena causam esse.

Fideles corpus et sanguinem Christi non in pane et vino coena Domini- XV. cae quaerere, sed oculos in coelum attollere et ibi corpus Christi quaerere 770 debere.

Infideles et impoenitentes Christianos in Coena Domini non verum XVI. corpus et sanguinem Christi, sed panem tantum et vinum sumere.

Dignitatem convivarum in hac coelesti Coena non ex sola vera in Chris- XVII. tum fide, sed etiam ex praeparatione hominum externa pendere.

775 Eos etiam, qui veram et vivam in Christum fidem habent eamque XVIII. retinent, nihilominus hoc sacramentum ad iudicium sumere posse, propterea quod in externa sua conversatione adhuc imperfecti sint.

| Externa visibilia Elementa panis et vini in sacramento adoranda esse. XIX. | 587

Praeter haec iusto Dei iudicio relinquimus omnes curiosas, sannis virulen- XX. 780 tis tinctas et blasphemas quaestiones, quae honeste, pie et sine gravi offensione recitari nequeunt, aliosque sermones, quando de supernaturali et coelesti Mysterio huius sacramenti crasse, carnaliter, capernaitice et plane abominan- dis modis, blaspheme et maximo cum Ecclesia offendiculo Sacramentarii loquuntur.

785 Prorsus etiam reiicimus atque damnamus Capernaiticam manducationem XXI. corporis Christi, quam nobis Sacramentarii contra suae conscientiae testimo- nium post tot nostras protestationes malitiose affingunt, ut doctrinam nostram apud auditores suos in odium adducant, quasi videlicet doceamus, corpus Christi dentibus laniari et instar alterius cuiusdam cibi in corpore 790 humano digeri. Credimus autem et asserimus, secundum clara verba Testa- menti Christi, veram, sed supernaturalem manducationem corporis Christi, quemadmodum etiam vere, supernaturaliter tamen, sanguinem Christi bibi docemus. Haec autem humanis sensibus aut ratione nemo comprehendere

858 CONCILIUM SAXONICUM – 1577

bens, 'gefangen genommen', und solch geheimnis anders nicht dann allein mit Glauben gefast und im Wort geoffenbaret wird.

820 VIII. Von der Person Christi

Aus dem streit von dem heiligen Abendtmal ist zwischen den reinen Theologen Augspurgischer Confession und den Calvinisten (welche auch etliche andere Theologen irre gemacht) ein uneinigkeit entstanden von der Person Christi, von beiden Naturen in Christo und iren eigenschafften.

825 Status Controversiae

Hauptstreit in dieser Zwispalt

Die Hauptfrage aber ist gewesen, ob die Göttliche und Menschliche natur umb der Persönlichen voreinigung willen Realiter, das ist, mit that und warheit in der Person Christi, wie auch derselben eigenschafften, miteinander
830 gemeinschafft haben und wie weit sich solche gemeinschafft erstrecke? Die Sacramentirer haben vorgeben, die Göttliche und Menschliche Natur in Christo sein also persönlich voreiniget, das keine mit der andern Realiter, das ist, mit der that und warheit, was einer jeden Natur eigen ist, sondern mehr nicht dann allein den Namen gemein haben. Dann Unio, sagen sie schlecht,
835 facit communia nomina, das ist, | die Persönliche vereinigung machet mehr 244v nicht, dann die Namen gemein, das nemlich Gott mensch und mensch Gott genennet wird, doch also, das Gott nichts mit der Menscheit und die Menscheit nichts mit der Gottheit, derselben Maiestet und Eigenschafften Realiter, das ist, mit der that und warheit gemein habe. Das widerspiel hat Doctor
840 Luther, und die es mit ime gehalten, wider die Sacramentirer gestritten.

Affirmativa

Reine lere der Christlichen Kirchen von der Person Christi

Solchen streit zu erkleren und nach anleitung unsers Christlichen Glaubens hinzulegen, ist unser Leer, Glaub und Bekentnis wie folget.

---

818 II Cor. 10, 15

EPITOME – 1577

potest, quare in hoc negocio, sicut in aliis fidei articulis, *intellectum nostrum in*
obedientiam Christi captivare oportet. Hoc enim mysterium in solo Dei verbo
revelatur et sola fide comprehenditur.

VIII. DE PERSONA CHRISTI.

Ex controversia superiore de Coena Domini inter sinceros Theologos
Augustanae Confessionis et Calvinistas, qui alios etiam quosdam Theologos
perturbarunt, dissensio orta est de persona Christi, de duabus in Christo natu-
ris et de ipsarum proprietatibus.

Status controversiae.

Principalis huius dissidii quaestio fuit, an divina et humana natura et
utriusque proprietates propter unionem personalem realiter, hoc est vere et
reipsa in persona Christi invicem communicent et quosque illa communicatio
extendatur?

Sacramentarii affirmarunt, divinam et humanam naturas in Christo eo
modo personaliter unitas esse, ut neutra alteri quicquam realiter, hoc est vere
et reipsa, quod cuiusque naturae proprium sit, communicet, sed nomina
tantum nuda communicari. Unio (inquiunt illi) facit tantum nomina communia, ut videlicet Deus dicatur homo et homo Deus appelletur, ita tamen, ut
Deus nihil cum humanitate commune habeat, et vicissim humanitas nihil cum
divinitate, quoad ipsius Maiestatem et proprietates, realiter, hoc est, revera et
reipsa, commune habeat. Contrariam vero huic dogmati sententiam D. Lutherus et qui cum ipso faciunt adversus Sacramentarios propugnarunt.

Affirmativa.

Sincera doctrina Ecclesiae Dei de persona Christi.

Ad explicandam hanc controversiam et iuxta analogiam fidei nostrae
Christianae decidendam, fidem, doctrinam et confessionem nostram piam
perspicue profitemur, videlicet:

860   CONCILIUM SAXONICUM – 1577

845   Das die Göttliche und Menschliche natur in Christo persönlich vereini- 1.
get, also das nicht zwene Christus, einer Gottes, der ander des Menschen Son,
sondern ein einiger Son Gottes und des Menschen Son sey, Luc. 1. Rom. 9.
       Wir gleuben, leren und bekennen, das die Göttliche und Menschliche 2.
Natur nicht in ein wesen vermenget, keine in die andere verwandelt, sondern
850 ein jede ire wesentliche eigenschafften behalte, welche der andern Natur eigenschafften nimmermehr werden.
       Die eigenschafft Göttlicher Natur sind: allmechtig, ewig, unendtlich 3.
nach eigenschafft der Natur und ires natürlichen wesens vor sich selbst allenthalben gegenwertig sein, alles wissen etc., welche der Menschlichen natur
855 eigenschafften nimmermehr werden.
       Die eigenschafften Menschlicher natur seind: ein leiblich Geschöpff oder 4.
Creatur sein, Fleisch und Blut sein, endtlich und umbschrieben sein, leiden,
sterben, auff- und niderfahren, von einem ort zum andern sich bewegen, hun-
ger, durst, frost, hitz leiden und dergleichen, welche der Göttlichen Natur
860 eigenschafft nimmermehr werden.
       Nachdem beide Naturen persönlich, das ist, in einer Person voreiniget, 5. | 2.
gleuben, leren und bekennen wir, das diese voreinigung nicht eine solche ver-
knüpffung und verbindung sey, das kein Natur mit der andern persönlich, das
ist, umb der persönlichen voreinigung willen etwas gemein haben sol, als
865 wann einer zwey breter zusammen leimet, do keines dem andern etwas gibet
oder von dem andern nimmet, sondern hie ist die höchste gemeinschafft,
welche Gott mit dem Menschen warhafftig hat, aus welcher persönlichen
voreinigung und der daraus erfolgenden höchsten und unaussprechlichen
gemeinschafft alles herfleust, was Menschlich von Gott und Göttlich vom
870 Menschen Christo gesaget und gegleubet wird, wie solche voreinigung und
gemeinschafft der Naturen die alten Kirchenlerer durch die gleichnis eines
feurigen Eysens wie auch der vereinigung Leibes und der Seelen im Menschen
erkleret haben.
       Daher gleuben, leren und bekennen wir, das Gott Mensch und Mensch 6.
875 Gott sey, welches nicht sein köndte, wann die Göttliche und Menschliche
natur allerdings keine gemeinschafft in that und warheit miteinander hetten.
Dann wie köndte der Mensch, Marien Son, Gott oder Gottes des allerhöchsten Son mit warheit genennet werden oder sein, wann seine Menscheit mit
Gottes Son nicht personlich vereiniget und also Realiter, das ist, mit der that
880 und warheit nichts, sondern nur den Namen Gottes mit im gemein hette.
       Daher gleuben, leren und bekennen wir, das Maria nicht ein blossen pur- 7.
lautern Menschen, sondern den warhafftigen Son Gottes empfangen und

---

845/847 die – Rom. 9.] Luc. 1, 31-35; Rom. 9, 5

EPITOME – 1577   861

Quod divina et humana natura in Christo personaliter unitae sint, ita I. | Luc. I.
prorsus, ut non sint duo Christi, unus filius Dei, alter filius hominis, sed ut Rom. 9.
unus et idem sit Dei et hominis filius.

Credimus, docemus et confitemur, divinam et humanam naturas non in II.
unam substantiam commixtas, nec unam in alteram mutatam esse, sed utram-
que naturam retinere suas proprietates essentiales, ut quae alterius naturae
proprietates fieri nequeant.

Proprietates divinae naturae sunt esse omnipotentem, aeternam, infini- III.
tam et secundum naturae naturalisque suae essentiae proprietatem, per se,
ubique praesentem esse, omnia novisse etc. Haec omnia neque sunt, neque
unquam fiunt humanae naturae proprietates.

Humanae autem naturae proprietates sunt: corpoream esse creaturam, IIII.
constare carne et sanguine, esse finitam et circumscriptam, pati, mori, ascende-
re, descendere, de loco ad locum moveri, esurire, sitire, algere, aestu affligi et si
quae sunt similia. Haec neque sunt, neque unquam fiunt proprietates divinae
naturae.

Cum vero divina et humana naturae personaliter, hoc est, ad constituen- V.
dum unum ὑφιστάμενον, sint unitae, credimus, docemus et confitemur, unionem illam hypostaticam non esse talem copulationem aut combinationem,
cuius ratione neutra natura cum altera personaliter, hoc est, pro|pter unionem 590
personalem, quicquam commune habeat, qualis combinatio fit, cum duo asse-
res conglutinantur, ubi neuter alteri quicquam confert aut aliquid ab altero
accipit. Quin potius hic summa communio est, quam Deus cum assumto
homine vere habet, et ex personali unione et summa ac ineffabili communione, quae inde consequitur, totum illud promanat, quicquid humani de Deo, et
quicquid divini de homine Christo dicitur et creditur. Et hanc unionem atque
communionem naturarum antiquissimi Ecclesiae Doctores similitudine ferri
candentis itemque unione corporis et animae in homine declararunt.

Hinc etiam credimus, docemus atque confitemur, quod Deus sit homo et VI.
homo sit Deus, id quod nequaquam ita se haberet, si divina et humana natura
prorsus inter se nihil revera et reipsa communicarent. Quomodo enim homo,
Mariae filius, Deus aut filius Dei altissimi vere appellari posset aut esset, si
ipsius humanitas cum filio Dei non esset personaliter unita atque ita realiter,
hoc est, vere et reipsa, nihil prorsus, excepto solo nudo nomine, cum ipso commune haberet?

862 CONCILIUM SAXONICUM – 1577

geboren habe, darumb sie auch recht die Mutter Gottes genennet wird und auch warhafftig ist.

885 Daher gleuben, leren und bekennen wir auch, das nicht ein purlauter 8. Mensch für uns gelidten, gestorben, begraben, gen Helle gefahren, von Todten erstanden, gen Himel gefahren und gesetzt zur Maiestet und Allmechtigen krafft Gottes, sondern ein solcher Mensch des menschliche Natur mit dem Son Gottes so eine tieffe, unaussprechliche vereinigung und gemeinschafft hat, 890 das sie mit im ein Person ist.

Darumb warhafftig der Son Gottes vor uns gelidten, doch nach eigen- 9. schafft der Menschlichen Natur, welche er in einigkeit seiner Göttlichen Person angenomen und im eigen gemacht, das er leiden und unser hoher Priester zu unserer versünung mit Gott sein köndte, | wie geschrieben stehet: 245ᵛ 895 Sie haben 'den Herren der herrligkeit gecreutziget', und: 'mit Gottes Blut seind wir erlöset worden', 1. Cor. 2., Actor. 20.

Daher gleuben, leren und bekennen wir, das des Menschen Son zur Rech- 10. ten der Allmechtigen Maiestet und Krafft Gottes Realiter, das ist, mit der that und warheit nach der Menschlichen natur erhöhet, weil er in Gott auffgeno- 900 men, als er von dem heiligen Geist in Mutterleib empfangen und sein Mensch- liche natur mit dem Son des allerhöchsten persönlich vereiniget.

Welche Maiestet er nach der persönlichen vereinigung allwegen gehabt 11. und sich doch derselben im standt seiner ernidrigung geeussert und der ursach warhafftig 'an aller weisheit und gnad bey Gott und den Menschen zugeno- 905 men', darumb er solche Maiestet nicht allezeit, sondern wann es ime gefallen erzeiget, biß er die Knechtsgestalt, und nicht die Natur nach seiner Aufferste- Phil. hung gantz und gar hingeleget und in den völligen gebrauch, offenbarung und erweisung der Göttlichen Maiestet gesetzet und also in sein herrligkeit eingan- gen, das er itzt nicht allein als Gott, sondern auch als Mensch alles weis, alles 910 vermag, allen Creaturen gegenwertig ist und alles was im Himel, auff Erden und unter der Erden ist, unter seinen füssen und in seinen henden hat, wie er selbst zeuget: 'Mir ist geben aller gewalt im Himel und auff Erden.' Und Ephe S. Paulus: Er ist 'uber alle Himel' gefahren, 'auff das er alles erfüllete', welchen seinen gewalt er allenthalben gegenwertig uben kan und im alles müglich und 915 alles wissendt ist.

Daher er auch vermag und im gantz leicht ist, sein warhafftigen Leib und 12. Blut im heiligen Abendmal gegenwertig mitzuteilen, nicht nach art oder

---

895 I Cor. 2, 8 895/896 Act. 20, 28 904 Luc. 2, 52 906 Knechtsgestalt] Phil. 2, 7 911 in – hat] Ioh. 13, 3 912 Matth. 28, 18 913 Eph. 4, 10

EPITOME – 1577

Eam ob causam credimus, docemus et confitemur, quod virgo Maria non nudum aut merum hominem duntaxat, sed verum Dei filium conceperit et genuerit: unde recte Mater Dei et appellatur et revera est. VII.

Inde porro credimus, docemus et confitemur, quod non nudus homo tantum pro nobis passus, mortuus et sepultus sit, ad inferos descenderit, a mortuis resurrexerit, ad coelos ascenderit et ad Maiestatem et Omnipotentem Dei virtutem evectus fuerit, sed talis homo, cuius humana natura cum filio Dei tam arctam ineffabilemque unionem et communicationem habet, ut cum eo una sit facta persona. VIII.

Quapropter vere filius Dei pro nobis est passus, sed secundum proprietatem humanae naturae, quam in unitatem divinae suae personae assumsit sibique eam propriam fecit, ut videlicet pati et Pontifex noster summus reconciliationis nostrae cum Deo causa esse posset. Sic enim scriptum est: | *Dominum gloriae crucifixerunt*. Et: *sanguine Dei redempti sumus*. IX.

591 | 1. Cor. 2.
Actor. 20.

Ex eodem etiam fundamento credimus, docemus et confitemur, filium hominis ad dextram omnipotentis Maiestatis et virtutis Dei realiter, hoc est, vere et reipsa, secundum humanam suam naturam esse exaltatum, cum homo ille in Deum assumtus fuerit, quam primum in utero matris a Spiritu sancto est conceptus eiusque humanitas iam tum cum filio Dei altissimi personaliter fuerit unita. X.

Eamque Maiestatem ratione unionis personalis semper Christus habuit, sed in statu suae humiliationis sese exinanivit, qua de causa revera aetate, sapientia et gratia apud Deum atque homines profecit. Quare Maiestatem illam non semper, sed quoties ipsi visum fuit, exeruit, donec formam servi, non autem naturam humanam, post resurrectionem plene et prorsus deponeret et in plenariam usurpationem, manifestationem et declarationem divinae maiestatis collocaretur et hoc modo in gloriam suam ingrederetur. Itaque iam non tantum ut Deus, verum etiam ut homo omnia novit, omnia potest, omnibus creaturis praesens est et omnia, quae in coelis, in terris et sub terra sunt, sub pedibus suis et in manu sua habet. Haec ita se habere, Christus ipse testatur, inquiens: *Mihi data est omnis potestas in coelo et in terra*. Et Paulus ait: *Ascendit super omnes coelos, ut omnia impleat*. Hanc suam potestatem ubique praesens exercere potest, neque quicquam illi aut impossibile est aut ignotum. XI.

Iohan. 13.

Matth. 28.
Ephes. 4.

Inde adeo et quidem facilime, corpus suum verum et sanguinem suum in sacra Coena praesens distribuere potest. Id vero non sit secundum modum et XII.

864   CONCILIUM SAXONICUM – 1577

eigenschafft der Menschlichen natur, sondern nach art und eigenschafft Göttlicher rechte, saget Doctor Luther aus unserem Christlichen Kinderglauben,
920 welche gegenwertigkeit nicht Irdisch, noch Capernaitanisch, gleichwol warhafftig und wesentlich ist, wie die wort seines Testaments lauten: 'Das ist, ist,
ist mein Leib' etc.

Durch diese unser Lere, Glauben und bekentnis wird die Person Christi
nicht getrennet, wie Nestorius gethan (welcher die Communicationem Idio-
925 matum, das ist, die warhafftige gemeinschafft der | eigenschafften beider natu-   246*
ren in Christo geleugnet und also die person getrennet, wie solches Lutherus
im Buch von den Conciliis erkleret), noch die naturen sampt iren eigenschafften miteinander in ein wesen vermischet, wie Eutyches geirret, noch die
menschliche natur in der person Christi verleugnet oder abgetilget wird, auch
930 keine natur in die ander verwandelt, sondern Christus ist und bleibet in alle   1. Tir
ewigkeit Gott und Mensch in einer unzertrenten Person, welches nach der
heiligen Dreifaltigkeit das höchste geheimnis ist, wie der Apostel zeuget, in
welchem unser einiger trost leben und seligkeit stehet.

Negativa

935   Widerwertige falsche lere von der Person Christi

Demnach vorwerffen und vordammen wir als Gottes wort und unserm
einfeltigen Christlichem Glauben zuwider alle nachfolgende irrige Artickel,
wann geleret wird:

921/922 Matth. 26, 26; Marc. 14, 22; Luc. 22, 19; I Cor. 11, 24   **930/932** sondern –
zeuget] I Tim. 3, 16

---

919 Doctor Luther] cfr M. Luther, 'Vom Abendmahl Christi. Bekenntnis (1528)', in
WA 26 (1909), p. 326, 29-p. 327, 20; 'Daß diese Worte Christi "Das ist mein Leib" noch
fest stehen wider die Schwarmgeister (1527)', in *WA* 23 (1901), p. 133, 19-p. 134, 11
924 Nestorius] († after 451), from Antioch, was the Patriarch of Constantinople. He
rejected the term 'God-bearer' for Mary and emphasized the human nature of Christ.
He therefore preferred to call her 'Christ-bearer'. The Council of Ephesus condemned
Nestorius in the year 431   **927** Conciliis] cfr M. Luther, 'Von den Konziliis und
Kirchen (1539)', in *WA* 50 (1914), 587, 29-591, 8   **928** Eutyches] in contrast to the
Antiochian school, Eutyches († after 454), Archimandrite of Constantinople and
advocate of the Alexandrian school, supported a unification of the natures in Christ
that included the divinisation of Christ's body. The resulting 'Eutychian controversy'
culminated in the terms of the Council of Chalcedon in the year 451. It defined the
relation between the divine and the human nature in Christ as 'inconfusedly',
'unchangeably', 'indivisibly' and 'inseparably'.

EPITOME – 1577

proprietatem humanae naturae, sed secundum modum et proprietatem dextrae Dei, ut Lutherus secundum analogiam fidei nostrae Christianae in Catechesi comprehensae loqui solet. Et haec Christi in sacra Coena praesentia neque physica aut terrena est neque Capernaitica, interim tamen verissima et quidem sub|stantialis est. Sic enim verba Testamenti Christi sonant: Hoc est, est, est corpus meum etc.

Hac nostra fide, doctrina et confessione persona Christi non solvitur, quod olim Nestorius fecit. Is enim veram communicationem Idiomatum seu proprietatum utriusque naturae in Christo negavit et hac ratione Christi personam solvit, quam rem D. Lutherus in libello suo de Conciliis perspicue declaravit. Neque hac pia nostra doctrina duae in Christo naturae earumque proprietates confunduntur aut in unam essentiam commiscentur (in quo errore Eutyches fuit), neque humana natura in persona Christi negatur aut aboletur, neque altera natura in alteram mutatur. Sed Christus verus Deus et homo in una indivisa persona est permanetque in omnem aeternitatem. Hoc post illud Trinitatis summum est mysterium, ut Apostolus testatur: in quo solo tota nostra consolatio, vita et salus posita est.

Negativa.

Contrariae et falsae doctrinae de persona Christi reiectio.

Repudiamus igitur atque damnamus omnes erroneos, quos iam recitabimus, articulos, eo quod verbo Dei et sincerae fidei nostrae Christianae repugnent, cum videlicet sequentes errores docentur:

866 CONCILIUM SAXONICUM – 1577

Das Gott und Mensch in Christo nicht eine Person, sondern ein anderer 1.
940 Gottes und ein anderer des menschen Son sey, wie Nestorius narret.

Das die Göttliche und menschliche natur miteinander in ein wesen 2.
vermischet und die menschliche natur in die Gottheit verwandelt, wie Eutyches geschwermet.

Das Christus nicht warhafftiger, natürlicher, ewiger Gott sey, wie Arrius 3.
945 gehalten.

Das Christus nicht eine warhafftige menschliche natur gehabt von Leib 4.
und Seel, wie Marcion gedichtet hat.

Quod unio personalis faciat tantum communia nomina, das ist, Das die 5.
persönliche vereinigung mache allein die Titel und Namen gemein.

950   Das es nur ein 'phrasis' und 'modus loquendi', das ist, nur wort und eine 6. | 2.
weise zu reden sey, wann man saget: Gott ist mensch, mensch ist Gott, dann
die Gottheit habe nichts mit der menscheit wie auch die menscheit nichts mit
der Gottheit Realiter, das ist, mit der that, gemein.

Das es nur 'Communicatio verbalis', das ist, nichts dann wort sey, wann 7.
955 gesaget wird: Gottes Son sey für der Welt Sünde gestorben, des Menschen
Son sey allmechtig worden.

Das die menschliche natur in Christo auff solche weise wie die Gottheit 8.
ein unendtlich wesen worden und aus solcher wesentlicher, mitgeteilter, in die
menschliche natur ausgegossen und von Gott abgesonderte krafft und eigen-
960 schafft auff solche weise wie die Göttliche natur allenthalben gegenwertig sey.

Das die menschliche natur der Göttlichen natur an irer substantz und 9.
wesen oder an derselben wesentlichen eigenschafften exaequiret und gleich
worden sey.

Das die menschliche natur Christi in alle ort des Himels und der Erden 10.
965 raumlich ausgespannet, welches auch der Göttlichen natur nicht zugemessen
werden soll.

Das Christo unmüglich sey von wegen der eigenschafft menschlicher 11.
natur, das er zumal mehr dann an einem ort sein köndte.

---

944 Arrius] († 336) taught that the Logos (the 'word' in terms of Ioh. 1, 1 seq. 14) was
a Creation of God and totally dissimilar and different to his essence. From this the
Arian dispute developed, which the First Ecumenical Council of 325 tried to mediate.
The *Creed* that was ratified in Nicaea excluded Arianism and was confirmed by the
Second Ecumenical Council of Constantinople (381)   **947** Marcion] was associated
with the Gnosis and lived in the middle of the second century. His dualistic teaching
led to the assumption of two gods and to a devaluation of the Old Testament, which
testified the adversary of God, the demiurge. Opposing him was the good God, who
sent Christ equipped with an illusory body to redeem the world

EPITOME – 1577

Quod Deus et homo in Christo non constituant unam personam, sed quod alius sit Dei filius et alius hominis filius, ut Nestorius deliravit. I.

Quod divina et humana naturae in unam essentiam commixtae sint et humana natura in Deitatem mutata sit, ut Eutyches furenter dixit. II.

Quod Christus non sit verus, naturalis et aeternus Deus, ut Arius blasphemavit. III.

| Quod Christus non veram humanam naturam anima rationali et corpore constantem habuerit, ut Marcion finxit. IIII. | 593

Quod unio personalis faciat tantum communia nomina et communes titulos. V.

Quod phrasis tantum et modus quidam loquendi sit, cum dicitur: Deus est homo et homo est Deus; siquidem divinitas nihil cum humanitate et humanitas nihil cum deitate realiter, hoc est vere et reipsa, commune habeat. VI.

Quod tantum sit verbalis sine re ipsa Idiomatum communicatio, cum dicitur, filium Dei pro peccatis mundi mortuum esse, filium hominis omnipotentem factum esse. VII.

Quod humana in Christo natura eo modo, quo est divinitas, facta sit essentia quaedam infinita, et ex hac essentiali, communicata, in humanam naturam effusa et a Deo separata virtute et proprietate eo modo, quo divina natura, ubique praesens sit. VIII.

Quod humana natura divinae ratione substantiae atque essentiae suae vel proprietatum divinarum essentialium exaequata sit. IX.

Quod humana natura in Christo in omnia loca coeli et terrae localiter expansa sit, quod ne quidem divinae naturae est tribuendum. X.

868 CONCILIUM SAXONICUM – 1577

Das allein die blosse Menscheit für uns gelidten und uns erlöset habe und 12.
970 das der Son Gottes im leiden mit derselben keine gemeinschafft mit der that
gehabt, als wann es in nichts angangen hette.

Das Christus allein nach seiner Gottheit bey uns auff Erden, im wort, 13.
Sacramenten und allen unsern nöten gegenwertig sey und solche gegenwertigkeit seine menschliche natur gantz und gar nichts angehe, nach welcher er
975 auch mit uns auff Erden, nachdem er uns durch sein leiden und sterben erlöset, nicht mehr zuschaffen habe.

Das der Son Gottes, so die menschlich natur angenommen, nachdem er 14.
Knechtsgestalt abgeleget, nicht alle werck seiner Allmechtigkeit in, durch und
mit seiner menschlichen natur verrichte, sondern nur etzliche und allein an
980 dem ort, da die menschliche natur raumlich sey.

Das er nach der menschlichen natur der Allmechtigkeit und anderer 15.|
eigenschafften Göttlicher natur allerding nicht vehig sey wider den aus-
gedruckten Spruch Christi: 'Mir ist gegeben aller gewalt im Himel und auff Matt
Erden.' Und S. Paulus: 'In im wonet alle fülle der Gottheit leibhafftig',
985 Colos. 2.

Das im grössere gewalt im Himmel und auff Erden gegeben, nemlich 16.
grösser und mehr dann allen Engeln und andern Creaturen, aber mit der
Allmechtigkeit Gottes habe er keine gemeinschafft, sey im auch dieselbige
nicht gegeben. Daher sie ein Mediam potentiam, das ist, ein solche gewalt
990 zwischen Gottes Allmechtigen gewalt und andern Creaturen gewalt tichten,
die Christo nach seiner menscheit durch die erhöhung gegeben, die weniger
denn Gottes Allmechtige gewalt und grösser dann anderer Creaturen gewalt
sey.

Das Christus nach seinem menschlichen Geist ein gewisse mas habe, 17.
995 wieviel er wissen sol, und das er nicht mehr wisse, dann im gebüret und von
nöten sey zu seinem Richterampt zu wissen.

Das Christus noch nicht vollkommene erkentnis Gottes und aller seiner 18.
werck habe, von dem doch geschrieben stehet, Das in im 'alle schetze der weis- Col.
heit und des erkentnis verborgen' seien.

1000 Das Christo nach seinem menschlichen Geist unmüglich sey zu wissen, 19.
was von ewigkeit gewesen, was jetzunder allenthalben geschehe und noch in
ewigkeit sein werde.

983/984 Matth. 28, 18   **984** Col. 2, 9   **998/999** Col. 2, 3

EPITOME – 1577

Quod Christo impossibile sit propter humanae naturae proprietatem, ut XI.
simul in pluribus quam in uno loco, nedum ubique, suo cum corpore esse
possit.

Quod sola humanitas pro nobis passa sit nosque redemerit et quod filius XII.
Dei in passione nullam prorsus cum humanitate (reipsa) communicationem
habuerit, perinde ac si id negocium nihil ad ipsum pertinuisset.

Quod filius Dei tantummodo divinitate sua nobis in terris, in verbo, XIII.
sacramentis, in omnibus denique aerumnis nostris praesens sit, et quod haec
praesentia prorsus ad humanitatem nihil pertineat. Christo enim, postquam
nos | passione et morte sua redemerit, secundum humanitatem suam nihil 594
amplius nobiscum in terris esse negocii.

Quod filius Dei, qui humanam naturam assumsit, iam post depositam XIIII.
servi formam non omnia opera omnipotentiae suae in et cum humanitate sua
et per eam efficiat, sed tantum aliqua et quidem in eo tantum loco, ubi humana natura est localiter.

Quod secundum humanitatem Omnipotentiae aliarumque proprietatum XV.
divinae naturae prorsus non sit capax. Idque asserere audent contra expressum
testimonium Christi: *Mihi data est omnis potestas in coelo et in terra.* Et contra- Matth. 28.
dicunt Paulo, qui ait: *In ipso inhabitat tota divinitatis plenitudo corporaliter.* Coloss. 2.

Quod Christo secundum humanitatem data quidem sit maxima potestas XVI.
in coelo et in terra, videlicet maior et amplior quam omnes Angeli et creaturae
acceperint, sed tamen ita, ut cum omnipotentia Dei nullam habeat communicationem neque omnipotentia illi data sit. Itaque mediam quandam potentiam inter omnipotentiam Dei et inter aliarum creaturarum potentiam
fingunt, datam Christo secundum humanam eius naturam per exaltationem,
quae minor quidem sit quam Dei omnipotentia, maior tamen omnium aliarum creaturarum potestate.

Quod Christo secundum spiritum suum humanum certi limites positi XVII.
sint, quantum videlicet ipsum scire oporteat, et quod non plus sciat quam ipsi
conveniat et ad executionem sui officii, iudicis nimirum, necessario requiratur.

Quod Christus ne hodie quidem perfectam habeat cognitionem Dei et XVIII.
omnium ipsius operum, cum tamen de Christo scriptum sit: In ipso *omnes* Coloss. 2.
thesauros sapientiae et scientiae absconditos esse.

Quod Christo secundum humanitatis suae spiritum impossibile sit scire, XIX.
quid ab aeterno fuerit, quid iam nunc ubique fiat et quid in omnem aeternitatem sit futurum.

870 CONCILIUM SAXONICUM – 1577

Da geleret und der Spruch Matth. 28.: 'Mir ist gegeben aller gewalt' etc. 20.
also gedeutet und lesterlich verkeret wird, das Christo nach der Göttlichen
1005 natur in der Aufferstehung und seiner Himmelfart restituiret, das ist, widerumb zugestellt worden sey, aller gewalt im Himmel und auff Erden, als hette
er im stand seiner niedrigung auch nach der Gottheit solche abgeleget und
verlassen. Durch welche Lere nicht allein die wort des Testaments Christi
verkeret, sondern auch der verdampten Arrianischen Ketzerey der weg berei-
1010 tet, das endlich Christus ewige Gottheit verleugnet und also Christus gantz
und gar sampt unserer seligkeit verloren, do solcher falschen Lere aus besten-
digem grundt Göttliches worts und unsers einfeltigen Christlichen Glaubens
nicht widersprochen würde.

IX. Von der Hellefahrt Christi

247

1015   Status Controversiae

Hauptstreit uber diesem Artickel

Es ist auch unter etzlichen Theologen, so der Augspurgischen Confeßion
zugetan, uber diesem Artickel gestritten worden: Wann und auff was weise
der Herr Christus, vermüge unsers einfeltigen Christlichen glaubens, gen Hel-
1020 le gefahren; ob es geschehen sey vor oder nach seinem Tode. Item, ob es nach
der Seel allein oder nach der Gottheit allein oder mit Leib und Seel geistlich
oder leiblich zugangen. Item, ob dieser Artickel gehöre zum Leiden oder zum
herrlichen Sieg und Triumph Christi.

Nachdem aber dieser Artickel, wie auch der vorgehende, nicht mit den
1025 sinnen noch mit der vernunfft begriffen werden kan, sondern mus allein mit
dem Glauben gefasset werden, ist unser einhellig bedencken, das solches nicht
zu disputiren, sondern nur auffs einfeltigste geglaubet und geleret werden
solle, inmassen D. Luther seliger in der Predigt zu Torgau Anno 33. etc.
solchen Artickel gantz Christlich erkleret, alle unnützliche, unnotwendige
1030 fragen abgeschnitten und zu Christlicher einfalt des Glaubens alle frome
Christen vermanet. Dann es ist gnug, das wir wissen, das Christus in die Helle
gefahren, die Helle allen Gleubigen zerstöret und sie aus dem gewalt des

---

1003 Matth. 28, 18

1028 Predigt zu Torgau Anno 33.] cfr M. Luther, 'Predigten des Jahres 1533. Dritte
Predigt, auff den Ostertag', in *WA* 37 (1910), p. 62, 22-p. 72, 12

EPITOME – 1577

Reiicimus etiam damnamusque, quod dictum Christi *Mihi data est omnis* XX. |
potestas in coelo et in terra horribili | et blasphema interpretatione a quibusdam Matth. 28.
975 depravatur in hanc sententiam: quod Christo secundum divinam suam natu- 595
ram in resurrectione et ascensione ad coelos iterum restituta fuerit omnis
potestas in coelo et in terra, perinde quasi, dum in statu humilitationis erat,
eam potestatem etiam secundum divinitatem deposuisset et exuisset. Hac
enim doctrina non modo verba Testamenti Christi falsa explicatione perver-
980 tuntur, verum etiam dudum damnatae Arianae haeresi via de novo sternitur, ut
tandem aeterna Christi divinitas negetur et Christus totus, quantus quantus
est, una cum salute nostra amittatur, nisi huic impiae doctrinae ex solidis verbi
Dei et fidei nostrae Catholicae fundamentis constanter contradicatur.

IX. De descensu Christi ad inferos.

985 Status controversiae.

Disceptatum fuit super hoc articulo inter quosdam Theologos, qui Augustanam Confessionem profitentur, quando et quo modo Dominus noster
Iesus Christus, ut testatur fides nostra Catholica, ad inferos descenderit: an id
ante vel post mortem eius factum sit. Praeterea quaesitum fuit, num anima
990 tantum, an divinitate sola, an vero anima et corpore descenderit, idque an
spiritualiter an vero corporaliter sit factum. Disputatum etiam est, num hic
articulus ad passionem, an vero ad gloriosam victoriam et triumphum Christi
sit referendus.
| Cum autem hic fidei nostrae articulus, sicut et praecedens, neque sensi- 596
995 bus neque ratione nostra comprehendi queat, sola autem fide acceptandus sit:
unanimi consensu consulimus de hac re non esse disputandum, sed quam sim-
plicissime hunc articulum credendum et docendum esse. Atque in hoc negocio sequamur piam D. Lutheri doctrinam, qui hunc articulum in concione
Torgae habita (Anno etc. XXXIII.) pie admodum explicuit, omnes inutiles et
1000 curiosas quaestiones praecidit atque ad piam fidei simplicitatem omnes Christianos adhortatus est.
Satis enim nobis esse debet, si sciamus Christum ad inferos descendisse,
infernum omnibus credentibus destruxisse nosque per ipsum e potestate mor-

872

Todes, Teufels, ewiger verdamnis des hellischen rachens erlöset habe; wie aber
solches zugangen, sollen wir sparen bis in die ander Welt, da uns nicht allein
1035 dis stück, sondern auch noch anders mehr geoffenbaret, das wir hie einfeltig
geglaubt und mit unser blinden vernunfft nicht begreiffen können.

X. Von Kirchengebreuchen, so man Adiaphora oder Mitteldinge nennet

Von Ceremonien oder Kirchengebreuchen, welche in Gottes Wort weder
1040 geboten noch verboten, sondern umb guter ordnung und wolstandts willen in
die Kirche eingeführet, hat sich auch zwischen den Theologen Augspurgischer
Confeßion ein Zwispalt zugetragen.

Status Controversiae

Der Hauptstreit von diesem Artickel

1045 Die Hauptfrage aber ist gewesen, ob man zur zeit der verfolgung und im
fall der bekentnis, wann die feinde des Evangelii sich gleich nicht mit uns in
der Lere vergleichen, dennoch mit unverletztem gewissen etzliche gefallene
Ceremonien, so an im selbst Mitteldinge und von Gott weder geboten noch
verboten, auff der Widersacher dringen und erfordern widerumb auffrichten
1050 und sich also mit inen in solchen Ceremonien und Mitteldingen vergleichen
möge. Der eine teil hat Ja, der ander hat Nein darzu gesagt.

Affirmativa

Die rechte warhafftige Lere und Bekentnis von diesem Artickel

Zu hinlegung auch dieser Zwispalt gleuben, leren und bekennen wir 1.
1055 einhellig, das die Ceremonien oder Kirchengebreuche, welche in Gottes wort
weder geboten noch verboten, sondern allein umb wolstandes und guter |
ordnung willen angestelt, an inen und für sich selbst kein Gottesdienst, auch
kein teil desselben seien; Matth. 15.: 'Sie ehren mich umbsonst mit menschlichen geboten.'

1058/1059 Matth. 15, 9

EPITOME – 1577

tis et Satanae, ab aeterna damnatione atque adeo e faucibus inferni ereptos.
Quo autem modo haec effecta fuerint, non curiose scrutemur, sed huius rei
cognitionem alteri seculo reservemus, ubi non modo hoc mysterium, sed et
alia multa in hac vita simpliciter a nobis credita revelabuntur, quae captum
coecae nostrae rationis excedunt.

X. DE CEREMONIIS ECCLESIASTICIS, QUAE VULGO ADIAPHORA SEU RES MEDIAE ET INDIFFERENTES VOCANTUR.

Orta est etiam inter Theologos Augustanae Confessionis controversia de
ceremoniis seu ritibus Ecclesiasticis, qui in verbo Dei neque praecepti sunt
neque prohibiti, sed ordinis tantum et decori gratia in Ecclesiam sunt intro-
ducti.

Status controversiae.

597

Quaesitum fuit, num persecutionis tempore et in casu confessionis
(etiamsi adversarii nobiscum in doctrina consentire nolint) nihilominus salva
conscientia aliquae iam abrogatae ceremoniae, quae per se indifferentes et a
Deo neque mandatae neque prohibitae sint, postulantibus id et urgentibus
adversariis, iterum in usum revocari possint et an hoc modo cum Pontificiis in
eiusmodi ceremoniis et adiaphoris conformari recte queamus. Una pars hoc
fieri posse affirmavit, altera vero negavit.

Affirmativa.

Sincera doctrina et confessio de hoc articulo.

Ad hanc controversiam dirimendam unanimi consensu credimus, doce-   I.
mus et confitemur, quod ceremoniae sive ritus Ecclesiastici (qui verbo Dei
neque praecepti sunt neque prohibiti, sed tantum decori et ordinis causa instituti) non sint per se cultus divinus aut aliqua saltem pars culutus divini. Scriptum est enim: *Frusta colunt me docentes doctrinas, mandata hominum.*   Matth. 15.

874 CONCILIUM SAXONICUM – 1577

1060 Wir gleuben, leren und bekennen, das die Gemeine Gottes jedes orts und 2.
jederzeit nach derselben gelegenheit macht habe, solche Ceremonien zu end-
ern, wie es der Gemeinen Gottes am nützlichsten und erbaulichsten sein mag.

Doch das hierinnen alle leichtfertigkeit und ergernis gemieden und son- 3.
derlich der schwachgleubigen mit allem fleis verschonet werde. 1 Cor
Rom.

1065 Wir gleuben, leren und bekennen, das zur zeit der verfolgung, wann ein 4.
runde bekentnis des Glaubens von uns erfordert, in solchen Mitteldingen den
Feinden nicht zu weichen, wie der Apostel geschrieben: 'So bestehet nun in Galat
der freiheit, damit uns Christus befreiet hat, und last euch nicht widerumb in
das knechtische joch fangen.' Item: 'Ziehet nicht am frembden joch; was hat 2. Co
1070 das Liecht vor gemeinschafft mit der Finsternis?' Item: 'Auff das die warheit Galat
des Evangelii bey euch bestünde, wichen wir demselben nicht eine stunde,
underthenig zu sein.' Dann in solchem fall ist es nicht mehr umb Mittelding,
sondern umb die warheit des Evangelii, umb die Christliche freyheit und umb
die bestetigung offentlicher Abgötterey, wie auch umb verhütung des Ergernis
1075 der schwachgleubigen zuthun, darin wir nichts zuvergeben haben, sondern
rund bekennen und darüber leiden sollen, was uns Gott zuschickt und uber
uns den feinden seines worts verhengt.
Wir gleuben, leren und bekennen auch, das kein Kirch die ander ver- 5.
dammen sol, das eine weniger oder mehr eusserlicher von Gott ungebotenen
1080 Ceremonien dann die andere hat, wann sonst in der Lere und allen derselben
Artickeln, wie auch im rechten gebrauch der heiligen Sacramenten miteinander einigkeit gehalten nach dem wolbekanten Spruch: 'Dissonatia ieiunii non
dissolvit consonantiam fidei. Ungleicheit des fastens sol die einigkeit im glauben nicht trennen'.

1063/1064 hierinnen – werde] I Cor. 8, 7-13; Rom. 14, 1.13-15   **1067/1069** Gal. 5, 1
1069/1070 II Cor. 6, 14   **1070/1072** Gal. 2, 5

1082/1084 a contemporary proverb. Cfr K. F. W. Wander, *Deutsches Sprichwörter-Lexikon*, vol. 1, Leipzig 1867 (ND: Aalen 1963), 937 (n. 18). According to Eusebius of Caesarea, this phrase originally came from Irenaeus of Lyon. Cfr Eusebius, *Historia ecclesiastica* V, 24, 13, hrsg. E. Schwartz – Th. Mommsen (*Eusebius Werke* 2, 1; *GCS* 9, 1), Leipzig 1903, p. 494, 15-25 (= *PG* 20, col. 500-504)

EPITOME – 1577

Credimus, docemus et confitemur, Ecclesiae Dei ubivis terrarum et quo- II.
cunque tempore licere pro re nata ceremonias tales mutare iuxta eam rationem, quae Ecclesiae Dei utilissima et ad aedificationem eiusdem maxime
accomodata iudicatur.

Ea tamen in re omnem levitatem fugiendam et offendicula cavenda, in- III. | 1. Cor.
primis vero infirmorum in fide rationem habendam et iis parcendum esse 8.
censemus. Rom. 14.

Credimus, docemus et confitemur, quod temporibus persecutionum, IIII.
quando perspicua et constans confessio a | nobis exigitur, hostibus Evangelii in 598
rebus adiaphoris non sit cedendum. Sic enim Apostolus inquit: *Qua libertate* Galat. 5.
Christus nos liberavit, in ea state et nolite iterum iugo servitutis subiici. Et alibi:
Nolite iugum ducere cum infidelibus etc. Quae enim est societas luci ad tenebras? 2. Cor. 6.
etc. Item: *Quibus neque ad horam cessimus subiectione, ut veritas Evangelii* Galat. 2.
permaneret apud vos. In tali enim rerum statu non agitur iam amplius de adiaphoris, sed de veritate Evangelii et de libertate Christiana sarcta tectaque con-
servanda et quomodo cavendum sit, ne manifeste Idololatria confirmetur et
infirmi in fide offendantur. In huiusmodi rebus nostrum certe non est aliquid
adversariis largiri, sed officium nostrum requirit, ut piam et ingenuam confessionem edamus et ea patienter feramus, quae Dominus nobis ferenda imposue-
rit et hostibus verbi Dei in nos permiserit.

Credimus, docemus et confitemur, quod Ecclesia alia aliam damnare non V.
debeat, propterea quod haec vel illa plus minusve externarum ceremoniarum,
quas Dominus non instituit, observet, si modo in doctrina eiusque articulis
omnibus et in vero sacramentorum usu sit inter eas consensus. Hoc enim vetus
et verum dictum est: Dissonantia ieiunii non dissolvit consonantiam fidei.

876 CONCILIUM SAXONICUM – 1577

Negativa

Falsche Lere von diesem Artickel

Demnach verwerffen und verdammen wir als unrecht und dem wort Gottes zuwider, wann geleret wird:

Das Menschen gebot und satzungen in der Kirchen vor sich selbst als ein Gottesdienst oder teil desselben gehalten werden sollen. 1.

Wann solche Ceremonien, gebot und satzungen mit zwang als notwendig der Gemein Gottes wider ire Christliche freiheit, so sie in eusserlichen dingen hat, auffgedrungen werden. 2.

Item, das man zur zeit der verfolgung und öffentlicher bekentnis den feinden des heiligen Evangelii (welches zu abbruch der warheit dienet) in dergleichen Mitteldingen und Ceremonien möge wilfaren oder sich mit inen vergleichen. 3.

Item, wann solche eusserliche Ceremonien und Mitteldinge also abgeschaffet werden, als solte es der Gemein Gottes nicht frey stehen, nach irer guten gelegenheit, wie es jederzeit der Kirchen am nützlichsten, sich eines oder mehr in Christlicher freiheit zu gebrauchen. 4.

XI. Von der ewigen Vorsehung und Wahl Gottes

Von diesem Artickel ist keine offentliche Zwispalt unter den Theologen Augspurgischer Confeßion eingefallen. Dieweil es aber ein tröstlicher Artickel, wann er recht gehandelt und deshalben nicht künfftiglich ergerliche disputation eingefürt werden möchte, ist derselbige in dieser Schrifft auch erkleret worden.

Affirmativa

Reine, warhafftige Lere von diesem Artickel

Anfenglich ist der unterscheid zwischen der 'Praescientia' et 'Praedestinatione', das ist zwischen der Versehung und ewigen Wahl Gottes, mit fleis zu mercken. 1.

Dann die Vorsehung Gottes ist anders nichts, dann das Gott alle ding weis, ehe sie geschehen, wie geschrieben stehet: 'Gott im Himel kan verbor- 2.

1114/1116 Dan. 2, 28

EPITOME – 1577

Negativa.

Falsae doctrinae de hoc articulo reiectio.

Repudiamus atque damnamus haec falsa et verbo Dei contaria dogmata:

Quod humanae traditiones et constitutiones in Ecclesiasticis rebus per se I. pro cultu Dei aut certe pro parte divini cultus sint habendae.

Quando eiusmodi ceremoniae et constitutiones Ecclesiae Dei coactione II. quadam tanquam necessariae obtrudun|tur, et quidem contra libertatem Christianam, quam Ecclesia Christi in rebus eiusmodi externis habet.

Cum asseritur, quod tempore persecutionis, quando clara confessio re- III. quiritur, hostibus Evangelii in observatione eiusmodi rerum adiaphorarum gratificari et cum ipsis pacisci et consentire liceat, quae res cum detrimento veritatis coelestis coniuncta est.

Cum externae ceremoniae, quae indifferentes sunt, ea opinione abrogan- IIII. tur, quasi Ecclesiae Dei liberum non sit pro re nata, ut iudicaverit ad aedificationem utile esse, hanc vel illam ceremoniam ratione libertatis Christianae usurpare.

XI. De aeterna praedestinatione et electione Dei.

De hoc articulo non quidem publice mota est controversia inter Augustanae Confessionis Theologos, sed tamen, cum hic articulus magnam piis mentibus consolalionem adferat, si recte et dextre explicetur, visum est eundem in hoc scripto declarare, ne forte temporis progressu disputationes aliquae cum offendiculo coniunctae de hac re exoriantur.

Affirmativa.

Sincera doctrina de hoc articulo.

Primum omnium est, quod accurate observari oportet, discrimen esse I. inter Praescientiam et Praedestinationem sive aeternam electionem Dei.

878 CONCILIUM SAXONICUM – 1577

1115 gen ding offenbaren; der hat dem König Nebucadnezar angezeiget, was in künfftigen zeiten geschehen sol.'

Diese Vorsehung gehet zugleich uber die frommen und bösen, ist aber 3. keine ursach des bösen, weder der sünden, das man unrecht thue (welche ursprünglich aus dem Teuffel und des menschen bösen, verkerten willen 1120 herkompt), noch ires verderben, daran sie selbst schuldig, sondern ordnet alleine dasselbig und steckt im ein ziel, wie lang es weren und alles unangesehen, das es an im selbst böse, seinen auserwehlten zu irem heil dienen solle.

Die Praedestination aber oder ewige Wahl Gottes gehet allein uber die 4. frommen, wolgefelligen Kinder Gottes, die eine ursach ist irer Seligkeit, 1125 welche er auch schaffet und was zur selbigen gehöret, verordnet; darauff Johan unser seligkeit so steiff gegründet, das sie die 'Pforten der Helle nicht uberwel- Matt tigen' können.

Solche ist nicht in dem heimlichen rath Gottes zu erforschen, sondern in 5. dem wort zu suchen, da sie auch geoffenbaret worden ist.

1130 Das wort Gottes aber füret uns zu Christo, der das 'buch des Lebens' ist, 6. in welchem alle die geschrieben und erwehlet seind, welche da ewig selig werden sollen, wie geschrieben stehet: 'Er hat uns durch denselben (Christum) Ephes erwehlet, ehe der Welt grundt geleget war.'

Dieser Christus ruffet zu im alle Sünder und verheisset inen erquickung 7. 1135 und ist ime ernst, das alle Menschen zu im kommen und inen helffen lassen sollen, denen er sich im wort anbeut und wil, das man es höre und nicht die ohren verstopffen oder das wort verachten sol, ver|heist darzu die krafft und 250r wirckung des heiligen Geistes, göttlichen beystand zur bestendigkeit und ewigen seligkeit.

1140 Derhalben wir von solcher unser Wahl zum ewigen Leben weder aus der 8. vernunfft noch aus dem Gesetz Gottes urteilen sollen, welche uns entweder in ein wild, wüst, epicurisch leben oder in verzweiffelung füren und schedliche gedancken in den hertzen der menschen erwecken, das sie bey sich selbst gedencken, auch solcher gedancken sich nicht recht erwehren können, so 1145 lange sie irer vernunfft folgen: Hat mich Gott erwehlet zur seligkeit, so kan ich nicht verdammet werden, ich thue was ich wölle; und widerumb: Bin ich nicht erwehlet zum ewigen Leben, so hilffts nichts, was ich gutes thue, es ist doch alles umbsunst.

1125/1126 darauff – gegründet] Ioh. 10, 27-29   **1126** Matth. 16, 18   **1130** Phil. 4, 3; Apoc. 3, 5   **1132/1133** Eph. 1, 4   **1134/1136** Dieser – sollen] Matth. 9, 35-38; 11, 28

EPITOME – 1577   879

| Praescientia enim Dei nihil aliud est, quam quod Deus omnia noverit,   II. | 600
antequam fiant, sicut scriptum est: *Est Deus in coelo, revelans mysteria, qui*   Dan. 2.
indicavit tibi, Rex Nabuchodonosor, quae ventura sunt in novissimis temporibus.

Haec Dei praescientia simul ad bonos et malos pertinet, sed interrim non   III.
est causa mali neque est cause peccati, quae hominem ad scelus impellat. Peccatum enim ex diabolo et ex hominis prava et mala voluntate oritur. Neque
haec Dei praescientia causa est, quod homines pereant; hoc enim sibi ipsis
imputare debent. Sed praescientia Dei disponit malum et metas illi constituit,
quousque progredi et quamdiu durare debeat, idque eo dirigit, ut, licet per se
malum sit, nihilominus electis Dei ad salutem cedat.

Praedestinatio vero seu aeterna Dei electio tantum ad bonos et dilectos   IIII.
filios Dei pertinet, et haec est causa ipsorum salutis. Etenim eorum salutem
procurat et ea, quae ad ipsam pertinent, disponit. Super hanc Dei praedestina-   Iohan. 10.
tionem salus nostra ita fundata est, ut *inferorum portae eam evertere nequeant.*   Matth. 16

Haec Dei praedestinatio non in arcano Dei consilio est scrutanda, sed in   V.
verbo Dei, in quo revelatur, quaerenda est.

Verbum autem Dei deducit nos ad Christum, is est Liber ille vitae, in quo   VI.
omnes inscripti et electi sunt, qui salutem aeternam consequuntur. Sic enim
scriptum est: *Elegit nos in Christo ante mundi constitutionem.*   Ephes. 1.

Christus vero omnes peccatores ad se vocat et promittit illis levationem.   VII.
Et serio vult, ut omnes homines ad se veniant et sibi consuli et subveniri
sinant. His sese redemptorem in verbo offert et vult, ut verbum audiatur et ut
aures non obturentur nec verbum negligatur et contemnatur. Et promittit se
largiturum virtutem et operationem spiritus sancti et auxilium divinam, ut in
fide constantes permaneamus et vitam aeternam consequamur.

De nostra igitur electione ad vitam aeternam neque ex rationis nostrae   VIII.
iudicio neque ex lege Dei iudicandum est, ne vel dissolutae et Epicureae vitae
nos tradamus, vel in despera|tionem incidamus. Qui enim rationis suae iudi-   601
cium in hoc negocio sequuntur, in horum cordibus hae perniciosae cogitationes (quibus aegerrime resistere possunt) excitantur: Si (inquiunt) Deus me ad
aeternam salutem elegit, non potero damnari, quicquid etiam designavero.
Contra vero, si non sum electus ad vitam aeternam, nihil plane mihi profuerit,
quantumcunque boni fecero, omnes enim conatus mei irriti erunt.

880 CONCILIUM SAXONICUM – 1577

Sondern es mus allein aus dem heiligen Evangelio von Christo gelernet 9.
1150 werden, in welchem klar bezeuget wird, wie 'Gott alles unter den unglauben
beschlossen, auff das er sich aller erbarme', und nicht wil, das jemand verloren
werde, sondern sich 'jederman zur busse bekehre' und an den Herrn Christum Ezec.
glaube. 1. Joh

Wer nun sich also mit dem geoffenbarten willen Gottes bekümmert und 10.
1155 der ordnung nachgehet, welche S. Paulus in der Epistel an die Römer gehalten,
der zuvor die menschen zur busse, erkentnis der sünden, zum Glauben an
Christum, zum Göttlichen gehorsam weiset, ehe er vom geheimnis der ewigen
Wahl Gottes redet, dem ist solche Lere nützlich und tröstlich.

Das aber 'viel beruffen und wenig auserwehlet' sind, hat es nicht diese 11.
1160 meinung, als wölle Gott nicht jederman selig machen, sondern die ursach ist,
das sie Gottes Wort entweder gar nicht hören, sondern mutwillig verachten,
die ohren und ir hertz verstocken und also dem heiligen Geist den ordentlichen weg verstellen, das er sein werck in inen nicht haben kan, oder, do sie es
gehört haben, widerumb in wind schlahen und nicht achten; daran nicht 2. Pe
Luc.
1165 Gott oder seine Wahl, sondern ire bosheit schuldig ist. Heb.
Und sofern sol sich ein Christ des Artickels von der ewigen Wahl Gottes 12.
annemen, wie sie im Wort Gottes geoffenbaret, welche uns Christum als das
'Buch des Lebens' vorhelt, das er uns durch die Predigt des heiligen Evangelii
auffschleust und offenbaret, wie geschrieben stehet: 'Welche er erwehlet hat, Rom
1170 die hat er auch beruffen'; indem wir die ewige Wahl des Vaters suchen sollen,
der in seinem ewigen Göttlichen rath beschlossen, das er ausserhalb denen, so
seinen | Son Christum erkennen und warhafftig an in gleuben, niemand wölle 250v
selig machen und sich anderer gedancken entschlahen, welche nicht aus Gott,
sondern aus eingeben des bösen Feindes herfliessen, dadurch er sich unterste-
1175 het, uns den herrlichen trost zu schwechen oder gar zu nemen, den wir in
dieser heilsamen Lere haben, das wir wissen, wie wir aus lauterer gnade one
allen unsern verdienst in Christo zum ewigen Leben erwehlet sein und das uns
niemand aus seiner handt reissen könne, wie er dann solche gnedige erwehl-
ung nicht allein mit blossen worten zusaget, sondern auch mit dem Eyde
1180 beteuret und mit den heiligen Sacramenten versiegelt hat, deren wir uns in
unsern höchsten anfechtungen erinnern und trösten und damit die feurigen
Pfeile des Teuffels ausleschen künnen.

1150/1151 Rom. 11, 32 **1152** Ez. 33, 11; 18, 23; I Tim. 2, 4; II Petr. 3, 9 **1157/
1158** Rom. 1-11 **1159** Matth. 20, 16; 22, 14 **1164/1165** nicht² – ist] II Petr. 2, 1; Luc.
11, 47-52; Hebr. 12, 15-17.25 **1168** Phil. 4, 3; Apoc. 3, 5 **1169/1170** Rom. 8, 30

EPITOME – 1577

Vera igitur sententia de Praedestinatione ex Evangelio Christi discenda IX.
est. In eo enim perspicue docetur, quod *Deus omnes sub incredulitatem conclu-* Rom. 11.
serit, ut omnium misereatur et quod nolit quenquam perire, sed potius ut Ezech. 18. 33.
omnes convertantur et in Christum credant. 1. Iohan. 2.

Qui igitur voluntatem Dei revelatam inquirunt, eoque ordine progre- X.
diuntur, quem D. Paulus in Epistola ad Romanos secutus est (qui hominem
prius deducit ad poenitentiam, ad agnitionem peccatorum, ad fidem in Christum, ad obedientiam mandatorum Dei, quam de aeternae praedestinationis
mysterio loquatur) iis doctrina de praedestinatione Dei salutaris est, et maxi-
mam consolationem affert.

Quod vero scriptum est: *multos quidem vocatos, paucos vero electos esse,* XI.
non ita accipiendum est, quasi Deus nolit, ut omnes salventur, sed damnationis impiorum causa est, quod verbum Dei aut prorsus non audiant, sed con-
tumaciter contemnant, aures obturent et cor indurent et hoc modo spiritui
sancto viam ordinariam praecludant, ut opus suum in eis efficere nequeat, aut
certe quod verbum auditum flocci pendant atque abiiciant. Quod igitur
pereunt, neque Deus neque ipsius electio, sed malitia eorum in culpa est. 2. Pet. 2.

Huc usque homo pius in meditatione articuli de aeterna Dei electione Luc.11.
tuto progredi potest, quatenus videlicet ea in verbo Dei est revelata. Verbum Heb. 12.
Dei enim nobis Christum *Librum vitae* proponit; is nobis per Evangelii prae- XII.
dicationem aperitur et evoluitur, sicut scriptum est: *Quos elegit, hos vocavit.* In Rom. 8
Christo igitur electio aeterna Dei pa|tris est quaerenda. Is in aeterno suo consi- 602
lio decrevit, quod praeter eos, qui filium eius Iesum Christum agnoscunt et in
eum vere credunt, neminem salvum facere velit. Reliquae cogitationes ex
animis piorum penitus excutiendae suntk, quia non a Deo, sed ex afflatu Satanae proficiscuntur, quibus humani generis hostis hoc agit, ut dulcissimam
illam consolationem vel enervet vel penitus e medio tollat, quam ex saluberrima hac doctrina haurire possumus: qua videlicet certi reddimur, quod mera
gratia sine ullo nostro merito in Christo ad vitam aeternam electi simus et
quod nemo ex ipsius manibus rapere nos possit. Et hanc clementissimam electionem non nudis verbis, sed interposito iureiurando Dominus contestando
confirmavit et venerabilibus sacramentis nobis obsignavit, quorum in summis
tentationibus meminisse et ex iis consolationem petere debemus, ut ignitia
diaboli tela extinguamus.

882 CONCILIUM SAXONICUM – 1577

Darneben sollen wir uns zum höchsten befleissigen, nach dem willen 13.
Gottes zu leben und unsern beruff, wie S. Petrus vermanet, 'veste zu machen' 2. Pe
1185 und sonderlich an das geoffenbarte wort uns halten, das kan und wird uns
nicht fehlen.

Durch diese kurtze erklerung der ewigen Wahl Gottes wird Gott seine 14.
Ehre gantz und völlig gegeben, das er allein aus lauter barmhertzigkeit one
allen unsern verdienst uns selig mache 'nach dem vorsatz seines willens'. Dar-
1190 neben auch niemands einige ursach zur kleinmütigkeit oder rohem, wilden
leben gegeben.

Antithesis oder Negativa

Falsche lere von diesem Artickel

Demnach gleuben und halten wir, welche die lere von der gnedigen Wahl
1195 Gottes zum ewigen leben also füren, das sich die betrübten Christen derselben
nicht trösten künnen, sondern dardurch zur kleinmütigkeit oder verzweife-
lung verursachet oder die unbusfertigen in irem mutwillen gestercket werden,
das solche Lere nicht nach dem wort und willen Gottes, sondern nach der
vernunfft und anstifftung des leidigen Sathans getrieben werde. Weil alles, 'was Rom
1200 geschrieben ist (wie der Apostel zeuget), uns zur lere geschrieben, auff das wir
durch gedult und trost der Schrifft hoffnung haben'. Demnach verwerffen wir
folgende irthumb:

Als wann geleret wird, das Gott nicht wölle, das alle Menschen busse 1. | 2
thun und dem Evangelio gleuben.

1205 Item, wann Gott uns zu sich beruffe, das es nicht sein ernst sey, das alle 2.
Menschen zu im kommen sollen.

Item, das Gott nicht wölle, das jederman selig werde, sondern unangese- 3.
hen ire sünde allein aus dem blossen rath, vorsatz und willen Gottes zum
verdamnis verordnet, das sie nicht können selig werden.

1184 II Petr. 1, 10 **1189** Eph. 1, 11 **1199/1201** Rom. 15, 4

1203/1204 Als – gleuben] cfr Calv., 'Institutio Christianae religionis (1559) III,
21, 5-6', in Peter Barth – Wilhelm Niesel (hrsg.), *Calvin, Opera selecta*. vol. 4, München
1968⁴, 373, 33-377, 18 **1207/1209** das¹ – werden] cfr *Gallican Confession* art. 12, ed.
Dingel, in *COGD* VI.1.1, p. 552

EPITOME – 1577 883

Interim tamen summo studio in eo elaboremus, ut ad normam voluntatis XIII.
divinae vitam nostram instituamus et *vocationem* nostram (ut D. Petrus loquitur) *firmam faciamus,* neque a Dei revelato verbo latum unguem recedamus; I. Pet. I.
illud enim nunquam nos fallet.

Hac brevi explicatione aeternae electionis divinae honos suus Deo plene XIIII.
et in solidum tribuitur, quod videlicet *secundum voluntatis suae propositum*
mera misericordia sine ullo nostro merito salvos nos faciat. Neque tamen hac
doctrina vel gravioribus illis animi perturbationibus et pusillanimitati vel
Epicurismo ansa praebetur.

Negativa.

Falsae doctrinae de hoc articulo reiectio.

Credimus igitur et sentimus, quando doctrina de electione Dei ad vitam
aeternam eo modo proponitur, ut | perturbatae piae mentes ex ea consolatio- 603
nem nullam capere queant, sed potius per eam in animi angustias aut desperationem coniiciantur aut impoenitentes in dissoluta sua vita confirmentur,
quod articulus hic non ad normam verbi et voluntatis Dei, sed iuxta humanae
rationis iudicium, et quidem impulsa Satanae, male et perperam tractetur.
Quaecunque enim scripta sunt (inquit Apostolus) *ad nostram doctrinam scripta* Rom. 15.
sunt, ut per patientiam et consolationem scripturarum spem habeamus. Reiicimus itaque omnes, quos iam enumerabimus, errores:

Quod Deus nolit, ut omnes homines poenitentiam agant et Evangelio I.
credant.

Quando Deus nos ad se vocat, quod non serio hoc velit, ut omnes homi- II.
nes ad ipsum veniant.

Quod nolit Deus, ut omnes salventur, sed quod quidam, non ratione III.
peccatorum suorum, verum solo Dei consilio, proposito et voluntate ad
exitium destinati sint ut prorsus salutem consequi non possint.

884 CONCILIUM SAXONICUM – 1577

1210 Item, das nicht allein die barmhertzigkeit Gottes und allerheiligste 4.
verdienst Christi, sondern auch in uns eine ursach sey der wahl Gottes, umb
welcher willen Gott uns zum ewigen leben erwehlet habe.

Welches alles lesterliche und erschreckliche irrige Leren sein, dadurch den
Christen aller trost genommen, den sie im heiligen Evangelio und gebrauch
1215 der heiligen Sacrament haben und derwegen in der Kirchen Gottes nicht
solten geduldet werden.

Diß ist die kurtze und einfeltige erklerung der streitigen Artickel, so eine
zeitlang von den Theologen Augspurgischer Confeßion widerwertig disputirt
und geleret worden. Daraus ein jeder einfeltiger Christ nach anleitung Gottes
1220 worts und seines einfeltigen Catechismi vernemen kan, was recht oder
unrecht sey. Do nicht allein die reine Lere gesetzt, sondern auch derselbigen
widerwertige, irrige lere ausgesetzt, verworffen und also die eingefallene,
ergerlichen spaltungen gründlich entscheiden seind. Der Allmechtige Gott
und Vater unsers Herren Jesu verleihe die gnade seines heiligen Geistes, das
1225 wir alle in im einig sein und in solcher Christlichen und ime wolgefelligen
einigkeit bestendiglich bleiben. Amen.

XII. Von andern Rotten und Secten, 251V
so sich niemals zu der Augspurgischen Confession bekant

Damit uns auch nicht stillschweigende solche zugemessen, weil wir
1230 derselben in vorgesatzter erklerung keine meldung gethan, haben wir zu ende
allein die blossen Artickel erzelen wöllen, darinnen sie sich irren und vielge-
dachtem unserm Christlichen glauben und bekentnis zuwider leren.

Irrige Artickel der Widerteuffer

Die Widerteuffer seind unter sich selbst in viel hauffen geteilet, do einer
1235 viel, der andere wenig irthumb bestreitet, ingemein aber füren sie solche Lere,
die weder in der Kirchen noch in der Policey und weltlichem Regiment, noch
in der Haushaltung zu dulden noch zu leiden.

1210/1212 das – habe] cfr P. Melanchthon, 'Loci praecipui theologici (1559)', in *CR*,
vol. 21 (1854), col. 916 = *MWA*, vol. 2/2, (1953), p. 597, 4-7 **1234/1237** Die – Haus-
haltung] This formulation mirrors the medieval teaching of the three standings
(*ecclesia, politia, oeconomia*), in which all human life is integrated

EPITOME – 1577

Quod non sola Dei misericordia et sanctissimum Christi meritum, sed IIII. etiam in nobis ipsis aliqua causa sit electionis divinae, cuius causae ratione Deus nos ad vitam aeternam elegerit.

Haec dogmata omnia falsa sunt, horrenda et blasphema, iisque piis mentibus omnis prorsus consolatio eripitur, quam ex Evangelio et sacramentorum usu capere deberent, et idcirco in Ecclesia Dei nequaquam sunt ferenda.

Haec brevis est et simplicissima articulorum controversorum explicatio, de quibus inter Theologos Augustanae Confessionis aliquandiu disceptatum et discrepantibus inter se sententiis disputatum est. Et ex hac declaratione homo pius quantumvis simplex secundum analogiam verbi Dei et Catechismi simplicem doctrinam deprehendere potest, quid verum sit, quid falsum. Non enim tantummodo sincera doctrina diserte est recitata, verum etiam contraria et falsa doctrina repudiata est et reiecta, et controversiae illae, offendiculorum plenae, solide sunt decisae atque diiudicatae.

| Faxit Deus omnipotens, pater Domini nostri Iesu Christi, ut per gratiam 604 Spiritus sancti omnes in ipso consentientes et concordes simus atque in consensu pio, qui ipsi probetur, constanter perseveremus. Amen.

XII. De aliis haeresibus et sectis, quae nunquam Augustanam Confessionem sunt amplexae.

Ne tacita cogitatione haereses illae et sectae nobis tribuantur, propterea quod earum in commemorata declaratione expressam mentionem non fecimus, visum est articulos earum ad calcem (ut dicitur) huius scripti nude recitare, in quibus nostri temporis haeretici a veritate dissentiunt et sincerae nostrae religioni et confessioni contrarium docent.

Errores Anabaptistarum.

Anabaptistae in multas sectas sunt divisi, quarum aliae plures, aliae pauciores errores defendunt. Generatim tamen omnes talem doctrinam profiten-

886 CONCILIUM SAXONICUM – 1577

Unleidliche Artickel in der Kirchen

Das Christus sein leib und blut nicht von Marien der Jungfrauen angenommen, sondern vom Himel mit sich gebracht. 1.

Das Christus nicht warhafftiger Gott, sondern nur mehr gaben des heiligen Geistes habe denn sonst ein heiliger Mensch. 2.

Das unser gerechtigkeit vor Gott nicht allein auff dem einigen verdienst Christi, sondern in der erneuerung und also in unser eigen frömmigkeit stehe, in deren wir wandeln, welche zum grossen teil auff eigene, sonderliche, selbst erwelte geistligkeit gesetzt und im grunde anders nichts dann eine neue Müncherey ist. 3.

Das die Kinder, so nicht getaufft, vor Gott nicht sünder, sondern gerecht und unschuldig sein, welche in irer unschuld, weil sie noch | nicht zu irem vorstand komen, one die Tauffe (derer irem vorgeben nach sie nicht bedürffen) selig werden; vorwerffen also die gantze Lere von der Erbsünde und was derselben anhanget. 4. 252r

Das die Kinder nicht sollen getauffet werden, bis sie zu irem verstandt komen und iren Glauben selbst bekennen können. 5.

Das der Christen kinder darumb, weil sie von Christlichen und gleubigen Eltern geboren, auch one und vor der Tauff heilig und Gottes kinder sein, auch der ursach der kinder Tauffe weder hoch halten noch beförden wider die ausgedrückte Wort der vorheissung Gottes, die sich allein auff die erstrecket, welche seinen Bund halten und denselben nicht verachten; Gen. 17. 6.

Das dis keine rechte Christliche gemeine sey, darinnen noch Sünder gefunden werden. 7.

Das man keine Predigt hören noch in den Tempeln besuchen solle, darinnen zuvor Bapistische Mess gehalten und gelesen worden. 8.

Das man nichts mit den Kirchendienern, so das Evangelium vermüge Augspurgischer Confeßion predigen und der Widerteuffer predigen und irthumb straffen, zu schaffen haben, inen auch weder dienen noch etwas arbeiten, sondern als die verkehrer Gottes worts fliehen und meiden sol. 9.

1259 Gen. 17.] Gen. 17, 4-8.19-21

EPITOME – 1577

tur, quae neque in Ecclesia neque in Politia neque in Oeconomia tolerari potest.

Articuli Anabaptistici, qui in Ecclesia ferri non possunt.

Quod Christus carnem et sanguinem suum non e Maria virgine assump- I.
serit, sed e coelo attulerit.

| Quod Christus non sit verus Deus, sed tantummodo caeteris sanctis sit II. | 605
superior, quia plura Spiritus sancti dona acceperit quam alius quispiam homo
sanctus.

Quod iustitia nostra coram Deo, non in solo Christi merito, sed in reno- III.
vatione atque adeo in nostra propria probitate, in qua ambulemus, consistat.
Ea vero Anabaptistarum iustitia magna ex parte electitia et humanitus excogi-
tata quadam sanctimonia constat, et revera nil aliud est quam novus quidam
Monachatus.

Quod infantes non baptizati coram Deo non sint peccatores, sed iusti et IIII.
innocentes et in illa sua innocentia, cum usum rationis nondum habeant, sine
baptismo (quo videlicet ipsorum opinione non egeant) salutem consequantur.
Et hoc modo reiiciunt totam de peccato Originali doctrinam, reliqua etiam,
quae ex ea dependent.

Quod infantes baptizandi non sint, donec usum rationis consequantur et V.
fidem suam ipsi profiteri possint.

Quod Christianorum liberi eam ob causam, quia parentibus Christianis VI.
et fidelibus orti sunt (etiam praeter et ante susceptum baptismum) revera sancti et in filiorum Dei numero sint habendi. Qua de causa etiam neque Paedo-
baptismum magnificiunt neque id operam dant, ut infantes baptizentur, quod
cum expressis verbis promissionis divinae pugnat; ea enim tantum ad eos
pertinet, qui foedus Dei observant, illudque non contemnunt. Gen. 17.

Quod ea non sit vera et Christiana Ecclesia, in qua aliqui adhuc peccato- VII.
res reperiuntur.

Quod conciones non sint audiendae ullae in iis templis, in quibus VIII.
aliquando Missae Pontificiae sunt celebratae.

Quod homo pius nihil prorsus commercii habere debeat cum Ecclesiae XI.
ministris, qui Evangelion Christi iuxta Angustanae Confessionis sententiam
docent et Anabaptistarum conciones ac errores reprehendunt, et quod
euismodi Ecclesiae ministris neque servire, neque operam locare liceat, sed
quod iidem ut perversores verbi divini vitandi et fugiendi sint.

Unleidentliche Artickel in der Policey

Das die Obrigkeit kein Gottgefelliger standt im Neuen Testament sey. 1.

Das ein Christen mensch mit gutem, unverletzten gewissen das Ampt der 2. Obrigkeit nicht tragen noch verwalten könne.

Das ein Christ mit unvorletztem gewissen das Ampt der Obrigkeit in 3. zufelligen sachen wider die bösen nicht gebrauchen noch derselben Underthanen iren habenden und von Gott empfangenen gewalt zum schutz und schirm anruffen mögen.

Das ein Christen mensch mit gutem gewissen kein Eyd schweren noch 4.|2 mit Eyde seinem Landesfürsten oder Oberherrn die Erbhuldung thun könne.

Das die Obrigkeit im Neuen Testament in unvorletztem gewissen die 5. Ubelthäter am leben nicht straffen könne.

Unleidentliche Artickel in der Haushaltung

Das ein Christ mit gutem gewissen nichts eigens behalten noch besitzen 1. könne, sondern schuldig sey dasselbe in die Gemein zugeben.

Das ein Christ mit gutem gewissen kein Gastgäber, Kauffman oder Mes- 2. serschmit sein könne.

Das Eheleut umb des Glaubens willen sich voneinander scheiden und 3. eines das ander verlassen und mit einem andern, das seines Glaubens ist, sich vorehelichen möge.

Irrige Artickel der Schwenckfeldianer

Das alle, die kein recht erkentnüs des regierenden Himelkönigs Christi 1. haben, welche Christum nach dem fleisch vor eine Creatur halten.

Das das Fleisch Christi durch die erhöhung also alle Göttliche eigen- 2. schafften angenomen, das er, Christus, als Mensch an macht, krafft, Maiestet, herrligkeit dem Vater und dem Wort allenthalben im grad und stell des wesens gleich, das nun mehr einerley wesen, eigenschafft, will und glori beider Natu-

---

1288 Schwenckfeldianer] The term 'Schwenckfeldianer' refers to the followers of the Silesian nobleman Caspar Schwenckfeld von Ossig († 1561). He had been heavily criticized by Luther for his spiritual understanding of Christ and his refusal of accepting preaching and sacraments as means of grace

EPITOME – 1577

Articuli Anbaptistici, qui in Politia sunt intolerabiles. 606

Quod Magistratus officium non sit sub novo Testamento genus vitae, I. quod Deo placeat.

Quod homo Christianus salva et illaesa conscientia officio Magistratus II. fungi non possit.

Quod homo Christianus illaesa conscientia officium magistratus, rebus III. ita ferentibus, adversus improbos administrare et exequi, et subditi potestatem illam, quam magistratus a Deo accepit, ad defensionem implorare non possint.

Quod homo Christianus sana conscientia iusiurandum praestare et iura- IIII. mento interposito obedientiam et fidem suo principi aut magistratui promittere nequeat.

Quod Magistratus sub Novo Testamento bona conscientia homines faci- V. norosos capitali supplicio afficere non possit.

Articuli Anabaptistici, qui in Oeconomia ferri non possunt.

Quod homo pius non possit conscientia salva proprium tenere et posside- I. re, sed quod is, quicquid omnino facultatum habeat, id totum in commune conferre debeat.

Quod homo Christianus illaesa conscientia neque cauponariam neque II. mercaturam exercere aut arma conficere possit.

Quod coniugibus propter diversam religionem divortium facere et cum III. alia persona, quae in religione non dissentiat, matrimonium contrahere liceat.

Errores Schwencofeldianorum. 607

Quod omnes illi, qui Christum, secundum carnem creaturam esse dicunt, I. non habeant veram regnantis coelestis Regis agnitionem.

Quod caro Christi per exaltationem eo modo omnes proprietates divinas II. acceperit, ut Christus, quantenus homo est, potentia, virtute, maiestate, gloria Patri et τῷ λόγῳ per omnia in gradu et statu essentiae omnino aequalis sit, ita,

CONCILIUM SAXONICUM – 1577

ren in Christo seien, und daß das Fleisch Christi zu dem wesen der heiligen Dreyfaltigkeit gehöre.

Das der Kirchendienst, das gepredigte und gehörte Wort, nicht sey ein 3. mittel, dadurch Gott, der heilige Geist, die Menschen lere, die seligmachende erkentnüs Christi, bekehrung, buß, glauben und neuen gehorsam in inen wircke.

Daß das Tauffwasser nicht sey ein mittel, dadurch Gott der Herr die 4.|2 Kindschafft versiegele und die Widergeburt wircke.

Das Brot und Wein im heiligen Abendtmal nicht mittel sein, dadurch 5. und damit Christus sein Leib und Blut austeile.

Das ein Christenmensch, der warhafftig durch den Geist Gottes widerge- 6. boren, das Gesetz Gottes in diesem leben vollkomen halten und erfüllen kön- ne.

Das keine rechte Christliche Gemein sey, da kein offentlicher Ausschlus 7. oder ordentlicher Process des Bannes gehalten werde.

Das der Diener der Kirchen andere leute nicht nützlich leren oder rechte, 8. warhafftige Sacrament austeilen könne, welcher nicht auch vor sein person warhafftig verneuert, widergeboren, gerecht und from sey.

Irthumb der neuen Arrianer

Das Christus nicht ein warhafftiger, wesentlicher, natürlicher Gott, eines ewigen Göttlichen wesens mit Gott, dem Vater, und dem heiligen Geist, son- dern allein mit Göttlicher Maiestet unter und neben Gott dem Vater gezieret sey.

Irthumb der Antitrinitarier

Das ist gar eine neue Secte, zuvorn in der Christenheit nicht erhöret, welche gleuben, leren und bekennen, das nicht ein einig, ewig, göttlich wesen sey des Vatern, Sons und heiligen Geists, sondern, wie Gott Vater, Son und heiliger Geist drey unterschiedliche Personen sein, also habe auch ein jede Person ihr unterschiedlich und von andern Personen der Gottheit abgeson-

---

1313 neuen Arrianer] The fathers of the Formula of Concord used the term 'new Arians' for those who, like the Arians in the fourth century, rejected the divinity of Christ. This included for example Johannes Campanus († after 1574) and the Socinian movement

EPITOME – 1577

ut iam utriusque in Christo naturae una sit essentia, eadem proprietates,
eadem voluntas eademque gloria, et quod caro Christi ad Sacrosanctae Trinitatis essentiam pertineat.

Quod ministerium verbi, praedicatum et auditu perceptum verbum non III.
sit instrumentum illud, per quod Deus Spiritus sanctus homines doceat saluta-
remque Christi agnitionem largiatur et conversionem, veram poenitentiam,
fidem et novam obedientiam in ipsis efficiat.

Quod aqua baptismi non sit medium, per quod Dominus adoptionem in IIII.
filiis Dei obsignet et regenerationem efficiat.

Quod panis et vinum in sacra Coena non sint organa, per quae et cum V.
quibus Christus corpus et sanguinem suum distribuat.

Quod homo pius, vere per Spiritum Dei regeneratus, legem Dei in hac VI.
vita perfecte servare et implere valeat.

Quod non sit vera Ecclesia Christi, in qua non vigeat publica excommu- VII.
nicatio et solennis aliquis excommunicationis modus seu, ut vulgo dicitur,
processus ordinarius.

Quod is Ecclesiae minister alios homines cum fructu docere aut vere VIII.
sacramenta dispensare non possit, qui ipse non sit vere renovatus, renatus et
vere iustus.

Error novorum Arianorum.

Quod Christus non sit verus, substantialis, naturalis Deus, eiusdem cum
Patre et Spiritu sancto essentiae, sed divina tantum Maiestate ita cum Patre
ornatus, ut Patre sit inferior.

Error Antitrinitariorum.

Haec prorsus nova haeresis, quae antehac Ecclesiis Christi ignota fuit,
eorum videlicet, qui opinantur, docent et profitentur, non esse unicam tantum
divinam et aeternam Patris, Filii et Spiritus sancti essentiam, sed quemadmodum Pater, Filius et Spiritus sanctus tres sunt distinctae personae, ita
unamquamque personam habere distinctam et a reliquis personis divinitatis

892   CONCILIUM SAXONICUM – 1577

dert wesen, die doch entweder alle drey, wie sonst drey unterschiedene und
voneinander in irem wesen | abgesonderte menschen, gleichs gewalts, weisheit,   253v
Maiestet und herrligkeit oder am wesen und eigenschafften einander ungleich,
das allein der Vater rechter warer Gott sey.

Diese und dergleichen Artickel allzumal und was denselben mehr
irthumb anhengig und daraus erfolget, verwerffen und verdammen wir als
unrecht, falsch, ketzerisch, dem wort Gottes, den dreyen Symbolis, der
Augspurgischen Confeßion und Apologi, den Schmalkaldischen Artickeln
und Catechismis Lutheri zuwider, vor welchen alle frome Christen hohes und
nidriges standes sich hüten sollen, so lieb inen irer Seelen heil und seligkeit ist.

Das dis unser aller Lehr, Glaub und Bekentnus sey, wie wir solches am
Jüngsten Tage vor dem gerechten Richter, unserm Herrn Jhesu Christo,
verantworten, darwider auch nichts heimlich noch offentlich reden oder
schreiben wollen, sondern gedencken vormittelst der gnaden Gottes darbey zu
bleiben, haben wir wolbedechtig in warer furcht und anruffung Gottes mit
eignen handen unterschrieben.

1339 unterschrieben] Andreae's manuscript bears the date 'Actum Berg, den 29ten
Maii 1577' and the signatures of the six fathers of the Formula of Concord: 'Iacobus
Andreae D. subscripsit. Nicolaus Selneccerus D. subscripsit. Andreas Musculus D.
subscripsit. Christophorus Cornerus D. subscripsit. Dauid Chytraeus. Martinus
Kemnicius. D.' The *Book of Concord* forgoes the imprint of these signatures

separatam essentiam. Et horum alii sentiunt, quod singulae personae in singulis essentiis aequali sint potestate, sapientia, maiestate et gloria, sicut alias tres
numero differentes homines, ratione essentiae suae, sunt a se invicem disiuncti
et separati. Alii sentiunt, tres illas personas et essentias ita inaequales esse ratione essentiae et proprietatum, ut solus Deus Pater verus sit Deus.

Hos atque his similes errores omnes et eos etiam, qui ab his dependent et
ex his consequuntur, reiicimus atque damnamus, utpote, qui falsi sint atque
haeretici et qui verbo Dei, tribus approbatis Symbolis, Augustanae Confessioni, eiusdem Apologiae, Smalcaldicis articulis et Catechismis Lutheri repugnent, quos etiam errores omnes pii, summi atque infimi cavere et vitare
debent, nisi aeternae suae salutis iacturam facere velint.

| Quod autem haec sit omnium nostrum fides, doctrina et Confessio (de
qua in novissimo illo die iudici Domino nostro Iesu Christo rationem reddere
parati sumus) et quod contra hanc doctrinam nihil vel occulte vel aperte dicere aut scribere, sed per gratiam Dei in ea constanter perseverare velimus, in
eius rei fidem re bene meditata in vero Dei timore et invocatione nominis eius
hanc epitomen propriis manibus subscripsimus.

CONCILIUM UPSALIENSE

1593

edidit
Oloph BEXELL

THE ASSEMBLY AND *DECRETUM* OF UPPSALA
1593

The *Decretum Upsaliense*, agreed upon at the Assembly of Uppsala (*Uppsala möte*) in 1593, is a document through which a Synod of the ecclesiastical province of Uppsala, in Sweden (at the time including Finland but not the current southern and south-western counties of Sweden, and two in the north, or the island of Gotland), officially adopted the *Confessio Augustana* as the creed of the Lutheran Church of Sweden, along with the *Apostles'*, the *Nicene* and the *Athanasian* creeds. This marked a watershed in the Swedish Reformation.

HISTORICAL BACKGROUND

The history of the Swedish Reformation began in the 1520s, when King Gustav I Vasa (1496-1560) sought to liberate Sweden from its dependency on Denmark and its King Christian II (1481-1559). Christian, King of Denmark and Norway, had occupied Sweden in 1520 and was determined to re-establish the Kalmar Union. After the Stockholm Bloodbath of 7-10 November 1520, Christian was deposed and exiled, and Gustav Vasa was elected King of Sweden in 1523. His intention was to build a Swedish nation with a Swedish royal dynasty. [1] To achieve his goal, he had to thwart the power of the Roman Church across the country. In 1527, with the so-called *Västerås Ordinantia*, the state confiscated massive amounts of wealth owned by the Church and large portions of its domains, and transformed ecclesiastical tithes in tax owed to

---

[1] See Wordsworth, *The National Church*, p. 183-271; Westman, *Reformationens genombrottsår*; Holmquist, *Svenska kyrkans historia*; G. Schwaiger, *Die Reformation in den nordischen Ländern*, München 1962; Andrén, *Reformationen i Norden*; Garstein, *Counter-Reformation in Scandinavia*, vol. 2 (1980); Brohed, *Reformationens konsolidering*; Nyman, *Förlorarnas historia*, p. 11-101; Andrén, *Sveriges kyrkohistoria 3: Reformationstid*, Stockholm 1999.

898 CONCILIUM UPSALIENSE – 1593

the civil authorities. ([2]) As a key ideological means to pursue his intentions, the King encouraged those theologically-motivated aspirations to reform the Church that had been spreading across the country. Advocates of Church reform were favoured and their activism was supported. ([3]) In 1531, Gustav appointed Laurentius Petri Nericius (1499-1573) archbishop of Uppsala without seeking prior approval from Rome, and declared himself the head of the Swedish Church. ([4]) The Diets of Örebro (1540) and Västerås (1544) completed the process of transformation into a hereditary monarchy with a national Church independent from Rome that Sweden had been undergoing in the previous years.

After Gustav I's death in 1560, a political struggle for the throne broke out between his three sons, each of whom became King of Sweden, but also held very different theological positions. ([5]) King Eric XIV (1533-1577), who was deposed by his brothers in 1569, was influenced by Calvinism and sought to reform the Church in a theologically radical direction, as opposed to his father, who was more religiously indifferent. Later on, this led to the so-called Liquorist Controversy between Lutherans and Calvinists in Sweden. ([6]) His brother, King John III (1537-1592) was, theologically speaking, a conservative. In his view, the reorganisation of the Church in Sweden should follow the principles of a conciliatory theology in order to achieve mutual understanding and agreement with the Roman Catholic and the Orthodox churches. A Swedish *Church Ordinance* was promulgated in 1571; ([7]) although they did not formally sanction it, the delegates at the Council of Uppsala (1572) swore

---

(2) 'Ordinantia som giordis j vesteras u herradagen anno XDXXVIJ', in *Handlingar rörande Sveriges historia*, Första serien, vol. 4 (1868), p. 247 ff.; Latin version also in Biblioteca Apostolica Vaticana, Bibl. Borghese, III, 89A. The *Decree* is printed in Tunberg, *Västerås riksdag 1527*, p. 31-39. See also S. Kjöllerström, *Kyrkolagsproblemet i Sverige 1571-1682* (*Samlingar och studier till Svenska Kyrkans Historia / Acta historico-ecclesiastica Suecana* 11), Stockholm 1944, p. 28-56; Id., 'Västerås ordinantia', *Scandia* 26 (1960), p. 41-98.

(3) Bergendoff, *Olavus Petri*; Kjöllerström, 'Gustav Vasa och reformatorerna', *Scandia* 36 (1970), p. 1-16.

(4) T. van Haag, 'Die apostolische Sukzession in Schweden', *Kyrkohistorisk årsskrift* 44 (1944), p. 1-168; Kjöllerström, *Kräkla och mitra*; also Kick, *Tel un navire sur la mer déchaînée*.

(5) Roberts, *The early Vasas*; L.-O. Larsson, *Arvet efter Gustav Vasa. En berättelse om fyra kungar och ett rike*, Stockholm 2005.

(6) Kjöllerström, *Striden kring kalvinismen i Sverige*, p. 147-264.

(7) *Then Swenska Kyrkordningen*, Stockholm 1571. Excerpts in English translation can be found in Yelverton, *The Mass in Sweden*, p. 58-63; Kjöllerström, *Den svenska kyrkoordningen 1571* includes the text in its entirety. On the sources, see E. Färnström, *Om källorna till 1571*; A. Thomson, 'Johan III', p. 345-354.

CONCILIUM UPSALIENSE – 1593

an oath to follow the *Church Ordinance*, to abide by its 'ceremonies and ecclesiastical practices', and to report those who promoted discord and division to the civil authorities. (8) In 1575, King John ordered the approval of a supplement to the *Ordinance*, the so-called *Nova Ordinantia*, (9) encouraging the reading of the Church Fathers and warning against the polemical pamphlets of the reformers. The purpose of the *Nova Ordinantia* was to restore the medieval ecclesiastical structures and offices (dioceses, bishops, provosts, etc.).

King John III himself, in collaboration with his theological advisor, Peter Michaelis Fecht († 1576), worked out a typographically-lavish Order of the Mass with Swedish and Latin parallel texts, the *Liturgia Svecanae Ecclesiae Catholicae et Orthodoxae Conformis* (1576), known as the *Red Book* (*Röda boken*) because of the colour of its headings. This Missal, adopted in 1577, (10) was immediately accused of containing the doctrine of the Eucharistic sacrifice by the supporters of the Reformation. The King, whose ideal was the early apostolic Church, wanted to reunite the Western Church on the foundations laid by the Church Fathers. In 1576, he sent an embassy to Rome to negotiate with Pope Gregory XIII. In exchange for the return of Sweden to the Roman Church as an ecclesiastical province with its own profile, John III pressed for a wide range of dispensations, including communion *sub utraque specie*, Mass in the vernacular (in accordance with the *Liturgia Svecanae Ecclesiae*), and clerical marriage. Not surprisingly, his demands were rejected. The papal nuncio Antonio Possevino (1533-1611) wrote that he himself secretly readmitted John III into the Roman Catholic Church during his visit to Stockholm in May 1578; however, the reliability of this piece of information is disputed. (11)

---

(8) For the text, see the edition below, 'Een copia af det som handlat bleff [...] i Concilio [...] MDLXXII'.

(9) *Nova Ordinantia ecclesiastica anno 75 conscripta et unanimi episcoporum consensu approbata*, first printed in *Handlingar rörande Sveriges historia*, Andra serien, vol. II/2 (1872), p. 181-351. On the King and the *Ordinance*, see Persson, *Johan III och Nova ordinantia*.

(10) The facsimile is printed in *Liturgia Svecanae ecclesiae catholicae & orthodoxae conformis (Johan III:s röda bok)*, Malmö 1953. A parallel edition with an English translation can be found in Yelverton, *The Mass in Sweden*. For a liturgical-historical interpretation, cfr. Serenius, *Liturgia Svecanae catholicae et orthodoxae conformis. En liturgihistorisk undersökning*. On the conflict, see Hammargren, *Den liturgiska striden*.

(11) The reliability of information found in A. Possevino, *Dilectioni Vestrae* (1579), Archivio Segreto Vaticano, Nunziatura di Germania, vol. XCII, fol. 3 is confirmed by Garstein, *Rome and the Counter-Reformation in Scandinavia*, p. 132-136, 141 ff. and 179 ff., as well as by Kjöllerström, *Kräkla och mitra*, p. 91. This is emphatically rejected by S. U. Palme, review of Garstein, 'Rome and the Counter-Reformation in Scandinavia', *Historisk Tidsskrift utgitt av Den norske historiske forening* 45 (1966), p. 136-137 and 158-160 as well as by V. Helk, review of Garstein, 'Rome and the Counter-

900 CONCILIUM UPSALIENSE – 1593

Meanwhile, opposition to King John's theological positions was growing in Sweden, spearheaded by his younger brother Charles (1550-1611), duke of Södermanland-Närke-Värmland (corresponding by and large to the old diocese of Strängnäs and the current diocese of Karlstad) and his circle of trusted ministers, educated in Rostock and influenced by Lutheran orthodoxy holding sway there. ([12]) Charles also wanted to reorganise the Church according to his own mind. Bitter tensions arose between the two brothers, and King John's reform programme was never implemented in Charles' duchy. The *Confessio Strengnensis* (1587), written by Charles' ministers, accused the supporters of the *Liturgia Svecanae Ecclesiae* of crypto-Catholicism; ([13]) the following year, John declared Charles' Lutheran ministers traitors and outlaws in the entire country. ([14]) Thus, the main reason underlying the calling of the Uppsala Assembly was the opposition between the conciliatory theology championed by King John and Lutheran orthodoxy favoured by Duke Charles, i.e. between liturgists and anti-liturgists.

THE ASSEMBLY

In 1590, it was suggested that this conflict should be resolved by a general Synod of the Swedish Church; the ministers on both sides should hold debates over liturgy – in which 'worldly authorities have no say' – in a 'friendly and humble manner'. ([15]) King John III, however, died in 1592; it was therefore Charles who summoned the Assembly in his capacity as regent. The heir-

---

Reformation in Scandinavia', *Historisk Tidsskrift utgitt av Den norske historiske forening* 45 (1966), p. 189-190. I. Montgomery, 'Den svenska religionspolitiken', p. 126 defines the information on his conversion as 'dubious'. The biography by L. Ericson Wolke, *Johan III. En biografi*, Lund 2004, p. 192-193, considers the historical circumstances and the King's personal reasons for a conversion as 'reasonable' elements to trust Possevino. See also Friedrich, 'Johan III – katholischer Gegenreformator oder protestantischer Ireniker?', p. 115-118.

(12) K. Henning, *Strengnäs stift under den liturgiska striden till Upsala möte 1593*, Stockholm 1893.

(13) *Confessio Cleri et Dioecesi Strengnensi de Liturgia*, Uppsala Universitetsbibliotek, MS K 57; *Clerkerijtz Bekennelse i Strengnäs Sticht om Liturgien*, Uppsala Universitetsbibliotek, MS Palmskiöld 112b, fol. 110r-130v. Printed in Chesnecoperus, *Fulkommelige skäl och rättmätige Orsaker*, fol. C3–G6. See also Andrén, 'Uppsala möte 1593'.

(14) *Konung Johans hårda Patent emot Prästerskapet uti Hertig Carls Furstendöme*, Riksarkivet Stockholm, MS Riksregistraturet 1588, fol. 39v-42r; translation in German by von Nettelbladt, *Schwedische Bibliothek*, vol. 4 (1730), p. 81-84. See also Jägerskiöld, 'Johan III:s aktion'.

(15) *Svenska riksdagsakter*, Avd. 1, vol. 2/3 (1899), p. 1040.

CONCILIUM UPSALIENSE – 1593

elect to the throne of Sweden, Charles' nephew Sigismund (1566-1632), who had been crowned King of Poland-Lithuania as Sigismund III (Zygmunt III Waza), was a Roman Catholic; however, he was still abroad and thus temporarily unable to assert his power. The anti-Catholic front had to be rallied before Sigismund could arrive in Sweden, and the Assembly was rapidly called unbeknown to him to meet on 1 March 1593. ([16]) Invitation letters were issued jointly by the duke and his state council (*rådet*) and were addressed to bishops, who were asked to show up accompanied by members of their diocesan chapters and ministers from individual deaneries. ([17]) Ministers began to arrive on 25 February and started preliminary talks. Sessions were held in the now-dismantled diocesan chapter house of Uppsala, near the cathedral. ([18]) The reference to 'a Christian and free Council and Assembly' found in the proceedings of the Synod placed emphasis on the shared view that the gathering was part of a historical continuum. Roughly, the attendance rate was inversely proportional to the distance to travel to Uppsala. The bishops of Linköping, Strängnäs, Västerås and Åbo (Turku) attended the Assembly along with 306 ministers; ([19]) nine state councillors were also present, but they did not have any right to vote. Duke Charles waited in the castle of Uppsala, at a stone's throw from the venue of the Assembly, to be constantly updated on the situation.

No official minutes were written down at the Uppsala Assembly; aside from the list of participants, only a handful working papers have been preserved. ([20]) On the other hand, there are several extensive chronicles of the

---

(16) The manuscript *Decree*, in Riksarkivet Stockholm, MSS no. 14-17, is printed in *Svenska riksdagsakter*, Avd. 1, vol. 3/1 (1894), p. 86-91; *Confessio Fidei. Uppsala mötes beslut 1593 om Svenska kyrkans bekännelse*, utg. L. Eckerdal – P. E. Persson, Stockholm 1993. For contemporary records of the Assembly together with the Decree and other documents, see *Svenska riksdagsakter*, Avd. 1, vol. 3/1 (1894), p. 26-116; Ahnfelt, 'Berättelse om Uppsala möte', p. 30-45; Latin and German translations in von Nettelbladt, *Schwedische Bibliothek*, vol. 4 (1730), p. 98-109. On the Assembly, see Kjöllerström, 'Die Nationalsynode zu Uppsala', p. 103-108; Cnattingius, *Uppsala möte*; Roberts, *The Early Vasas*, p. 327-338; Montgomery, *Värjostånd och lärostånd*, p. 83-100; Id., 'Uppsala möte 1593'; Garstein, *Rome and the Counter-Reformation in Scandinavia*, p. 94-109.

(17) *Svenska riksdagsakter*, Avd. 1, vol. 3/1 (1894), p. 16.

(18) Carlsson, 'Nuvarande domkyrkans omgivningar', p. 106-115.

(19) Due to their advanced age and the harsh Scandinavian winter, the bishops of Skara and Växjö did not attend.

(20) The ministers at the Assembly handed a joint request to the duke and council of state asking that the University of Uppsala, founded in 1477 but closed during the 1500s, be re-established. This happened in 1595.

CONCILIUM UPSALIENSE – 1593

Assembly, written later on by representatives of the successful majority; ([21]) reports authored by the defeated group of supporters of the *Red Book* are not available. The archiepiscopal see of Uppsala was at that time vacant after the death of its latest officeholder, and the regent insisted on postponing the election of a new archbishop until after the Assembly; thus, the latter had no obvious president. The first session, held on 3 March, was introduced by the seneschal of the Kingdom (*riksdrotsen*), who spoke on behalf of the duke and presided over the election of the moderator of the Synod. ([22]) The bishop of Linköping, the obvious candidate to the role, had once been a supporter of King John's *Liturgia Svecanae Ecclesiae*; the duke therefore favoured a free election of somebody who was not a bishop. Professor Nicolaus Olai Bothniensis († 1600), the product of an orthodox Lutheran education in Rostock, was elected moderator of the Assembly. Six years later, he was appointed archbishop of Uppsala.

Synodal works began with a speech by the moderator, who reminded the Assembly of how the Church had always settled disputes through councils. He also aired a number of theses, written by himself, on the Holy Scriptures and on how the Church Fathers as well as the early Christian creeds were closely related to the former. ([23]) In the following sessions, the *Confessio Augustana* was read aloud in Latin and in Swedish, article by article, and everyone was invited to speak and to vote on each and every single article. On 5 March, the Assembly approved the *Augustana*; delegates declared to be prepared to defend the Christian faith with their 'life and blood', as was written in the confession. On this occasion, the moderator is believed to have uttered the well-known phrase 'Now Sweden has become as one man and we all have one Lord and God'. ([24])

Later on, the delegates considered those liturgical issues which represented matters of debate. By that moment, nobody was any longer willing to stand up for the late King John's *Liturgia*: the Synod rejected it unanimously. Many among those who used to be supporters of the *Red Book* requested – more or

---

(21) *Svenska riksdagsakter*, Avd. 1, vol. 3/1 (1894), p. 1-149; a report of the Assembly is also printed in Cnattingius, 'D-källan till Uppsala möte', p. 328-339.

(22) The seneschal of the Kingdom was baron Nils Gyllenstierna (af Lundholm) (1526-1601); he enrolled at the universities of Wittenberg (1542) and Rostock (1563).

(23) Cnattingius, 'Nicolaus Bothniensis' teser om Skriften 1584 och Uppsala mötes beslut', *Kyrkohistorisk årsskrift* 34 (1934), p. 161-196.

(24) *Svenska riksdagsakter*, Avd. 1, vol. 3/1 (1894), p. 51, also printed in Cnattingius, 'D-källan till Uppsala möte', p. 334. In general on the sources, see K. Hildebrand, 'Undersökningar'. On the authenticity of the quotation, see Ahnlund, *Tradition och historia*, p. 54-62.

less voluntarily – to speak, and one by one they offered their own humblest apologies for having upheld erroneous positions in the past. On 12 March, a draft version of the *Decretum* was submitted to the regent's attention for approval. Charles managed to sneak in some amendments to several formulations, but he was ultimately forced to make considerable concessions to the Assembly, and the result was a compromise. For example, against the regent's wishes, the final version of the *Decretum* featured condemnations of 'Papists' and 'Sacramentarians', but crucially also of Zwinglians, Calvinists, and 'all other Heretics'. The Assembly also elected Abraham Angermannus (*c.* 1540-1607) archbishop of Uppsala. Angermannus had been the leading adversary of the *Liturgia* and had suffered exile under the reign of John III. ([25])

THE *DECRETUM*

The *Decretum Upsaliense* constitutes a *summa* of the final decisions of the Assembly. ([26]) In this document, Duke Charles made known, along with the state councillors, bishops and 'ordinary ministers' who had 'gathered [...] at Uppsala', the result of the Assembly's deliberations. It was 'a Christian, general, free, domestic assembly as has always been the custom since the time of the Apostles and ever since', and the document referred to the fact that King John himself had been planning to summon such a gathering.

The Assembly, through Article 1 of its *Decretum*, expressed the desire to uphold 'the pure and sanctifying Word of God' as the fundamental rule of Christian faith and doctrine. In the parishes of Sweden 'it should be taught, believed and made known that the Holy Scriptures derive their origin from the Holy Spirit and contain all the necessary Christian knowledge of God Almighty, our salvation and of good deeds and actions'. The Bible was the foundation of faith and the guiding light for preventing or settling any dispute over religion. Neither 'the holy Fathers' nor anyone else, with whatever authority – and this might be a reference to Duke Charles – may add anything

---

(25) R. Ohlsson, *Abraham Angermannus. En biografisk studie* (*Samlingar och studier till Svenska Kyrkans Historia / Acta historico-ecclesiastica Suecana* 13), Stockholm 1946; cfr. the review by S. U. Palme, *Kyrkohistorisk årsskrift* 46 (1946), p. 329-345. See also Montgomery, 'Frihet, politik och religion. Självständighetens problematik 1593-1608. Problemet mäster Abraham', in A. Laine – A. Laitinen (toim.), *Yliopisto, kirkko ja yhteiskunta. Aila Lauhan juhlakirja* (*Suomen kirkkohistoriallisen seuran toimituksia / Finska kyrkohistoriska samfundets* handlingar 218), Helsinki 2011, p. 143-154.

(26) Facsimile in *Svenska riksdagsakter*, Avd. 1, vol. 3/1 (1894), p. 96-97. A German translation of the *Decretum Upsaliense* can be found in Rango, *Svecia Orthodoxa*, p. 39-46.

to the Word of God at his own discretion or pleasure. Article 2 accepted (*bejake och wederkännes*) the three creeds (*symbola*) of the early Church and the 'earliest, truthful and unadulterated' version of the *Confessio Augustana*, i.e. the one written in 1530.

Article 3 declared that the Church of Sweden abode by 'the religion that existed at the end of the reign of King Gustav' and that was 'written down by Archbishop Laurentius Petri Nericianus in his Church Ordinance of 1571', which was 'issued from the printers in the year [15]72' and later 'agreed upon and accepted'. Certain liturgical practices used in the celebration of baptism and of the Eucharist accepted by the *Church Ordinance* were discussed: the use of salt and candles, the elevation, the moving of the Missal 'from one corner [of the altar] to the other', and bell-tolling during the elevation. According to the *Decretum*, these liturgical practices had not led to any abuse. These rites had already been withdrawn by most Evangelical churches, as 'more evils [came] from the[ir] abuse than good from the[ir] use'. Bishops and ministers should therefore teach the people so that abuses disappear. If that is not possible, bishops, diocesan chapters and ministers should discuss how these ceremonies could eventually be abolished without upsetting their flocks. Article 4 stated that the performance of an exorcism rite was not a precondition for the validity of baptism. However, it was a reminder of the state of the human soul, tarnished by original sin, and a testimony to the powerful effects of baptism. On this particular point, the *Decretum* left individual parishes free to make exorcism optional. In order not to upset the common folk, and to remind that in any case the children's bodies were beset by the devil, the words 'Get out of here' should be replaced by 'Turn away from here'. As long as the unity of faith was preserved, this article did not condemn any 'parishes in foreign countries or mighty people in this country' unwilling to change this rite. Finally, Article 5 rejected and condemned King John's *Liturga Svecanae Ecclesiae* as far too 'similar to the Pope's Mass' and as 'the root and cause of much anxiety'. All 'Popish, Sacramentarian, Zwinglian, Calvinist, Anabaptist, and all other Heretical delusions' were refuted. Christians of other confessions should not be exiled on account of their 'actions and conduct' but were not allowed to worship publicly and must not revile the national Church. Ecclesiastical discipline should follow the *Church Ordinance* of 1571 and should be administered by bishops and chapters.

The purpose of the *Decretum* was to clarify the confessional tenets of the Church of Sweden and to affirm the authority of the 1571 *Church Ordinance*. The *Decretum* had to be printed and disseminated as quickly as possible, as it had been adopted unanimously with the gracious help and assistance of the Almighty God. The delegates had also promised not to allow themselves to be

CONCILIUM UPSALIENSE – 1593

'lured, forced, or give in to pressure', whether through gifts, favours, friendship, family affinity, threats, antipathy or curses. In 1593, a book containing the *Decretum* along with all the other previous theological documents that the *Decretum* had endorsed was published. It included an extensive subtitle, of which the first part reads as follows in English: *Confessio Fidei. That is: The Christian creed, which the Church of God in the Kingdom of Sweden has generally believed and professed since the truth of the Gospel through the grace of God, during [...] the reign of [...] King Gustav, was brought back from Papal darkness to light [...].* (27) This book was widely disseminated and has since been reprinted in a number of new editions, of which the latest appeared in 1993. On the 1693 centenary, this book was also translated into Finnish. (28) The president of the Assembly, Nicolaus Bothniensis, and the newly-elected archbishop, Abraham Angermannus, took care of the publication of the *Confessio Fidei*. Most probably, they were the authors behind the anonymous foreword and postscript of the *Confessio* and might also have prepared the Swedish translation of the theological articles.

The *Decretum*'s foreword ('Allom och serdeles'), dated 30 June 1593, declared that the Uppsala Assembly was summoned as 'a free Christian Council' (*Concilium*) in order to prevent divisions and discord and to abolish everything that nobody 'who kept close to God and to the truth' could possibly want to preserve. It then described how the *Decretum* was approved unanimously and was immediately sent off to all parishes of Sweden to be read, signed and sealed. In order to persuade the reader that 'our confession of faith is not founded on anything other than the writings of the Prophets and the Apostles, and is testified by the Teachers of the Ancient Church, as they desired to keep to the Holy Scriptures', the book also included the creeds of the early Church as well as 'the unaltered Augsburg Confession [...] as it was offered to Emperor Charles V'. The Swedish Church's confession of faith contained, in short, 'the core and sum of our Christian religion', as it was 'more extensively testified by the Holy Spirit and described in the writings of the Prophets and the Apostles'. In this edition of documents, the *Decretum* was

---

(27) *Confessio fidei, Thet är.* It has since been published in a number of editions (the latest one in 1993). The *Decree* of the Uppsala Assembly is also reprinted in current editions of the Church of Sweden's confessional documents, including the *Book of Concord*. The latest edition is found in *Svenska kyrkans bekännelseskrifter*, utg. Samfundet Pro Fide et Christianismo, Stockholm 2005, p. 703-710.

(28) *Confessio fidei, Se on.* For a facsimile edition with commentaries and a summary in German, see M. Parvio (toim.), *Confessio fidei. Suomen luterilaisuuden ensimmäinen tunnustuskirja* (*Suomen kirkkohistoriallisen seuran toimituksia* 162.), Helsinki 1993, p. 1-159.

906 CONCILIUM UPSALIENSE – 1593

thus complemented by the full texts of the *Confessio Augustana* and the *Credo Apostolicum, Nicaenum* and *Athanasianum* as well as by the resolutions of the Synod of Uppsala of 1572. The proceedings of the 1572 Synod stated that the Church of Sweden accepted the Christian doctrine as found in the writings of the prophets and of the Apostles; that marriage between cousins was prohibited; that it ratified the practices and ceremonies mentioned in the 1571 *Church Ordinance*; that ministers were encouraged to be mindful of itinerant preachers who stirred division and rebellion. The book also included a short postscript discouraging the dissemination of any heretical 'books or libellous pamphlets' or the transgression or defamation of the decisions taken by the Church assembled. If anyone wanted to discuss the latter, this debate should take place at 'ordinary meetings and *Academiae Consistorio*', where anyone could be interrogated and appropriately judged. '[G]eneral and authoritative' visitations across Sweden should be undertaken by archbishops and bishops; if need arose, they should seek the 'Governor' (*Gubernator*) and the civil authorities' assistance. (29)

The Assembly requested the Duke – the 'gracious promoter of the Assembly' – and his state council to sign the *Decretum* and required 'other Estates, the Aristocracy, the Burghers, the Officers' to do the same. As the Foreword declared, copies of the *Decretum* were sent off to the diocesan chapters for approval. It was signed by both Duke Charles and Duke Gustav of Saxony-Angria-Westphalia (Gustav Vasa's nephew, who resided in Sweden) as well as by 14 state councillors, 7 bishops, 1556 ministers, 218 noblemen, and 157 officers, along with the mayors and magistrates of 36 cities and the delegates of 197 deaneries (*härader*) and counties.

During his coronation ceremony, King Sigismund had to swear an oath that he would not attempt to overthrow the *Decretum* of the Uppsala Assembly. The implementation of the *Decretum* was reinforced when he was deposed in 1599. His uncle, Duke Charles of Södermanland-Närke-Värmland, was crowned King in 1609 with the name of Charles IX.

NOTE ON THE EDITION

The text of the Foreword, *Decretum*, Postscript and Appendix is offered below in accordance with the official printed edition, *Confessio fidei. Thet är:*

---

(29) A few years later, Archbishop Angermannus carried out visitations across the entire country as the official delegate of the duke. See *Ärkebiskop Abrahams räfst. Efter originalakterna*, utg. O. Holmström (*Skrifter utg. av Svenska Kyrkohistoriska Föreningen* 4/1-2.), 2 vols, Uppsala 1901-1902; Ohlsson, *Abraham Angermannus*, p. 268-284.

then christeligha troos bekännelse, hwilka Gudz försambling, vthi Sweriges Rijke almänneligha trodt och bekänt hafwer [...] Stockholm 1593-1594. In this edition, an appendix, consisting of 'a copy of the Resolution that was passed and signed by the clergy at a Council held at Uppsala in August 1572', was added. The text is also reprinted here in accordance with that edition.

BIBLIOGRAPHY

Sources (and Their Abbreviations)

Biblioteca Apostolica Vaticana

Bibl. Borghese III, 89 A *Constitutiones Sueticae in publicis comitijs regnorum Sueciae et Gothiae factae, anno Dni Millesimo quingentesimo septimo circa Dominicam Trinitatis in civitate Arosiensi per Gustavum eorundem regnorum regem et eius proceres ad subvertendam in illis terris omnem catholicae ecclesiae et Sanctae Sedis Apostolicae auctoritatem,* fol. 39v-42r.

Riksarkivet Stockholm

MS no. 15	*Decretum Upsalense,* 'Ständernas beslut och försäkringar'.
MSS no. 14-17	*Decretum Upsalense,* 'Ständernas beslut och försäkringar'.
MS Riksregistraturet 1588	*Konung Johans hårda Patent emot Prästeskapet uti Hertig Carls Furstendöme,* fol. 39v-42r.

Uppsala Universitetsbibliotek

MS K57	*Confessio Cleri et Diocesi Strengnenses de Liturgia.*

908   CONCILIUM UPSALIENSE – 1593

OTHER SOURCES

N. Chesnecoperus, *Fulkommelige skäl och rättmätige Orsaker, Så och sanfärdige Berättelser, Hwarföre Samptlige Sweriges Rijkes Ständer hafwe medh all fogh och rätt afsagdt konung Sigismundum vthi Polen och storfurste j Littowen, etc. sampt alle hans efterkommande lijfsarwingar ewärdeligen ifrå Sweriges Rijkes Crona och Regemente, och all then hörsamheet och lydhno, som the honom efter Arfföreeningen hafwe skyldige och plichtige warit, och vthi stadhen igen vthkorat, anammat och crönt* [...] *Then Stormächtigste, Höghborne Furste och Herre, Her Carl then nijonde, Sweriges, Göthes, Wendes, Finnars, Carelers, Lapers j Norlanden, the Cajaners och Esters j Lifland, etc. Konung, sampt alle H.K.M.s efterkommande LifsArwingar, til deres och Sweriges Rijkes rätte Konunger och Herrer. Allom och hwariom och eenom, som sanningen begäre at wetta, til rättelse och vnderwijsning,* Stockholm 1607 [= Chesnecoperus, *Fulkommelige skäl och rättmätige Orsaker*].

Confessio fidei, Se on: Sen Christillisen Uscon Tunnustus, jonga Jumalan Seuracunda Ruotzin Waldacunnas, yhteisest' usconut ja tunnustanut on, sijtä Ajasta, cuin Evangeliumin Totuus, corkiasa Cunnia-Muistos ylistetyn Cuningas Gustawin hallituxen Aicana, Pawilaisesta pimeydestä, Jumalan Armon cautta, jällens Walkeuteen tuli. Ja sitte Wuona 1572. Cuningas Johan wainan Hallituxen alla, Upsalan yhteisesä Pappein-Cocouxesa wast'udest wahwistettu. Ja wielä edespäin Wuonna 1593. sijnä Christilisesä ja wapasa Conciliumis, joca samasa paicasa pidettin, caikilda Waldacunnan Säädyildä, alakirjoituxilla ja Sineteillä tuli wahwistetuxi ja tuetuxi, caikille Christin-Uscowaisille ja jälken tulewaisille uscollisexi Neuwoxi, terwellisexi wahwistamisexi, ja muttamattomaxi Testamentixi. Mutta nyt wast'udesta Cuningallisen Majestetin Armollisimman Käskyn jälken ylöspandu ja Prändistä ulosannettu, tänä sisäll'olewaisna Wuonna, joca on se Sadas Upsalan Cocouxen jälken, Turku 1693 [= *Confessio fidei, Se on*].

Confessio fidei. Suomen luterilaisuuden ensimmäinen tunnustuskirja, toim. M. Parvio (*Suomen kirkkohistoriallisen seuran toimituksia* 162), Helsinki 1993.

Confessio fidei. Thet är: Then Christeligha Troos Bekännelse, hwilka Gudz Försambling, vthi Sweriges Rijke almänneligha trodt och bekänt hafwer, ifrå thet Euangelij sanning, vthi Konung Gvstafs, höghlofligh ihughkommelse, Regementz tijdh, vthur thet Påweska mörkret, igenom Gudz nådh, åter kom j liuset igen. Och sedhan Anno etc. 72 vnder saligh Konung Jahans Regering, j Vpsala almänne Prestemöte på nytt bekräftighat. Men nu yterlighare och fornemligest genom then Högborne Furstes och Herres, Her

CONCILIUM UPSALIENSE – 1593

Carls, Sweriges Rijkes Arffurstes Hertigz til Sudermanland, Näricke och Wärmelandh: Christelighe omwårdnet och trogne förfordran j thetta åhr etc. 93 vthi thet christeligha och frija Concilio som genom Hans F: rådh och bijståndh thärsammestädz hållet, af alle Rijkesens Ständer, medh Vnder-skrifning och Insighel wardt stadfäst och confirmerat, allom Christroghnom och wårom efterkommandom til troghna vnderwijsning, helsosamma styrkio och oryggelighit Testament. Stockholm 1593-1594 [= *Confessio fidei. Thet är*].

Confessio Fidei. Uppsala mötes beslut 1593 om Svenska kyrkans bekännelse, utg. L. Eckerdal – P. E. Persson, Stockholm 1993.

C. von Nettelbladt, *Schwedische Bibliothec, in welcher verschiedene sowol zur alten als neuern schwedischen Civil- Kirchen- und gelehrten Historie gehöri-ge, theils gedruckte und rare, theils ungedruckte Schrifften, Uhrkunden, Diplomata, Observationes, Inscriptiones, &c. als auch alle Disciplinen und Facultäten betreffende alte und neue Erfindungen, Erläuterungen, Verbesse-rungen, u.d.g. Wie nicht weniger die Lebens-Beschreibungen berühmter schwedischer Helden und gelahrter Männer, Relationes von merckwürdigen Begebenheiten, curieuse Müntzen und Schau-Pfenninge, &c. Samt den Novis literariis Sveciæ, mit gebührendem Fleisz gesammlet, und zum Beweisz der blühenden Gelehrsamkeit in Schweden dargeleget werden*, 4 vols, Stockholm – Leipzig 1728-1730 [von Nettelbladt, *Schwedische Bibliothec*].

C. T. Rango, *Svecia Orthodoxa, das ist: Das rechtgläubige nordische Königreich Schweden, wie dasselbe, von Zeit der Reformation Gustavi Erici immerdar der Lehre der einmahlangenommenen Augspurgischen Confession, und wie dieselbe hernach in den übrigen Büchern Libri Concordiae erkläret ist, eifrig zugethan geblieben sey und bleiben wolle, als ein der Schwedischen Kirchen-Historien Kurtzer Ausszug mit Anziehung der ins Teutsche übersetzen Königl. Versicherungen, Diplomatum und Urkunden nebst einigen Historischen und Theologischen Digressionibus*, Stettin 1688 [= Rango, *Svecia Orthodoxa*].

Then Swenska Kyrkeordningen, Stockholm 1571.

LITERATURE (AND ITS ABBREVIATIONS)

O. Ahnfelt, 'Berättelse om Uppsala möte i Linköpingshandskriften T 136', *Kyrkohistorisk årsskrift* 3 (1902), p. 30-45 [Ahnfelt, 'Berättelse om Uppsala möte'].

N. Ahnlund, *Tradition och historia*, Stockholm 1956 [= Ahnlund, *Tradition och historia*].

Å. Andrén, *Reformationstid*, in L. Tegborg (utg.), *Sveriges kyrkohistoria*, 8 vols, Stockholm 1998-2005, vol. 3 (1999).

—, 'Uppsala möte 1593 och Strängnäsbeslutet "om ceremoniernas bortlegning"', *Kungliga Humanistiska vetenskapssamfundet i Lund. Årsberättelse* 53/3 (1952), p. 97-120 [= Andrén, 'Uppsala möte 1593'].

C. Bergendoff, *Olavus Petri and the Ecclesiastical Transformation in Sweden 1521-1552: A Study in the Swedish Reformation*, Philadelphia 1956 [= Bergendoff, *Olavus Petri*].

R. Carlsson, 'Nuvarande domkyrkans omgivningar', in R. Carlsson et al. (utg.), *Uppsala domkyrka*, 9 vols, Uppsala 2010-2016, vol. 2 (2010), p. 65-378 [= Carlsson, 'Nuvarande domkyrkans omgivningar'].

H. Cnattingius, 'Författarskapet till Uppsala mötes D-källa', *Kyrkohistorisk årsskrift* 48 (1948), p. 155-162.

—, 'D-källan till Uppsala möte', *Kyrkohistorisk årsskrift* 44 (1944), p. 292-339 [= Cnattingius, 'D-källan till Uppsala möte'].

—, *Uppsala möte. Konturerna av en kyrkokris,* Stockholm 1943 [= Cnattingius, *Uppsala möte*].

L. Ericson Wolke, *Johan III. En biografi*, Lund 2004

E. Färnström, *Om källorna till 1571 års kyrkoordning med hänsyn till tyska kyrkoordningar*, Uppsala 1935 [= Färnström, *Om källorna till 1571*].

M. Friedrich, 'Johan III – katholischer Gegenreformator oder protestantischer Ireniker? Ein hinweis auf eine bislang unbeachtete Quelle', *Kyrkohistorisk årsskrift* 96 (1996), p. 115-118 [= Friedrich, 'Johan III – katholischer Gegenreformator oder protestantischer Ireniker?'].

O. B. Garstein, *Rome and the Counter-Reformation in Scandinavia until the Establishment of the* S. Congregatio de Propaganda Fide *in 1622: Based on the Source Material in the Kolsrud Collection*, 2 vols, Oslo 1964-1980 [Garstein, *Counter-Reformation in Scandinavia*].

G. Gaßmann, 'Synode III/3', in *Theologische Realenzyklopädie*, 36 vols, Berlin – New York 1976-2004, vol. 32 (2001), p. 583.

G. Göransson, 'Schweden', in *Evangelisches Kirchenlexikon. Internationale theologische Enzyklopädie*, 5 vols, Göttingen [3]1986-1997, vol. 4 (1996), col. 143-144.

—, 'Schweden. I. Kirchengeschichte', in *Die Religion in Geschichte und Gegenwart*, 6 vols, Tübingen [3]1957-1962, vol. 5 (1961), col. 1594.

CONCILIUM UPSALIENSE – 1593   911

T. van Haag, 'Die apostolische Sukzession in Schweden', *Kyrkohistorisk årsskrift* 44 (1944), p. 1-168.

A. Hammargren, *Den liturgiska striden under konung Johan III*, Uppsala 1898 [= Hammargren, *Den liturgiska striden*].

Handlingar rörande Sveriges historia. På Kongl. Majt:s nådiga befallning med understöd af statsmedel utgifna av Kongl. Riks-Arkivet, utg. Kongl. Riksarkivet, 50 vols, Stockholm 1861-1959 [= *Handlingar rörande Sveriges historia*].

K. Hildebrand, 'Undersökningar till Uppsala mötes historia', *Historisk tidskrift* 13 (1893), p. 89-122 [= Hildebrand, 'Undersökningar'].

H. Holmquist, *Svenska kyrkans historia. Reformationstidevarvet. 1521-1611*, Stockholm 1933 [= Holmquist, *Svenska kyrkans historia*].

O. Jägerskiöld, 'Johan III:s aktion mot prästerskapet i hertig Karls furstendöme 1588', in S. Grauers – Å. Stille (utg.), *Historiska studier tillägnade Nils Ahnlund 23/8/1949*, Stockholm 1949, p. 105-117 [= Jägerskiöld, 'Johan III:s aktion'].

A. Jarlert, 'Schweden II', in *Theologische Realenzyklopädie*, 36 vols, Berlin – New York 1976-2004, vol. 30 (1999), p. 654-655.

R. Kick, *Tel un navire sur la mer déchaînée: La communauté chrétienne dans l'oeuvre de Laurentius Petri, archevêque d'Uppsala (1531-1573)* (*Bibliotheca Theologica Lundensia* 52), Lund 1997 [= Kick, *Tel un navire sur la mer déchaînée*].

S. Kjöllerström, 'Gustav Vasa och reformatorerna', *Scandia* 26 (1970), p. 1-19.

—, *Kräkla och mitra. En undersökning om biskopsvigningar i Sverige under reformationstiden* (*Bibliotheca Theologiae Practicae* 19), Lund 1965 [= Kjöllerström, *Kräkla och mitra*].

—, 'Västerås ordinantia', *Scandia* 26 (1960), p. 41-98.

—, 'Das Bekenntnis in der schwedischen Reformationskirche', in G. Aulén (hrsg.), *Ein Buch der Kirche. Unter Mitarbeit schwedischer Theologen*, Göttingen 1951, p. 212-233.

—, 'Vår kyrkas bekännelseskrifter i svensk språkdräkt', *Svensk Teologisk Kvartalskrift* 21 (1945), p. 251-256.

—, 'Die Nationalsynode zu Uppsala. Eine schwedische Dreihundertfünfzigjahrfeier', *Protestantische Rundschau* 20 (1943), p. 193-208. [= Kjöllerström, 'Die Nationalsynode zu Uppsala'].

—, *Striden kring kalvinismen i Sverige under Erik XIV. En kyrkohistorisk studie*, Lund 1935 [Kjöllerström, *Striden kring kalvinismen i Sverige*].

912 CONCILIUM UPSALIENSE – 1593

Liturgia Svecanae Ecclesiae Catholicae & Orthodoxae Conformis (Johan III:s röda bok). Tryckt i Stockholm 1576. Faksimiledition, utg. S. Kroon, Malmö 1953.

I. Montgomery, 'Uppsala möte 1593', *Kyrkohistorisk årsskrift* 93 (1993), p. 13-19 [= Montgomery, 'Uppsala möte 1593'].

—, 'Den svenska religionspolitiken', in I. Brohed (utg.), *Reformationens konsolidering i de nordiska länderna*, Oslo 1990, p. 119-136 [= Montgomery, 'Den svenska religionspolitiken'].

—, *Värjostånd och lärostånd. Religion och politik i meningsutbytet mellan kungamakt och prästerskap i Sverige 1593-1608 (Acta Universitatis Upsaliensis. Studia Historico-Ecclesiastica Upsaliensia* 22), Uppsala 1972 [= Montgomery, *Värjostånd och lärostånd*].

M. Nyman, *Förlorarnas historia. Katolskt liv i Sverige från Gustav Vasa till drottning Kristina*, Stockholm 1997 [= Nyman, *Förlorarnas historia*].

R. Persson, *Johan III och Nova ordinantia (Bibliotheca theologiae practicae* 30), Lund 1973 [= Persson, *Johan III och Nova ordinantia*].

H. Pleijel, *Svensk lutherdom. Studier i luthersk fromhet och svensk folkkultur*, Stockholm 1944.

Reformationen i Norden. Kontinuitet och förnyelse, utg. C.-G. Andrén (*Skrifter utg. av Nordiskt institut för kyrkohistorisk forskning* 3), Lund 1973 [= Andrén, *Reformationen i Norden*].

Reformationens konsolidering i de nordiska länderna 1540-1610, utg. I. Brohed (*Skrifter utg. av Nordiskt institut för kyrkohistorisk forskning* 6), Oslo 1990 [= Brohed, *Reformationens konsolidering*].

M. Roberts, *The Early Vasas: A History of Sweden 1523-1611*, Cambridge 1968 [= Roberts, *The Early Vasas*].

S. Serenius, *Liturgia Svecanae catholicae et orthodoxae conformis. En liturgihistorisk undersökning med särskild hänsyn till struktur och förlagor (Acta Academiae Aboensis: Humaniora* 33:1), Åbo 1966 [= Serenius, *En liturgihistorisk undersökning*].

Den svenska kyrkoordningen 1571 jämte studier kring tillkomst, innehåll och användning, utg. S. Kjöllerström, Lund 1971 [= Kjöllerström, *Den svenska kyrkoordningen 1571*].

Svenska riksdagsakter jämte andra handlingar som höra till statsförfattningens historia under tidehvarfvet 1521-1718, utg. E. Hildebrand et al., 15 vols, Stockholm 1887-1954 [= *Svenska riksdagsakter*].

CONCILIUM UPSALIENSE – 1593

A. Thomson, 'Johan III och stadfästelsen av 1571 års kyrkoordning', *Scandia* 31 (1965), p. 345-354 [= Thomson, 'Johan III'].

S. Tunberg, *Västerås riksdag 1527. Några kritiska anmärkningar* (*Uppsala universitets årsskrift 1915: Filosofi* 1), Uppsala 1915 [= Tunberg, *Västerås riksdag 1527*].

K. B. Westman, 'Ett par fynd i Strängnäs domkapitels arkiv. 2. Strängnensiska prästmötesföredrag från tiden 1585-1601', *Kyrkohistorisk årsskrift* 20 (1919), p. 349-353.

—, *Reformationens genombrottsår i Sverige*, Stockholm 1918 [= Westman, *Reformationens genombrottsår*].

J. Wordsworth, *The National Church of Sweden*, London 1911 [= Wordsworth, *The National Church*].

E. E. Yelverton, *The Mass in Sweden: Its Development from the Latin Rite from 1531 to 1917* (*Henry Bradshaw Society Lectures* 57), London 1920 [= Yelverton, *The Mass in Sweden*].

MONITUM

Confessio fidei. Thet är: Then Christeligha Troos Bekännelse, hwilka Gudz Försambling, vthi Sweriges Rijke almänneligha trodt och bekänt hafwer, ifrå thet Euangelij sanning, vthi Konung Gvstafs, höghlofligh ihughkommelse, Regementz tijdh, vthur thet Påweska mörkret, igenom Gudz nådh, åter kom j liuset igen. Och sedhan Anno etc. 72 vnder saligh Konung Jahans Regering, j Vpsala almänne Prestemöte på nytt bekräftighat. Men nu yterlighare och fornemligest genom then Högborne Furstes och Herres, Her Carls, Sweriges Rijkes Arffurstes Hertigz til Sudermanland, Näricke och Wärmelandh: Christeligbe omwårdnet och trogne förfordran j thetta åhr etc. 93 vthi thet christeligha och frija Concilio som genom Hans F: rådh och bijståndh thärsammestädz hållet, af alle Rijkesens Ständer, medh Vnderskrifning och Insighel wardt stadfäst och confirmerat, allom Christroghnom och wårom efterkommandom til troghna vnderwijsning, helsosamma styrkio och oryggelighit Testament, Stockholm 1593-1594, p. 1-13, 164-170.

CONCILIUM UPSALIENSE
1593

CONFESSIO FIDEI.

Thet är: Then Christeliga Troos Bekännelse, hwilka Gudz försambling uthi Sweriges Rijke almänneliga trodt och bekändt hafwer, ifrå thet Euangelij sanning, uthi Konung GUSTAFS, höghlofligh ihughkommelse, Regementz tijdh, uthur thet Påweske mörkret, igenom Gudz nådh, åter kom j liwset igen.

Och sedhan Anno etc. 72 under saligh Konung IAHANS Regering, j Upsala almänne Prestemöte på nytt bekräftighat.

Men nu yterligare och förnemligest genom then Högbome Furstes och Herres, Her CARLS, Sweriges Rijkes Arffurstes, Hertigz til Sudermanlandh, Näricke och Wärmelandh: Christelighe omwårdnet och trogne förfordran, j thetta åhr etc. 93, uthi thet Christeligha och frija Concilio, som genom hans F: rådh och bijståndh, thär sammestädz hållet, och sedhan aff alle Rijkesens Ständer, medh Underskriffning och lnsigel wardt stadfäst och confirmerat, allom Christtrognom och wårom effterkommandom til troghna underwijsning, helsosamma styrkio och oryggeligit Testament.

Tryckt j Stockholm, aff Andrea Gutterwitz. Anno Christi M.D.XCIII.

| 2. Paralip: 15.

Och the trädde uthi förbundet, at the skulle sökia HERRAN, theras Fäders Gudh aff alt hierta, och aff allo siäl, Och hwilken somicke sökte HERRAN Israels Gudh, han skulle döö, bådhe liten och stoor, bådhe man och qwinna. Och the sworo HERRANOM medh högha röst, medh roop, medh trommeter och basuner. Och hela Juda frögdadhe sigh öffuer eedhen, ty the hadhe sworit aff alt hierta, och the sökte honom aff allom wilia, och han lät sigh aff them finna. Och HERREN gaff them roo alt om kring.

23/29 Och – kring] II Par. 15, 12-15

918 CONCILIUM UPSALIENSE – 1593

30 [FOREWORD]

Allom och serdeles hwariom och enom Christrognom, som thenna näst-
följande Bekännelse läsandes eller hörandes warder, tilbiude och önske wij
underskrifne, hwar j sitt stånd och wärdigheet, Gudz nådhe och barmhertig-
heet, genom Frelsaren IEsum CHristum, etc.

35 Efter thet at then splijt och oenigheet, som j förledne åhr hafwer waridt
på färde uthi Religions sakerne, j wårt käre Fädernes-Rijke, är nu medh thens
Alzmächtiges nådige tilhielp, j thet Christelige, frije *Concilio* och Möte, som
stodh j Upsala, åhr etc. 93, medh samhål|ligt rådh, och alles theres betäncken 2
och samtycke, som thär tilstädes wore, medh sådan grundeligh skäl, afskaffat
40 och uthaff wägen lagdt, at ingen som widh Gudh och sanningen blifwe will,
kan annat betyga eller medh godt samwet, thet som giordt och beslutit är,
någen tijdh ryggia. Och wardt på samma tijdh ehn Religions förehning och
Bekännelse skrifteligen författat, och medh Underskrifning och Insegel stadfäst och bekräftiget, hwilken ock nu sedan är almänneligen j alle Landzendar
45 uthi wårt käre Fädernes Rijke, för alle Ständer upläsin och förkunnet, och aff
them gilledt och wedertagin, såsom ock underskrifwin och försegld.

Och på thet at samme Religions Bekännelse, må så wäl främmande som
infödde kunnigh ware, Therföre wardt j sielfwe *Concilio* beslutit, såsom wij
ock nu för nyttigt, nödigt och rådhsampt achte, at late förbenämde Christeli-
50 ge Religions och wår Lärdoms förehning, sampt medh the tre Gudz Församb-
lings troos Bekännelser, hwilke *Symbola* kallas, såsom ock then rette, reene
och oförandrede Augzburgiske *Confession*, hwilken Anno etc. 30, på then store
Rijksdagh, som tå af Chur-Furster och Städher hållen bleff, wardt öfwerant-
wardet Keyser Carl then | Femte, aff Trycket late uthgå: På thet hwar och en 3
55 kan them bekomme, och ther aff läre och wete, att wår troos Bekännelse är på
intet annat grundat, än på Propheternes och Apostlernes Skrifter, och hafwer
witnesbyrd aff the rätte och gamble Kyrkiones Lärare, när the sigh widh then
helghe Skrift hålledt hafwe, och all falsk läre hafwe wij platt ogilledt och
förkastet, ehwadh nampn the helst hafwe kunne.

60 Begäre förthenskuld aff alle frome och Christtrogne menniskior, at the
wele thenne Bekännelse icke annorledes förstå eller uthtyde, än som orden och
meningen lyde, som theruthinnen författede äre, och alzintet achte wåre mot-
ståndares orätwijse förtalande och fördömande, som ingen sanning wele eller
kunne höre eller lyde: Uthan mykit heller, sådanne Förehning och the medh-
65 följende *Symbola*, sampt then rätte och oförfalskede Augsburgiske *Confession*,

---

51/52 then – Confession] cfr *Formula concordiae*: 'Augustanam, primam illam et non
mutatam [...] nostri temporis symbolum iudicamus'

CONCILIUM UPSALIENSE – 1593

hwilke korteligen innehålle, kärnan och Summan aff wår Christelige Religion, som elliest uthi Propheternes och Apostlernes Böker aff Gudz Ande widhlyftigt författet och skrifwit är, fliteligen öfwerläse, läre och betänckie, sine barn och wårdnedt, at the thet samme göre, troligen och idkeligen förmane: och sedan uthi samme troos Bekännelse, | medh Gudz milde tilhielp, in j dödhen sigh fast och stadeligen förhålle. Ther til then ewige och alzmächtige Gudh, för sin älskelige enfödde Sons Iesu Christi förskyllen, werdiges hwar och en Christen menniskie sin helge Ande nådeligen förläne, och oss wår Christendoms ähronampn ewinnerligen at niuta late, Amen.

Datum Stockholm, den 30 Julij, *Anno &c.* 1593.

| DECRETUM UPSALIENSE.*

Decretvm Vpsaliense. Eller Beslwt, som j thet almänneligha Concilio och Möte uthi Upsala wardt samtyckt och underskrifwit, uthi Februarij och Martij Månadher. Åhr efter Christi börd, 1593.

Wi Carl medh Gudz nåde, Sweriges Rijkes Arffurste, Hertigh til Sudermanland, Näricke och Wärmeland, Och wij efterskrefne Sweriges Rijkes Rådh, Biscopar och menige Presterskap, som nu här j Upsala, til thette Möte hafwe waridt församblade: Göre wetterligit och uppenbarligen bekänne, så wäl för oss närwarande, som them the frånwarande äre, at eftersom allom noghsampt kunnigt är, hwad twist och oenigheet, som på nästförledne åhr, här uthi wårt Fäder|nesland Swerige, uthi Religions saker warit hafwer, therigenom mykin splijt och förargelse sigh hafwer j monge måtte förorsaket, och man både aff Exempel, så wäl som af förfarenheten, både uthi främmende Land, såsom elliest hafwer förnummit ingen ting skadeligere ware uthi något Konunge-Rijke, än twist och oenigheet: och intet nyttigere och gagneligere, eller thet som meere förbinder hiertan tilsamman, än sämie och enigheet, och serdeles j Religionen, Therföre, på thet at sådane enighet måtte ock så wäl här j Rijket uthi Religionen uprättet och förmehrat warda, som elliest j andre måtte, Och thet icke elliest hafwer kunnet skee, än genom itt Christeligit, almänt, frijt inrijkes Möte, efter som ifrån Apostlarnes tijdh och alt sedan hafwer brukeligit waridt, Såsom ock Kong: Majest: wår älskelige käre Broder, och alles wår nådige Herre, Christeligh och högloflig ihughkommelse, alrede för någre åhr sedan, och något för sitt Christelige aflidende nådeligen samtykte, at itt sådant möte skulle hållit warda, etc.

Är forthenskul nu uthaff alles wåre samdrechtige åstundan och bewiljelse beramat blifwit, at een Sammankommelse, aff the förnämste Ständer, här j Rijket, högre och nidrige, lärde och lekte, måtte hållen blifwe, nu på närwa-

920 CONCILIUM UPSALIENSE – 1593

randes åhr, efter Christi | börd, etc. 1593, *Dominica Esto mihi*, som war then 25   7
Februarij, här j Upsala, til att göre ehn Förehning uthi then Christelige Läro,
105 såsom ock Kyrkesedher, Församblingenes Disciplin, och laghligit Archie-
biscops och andre Biskopers wahl, medh flere nödige Puncter, som hafwe
synts nyttige och rådelige ware. Hwarföre ock nu j the helghe Trefaldigheetz
nampn, på förnämde dagh och tijdh, näst ehn innerligh åkallan til Gudh then
alzmächtigeste, efter ehn gudeligh, noge och flitigh öfwerwägning aff oss
110 samptligen, frijwilligen, onödhgede och aff wälbetänckt och berådt mode, om
thesse efterskrefne Puncter, så ehndrächteligen förehnt och beslutit är, som här
efter folier:

[1] Först, at wij alle widh Gudz rehne och salighgörende Ord, hwilket j
the helge Propheters, Euangelisters och Apostlers Skrifwelser författet är, sam-
115 hålligen blifwe wele, och at j wåre Församblinger, skal lärdt, trodt och bekändt
warde, at then helge Skrift aff then helige Ande sitt ursprung hafwer, och
innehåller fulkomligen, alt thet som then Christelige Lärdom, om Gudh then
alzwåldigeste, och wår saligheet, sampt gode gärninger och dygder tilkommer,
och är ehn grund och stödh til ehn rätt Christen Troo, och itt rättesnöre til at
120 döme, åtskilie och förekomme all twist uthi Religionen, och ingen förklarning
aff androm behöfwes, anten aff the helige Fäder eller an|dre, som aff egen   8
godhtycke något thet til satt hafwe, thet icke är medh then helge Skrift, ehoo
the ock helst ware kunne, Althenstund ingen menniske efterlatit är, att tyde
Gudz ord efter egit sinne, och theruthinnen skal ingen persohns anseende,
125 högheet, eller *authoritet*, achtedt eller gilledt warde, uthan then helge Skrift
allene, som förbemält är, etc.

[2] Thernäst, bejake och wederkännes wij oss aldeles wele hålle widh the
Apostoliske, Niceniske och Athanasij *Symbola* såsom ock widh then äldste

---

113/114 Gudz – är] cfr *Epitome Formulae concordiae*, p. 807, 9-12, 'Credimus confitemur et docemus unicam regulam et normam, secundum quam omnia dogmata omnesque doctores aestimari et iudicari oporteat, nullam omnia aliam esse, quam prophetica et apostolica scripta cum Veteris tum Novi Testamenti' **115/116** lärdt – warde] cfr *Epitome Formulae concordiae*, p. 807, 9 et passim, 'Credimus, confitemur et docemus' **127/128** Thernäst – Symbola] cfr *Formula concordiae*, 'Solida Declaratio', in I. Dingel et al. (hrsg.), *Die Bekenntnisschriften der evangelisch-lutherischen Kirche. Vollständige Neuedition*, Göttingen 2014, p. 1311: 'amplectimur etiam [...] Athanasii' **128/129** then – Confession] cfr *Formula concordiae*, 'Solida Declaratio', in Dingel et al. (hrsg.), *Bekenntnisschriften*, p. 1311: 'Augustanam, primam illam et non mutatam [...] nostri temporis Symbolum esse iudicamus'. The *Confessio Augustana Invariata* is considered here to have the status of a creed, parallel to the *Apostolicum*, *Nicoenum* and *Athanasianum*

103 Dominica – mihi] *intellege* Quinquagesima   **120/126** och² – är] *dux Carolus add.* (cfr *Svenska riksdagsakter*, Avd. 1, vol. 3/1, p. 97)

CONCILIUM UPSALIENSE – 1593   921

rette och oförandrede Augzburgiske *Confession*, hwilken som aff Chur-Furster
och Städer bleff öfwerantwardet Keyser Carl then Femte, på then store Rijksdagh j Augzburgh, åhr efter Christi börd, 1530.

[3] Theslikest widh then Religion, som j saligh och höghlofligh hoos
Gudh j åminnelse, saligh Konung Gustafs sidste Regementz, och salige
Archiebiscop Lars *Petri Nericiani*, then äldres lijfztijdh, både j Lärdom och
Kyrkeseder här j Rijket hållet och igenom then präntede Kyrkeordningen j
Trycket uthgången, Anno, etc. 72 är samtyckt och bejaket blefwen. Men efter
theruthinnen äre någre Ceremonier beholdne, som både widh Döpelsen och
Herrens Jesu Christi Natward brukede blifwe, som är salt, liws och uphöyel-
sen, Item flytie medh Messeboken ifrå thet ene hörnet til thet andre på Alta-
ret: Item klempe | när uphöyes, hwilke ock j mästeparten aff the Euangeliske   9
Församblinger alrede äre aflagde, efter the fast, och j itt stoort misbruuk kom-
ne äre, så at mehre ondt uthaff misbruket, än godt aff Ceremonierne blifwer
förorsaket. Therföre är almänneligen och samdrächteligen, ther til bejaket och
bewiliet, at Soknepresterne, så ock Bisperne j Visiterningerne, på thet fliteli-
geste Almogen här om läre, underwijse och til at misbruket falle late, troligen
skole förmane, och när the bewijsligen och noghsambligen förnimme misbruket icke kunne borttages, medh mindre, at sielfwe Ceremonierne förfalle och
uthur ögonen förskaffes, mage Bisperne medh någre aff hwart Capitel j alle
Sticht sampt andre the Iärdeste aff Presterskapet sammankomme, och om
fogeligeste medel och wäger sigh betänckie, rådhslå, och endrächteligen sam-
mansättie, huruledes thesse förnämde Ceremonier medh tijdhen (dogh uthan
någen förargelse och buller) j stillheet kunde aflägges.

[4] Ehwad *Exorcismum* anlanger, bekänne wij honom icke ware så nödigh
widh Dopet, at then föruthan, Dopet icke skulle wara fulkomligit, uthan efter
thenne Ceremonien wäl öfwerehns stemmer medh Dop|sens handel, påmin-   10
nendes icke barnet, uthan them som tilstädes äre, om alle menniskers lägenhe-
et, för än the til Dopet komme, och om Dopsens kraft. Therföre måge wij then
j wåre Församblinger efter ehn Christen frijheet wäl bruke. Men om the ord,
som synes alt förhårde ware, på thet at icke någen sigh ther öfwer skulle förar-
ge, menendes, at någen lekamligh besättielse skal ther medh mehnt warde,
hafwe wij sampligen bewiliet, at man the orden, Fahr här uth, etc. lindre må,

---

153 4] baptismal exorcism became optional after the 1572 *Ordinance*. The *Order of Baptism* (*Ordning medh Döpelsen*) declared that exorcism had been performed for more than 1300 years, 'as we have clearly learnt from the works of St Cyprian, St Augustine and from the writings of other ancient teachers'. However, the congregations that chose not to administer it were never condemned. In these congregations, it was normally not administered even in the event of an emergency baptism

922 CONCILIUM UPSALIENSE – 1593

Och j then staden insattie, Wijk här ifrå, *etc.* Dogh så, at man här medh icke
thes heller fördömer the Församblinger j främmendeland, eller höge Personer
här inrijkes, som thenne icke så bruke, uthan sigh hafwe then förbehållen, och
165 elliest medh oss äre ehns j Trone.

[5] Om then *Liturgia*, som någre aff Presterskapet här j Rijket wedertagit
hafwe, althenstund hon är j sanning befunnen ehn root och orsaak til mykin
oroo, som sigh uthi Religions saker, här j Rijket hafwer tildragit, och elliest
medh Skriftennes grund bewijst, at hon j alle motte är wijskepeligh och j
170 sielfwe grunden aldeles lijkformigh then Påweske Messe, hwilken är förargeligh, och aldeles gehnsträfwer och förringer Christi wår Frelsares fertienst, och
såsom een port och ingång til all annen Påwesk grufweligh wilfarelse. Therföre
hafwe wij ock samptligen och j synderheet, förbenämde *Liturgiam*, och alt
hennes onde medhfölie, j Läre, Ceremonier och Disciplin, ehwadh nampn
175 thet helst hafwe kan, aldeles ogilledt, och aff | Christeligit alfwar, medh hierta 11
och mun wedersaket, och oss ehndrächteligen, ther til, alfwarligen förplichtet,
at wijj henne aldrigh mehre annamme, gille eller bruke wele. Såsom icke heller
något annet aff the Påweskes lärdom eller wilfarelser, ehwadh nampn the helst
hafwe kunne, någen tijdh gille eller wedertage, uthan them aldeles förkaste,
180 såsom menniskiestadger, för werldzlig högheet, wälde, macht, och rijkedomer
uptänckte, igenom hwilke monge menniskior ofte äre bedragne wordne. Theslikest och aldeles afsäioms wij alle Sacramenterers, Zwinglianers och Calvinis-
ters wilfarelser, så ock Wederdöpere och alle andre Kättere, ehwadh nampn
the helst hafwe kunne, någen tijdh til at inryme, gille eller samtyckie.

185 Yterligere om Disciplin och skäligh Kyrkeaga, hafwe wij ock befunnit, at
hon uthi wår förnämde tryckte Kyrkeordning til sielfwe grunden mästedehls
är författet. Och efter hon en tijdhlong myckit försumedt är, hafwer hwar efter
sitt stånd och wärdigheet lofwedt ther til förhielpe, at hon här efter må fliteli-
gere warde efterkommen, och troligere sampt alfwarsamligere uthi wercket
190 stelt. Och ther som sielfwe saken så kräfwer, må thet som ytermehre behöfwes,
medh Bispernes och Capitelens gemene samtyckie, blifwe tillagdt och förmeh-
ret. Och ändogh them icke borde lidhne, eller efterlatit warde, sigh här j | 12
Rijket nedhsättie, som medh någen falsk Lärdom umgå, och medh oss uthi
Lären icke ehns äre, på thet the andre medh sigh icke förföre måtte: Lijkwäl
195 efter sådant för handel och wandel skul icke wäl kan förhindret warde, så är så
widt samtyckt, at them som någen Kättersk lärdom hafwe, icke skal tilstadt

---

185/187 Yterligere – författet] the Assembly referred here to Chapter 10 of the 1572
Ordinance, dealing with excommunication ('Om bann'): cfr *Then Swenska
Kyrkeordningen*, Stockholm 1571, p. 31v; Kjöllerström, *Den svenska kyrkoordningen 1571*,
p. 81; *Handlingar rörande Sveriges historia*, Andra serien, vol. II/2 (1872), p. 73-76

CONCILIUM UPSALIENSE – 1593

eller efterlatit ware, at hålle någre uppenbare Samqwemder j huus eller anner-
städz, så frampt hwar någre ther medh befinnes, eller the som elliest försmäde-
ligen tale om wår Religion, the skole tilbörligen straffede blifwe.

200   Och på thet, at allom må kunnigt och wetterligit warde, hwadh wij yterligere uthi thenne Samqwemd handlet och oss hafwe förehnet om, uthi alle
Puncter och Artickler, så skal sådant med förste aff Trycket uthgå. Medh hwilke, så wäl som thet ock här uthi författet är, wij igenom Gudz then alrehögstes
nådige hielp och bijstånd enhålleligen lofwet, tilsagdt och förplichtet hafwe,
205 oss in j dödhen wele faste och ståndachtige blifwe, och therifran aldrigh någen
tijdh låcke, twinge eller tränge late, hwarken igenom gåfwer, gunst, wenskap,
mågsämie, hoot, ogunst eller undsäyelse, uthan oss och then saken Gudh then
alzmächtige j händer befale, hwilken hon allene tilhörer, hans Guddomlige
Majestet warder oss ther widh wäl nådeligen behållendes och krafteligen för-
210 swarendes.

   | Til ytermehre wisse och stadfästelse, at alt thette widh then mening som   13
widh hwar Punct beslutit är, ährligen, uprichteligen och Christeligen, fast,
stadigt och oryggeligen må hållet och efterkommet warde, och at thet ene
Ståndet til thet andre, icke annet måtte sigh hafwe til at försee, än troheet,
215 tryggheet, rätrådigheet, hielp och bijståndigheet uthi thenne samtyckte
Bekännelse, så hafwe wij Carl medh Gudz nåde, etc. och wij underskrefne
Sweriges Rijkes Rådh, Biscopar, Riddersmän och Adel, Presterskap och Köp-
stadzmän, så wäl för oss, som wåre efterkommende, thenne Bekännelse, frijwilligen och aff troofast hierte, medh egne händer underskrifwit, och wår Secret
220 och Insigle här neden före tryckie latidt: Hwilket och the så wäl Andelige som
Werldzlige, som ock nu icke närwarende äre, medh oss ehnse wälwilleligen
warde görende. *Actum Vpsaliae*, then 20 Martij, åhr etc. 1593. [...]

[POSTSCRIPT]

   Altså är nw, genom Gudz nådige tilhielp, föreskriffne almännelighe *Con-*
225 *cilij* Beslwt, sampt medh then rätta Augzburgeska Bekännelsen, wår Christ-
troghna Swenska Försambling til godho på Prent uthgången: Men at samma
thes helgha Euangelij saliggörande Lära och Religions Form, må Christeligha
och longwaright widh macht hållas, och oförkränckt, bådhe hoos oss och
wårom effterkommandom bewaras och behållas: Skal ingom tilstadt wara,
230 kätterska Böker eller och Smädeschriffter j Rijket at föra och uthsprijdha:

---

222 Actum – 1593] in the printed edition of the *Decretum*, the *Credo Apostolicum*,
Credo Nicaenum, *Credo Athanasianum*, as well as the *Confessio Augustana* are
reproduced before the Postscript

924 CONCILIUM UPSALIENSE – 1593

änsijdher eenighetennes Beslwt öffuerträdha heller förtala, och oenigheet och
obestånd ther medh åstadh komma: ey heller någhrom loflighit, disputerlige
Spörsmål j Tronnes Läro upwäckia och drijffua, föruthan j gemene Möter och
Academiae Consistorio, thär the laghligha förhöras, och medh Gudhz ord
235 rättas och dömas skole. Theslikes och, til at affwäria, hwad som förargheligit,
antingen uthi Lära eller leffuerne finnes, eller sigh inträngia kan, skal een
almänneligh myndigh *Visitation*, uthöffuer heela Rijket aff Ärchiebiscopen
sampt Biscopen uthi Stichtet, hållen warda, när saken så tyckies kräffia, och
lägenheeten medhgiffuer, ther til och Landzens *Gubernator* och Lagman,
240 sampt medh Befalningzmannom, them skal bijståndigh wara, uppå thet, at
alle the, som j någhon sådana saak retteligha bör tiltalas, måge til lydhno och
hörsamheet holdne warda. Såsom och uthi saligh och höghlofligh ihugkom-
melse, Konung Göstaffz Regementz tijdh, sådan almänneligh *Visitation*, effter
Schrifftennes exempel och Församblingennes gemeene bruuk, är wordet
245 hållen. [...]

| [Appendix: Resolution of the Council of Uppsala, 1572]   164

*Een Copia aff thet som handlat, beslutit, beseglat och underschriffuit bleff
aff Clerkerijt j Concilio som stodh j Upsala, Anno M.D.LXXII. Mense Augusto.*
Wi effterschriffne, LAURENTIUS Archiebiscop j Upsala, *Martinus* j Lin-
250 köping, *Iacobus j Schara, Nicolaus* uthi Strengnäs, och *Iohannes* j Westerås,
Biscopar.
Aff Upsala Stichts Clerkerij: *Ericus Nicolai* Domprost, *Laurentius Petri
Gothus Rector Academiæ: Upsaliensis. Olaus Ionae, Petrus Benedicti, Professores,
Ioachimus Olai* Kyrkioheerde j Upsala, *Olaus Andreae* Scholemestare. Aff
255 Stockholms Stadh: *Olaus Petri* Kyrkioheerde, *Abrahamus Andreae* Schole-
mestare och Predicant thär sammestadz. Aff Geffle Stadh: *Andreas Laurentij*
Kyrkioheerde och Landzproste j Gestrikeland, *Iacobus Matthaei* Kyrkioheerde

---

242/245 Såsom – hållen] we omitted the signatures of dukes Carl and Gustav, the
members of the state council (*Sweriges Rijkes Rådh*), Archbishop Laurentius Petri, the
bishops, the nobility, and of the ministers, mayors and councillors of town and cities, as
well as of the representatives of counties and deaneries **243/245** effter – hållen] in
the omitted passage, the 1593 *editio princeps* lists all the personal signatures, written
after the end of the *Concilium* and before the *Decretum* was disseminated across
Sweden **249/251** Wi – Biscopar] Laurentius Petri Nericius (1499-1573), archbishop
of Uppsala; Martinus Olai Gestritius († 1585), bishop of Linköping; Jacobus Johannis
Vestrogothus († 1607), bishop of Skara; Nicolaus Olai Helsingius († 1585), bishop of
Strängnäs; Johannes Nicolai Ofeegh, bishop of Västerås

CONCILIUM UPSALIENSE – 1593

och Landzproste j Delsbo, *Iohannes Petri* Kyrkioheerde och Landzproste j
Wendel, *Iacobus Gislonis* Kyrkioheerde och Landzproste j Wekol.

260 Aff Linköpungs Stichts Clerkerij: *Iesperus Marci* Kyrkioheerde j Wadste-
na, *Petrus Benedicti* Kyrkioheerde j Säby, *Nicolaus Arvidi* Kyrkioheerde j Eedh,
Laurentius Laurentij Kyrkioheerde j Hershammar.

| Aff Schara Stichts Clerkerij: *Catillus Iohannis* Kyrkioheerde j Dala, 165
Iohannes Laurentii Kyrkioheerde j Åklinga, *Georgius Eschilli* Kyrkioheerde j
265 Herliunga, *Halvardus Petri* Kyrkioheerde j Wonga, *Andreas Magni* Kyrkioheerde j Gökim.

Aff Strengnäs Stichts Clerkerij: *Reginoldus Ragvaldi* Kyrkioheerde j
Strengnäs, *Andreas Iohannis* Kyrkioheerde j Bäling, *Nicolaus Erici* Kyrkioheerde j Tälge, *Elaus Pauli* Kyrkioheerde j Ordala, *Laurentius Thomae* Kyrkioheer-
270 de j Ytresela, *Iohannes Nicolai* Kyrkioheerde j Mädelösa, *Canutus Iohannis*
Kyrkioheerde j Östmo.

Aff Westerårs Stichts Clerkerij: *Erasmus Nicolai* K:M:Predicant och
Domprost j Westerårs, *Salomon Birgeri* Scholemestare thär sammestädz, *Laurentius Torchilli* Kyrkioheerde j Irestadh, *Iohannes Andreae* Kyrkioheerde j
275 Romfertuna.

Aff Wäghsiö Stichts Clerkerij: *Nicolaus Stephani* Domprost j Wäghsiö,
och *Dn: Episcopi* uthi samma Wäghsiö fulmynduga Sendebudh, medh andre
flere Clerker,

genom then Stormächtigstes Höghborne Förstes och Herres Her Johans
280 then Tridie, Sweriges, Göthes och Wendes etc. Konungz wår Allernådigste
Herres Mandat och befalning, nu åhr etc. 1572 til at uthi then helgha Treefal-
ligheetz nampn, hålla itt almänneligit *Provincial Concilium* j Upsala
församb|lade, göre witterlighit, at wij alle eendrächteligha samtyckt haffue, 166
och medh thenna wår schriffteligha *Protestation* och Betygelse, samtyckie och
285 beslute,

[6] at wij fast och owijkeligha, så hädhan ifrå som här til, widh then retta
Christeligha Läron, som författat är uthi Prophetiska och Apostoliska Schrif-
ter, then ock här j Rijket nu en godh tijdh haffuer (Gudh thes loff) warit
predicat, uthi alla Artikler och Puncter uthan all fåfeng och falsk bijläro,
290 bliffua, och henne fordra och utbredha wilie, Gudhi til ähro och hans Försam-
ling til tröst och saligheet. Och wilie twert emoot fly, affskaffa och affwäria
allahanda falsk och kettersk läro, genom hwilka thenna retta och sanskylligha
läran, må förkrenckt och förhindrat warda.

[7] Theslikest haffue wij och eendrächteligha beslutit, at wij hwar j sin
295 stadh skole oss ther om beflijta, at hwadh som hörer til ährligheet, tucht och
godha sedher styrckt, fordrat och fremiat, Och twert emoot hwadh oährlighit,
lastelighit och förargelighit är, genom Gudz nådhiga bijstånd, förnedhrat och

926 CONCILIUM UPSALIENSE – 1593

affskaffat warda må, och thet uthi allahanda saker, men synnerligha uthi Ech-
tenskaps handligar: Så at ingen aff oss ther uthinnan någhot thet wara kan
300 emoot then helgha Schrifft, antingen klarlighare eller oklarligare, emoot
ährligheet, Christeligh tucht och godha sedher effterlåter. Såsom thet sigh
haffuer medh Echtenskap j then | andra ledhen *aequalis lineae*; ther om nu 167
emellan någhra aff oss haffuer warit twist och misdrächt. Men j thenna
samqwemd så fördraghet, at ingom sådana olofligh och förargeligh gifftermål
305 skal warda effterlåtet, oanseedt at någhorstädz j fremmandeland annorlunda
kan lärdt och practicerat warda. Ty ehwadh man uthi thenna sakenne disputerar
eller handlar, så kunne wij dogh aldrig ther på retteligha försäkradhe warda, at gifftermål uthi annan ledh, ther är, sydzkonabarn emellan, icke är bådhe
emoot naturligh och Gudz beschriffna Lagh, nemligha thenna, Ingen skal ingå
310 til sijn nästa blodzfrencko, til at blotta hennes blygd. Så moste och hwar och
en bekenna, at ährlighare, Christelighare och tryggare är, haffua slijk gifftermål
fördragh (såsom alle rettsinnighe Christne uthi hela Christenhetenne, bådhe
aff högre och läghre ständer, alt in til thenna dagh giordt haffua) än sigh ther
til begiffua, thet dogh någhre nu hoos oss haffua sigh företaghet begära och
315 göra.

[8] Sedhan haffue wij ock så samfält föreenat oss, at man uthi alla landzendar här j Rijket bliffua skal widh the Ceremonier och Kyrkiosedher, som här
tildags ibland oss Swenska och uthi wåra Församblingar haffua warit j bruuk,
och nu författadhe äro uthi wår genom Trycken uthgångna Kyrkeordning,
320 och ingalunda lijdha eller tilstädhia wilie, at någhor andre | Ceremonier, 168
antingen aff sigh sielff dichtar, eller the som fremmande äro, j bruket införer.
Ther medh han må åstadh komma Stichten, eller ock Församlingarna emellan,
twist, buller och oenigheet, såsom man thetta aff fremmande land, för slijka
orsaker skul, wel hördt och spordt haffuer.

325 [9] På thet sidsta, effter thet år j sanningenne befunnet, at någhre stadhe-
lighe menniskior, som aff och til dragha j landet, sigh bådhe medh ord och
gerningar så förhålla, at the twedrächt och uproor mågha komma til wägha.
Therföre skole wij Biscoparna flijteligha förmana menigha Clerkrijt, at hwar
och en j sin Sokn haffuer här på granna acht, och ther någhor någhot slijkt
330 kunde förnimma, at han tå thet ingalunda hoos sigh haffuer fördolt, uthan j
tijdh giffuer thet K.M. befalningsmän tilkenna, at the maghe slijka skalkar
angrijpa, och såledhes farligheet och skadha förekomma.

Nu thes til wisso, at wij alle thetta så beleffuat och samtyckt haffue,
Underscriffue wij hwar och en medh sijn egen hand, och henge här före wår
335 Insigel. Giffuit i föreschriffne Upsala, then 22. *Augusti* Åhr etc. såsom före-
scriffuit står.

CONCILIUM UPSALIENSE – 1593

| PROVER: XXX.

All Gudz ord äro igenomluttradt, och äro en skiöld them som troo uppå honom.
Lägg intet til hans ord, at han icke skal straffa tigh, och tu warder lögnachtigh
funnen.

PSALM: CXIX.

Medh titt bodh gör tu migh wijsare än mina fiender,
Ty til ewigh tijdh är thet mitt eghit.
Jagh är lärdare än alle mine Lärare, Ty iagh haffuer
mitt taal om tina witnesbyrder.
Jagh är förståndighare än the gamble, Ty iagh håller tina befalningar.
Jagh håller mina fötter ifrå alla onda wäghar, at iagh må bliffua widh titt ord.
Jagh wijker icke ifrå tina rätter. Ty tu lärer migh.
Tijn ord äro migh sötare j munnen, än hånogh.
Jagh warder aff tinna befalningar förståndigh,
Therföre hatar iagh alla falska wäghar.
Titt ord är een lychta för mina fötter, och itt liws på mina wäghar.

| PSALM: XCV.

J dagh om j hören HERRENS *röst, så förhärder icke idhor hjerta.*
Underscriffuit aff migh *Andrea Gutterwitz.*
Och fulbordat j Julij Månadt,
Anno Domini
M. D. XCIV.

338/340 Prou. 30, 5-6 **342/352** Ps. 119, 98-105 **354** Ps. 95, 7-8

ARTICULI LAMBETHANI

1595

edidit
Torrance KIRBY

THE *LAMBETH ARTICLES*
1595

The canonically-approved doctrine of predestination in the Church of England is articulated in Article 17 of the *Articles of Religion* (1563/1571). Originally composed in 1553 and included among the *Forty-Two Articles* of Edward VI – where it was also numbered 17 – the article 'Of Predestination and Election' was already much the longest in the formulary. (1) A modestly-revised version of the *Articles*, reduced in number to thirty-eight, was agreed upon in Convocation by the bishops and clergy of the province of Canterbury held in 1563. Eight years later, the final recension of the *Articles* – now thirty-nine in number – was confirmed again by both houses of Convocation, authorised by statute of Parliament, and promulgated following royal assent on 29 May 1571. (2) The Act required formal subscription to the *Articles* by all candidates for ordination, by all clergy upon presentation to a benefice, as well as by all who had been previously ordained during the reign of Queen Mary (1553-1558). (3) Throughout this period, the doctrine of predestination had been the subject of much-heated dispute, as evidenced by an account given under the heading 'De Haeresibus' in the draft reform of English canon law known as

(1) The *Forty-Two Articles* received royal authorisation just weeks before the young King Edward VI's death on 6 July of that year. See *Articles agreed on by the Bishops and other learned men in the Synod at London in the year of our Lord God 1552, for the avoiding of controversy in opinions, and the establishment of a godly concord, in certain matters of Religion. Published by the King's Majesty's commandment, in the Month of May A.D. 1553*, London 1553.

(2) *Articles whereupon it was agreed by the archbishoppes and bishoppes of both prouinces and the whole cleargie, in the conuocation holden at London in the yere of our Lorde God. 1562. according to the computation of the Churche of Englande, for the avoiding of the diuersities of opinions, and for the stablishyng of consent touching true religion. Put foorth by the Queenes aucthoritie*, London 1571.

(3) 13 Eliz. I cap. 12, 'An Act to reform certain disorders touching Ministers of the Church', in *Statutes of the Realm*, vol. 4/1 (1819), p. 310-312.

the *Reformatio legum ecclesiasticarum* (1571). (4) The canonical formula of the article as approved in 1571 reads as follows:

OF PREDESTINATION AND ELECTION

Predestination to lyfe, is the euerlastyng purpose of God, whereby (before the foundations of the world were layd) he hath constantly decreed by his (1) own judgement (1) *councell* secrete to vs, to deliuer from curse and damnation, those whom he hath chosen *in Christe* out of mankynd, and to bryng them *by Christe* to euerlastyng saluation (2) by Christ (2), as vessels made to honour. (3) Whereupon such as have (3) Wherefore they which be indued with so excellent a benefite of God, (4) given unto them (4) be called accordyng to Gods purpose by his spirite workyng in due season: they through grace obey the callyng: they be iustified freely: they be made sonnes of God by adoption: they be made lyke the image of his onelye begotten sonne Jesus Christe: they walke religiously in good workes, and at length by Gods mercy, they attaine to euerlastyng felicitie. (5)

As the godly consyderation of predestination, and our election in Christe, is full of sweete, pleasaunt, and vnspeakeable comfort to godly persons, and such as feele in themselues the working of the spirite of Christe, mortifying the workes of the fleshe, and their earthlye members, and drawing vp their mynde to hygh and heauenly thinges, as well because it doth greatly establyshe and confirme their fayth of eternal saluation to be enjoyed through Christe, as because it doth feruently kindle their loue towardes God. So, for curious and carnal persons, lacking the spirite of Christe, to haue continually before their eyes the sentence of Gods predestination, is a most daungerous downefall, whereby the deuyll (5) may (5) (6) *doth* thrust them either into desperation, or into rechelesnesse of most vncleane liuing, no lesse perilous then desperation.

---

(4) *Reformatio legum ecclesiasticarum ex authoritate primum Regis Henrici. 8. inchoata: deinde per Regem Edouardum 6. provecta, adauctaq. in hunc modum, atq. nunc ad pleniorem ipsarum reformationem in lucem aedita*, Londini 1571, Chapter 2, par. 22 ('De Haeresibus'). See G. Bray, *Tudor Church Reform: The Henrician Canons of 1535 and the* Reformatio legum ecclesiasticarum, Woodbridge 2000, p. 211-212, as well as T. Kirby, 'Lay Supremacy: Reform of the Canon Law of England from Henry VIII to Elizabeth I (1529-1571)', *Reformation and Renaissance Review* 8/3 (2006), p. 349-370.

(5) The matter marked between the marker (1) through (4) was deleted in the 1571 revision. The italicised matter was inserted in its stead.

(6) The subjunctive mood (5) was replaced by the indicative (*doth*) in the 1563 revision. Phrase (6) was deleted in the 1563 revision.

ARTICULI LAMBETHANI – 1595

Furthermore, (6) although the decrees of predestination are unknown to us, yet (6) we must receaue Gods promises in such wyse, as they be generally set foorth to vs in holy scripture: and in our doynges, that wyl of God is to be folowed, which we haue expreslye declared vnto vs in the worde of God.

It is noteworthy that this formulation of predestination in the *Articles of Religion* makes no reference to the corollary concept of reprobation, or to the so-called double decree. In this respect, the article is in basic agreement with Heinrich Bullinger's highly-influential, classical statement of the Reformed doctrine in the *Second Helvetic Confession* (1566). (7) Early in the 1550s, Calvin had engaged the French Carmelite theologian, Jérôme Bolsec, on this question, (8) and this atmosphere of controversy on the continent was communicated across the English Channel with increased intensity following the return of the Marian exiles at the accession of Queen Elizabeth I. Polemics on the subject were to become even more pronounced in England as the reign of Elizabeth advanced.

The controversy became especially acute at the University of Cambridge where, in a lecture on the Book of Jonah in 1579, Peter Baro, then Lady Margaret Professor of Divinity, maintained that 'it is the will of God we should have eternal life, if we believe and persevere in the faith of Christ; but if we do not believe, or believing only for a time, do not persevere, then it is not the will of God we should be saved'. (9) Later, in a sermon preached at the University Church of Great St Mary's in 1595, Baro set out a position tantamount to universal atonement. According to Baro, 'God created all men according to His own likeness in Adam, and so consequently, to eternal life; Christ died sufficiently for all [...]; the promises of God made to us, as they are generally propounded [*generaliter propositae*] to us, were to be generally understood, as it is set down in the seventeenth Article'.

For this interpretation of Article 17 'On predestination', Baro was referred to the Vice-Chancellor of the University; although proceedings against him were stayed at the instigation of his patron – William Cecil, Lord Burghley – Baro resigned his chair the following year. Meanwhile, William Barrett, a fellow of Gonville and Caius College, took up the struggle and preached a robust sermon on 29 April 1595 in defense of Baro's position, which included a direct attack on Calvin, Theodore Beza, and Peter Martyr

(7) In Chapter 10.

(8) P. C. Holtrop, *The Bolsec Controversy on Predestination, from 1551 to 1555*, Lewiston (NY) 1993.

(9) P. Baro, *In Jonam prophetam praelectiones 39* [...], Londini 1579, p. 217, quoted by Hardwick, *A History of the Articles*, p. 166.

Vermigli, all of whom had endorsed an unconditioned decree of reprobation. A party within the University took up the defense of a thoroughly Augustinian stance on the matter of the double decree, and included such heavy-weights as William Perkins, Laurence Chaderton, and at their head William Whitaker, then Regius Professor of Divinity. (10) Barrett was dealt with more severely than Baro by the vice-Chancellor and heads of houses, and was compelled to make a formal retraction of his denial of the decree of reprobation at the University church on 10 May. This Cantabrigian controversy precipitated a complaint to John Whitgift, Archbishop of Canterbury, by Whitaker and his allies while Barrett in his turn appealed from the Vice-Chancellor to Whitgift.

Thus, both parties of this increasingly fraught doctrinal dispute sought clarification and mediation from the primatial see. By September 1595, Dr Whitaker had drafted a series of eight questions to be put to Barrett at a meeting attended by a University delegation together with certain bishops, and held at Lambeth Palace, the archbishop's residence in London. Under considerable pressure, Barrett subsequently agreed to make a formal retraction. By late November, Whitaker and his allies had drafted the original version of the doctrinal statement which came to be known as the *Lambeth Articles*, with a view to settling doctrinal disagreements in the University once and for all. In principle, the *Lambeth Articles* were formulated as an attempt at clarifying the interpretation of Article 17 of the *Articles of Religion* (1571) within the context of the University. In broader terms, they represent a struggle between two adversarial schools of theological opinion for the high ground of reputed doctrinal orthodoxy. Whitgift, assisted by Bishop Richard Fletcher – recently translated to the see of London and supported by Archbishop Hutton of York – was sympathetic in no small degree to Whitaker and his party. Nonetheless, the meeting of prelates and divines at Lambeth achieved some modification of the original draft, with the general thrust of rounding off the harder edges of Whitaker's so-called *Orthodoxal Propositions* concerning the double decree.

The *Lambeth Articles*, however, have never held the status of canonically-authorised teaching within the Church of England. Indeed Whitgift was careful in his instructions to the University that the *Articles* 'must be so taken and used as the private judgements' of the compilers, who thought 'them to be true and correspondent to the doctrine professed in the Church of England,

---

(10) For an account of the Cambridge predestinarian controversy of the 1590s, see Lake, *Moderate Puritans*, p. 201-242.

ARTICULI LAMBETHANI – 1595

and established by the laws of the land, and not as laws and decrees'. ([11]) Moreover, both Burghley and the Queen herself expressed their displeasure with the constitutional form of the proceedings. In a formal oration before the Supreme Governor of the Church of England, Burghley is reported to have argued that

> in such things as did appertain to the State of Religion no body could by the Laws of *England* determine any thing, but by the Authority of the Queen, and that too with the Consent of Parliament. And this was a wise Institution; for there is generally a furious Zeal of Religion in Mens Minds, which, when it is once raised, makes them easily run into Parties and Factions: But now here are a few Divines, that have dared to make Decrees and Determinations concerning the most important Questions, which Learned Men for many Ages since could never yet agree about. ([12])

Elizabeth, ever protective of her royal prerogative in matters ecclesiastical, forbade publication of the document inasmuch as the assembly of prelates and divines at Lambeth was convened without due royal sanction. It is reported by Ellis that the Queen, only half in jest, accused her archbishop of violating the medieval statute of *Praemunire* of 1392 (16 Ric 2, cap.5). ([13]) Consequently, the *Lambeth Articles* more or less drop from view until the Hampton Court Conference of 1604, when John Rainoldes, moderate Puritan and sometime fellow of Corpus Christi College, Oxford, unsuccessfully urged formal amendment of the thirty-nine *Articles of Religion* by way of inclusion of the *Lambeth Articles*. Richard Hooker, Rainoldes' erstwhile pupil at Corpus Christi, continued the theological reflection on the substance of the controversy with his splendidly-erudite draft of a response to 'The Tenth Article touching predestination' contained in *A Christian Letter of certaine Englishe Protestantes* (1599), a polemical pamphlet critical of Hooker's supposed deviation from the stan-

---

(11) Whitgift, *Works*, vol. 3 (1853), p. 611-612; Hardwick, *A History of the Articles*, p. 175-176.

(12) Ellis, *A defence*, p. 98-99. This post-Restoration edition of doctrinal formularies, reprinted in 1671, 1675, 1684, 1699, and 1846 is remarkable for its omission of the *Lambeth Articles*.

(13) 21 Henry VIII, cap. 13, in *Statutes of the Realm*, vol. 3, p. 292-296. *Praemunire* was an offence under statute law which received its name from the writ of summons to the defendant, charged with appealing to a power outside of the realm for resolution of a situation within England that was under the jurisdiction of the Crown. The original fourteenth-century statute was invoked in the reign of Elizabeth's father in order to prevent appeals to the authority of the papacy.

936 ARTICULI LAMBETHANI – 1595

dard of Reformed orthodoxy as defined by the *Thirty-Nine Articles*. (14) Near the conclusion of his discussion of the points at issue, Hooker offered his own subtle reformulation of the Lambeth. (15)

In 1615, the Parliament of the Kingdom of Ireland, together with the Convocation of the archbishops, bishops, and clergy of the Church of that realm, agreed to a doctrinal formula, commonly called the *Irish Articles*, which relied heavily upon the *Articles of Religion* of the Church of England and incorporated the *Lambeth Articles* virtually in their entirety, although not in the same sequence. (16) Even this single instance of canonical status for the Lambeth document was short-lived. Twenty years after their adoption, the Irish Parliament and Convocation of 1635 reaffirmed the English *Articles* of 1563/1571, which have since remained the standard of doctrine in the Church of Ireland. Apart from their inclusion in the Irish formulary, the *Lambeth Articles* would have to wait for more than half a century before their first publication in 1651. They subsequently went through multiple printings in an edition by John Ellis after the Restoration, while the first English translation of Ellis' Latin version only appeared in 1700.

BIBLIOGRAPHY

Sources (and Their Abbreviations)

A collection of articles, injunctions, canons, orders, ordinances, and constitutions ecclesiastical with other publick records of the Church of England; chiefly in the times of K. Edward. VIth, Q. Elizabeth. and K. James. Published to vindicate the Church of England and to promote uniformity and peace in the same. And humbly presented to the Convocation, London 1661 [= *A collection of articles*].

Articuli Lambethani id est, I. Articulorum Lambethae exhibitorum historia, II. Articuli de praedestinatione, & annexis capitibus à D. Whitakero Lambethae propositi, III. Iidem prout ab episcopis theologisque concepti & admissi, IV. Lanceloti Andrewes tou panu Wintoniensis episcopi, de synodo

---

(14) Trinity College Dublin, MS 121, fol. 66v. See 'Dublin Fragments', in J. Booty (ed.), *The Folger Library Edition of the works of Richard Hooker*, 5 vols, London – Cambridge (MA) 1977-1990, vol. 4 (1982), p. 123-167.

(15) 'Dublin Fragments', p. 166-167.

(16) See p. 967-998.

ARTICULI LAMBETHANI – 1595

oblatis Articulis judicium, unà cum ejusdem censurâ censurae D. Barreti, de certitudine salutis, quibus annexa est, V. Sententia D. Overal theologiae in Academia Cantabrigiensi professoris olim regii, de praedestinatione kai tois echomenois [...], Londini 1651 [= *Articuli Lambethani*].

J. Ellis, *A defence of the thirty nine articles of the Church of England. Written in Latin by J. Ellis, S.T.D. Now done into English. To which are added the Lambeth articles*, London 1700 [= Ellis, *A defence*].

—, *Articulorum XXXIX Ecclesiae Anglicanae defensio unaà cum novâ eorundem versione authore Jo. Ellis* [...]; *his accedunt Articuli Lambethani, unà cum rev. & doct. virorum in eos censurâ &c.*, Cantabrigiae 1694 [= Ellis, *Articulorum defensio*].

P. Heylyn, *Historia quinqu-articularis: or, A declaration of the judgement of the Western Churches, and more particularly of the Church of England, in the five controverted points, reproched in these last times by the name of Arminianism collected in the way of an historicall narration, out of the publick acts and monuments, and most approved authors of those severall churches*, London 1660.

The Statutes of the Realm: Printed by Command of His Majesty King George the Third, in Pursuance of an Address to the House of Commons of Great Britain, ed. J. Raithby, 11 vols, London 1810-1828 [= *Statutes of the Realm*].

LITERATURE (AND ITS ABBREVIATIONS)

B. Cummings, *The Literary Culture of the Reformation: Grammar and Grace*. Oxford 2002.

C. Hardwick, *A history of the Articles of Religion: to which is added a series of documents, from AD 1536 to AD 1615; together with illustrations from contemporary sources*, London 1895 [= Hardwick, *A History of the Articles*].

P. Lake, *Moderate Puritans and the Elizabethan Church*, Cambridge – New York 1982 [= Lake, *Moderate Puritans*].

V. C. Miller, *The Lambeth Articles: Doctrinal Development and Conflict in Sixteenth-Century England*, Oxford 1994.

H. C. Porter, *Reformation and reaction in Tudor Cambridge*, s.l. [but Hamden (CT)] 1972.

J. Strype, *The life and acts of John Whitgift, DD: the third and last Lord Archbishop of Canterbury in the reign of Queen Elizabeth: the whole digested, compiled and attested from records, registers, original letters, and other authentic MSS*, Oxford 1822.

N. Tyacke, *Anti-Calvinists: The Rise of English Arminianism, c. 1590-1640*, Oxford 1987.

J. Whitgift, *The Works of John Whitgift, DD, Master of Trinity College* [...] – ed. J. Ayre, 3 vols, Cambridge 1851-1853 [= Whitgift, *Works*].

Monitum

The Latin text is from John Strype, *Life and Acts of John Whitgift* (Oxford: Oxford University Press, 1822), vol. II. p. 280. Strype states that he copied it from the original MS of the Lord Treasurer, Lord Burghley (probably presented to him by Dr Whitaker, Regius Professor of Divinity at Cambridge).

The English text is from Thomas Fuller, *Church History of Britain* (Oxford: Oxford University Press, 1845), vol. V. p. 220.

ARTICULI LAMBETHANI
1595

ARTICULI APPROBATI A REVERENDISSIMIS DOMINIS DD JO-ANNE ARCHIEPISCOPO CANTUARIENSI, ET EPISCOPO LON-DINENSI, ET ALIIS THEOLOGIS, LAMBETHAE, NOVEMBRIS 20, ANNO 1595.

I.

Deus ab aeterno praedestinavit quosdam ad vitam, et quosdam ad mortem reprobavit.

2.

Causa movens aut efficiens praedestinationis ad vitam non est praeviso fidei, aut perseverantiae, aut bonorum operum, aut ullius rei, quae insit in personis praedestinatis, sed sola voluntas beneplaciti Dei.

3.

Praedestinatorum praefinitus et certus numerus est qui nec augeri nec minui potest.

4.

Qui non sunt praedestinati ad salutem necessario propter peccata sua damnabuntur.

5.

Vera, viva et justificans fides, et Spiritus Dei sanctificans non extinguitur, non excidit, non evanescit in electus, aut finaliter aut totaliter.

6.

Homo vere fidelis, id est, fide justificante praeditus, certus est plerophoria fidei, de remissione peccatorum suorum, et salute sempiterna sua per Christum.

---

19 et¹] *addidi*

ARTICULI LAMBETHANI – 1595

7.

Gratia salutaris non tribuitur, non communicatur, non conceditur universis hominibus, qua servari possint, si voluerint.

8.

Nemo potest venire ad Christum, nisi datum ei fuerit, et nisi Pater eum traxerit. Et omnes homines non trahuntur a Patre, ut veniant ad Filium.

9.

Non est positum in arbitrio aut potestate uniuscuiusque hominis servari.

ARTICLES APPROVED BY JOHN, THE MOST REVEREND LORD ARCHBISHOP OF CANTERBURY, DD, AND RICHARD BISHOP OF LONDON, AND OTHER THEOLOGIANS, AT LAMBETH, ON 20 NOVEMBER 1595.

1.

God from eternity hath predestinated certain men unto life; certain men he hath reprobated.

2.

The moving or efficient cause of predestination unto life is not the foresight of faith, or of perseverance, or of good works, or of any thing that is in the person predestinated, but only the good will and pleasure of God.

3.

There is predetermined a certain number of the predestinate, which can neither be augmented nor diminished.

4.

Those who are not predestinated to salvation shall be necessarily damned for their sins.

ARTICULI LAMBETHANI – 1595

5.

A true, living, and justifying faith, and the Spirit of God justifying, is not extinguished, falleth not away; it vanishet not away in the elect, ether finally or totally.

6.

A man truly faithful, that is, such a one who is endued with a justifying faith, is certain, with the full assurance of faith, of the remission of his sins and of his everlasting salvation by Christ.

7.

Saving grace is not given, is not granted, is not communicated to all men, by which they may be saved if they will.

8.

No man can come unto Christ unless it shall be given unto him, and unless the Father shall draw him; and all men are not drawn by the Father, that they may come to the Son.

9.

It is not in the will or power of every one to be saved.

APPENDIX

RICHARD HOOKER'S DRAFT REVISION OF THE LAMBETH ARTICLES
in Trinity College Dublin, MS 121, fol. 66v

I.

That God hath predestinated certain men, not all men.

---

51 justifying²] *vide versionem latinam*, fides [...] sanctificans

2.

That the cause moving him hereunto was not the foresight or any virtue in us at all.

3.

That to him the number of his elect is definitely known.

4.

That it can not be but their sins must condemn them to whom the purpose of his saving mercy doth not extend.

5.

That to God's foreknown elect final continuance of grace is given.

6.

That inward grace whereby to be saved is deservedly not given unto all men.

7.

That no man cometh unto Christ whom God by the inward grace of his Spirit draweth not.

8.

And that it is not in every, no, not in any man's own mere ability, freedom, and power, to be saved, no man's salvation being possible without grace. Howbeit, God is no favorer of sloth; and therefore there can be no such absolute decree touching man's salvation as on our part includeth no necessity of care and travail, but shall certainly take effect, whether we ourselves do wake or sleep.

---

82 6.] Hooker omitted Chapter 6 of the *Lambeth Articles* entirely

CONCILIUM TUISCOBURGENSE

1610

edidit
Andreas MÜHLING

THE FIRST GENERAL SYNOD OF
THE REFORMED CHURCH AT DUISBURG
1610

The Political Context

From a political point of view, the general Synod of the Reformed Church met in a tumultuous period for the United Duchies of Jülich-Berg-Cleves-Mark. ([1]) Until the end of the sixteenth century, two dukes held political and ecclesiastical sway in Jülich-Berg: John III (1521-1539), who was the first to unite the duchies of Jülich and Berg with the imperial fief of Cleves-Mark, and his son and successor William V (1539-1592). Jülich-Berg was the centre of a border area relevant both in economic and cultural terms. The consolidation of these territories quickly made it one of the most important conglomerates of the Imperial system. The events that took place here had repercussions in every corner of the Empire. ([2])

At the time, the modernisation of a political regime involved, at least in principle, changes to ecclesiastical policy. As early as John III's rule, the fundamental outline of political reform was drawn in this specific context. This shift could be seen, for example, with the *Ecclesiastical Ordinance* of 1532/1533, which also garnered praise from Erasmus of Rotterdam. The *Ordinance* appeared moderate in tone, inclined to limit the jurisdiction of the clergy and to avoid extreme positions concerning Lutheranism. It shied away from controversial theological issues, but at the same time it adopted a number of crucial stances of the Reformed Church: for example, that the Bible must be the guiding principle for preaching and for Christian life in general. ([3]) What political objectives did John III pursue with the promulgation of such an *Ordinance*? The objective was to safeguard political power, and in many ways,

---

([1]) See H. Smolinsky, 'Jülich-Kleve-Berg', in A. Schindling – W. Ziegler (hrsg.), *Die Territorien des Reichs im Zeitalter der Reformation und Konfessionalisierung: Land und Konfession 1550-1650*, 7 vols (*Katholisches Leben und Kirchenreform im Zeitalter der Glaubensspaltung 49-53* and 56-57), Münster ²1995, vol. 3, p. 86-106.

([2]) See Szameitat, *Konrad Heresbach*, as well as Flesch, 'Konfessionalisierung im Rhein-Maas-Raum' with related bibliography.

([3]) Text in Teschenmacher, *Annales*, p. 26-44.

this was the reason – and not purely for religious conviction – why several princes of the Holy Roman Empire supported the Reformation.

John III, duke of Cleves died in 1539. William sought to carry on the policies of his father, or at least his most fundamental stances. Emperor Charles V deftly began to impose strict limitations on the young duke with the aim of limiting his political agency. Both claimed hereditary rights over Geldern, and when William led his troops to defeat in 1543, his reformist enthusiasm waned significantly. Bound by severe conditions under the Treaty of Venlo (1543), he had to commit himself to abolishing any and all religious innovations and to remain faithful to the Roman Church. The duke found himself having to manage internal politics with extreme caution, so as not to provoke Charles V for political or religious reasons, either through specific resolutions or as a result of socio-political events that might take place within the United Duchies. That being said, the early 1550s saw a radical shift in the imperial political landscape. Charles V, with the Diet of Augsburg (1555), recognised both the so-called old faith and the Lutheran faith inspired by the *Confessio Augustana* and, eleven years later, the Reformed faith.

Following the Diet of Augsburg, the notion of carrying out ecclesiastical reform in Jülich-Berg resurfaced with a certain intensity. Furthermore, any ecclesiastical reform would necessarily involve political steps as well. In 1565, the right to partake in the *Abendmahl* (i.e. the Lord's Supper) was extended to all believers in both kinds ('in beiderlei Gestalt'). The same year, a commission was established to reform the old *Ecclesiastical Ordinance* of 1532. The draft of the new *Ordinance* was presented in October 1566. It stipulated that the Gospel be announced in a pure ('rein') and authentic ('lauter') manner, the Mass be in German, and the chalice of sacred wine be shared ('Laienkelch'). The theological framing of baptism and the Eucharist was also more similar to that of Lutheranism. (4)

This ecclesiastical-political momentum seemed unstoppable, but a series of apoplectic strokes significantly reduced the duke's presence in the governance of the United Duchies from 1567 onward. Repercussions were equally serious: the Jülich-Berg progressively fell prey to the political games of foreign powers. The Counter-Reformation appeared on the scene. From 1583 on, the war of Cologne (known as the Seneschal Upheaval), followed by the Dutch wars against Spain, found the United Duchies increasingly traversed by foreign soldiers. The Thirty Years' War ultimately started here. The ruling family seemed to be born under a bad sign. This went hand-in-hand with its adverse fate. In this age, individual personalities influenced social, economic

(4) Mühling, 'Obrigkeit und « Secterei »', p. 13-15.

and political events – more specifically, those of an ecclesiastical-political nature – to a great extent, with fatal consequences for Jülich-Berg. A number of unhappy circumstances were less than ideal for political stability: the serious illness that struck the duke in 1567, the *Geistesschwäche* (i.e. dementia) – with which John William, successor to the throne, was diagnosed in 1589/1590 – the death of his father in 1592, and the vain attempt by duchess Jakobea of Baden to govern the territories. From 1592 to 1609 – the year of the last duke's death – the territory was governed by a committee of counsellors. This exposed Jülich-Berg to external political interference (e.g. the Emperor). Counter-Reformation measures were also promulgated by the Spanish during the occupation of the city of Wesel.

The Ecclesiastical-Political Context

Until 1567, the openness of Jülich-Berg to evangelical influences was remarkable. This fostered the socio-political stability of the United Duchies and, at the same time, the modernisation of their government on a social, economic, and cultural-political level. Duke William also scrupulously followed the provisions against heresy (*Ketzerbestimmungen*) of the imperial jurisdiction, as he could not afford to show the slightest weakness on such delicate issues of ecclesiastical-political significance. As a result, any measures taken by authorities against the so-called *Sakramentierer* – a broad derogative term referring to witches, reformists, and Anabaptists – were politically induced. In the delicate context of the Holy Roman Empire, the duchy's policy was to convey the impression of not extending any form of favour to these communities or religious groups. (5) Nonetheless, the political declarations of intent and their actual implementation did not always coincide. In fact, there was no witch-hunt in the United Duchies, and, from 1550 onwards, even the communities of Reformed refugees and the German Reformed congregations from the Netherlands were largely tolerated. These minorities, from 1567 on, were subjected to greater political pressure. (6)

The ecclesiastical-political shift must have significantly affected the synodical statute. The organisation of Reformed congregations under a synodical system began in the city of Jülich in 1570. In the framework of the soon-to-be-prepared *Ecclesiastical Ordinance*, this should be seen as a clear response to the checks that political authorities were laying out and to the risk of losing its place of value in the public arena. In fact, even as early as 21 July 1589, the

---

(5) Mühling, 'Obrigkeit und «Secterei»', p. 15-19.
(6) Mühling, 'Der Weseler Konvent von 1568', p. 177.

duchy of Berg instituted the first of its own Reformed synods. The dukes exercised their political power rather mildly even after 1567, and no criminal measures were enacted against Lutherans. Given these favourable circumstances, the congregations organised themselves at a provincial level starting from 1609.

As mentioned above, the political climate drastically changed in 1567 as a direct consequence of the apoplectic strokes that inhibited the duke from fully exercising his will. Following his serious stroke on 29 September 1566, he was capable at best of confused stuttering. This political vacuum gave rise to Counter-Reformation leanings, and strategic positions in the political hierarchy were gradually taken up by Catholics. After 1567, not only was there a renewed witch hunt and persecution of Anabaptists, but Calvinists and Lutherans were targeted by increasingly intolerant authorities from 1570 onwards. These circumstances had a variety of consequences, including the emergence of parallel ecclesiastical structures. This leads us to a twofold consideration: if we examine the historical and territorial context, from a confessional perspective the history of the Rhenish church includes an extremely particular episode; and the reformist path initiated by the duchies of Jülich-Berg was jeopardised. (7)

The General Synod of Duisburg

The last duke of Jülich-Cleves-Berg, John William, died without an heir in the spring of 1609. Succession to the throne was uncertain, and so were the prospects for the United Duchies in political and ecclesiastical terms. The Empire fell into deep conflict. In order to avoid military occupation by imperial troops temporarily quartered in Jülich, the Brandenburg Electorate and Palatinate-Neuburg, both evangelical in orientation – the two regents were married to the daughters of duke John William – agreed to rule Jülich-Berg jointly. This decision was officialised with the Treaty of Dortmund on 10 June 1609. The two regents promptly assigned troops to be stationed in the territories of Jülich and Cleves. (8) For the issue at hand, one aspect is of particular importance: in June 1609, the duchies of Cleves-Mark and Jülich-Berg swore loyalty to the two regents, and in response the regents granted them confessional liberty. In so doing, an important ecclesiastical-political question remained unanswered: which specific confessions would benefit from this public liber-

---

(7) Mühling, 'Obrigkeit und «Secterei»', p. 23-26.
(8) See Engelbrecht, 'Die konfessionelle Problematik im jülisch-klevischen Erbfolgestreit'; Teschenmacher, *Annales*, p. 348-402.

CONCILIUM TUISCOBURGENSE – 1610

ty? Certainly Catholics and Lutherans; but what about the Reformed? According to imperial jurisdiction, they were tolerated in the best of circumstances: thus, the issue remained as to whether religious freedom could be extended to them as well.

Reformed communities – that had remained clandestine until then – were indifferent to any eventual juridical objections and held themselves to be included in the concession. They took this opportunity to exploit the legal ambiguity and to come out into the open. New communities were founded in rapid succession in a number of towns and villages. Their numbers grew, the need for pastors increased, and, given the growing number of communities, it became necessary to make certain organizational modifications on a statutory level.

On 17 August 1610, an extraordinary preparatory assembly was held in Düren. (⁹) This assembly called the first Reformed general Synod in Duisburg in September 1610. Duisburg belonged to the duchy of Cleves and had been open to the Reformation since 1543. The city's location was advantageous as it was easy to reach, and its Church of the Savior was a suitable meeting place. The meeting was held on 7-11 September 1610 and constituted the first 'General Synod of All the Reformed Churches of the Three Principalities of Jülich, Cleves and Berg'. Thirty-six pastors and elders met under the guidance of two renowned theologians, Abraham Scultetus and Johannes Fontanus, with the aim of consulting and making important decisions regarding the future of their churches.

THE SYNOD'S MOST SIGNIFICANT RESOLUTIONS

Alongside the renewed affirmation of the Holy Scriptures as the 'sole guiding principles of faith and doctrine', the general Synod held the *Heidelberg Catechism* (§ 4) to be exegetically binding. Any theological differences would have to be dealt with and resolved in a communal perspective and in the context of the Synod (§ 4), which would be periodically called and organised with the presence of deacons and pastors (§ 9, 4). Significant import was reserved to the high pedagogical and theological preparation that pastors and doctors (§ 8) had to possess in order to be able to implement the cultural and political reforms that the Synod wished to propose. In particular, the institution of compulsory primary school was an ambitious, broad objective of the Synod: each congregation would have to appoint a school teacher whose duty

(9) Text in Rosenkranz, *Generalsynodalbuch*, p. 15-16.

was to teach the *Heidelberg Catechism* (§ 8). Ultimately, the Synod explicitly abided by the presbyterian-synodal principle (§ 9).

However, another article (§ 4) stated:

> With this resolution, however, the brethren present do not intend to prejudice in any way with the Word of God, and therefore with this confession, other churches within or outside of the confines of the German nation. ([10])

This article was held as equally important by the Synod advocates. No threatening theological stances were taken to impose the Duisburg resolution upon other churches.

The decisions of the Synod of Duisburg spread far and wide throughout the territories of the Lower Rhine. It significantly contributed to the consolidation of the Reformed communities in Jülich-Berg-Cleves-Mark. Enduring ecclesiastical institutions were established and the educational and formative responsibility that the Church must exercise was made explicit. A significant presbyterian-synodal principle was the guiding, coordinating role assigned to the Church itself. However, it is remarkable that this presbyterian-synodal role was not considered by Synod advocates as the distinguishing mark of the Church's authenticity, but rather an *interim*; that is, a valid but temporary reference while waiting for an agreement upon the matter with political authorities. The idea that this principle would assume such relevance for all evangelical communities was neither foreseen nor wished for by the Synod of Duisburg. However, for the first time, it represented the intentional affirmation of the symbolic nature of the Holy Scriptures and the *Heidelberg Catechism*. In this sense, the Synod of Duisburg provided a valuable contribution to the consolidation of the *Heidelberg Catechism* throughout the territories of the Empire. ([11])

---

(10) 'Mit dieser Erklerung aber wollen die anwesenden Brüder anderen Kirchen in und außerhalb teutscher Nation mit Gottes Wort und also dieser Bekentnis mit einstimmenden confessionibus in keinem Wege ichts prejudicirt haben'. See the edition below.

(11) Mühling, 'Anmerkungen zur reformierten Katechismusbildung'.

BIBLIOGRAPHY

SOURCES

Generalsynodalbuch. Die Akten der Generalsynoden von Jülich, Kleve, Berg und Mark 1610-1793. 1 Teil. Die Akten der Generalsynoden von 1610-1755, hrsg. A. Rosenkranz (*Schriftenreihe des Vereins für Rheinische Kirchengeschichte* 20 / *Urkundenbuch zur Rheinische Kirchengeschichte* 2/1), Düsseldorf 1966 [= Rosenkranz, *Generalsynodalbuch*].

LITERATURE (AND ITS ABBREVIATIONS)

S. Becker, *Zwischen Duldung und Dialog. Wilhelm V. von Jülich-Berg als Kirchenpolitiker* (*Schriften des Vereins für Rheinische Kirchengeschichte* 184), Bonn 2014.

J. Engelbrecht, 'Die konfessionelle Problematik im jülisch-klevischen Erbfolgestreit', in S. Flesch – B. Magen – A. Mühling (hrsg.), *Die 1. Reformierte Generalsynode 1610 – aus der Sicht der Wissenschaft*, Bonn 2010, p. 93-102 [= Engelbrecht, 'Die konfessionelle Problematik im jülischklevischen Erbfolgestreit'].

S. Flesch, 'Konfessionalisierung im Rhein-Maas-Raum', in S. Flesch – B. Magen – A. Mühling (hrsg.), *Die 1. Reformierte Generalsynode 1610 – aus der Sicht der Wissenschaft*, Bonn 2010, p. 1-56 [= Flesch, 'Konfessionalisierung im Rhein-Maas-Raum'].

H. Frost, 'Gedanken über das reformierte Kirchenrecht am Niederrhein zwischen Emden (1571) und Duisburg (1610)', *Monatshefte für Evangelische Kirchengeschichte des Rheinlandes* 23 (1974), p. 33-49.

I. Hantsche, 'Die politischen und wirtschaftlichen Auswirkungen des niederländischen Freiheitskampfes auf den Niederrhein vor der Synode 1610', in S. Flesch – B. Magen – A. Mühling (hrsg.), *Die 1. Reformierte Generalsynode 1610 – aus der Sicht der Wissenschaft*, Bonn 2010, p. 57-89.

A. Mühling, 'Das theologische Umfeld der Synode von 1610', in S. Flesch – B. Magen – A. Mühling (hrsg.), *Die 1. Reformierte Generalsynode 1610 – aus der Sicht der Wissenschaft*, Bonn 2010, p. 103-114.

—, 'Obrigkeit und «Secterei». Politik und Religion in Jülich-Berg im 16. Jahrhundert', *Monatshefte für Evangelische Kirchengeschichte des Rheinlandes* 58 (2009), p. 13-26 [= Mühling, 'Obrigkeit und «Secterei»'].

—, 'Der Weseler Konvent von 1568', in J. Conrad (hrsg.), *Evangelisch am Rhein. Wesen und Werden einer Landeskirche*, Düsseldorf 2007, p. 175-177 [= Mühling, 'Der Weseler Konvent von 1568'].

—, 'Anmerkungen zur reformierten Katechismusbildung', in Gemeinschaftswerk der Evang. Publizistik (hrsg.), *Katechismen der Reformationszeit. Beiträge des Theologischen Arbeitskreises für reformationsgeschichtliche Forschung der Union Evangelischer Kirchen in der Evangelischen Kirche in Deutschland zum Thema Katechismen (EPD-Dokumentation 39)*, Frankfurt am Main 2012, p. 37-41 [= Mühling, 'Anmerkungen zur reformierten Katechismusbildung'].

M. Szameitat, *Konrad Heresbach – Ein niederrheinischer Humanist zwischen Politik und Gelehrsamkeit*, Bonn 2010 [= Szameitat, *Konrad Heresbach*].

W. Teschenmacher, *Annales Ecclesiatici*, Düsseldorf 1962 [= Teschenmacher, *Annales*].

H. Zschoch, 'Kirchenordnung der Freiheit. Die presbyterial-synodale Ordnung im Wandel politischer Konstellationen', in S. Flesch – B. Magen – A. Mühling (hrsg.), *Die 1. Reformierte Generalsynode 1610 – aus der Sicht der Wissenschaft*, Bonn 2010, p. 115-134.

MONITUM

Generalsynodalbuch. Die Akten der Generalsynoden von Jülich, Kleve, Berg und Mark 1610-1793. 1 Teil. Die Akten der Generalsynoden von 1610-1755, hrsg. A. Rosenkranz (*Schriftenreihe des Vereins für Rheinische Kirchengeschichte 20 / Urkundenbuch zur Rheinische Kirchengeschichte 2/1*), Düsseldorf 1966, p. 17-24.

CONCILIUM TUISCOBURGENSE
1610

| ACTA DES ERSTEN GENERALSYNODI DER GESAMPTEN REFORMIRTEN KIRCHEN IN DEN DRIEN FURSTENTUMBEN GULICH, CLEVE UND BERGE IM JAR 1610 DEN 7. SEPTEMBRIS ZU DUISBERG GEHALTEN.

Deputirte zu diesem Synodo seint gewesen

GULICHSCHER KIRCHEN:

Dominus Theodorus Hordaeus von Sittert, D Wernerus Lachius von Wassenberg, Johannes de Lünenschlad von Heinsberg, Daniel Telones von Dueren, D Servatius Kuchenius, Eltister von Duiren, Leonhart Haneman, Eltister von Linnich

CLEVISCHER:

Wilhelm ter Porten, Eltister von Cleve, Dr Wilhelmus Stephani et Georgius Scheutzlichius von Wesel, Petrus Ceporinus von Goch, Theodorus Dunckius von Emmerich (obiit anno 1613), Philippus Eilbracht anstat eines Eltisten von Xanten

BERGISCHER:

Philippus Popinghusen von Duisseldorp, Gerhard Froman, ein Eltister von Ratingen, Petrus Curtenius von Elverfeld, Petrus Wirtzius von Mulheim, Jeronimus Banfius von Solingen, Christianus Villanus anstat eines Eltisten von Siburg, so nit erschienen

AUS DER REICHSSTAT AACH:

Engelbertus Breberenus, Prediger der deutschen Kirchen, Petrus Niset, Eltister der franzosischen Gemeine daselbst

AUS DER REICHSSTAT DUISBERGH:

Wilhelmus Rongius und Petrus Scriverius

AUS BENACHBARTEN HERRSCHAFTEN:

von Wevelinckhoven: Andreas Rotarius, Prediger, und Dietrich Overlach, Eltister

von Wickratbergh: Johannes Sylvius

von Reid: Casparus Wachendorf

von Odenkirchen: Casparus Eilbracht

wegen der Herlichkeit Hardenberg: Rutgerus Topander

| FREIWILLIGE AUS DER GRAFSCHAFT MOERS:

Conradus Velthusius von Moers, Johannes Eilbracht von Hohen-Emmerich, Reinerus Sohnius von Freymersheim

958   CONCILIUM TUISCOBURGENSE – 1610

Clevische Adjuncten, jedoch mit gnugsamen Credenzen erschenen:
Bernhardus Brantius von Büderich, Johannes Damius von Goch, Henrich von der Elburgh von Emmerich.

40 Auch seint auf mund- und schriftlich Ersuchen der gesambten reformirten Kirchen in den dreien Fürstentumben erschenen und praesentes gewesen Dominus Johannes Fontanus et Dominus Abrahamus Scultetus.

§ 1. Anfenglich nach getaenem Gebet haben die Deputirte ihre Credenzbrief aufgelegt, welche allermaßen richtig befunden.

45 § 2. Folgentz sein nach Gewohnheit zu guter Ordnung in Praesidem Doctor Wilhelmus Stephani, in Assessorem Petrus Curtenius, in Scribam M Petrus Scriverius erwehlet worden.

§ 3. Darauf seint folgende Puncten zu verhandlen vorgenommen:

1. Weil sich fast allerhand Neuerung in Religionssachen hin und wieder 50 ereugen wollen, wie dieser Landen Kirchen vor denselben verwahret und die reine evangelische Lehr, wie sie bis anhero darinnen getrieben, moge erhalten werden.

2. Weil bis anhero dieser Landen reformirte Kirchen, aldweil sie unter dem Creuz gesteckt, in Ungleichheit der Ceremonien geraten, auch die notige 55 Disciplin allerwegen nit der Gebeur hat konnen bestellt und geübt werden, und dan sie nunmehr durch sonderliche Schickung Gottes unter ihrer christlichen Obrigkeit Schutz frei offentlich moge zusamenkommen, wie sie soviel möglich zu Gleichformigkeit derselben und Beforderung der Disciplin gelangen mogen.

60 3. Weiln auch viel am ordentlichen Beruf der Kirchendiener gelegen, wie damit dergestalt zu verfahren, daß alle Unordnung vermitten bleibe.

4. Weil viel Mangels im Unterhalt des Predigamts gespueret, wie demselben abzuhelfen sei.

5. Weil hochnotig, daß die Jugend bei Zeit zu der Erkentnis und Furcht 65 Gottes vornemlich erzogen, wie die Gemeinen mit notigen Schulen und Schuldiener hin und wider mochten versehen werden.

6. Weil zu Beforderung der Kirchen Gottes und seiner heilsamen Wahrheit bis hinzu in diesen Landen üblich gewesen die Synodi und Beikumpsten der Kirchendiener und Eltisten, wie dieselbe ferner am frucht-70 barlichsten zu continuiren.

§ 4. Vom ersten Puncten: Belangend den ersten Puncten halten die anwesende Brüder nach wie vor das heilige Wort Gottes, in prophetischen und apostolischen Schriften vollkommentlich begriffen, für die einige Regul | und   19 Richtschnur ihres Glaubens und Lehre. Vors ander halten sie auch dafür, daß 75 die Summa der in Gottes Wort gegrundten Religion im Heidelbergischen

CONCILIUM TUISCOBURGENSE – 1610

Catechismo wol gefaßt und derentwegen derselb Catechismus, wie vor diesem, also auch hinfüro in Schulen und Kirchen zu behalten und zu treiben sei; soll derhalben niemanden gestattet werden, einige novitates oder besondere Catechismos einzuführen. So aber jemand were, der sich inskünftig an dem einen oder andern Puncten des Catechismi in seinem Gewissen zweifelhaftig und beschwert befinden mochte und dasselbe in Gottes Wort klarer und deutlicher ausgedruckt zu sein vermeinte, derselb in Gottes Wort klarer und deutlicher ausgedruckt zu sein vermeinte, derselb soll solchs nit alsbald auf die Canzel bringen und den Catechismum tadeln, sondern sich davon freund- und bruderlich mit seiner Classe besprechen; so ihme daselbst nit gnug geschege, sol man's zum Synodo gelangen lassen, daselbst dann dergestalt ferner zu handeln, damit dies zwei extrema vur all verhütet werden, nemblich licentia novitatum und servitus conscientiarum. – Mit dieser Erklerung aber wollen die anwesenden Brüder anderen Kirchen in und außerhalb teutscher Nation mit Gottes Wort und also dieser Bekentnis mit einstimmenden confessionibus in keinem Wege ichts prejudicirt haben.

§ 5. Vom andern: Betreffend den andern Puncten von Gleichheit der Kirchenceremonien halten die anwesenden Brüder davor, daß diejenige Kirchen, so bishero der churfürstlichen Pfaltz Agenden gefolget, hinfurter auch dabei verbleiben; wie imgleichen die Kirchen im Clevischen Lande, so der Niderlendischen Agenden sich gebrauchet, weil sie einander nit sehr ungleich, auch hinfort dabei gelassen werden sollen. Was aber die Bilder, Altaer und andere abgottische Reliquien anlangt, soll bei der Obrigkeit umb Abschaffung derselben zu bequemer und gelegener Zeit undertenig angehalten werden. – Daß die Kirchendisciplin vermoge des Spruchs Christi Matth. 18. V. 17 und desselben Erklerung, im Heidelbergischen Catechismo begriffen, geübet und unterhalten werden solle. Wo auch in einigen Kirchen dieselbe nit angestelt oder aber verfallen were, daß die Prediger daran sein und bei ihrer Obrigkeit mit gebuerender Bescheidenheit dahin sich bearbeiten sollen, daß sie soviel moglich angericht und befordert werde.

§ 6. Vom dritten: Angehend vors dritte den ordentlichen Beruf der Kirchendiener in den Gemeinden, welche noch zur Zeit bis auf bessere Verordnung unserer gnedigen Landsfursten ihre Kirchendiener selbsten unterhalten und derentwegen berufen, halten die anwesende Brüder dafür, daß von diesen Gemeinen zum Kirchendienst solche Personen sollen berufen werden, die wegen ihrer Wissenschaft und Geschickligkeit dazu tüchtig und bequem seint und die ein gutes Zeugnis ihrer Lehr von den Academiis und Schulen, da sie studiret, wie auch ihres vorigen Wandels und | Abzuges mitbringen, sie seien vorhin in Ministerio gewesen oder nit. – Daß auch gemelte Gemeinden in Berufung ihrer Diener mit Vorwissen und Gutachten ihrer Class verfaren und, da einige Berufene noch nit zum Ministerio ordinirt weren, daß die von selbiger Class oder aber in dem Provinciali Synodo der Gebuer examinirt und nach befundener Geschickligkeit ordinirt und confirmirt werden sollen. – Daß alle Ministri, auch ehe sie admittirt und aufgenommen werden, sie seien in Ministerio vorhin gewesen oder nit, dieser Conformitet oder Synodalverei-nigung unterschreiben, auch nit angenommen werden sollen, so sie sich der Unterschreibung weigeren würden, in maißen dan die itzo anwesende Herren Fratres diese Conformitet alle unterschrieben. Und daß endlich allen Kirchen anzuzeigen, daß sie keinen zum Prediger fordern oder annehmen sollen ohne vorgehende sothane Approbation und Unterschreibung.

§ 7. Vom vierten: 1) Die Unterhaltung der Kirchendiener angehend halten die anwesenden Bruder dafür, daß bis auf bessere Anordnung unserer gnedigen Fürsten und Herren, wie bishero ein jede Kirch oder Gemeine ihre Diener soll erhalten. Soverne aber einige Kirch des Vermogens nit were, sollen die benachburte Kirchen wie auch die ganze Class derselben mit treuer brü-derlicher Hilf beistehen und darinnen nottdurftige Versehenung tun helfen, bis zur Zeit, daß man von der landsfürstlicher Obrigkeit durch einige Suppli-cation mit Vorbringung allerhand Kirchenbeschwernis etwas Besseres erlan-gen mochte. – 2) Daß keinem Ministro, der sein ordenlich Unterhalt an einem Ort hat, soll freistehen, da etwan zwei, drei oder mehr Kirchen zu Unterhaltung eines Dieners sich zusammengetan hetten, denselben also verei-nigten Kirchen einige davon abzustricken und neben der seinen zu bedie-nen. – 3) Daß, so ein Prediger an einigem Ort Tods verfahren wurde, alsdan dessen hinterlassene Wittib das ganze folgende Jahr das stipendium genießen und die negst gelegene und benachbarte Kirchendiener des Orts oder der Class inmittels den Dienst vertreten sollen, dazu sich alle und jede anwesende Bruder habe willig anerboten.

§ 8. Vom fünften: Die Schuelen und derselben Diener Underhalt con-cernirend, halten die anwesende Brüder dafür, daß es in alle Wege notig, daß eine jede Gemein, sofern es immer moglich, neben dem Prediger auch einen Schulmeister für die Jugend habe und anstelle; so aber eine Gemeind für sich allein einen zu underhalten und zu bestellen nit vermochte, daß alsdann zwo, drei oder mehr benachbarte Gemeinden sich darin zusamentun und zugleich einen Schuldiener bestellen und erhalten, auch die Prediger die Zuhorer in denselben Gemeinten vermahnen, daß sie ihre Kinder bei dieselbe ihre bestel-te Schulmeister und bei keine andere zu schicken schuldig und gehalten sein sollen. Daß die Prediger und Eltisten wegen des Schuldieners, der bestelt wur-de, sich erkundigen sollen, ob er in der christlichen Lehr gesund und rein und mit der Kirchen einig sei, wie auch von ihme forderen, daß er keinen anderen Catechismum, als der in diesen Kirchen ublich, der Jugend vortrage.

CONCILIUM TUISCOBURGENSE – 1610

| § 9. Vom sechsten: Ferners halten die anwesende Brüder dafür, daß zu
Vortpflanzung und Erbauung der Kirchen sehr dienlich, daß die bis anhero
unter dem Creuz geubte Zusammenkunften der Kirchendiener und Eltisten
auf folgende Weise soll continuirt werden:

1. (species Conventuum) Irstlich daß eine jede Gemeine ihr Presbyterium oder Consistorium habe und underhalte; oder wo eine Gemeinde allein
zu schwach oder gering darzu were, sich zwo, drei oder mehr zusamentuen
und unter ihnen ein gemeines Consistorium anstellen. – Zum anderen daß
alle Kirchen in gewisse Classes geteilt und in jede Class gewisse Kirchen gezogen werden, die ihre Classicos Conventus haben und zu bestimbten Zeiten
besuchen sollen. – Zum dritten daß die Classes den Provincialibus Synodis zu
gebuerlichen Zeiten beiwohnen, und zum vierten die Provinciales die Generales Synodos auch besuchen sollen.

2. (tempus) Daß die Presbyteria allen acht oder 14 Tagen (nach Gelegenheit und Nottdurft jedes Orts) gehalten werden, die Classici Conventus
zweimal im Jahr, die Provinciales Synodi alle Jahr einmal, die Generales Synodi zu dreien Jahr einmal, allein daß aus hochwichtigen Ursachen und Notturft der erste Generalsynodus über ein Jahr wiederumb gehalten werde.
Damit aber die Provinciales Synodi nit auf eine Zeit infallen mochten: daß
die Juliacenses ihren Provincialsynodum des Dinstags post dominicam Cantate, die Clivenses post dominicam Trinitatis, Montenses Dinstags post dominicam quintam Trinitatis halten sollen; und daß, so oft ein Provincialsynodus in
einem dieser dreien Landen gehalten wird, von wegen der andern Fürstentumben aus jedem einer darzu deputirt und abgefertigt werde, der demselben
beiwohne, und also bruderliche Correspondenz und Einigkeit erhalten werden moge.

3. (locus) Daß der negst Provinzialsynodus im Fürstentumb Gulich zu
Linnich, im Fürstentumb Cleve zu Wesel, im Fürstentumb Berge zu Düsseldorf, der Generalsynodus aber wiederumb alhie zu Duißberg den ersten Dinstag in Septembri 1611 gehalten werde.

4. (personae) Daß zu Besuchung dieser vorschreven Conventen die
Deputierten folgender Weise verordnet werden: aus jedem Consistorio ein
Prediger und ein Eltister zum Classico Conventu; aus jeder Claß zwei Prediger und zwei Eltisten zum Provinciali Synodo; aus jedem Provincialsynodo
vier Prediger und zwei Eltisten zum Generalsynodo. Daß auch in Anordnung
der Deputirten in Achtung genommen werde, daß darzu halb alten (so dem
nechsten vorigen Generalsynodo beigewohnt haben) und halb neue (so bei
dem vorigen nit gewesen) im Provinciali Synodo erwehlet werden. – Die
benachbarte Nebenherrlichkeiten belangend, daß mit Belieben ihrer Oberen

962 CONCILIUM TUISCOBURGENSE – 1610

195 von jederer einen Prediger und einen Eltisten zu schicken, oder anderen ihre Notturft zu bevehlen ihnen freistehen solle.

5. (sumtus) Daß die Unkosten, so zu Besuchung der Provincial- und Generalsynoden aufgewendet werden, ein jede Kirch jedes Lands, wie vorhin, vor sich selbsten trage.

200 | 6. (materialia) Daß auf allen furbenenten Beikumpsten und Synoden 22 allein Kirchensachen nach christlicher Weise, und keine politische Dingen fürbracht und verhandelt und in diesem Stück folgende gradus in Acht genommen werden: daß nichts ad Classicum Conventum bracht werde, welches nit zuvor in Presbyterio, wie auch in Provinciali Synodo nichts, das 205 nit vorhin in Classico Conventu, im gleichen zum Generali Synodo nichts, das nit zuvor in Provinciali were fürbracht und nit hette konnen erortert werden; daß auch dieser gedachten Beikumpsten einer dem andren unterworfen seie, als Presbyterium Classico Conventui, Classis Provinciali Synodo, Provincialis Generali.

210 7. (formalia) Daß die Synodi angefangen und gehalten werden nachfolgender weise: 1. daß die, so zum anstehenden Synodo deputirt seint, des Abends für dem bestimbten Tag an den benanten Ort mit genugsamen Credenzen von ihren Kirchen ankommen; 2. daß hernacher mit gemeinem Rat bei gewisser Straff die Stund, zu welcher man folgendes Tags anfangen 215 soll, vom letztgewesenen Praeside ernent und eingebunden werde; 3. daß, sobald man umb ernente Stund zusamen kommen, nach vorgehendem Gebet auf Anmahnung letztgewesenen Praesidis durch schriftliche suffragia ein ander Praeses, Assessor et Scriba erwehlet werden; 4. daß derselb Praeses das Gebet tue, die Brüder der Stille, guter Ordnung, Kurze und Deutlichkeit im 220 Reden ermahne, von jeglichen Deputirten Credenzbrief fordere, die deutlich vorlese, sie mit den anwesenden Fratribus examinire, die absentes verzeichne, pro Synodi membris die Diener, so erstlich erscheinen und noch nit aufgenommen seint, formlich aufnehme; 5. daß er des vorigen Synodi acta verlesen lasse, ob alles verrichtet seie, nachfrage, die Predig durch den, dem sie im vori-225 gen Synodo auferlegt, geschehen lasse, durch ergangene Umbfrage jedes Bedenken erforsche und vernehme, dasselb dem, der gepredigt, brüderlich anzeige; 6. daß er frage, wie es in jeder Kirche stehe mit der Predig gottliches Worts, Bedienung der Sacramenten, Catechesatio, Kirchendisciplin, Armenverpflegung und Schulen; 7. daß er fordere die mitgegebene instructiones und 230 die darinnen begriffene Sachen erortere; 8. daß man handle von Fast- und Bettagen, wo man den künftigen Synodum halten soll, wer predigen, wem das Synodalhandbuch zu vertrauen; 9. daß er die acta und Handlung deutlich verlesen, auch unterschreiben lasse, jedem copiam actorum vor seine Kirch mitzunehmen bevehle, die Handlung mit dem gebet schließe, niemanden

CONCILIUM TUISCOBURGENSE – 1610

963

ohne Erlaubnis abscheiden lasse; 10. und endlich daß nach geendigtem Synodo und Beikumpst der Praeses und Assessor vor alle Sachen, den Generalem Synodum betreffend, Sorge tragen sollen, und daß sie beide solches Lastes nit zu erlassen, bis im folgenden Synodo durch gemeine Wael unter den alsdann anwesenden Brüderen ein ander Praeses und Assessor erwehlet seie.

8. Jede Claß soll auch ihren besonderen Inspectorem haben und daß derselbe in einem jeglichen Classico Conventu erwelet werde.

| § 10. 1. Ist auch einhelliglich beschlossen, einen allgemeinen Fast- und Bedtag in allen Kirchen dieser dreien Fürstentumben und anderen benachbarten Kirchen auf dominicam primam Adventus anzustellen.

2. Item daß die reformirte Kirchen in der Grafschaft Marck, wie zu Duiren beschlossen, sich dieser unser Conformitet gemäß zu verhalten, schriftlich ersucht werden.

Endlich daß keinem freistehen solle, weder diese vorgemelte beschlossene Puncten etwas zutuen oder dieselbe zu verenderen, es seie in Presbyterio, Classico Conventu oder Provinciali Synodo, es werde dan von dem Generalsynodo beschlossen, welcher ihme dan Gewalt, davon und darzu zu tuen, zu minderen und zu vermehren, nachdem es der Kirchen Nutz zu sein gespueret werden mochte, hiemit woll vorbehalten haben.

Und ist diese ganze Beratschlagung auf ein Interim gestelt, solang nemblich Kirchen und Schulen dieser Landen in itzigem Zustand pleiben, bis Gott der Herr Gnad verleihet, daß sich unsere gnedige Landsfürsten derselben mit mehrem mogen annehmen.

Ist auch Petrus Wachendorpius auf Anhalten der Kirchen zu Linnich examinirt und ordinirt worden.

§ 11. (Gravamina) Nachdem allerhand Gravamina und Beschwernis der Kirchen von den Brüdern proponirt, als nemblich, daß ihr Begerte were, von ihren fürstlichen Gnaden zu erlangen:

1. daß ortodoxi Ministri bei den Collatoribus von wegen ihrer Confession nit verworfen oder ihnen die Placaten verweigert wurden;

2. daß keiner Gemeind, so sich zu diesem Synodo bekennen, einiger Diener, der dem Synodo nit vorhin unterschrieben, aufgedrungen werde;

3. daß die geistliche Closter oder Prelaten in und außerhalb diesen Fürstentumben von den Renten und Zehenden, wie auch Vicarien und Canonicaten den Kirchen und Schuldienern zu ihrer besseren Unterhaltung contribuiren und helfen sollen;

4. daß Vicarien den Unwirdigen und denen sie nit gebueren, als Kriegsknechten und anderen, insonderheit die auf Jesuitischen Schulen seint, wider derselbigen, so jus conferendi haben, Willen widerumb benomen und anderen, so auf orthodoxis Academiis studiren, conferirt werden mochten;

964   CONCILIUM TUISCOBURGENSE – 1610

275   5. daß die Gemeinten, so das exercitium publicum vorhin gehabt, ihnen aber wider Verheischung entzogen worden, widerumb restituirt und darzu verholfen werden;

     6. daß den Gemeinten, so keine bequeme Platz und Orter haben, ihr exerxcitium des Predigambts zu treiben, solche vergünstiget und sie damit 280 versehen werden mochten, und daß hierüber eine algemeine Supplication in Namen aller reformirten Kirchen ihre fürstliche Gnaden gnedigst hierin zu bewilligen, offerirt werde, welches von den anwesenden Fratribus für ratsam und hochnotig angesehen worden.

     | Es ist auch von den anwesenden Herren Brüdern eine bitliche Vorschrift 24 285 von wegen der Kirchen zu Aach und zu Colln an die churfürstliche Pfaltz und Landgraven Moritz im Namen des Synodi, damit si publicum exercitium haben mochten, abgehen zu lassen beschlossen.

     Ferner daß an jedem Ort, da es notig, die Vornehme vom Adel und Beambten ersucht werden sollen, die Religion in eines jeden seinem Gebiet zu 290 befördern. Item daß bei denen Beambten und adlichen Personen, bei welchen dieser Synodus traducirt, Entschuldigung beschehe durch diejenige, denen darzu Gelegenheit mochte vorstehen.

     Und ist also dieser Synodus nach gethaenem Gebet beschlossen, und seint auch darauf die sembtlichen Brüder in Fried, Lieb und Einigkeit von einander 295 gescheiden. Anno 1610 den 11. Septembris.

     Unterschriften:

     Wilhelmus Stephani, Petrus Curtenius, Petrus Scriverius,

     aus Jülicher Synode: Theodorus Hörden (Sittard), Wernerus Lach (Wassenberg), Johannes de Leunesladt (Heinsberg), Daniel Telones (Düren), 300 Servatius Keuchenius (Düren), Lonhardt Haneman (Linnich).

     aus Klever Synode: Georgius Scheutzlichius (Wesel), Petrus Ceporinus (Goch), Theodorus Dunckius (Emmerich), Philippus Eilbracht (Xanten), Aelt Wilhelm ter Porten (Kleve), Johannes Damius Adjunctus, Ministri nomine (Goch), Bernhardus Brantius (Büderich).

---

298 Jülicher Synode] *supplevi*; *a.c.* JS   Sittard] *supplevi*   Wassenberg] *supplevi*
299 Heinsberg] *supplevi*   Düren] *supplevi*   **300** Düren] *supplevi*   Linnich] *supplevi*
301 Klever Synode] *supplevi*; *a.c.* KS   Wesel] *supplevi*   **302** Goch] *supplevi*
Emmerich] *supplevi*   Xanten] *supplevi*   **303** Kleve] *supplevi*   **304** Goch] *supplevi*
Büderich] *supplevi*

CONCILIUM TUISCOBURGENSE – 1610

305   aus Bergische Synode: Philippus Popinghusius (Düsseldorf), Petrus Wirtzius (Mülheim), Hieronymus Banffius (Solingen), Aelt Gerhardus From (Ratingen), Rutgerus Topander (Langenberg).

   von Duisburg: Wilhelmus Rongius; von Aachen: Engelbertus Breberenus (germanicae et gallicae ecclesiae nomine), Pierre Nizet ancien; von
310 Wickrathberg: Johannes Sylvius; von Wevelinghoven: Andreas Rotarius und Aelt Dierich Averlach.

---

305 Bergische Synode] *supplevi*; *a.c.* BS   Düsseldorf] *supplevi*   **306** Mülheim]
supplevi   Solingen] *supplevi*   Ratingen] *supplevi*   **307** Langenberg] *supplevi*

CONCILIUM HIBERNICUM

1614/1615

edidit
Torrance KIRBY

THE *ARTICLES OF RELIGION* OF THE CHURCH OF IRELAND, COMMONLY CALLED THE *IRISH ARTICLES*
1614/1615

The reformed Church of Ireland came into being in 1536 when the Irish Parliament, following the example set by the Parliament at Westminster in 1534 with the enactment of the statute of Royal Supremacy – which notably declared England to be 'an empire' ([1]) – declared King Henry VIII to be supreme head of the Church. The case of Ireland was somewhat complicated by the fact that Henry was not constitutionally recognised in Ireland as sovereign until 1542. Prior to that date Henry's title to rule was based on the Lordship of Ireland, a feudal status which dated back to the Norman invasion of the twelfth century. Moreover, the Lordship of Ireland was designated a papal possession which the King of England held in fief as the Pope's Lord Lieutenant. Technically, while Henry ruled the Church of Ireland as its Supreme Head he remained a vassal of the 'Bishop of Rome', as the Pope was now officially designated according to English statute. This anomalous status was rectified under the so-called Crown of Ireland Act passed by the Irish Parliament in 1541, at which time Henry assumed for the first time the title of King of Ireland accompanied by the renaming of the territory the Kingdom of Ireland. ([2]) Consequently, his ecclesiastical headship of the realm preceded his full sovereignty as King by eight years. Such were the intricate constitutional origins of the independent and reformed Church of Ireland.

During the latter years of the reign of Henry VIII, and into that of Edward VI, the Irish prelacy relied upon the determinations of the English

---

([1]) The parliamentary sessions of 1533 and 1534 made decisive moves against the papacy with the formal enactment of the Royal Supremacy. In strictly constitutional terms, a series of statutes beginning with the *Act in Restraint of Appeals to Rome* of 1533 (24 Hen. 8, *c.* 12), followed by the *Act of Supremacy* of 1534 (26 Hen. 8, *c.* 1), and culminating with an *Act Extinguishing the Authority of the Bishop of Rome* in 1536 (28 Hen. 8, *c.* 10) accomplish the revolution which established Henry VIII's headship of the Church. The preamble of the *Act of Supremacy* famously declares that England is an 'empire', governed by one supreme head, namely the King, and that under his rule the Church is wholly self-sufficient 'without the intermeddling of any exterior person or persons'.

([2]) 33 Hen. 8, *c.* 1, *An Act that the King of England, his Heirs and Successors, be Kings of Ireland* (1542).

Convocation, and received their formularies of doctrine and worship which were established in the larger Kingdom under the authority of the royal ecclesiastical supremacy. (3) The reformed clergy of the Irish Church accepted the liturgy of the *Book of Common Prayer* (1559) in 1560 following the accession of Queen Elizabeth I. It remains unclear what status the *Articles of Religion* (1563/1571) of the Church of England held within the Church of Ireland during this period. The first Convocation of the archbishops, bishops and clergy of Ireland – held on the model of the Convocation of the province of Canterbury in 1563 – was not convened until 1614 when it sat in conjunction with the Irish Parliament. In a sermon preached before the English House of Commons some years later on 16 February 1620, James Ussher (1581-1656) notably observed that '[w]e all agree that the Scriptures of God are the perfect rule of our faith; we all consent in the main grounds of religion drawn from thence; we all subscribe to the Articles of doctrine agreed upon in the synod of the year 1562, for the avoiding of diversities of opinions'. (4) This is indeed a revealing statement from the principal putative author of the *Irish Articles* of 1615 who, at that time, had recently been appointed vice-Chancellor of Trinity College Dublin, and would later, in 1625, be consecrated archbishop of Armagh and primate of all Ireland. (5)

Close inspection of these *Articles* approved by the Convocation of the Church of Ireland shows a marked dependence upon the Elizabethan formulary as doctrinal paradigm. Fully thirty-six of the *Thirty-Nine Articles of Religion* are rehearsed more or less verbatim, although their order is considerably altered. (6) In addition to their reflection of heavy influence of the doctrinal substance of the *Thirty-Nine Articles*, the *Irish Articles* have the noted feature of incorporating in their entirety – but once again not in the same precise order – the rigorous Calvinist teaching concerning the doctrine of predestination set forth in Archbishop John Whitgift's *Lambeth Articles* of 1595, (7) a considerably more expanded treatment of this doctrine than is found in Arti-

---

(3) Worship according to the order of the first Edwardine *Book of Common Prayer* (1549) was first held in Ireland on Easter Sunday 1551. Hardwick, *A History of the Articles of Religion*, p. 181.

(4) J. Ussher, 'A Sermon preached before the Commons House of Parliament', in Elrington, *Works of James Ussher*, p. 421. This sermon was first printed in 1621.

(5) According to N. Bernard, *Life of Ussher*, London 1793: 'Anno 1615 there was a [...] convocation of the clergy, then those learned articles of Ireland were composed and published, [Ussher] being a member of the Synod was appointed to draw them up', quoted in Ford, *James Ussher*, p. 86.

(6) See p. 567-631

(7) See p. 929-944. See V. C. Miller, *The Lambeth Articles: Doctrinal Development and Conflict in Sixteenth-Century England*, Oxford 1994.

cle XVII of the Elizabethan *Articles of Religion*. Another instance, namely the omission from the *Irish Articles* of Article XXXVI ('On the consecration of Bishops and ministers') of the 1563/1571 formulary, is possibly indicative of an attempt in the Irish document to accommodate Puritan nonconformity to some degree. (8) Moreover, and perhaps of even greater lasting significance, the *Articles* of 1615 resolutely reflect continental patterns of Reformed dogma by displacing the primary doctrine concerning the Trinity and the divine essence in the opening articles with the locus concerned with the authority of Scripture, an order found, for example, in the *Second Helvetic Confession* (1566), and which anticipates the order of the *Westminster Confession* (1647). (9) The *Irish Articles* also present a formulation of covenant theology which is more closely aligned with *Westminster* than with the Elizabethan *Articles*. In the light of such distinctive marks, the *Irish Articles* have come to be viewed as a bridge of sorts connecting the doctrine of the sixteenth-century Church of England with the more robust Calvinist reform of the mid-seventeenth century.

The *Irish Articles* of 1615 number 104 in all. Articles 1 through 7 treat the authority of the Holy Scripture and the three ancient creeds – i.e. the *Apostles'*, *Nicene*, and *Athanasian*. In articles 8 to 10 there is a treatment of the doctrine of the Holy Trinity, followed by a decidedly prelapsarian emphasis on the doctrine of predestination in articles 11 through 17. It is not until Article 18 that the subjects of creation and providence put in an appearance (articles 18 to 21). There then follows a series of articles (22 to 28) on matters of theological anthropology, i.e. 'Of the fall of man, originall sinne, and the state of man before justification'. Articles 29 and 30 treat the objective accomplishment of the redemption of humanity through the sole mediatorship of Christ, and 31 through 33 consider the communication to humanity of the gifts of this redemption by means of the divine grace. The soteriological theme continues with a treatment of faith and the grace of justification in articles 34 through 38, followed by good works and the grace of sanctification in 39 through 45. Articles 46 to 56 explore the consequent duty of service owed by humanity to God in the form of prayer and worship. 57 through 62 consider the authority of the civil magistrate and the duty of obedience owed to him by subjects, while 63 to 67 examine the duty owed by every man to his neighbour. The following section turns to matters of ecclesiology with a consideration of the distinction between the visible and invisible Church, followed by a series of articles (75 to 80) on the limits of the authority of the institutional Church, in

(8) On this point see Ford, *James Ussher*, 90-91.
(9) See *Westminster Confession*, in *COGD* VI.2 (forthcoming).

particular concerning the due subordination of episcopal to royal authority. Articles 81 through 84 address the theme of the double covenant as revealed in the Old and New Testament, while 85 to 88 provide a bridge to a broader discussion of the nature of the sacraments with three articles (89 to 91) on baptism, and nine (92 to 100) on the Lord's Supper including a noteworthy excursus on the hermeneutics of sacramental presence. The concluding four articles exhibit a distinctly eschatological emphasis: 'Of the state of the soules of men, after they be departed out of this life; together with the generall Resurrection, and the last Judgement'.

Appended to the *Articles* is a formal decree of the Synod which states that any minister of the Church of Ireland who publicly contradicted any aspect of this doctrine and who, after due admonition failed to conform, was subject to being 'silenced and deprived of all spirituall promotions'. It should be noted that these *Articles* were set aside by a Convocation of the Irish Church summoned at the instigation of Archbishop William Laud in 1635 under the leadership of the earl of Strafford, then Lord-Lieutenant of Ireland, and his chaplain, John Bramhall, a leading Laudian high-churchman. This Convocation reaffirmed the *Thirty-Nine Articles* of 1563/1571 which have since remained the standard of doctrine within the Church of Ireland.

BIBLIOGRAPHY

Sources (and Their Abbreviations)

Articles of religion agreed vpon by the archbishops, and bishops, and the rest of the cleargie of Ireland, in the conuocation holden at Dublin in the yeare of our Lord God 1615. for the avoyding of diuersities of opinions: and the establishing of concent touching true religion, Dublin 1615.

Articles of religion [...] for the avoyding of diuersities of opinion and the establishing of concent touching true religion, London 1628. Repr. London 1629; London 1681.

G. Bray, *Documents of the English Reformation*, Cambridge 1994.

T. Kirby, 'The Articles of Religion of the Church of England (1563-1571), commonly called the *Thirty-Nine Articles*', in *RefBK*, vol. 2/1 (2009), p. 371-410 [= *Articles of Religion*].

P. Schaff, *The Creeds of the Evangelical Protestant Churches*, London 1877.

CONCILIUM HIBERNICUM – 1614-1615

LITERATURE (AND ITS ABBREVIATIONS)

The Life of the Most Rev. James Ussher, D.D., Lord Archbishop of Armagh, and Primate of All Ireland: With an Account of His Writings, ed. C. R. Erlington, Dublin 1848.

The Whole Works of the Most Rev. James Ussher, D.D., Lord Archbishop of Armagh, and Primate of All Ireland: Now for the First Time Collected, with a Life of the Author, and an Account of His Writings, ed. C. R. Erlington, Dublin 1864 [= Elrington, *Works of James Ussher*].

G. H. Fitzgerald, *The Irish Articles of Religion and the Westminster Confession of Faith*, ThD Thesis, Union Theological Seminary 1962.

A. Ford, *James Ussher: Theology, History, and Politics in Early Modern Ireland and England*, Oxford 2007 [= Ford, *James Ussher*].

C. Hardwick, *A History of the Articles of Religion: To which is Added a Series of Documents, from A.D. 1536 to A.D. 1615*, London ²1895 [= Hardwick, *A History of the Articles of Religion*].

G. Stokes, *Essay on the Nature and Import of Subscription to the Thirty-Nine Articles in Ireland*, Dublin 1799.

MONITUM

Articles of religion agreed vpon by the archbishops, and bishops, and the rest of the cleargie of Ireland, in the conuocation holden at Dublin in the yeare of our Lord God 1615. for the avoyding of diuersities of opinions: and the establishing of concent touching true religion, Printed at Dublin by Iohn Franckton printer to the Kings most excellent Maiestie, 1615.

CONCILIUM HIBERNICUM
1614-1615

ARTICLES OF RELIGION AGREED VPON BY THE ARCH-
BISHOPS, AND BISHOPS, AND THE REST OF THE CLEARGIE OF
IRELAND, IN THE CONUOCATION HOLDEN AT DUBLIN IN
THE YEARE OF OUR LORD GOD 1615. FOR THE AVOYDING OF
5 DIUERSITIES OF OPINION, AND THE ESTABLISHING OF CON-
SENT TOUCHING TRUE RELIGION.

Printed at Dublin by Iohn Franckton printer to the Kings most excellent
Maiestie, 1615.

OF THE HOLY SCRIPTURE AND THE THREE CREEDES.

10   1. The ground of our Religion, and rule of faith and all saving trueth is the
word of God, contained in the holy scripture.

2. By the name of holy Scripture wee understand all the Canonicall
Bookes of the Old and New Testament, viz.

Of the Old Testament.   Of the New Testament

15   *The 5 Books of Moses.*   *The Gospels according to*

---

10 1.] the first article's pronouncement of the Scripture as the *regula fidei* follows the
order of the *Second Helvetic Confession* (1566). Composed by Heinrich Bullinger, this
formulary has long been regarded as among the most authoritative in the Reformed
tradition, having been the most widely received and formally approved. In this highly
significant respect the order of the *Irish Articles* departs from the model of the *Thirty-
Nine Articles of the Church of England* (1563-1571) on which it depends substantially in
content. In the latter formulary, the first five articles address the substance of the faith
in the doctrine of the Holy Trinity, whereas the article concerning 'the sufficiency of
the Holy Scriptures to salvation' is numbered sixth. This latter approach to
confessional *ordo,* modelled upon the *Augsburg Confession* (1530) composed by Philipp
Melanchthon, is found in Thomas Cranmer's early draft of *Thirteen Articles* of 1538
(Henry VIII) and continues in all of Cranmer's subsequent drafts including the *Forty-
Two Articles* of 1553 (Edward VI) and culminating in the *Thirty-Nine Articles* (Elizabeth
I). The *Westminster Confession* (1647) observes the same order as the *Irish Articles*
12 2.] cfr Article VI 'Of the sufficiency of the Scriptures for salvation' in the *Articles of
Religion* (1563-1571). The English formulary was agreed by 'the Archbishoppes and
Bishoppes of both prouinces and the whole cleargie, in the Conuocation [of the
Province of Canterbury] holden at London in the yere of our Lorde God, 1562,
according to the computation of the Churche of Englande [i.e. 1563 New Style]', but
only received full canonical status 1571 when it was formally approved by an Act of
Parliament and received royal assent **14** New Testament] Article VI (1563-1571) does
not specifically list these books but states that '[a]ll the bookes of the newe Testament,
as they are commonly receaued, we do receaue, and accompt them for Canonicall'

Josua.	*Matthew.*
Judges.	*Mark.*
Ruth.	*Luke.*
The first and second of Samuel.	*John.*
The first and second of Kings. |	*The Acts of the Apostles.*
The first and second of Chronicles.	*The Epistle of S. Paul to the Romaines.*
Ezra.	*Corinthians, 2.*
Nehemiah.	*Galathians.*
Esther.	*Ephesians.*
Job.	*Philippians.*
Psalmes.	*Colossians.*
Proverbs.	*Thessalonians, 2.*
Ecclesiastes.	*Timothie, 2.*
The Song of Solomon.	*Titus.*
Isaiah.	*Philemon.*
Jeremiah, his prophecie	*Hebrewes.*
and Lamentation.	
Ezechiel.	*The Epistle of S. James.*
Daniel.	*Saint Peter, 2.*
The 12 lesse Prophets.	*Saint John, 3.*
	Saint Jude.
	The Revelation of Saint John.

All which wee acknowledge to be given by the inspiration of God, and in that regard to be | of most certaine credit and highest authority.

3. The other Bookes commonely called *Apocryphall,* did not proceede from such inspiration, and therefore are not of sufficient authoritie to establish any point of doctrine, but the Church doth reade them as Bookes containing many worthy things for example of life and instruction of maners.

Such are these following.

The third booke of Esdras.
The fourth booke of Esdras.
The booke of Tobias.
The booke of Judith.
Additions to the booke of Esther.
The booke of Wisdome.
The booke of Jesus the Sonne of Sirach, called Ecclesiasticus.
Baruch with the Epistle of Jeremiah.
The song of the three Children.
Susanna.

CONCILIUM HIBERNICUM – 1614-1615

Bell and the Dragon.
The praier of Manasses.
The First booke of Maccabees.
The Second booke of Maccabees.

60   4. The Scriptures ought to be translated out of the originall tongues into all languages for the common use of all men: neither is any person to be discouraged from reading the Bible in such a lan|guage, as he doth under-   A4v stand, but seriously exhorted to read the same with great humilitie and reverence, as a special meanes to bring him to the true knowledge of God and of his
65 owne duty.

    5. Although there be some hard things in the Scripture (especially such as have proper relation to the times in which they were first uttered, and prophesies of things which were afterwardes to bee fulfilled), yet all things necessary to bee known unto everlasting salvation are clearly delivered therein: and
70 nothing of that kinde is spoken under dark mysteries in one place, which is not in other places spoken more familiarly and plainely to the capacitie of learned and unlearned.

    6. The holy Scriptures containe all things necessary to salvation, and are able to instruct sufficiently in all points of faith that wee are bound to beleeve,
75 and all good duties that wee are bound to practice.

    7. All and everie the Articles contained in the *Nicen Creed*, the *Creede* of *Athanasius*, and that which is commonely called the *Apostles Creede* ought firmly to be receaved and beleeved, for they may be proved by most certaine warrant of holy Scripture.

80 | OF FAITH IN THE HOLY TRINITIE.   B1r

    8. There is but one living and true God, everlasting, without body, parts, or passions, of infinite power, wisedom, and goodnes, the maker and preserver of all things, both visible and invisible. And in unitie of this Godhead there be

---

60 4.] cfr Article XXIV 'Of speakyng in the congregation' (1563-1571), where the use of the vernacular is maintained in the context of prayer and the sacraments   **73** 6.] this article invokes the Reformed concept of the *tertius usus legis*, the so-called moral use of the law revealed in Scripture. Emphasis on Scripture as instructive in 'all good duties that wee are bound to practice' reveals a pronounced influence of Calvin's soteriology. The 'sufficiency of Scripture to Salvation' is the chief focus of Article VI concerning Scripture in the *Articles of Religion* of 1563-1571. The latter makes no mention of the authority of Scripture in matters of practice and discipline   **76** 7.] Article VII is closely modelled upon Article VIII 'Of the three Credes' (1563-1571)   **81** 8.] Article I 'Of fayth in the holie Trinitie' in the *Articles of Religion* (1563-1571)

980　CONCILIUM HIBERNICUM – 1614-1615

three persons of one and the same substance, power, and eternitie: the Father,
85　the Sone, and the holy Ghost.

9. The essence of the Father doth not begett the essence of the Sonne; but
the person of the Father begetteth the person of the Sonne, by communicating
his whole essence to the person begotten from eternitie.

10. The holy Ghost, proceeding from the Father and the Sonne, is of one
90　substance, majestie, and glory, with the Father and the Sonne, very and eternall God.

Of Gods eternall decree, and Predestination.

11. God from all eternitie did by his unchangeable counsell ordaine whatsoever in time should come to passe: yet so, as thereby no violence is offred to
95　the wills of the reasonable creatures, and neither the libertie nor the con-
tin|gencie of the second causes is taken away, but established rather.　Biv

---

89　10.] cfr Gal. 4, 6; Act. 16, 7; Rom. 8, 9; praecipue Ioh. 25, 26

86　9.] cfr Article II 'Of the worde or sonne of God which was made very man' in the
Articles of Religion (1563-1571). Unlike the *Irish Articles*, the English formulary's
sequence of three separate articles on Christology emphasise the incarnation (Article
II), Christ's descent into hell (Article III), and the resurrection (Article IV). The
Christology here places stronger Trinitarian emphasis on the divine Sonship, the unity
of essence with the Father　**89**　10.] this article is identical to Article V 'Of the holy
ghost' (1563-1571). It is notable for its affirmation of the *filioque* clause added to the
Nicene Creed at the provincial Synod of Toledo (589). The *Articles* are thus committed
to this distinctive formula of Western Christendom. While the Father is alone the
'fountain' of godhead – which the Son, as begotten, is not – the *filioque* serves to
reinforce the co-equality and consubstantiality of these two persons in relation to the
procession of the third　**92**　Of – Predestination] cfr Article XVII (1563-1571), where
the doctrine of predestination is treated at the conclusion of a soteriological sequence
of articles touching on grace through faith or justification, good works or
sanctification, and salvation by Christ alone. The *Irish Articles* once again depart
significantly from the order of 1563-1571 by placing the treatment of predestination
adjacent to the articles on the doctrine of the divine being and prior to the treatment
of creation, the fall, and the means of salvation　**93**　11.] the content of this sequence
of articles is largely derived from the *Lambeth Articles* (see p. 942-944). Queen
Elizabeth I refused to give sanction to the *Articles* on the ground that the convening of
a Synod without her express permission was in violation of her royal prerogative

CONCILIUM HIBERNICUM – 1614-1615 981

12. By the same eternall counsell God hath predestinated some unto life, and reprobated some unto death: of both which there is a certaine number, knowen onely to God, which can neither be increased nor diminished.

13. Predestination to life, is the everlasting purpose of God, whereby, before the foundations of the world were layed, he hath constantly decreed in his secret counsell to deliver from curse and damnation, those whom he hath chosen in Christ out of mankinde, and to bring them by Christ unto everlasting salvation, as vessels made to honor.

14. The cause moving God to predestinate unto life, is not the foreseeing of faith, or perseverance, or good workes, or of any thing which is in the person predestinated, but onely the good pleasure of God himselfe. For all things being ordained for the manifestation of his glory, and his glory being to appeare both in the workes of his Mercie and of his Justice; it seemed good to his heavenly wisdome to choose out a certaine number towards whome he would extend his undeserved mercie, leaving the rest to be spectacles of his justice.

15. Such as are predestinated unto life, be called according unto Gods purpose (his Spirit working in due season) and through grace they obey the | B2r calling, they bee justified freely, they bee made sonnes of God by adoption, they be made like the image of his onely begotten Sonne JESUS CHRIST, they walke religiously in good workes, and at length, by Gods mercie they attaine to everlasting felicitie. But such as are not predestinated to salvation shall finally be condemned for their sinnes.

97/98 By – death] the first clause of Article 12 derives from Article 1 of the *Lambeth Articles* **98/99** of – diminished] the second clause of Article 12 repeats Article 3 of the *Lambeth Articles* **100** 13.] see R. Hooker, *Of the Lawes of Ecclesiasticall Politie*, London 1597, Book 5, 56, 5: 'whatsoever wee doe behold now in this present world, it was inwrapped within the bowells of divine mercie, written in the booke of eternall wisdom, and held in the handes of omnipotent power, the first foundations of the world being as yeat unlaide. So that all thinges which God hath made are in that respect the ofspringe of God, they are *in him* as effects in their highest cause, he likewise actuallies is *in them*, thassistance and influence of his deitie is *their life*' **105/107** The – himselfe] this first sentence of Article 14 reiterates *Lambeth Articles*, Article 2 **109/112** it – justice] according to Article 4 of the *Lambeth Articles*, 'Those who are not predestinated to salvation shall be necessarily damned for their sins' **113/118** Such – felicitie] the formulation of the first sentence of Article 15 is derived from Article XVII 'Of Predestination' (1563-1571) **118/119** But – sinnes] the final sentence of Article 15 reiterates the *Lambeth Articles*, Article 4. Cfr R. Hooker, *Of the Lawes of Ecclesiastical Politie*, Book V, 56, 7: 'Wee are therefore in God through Christ eternallie accordinge to that intent and purpose whereby wee were chosen to be made his in this present world before the world it selfe was made, wee are in God through the knowledge which is had of us and the love which is borne towards us from everlastinge'

982   CONCILIUM HIBERNICUM – 1614-1615

120   16. The godly consideration of Predestination and our election in CHRIST
is full of sweete, pleasant, and unspeakable comfort to godly persons, and such
as feele in themselves the working of the spirit of CHRIST, mortifying the
workes of the flesh, and their earthly members, and drawing up their minds to
high and heavenly things: as well because it doth greatly confirme and estab-
125 lish their faith of eternall salvation to be enjoyed through CHRIST, as because
it doth fervently kindle their love towardes God: and on the contrary side, for
curious and carnall persons, lacking the spirit of CHRIST, to have continually
before their eyes the sentence of Gods predestination is very dangerous.

17. Wee must receave Gods promises in such wise as they be generally set
130 forth unto us in holy Scripture; and in our doings, that will of God is to be
followed, which wee have expressly declared unto us in the word of God.

| OF THE CREATION AND GOVERNMENT OF ALL THINGS.   B2v

18. In the beginning of time, when no creature had any being, God by his
word alone, in the space of six dayes, created all things, and afterwardes by his
135 providence doth continue, propagate, and order them according to his owne
will.

19. The principall creatures are Angels and men.

20. Of Angels, some continued in that holy state wherein they were created, and are by Gods grace for ever established therein: others fell from the
140 same, and are reserved in chaines of darknesse unto the judgement of the great
day.

21. Man being at the beginning created according to the image of God
(which consisted especially in the Wisdome of his minde, and the true Holy-
nesse of his free will) had the covenant of the lawe ingrafted in his heart:
145 whereby God did promise unto him everlasting life, upon condition that he
performed entire and perfect obedience unto his Commaundments, accord-

---

142/144 Man – heart] cfr Rom. 2, 14

120 16.] the formulation of Article 16 is closely modelled upon the second paragraph
of Article XVII (1563-1571)   **129** 17.] Article 17 reiterates the final statement found in
Article XVII (1563-1571). There is no mention of *Lambeth*, Article 6 in the *Irish Articles*
until Article 37 (see below)   **132** Of – things] there is no corresponding treatment of
the doctrines of creation and providence in the *Articles of Religion* (1563-1571) as we
find here in Articles 18 through 21. In this respect, the *Irish Articles* owe something to
the *Second Helvetic Confession*, chapters 6 'Of the Providence of God' and 7 'Of the
Creation of all things: of Angels, the Devil, and man'   **138** 20.] cfr *Second Helvetic
Confession*, Chapter VII

CONCILIUM HIBERNICUM – 1614-1615

ing to that measure of strength wherewith hee was endued in his creation, and
threatened death unto him if he did not perform the same.

| OF THE FALL OF MAN, ORIGINALL SINNE, AND THE STATE OF MAN BEFORE JUSTIFICATION.

22. By one man sinne entered into the world, and death by sinne: and so
death went over all men, for as much as all have sinned.

23. Originall sinne standeth not in the imitation of Adam (as the Pelagians dream) but is the fault and corruption of the nature of every person that
naturally is ingendred and propagated from Adam: whereby it commeth to
passe that man is deprived of originall righteousnes, and by nature is bent unto
sinne. And therefore, in every person borne into the world, it deserveth Gods
wrath and damnation.

24. This corruption of nature doth remaine even in those that are regenerated, whereby the flesh alwaies lusteth against the spirit, and cannot bee made
subject to the lawe of God. And howsoever, for Christs sake there bee no condemnation to such as are regenerate and doe beleeve: yet doth the Apostle
acknowledge, that in itselfe this concupiscence hath the nature of sin.

25. The condition of man after the fall of Adam is such that he cannot
turne and prepare himselfe by his owne naturall strength and good | workes, to
faith and calling uppon God. Wherefore wee have no power to doe good
workes pleasing and acceptable unto God without the grace of God preventing us, that wee may have a good will, and working with us when wee have that
good will.

26. Workes done before the grace of Christ and the inspiration of his spirit are not pleasing unto God, for as much as they spring not of faith in Jesus
Christ, neither doe they make men meete to receave grace, or (as the Schoole
Authors say) deserve grace of congruitie: yea rather, for that they are not done
in such sorte as God hath willed and commaunded them to be done, wee
doubt not but they are sinfull.

149/150 Of – justification] cfr Article IX 'Of originall or birth sinne' (1563-1571)
159/169 This – will] Articles 23 and 24 closely reiterate the formulation of Article IX
'Of originall or birth sinne' (1563-1571)   **164** 25.] Article 25 is an exact rendering of
Article X 'Of free wyll' (1563-1571)   **170** 26.] Article 26 renders Article XIII 'Of
workes before iustification' (1563-1571). The soteriological matter of the intervening
English Articles, XI 'Of the iustification of man' and XII 'Of good workes', are treated
below in sections devoted to justification (Articles 34-38) and sanctification
respectively (Articles 39-45)

984 CONCILIUM HIBERNICUM – 1614-1615

27. All sinnes are not equall, but some farre more heynous than others yet the very least is of its owne nature mortall, and without Gods mercie maketh the offender lyable unto everlasting damnation.

28. God is not the Author of sinne: howbeit he doth not onely permit, but also by his providence governe and order the same, guiding it in such sort by his infinite wisdome, as he turneth to the manifestation of his owne glory and to the good of his elect.

| Of Christ, the mediator of the second Covenant. B4r

29. The Sonne, which is the Word of the Father, begotten from everlasting of the Father, the true and eternall God, of one substance with the Father, tooke mans nature in the wombe of the blessed Virgin, of her substance: so that two whole and perfect natures, that is to say, the Godhead and Manhoode, were inseperably joined in one person, making one Christ very God and very man.

30. Christ in the truth of our nature was made like unto us in all things, sinne onely excepted, from which he was cleerely voyd, both in his life and in his nature. He came as a Lambe without spott to take away the sinnes of the world by the sacrifice of himself once made, and sinne (as *Saint John saith*) was not in him. He fulfilled the lawe for us perfectly: For our sakes he endured most greivous torments immediately in his soule, and most painefull sufferings in his body. He was crucified, and dyed to reconcile his Father unto us, and to be a sacrifice not onely for originall guilt, but also for all our actuall transgressions. He was buried and descended into hell, and the third day rose from the dead, and tooke againe his body, with flesh, bones, and all things appertaining to the perfection of mans nature: wherewith he ascended into Heaven, and there sitteth at | the right hand of his Father, untill hee returne to B4v judge all men at the last day.

---

176 27.] cfr Article XVI 'Of sinne after Baptisme' (1563-1571)   **179** 28.] cfr *Westminster Confession*, Chapter III, Article 1, 'Of God's Eternal Decree' (see *COGD* VI.2, forthcoming)   **184** 29.] restates Article II 'Of the worde or sonne of God which was made very man' of the *Articles of Religion* (1563-1571)   **190/194** Christ – him] combines the first portion of Article XV 'Of Christe alone without sinne' with the last part of Article II, both in the *Articles of Religion* (1563-1571)   **194/198** He – transgressions] expands on the *Articles of Religion* (1563-1571)   **198/202** He – day] the last sentence of Article 30 combines the remainder of Article III with Article IV, *Articles of Religion* (1563-1571)

CONCILIUM HIBERNICUM – 1614-1615   985

Of the communicating of the grace of Christ.

31. They are to be condemned, that presume to say that every man shalbe saved by the lawe or sect which he professeth, so that he be diligent to frame his life according to that lawe and the light of nature. For holy scripture doth set out unto us onely the name of Jesus Christ whereby men must be saved.

32. None can come unto Christ, unlesse it bee given unto him, and unlesse the Father drawe him. And all men are not so drawen by the Father that they may come unto the Sone. Neither is there such a sufficient measure of grace vouchsafed unto everie man whereby he is enabled to come unto everlasting life.

33. All Gods elect are in their time inseparablye united unto Christ by the effectuall and vitall influence of the holy Ghost, derived from him as from the head unto every true member of his mysticall body. And being thus made one with Christ, they are truly regenerated and made partakers of him and all his benefits.

| Of Justification and Faith.   C1r

34. Wee are accounted righteous before God, onely for the merit of our Lord and Saviour Jesus Christ, applied by faith: and not for our owne workes or merits. And this righteousnes, which wee so receave of Gods mercie and Christs merits, imbraced by faith, is taken, accepted, and allowed of God for our perfect and full justification.

35. Although this justification be free unto us, yet it cometh not so freely unto us that there is no ransome paid therefore at all. God shewed his great

---

204 31.] restates Article XVIII of the *Articles of Religion* (1563-1571), 'Of obtaynyng eternall saluation, only by the name of Christe'   **208** 32.] based on Article 8 of the *Lambeth Articles*. The *Westminister Confession*, Chapter X, Article 4, 'Of Effectual Calling' also resembles this article   **213** 33.] Article 33 sums up Calvin's conception of salvation as a participation in the *beneficia Christi* through an *insitio in Christum*. See Calv., *Instit.* (1559), 3. 2. 24 (vol. 1, p. 369-370). For further discussion of this teaching see A. E. McGrath, *Iustitia Dei: A History of the Christian Doctrine of Justification*, 2 vols, Cambridge 2005, vol. 2, p. 256   **219** 34.] Article 34 restates *Articles of Religion* (1563-1571), Article XI 'Of the iustification of man'   **224** 35.] Article 35 is based on 'A Sermon of the Salvation of Mankynd by onely Christ our Saviour, from sinne and death everlastyng', third sermon in the authorised *Book of Homilies*. Cfr *Certaine sermons appoynted by the Quenes Maiestie, to be declared and read, by all persons, vicars, and curates, euery Sundaye, holy daye, in theyr churches: and by her Graces aduise perused and ouersene, for the better vnderstandyng of the simple people*, London 1562, fol. D2r seq. The *Homilies* are authorised by the *Articles of Religion* (1563-1571), Article 35, as

mercie in delivering us from our former captivitie, without requiring of any ransome to be payd, or amends to be made on our parts; which thing by us had been unpossible to bee done. And whereas all the world was not able of themselves to pay any part towards their ransom, it pleased our heavenly Father of his infinite mercie without any desert of ours, to provide for us the most precious merits of his owne Sonne, whereby our ransome might be fully payd, the lawe fulfilled, and his justice fully satisfied. So that Christ is now the righteousnes of all them that truly beleeve in him. Hee for them payd their ransome by his death. Hee for them fulfilled the lawe in his life. That now in him, and by him everie true Christian man may be called a fulfiller of the lawe: forasmuch as | that which our infirmitie was not able to effect, Christs justice C1v hath performed. And thus the justice and mercie of God doe embrace each other: the grace of God not shutting out the justice of God in the matter of our justification; but onely shutting out the justice of man (that is to say, the justice of our owne workes) from being any cause of deserving our justification.

36. When wee say that wee are justified by Faith onely, wee doe not meane that the said justifying faith is alone in man, without true Repentance, Hope, Charity, and the feare of God (for such a faith is dead, and cannot justifie), neither doe wee meane that this our act to beleeve in Christ, or this our faith in Christ, which is within us, doth of it selfe justifie us, nor deserve our justification unto us, (for that were to account our selves to be justified by the vertue or dignitie of some thing that is within ourselves:) but the true understanding and meaning thereof is that although wee heare Gods word & beleeve it, although wee have Faith, Hope, Charitie, Repentance, and the fear of God within us and add never so many good workes thereunto: yet wee must renounce the merit of all our said virtues, of Faith, Hope, Charitie, and all our other vertues, and good deeds, which wee either have done, shall doe, or can doe, as things that be farre too weake and imperfect, and unsufficient to deserve remission of our sinnes, and our justification: and therefore wee must trust onely in Gods mercie, and | the merits of his most dearely beloved Son, C2r our onely Redeemer, Saviour, and Justifier, Jesus Christ. Neverthelesse, because Faith doth directly send us to Christ for our justification, and that by faith given us of God wee embrace the promise of Gods mercie, and the remission of our sinnes, (which thing none other of our vertues or workes properly

---

containing 'godly and wholesome doctrine, and necessarie for these tymes' **242** When – onely] see 'A Sermon of the Salvation of Mankynd' **251/257** yet – Christ] see the second part of 'A Sermon of the Salvation of Mankynd', fol. D4v seq.

CONCILIUM HIBERNICUM – 1614-1615

doth:) therefore the Scripture useth to say, that *Faith without workes*: and the auncient fathers of the Church to the same purpose, that onely Faith doth justify us.

37. By justifying Faith wee understand not onely the common belief of the Articles of Christian Religion, and a perswasion of the truth of Gods worde in generall: but also a particular application of the gratious promises of the Gospell, to the comfort of our owne soules: whereby wee lay hold on Christ with all his benefits, having an earnest trust and confidence in God that he will be mercifull unto us for his onely Sonnes sake. So that a true beleever may be certaine, by the assurance of faith, of the forgivenesse of his sinnes, and of his everlasting salvation by Christ.

38. A true lively justifying faith, and the sanctifying Spirit of God, is not extinguished, nor vanisheth away in the regenerate, either finally or totally.

| OF SANCTIFICATION AND GOOD WORKES.   C2v

39. All that are justified, are likewise sanctified: their faith being alwaies accompanied with true Repentance and good Workes.

40. Repentance is a gift of God, whereby a godly sorrow is wrought in the heart of the faithfull for offending God their mercifull Father by their former transgressions, together with a constant resolution for the time to come to cleave unto God and to lead a new life.

41. Albeit that good workes, which are the fruits of faith, and follow after justification, cannot make satisfaction for our sinnes, and endure the severitie of Gods judgement: yet are they pleasing to God, and accepted of him in Christ, and doe spring from a true and lively faith, which by them is to be discerned as a tree by the fruite.

42. The workes which God would have his people to walke in are such as he hath commaunded in his holy Scripture, and not such workes as men have

---

261 Eph. 2, 8-9; Tit. 3, 5; II Tim. 1, 9; Iac. 2, 26

262/263 onely – us] see the third part of 'A Sermon of the Salvation of Mankynd', fol. E3v; Augustinus, *De spiritu et littera* 22, hrsg. C. F. Vrba – J. Zycha (*CSEL* 60), Wien – Leipzig 1913, p. 176, 13-17   **264** 37.] the last statement in Article 37 is based upon the *Lambeth Articles* 6: 'man truly faithful, that is, such a one who is endued with a justifying faith, is certain, with the full assurance of faith, of the remission of his sins and of his everlasting salvation by Christ'   **272** 38.] cfr *Articles of Religion* (1563-1571), Article XVI 'Of sinne after Baptisme'   **277** 40.] this article expresses the teaching concerning repentance in the *Second Helvetic Confession*, Chapter 14, 1   **281** 41.] reiterates *Articles of Religion* (1563-1571), Article XII 'Of good workes'   **286** 42.] cfr *Second Helvetic Confession*, Chapter 16 'Of faith and good works, and of their reward'

988 CONCILIUM HIBERNICUM – 1614-1615

devised out of their owne braine, of a blinde zeal and devotion, without the warrant of the word of God.

290   43. The regenerate cannot fulfill the lawe of God perfectly in this life. For in many things wee offend all: and if wee say, wee have no sinne, wee deceave our selves, and the truth is not in us.

    44. Not everie heynous sinne willingly commit|ted after baptisme is sinne   C3r against the holy Ghost and unpardonable. And therefore to such as fall into 295 sinne after baptisme, place for repentance is not to be denied.

    45. Voluntary workes besides, over, and above Gods commaundments, which they call workes of Superrogation, cannot be taught without arrogancie and impietie. For by them men doe declare that they doe not onely render unto God as much as they are bound to do, but that they doe more for his sake 300 than of bounden duty is required.

Of the seruice of God.

    46. Our duty towards God is to beleeve in him, to feare him, and to love him with all our heart, with all our minde, and with all our soule, and with all our strength to worship him, and to give him thankes, to put our whole trust 305 in him, to call upon him, to honour his holy Name and his word, and to serve him truely all the dayes of our life.

    47. In all our necessities wee ought to have recourse unto God by prayer: assuring ourselves that what soever wee aske of the Father in the name of his Sonne (our onely mediator and intercessor) Christ Jesus, and according to his 310 will, he will undoubtedly grant it.

    | 48. Wee ought to prepare our hearts before wee pray, and understand   C3v the things that wee ask when wee pray: that both our hearts and voyces may together sound in the eares of Gods Majestie.

    49. When almightie God smiteth us with affliction, of some great calami-315 tie hangeth over us, or any other weighty cause so requireth; it is our dutie to humble ourselves in fasting, to bewaile our sinnes with a sorowful heart, and

---

290 43.] this article recalls Martin Luther's formulation of the human condition after the gift of grace as *simul justus, simul peccator*   **293** 44.] cfr *Articles of Religion* (1563-1571), Article XVI   **296** 45.] this article restates all but the final sentence of the *Articles of Religion* (1563-1571), Article XIV 'Of workes of supererogation', which reads: '[w]hereas Christe sayth playnly, When ye have done al that are commaunded to you, say, We *be* vnprofitable seruantes'   **314** 49.] 'Of Publique Solemn Fasting', in *A Directory for the publique worship of God throughout the three kingdoms of England, Scotland, and Ireland*, London 1645, p. 74-79 (see *COGD* VI.2, forthcoming)

CONCILIUM HIBERNICUM – 1614-1615   989

to addict ourselves to earnest prayer, that it might please God to turne his wrath from us, or supplie us with such graces as wee greatly stand in neede of.

50. Fasting is a with-holding of meate, drincke, and all naturall foode, with other outward delights, from the body for the determined time of fasting. As for those abstinences which are appointed by publike order of our state, for eating of fish and forbearing of flesh at certaine times and daies appointed, they are no wayes meant to bee religious fastes, nor intended for the maintenance of any superstition in the choice of meates, but are grounded merely upon politicke considerations for provision of things tending to the better preservation of the Common-wealth.

51. Wee must not fast with this perswasion of minde, that our fasting can bring us to heaven, or ascribe holynesse to the outward worke wrought. For God alloweth not our fast for the worke sake (which of it selfe is a thing meerely indifferent) | but chiefly respecteth the heart, how it is affected there- C4r in. It is therefore requisit that first before all things wee clense our hearts from sinne, and then direct our fast to such ends as God will allow to bee good: that the flesh may thereby be chastised, the spirit may be more fervent in prayer, and that our fasting may bee a testimony of our humble submission to Gods majestie, when wee acknowledge our sinnes unto him, and are inwardly touched with sorrowfulnesse of heart, bewailing the same in the affliction of our bodies.

52. All worship devised by mans phantasie, besides or contrary to the Scriptures (as wandring on Pilgrimages, setting up of Candles, Stations, and Jubilies, Pharisaicall sects and fained Religions, praying upon Beades, and such like superstition) hath not onely no promise of reward in Scripture, but contrariwise threatnings and maledictions.

53. All manner of expressing God the Father, the Sonne, and the holy Ghost in an outward forme is utterly unlawfull. As also all other images devised or made by man to the use of Religion.

54. All religious worship ought to be giuen to God alone: from whome all goodnesse, health, and grace ought to be both asked and looked for, as from the very author and giver of the same, and from none other.

---

327 51.] Article 51 is based on extracts from 'Of good woorkes: And first of fasting, ii. Partes', in *The second tome of homilies of suche matters as were promised, and intituled in the former part of homilies. Set out by the aucthoritie of the Queenes Maiestie: and to be read in euery parish church agreeably*, London 1574   **343** 53.] Articles 52 and 53 loosely express the sentiments of Article XXII of the *Articles of Religion* (1563-1571)

990 CONCILIUM HIBERNICUM – 1614-1615

55. The name of God is to be used with all reverence | and holy respect: C4v
350 and therefore all vaine and rash swearing is utterly to be condemned. Yet
notwithstanding upon lawfull occasions, an oath may be given, and taken
according to the word of God, *justice, judgment, and truth.*

56. The first day of the weeke, which is the *Lords day*, is wholly to be dedi-
cated unto the service of God: and therefore wee are bound therein to rest
355 from our common and dayly business, and to bestow that leasure upon holy
exercises, both publike and private.

Of the Civill Magistrate.

57. The King's Majestie under God hath the Soveraigne and chiefe power
within his Realmes and Dominions over all manner of persons of what estate,
360 either Ecclesiasticall or Civill, soever they bee; so as no other forraine power
hath or ought to have any superiority over them.

58. Wee doe profess that the supreame governement of all estates within
the said Realmes and Dominions in all causes, as well Ecclesiasticall as Tempo-
rall, doth of right appertaine to the King's highnes. Neither doe wee give unto
365 him hereby the administration of the Word and Sacraments, or the power of
the Keyes: but that prerogatiue onely which wee see to have beene alwaies
given | unto all godly Princes in holy Scripture by God himselfe; that is, that D1r
hee should containe all estates and degrees committed to his charge by God,
whether they be Ecclesiasticall of Civill, within their duty, and restraine the
370 stubborne and evill doers with the power of the Civill swoorde.

59. The Pope neither of himselfe, nor by any authoritie of the Church or
Sea of Rome, or by any other meanes with any other, hath any power or
authoritie to depose the King, or dispose any of his Kingdomes or Dominions,
or to authorise any other Prince to invade or annoy him, or his Countries, or
375 to discharge any of his subjects of their allegeance and obedience to his
Majestie, or to give license or leave to any of them to beare arms, raise tumult,

---

349 55.] based on Article XXIX, 'Of a Christian mans othe', of the *Articles of Religion*
(1563-1571)   **353** 56.] cfr 'Of the sanctification of the Lords Day', *A Directory of
publique worship*, p. 56-57   **358** 57.] based on Article XXXVII, 'Of the civill
Magistrates', of the *Articles of Religion* (1563-1571), where that article reads: '[t]he
Queenes Maiestie hath the cheefe power in this Realme of Englande, and other her
dominions'   **362** 58.] also based on the continuation of Article XXXVII of the
Articles of Religion (1563-1571)   **371** 59.] this article expands on the brief observation
in Article 37 of the *Articles of Religion* (1563-1571): '[t]he bishop of Rome hath no
iurisdiction in this Realme of Englande', perhaps owing to the circumstance of the
Protestant population being in a minority in the Kingdom of Ireland

CONCILIUM HIBERNICUM – 1614-1615

or to offer any violence or hurt to his Royall person, state, or governement, or to any of his subjects within his Majesties Dominions.

60. That Princes which be excommunicated or deprived by the Pope, may be deposed or murdered by their subjects, or any other whatsoever, is impious doctrine.

61. The lawes of the Realme may punish Christian men with death, for heynous and grievous offences.

62. It is lawfull for Christian men, at the commaundment of the Magistrate, to beare arms, and to serve in just warres.

| OF OUR DUTY TOWARDS OUR NEIGHBOURS.   Div

63. Our duty towards our neighbours is, to love them as ourselves, and to do to all men as wee would they should doe to us; to honour and obey our Superiors; to preserve the safetie to mens persons, as also their chastitie, goodes, and good names; to beare no malice nor hatred in our hearts; to keepe our bodies in temperance, soberness, and chastitie; to be true and just in all our doings; not to covet other mens goodes, but labour truly to get our owne living, and to doe our duty in that estate of life unto which it pleaseth God to call us.

64. For the preservation of the chastitie of mens persons, wedlocke is commaunded unto all men that stand in neede thereof. Neither is there any prohibition by the word of God, but that the ministers of the Church may enter into the state of Matrimony: they being nowhere commaunded by Gods Law, either to vow the estate of single life, or to abstain from marriage. Therefore it is lawfull also for them, as well as for all other Christian men, to marrie at their owne discretion, as they shall judge the same to serve better to godliness.

65. The riches and goodes of Christians are not common, as touching the right, title, and possession of the same: as certaine Anabaptists falsely affirm. Notwithstanding everie man ought of such things as hee possesseth, liberally to give almes to the poor, according to his abillity.

| 66. Faith given is to be kept, even with Hereticks and Infidells.   D2r

67. The Popish doctrine of Equivocation & mental Reservation is most ungodly, and tendeth plainely to the subversion of all humaine society.

382/385 The – warres] Articles 61 and 62 reiterate the two final provisions of Article XXXVII of the *Articles of Religion* (1563-1571)   **395** 64.] restates elements of Article XXXII of the *Articles of Religion* (1563-1571)   **403** 65.] reiterates Article XXXVIII, *Articles of Religion* (1563-1571)

992 CONCILIUM HIBERNICUM – 1614-1615

410 OF THE CHURCH, AND OUTWARD MINISTERY OF THE GOSPELL.

68. There is but one Catholike Church (out of which there is no salvation) containing the universall company of all the Saints that ever were, are, or shalbe, gathered together in one body, under one head Christ Jesus: part whereof is already in heaven *triumphant*, part as yet *militant* heere upon earth.
415 And because this Church consisteth of all those, and those alone, which are elected by God unto salvation, & regenerated by the power of his spirit, the number of whome is knowen onely unto God himselfe; therefore it is called *Catholike* or universal, and the *Invisible* Church.

69. But particular and visible Churches, (consisting of those who make
420 profession of the faith of Christ, and live under the outward meanes of salvation) be many in number wherein the more or less sincerely according to Christs institution, the word of God is taught, the Sacraments are administered, and the authority of the Keyes is used, the more or less pure are such Churches to be accounted.

425 | 70. Although in the visible Church the evill bee ever mingled with the D2v
good, and sometimes the evil have chiefe authoritie in the ministration of the word & Sacraments: yet, for as much as they doe not the same in their owne name, but in Christs, and minister by his commission and authority; wee may use their ministry both in hearing the word, and in receaving the Sacraments.
430 Neither is the effect of Christs ordinance taken away by their wickednesse: nor the grace of Gods gifts diminished from such as by faith and rightly doe receave the Sacraments ministered unto them; which are effectual, because of Christs institution and promise, although they be ministered by evill men. Neverthelesse it appertaineth to the discipline of the Church, that inquiry be
435 made of evill ministers, and that they be accused by those that have knowledge of their offences, and finally being found guiltie, by just judgement bee deposed.

71. It is not lawful for any man to take upon him the office of publike preaching or ministring the Sacraments in the Church, unlesse hee bee first
440 lawfully called and sent to execute the same. And those wee ought to judge lawfully called and sent which be chosen and called to this worke by men who have publike authoritie given them in the Church, to call and send ministers into the Lords vineyard.

---

419 69.] cfr Article XIX, 'Of the Church', *Articles of Religion* (1563-1571)   **425** 70.] reiterates Article XXVI, *Articles of Religion* (1563-1571)   **438** 71.] reiterates Article XXIII, 'Of Ministryng in the congregation', of the *Articles of Religion* (1563-1571)

CONCILIUM HIBERNICUM – 1614-1615   993

72. To have public prayer in the Church, or to | administer the Sacra-   D3r
ments in a tongue not understoode of the people, is a thing plainely repugnant
to the word of God and the custome of the Primitive Church.

73. That person which by publike denunciation of the Church is rightly
cut off from the unitie of the Church, and excommunicate, ought to be taken
of the whole multitude of the faithfull, as a Heathen and Publican, untill by
Repentance he be openly reconciled and receaved into the Church by the
judgement of such as have authoritie in that behalfe.

74. God hath given power to his ministers, not simply to forgive sinnes
(which prerogative hee hath reserved onely to himself), but in his name to
declare and pronounce unto such as truely repent and unfainedly beleeve his
holy Gospell, the absolution and forgivenesse of sinnes. Neither is it Gods
pleasure, that his people should be tyed to make a particular confession of all
their known sinnes unto any mortal man: howsoever any person grieved in his
conscience, upon any speciall cause may well resort unto any godly and
learned Minister to receave advise and comfort at his hands.

| OF THE AUTHORITIE OF THE CHURCH,   D3v
GENERALL COUNCELLS, AND BISHOP OF ROME.

75. It is not lawful for the Church to ordaine any thing that is contrary to
Gods word: neither may it so expound one place of Scripture, that it be repugnant to another. Wherefore although the Church bee a witness, and a keeper
of holy writt: yet as it ought not to decree any thing against the same, so
besides the same ought it not inforce any thing to be beleeved upon necessitie
of salvation.

76. Generall Councells may not be gathered together without the commaundment and will of Princes; and when they be gathered together (for as
much as they be an assembly of men and not alwaies governed with the spirit
and word of God) they may erre, and sometimes have erred, even in things

---

444 72.] cfr Article XXIV, 'Of speakyng in the congregation', *Articles of Religion*
(1563-1571)   **447** 73.] a slight rephrasing of Article XXXIII, 'Of excommunicate
persons', *Articles of Religion* (1563-1571)   **452/455** God – sinnes] the first part of this
article derives from the formula of 'Absolution in the Office of Morning (and Evening)
Prayer' according to the use of the *Book of Common Prayer* (1559)   **462** 75.] this article
restates Article XX of the *Articles of Religion* (1563-1571), 'Of the Aucthoritie of the
Church', but omits the first sentence of that article, which reads: '[t]he Church hath
power to decree Rites or Ceremonies, and aucthoritie in controversies of fayth'
468 76.] reiterates Article XXI of the *Articles of Religion* (1563-1571), 'Of the
aucthoritie of generall Counselles'

994 CONCILIUM HIBERNICUM – 1614-1615

pertaining to the rule of pietie. Wherefore things ordained by them, as necessary to salvation, have neither strength nor authority, unlesse it may be shewed
that they bee taken out of holy Scriptures.

475 77. Every particular Church hath authority to institute, to change, and
cleane to put away ceremonies and other Ecclesiasticall rites, as they be super-
fluous, or be abused; and to constitute other, making more to seemlyness, to
order, or edification.

78. As the Churches of *Jerusalem, Alexandria*, and *Antioch* have erred: so
480 also the Church of *Rome* hath erred, not onely in those things which concerne
matter of practice and point of ceremonies, but also in matters of faith.

| 79. The power which the Bishop of *Rome* now challengeth, to be D4r
Supreame head of the universall Church of Christ, and to be above all Emper-
ours, Kings and Princes, is an usurped power, contrary to the Scriptures and
485 word of God, and contrary to the example of the Primitive Church: and
therefore is for most just causes taken away and abolished within the Kings
Majesties Realmes and Dominions.

80. The Bishop of *Rome* is so far from being the Supreame head of the
universall Church of Christ, that his workes and doctrine doe plainely discov-
490 er him to be *that man of sin*, foretold in the holy Scriptures, *whome the Lord*
shall consume with the Spirit of his mouth, and abolish with the brightness of his
comming.

OF THE STATE OF THE OLD AND NEW TESTAMENT.

81. In the Old Testament the Commaundments of the Law were more
495 largely, and the promises of Christ more sparingly and darkely propounded;
shaddowed with a multitude of types and figures, and so much the more generally and obscurely delivered, as the manifesting of them was further off.

82. The Old Testament is not contrary to the New. For both in the Old
and New Testament | everlasting life is offred to mankinde by Christ, who is D4v
500 the onely mediator betweene God and man, being both God and man.
Wherefore they are not to be heard, which faine that the old Fathers did look
onely for transitory promises. For they looked for all benefits of God the

---

490/492 II Thess. 2, 8

---

479 78.] restates the latter part of Article XIX, 'Of the Church', *Articles of Religion*
(1563-1571)   **482** 79.] see Article XXXVII of the *Articles of Religion* (1563-1571)
498 82.] the first portion of Article 82 is derived from Article VII, 'Of the Olde
Testament', *Articles of Religion* (1563-1571)

CONCILIUM HIBERNICUM – 1614-1615

Father through the merits of his Sonne Jesus Christ, as wee now doe: onely they beleeved in Christ which should come, we in Christ already come.

83. The New Testament is full of grace and truth, bringing joyful tidings unto mankinde, that whatsoever formerly was promised of Christ, is now accomplished: and so instead of the auncient types and ceremonies, exhibiteth the things themselves, with a large and cleere declaration of all the benefits of the Gospell. Neither is the ministry thereof restrained any longer to one circumcised nation, but is indifferently propounded unto all people, whether they be Jewes or Gentils: so that there is now no Nation which can truly complaine that they be shut forth from the communion of Saints and the liberties of the people of God.

84. Although the Law given from God by Moses, as touching ceremonies and rites be abolished, and the Civill precepts thereof be not of necessity to be receaved in any Commonwealth: yet notwithstanding no Christian man whatsoever is freed from the obedience of the Commaundments, which are called Morall.

| OF THE SACRAMENTS OF THE NEW TESTAMENT.　　Eɪɪ

85. The Sacraments ordained by Christ, be not onely badges or tokens of Christian mens profession: but rather certaine sure witnesses, and effectual or powerful signes of grace and Gods good will towards us, by which he doth worke invisibly in us, and not onely quicken but also strengthen and confirm our faith in him.

86. There be two Sacraments ordained of Christ our Lord in the Gospel, that is to say, *Baptisme* and the *Lords Supper*.

87. Those five which by the Church of *Rome* are called Sacraments, to witt, *Confirmation, Penance, Orders, Matrimony*, and *Extreame unction*, are not to be accounted Sacraments of the Gospell: being such as have partly grown from corrupt imitation of the Apostles, partly are states of life allowed in the Scriptures, but yet have not like nature of Sacraments with *Baptisme* and the *Lords Supper*, for that they haue not any visible signe or ceremonie ordained of God, together with a promise of saving grace annexed thereunto.

88. The Sacraments were not ordained of Christ to be gazed upon, or to be carried about; but that wee should duly use them. And in such onely as worthily receave the same, they have a wholesome effect and operation; but

---

514 84.] this article reiterates the second portion of Article VII of the *Articles of Religion* (1563-1571)　　**534** 88.] restates Article XXV and the final statement in Article XXVIII, 'Of the Lordes Supper', *Articles of Religion* (1563-1571)

they that receave | them unworthilie, thereby draw judgement upon them- Eıv
selues.

Of Baptisme.

540   89. Baptisme is not onely an outward signe of our profession, and a note
of difference whereby Christians are discerned from such as are no Christians;
but much more a Sacrament of our admission into the Church, sealing unto us
our new birth (and consequently our Justification, Adoption, and Sanctification) by the communion which wee have with Jesus Christ.

545   90. The Baptisme of Infants is to be retained in the Church as agreeable
to the word of God.

91. In the administration of Baptisme, *Exorcism, Oile, Salte, Spittle*, and
superstitious *hallowing of the Water*, are for just causes abolished: and without
them the Sacrament is fully and perfectly administered, to all intents and pur-

550 poses agreeable to the institution of our Saviour Christ.

Of the Lords Supper.

92. The Lords Supper, is not onely a signe of the mutuall love which
Christians ought | to bear one towards another, but much more a Sacrament E2r
of our preservation in the Church, sealing unto us our spirituall nourishment

555 and continuall growth in Christ.

93. The change of the substance of bread and wine into the substance of
the Body and Bloud of Christ, commonely called *Transubstantiation*, cannot
be proved by holy writt; but is repugnant to plaine testimonies of the Scripture, overthroweth the nature of a Sacrament, and hath given occasion to most

560 grosse Idolatry and manifold superstitions.

540/546 Baptisme – God] Articles 89 and 90 derive from Article XXVII, 'Of
Baptisme', *Articles of Religion* (1563-1571)   **547** 91.] this article calls for the abolition
of ancient ritual practices associated with baptism which were still widely practiced by
the majority of the Roman Catholic population of the Kingdom of Ireland   **556** 93.]
Articles 92 and 93 reiterate the formula of Article XXVIII, 'Of the Lordes Supper',
Articles of Religion (1563-1571)

CONCILIUM HIBERNICUM – 1614-1615   997

94. In the outward part of the holy Communion, the Bodie and Bloud of Christ is in a most lively manner *represented*: being no otherwise present with the visible elements, then things signified and sealed are present with the signes and seales, that is to say, symbolically and relatively. But in the inward and spirituall part, the same Body and Bloud is really and substantially *presented* unto all those who have grace to receave the Sonne of God, even to all those that beleeve in his name. And unto such as in this maner doe worthylie and with faith repaire unto the Lords table, the Bodie and Bloud of Christ is not onely signified and offered, but also truly exhibited and communicated.

95. The Bodie of Christ is given, taken, and eaten in the Lords Supper, onely after an heavenly and spirituall manner; and the meane where|by the Body of Christ is thus receaved and eaten is Faith.   E2v

96. The wicked, and such as want a lively faith, although they doe carnally and visibly (as *Saint Augustine* speaketh) presse with their teeth the Sacrament of the body and bloud of Christ: yet in no wise are they made partakers of Christ; but rather to their condemnation, doe eat and drink the signe or Sacrament of so great a thing.

97. Both the parts of the Lords Sacrament, according to Christs institution and the practise of the auncient Church, ought to be ministred unto Gods people; and it is plain sacriledge to rob them of the mysticall cup, for whom Christ hath shed his most precious blood.

98. The Sacrament of the *Lords Supper* was not by Christs ordinance reserved, carried about, lifted up, or worshipped.

99. The sacrifice of the Masse, wherein the Priest is said to offer up Christ for obtaining the remission of painr or guiltr for the quickr and the dead, is neither agreeable to Christs ordinance, nor grounded upon doctrine Apostolike; but contrarywise most ungodly, and most injurious to that all-sufficient

---

561 94.] this is the high realist doctrine of sacramental presence taught by Calvin and Peter Martyr Vermigli. See the latter's definitive exposition of this position in his *Tractatio de sacramento Eucharistiae*, Oxonium 1549; see also P. M. Vermigli, *The Oxford Treatise and Disputation on the Eucharist, 1549* – ed. and transl. J. C. McLelland (*Sixteenth Century Essays & Studies* 56), Kirksville (MO) 2000   **571** 95.] Article 95 reiterates the formula of Article XXVIII 'Of the Lordes Supper', *Articles of Religion* (1563-1571)   **574** 96.] restates Article XXIX 'Of the wicked which do not eate the body of Christe in the vse of the Lordes Supper', *Articles of Religion* (1563-1571); see Augustinus, *In Iohannis evangelium tractatus CXXIV* 26, 12, ed. R. Willems (*CC SL* 36), Turnhout 1954, p. 266, 20-22   **579** 97.] based on Article XXX 'Of both kindes', *Articles of Religion* (1563-1571)   **583** 98.] based on Article XXVIII of the *Articles of Religion* (1563-1571)   **585** 99.] based on Article XXXI, 'Of the one oblation of Christe', *Articles of Religion* (1563-1571)

sacrifice of our Saviour Christ, offered once for ever upon the Crosse, which is
590 the onely propitiation and satisfaction for all our sinnes.

100. Private Mass, that is, the receaving of the Eucharist by the Priest
alone, without a competent | number of comunicants, is contrary to the insti-   E3r
tution of Christ.

Of the state of the soules of men, after they be departed out
595 ### of this life; together with the generall Resurrection, and
the last Judgement.

101. After this life is ended, the soules of Gods children be presently
receaved into Heaven, there to enjoy unspeakable comforts; the soules of the
wicked are cast into Hell, there to endure endless torments.

600 102. The doctrine of the Church of *Rome*, concerning *Limbus Patrum,
Limbus Puerorum, Purgatorie, Prayer for the dead, Pardons, Adoration of
Images and Relickes*, and also *Invocation of Saints* is vainely invented without
all warrant of holy Scripture, yea and is contrary unto the same.

103. At the end of this world, the Lord Jesus shall come in the clouds with
605 the glory of his Father: at which time, by the almightie power of God, the
living shalbe changed, and the dead shalbe raised; and all shall appeare both in
body and soule before his judgement seate, to receave according to that which
they have done in their bodies, whether good or evill.

104. When the last judgement is finished, Christ shall deliver up the
610 Kingdome to his Father and God shalbe all in all.

| The Decree of the Synod.   E3v

If any Minister, of what degree of qualitie soever he be, shall publikely
teach any doctrine contrary to these Articles agreed upon; If after due admonition he does not conforme himselfe, and cease to disturbe the peace of the
615 Church, let him be silenced and deprived of all spirituall promotions he doth
enjoy.

FINIS.

---

591 100.] cfr *Westminster Confession*, Chapter XXIX, par. 4, 'Of the Lords Supper'
600 102.] reiterates Article XXII, 'Of Purgatorie', *Articles of Religion* (1563-1571)
609 104.] this concluding eschatological flourish of the *Irish Articles* is repeated in
Chapter XXXIII of the *Westminster Confession*. The *Articles of Religion* (1563-1571)
draw to a close with a decidedly this-worldly emphasis (and by comparison perhaps
more prosaically) in a prohibition of rash oath-taking, but allowing that 'a man may
sweare when the Magistrate requireth'

CONCILIUM ABERDONIENSE
ECCLESIAE SCOTICANAE

1616

edidit
Ian HAZLETT

THE GENERAL ASSEMBLY OF
THE CHURCH OF SCOTLAND,
ABERDEEN, 1616*

CONTEXT OF THE 1616 GENERAL ASSEMBLY

The General Assembly of the Church of Scotland, chaired by a moderator who was deemed to be *primus inter pares*, possessed the highest authority in the presbyterian system of hierarchical Church courts. This polity was ultimately understood as being not just in conformity with Scriptural paradigms, but also *de iure divino*, and so a matter of belief in shaping the visible Church. These concepts were influentially represented in Scotland by Andrew Melville (1545-1622). (1) The idea was designed to replace the traditional – but perceived by radical presbyterians as un-Scriptural – order of monarchical episcopacy with its focus on individual hierarchy rather than corporate presbyterate and authority. (2) Late-sixteenth-century controversial discussions on the matter in Scotland, England, and Geneva had polarised the issue beyond what had been a matter of indifference in the earlier phase of the Reformation. Yet there were still many in the middle of the spectrum who were content with a pragmatic and *ad hoc* approach which would cater for a mixed system of episcopacy or superintendence and presbytery in the interest of the Church's immediate wellbeing. (3) The first generation of post-1560 Scottish reformers had not been averse to this; however, from the late-1570s to the mid-1590s in Scotland, exclusivist presbyterian thinking was gaining the upper

---

(*) We decided not to capitalise 'presbyterian' and 'episcopalian' in light of the principle of premature reification. In the sixteenth and early seventeenth centuries, no individuals, parties or churches actually designated themselves as Presbyterian or Episcopal(ian), even if they advocated those ecclesiologies theoretically and sometimes used such adjectives to represent their thought. Lower-case *p* and *e* are standard practice in modern Scottish pre-1638 Reformation historiography.

(1) See *ODNB* and *DSCHT*, *ad vocem*.

(2) See Mechie, 'Episcopacy'; Mullan, *Episcopacy in Scotland*; Selwyn, 'The First Scottish Episcopacy'; Henderson, *Presbyterianism*; Cameron, 'Presbyterianer'; Maruyama, *The Ecclesiology of Theodore Beza*, especially p. 174-194; Kirk, '«The Polities of the Best Reformed Churches»'; Mason – Reid, *Andrew Melville*, p. 127-154; Mullan, 'Revolution, Consensus, and Controversy', p. 157-160.

(3) See Foster, *The Church*, p. 6-31 and 119-126.

hand, even though there were still some titular or nominal bishops, always appointed by the crown, but of little authority. The subsequent reaffirmation and fuller imposition of episcopacy meant that tension, confrontation and collision between the two concepts were chronic features of the Scottish Church up to 1690. (4)

The chief factor impeding presbyterian development was King James VI, especially after he also became King of England (as James I) in 1603, and thereby Supreme Governor of the episcopalian Church of England (and of Ireland), a role he claimed for himself in the Church of Scotland, but for which there was no statutory enactment. It had been the Catholic Mary Stewart who was monarch at the inception of the Reformed Church of Scotland in 1560. And while Scottish Protestant reformers hoped that their monarch would be godly, they did not envisage him or her to be god-like. Although James was personally committed to specifically Reformed and Calvinist doctrine, it was in the areas of ecclesiastical polity and Church-state relations that his stance was controversial in Scotland; but he had support from cross-sections in the Kirk, especially in conservative areas outside central Scotland. His theories of the divine right of kings, royal prerogative, and patriarchal government meant that he saw himself as having supreme authority in both state and Church, akin, as he understood it, to the ancient Christian emperors. He characterised the essential Reformed and presbyterian concept of ministerial parity (i.e. equality of ministers and elders) as 'the mother of confusion and enemy to unity [...] and which cannot agree with a monarchy'. (5) Hence his famous axiom: 'no bishop, no King'. (6) Yet it would be wrong to see James's religious policies merely as a conservative reaction, given that he was also strongly motivated by a concern for the relative modernisation of the Church and of religious texts, as reflected in his concern for a new English translation of the Bible, which appeared in 1611.

From 1596 onwards in Scotland, James's declared strategy was both to restore full episcopacy into the Kirk and to attempt to exercise a caesaropapist or quasi-Erastian authority over it. He attended several Church general assemblies in person. To those ends, he declared opposition to presbyterian practices in Scotland and planned a *remaniement* of the Church of Scotland along the lines of the Church of England not just in governance, but in most other aspects. A General Assembly of the Church should not have supreme author-

---

(4) Lee, 'James VI and the Revival of Episcopacy'; MacDonald, *The Jacobean Kirk*, p. 148-153; Id., 'James VI and the General Assembly'.

(5) Foster, *The Church*, p. 11.

(6) Wormald, 'The Scottish Jacobean Episcopate'; Id., 'The Headaches of Monarchy'.

ity in religious affairs and was subordinate to the divinely-authorised royal will, including a right to summon it. Moreover, anglicisation of the Scottish Kirk in most aspects was another major plan in the King's programme under the guise of pan-British uniformity and assimilation.

While James had supporters in Scotland, there was sufficient opposition to make the general Church situation volatile. From 1606 to 1618, there were six royally-convened (and episcopalian) general assemblies in Scotland. These were not due to any commitment to an experiment of a mixed system, but rather to the realities of the balance of the ecclesiastical parties. For James, it could only be transitional. The two best-known assemblies were the ones at Glasgow in 1610 and at Perth in 1618. It was at the Glasgow Assembly that full jurisdictional episcopacy with thirteen dioceses was restored in the Scottish Kirk; also created was an episcopal Court of High Commission that would undermine the ecclesial authority of regional presbyteries and national general assemblies. The pro-episcopalian aspiration was that, in time, the General Assembly would mutate into something like a Synod of the Church of England or an Anglican House of Convocation, all subordinate to Crown and Parliament. The 1618 Perth Assembly, however, witnessed such massive presbyterian and public opposition on liturgical matters in the context of disputable 'traditions' that no General Assembly was convened for another twenty years. However, the see-saw battles between episcopacy and presbytery continued for the rest of the century, extending even to turf wars for control of the Church's archival records, that continued up to the nineteenth century. This, as will be explained below, had noxious – if not wholly catastrophic – consequences for the manuscript sources-history of these assemblies, and for the Aberdeen one in particular.

The 1616 Aberdeen Assembly can be placed as a significantly transitional synod among the six quasi-episcopalian ones from 1606 to 1618. Unlike the others, it dealt with general religious issues in both a global and specific manner, but presented as the King's agenda. In mind was not just reform in the Church, but reform of the Scottish Reformation. James had hopes to dispense with a General Assembly and simply issue decrees to be implemented by bishops. However, they, and especially his chief Church agent in Scotland, John Spottiswoode (1565-1639) (7) – Glasgow university graduate, ex-presbyterian, but like the King a subscriber to Calvinist orthodoxy, until recently archbishop of Glasgow and now archbishop of St Andrews – advised the King against proceeding without an Assembly as being impolitic. Anyway, the gen-

---

(7) See *ODNB* and *DSCHT, ad vocem*. See also Goodare, 'How Archbishop Spottiswoode became an episcopalian'.

eral assemblies of the Scottish Kirk were not just synods: they were, as the royal proclamation (approved by the Privy Council) summoning the Aberdeen Assembly said, 'national' assemblies, that is, of Church and state, or Christendom in Scotland. However, as was alleged at the time, the very short notice given of the Assembly and its venue in the far north-east of Scotland at Aberdeen were arguably disincentives to strong participation by presbytery commissioners from central, southern, and western Scotland. The King's reform plans – in consultation with higher clergy – were delivered to the Assembly in the form of fourteen *Instructions* by his personal representative, the Lord High Commissioner, and his team of advisers and assistants. These *Instructions* formed the Assembly's agenda and order of business and are incorporated in the text of the proceedings below. They reveal that the chief concerns were a perceived decay in religion, inadequate (Protestant) evangelisation, surviving and growing Catholicism among certain parts of the population and in certain regions, outdated and prolix doctrinal or confessional statements, ineffective preaching and religious instruction, inefficient provision of theological education in the four universities, lack of liturgical uniformity in Church services, incompetent ecclesiastical discipline and management, and financial impoverishment of the Church due to the secularisation and plundering of many benefices of the 'patrimony of the Kirk' at the Reformation. As will be seen below, the Aberdeen Assembly did not provide ready-made remedies, with one exception: a new confession of faith. Instead, the Assembly was diagnostic and mostly initiated specific solutions and measures, many of which were drawn from English examples.

The Proceedings of the Aberdeen Assembly

There were six sessions of the Aberdeen Assembly, held between 13 and 21 August 1616 in the city church of St Nicholas, also known as the 'New Kirk'. (8) The first session was constitutive, dealing with preliminaries. In line with the royal proclamation convening the Assembly, the main general business item intimated at this stage was religious decline and the need to tighten measures against survivalist Roman Catholicism and against recusancy. Also in mind were defections (or 'apostasy') from the Reformed faith and so reviving Catholicism due to the palpable impact of the Counter-Reformation in

---

(8) For a report outlining the Assembly's enactments and the King's reaction, see *RPCS*, vol. 10, p. 598-601, no. 1. For other summaries of the Assembly's proceeding, see for example *Scottish Liturgies*, p. xviii-xxv and 146-149; Foster, *The Church*, p. 126-132; Lee, *Government by Pen*, p. 155-161.

CONCILIUM ABERDONIENSE ECCLESIAE SCOTICANAE – 1616

the country, especially in the north of Scotland. (9) This reflected a phase between 1613 and 1616 in Scotland, England and elsewhere in Protestant Europe of anti-Catholic zeal and tougher government legislation. (10)

In response, the second session saw the passing of eleven enactments on the ways and means of: firstly, countering laxity in the enforcement of existing anti-Catholic legislation; secondly, detecting crypto-Catholics; and thirdly, persuading all exposed and known Catholics to conform to the Reformed Kirk by a programme of religious re-education through preaching and instruction. The influence of itinerant Jesuits and seminary priests trained abroad was highlighted. The remedy is seen largely as a pastoral and practical theological one: while Catholicism was legally prohibited and known Catholics were liable to judicial discrimination and penalties, physical persecution of the person in the traditional sense was not on the royal agenda. In Scotland, severe penal sentences were mostly suspended, the notable exception (1615) being the case of the Jesuit John Ogilvie in Glasgow, Scotland's only Catholic martyr. King James had an aversion to such measures, bearing in mind his vision of ultimate reconciliation with a reformed Catholicism. (11)

The third session continued in similar vein. A group was appointed to compose tracts replying to Catholic literature in circulation. Furthermore, measures were agreed on taking action about continuing public manifestations of popular Catholic piety and other 'superstitions' in the localities. Also, warnings were expressed about Catholic clergy circulating in the guise of physicians and apothecaries, as well as some who infiltrated schools run by sympathetic upper-class women in order to give Catholic instruction to young people. But the main business of this session was the delicate question of one of the chief Catholic magnates in Scotland, George Gordon, First Marquis of Huntly (1561/1562-1636) (12) and privy councillor, whose power base was in the north of Scotland and in Aberdeenshire, areas of some Catholic resis-

---

(9) See King James to Archbishop John Spottiswoode, 22 June 1616, in *Original Letters*, vol. 2, p. 471-472; see also King James to Andrew Murray, 18 July 1616, in *Original Letters*, vol. 2, p. 489; Roberts, 'Jesuit Missions in the Highlands'; Spurlock, 'Post-Reformation Scottish Catholic Revival'; Spurlock, 'Catholicism in Scotland to 1603'.

(10) For a comprehensive survey of the general religious situation in Scotland at the time, see *RPCS*, vol. 11 (1894), p. xliii-lxxv; for government enactments and declarations in 1613-1616 against perceived Catholic resurgence, see *RPCS*, vol. 10 (1891), p. xcvii-cii; on the Aberdeen General Assembly 1616 in this context, see *ibid.*, p. cii-cx.

(11) See Patterson, *King James*; McCoog, *The Society of Jesus*, chapters 1 and 2.

(12) See *ODNB*, entry 'Gordon, George'.

tance. ([13]) He had a history of prudential zig-zagging between the Catholic and Reformed faiths, multiple excommunications by the Church of Scotland, and exile. Since Huntly was needed by the government to help implement general royal policies in the north of Scotland, the authorities vacillated between prosecuting and reconciling him. He was at this time in England, where on conforming to the Church of England he had been absolved from excommunication by the archbishop of Canterbury, George Abbott, in association with the primate of the Church of Ireland and the bishop of London. This alarmed the Scottish bishops. A close Calvinist friend of King James, Abbott was alert to Scottish sensitivities over perceived usurpation of the independence of the Church of Scotland. Reassuring correspondence in this sense between the archbishop of Canterbury, the archbishop of St Andrews, and the King was read out in the Assembly, acknowledging that the Scottish Kirk was indeed under no automatic obligation to recognise Huntly's absolution. Accordingly, an agent for Huntly at the Assembly indicated the willingness of the marquis to appear in person at the Assembly to have his release from excommunication endorsed on whatever terms of submission were required. The Assembly agreed, and it was arranged for Huntly present himself at the Assembly's final session in the following week. ([14])

The fourth session saw the eagerly awaited announcement of the royal *Instructions* specifying in detail the provision of remedies for the problem of defections to Roman Catholicism. This was at least the pretext. For the King's ulterior motive was to try to align in form and substance the Church of Scotland more to the Church of England, whose supreme governor he was. The keynotes were 'congruity' and 'convergence' within an episcopalian and pseudo-Erastian format as a means of correcting the 'inordinate' – as he perceived it – character of the Scottish Reformation. ([15]) The royal *Instructions* for the Aberdeen Assembly, fourteen in total, embodied further steps in that general direction, particularly in the areas of doctrine, Church discipline, worship and ceremonies, religious instruction of the young, and theological edu-

(13) Other leading Catholic sympathisers among the nearby Scottish aristocracy at this time were the earl of Errol (Francis Hay), ally of Huntly, the earl of Sutherland (John Gordon), kinsman of Huntly, the earl of Caithness (George Sinclair), Andrew Lord Gray, the countess of Linlithgow (Elizabeth Gordon, daughter of Huntly) among others. See also *Synod of Fife*, p. 36-38, 54-55, 57-58, 58-59, 70-71, 74-75, 76-77. For other nonconforming nobility and gentry in the country, see below in text of the Aberdeen Assembly's fifth session, item 4. Spurlock, 'The Laity and the Structure of the Catholic Church in Early Modern Scotland', p. 235.

(14) For further background details on the Huntly affair, see *RPCS*, vol. 10 (1891), p. civ-cv and 561-564, no. 1; Spottiswoode, *History*, vol. 3 (1851), p. 208 and 230-235.

(15) See Croft, *King James*, p. 163-165; MacDonald, 'James VI and I'.

cation. The first three of these figured prominently in a memorandum on the current needs of the Church of Scotland penned in June of the previous year by Spottiswoode while still archbishop of Glasgow. (16) In the following Assembly session, enactments were made in respect of the specific instructions.

The fifth session's most notable resolutions related accordingly to a new confession of faith, a catechism, a revised liturgy, a book of canons on church law, and higher theological education. The groundwork for a new confession had been done a few years previously when alternatives to the traditional *Scots Confession* (1560) and its subsequent, more explicitly anti-Catholic supplement, the *King's Confession* (1581), were being discussed in Scotland. (17) In 1611 it was a topic of discussion between the King and the bishops. (18) In 1612, a draft of a new confession – which had been examined in England – was sent by the Scottish secretary of state, Sir Alexander Hay, to the archbishops of Glasgow and St Andrews for approval. (19) In April of the same year at the St Andrews diocesan Synod of Fife, a committee including the St Andrews university theologian, Robert Howie (*c.* 1568-1646) (20) was asked to revise the existing confessions; the articles should be 'short and clear'. (21) A draft confession of twenty-four articles in succinct form was submitted. Its precise relationship, if any, to the evolving *New Confession* of 1616 remains to be determined, since not only have the Fife Synod articles never been published, but no transcription in full from the original manuscript synodal minutes is readily available. (22) And while the 'true and simple' *Aberdeen Confession* appears to have been subject to drafts and revision before and after 1616, its primary authors – according to the contemporary historian David Calderwood (1575-

---

(16) *Original Letters*, vol. 2, p. 445-446.

(17) The *New Confession* or *Aberdeen Confession*, first published in 1678/1679 in David Calderwood's *True History*, has never been the subject of major historical or theological investigation due to its redundancy and submergence. For some brief analyses see Cooper, *Confessions of Faith*, p. 32; McCrie, *The Confessions of the Church of Scotland*, p. 27-35; Foster, *The Church*, p. 128-130; Donaldson, *The Faith of the Scots*, p. 82-83; Hazlett, 'Vestures of the Faith', especially p. 21-25; Hazlett, 'Reformed Theology in Confessions and Catechisms', p. 202-204.

(18) See King James to the Scottish bishops, 2 March 1611, in *Memoirs of the Maxwells of Pollok*, vol. 2, p. 13.

(19) On 4 July 1612, as in *Original Letters*, vol. 1, p. 293.

(20) See *ODNB* and *DSCHT, ad vocem*; see also Lippe, *Selections*, p. 235-244.

(21) *Synod of Fife*, p. 44-45.

(22) *Minutes of the Synod of Fife, 1610-1636*, National Records of Scotland, General Register House, GD 16 / 46 / 39 (previously CH2 / 154 / 1), p. 95-98. The text was not included in the published minutes cited in previous note. Three comparative parallel passages of the 1612 and 1616 confessions are supplied by Foster, *The Church*, p. 129, no. 84.

1650) (²³) – were said to have been John Hall (*c.* 1559-1627) and John Adamson (1576-*c.* 1651), who was later appointed principal of the University of Edinburgh. (²⁴)

The *New Confession* (fifth session, item 6) took the form of fifty-three unnumbered articles, without headings, concisely and systematically presented. It was meant to provide a modernised and more convenient statement of beliefs than the expansive and sometimes impassioned *Scots Confession* of 1560 and the more manifestly anti-Catholic *King's Confession* of 1581. A primary objective, nonetheless, was disciplinary: presenting the Reformed faith in purely positive and more comprehensible terms to both Roman Catholics and indifferent conformers to the Kirk was considered to be less intimidating. The model in mind in this respect was, as Spottiswoode had stated in his 1615 memorandum, 'the Confession of the English Church', (²⁵) i.e. the low-key *Thirty-Nine Articles.* This anglicisation was maybe true in the form, but the content reflected unmistakeable trends in international Reformed orthodoxy also evident in the Church of England and the Church of Ireland at the time, e.g. the *Lambeth Articles* (1595), the *Irish Articles* (1615), and the Synod of Dordrecht (1619). (²⁶) Here we will refer to just four examples: first, the Genevan doctrine of double-decree predestination, particularly as formulated by Theodore Beza, is explicitly introduced and given priority in the first article; second, the *Consensus Tigurinus* (1549) between Zurich and Geneva on the sacraments in the framework of a maturing covenant theology is conspicuously evident in articles 30 to 43, where the sacraments are subordinate to predestination and 'God's eternal covenant' as 'seals' of it (Article 32); third, there are emphases on evidence of sanctification following justification (Article 27), and on the certainty of salvation (Article 29) as befits the elect who, belonging to the true Catholic Church, are (effectually) called to eternal life in Christ (Articles 6 and 5); fourth, there is implicit repudiation of soteriological heterodoxy in some Reformed milieus such as Arminian circles (Articles 24 to

(23) Calderwood, *History*, vol. 7 (1845), p. 226. On Calderwood, see *ODNB* and *DSCHT, ad vocem.*

(24) Minister of Liberton, near Edinburgh. He had neo-Latin poetry interests and was flexible on Church government. See *ODNB, ad vocem*; *Scottish Liturgies*, p. xxi-xxii, no. 1; S. J. Reid, 'Melville's Anti-Episcopal Poetry', in Mason – Reid, *Andrew Melville*, p. 131-137. Reid, *ibid.*, p. 134, and Foster, *The Church*, p. 129, suggest plausibly that Hall and Adamson might have availed of the Synod of Fife's text as their point of departure. John Hall was an Edinburgh minister, expelled by the King in 1619 for his opposition to liturgical changes. See also *Scottish Liturgies*, p. xxi-xxii, no. 1.

(25) *Original Letters*, vol. 2, p. 445.

(26) See p. 929-944, p. 967-998, and the *Synod of Dordrecht*, in *COGD* VI.2 (forthcoming).

26), which may have had an incipient presence at this time in Scottish Protestant groups less wholly inimical to Catholic tradition. (27)

We do not know if the *Confession* was debated at the Aberdeen Assembly. It was evidently not yet seen as the finished article, given that at the end of the Assembly minutes there was provision made for its revision by the reform commission (29 members) or a subcommittee drawn from that (5 members), as testified by Calderwood. (28) The one person named as a member of that commission, of the subcommittee, and as a co-author of the confession agreed upon at the Synod of Fife was Robert Howie from St Andrews. His influence on the substance of the *New Confession* must have been substantial, particularly on Christology – on which he had published a book in Switzerland – and on the Eucharist; on the latter, a short, handwritten discussion of his has survived. (29) He had spent seven or eight years studying theology on the Continent and especially in Basel, where his teacher, Johann Jakob Grynaeus, was an influential proponent of Reformed orthodoxy of the Calvinist hue. (30) Thereafter, however, the *New Confession* was not published at the time and virtually disappeared into oblivion, although it seems to have been used occasionally by episcopalian Church courts after 1616. (31) Its association with episcopacy and royal interventionism in the Church sealed its rejection in presbyterian thinking. This was because the final article (Article 53) implicitly ruled out the axioms of presbyterian ecclesiology embodied in the normative Second Book of Discipline, (32) and because it also implied the validity of coercively imposed liturgical and ceremonial practices, which were seen as novelties; in addition, the royal *Instructions* had stipulated compulsory subscription by everyone admitted to civil or ecclesiastical offices and by all university students. On the restoration of episcopacy in 1660-1689, however, the *Aberdeen Confession* seems simply to have been forgotten about (or lost) as it had not been copied into the Church's official *Registers* in the absence of a final version.

Item 7 in the fifth session was a proposal for a new catechism. Various catechisms used previously included the *Genevan Catechism*, the long and short catechism of John Craig (*c.* 1512-1600), and new English translations of

---

(27) Henderson, 'Arminianism in Scotland'; Mullan, *Scottish Puritanism*, p. 208-243.

(28) Calderwood, *History*, vol. 7 (1845), p. 226; see also the end of the sixth session of the Aberdeen Assembly in the text below.

(29) Howie, *Accuratus*.

(30) See 'Introduction', in Cameron, *Letters*, p. xvii-xx, xxiii-xxvii, and xliii-xlvii.

(31) Foster, *The Church*, p. 130.

(32) See *The Second Book of Discipline, with Introduction and Commentary*, ed. J. Kirk, Edinburgh 1980; *DSCHT*, 'Second Book of Discipline'.

the *Heidelberg Catechism* (1563) were authorised for use in the Scotland in 1591 and 1615, as well as strongly promoted by the King. (33) Most of these, however, were considered to be still too extensive and complex for common use. At the Aberdeen Synod it was agreed that a new Scottish 'easy, short and compendious' catechism for ordinary people be composed. A subcommittee consisting of John Hall, John Adamson, and Patrick Galloway (*c.* 1551-1626) (34) was entrusted with the task. The aim was to have it ready for printing soon as the only catechism authorised in Scotland. While a royal license to publish it was issued to an Edinburgh bookseller, Gilbert Dick – and the General Assembly at Perth in 1618 ratified the catechism as 'printed with privilege' – the publishing history of the *Catechism* is obscure and seems to have been controversial in regard to publishing infringements. (35) The result is that no incontestable proof of its publication can be produced, as it may not have been more than a broadsheet. However, in an extant handwritten draft of the revised order of service or liturgy, also commissioned by the 1616 Assembly, the text of the *Catechism* was inserted in the section on confirmation. It can now be read in the draft form of service that was published in the nineteenth century. (36) However, another nail in the coffin of the 1616 *Catechism* was that Church opinion did not rate it either as suitable for all its intended beneficiaries. At the Synod of Fife in October 1620, a committee led by Robert Howie was set up to peruse the *Aberdeen Catechism* and compose an alternative which should be 'intelligible and edifying for the rude and younger sort'. (37)

In 1615, Archbishop Spottiswoode stated that '[t]here is lacking in our Church one form of divine service'. (38) He was referring to perceived bad practice rather than provision. Accordingly, it was agreed in the Assembly's fifth session (item 8) to revise the order of divine service or worship and make

---

(33) [C. Olevianus – Z. Ursinus], *Catechisme of Christian religion*, Edinburgh 1615. Cfr. *DSCHT*, entry 'Catechisms'; Foster, *The Church*, p. 130-131; *Scottish Liturgies*, p. xxi; *The School of Faith: The Catechisms of the Reformed Church*, ed. T. F. Torrance, London 1959.

(34) From 1607 minister of St Giles, Edinburgh, Galloway had a strongly Protestant and presbyterian background, but a later readiness to accommodate to the King on liturgy made him suspect to strict presbyterians. He had already published *A Catechisme: Conteyning Summarely the Chief Points of Christian Religion*, London 1588. See *ODNB* and *DSCHT*, *ad vocem*; *Scottish Liturgies*, p. xxi-xxii, no. 1.

(35) King James to the Privy Council, February 1618, in *Original Letters*, vol. 2, p. 817; *Scottish Liturgies*, 'Notes', p. 146-148; Foster, *The Church*, p. 131.

(36) *Scottish Liturgies*, p. 79-85.

(37) *Synod of Fife*, p. 94.

(38) *Original Letters*, vol. 2, p. 445.

CONCILIUM ABERDONIENSE ECCLESIAE SCOTICANAE – 1616   1011

it prescriptive before the sermon, so that 'the common people may learn it and by custom serve God rightly'. (39) Further reform and revision of worship had been talked about since 1584. The traditional and official *Book of Common Order* (or *Psalm Book*), based on the Genevan service, had divided opinion and was not being uniformly used due to some latitude it granted to the minister or reader conducting the Sabbath service. (40) The influence of English puritan notions of free order of worship and extemporisation was also reinforcing such a tendency. Nor did the Scottish *Psalm Book* have the same statutory authority as the *Book of Common Prayer* in England and Ireland. This caused a diversity which was defended by some and denounced by others. An Assembly committee which included John Adamson, Patrick Galloway, and Peter Hewat was entrusted with the task of revision to be submitted for scrutiny to the post-assembly reform commission. The outcome was the draft *A Forme of Service*, (41) which in substance did not depart radically from the existing *Book of Common Order*. This was the first of three drafts, (42) the third of which was approved at the Perth General Assembly and by the King in 1618, but was not enforced due to the strength of presbyterian opposition. The ultimate outcome was the published *Scottish Prayer Book* in 1637, which as a pseudo-Anglican liturgy sponsored by the Crown only provoked widespread revolt in Scotland, helping to activate the National Covenant in 1638.

Item 9 of the fifth session dealt with the lack of uniform and easily accessible regulations in Church discipline, in the sense of practice and procedure in all areas of the Church's order, worship, organisation and administration. Various precedents and customs were embedded in the accumulated Church Registers or Books which were in unrevised manuscript form and not disseminated. The need of a printed code was obvious. The Aberdeen Assembly adopted the royal instruction in this respect, namely to commission a book of canons (similar to the Church of England one of 1603) extracted from Assembly records. Two people – including the new archbishop of Glasgow, James Law – were entrusted with the task and charged (optimistically) to present a draft to the Assembly's reform commission on the following 1 December. This

---

(39) See the royal *Instructions* in the Assembly's fourth session below, no. 8.

(40) See Donaldson, *The Making of the Scottish Prayer Book*, p. 24-26; Id., 'Reformation to Covenant'; *Scottish Liturgies*, p. ix-lxxii; Maxwell, *A History of Worship*, p. 70-73; McMillan, *The Worship*, p. 69-70 and 102-104; Spinks, 'Emergence of a Reformed Worship Tradition', p. 258-265.

(41) Text in *Scottish Liturgies*, 'Appendix'; see also *Scottish Liturgies*, 'Introduction', p. xxiii-xxiv.

(42) See Donaldson, 'Reformation to Covenant', p. 48-52; on the second and third drafts, see Donaldson, 'A Scottish Liturgy', p. 89-91.

did not happen, as was complained about by the contemporary presbyterian writer, member of the Aberdeen Assembly, and its reform commission, William Scot (1558-1642). (43) Apart from the daunting literary task, part of the problem was that episcopalian and presbyterian notions of authority and procedure were incompatible. Another difficulty was that just after the Aberdeen Assembly, the King wanted five further liturgical and ceremonial practices simply inserted into the new book of canons; but Archbishop Spottiswoode resisted on the grounds that they would need to be discussed by a Church assembly. (44) A book of canons on the English model eventually appeared in 1636/1637, but was rejected – along with the Scottish *Booke of Common Prayer* – in Scotland after presbyterian restoration at Glasgow in 1638.

A final item of note at the 1616 Assembly was on ministerial training and theological education. On the latter, it was resolved that the divinity college (St Mary's) at St Andrews should be the sole Church seminary in Scotland; till then there had been four, i.e. at the ancient universities of St Andrews, Glasgow, and Aberdeen, and at the new Edinburgh College, founded in 1583. (45) The Assembly decision was at variance from the eleventh item of the royal *Instructions*. These had made the provisos that the Glasgow College should be still retained for bachelor-level theology in western Scotland, but that anyone proceeding to doctoral studies should move to St Andrews. Also decided was that each of Scotland's thirteen dioceses should fund two divinity students of no private means at St Andrews. Various factors lay behind these developments. One was a continuing shortage of ministers in the post-Reformation era, and to which the Aberdeen Assembly intermittently alluded. Another was the need to rationalise and centralise the provision of theological education in respect of resources, human and material, in a country that was small and not rich, but had twice as many universities as England. In addition, there was the negative effect on Church finance of the 'dilapidation of benefices' (cited in the Assembly as an overriding issue) due to the diversion of much of the Church's patrimony at the Reformation to the Crown and the aristocracy. Further, behind the intention to envisage a pre-eminence of St Andrews along with St Mary's theological college was the royal plan to reshape Scottish universities and degrees according to the Oxbridge model and some

(43) Scot, *Apologetical Narration*, p. 245.

(44) Spottiswoode, *History*, vol. 3 (1851), p. 236-238. These were later known as the controversial *Five Articles of Perth*, after the contentious General Assembly there in 1618. See *DSCHT, ad vocem*.

(45) See *DSCHT*, entry 'Education, Theological'; Whytock, *Scottish Theological Education*.

CONCILIUM ABERDONIENSE ECCLESIAE SCOTICANAE – 1616   1013

Continental models, thus reintroducing degree titles in theology (which, as happened in Scotland, Reformed academies in Europe had shunned). Future bishops would be required to be doctors of theology. ([46]) The entire strategy was not adopted by the Assembly, and the vision was never to be completely realised.

THE MANUSCRIPT TRADITION

Historically, the official records of the general assemblies of the reformed Church of Scotland from 1560 to 1616 have been referred to variously as 'The Register(s) of the Kirk', 'The Book(s) of the Assembly', 'The Acts and Proceedings of the General Assembly of the Church of Scotland', 'Acts of the Assemblie', 'The Book of the Universal Kirk of Scotland', 'The Book of the Kirk', 'The Book', and so forth. ([47]) In the sources and literature, such variety of designation can be perplexing, as it does not always refer to the same records; on top of this, most of them no longer exist in their original forms. However, basically three categories of original witness can be distinguished. The first were the authoritative 'Registers'. These contained comprehensive records up to 1616 in eight manuscript in-folio tomes, sometimes with accompanying files or 'scrolls'. The second was a substantial abridgement or compendium in one manuscript volume extracted from the copious Register, intended for convenient use by local presbyteries and regional synods. This was called the *Book of the Universal Kirk* (hereafter abbreviated as *BUK*). There was more than one version of this. The third was a genre of manuscript abstracts or excerpts called 'Abbreviates' of 'general actes' of the assemblies, which were a short collection of assembly decisions that served as a quick reference handbook or checklist. ([48])

The sole pre-1616 version of the *BUK* known to be extant is now held in the Aberdeen University Library (MS 227), and is referred to in the literature as the Carmichael MS. ([49]) It is incomplete – as it only goes up to 1590 – and

---

(46) For further details of the strategy apart from the royal *Instructions* delivered at the fourth session, see 'Articles set down by His Majesty concerning the University of St Andrews', in *Original Letters*, vol. 2, p. 807-809. Cfr. Reid, *Humanism and Calvinism*, p. 245-248.

(47) For further information on the turbulent history of the Assembly records of 1560-1618, see *DSCHT*, entry '*Booke of the Universall Kirk*', p. 87; Shaw, *General Assemblies*, p. 1-8; *BUK* (Peterkin), p. vi-viii and 599-600; *BUK* (Thomson), vol. 3 (1845), p. xii-xiv and especially the 'Appendix', p. xvii-li.

(48) *BUK* (Peterkin), p. ii.

(49) Shaw, *General Assemblies*, p. 6-7.

was later continued to 1602. Another early version of the *BUK* that was continued (according to reports) up to 1616, is cited as the Crawford MS. It is not currently traceable and thus presumably not extant. (50) The only extant version extending to 1616 was created in the first four months of 1638. (51) This was six months before the General Assembly at Glasgow in November and December of that year inquired into the Church's official Registers, into which it was discovered that the 1616 Aberdeen Assembly records had actually not yet been inserted (see below). The source – or sources – which the uniquely extant version of the *BUK* was copied from is a matter of speculation due to the absence of any other original texts, including the full 1616 record. (52) It could have been from an existing *BUK* expanded up to 1616. It could also have been partly from a *BUK* which did not extend to 1616, (53) and partly from the accessible minutes of the 1616 Aberdeen Assembly not yet in the Register. According to an eyewitness report in 1834, the extant version of the *BUK* up to 1616 was estimated to amount to about one third of the complete Registers; (54) the latter were still extant in 1834, but soon to be destroyed. That surviving *BUK* (an abridgement, like all *BUKs*) constitutes Tradition 1 among present-day manuscripts and editions. It is the major source of the records of the Aberdeen Assembly.

However, as will be described more fully below, there were also two other streams of transmission independent of the *BUK*. These are here characterised as Traditions 2 and 3. In the nineteenth-century printed edition which has been standard till now (*BUK* - ed. Thomson), significant elements of Tradition 2 were grafted into the text of Tradition 1 to make a composite text. This second manuscript tradition derived from the extensive and mostly extant manuscript collections of contemporary presbyterian historian, David Calderwood (*c.* 1575-1650). (55) There are – as it were – two *textus principes* or a twofold source for any edition. The third manuscript tradition represents an epitome of assemblies' acts, and is thus an Abbreviate. In earlier times there were multiple copies, but only one copy is known now to have survived (see Tradition 3 below).

---

(50) Shaw, *General Assemblies*, p. 10; *BUK* (Thomson), vol. 3 (1845), p. xiii and no. 13; *Analecta Scotica.*, vol. 2 (1837), p. 144.

(51) See below, Tradition 1, no. 1.

(52) Shaw, *General Assemblies*, p. 9; *Analecta Scotica*, p. 312 and 323.

(53) *BUK* (Thomson), vol. 3 (1845), p. xiii-xiv.

(54) *BUK* (Thomson), vol. 3 (1845), p. xiv.

(55) On him, see the relevant entries in *DSCHT* and *ODNB*.

Impact of Conflict and Natural Disasters

The monumental lacuna in respect of the pre-1638 original manuscript records of the general assemblies is that they no longer exist, be it in the form of minutes (the 'scrolls') drafted initially by the Assembly clerk, or of the large folio volumes of the Register into which they were engrossed. In addition, apart from the incomplete manuscript of the *BUK* now in Aberdeen, all pre-1638 copies of the *BUK* have gone astray as well. (⁵⁶) This loss was cumulative. It was due partly to the seventeenth-century British civil wars; partly to the loss of some at sea (it is surmised) when being returned to Scotland from London at the end of the Cromwellian Protectorate on the restoration of the monarchy in 1660; partly to their seizure from presbyterians and to book burnings in 1662 after episcopalian re-establishment following a presbyterian interlude (1638-1660); partly to destruction by fire at Edinburgh in 1701; partly to a degree of ennui about the turbulent past manifested by the established presbyterian Church of Scotland in the Enlightenment era; but chiefly to the accidental incineration of the surviving original records at the Westminster Parliament in 1834. Some original Registers had been in the hands of Scottish bishops between the 1590s and 1638, when they were surrendered to the Glasgow General Assembly on its abolition of ecclesiastical episcopacy. They came into the hands of the episcopalian hierarchy again post-1660, when presbyterian polity was dismantled and episcopacy reinstalled by King Charles II. Some abridged transcripts of various kinds remained in the hands of pro-presbyterian individuals. However, even after the definitive establishment of presbyterian church government in 1690, what survived of the original Registers was still retained by episcopalian nonconformists refusing to surrender them. One of their number, a dissenting titular bishop, Archibald Campbell († 1744), suggested offering them for sale, and that the Church could buy them for £100. (⁵⁷) The Church did not pay up, so Campbell eventually deposited them (1737) in the library of Sion College, London. Access to these Registers was denied to presbyterians and the Church of Scotland.

When in 1834 the Kirk petitioned the Westminster Parliament for these originals to be returned, the three (out of originally eight) surviving manuscript volumes of the Registers were produced for judicial verification. However, in the course of an adjournment of the House of Commons' select committee dealing with the matter, the Houses of Parliament were burnt

---

(56) Shaw, *General Assemblies*, p. 7-10.
(57) The Procurator of the Church to the Moderator, 3 May 1733, in *BUK* (Thomson), vol. 3 (1845), 'Appendix', p. xl.

down. This completed the total loss of all original Registers of the Church of Scotland up to 1616. Therefore, the registered version of the minutes of the 1616 Aberdeen General Assembly, only incorporated into the Registers in 1638 or afterwards, also perished in that conflagration. From 1834 onwards, the only means to access the original record of the Kirk's General Assemblies, including that of Aberdeen, was via surviving abridgements such as the *BUK*, some Abbreviates, and the seventeenth-century transcripts by David Calderwood. Other contemporary and later (but pre-1834) historians – such as James Melville, John Row, William Scot, Alexander Petrie, and Jeremy Collier – included documentary illustrations directly from the Register. [58] Nonetheless, it is only from the historiographical work of the Moderator-Archbishop John Spottiswoode, [59] a key figure in the 1616 Assembly, that anything extra on the Aberdeen Assembly from the lost Register can be cited. [60]

This sequence of accident, dispersion, calamity, destruction and lack of access – 'injury of times and cross-providences' [61] – was obviously related to the vicissitudes of the chronic ecclesiological struggles in the post-Reformation era between the presbyterian and episcopalian parties in Scotland, as well as between Church and state, for control of the Scottish Kirk. A symptom of this was rivalry between presbyterians, episcopalians, and even the government for the ownership and custodianship of Assembly records, therefore for control of the memory and documented history of the supreme court of the Church. For presbyterians, the Registers as a whole were of totemic value, since they embodied the 'Kirk of Scotlands Magna Carta, containing all her priveledges and liberties since the Reformation'. [62] This related crucially to the presbyterian constitution of the *Second Book of Discipline* of 1578, [63] which was inserted into the Church Registers in 1581 and ratified by the Scottish Parliament in 1592 (albeit denied royal assent).

In those times, the Scottish Kirk had no fixed headquarters with archives. The keeper of the records was normally the Clerk of the Church (or of the Assembly), who prepared the minutes of the proceedings of assemblies and

---

(58) See *BUK* (Peterkin), p. vii-viii; Shaw, *General Assemblies*, p. 10-12.

(59) See note 7 above. He began historical writing in the 1620s at James' request.

(60) Spottiswoode, *History*, vol. 3 (1851), p. 235-236.

(61) *Analecta Scotica*, p. 364.

(62) According to Alexander Henderson, moderator of the Glasgow General Assembly of 1638, as in *BUK* (Thomson), vol. 3 (1845), 'Appendix', p. xviii.

(63) On its essence as conciliar self-government and parity of ministers and elders see Foresta, 'Transregional Reformation', p. 199. Cfr. Henderson, *Presbyterianism*; Cameron, 'Presbyterianer'; *Second Book of Discipline*, ed. J. Kirk.

inserted their filtered contents into the Register tomes. But the Registers sometimes came into the hands of archbishops inclined to suppress or edit material of a pro-presbyterian nature. There was also presbyterian reluctance over suggestions by the government to entrust the assembly records to its care in the office of the Lord Privy Seal, close to the King. (64) Inevitably, there were serious presbyterian complaints about pages in the assembly records that were mutilated, amended or torn out by figures in the episcopalian hierarchy, most notoriously by Archbishop Patrick Adamson (1537-1592). (65) Therefore, even if the defective and damaged eight in-folio volumes of the Register had all survived into our times, retrieving or reconstructing the pure urtexts in their entirety would still be impossible. Even the surviving versions of the Aberdeen Assembly records must be categorised ultimately as the best possible record (rather than an absolutely true record) in view of episcopal editing of the minutes, referred to below.

The Original Aberdeen Assembly Minutes and Their Register Record

Following the Scottish National Covenant of resistance to the English episcopalian model and to direct royal involvement in ecclesiastical affairs, an exclusively presbyterian General Assembly was convened at Glasgow Cathedral in 1638. It set up a committee of inquiry into the whereabouts of the dispersed Registers and called them in. On inspection by the Assembly, the records of the first three of six episcopacy-dominated general assemblies (1606, 1608, 1610) had been already entered. (66) Even though they declared all episcopally managed assemblies null and void, presbyterians were still content to retain them on the record as evidence of episcopal and royal tyranny. A special case was the minute of the proceedings of the Aberdeen Assembly. As will be illustrated in the textual apparatus, there were allegations of some episcopal manipulation. The Glasgow Assembly noted the following: that with regard to the 1616 Aberdeen Assembly acts and proceedings, its moderator, Archbishop John Spottiswoode, 'with his own hand did interline, adde, change, vitiate, direct to be extracted or not extracted, as he pleased, as the scrolls themselves doe show', to the extent that 'the clerk did not registrate the acts of that Assembly in the books of the Assemblies, as may be easily seen by

(64) Shaw, *General Assemblies*, p. 1-2.
(65) Shaw, *General Assemblies*, p. 3-4.
(66) For the Glasgow Assembly's report of its complex proceedings 'relative to the Registers of the Church', see *BUK* (Thomson), vol. 3, 'Appendix', p. xvii-xxvii.

the blank in the register left for them remaining unfilled'. (⁶⁷) In short, the 1616 Assembly record was still in the form of 'scrolls' and loose papers – i.e. the original minutes – or a preliminary draft by the clerk for the Register, but sub-edited to some extent by the moderator-archbishop. (⁶⁸) Their provisional character is also suggested by the occasional rubric in the transmitted text of Tradition 1 of 'Here to insert'.

Complete corroboration of this general situation is provided by an earlier observation by the Glasgow Assembly: '[t]he Moderator said that the books and acts of all former Assemblies should be produced [...] [it was answered that there were] onlie two bookes containing some Acts from the year 1590 till the Assemblie at Aberdeen holden *anno* 1616, which therein is onlie begunne, with the minuts of the acts of the said Assemblie of Aberdene *in a paper apairt*'. (⁶⁹) In other words, space left explicitly in the Register for the Aberdeen record had not yet been filled in, but fortunately a draft of that Assembly's minutes was still to hand in a separate folder. Accordingly, the Aberdeen Assembly record was not inserted into the Register until late in 1638 or even later. This is the assumption, since it cannot be proven on the basis of direct evidence. However, other circumstantial evidence makes it a certainty. First, in the course of condemning the 'six late pretended assemblies' – i.e. episcopalian assemblies – from 1606-1618, (⁷⁰) the Glasgow Assembly of 1638 noted that their invalid status was 'confirmed by the registers of the Assembly'. This suggests that by that point, the Aberdeen records had been, or would soon be, inserted into the Register. Secondly, and more convincingly: a failed proposal by the General Assembly in 1733 to have the surviving registers – which the Church no longer possessed – published, described them as '[t]he Acts of the General Assembly of the Church of Scotland from the Reformation to 1616 *inclusive*'. (⁷¹) This looks like decisive evidence that the Aberdeen Assembly records had been copied into the old Registers.

Current Availability of Main Sources in Manuscript and Print

The original official record of the Aberdeen General Assembly in the Church Register has been lost forever. But as already mentioned, a version of

---

(67) *Ibid.*, p. li.

(68) In the first published version of Calderwood's text-collections, he noted: '[t]hus far out of the Scrolles, together with the Bishops additions and alterations'. Calderwood, *True History*, p. 667.

(69) *BUK* (Thomson), vol. 3, 'Appendix', p. xvii.

(70) *Ibid.*, p. xlix.

(71) *Ibid.*, p. xli.

CONCILIUM ABERDONIENSE ECCLESIAE SCOTICANAE – 1616

it was incorporated into a new copy of the *BUK* early in 1638 and, being extant, is the basis of Tradition 1. As regards the two surviving versions of David Calderwood which form Tradition 2 (see below), a complication is that his material on the Aberdeen Assembly takes two different forms. One manuscript seems to have been taken in part from pre-existing Abbreviates and other documents associated with the assembly; hence his reference to 'some copies' or 'another copie'. (72) The other version (1679 published text only) was stated by him to incorporate what was 'extant in the Clerk's scrolls', (73) i.e. the minutes of the Aberdeen assembly in the *'paper apairt'*. Calderwood was present at the Glasgow Assembly in 1638 where these minutes were accessible. Since some features of both his surviving versions of the Aberdeen Assembly proceedings are not in the *BUK,* (74) his manuscripts for that Assembly are complementary. From subsequent historical allusions, one can guess that all in all about sixteen copies of Assembly proceedings up to 1616 in various formats (including Abbreviates) were still extant in the nineteenth century. Early in that century, two different editions of the Assembly records – which included the 1616 Aberdeen Assembly – were published almost simultaneously (see the list of *Printed editions* below). Unfortunately, no systematic list, catalogue, stemma, analytic or comparative description of surviving manuscripts was provided in the 1840s. While the editors identified the one or two manuscripts used by them, they (like Calderwood before them) only alluded vaguely to other copies. The editors' interest was more in reporting on records and copies in the past which had been destroyed or lost. One editor, Alexander Peterkin, used just one manuscript – the existing 1638 *BUK* version in the former Advocates' Library copied from the primary copy in Glasgow University Library – but then he also referred to 'the copies' of the *BUK* in the Advocates' Library, whereas we know of only one. Yet Peterkin did intimate a supplementary volume of 'Notes' with a survey of surviving manuscripts and their collation on completion of the volume; but this did not materialise. (75) The other editor of the *BUK,* Thomas Thomson, did discuss briefly the two different manuscripts used for his edition (1638 *BUK* and a copy of an extant Calderwood MS). He also alluded to 'various copies' and 'collation with other copies', (76) but nothing specific was mentioned. As he

(72) See Calderwood, *History,* vol. 7 (1845), p. 224-225.
(73) Calderwood, *True History,* p. 657. On p. 665 he also refers to a 'leafe or page loose among the Acts of this Assembly [and] Scrolles'.
(74) *BUK* (Peterkin), p. vii (item 5 there).
(75) *BUK* (Peterkin), p. vi, 599, and 600.
(76) *BUK* (Thomson), vol. 3 (1845), 'Preface', p. xiii-xiv.

stated, rather than being the actual editor, he was content to declare that his research assistant knew more than anyone else about these matters. (⁷⁷)

Accordingly, information in the editions of Peterkin and Thomson on the specific manuscripts they used is minimal, being confined basically to their current location and information about their collation. Issues of provenance and transmission were not explored, and the special history of the Aberdeen Assembly record in Tradition 1 was not mentioned. The physical and internal characteristics (including the script of the manuscripts) were not described, although, of course, the interest of these editors was to make available a whole corpus of material with no focus on any individual General Assembly record. And while the Calderwood material used for Thomson's edition of the *BUK* was identified, there was no reference in his preface to volume 3 of another and better Calderwood MS which was still extant at that time; it contained an even fuller version of the Aberdeen Assembly record. (⁷⁸)

Some manuscript copies known when those editions appeared (1839-1845) have vanished (⁷⁹); in addition, there have been library mergers, changes of library location and library names. Peterkin did refer to a list of manuscripts drafted by the then Clerk of the Church of Scotland, Dr John Lee (1779-1859), who had been very active in trying to retrieve the originals from London. Peterkin expressed the hope that all extant manuscripts would be re-located to Edinburgh, and that the General Assembly would have Lee's list published. (⁸⁰) All this came to nought, and Lee's list is so far untraceable. Consequently, a modern editor has to start from scratch to establish the existence, whereabouts, and authenticity of most surviving copies which include the 1616 Assembly along with their relationship to each other as well as to originals and lost copies. Today, eight of the various manuscript copies of Kirk records made from the 1620s onwards that include the 1616 Assembly record are known to be extant and accessible. Among these, there are two independent primary copies (*BUK* and in Calderwood's large version). From the first there are two later transcripts; from the other there are three subsequent copies. In addition, there is one early Abbreviate, containing excerpted assembly decisions or acts. These surviving manuscripts may be sub-divided into three families with the common ultimate source which is no longer extant, to be designated with the siglum (*O*).

(77) *BUK* (Thomson), p. xv.

(78) See no. 89 and no. 90 below. Thomson presently became aware of it in connection with his edition of Calderwoods's *History*, but still did not avail himself of it.

(79) See Shaw, *General Assemblies*, p. 4-10.

(80) *BUK* (Peterkin), p. x-xi.

CONCILIUM ABERDONIENSE ECCLESIAE SCOTICANAE – 1616   1021

a.   MS Tradition I

1. This group derives from a copy of a pre-1638 *BUK* that was made in the first quarter of 1638 by a Church reader, William Laing. Laing's copy includes the acts and proceedings of the Aberdeen General Assembly before they were produced at the Glasgow Assembly at the end of that year, and before they were inserted into the Church Registers. All else is speculation. Its subsequent itinerary is uncertain, but since 1697 the transcript has been located at Glasgow University Library (MS Gen 1122). Acquired for the library by Robert Wodrow (1679-1734), Church minister in Eastwood near Glasgow, historian and university librarian from 1697 to 1701, he had purchased it from a Scottish ex-bishop, John Sage (1652-1711). ([81])

Title: *The book of all the General Assemblies of the Church of Scotland since the Reformatione: wherein the heidis and conclusionis devysit be the ministers and commissioneris of the particular kirks therof are speciallie expressed and contenit for the setting foorth of gods glorie and the furderance of trew religion within this our Kingdome. Begun in the yere of remembrance 1560.* Bound folio volume, 30 × 18 cm. 351 pages, manually paginated. At the bottom of p. 349 there is a note by the copyist, William Laing: 'Begune by me Wm Layng reider of Ebdie [Abdie, in Fife] kirk upone ye 15 of Januar 1638 and completed upon ye 23 of Apryll in ye samme year'. The title of the 1616 Aberdeen Assembly record is 'The general assembly of the Kirk of Scotland halden at Aberdeen the 13 of August 1616 yeirs', manually paginated 324-331. The script, crabbed and hurried and so not easily legible, is in the standard European secretary hand, with frequent abbreviations plus Old English or Scots letters, namely *3 (yogh)* for 'y' or 'ng', and *þ* or *y (thorn)* for 'th'. The ink is oak gall. Sole marginalia are numbering from 1-5 on p. 330. Its siglum in this edition will be '*L*'.

2. A late-seventeenth-century copy (MS Gen 1132) transcribed directly from the previous item has been also held in Glasgow University Library since 1699 or 1700. Older literature cited a previous reference still inscribed on the volume's bookplate (BE9-x.18). It is another copy of the entire *Book of the Assembly (BUK)* commissioned by the Principal of Glasgow University, William Dunlop (*c.* 1649-1700). Bound folio volume, 39 × 22.25 cm.

Its anglicised title is: *The book of all the General Assemblies of the Church of Scotland since the Reformation, wherein the heads and conclusions devised by the ministers and commissioners of the particular kirks thereof are specially*

---

(81) For his account of the matter, see Sage, *Works*, vol. 1 (1844), p. 4-7. On him cfr *ODNB*.

1022 CONCILIUM ABERDONIENSE ECCLESIAE SCOTICANAE – 1616

express'd & contain'd [...] *Begun in the year of remembrance 1560.* The title page is highly stylised and artistic in a naïve way, framed, with liberal use of ornate capitals, especially the initial 'T' of the incipit that is very large and semi-illuminated. This page also bears the ownership inscription of 'Principal William Dunlop, 1699', who presumably bequeathed it to the college library. The title of the 1616 Aberdeen record therein is 'The General assemblie of the Kirk of Scotland halden att Aberdene the 13 of August 1616 yeirs', manually paginated 465-476. The script is a mixture of secretary hand (predominant) and cursive italic, also with use of the letters *yogh* and *thorn*. The abbreviations of '*L*' are replicated, but the orthography occasionally varies. There is increased use of capitalisation, sometimes extraordinarily ornate and random. Catchwords; sole marginalia are numbering 1-5 on p. 474. A list of corrections and addenda, based on a comparison with David Calderwood's MS *History of the Kirk of Scotland*, to the entire volume is in a letter of 20 December 1791 from a local scholarly minister and Glasgow University Dean of Faculties, the Reverend Dr James Meek (1742-1810), (82) to George Jardine, professor of Greek and Logic. The letter was attached to the volume by order of the Glasgow University Senate; just one minor addendum is suggested for the Aberdeen Assembly record. The siglum of this copy in our edition will be '*D*'.

3. A third and important version of the text is another copy of '*L*' (Adv.17.11.8 or MS 1766) made in Glasgow that came later to the former Faculty of Advocates Library, Edinburgh. Its non-law holdings became the core of the modern National Library of Scotland in 1925. Front page has: *Ex Libris Bibliothecae Juridicae Edinburgi. Anno Domini 1766.* Title page has: *The Booke of the universall Kirk of Scotland Wherein the heades and conclusions devysit be the ministers and commissionarios of the particular Kirk's Thereof are specially expressed and contained.* An eighteenth-century manuscript note on the title page affirms that this title is authentic, since it was based on older *BUK* manuscripts (pre-1638); one, up to 1602, was owned by the Earl of Cromarty, George Mackenzie (the Carmichael MS, mentioned above), and the other

---

(82) See J. Frame, *A narrative of the case of the parish of Cambuslang; containing a true state of the process concerning the settlement of Mr Meek in that parish; with an account of the foundation and grounds of the opposition to his admission* [...], Glasgow 1775 (Glasgow University Library, Special Collections, Sp Coll Mu2–c. 10); *An abstract of the proceedings of the General Assemblies of the Church of Scotland, from 1560 to approximately the 1630s* (Glasgow University Library, GB 0247, MS Gen 1132); *Register of the actings and proceedings of the General Assembly of the Church of Scotland. 1793 to 1797* (Glasgow University Library, GB 0247, MS Gen 1159); W. H. Porter, *Cambuslang and its Ministers* (Mitchell Library, Glasgow, Glasgow Collection, GC941.433, CAM 188520, Box 952).

CONCILIUM ABERDONIENSE ECCLESIAE SCOTICANAE – 1616   1023

(reportedly up to 1616) by the Earl of Crawford, William Lindsay, now missing. (83) This National Library text was to some extent collated with those two
manuscripts as well as with a Calderwood MS (Tradition 2 below). These
collations had little bearing on the 1616 Aberdeen Assembly record in the
MS. Also inscribed on the title page is *Vetusta bona quam amena* [How
delightful are the good old things]. Bound folio volume, 37 × 23 cm; manual
pagination of 355 pages, plus seventeen unnumbered pages of appendices. The
volume most likely came to the Advocates Library with the bequest of the
extensive manuscript collection belonging to Robert Wodrow after his death
in 1734, since the annotations and collations on the manuscript are actually in
his hand, including an alert that some dates (years) may confuse modern readers due to the difference between the Julian and Gregorian calendars. We
know that this volume was a second copy (for Wodrow's own use) of the Glasgow text '*L*', since a Wodrow note on the title page refers to 'the copy in the
Glasgow Library from whence this is transcribed'. The last page in the volume
also states 'This book is transcribed'. Various copyists were involved. The title
of 1616 Aberdeen Assembly minutes is 'The Generall Assembly of the Kirk of
Scotland halden at Aberdeen the 13 of August i6i6 yeares', p. 346–[353], 350-
353 wrongly numbered as '250', '251', '252', '253', manually paginated. Adjacent
to each page number is 'i6i6'. The neat script of the Aberdeen Assembly material is a mixture of secretary hand and cursive italic with continuing use of
the letter *thorn*, but not of *yogh*. Increased capitalisation, less abbreviation, but
the orthography is very faithful to the original. Catchwords; sole marginalia
are numbering from 1-5 on p. [352]. Its siglum within this edition will be '*N*'.

> b.   *MS Tradition 2*

This is connected with the name of David Calderwood, minister, Church
historian and chronicler, committed presbyterian apologist and controversial-
ist expelled by the King to the Continent in 1617 for disobedience. In the
Netherlands, and after his return to Scotland in 1625, Calderwood planned
and worked on his collection of source materials for a history of the Kirk from
the early-sixteenth century to 1625, when James VI died. His approach was
from a strict Reformed and presbyterian point of view on Church polity and
Church-state relations, to which the monarchy and sometimes the Scottish
Parliament were antipathetic. In 1638, the General Assembly granted Calderwood a pension to help fund his project of a history of the Scottish Church
from the early-sixteenth century. His manuscript files are a huge autograph

(83) See above, notes 48-49.

1024   CONCILIUM ABERDONIENSE ECCLESIAE SCOTICANAE – 1616

collection and database of copies and summaries of accessed sources and commentary. These include the unprocessed minutes of the Aberdeen Assembly. The supreme value of Calderwood's presentations of the Assembly is that they include the sole source-text of the *New Confession of Faith* (which was only later printed), something not remarked upon in scholarly literature. Calderwood's surviving and copious manuscript originals in two different formats (84) were subsequently published (see below).

The first manuscript collection (= *cura* 1) of Calderwood in three volumes is now in the British Library, London, where it is designated as *Materials for a History of the Church of Scotland*. It was a vast commonplace book which accumulated sources for a Scottish Church history from 1504 (year of birth of the Scottish Lutheran martyr, Patrick Hamilton). It comprised over 3,100 folio pages, but only a third survived, namely up to the year 1586, so that it has no relevance for the 1616 Aberdeen Assembly. However, one can confidently assume that the missing volumes contained materials on that Assembly that are absorbed in one form or another in the abstracted second, also three-volume, series of Calderwood manuscripts (= *cura* 2). This second Calderwood recension is a relatively shorter and systematic rearrangement of his (now mostly lost) first set of materials. Since it does contain some Aberdeen Assembly sources, the manuscript constitutes the copy-text of Tradition 2, thus serving as MS no. 1 below:

1. This comparatively condensed, but still comprehensive version going up to 1625 was completed by 1627. It is a chronologically ordered, narrative history by Calderwood with extensive, illustrative sources embedded in the text. He did not identify his sources for the Aberdeen Assembly beyond vague references to 'other copies', referring probably to Abbreviates and possibly a contemporary copy of the *BUK* which had some material on the 1616 Assembly. During the creation of this version of his *History*, Calderwood must also have had access to at least some Aberdeen Assembly original papers, for among other information supplied is a copy of the *New Confession* that is the unique witness. This MS, *cura* 2, is also now located in the British Library, London, gifted (along with *cura* 1) to it in 1765 by a descendant of Calder-

---

(84) For a basic overview of the relationship between his MSS, see the Calderwood entry in *ODNB*. For further information on that and on the history of the MSS, see Calderwood, *History*, vol. 1 (1842), p. vi-vii, but especially vol. 8 (1849), p. viii-xii and 'Second Appendix', p. [3]–[5] and 129-132. See also *Early Letters of Robert Wodrow, 1698-1709*, ed. D. W. Sharp (*Publications of the Scottish History Society* 3/24), Edinburgh 1937, p. 25, 30-31, 39-48, and 46-47; *Analecta Scotica*, vol. 2 (1837), p. 195; Wodrow, *Correspondence*, vol. 3, p. 265-266; Chalmers, *General Biographical Dictionary*, vol. 8 (1813), p. 56, note *.

CONCILIUM ABERDONIENSE ECCLESIAE SCOTICANAE – 1616   1025

wood's grand-nephew (Judge William Calderwood, Lord Polton) who had inherited it. Library reference: Add MS 4737-4739. Title: *The Historie of the Kirk of Scotland beginning at Mr Patrick Hammiltoun and ending at the death of James the sixt.* Three bound and very large folio volumes, this manuscript amounts to 2,013 pages. On the first leaf of each volume is the inscription: *Ex Libris Dom. Guilelmi Calderwood de Poltoun.* The Aberdeen Assembly record (interwoven with Calderwood's supplementary data and commentary), is in volume 3, under the year 1616. Library reference: Add MS 4739. Title of the 1616 Assembly section is 'The generall assemblie holden at Aberdeene'. Script is very neat secretary hand including letters *thorn* and *yogh*. Running short title: 'King James 6'; catchwords; some marginalia functioning as sub-headings; top left of each page is '*an 1616*'. This MS was used for Calderwood's *History of the Kirk of Scotland* edited by Thomas Thomson and published by the Wodrow Society in 1842-1849 (see note 38 and *Printed editions* in Tradition 2, no. 2 below). The MS shall be indicated by the siglum '*C*'. There are also three later manuscript copies elsewhere of this so-called *Large* or *Larger History* by Calderwood of which only the first was directly transcribed from *C*. These versions date from the late-seventeenth, the eighteenth and early nineteenth centuries.

2. The first copy of *C*, which was still in Scotland at the time, is in Glasgow University Library, ([85]) six large volumes amounting to 3,981 pages (MS Gen 1190-1195). The transcript was sponsored and acquired by the university in 1692 through the offices of its Principal and zealous presbyterian, William Dunlop (*c.* 1649-1700). The relevant volume 6 (MS Gen 1195) comprises 537 pages. Its title page is *Part of Calderwood's Large History vol: 6 Comprehending the History of Church and State from Janurij 1607 to K. James the sixths death 1625.* Bound folio volume, 33 × 20 cm. Inscribed on the title page is *Ex libris Bibliothecae Universitatis Glasguensis, propriis Academiae sumptibus, cum 5 sociis voluminibus, An. Dom. 1692*, with William Dunlop's signature. The Aberdeen Assembly material has as title or incipit: 'The general assemblie holdin at Aberdeen beganne the 13 of Augustj', manually paginated 270-281. Running short title: 'King James 6'. Beside each page number is '*an 1616*'. Catchwords; marginalia on p. 273-274, acting as sub-headings. Script is secretary hand with some cursive italic tendencies; the binding tends to distort or obscure text in the guttering; use of the letter *thorn* in lower case only. A manuscript index to the *History* was prepared in 1836 by the Reverend James Inglis (1767-1847), catalogued separately in the library as MS Gen 1196. The siglum of this copy of the will be '*G*'.

(85) See Calderwood, *History*, vol. 8 (1849), 'Second Appendix', p. 130-131.

3. Another copy, based on *G*, was done in 1724 by an amanuensis of Robert Wodrow, former Glasgow University librarian, for his personal use. (⁸⁶) By 1728, Wodrow himself had collated it with the Calderwood originals (*C*) in the possession of the Calderwood family. The copy was subsequently purchased in 1742 by the then Church of Scotland General Assembly Library, which since 1958 became part of the Library of New College, Edinburgh (now administratively part of Edinburgh University Library), reference: MS CALD. Six bound volumes, large folio size, manually paginated. At the end of volume 6 there is a note by Wodrow: 'Eastwood Agust 28, 1728. This with the other five volumes, are collated with the originall copy, of Mr David Calderwoods History, belonging to my Lord Polton, Sir William Calderwood, the authors grand = nepheu By me R Wodrow'. Each volume is stamped with *Bibliotheca Ecclesiae Scoticanae*. Volume 6,624 folio pages, contains the Aberdeen Assembly records at p. 364-378. Script is largely cursive italic; orthography increasingly anglicized; catchwords; running short title: '*James 6*'; occasional corrections and insertions by Wodrow; marginalia on p. 368-370 only, partly Calderwood's originals (underlined), partly Wodrow's. A note on the front page of volume 1 states: 'The margins [marginalia] in this volume without lines under them are not in the original but my adding. R[obert] W[odrow]'. This Calderwood manuscript was partially incorporated into the Maitland and Bannatyne Clubs edition of the *BUK* edited by Thomson (see *Printed editions* below). This manuscript will be designated as '*W*'.

4. The third copy, originally in the Advocates Library, Edinburgh, is now located in the National Library of Scotland (Adv. 33.36.1). (⁸⁷) This consists of fourteen beautifully-bound folio volumes plus an indices volume, all in-quarto, 21 × 16 cm. The Aberdeen Assembly material is in volume 14, manually paginated 558-587. The provenance of this manuscript is uncertain. It seems to be basically another copy of the *G* at a much later stage, and a note on p. 589 of vol. 14 states: 'Collated with the MSS in the possession of the Church of Scotland by J. J. [i.e. James Inglis]'. That is to say, it was collated with *W* above. That there were several copyists, one of whom was also Inglis, is borne out by the various scripts, sometimes cursive italic, sometimes copperplate (English round hand), and which suggest an early-nineteenth-century transcription. Orthography is partially anglicised, and with no use of letters *yogh* and *thorn*. Running short title: '*King James 6*'; catchwords; top of each page is also '1616'; marginalia on p. 558, 564, 566, 567, 568, 569, 570, but transferred from *W*; intermittent minor corrections made by the collator, but *Item*

---

(86) Calderwood, *History*, vol. 8 (1849), 'Second Appendix', p. 131.
(87) Calderwood, *History*, vol. 8 (1849), 'Second Appendix', p. 132.

CONCILIUM ABERDONIENSE ECCLESIAE SCOTICANAE – 1616   1027

is regularly misspelt as *Ittem*. The MS in volume 15 is entitled: 'A Descriptive Index to the Reverend David Calderwood's History of the Church of Scotland in the Advocates Library'; in addition there is a second index, separately paginated 1-74, entitled 'Index to the proceedings of General Assemblies 1560-1618'. At the end of these indices is: 'James Inglis 1838'. This is equivalent to the manuscript index volume (siglum *G*) by the same author located in Glasgow University Library (see above, no. 2). The siglum of this copied version of the *History* is '*T*'.

c.   Calderwood's abridgement of *C*

In addition, it is appropriate here to cite another primary Calderwood manuscript which includes the 1616 Assembly, but which seems to be no longer extant or accessible; yet it is relevant for the first of the Calderwood *Printed editions* below. This is the MS of *cura* 3 which, commencing in 1631, Calderwood prepared for publication – the so-called *Short, Shorter*, or *The True History* – so that is relevant for the *stemma siglorum* of manuscripts and editions. The *True History* had been long thought to be largely pseudo-Calderwood manufactured by presbyterian apologists. However, according to the early-nineteenth-century editors and rediscovered correspondence from the seventeenth century, the source manuscript, a Calderwood autograph with his own marginal corrections, was still extant at Cavers Castle in the Scottish Borders, the home of the traditionally presbyterian Clan Douglas. At a time when presbyterianism was outlawed (post-1660), and when the Church Registers had been appropriated by the episcopal establishment, the manuscript was discreetly copied by committed presbyterians and smuggled out of the country to a like-minded Scottish minister in Rotterdam, Robert McWard (*c*. 1628-1681) ([88]) for publication. ([89]) The Cavers MS, also now missing, was an abridged version of *C*, but with fuller material on the Aberdeen Assembly, ([90]) in a single volume crafted by Calderwood explicitly for publication (printed posthumously in 1678). Representing the third version of Calderwood's threefold set of resources, this non-extant MS will be represented with the siglum (*C³*).

(88) See *ODNB*; *DSCHT, ad vocem*.
(89) Calderwood, *History*, vol. 1 (1842), p. vii, and especially vol. 8 (1849), 'Second Appendix', p. [5]-[9]; Wodrow, *Correspondence*, vol. 3, p. 265-266.
(90) Calderwood, *History*, vol. 8 (1849), 'Second Appendix', p. 95.

1028   CONCILIUM ABERDONIENSE ECCLESIAE SCOTICANAE – 1616

d.   MS Tradition 3

The sole witness to this is a mid-seventeenth-century Abbreviate of excerpts in the form of a catalogue of summarised enactments and resolutions taken from the *BUK*. According to the 1638 Glasgow General Assembly, there were 'many' such briefer digests in circulation (⁹¹) but currently known to be extant is just one example. MS Dc.3.54 is located in Edinburgh University Library. Bound volume, in-quarto, 23 × 17.15 cm. On the inside of the front cover is '1744', but the manuscript was not acquired by the library until the nineteenth century. Below '1744', what may have been an earlier *ex libris* inscription or date of copying has been scrubbed out, for '1643' is still just about detectable. Title: *Acts of the General assemblies of the Church of Scotland Takin out of the register therof*, and then in later hand: *from 1560-1618*. In fact the MS begins in 1562 and ends in 1617. Unlike either the original Registers or the *BUK*, this manuscript contains a record of the St Andrews General Assembly of 1617. Manual signatures [A]–I⁵. The heading for the Aberdeen Assembly material is simply: 'i6i6 15 august aberdeine', within four leaves: H[8v]–I[3v]. Script is in pure secretary hand, suggesting a mid-seventeenth-century date like '1643'; ink is fading and pages are partly water damaged. The contents are – in abstracted chronological form – ten of the eleven resolutions of the Aberdeen Assembly's second session, the five resolutions of the third session, and the fourteen resolutions of the fourth session, although the sessions are not differentiated. This manuscript's siglum will be '*E*'.

SURVEY OF PREVIOUS EDITIONS

The 1616 Aberdeen Assembly record has been published on five different occasions in different formats (excluding two reissues). For MS Tradition 1 there are three instances, and for MS Tradition 2 there are two, or three (see note 105 below).

a.   Editions in Tradition 1

1. The pioneer publication (1839) of the *Book of the Universal Kirk* was edited by Alexander Peterkin (1780-1846), an advocate, man of letters, churchman, and journalist. (⁹²) The Aberdeen Assembly material is on p. 589-

---

(91) *BUK* (Thomson), vol. 3 (1845), 'Appendix', p. xxv, xli.
(92) See *Dictionary of National Biography*, 63 vols, London, 1885-1900, vol. 45 (1896), p. 67.

599, in the section of the edition entitled 'Rescinded Acts of Assembly'; this refers to the retrospective annulment by the presbyterian Glasgow General Assembly (1638) of the proceedings of the six episcopalian 'pretended' assemblies from 1606 to 1618. (93) Peterkin's preface is largely an account of the troubled and tragic history of the original Assembly records (destroyed just five years before in London). He indicated that the edition would be 'from the copies in the Advocates' Library' (p. vi), now held in the National Library of Scotland. He said nothing else about these copies, but he meant presumably not only MS *N* of Tradition 1 but also MS *I* of Tradition 2; for subsequently (p. vii) he referred to Calderwood's MS *History* (*cura* 2, or the *Larger*) of which *I* was a copy also in that library. Yet this is speculation and inconsequential, since Peterkin's edition is just a printed replication of MS *N*. There is no mention of the primary copy in Glasgow, *L*. At the very end of his text, Peterkin acknowledged many mistakes and transcription errata which might seem like variants. The several 'Here to insert' rubrics in the text are not filled in: for example, the text of the *New Confession of Faith* is not supplied. As was usual in that period, there are no apparatuses apart from a modicum of footnotes. Yet Peterkin's stated purpose was to present an interim edition. He indicated that in an appendix volume of 'Notes and Illustrations' he intended not only to offer a copious index, a glossary of obsolete words, and corrigenda for the whole *Book*, but also 'to supply from other sources the portions which are wanting in the text – and to note any seeming discrepancies among the *several transcripts* and Abbreviates'. (94) This did not happen, even if the intention related more to content rather than identifying all specific manuscript copies and their locations. The siglum for this edition will be '*p*'.

2. Not long after *p*, a new, more authoritative edition in three volumes (1839-1845) appeared. Its first volume appeared in same year when Peterkin's *BUK* was published. Once volume 3 of the new edition was published in 1845, Peterkin's edition was superseded, although it has continued to be used up to modern times. The title of the new *BUK* edition – jointly sponsored by the Maitland and Bannatyne Clubs – was *Acts and Proceedings of the General Assemblies of the Kirk of Scotland from the year MDLX [–1618] [...].* The editor was Thomas Thomson M.A., B.D. (1768-1852), lawyer, archivist, and Deputy-Clerk Register of Scotland. (95) The three parts or volumes amount to 1,167 pages in one pagination plus sixty-one more pages of an index (by Mr David

---

(93) See *BUK* (Thomson), vol. 3 (1845), 'Appendix', p. xlix-li.
(94) *BUK* (Peterkin), p. vi and 599-600.
(95) See *ODNB*, *ad vocem*.

1030   CONCILIUM ABERDONIENSE ECCLESIAE SCOTICANAE – 1616

Meek) as well as five more pages of 'Additions and Corrections to the Index'.
The 1616 Aberdeen Assembly record is in Part 3, p. 1116-1139.

Thomson's edition was innovative and valuable. Recognising that no
single existing manuscript provided a complete version of the proceedings of
any General Assembly (as had been in the lost Registers), he synthesised
Tradition 1 and Tradition 2 to make a fuller version. His composite version
was, accordingly, based on available transcripts in Edinburgh, namely *N* and
the Calderwood *W*. The procedure was simply to graft here and there on to *N*
some select material from *W*, 'the unprinted History of the Church by Calderwood, which embraces much larger and more authentic selections from the
Register than any other existing Manuscript'. (⁹⁶) In his text of the Aberdeen
Assembly, this is visible with use of square brackets and then 'C' at the end.
Since both texts had been collated with each other and with others (including
the original *C* by Wodrow a century before), these were good choices. Curiously, Thomson only mentioned this collation explicitly with respect to *W*, on
which Wodrow's signature appears; whereas while the notes on *N* are in
Wodrow's handwriting, his signature is absent. There is an apparent complication: while Thomson stated that the main copy-text for his edition was 'the
copy preserved in the Advocates Library', (⁹⁷) like Peterkin he also referred
(on two occasions) to 'two MS copies of the B.U.K. in the Advocates
Library'. (⁹⁸) There may well have been, but only one still exists; and for the
Aberdeen Assembly it is of no consequence, since *N* – like the other two
MSS in Tradition 1 – represented the only tradition that extended to 1616. As
with Peterkin, there is no mention of the copy in Glasgow from which *N* is
derived: *L*, a fact that was known in the public domain. (⁹⁹) The fact of the
matter is that Thomson oversaw rather than actually prepared the edition. The
ground work for the edition, limited to manuscript sources in Edinburgh, was
done by his assistant, the Reverend William B. Smith, military chaplain in
Edinburgh. '[D]eep obligations' were expressed to him for his 'zealous and
long sustained efforts'. (¹⁰⁰) There are no detailed descriptions of the manuscripts used in Thomson's edition. There is no speculation about their origins.

(96) *BUK* (Thomson), vol. 1 (1839), [Foreword], p. [i].
(97) *BUK* (Thomson), vol. 3 (1845), 'Preface', p. xiv.
(98) *BUK* (Thomson), vol. 1 (1839), [Foreword], p. [i]; vol. 3 (1845), p. 1121, note *.
(99) Chalmers, *General Biographical Dictionary*, vol. 8 (1813), p. 56, note *.
(100) *BUK* (Thomson), vol. 3 (1845), 'Preface', p. xv. Cfr. Alexander Peterkin to
David Laing, 1839, in D. Laing, *Laing Correspondence*, Edinburgh University Library,
MS La.iv.17, fol. 7393: 'I saw the manuscript [?] to which you refer [...] in the possession of Mr Smith who is engaged in transcribing the Booke of the Kirk for the Club'.
See also at note 76 above.

CONCILIUM ABERDONIENSE ECCLESIAE SCOTICANAE – 1616

There are no textual apparatuses apart from occasional minor footnotes. And as in Peterkin, there are no introductions to the Aberdeen Assembly, just as there are none to any other one. The primary concern is to provide a bald text. The siglum for this standard edition will be '*t*'.

3. In modern times, the text of *t* has been made available again in print. Edited by Rev. Dr. Duncan Shaw, with a brief general introduction, this is *The Acts and Proceedings of the Church of Scotland 1560 to 1618*, published in three volumes for the Scottish Record Society in 2004. This is not a facsimile, since the text has been reset. Now it is in two volumes, and like in *t*, it is continuously paginated. Volume 3 is an *Index* based on the one in *t*, but much expanded. The Aberdeen Assembly record is in volume 2, p. 1509-1537. Like the others, Shaw's edition is not a text-critical one in the strict sense, and the actual text is completely modernised in matters of orthography, capitalisation and punctuation. Old Scots vocabulary and idioms are nonetheless retained. There are no footnotes, although in the introduction there are some bibliographical references. The siglum of this edition is '*s*'.

b. Editions in Tradition 2

1. The first of these is David Calderwood's *True History*. It was taken from MS (*C³*). This text, commenced in 1631, was published posthumously in 1678/1679 in Rotterdam and reissued in 1678 and 1704. It could not have been published in Scotland at the time due to the clampdown on presbyterians by the Restoration episcopalian regime of the time. The text is from a copy of Calderwood's much reduced *cura* 3, which he intended for publication should his large manuscript collections fall into the wrong hands and be destroyed. The suspenseful background leading up to this publication has been outlined above at MS Tradition 2: 'Calderwood's abridgement of *C*', with reference to (*C³*), but no longer extant. The text amounts to 814 pages, with the Aberdeen Assembly material on p. 656-673. This includes the prudentially anonymous epistle or preface 'To the Reader' ([101]) by the editors, now known to have been Robert McWard ([102]) in Rotterdam and John Carstairs, a minister in Scotland. ([103]) This preface is a statement of the political and religious presbyterian interest, which is corroborated by Calderwood's text. There is no means of knowing how far the verbose title was Calderwood's or the editors'; it also suggests that this was an official presbyter-

(101) Reprinted by Laing in Calderwood, *History*, vol. 8 (1849), 'First Appendix', p. 13-22.
(102) See note 87 above.
(103) See Calderwood, *History*, vol. 8 (1849), 'First Appendix', p. [5]-[10].

ian history, since it implies that it is the account that Calderwood was encouraged to complete at the Glasgow General Assembly in 1638. It also states that the *True History* was 'examined, revised, and approved' by one or other General Assembly; it is now impossible to know if the increased anglicisation of the text and its expanded capitalisation was done by Calderwood or by the revisers or editors. The Church *imprimatur* must have been given before 1653, when the General Assembly was dissolved in the Cromwellian era; and following the 1660 restoration of both monarchy and episcopacy, no other Assembly was convened until 1690. These unfavourable circumstances help account for the delay in the publication of the *True History* on the continent in 1678/1679. The chief significance of the book for the edition here is that while it embodies a radical abridgement of *C*, the *Large History*, its transcript of the records of the Aberdeen Assembly is much fuller due to the unrestricted access Calderwood had at Glasgow in 1638 to the minutes of that Assembly. (104) The earlier version of *C* on the 1616 Assembly reflected rather the use of abbreviates and other abridgments along with only limited access to the complete minutes. As will be seen in the next item, the Aberdeen record here is reprinted in an appendix of the next item. The expanded version resembles more the account in *BUK* as in Tradition 1. The siglum of this edition will be '*r*'.

2. This is the nineteenth-century edition of Calderwood's *History of the Kirk of Scotland*, taken from MS *C*, edited by Thomas Thomson, and published by the Wodrow Society in 1842-1849. Extending over seven volumes, the text is reproduced from the original *verbatim et literatim*, so that Calderwood's spelling and phraseology is strictly preserved. The only difference is that the edition uses as subheadings what Calderwood had placed as marginalia. While Thomson's preface in volume 1 offers a brief and general introduction, it is just the bare text that is given throughout, with no notes or any other information. Volume 8, edited by David Laing, is devoted to providing many of the background details about Calderwood himself, his manuscripts, a general index to the seven volumes, plus an index to volume 8. Additionally, he listed all the MSS of Tradition 2 and their locations at the time of the edition. Most significantly, there is in this volume wide-ranging collation between Calderwood's edited *History* and the *True History* – that is, Calderwood's *cura* 2 and *cura* 3 – within the second Appendix. This is important for the Aberdeen Assembly above all. On noting that the version of its record in the *True History* is much fuller than in *C* and is more closely taken the from the Assembly minutes, Laing proceeds there to reproduce from the 1678 book

---

(104) See notes 70-73 above.

CONCILIUM ABERDONIENSE ECCLESIAE SCOTICANAE – 1616   1033

the entire text of the Assembly record. ([105]) This underlines the fact that the Aberdeen Assembly record in Calderwood's *History* – being largely an abbreviated patchwork drawn from various sources with commentary – was superseded by the account in the *True History*, albeit not completely; for there is relevant further information in the former which is not found in the latter (also not in Tradition 1, as we have seen above), so that the two accounts complement each other. In short, no one MS or edition of Calderwood can give the fullest account. The edition of Calderwood's *History* will have the siglum '*c*'.

PRINCIPLES APPLIED IN THE EDITION

The copy-text of this edition will be essentially the version already presented by Thomas Thomson in his edition of the *BUK*, indicated above under *Printed editions*, no. 2, siglum *t*. Since no individual surviving MS or any one manuscript tradition provides a full picture of the proceedings of the 1616 Aberdeen General Assembly, and since Thomson's text constitutes a conflation of the two traditions, it is not possible to do much better than that in the current circumstances. There will, however, be some differences in the text below.

First, while the material from Calderwood (Tradition 2) that Thomson grafted on to the lead MS from Tradition 1 was marked within square parentheses and then 'C' within the text, we will simply refer to the original format in the textual apparatus. This will include the *New Confession*, bearing in mind that Calderwood's inclusion of it is the unique witness to it.

Second, we will insert small bits of information in Calderwood on the Assembly that were excluded or overlooked by Thomson. This will also be specifically indicated in the apparatuses.

Third, we will insert into session 3 of the Assembly two letters, one from the archbishop of Canterbury to the archbishop of St Andrews, the other (paraphrased in the source) from King James to the archbishop of St Andrews. These were omitted by the seventeenth-century copyists and the nineteenth-century editors because such letters were not readily accessible at the time. Yet their inclusion into the minutes was the intention of the General Assembly's

---

(105) Calderwood, *History*, vol. 8 (1849), 'Second Appendix', p. 95. Here Laing quotes Calderwood in *True History*, p. 657: 'I have here subjoined the Proceedings and Acts of this Assembly, as they are extant in the Clerk's scrolles'. The text reproduced by Laing is on p. 95-111 and constitutes in reality a third printing of the Aberdeen Assembly record in Tradition 2.

1034 CONCILIUM ABERDONIENSE ECCLESIAE SCOTICANAE – 1616

Clerk at the time, Thomas Nicholson of Cockburnspath, an elder. (106) His minutes have the typical rubric: 'Heir to insert the two letters quhilk is to be found afterward'. Since these letters were only found in the mid-nineteenth century, they can be included here.

Fourth, at the head of the minutes we will include the royal proclamation of James VI, since it also reflects his conception of a General Assembly or of what it should be.

Fifth, at each individual item of business we will insert numbers in square brackets, to assist references. The royal instructions were already numbered. The 53 unnumbered articles of the *Confession* will also be enumerated.

Sixth, the discreetly anglicising orthography of the text in the Thomson edition will be mostly retained. To indicate all differences in all the manuscripts would result in several hundreds of variants. These differences magnified over time with each new transcript due to increasing anglicisation of spelling and capitalisation. The one exception where I will change the orthography tacitly will be the *Confession*. All printed versions of it reflect increasing degrees of anglicisation; but I have realigned the orthography there to the earliest copy (*G*, *c.* 1690) of Calderwood, in Glasgow, which is very close to the original in London. The fact that modernised English renderings of the text are now available in fairly recent editions (*s*) published by Duncan Shaw and James Dennison (107) has made that decision easier.

Seventh, to avoid overloading the edited text with an excess of contextual information and notes, I have provided the bulk of this information above. Any information, mostly minor, not found there will be supplied in the Apparatus 2.

Eighth, Archbishop Spottiswoode's *History* contains one decision of the Assembly that was not recorded in any other source. In addition, in his *True History* Calderwood reported some emendations of Spottiswoode on the original Assembly minutes. In the critical apparatus, these Spottiswoode sources will be indicated with *Spott.*

Lastly, since seventeenth-century vernacular writing in Scotland was a mixture of late-medieval Scots and early-modern English, not only orthography but also vocabulary and phraseology differ considerably from modern standard English. To assist readers, a translation of Scots and archaic earlymodern English words and phrases has been provided in the third apparatus.

---

(106) Professor of Civil Law at King's College, Aberdeen, and Commissary of Aberdeen, he was the Clerk of Assembly from 1594 to 1618. See Shaw, *General Assemblies*, p. 147-159.

(107) See Dennison, 'Scottish Confession (1616)'.

BIBLIOGRAPHY

Sources (and Their Abbreviations)

Other Manuscripts

Centre for Research Collections, Edinburgh University Library

MS La. IV. 17 · D. Laing, *Laing Correspondence.*

Glasgow University Library, Special Collections

MS Gen 1196 · J. Inglis, *Index to David Calderwood's History of the Church of Scotland* [*c.* 1835].

MS Gen 1197-1218 · R. Wodrow, *Biographical Collections*, 21 vols.

National Library of Scotland, Edinburgh

Adv. 33. 6. 1 · J. Inglis, *A Descriptive Index to the Reverend David Calderwood's History of the Church of Scotland in the Advocates Library.*

Adv. 33. 6. 2 · —, *Index to the Proceedings of General Assemblies 1560-1618.*

National Records of Scotland, General Register House, Edinburgh

GD 16 / 46 / 39 (previously CH2 / 154 / 1) · *Minutes of the Synod of Fife, 1610-1636.* (contains material excluded from the printed version offered below).

St Andrews University Library

MSS BV 8 24 H7 · R. Howie, *Accuratus de coenae domini tractatus* [= Howie, *Accuratus*].

1036 CONCILIUM ABERDONIENSE ECCLESIAE SCOTICANAE – 1616

Published Primary Sources

The Acts and Proceedings of the Church of Scotland, 1560 to 1618, ed. D. Shaw (*Scottish Record Society – New Series* 26-28), 3 vols, Edinburgh 2004 [= Shaw, *Acts and Proceedings*].

Acts and Proceedings of the General Assemblies of the Kirk of Scotland, from the year MDLX [–1618] *collected from the most authentic manuscripts.* [Title in text]: *The Booke of the Universall Kirk of Scotland: wherein the headis and conclusiouns devysit be the ministeris and commissionares of the particular kirks thereof are specially expressed and contained*, ed. T. Thomson (*Maitland Club Publications* 49; *Bannatyne Club* 81), 3 pts. in 3 vols, Edinburgh 1839-1845 [= *BUK* (Thomson)].

The Acts of the Parliaments of Scotland, ed. C. Innes – T. Thomson, 12 vols, Edinburgh 1814-1875 = *Records of the Parliaments of Scotland*, ed. G. H. MacIntosh – A. J. Mann – R. J. Tanner, St Andrews 2007-2012 (online resource) [= *Act. Scot. Parl.*].

Analecta Scotica: Collections Illustrative of the Civil, Ecclesiastical and Literary History of Scotland, ed. J. Maidment, 2 vols, Edinburgh 1834-1837 [= *Analecta Scotica*].

The Booke of the Universall Kirk of Scotland: wherein the Headis and Conclusionis Devysit be the Ministers and Commissionaris of the Particular Kirks thereof are specially expressed and contained, ed. A. Peterkin, Edinburgh 1839 [= *BUK* (Peterkin)].

[D. Calderwood], *The History of the Kirk of Scotland. By David Calderwood, some time minister of Crailing. Edited from the original manuscript preserved in the British Museum, by the Rev. Thomas Thomson* (*The Wodrow Society for the Publication of the Works of the Fathers and Early Writers of the Reformed Church of Scotland*), 8 vols – vol. 8 ed. D. Laing, *Appendices and General Index*, Edinburgh 1842-1849 [= Calderwood, *History*].

D. Calderwood, *The True History of the Church of Scotland, From the beginning of the Reformation, unto the end of the Reigne of King James VI. Wherein* [...] *there is not only a series of the Assemblies, and of the Principal of their Actings recorded; but also a full and plaine Relation of the Trials and Troubles, which the Church did meet with from Enemies to the Purity of here Doctrine, Worship, Discipline and Government;* [...] *of the faithful contendings* [...] *for the Prerogatives of Christ, as the alone Head of the Church, for the purity of His Institutions, and for the Liberty and Privileges of His Church and Kingdom, against all the Enemies thereof; and particu-*

CONCILIUM ABERDONIENSE ECCLESIAE SCOTICANAE – 1616   1037

larly against Erastianisme and Prelacy, the two grand Enemies of the Discipline and Government of the Church of Christ [...] Written by That learned and laborious servant of Christ Mr David Calderwood. At the Appointment of the General Assembly by whom his labours herein were several revised and examined, and at length approved for the presse, [ed. J. Carstairs – R. McWard, Rotterdam 1678] [= Calderwood, *True History*].

'Confessio Scotica 1560', ed. I. Hazlett, in *RefBK*, Band 2/1 (2009), p. 209-299 [= 'Confessio Scotica'].

Corpus iuris canonici, editio lipsiensis secunda, ed. E. Friedberg – L. Richter, 2 vols, Lipsiae ²1879-1881 [= *Corpus iuris canonici, editio lipsiensis secunda*].

J. T. Dennison Jr, 'Scottish Confession (1616)', in J. T. Dennison Jr (ed.), *Reformed Confessions of the 16th and 17th Centuries in English Translation*, 4 vols, Grand Rapids 2014, vol. 4, p. 108-116 [= 'Scottish Confession (1616)'].

Ecclesiastical Records: Selections from the Minutes of the Synod of Fife, M.DC.XI-M.DC.LVII, ed. G. R. Kinloch (*Abbotsford Club Publications* 8), Edinburgh 1837 [= *Synod of Fife*].

Letters of John Johnston (c. 1565-1611) and Robert Howie (c. 1565–c. 1645), ed. J. K. Cameron(*St Andrews Publications* 54), Edinburgh – London 1963 [= Cameron, *Letters*].

Memoirs of the Maxwells of Pollok, ed. W. Fraser, 2 vols, Edinburgh 1863 [= *Memoirs of the Maxwells of Pollok*].

R. Mocket, *God and the King: or, a dialogue shewing that our Soueraigne Lord King Iames, being immediate vnder God within his dominions, doth rightfully claime whatsoeuer is required by the Oath of allegiance, Imprinted by his Maiesties speciall privilege and command to the onely use of Mr Iames Primrose, for the kingdome of Scotland*, London 1616.

[C. Olevianus – Z. Ursinus], *Catechisme* [i.e. Heidelberg] *of Christian religion*, Edinburgh 1615.

Original Letters on Ecclesiastical Affairs chiefly written by, or addressed to His Majesty King James the Sixth, after his accession to the English throne, ed. D. Laing (*Bannatyne Club* 92), 2 vols, Edinburgh 1851 [= *Original Letters*].

Register of the Privy Council of Scotland, A.D. 1545-1625. Series I, ed. J. H. Burton – D. Masson, 14 vols, Edinburgh 1877-1898 [= *RPCS*].

1038 CONCILIUM ABERDONIENSE ECCLESIAE SCOTICANAE – 1616

J. Row, *The historie of the Kirk of Scotland, M.D.LVIII.-M.DC.XXXVII with additions and illustrations, by his sons* (*Maitland Club Publications* 55.51/2) – ed. W. Fleming, Edinburgh 1842.

J. Sage, *The Works of the Right Rev. John Sage, a Bishop of the Church in Scotland* (*Spottiswoode Society* 2), 3 vols, Edinburgh 1844-1846 [= Sage, *Works*].

W. Scot, *An Apologetical Narration of the State and Government of the Kirk of Scotland since the Reformation* (*Wodrow Society*) – ed. D. Laing, Edinburgh 1846 [= Scot, *Apologetical Narration*].

Scottish liturgies of the reign of James VI: The Booke of common prayer and administration of the sacraments with other rites and ceremonies of the Church of Scotland as it was sett down […], ed. G. W. Sprott, London 1901 [= *Scottish Liturgies*].

J. Spottiswoode, *History of the Church of Scotland, beginning the year of our Lord 203, and continued to the end of the reign of King James VI* (*Bannatyne Club* 93), ed. M. Napier – M. Russell, 3 vols, Edinburgh 1847-1851 [= Spottiswoode, *History*].

LITERATURE (AND ITS ABBREVIATIONS)

Andrew Melville (1545-1622): Writings, Reception and Reputation, ed. R. A. Mason – S. J. Reid, Ashgate 2014 [= Mason – Reid, *Andrew Melville*].

J. A. Beaton, *Scots Law: Terms and Expressions*, Edinburgh 1982.

G. B. Burnet, *The Holy Communion in the Reformed Church of Scotland*, Edinburgh – London 1960 [= Burnet, *The Holy Communion*].

R. Burns, 'Enforcing Uniformity: Catholics and Kirk Sessions in Early Modern Scotland', *Innes Review* 69 (2018), p. 111-130 [= Burns, 'Enforcing Uniformity'].

J. K. Cameron, 'Presbyterianer', in *Theologische Realenzyklopädie*, 36 vols, Berlin – New York 1976-2004, vol. 27 (1997), p. 340-359 [= Cameron, 'Presbyterianer'].

A. Chalmers, *The General Biographical Dictionary: Containing an Historical and Critical Account of the Lives and Writings of the Most Eminent Persons in Every Nation*, 32 vols, London 1812-1817 [= Chalmers, *General Biographical Dictionary*].

The Concise Scots Dictionary, ed. M. Robinson, Aberdeen 1987.

J. Cooper, *Confessions of Faith and Formulas of Subscription in the Reformed Churches of Great Britain and Ireland especially in the Church of Scotland*, Glasgow 1907 [= Cooper, *Confessions of Faith*].

W. Coster, *Baptism and Spiritual Kinship in Early Modern England*, Aldershot 2002 [= Coster, *Baptism and Spiritual Kinship*].

P. Croft, *King James*, Basingstoke – New York 2003 [= Croft, *King James*].

Dictionary of National Biography, 63 vols, London 1885-1900.

Dictionary of Scottish Church History & Scottish Theology, ed. N. M. de S. Cameron – D. Wright et al., Edinburgh 1993 [= *DSCHT*].

A. C. Denlinger, 'The Aberdeen Doctors and Henry Scougal', in D. Fergusson – M. W. Elliott (eds), *The History of Scottish Theology*, 3 vols, Oxford – New York 2019, vol. I., p. 279-295 [= Denlinger, 'The Aberdeen Doctors'].

G. Donaldson, 'Reformation to Covenant', in D. Forrester – D. Murray (eds), *Studies in the History of the Worship in Scotland*, Edinburgh, ²1996, p. 37-57 [= Donaldson, 'Reformation to Covenant'].

—, *The Faith of the Scots*, London 1990 [= Donaldson, *The Faith of the Scots*].

—, 'A Scottish Liturgy in the Reign of James VI', *Miscellany of the Scottish History Society* 10 (1965), p. 89-117 [= Donaldson, 'A Scottish Liturgy'].

—, *The Scottish Reformation*, Cambridge 1960 [= Donaldson, *Scottish Reformation*].

—, *The Making of the Scottish Prayer Book of 1637*, Edinburgh 1954 [= Donaldson, *The Making of the Scottish Prayer Book*].

Fasti Ecclesiae Scoticanae medii aevi ad annum 1638. Revised Edition, ed. D. E. R. Watt – A. L. Murray (*Publications of the Scottish Record Society – New Series* 25), Edinburgh 2003.

Fasti Ecclesiae Scoticanae: The Succession of Ministers in the Church of Scotland from the Reformation, ed. H. Scott et al., Edinburgh ²1981.

P. Foresta, 'Transregional Reformation: Synods and Consensus in the Early Reformed Churches', *Journal of Early Modern Christianity* 2 (2015), p. 189-203 [= Foresta, 'Transregional Reformation'].

W. R. Foster, *The Church before the Covenants: The Church of Scotland 1596-1638*, Edinburgh - London 1975 [= Foster, *The Church*].

E. B. Fryde et al., *Handbook of British Chronology*, Cambridge 2003.

J. Goodare, 'How Archbishop Spottiswoode became an episcopalian', *Renaissance and Reformation Review* 32 (2006), p. 83-103 [= Goodare, 'How Archbishop Spottiswoode became an episcopalian'].

P. Ha, *English Presbyterianism 1590-1640*, Stanford (CA) 2011.

I. Hazlett, 'Reformed Theology in Confessions and Catechisms to c. 1620', in D. Fergusson – M. Elliot (eds), *History of Scottish Theology*, 3 vols, Oxford – New York 2019, vol. 1, p. 189-209 [= Hazlett, 'Reformed Theology in Confessions and Catechisms'].

—, 'Church and Church/State Relations', in U. L. Lehner – R. A. Muller – A. G. Roeber (eds), *The Oxford Handbook of Early Modern Theology, 1600-1800*, New York 2016, p. 242-258.

—, 'Vestures of the Faith: Three Scottish Confessions, 1560-1616', in J. C. Stewart (ed.), *A Useable Past? Belief, Worship, and Song in Reformation Context*, Edinburgh 2013, p. 1-30 [= Hazlett, 'Vestures of the Faith'].

—, 'Playing God's Card: Knox and Fasting, 1565-66', in R. Mason (ed.), *John Knox and the British Reformations*, Aldershot 1998, p. 176-198 [= Hazlett, 'Playing God's Card'].

G. D. Henderson, *Presbyterianism*, Aberdeen 1954 [= Henderson, *Presbyterianism*].

—, 'Arminianism in Scotland', *London Quarterly and Holborn Review* 157 (1932), p. 493-504 [= Henderson, 'Arminianism in Scotland'].

H. Jedin, *Geschichte des Konzils von Trent,* 3 vols, Freiburg 1951 [= Jedin, *Geschichte*].

J. Kirk, '«The Polities of the Best Reformed Churches»: Scottish Achievements and English Aspirations in Church Government after the Reformation', in J. Kirk (ed.), *Patterns of Reform: Continuity and Change in the Reformation Church*, Edinburgh 1989, p. 334-367 [= Kirk, '«The Polities of the Best Reformed Churches»'].

M. Lee Jr, *Government by Pen: Scotland under James VI and I*, Urbana – London 1980 [= Lee, *Government by Pen*].

—, 'James VI and the Revival of Episcopacy in Scotland, 1596-1600', *Church History* 43 (1974), p. 50-64 [= Lee, 'James VI and the Revival of Episcopacy'].

J. C. Lees, *The Abbey of Paisley from its Foundation till its Dissolution*, Paisley 1878 [= Lees, *The Abbey of Paisley*].

A. R. MacDonald, 'Church and State in Scotland from the Reformation to the Covenanting Revolution', in I. Hazlett (ed.), *A Companion to the Reformation in Scotland, ca. 1425-1638*, Leiden – Boston 2022, p. 607-629.

CONCILIUM ABERDONIENSE ECCLESIAE SCOTICANAE – 1616

—, 'James VI and I, the Church of Scotland, and British Ecclesiastical Convergence', *Historical Journal* 48/44 (2005), p. 885-903 [= MacDonald, 'James VI and I'].

—, 'James VI and the General Assembly, 1586-1625', in J. Goodare – M. Lynch (eds), *The Reign of James VI*, East Linton 2000, p. 170-185 [= MacDonald, 'James VI and the General Assembly'].

—, *The Jacobean Kirk, 1567-1625: Sovereignty, Polity, and Liturgy*, Ashgate 1980 [= MacDonald, *The Jacobean Kirk*].

D. MacMillan, *The Aberdeen Doctors: A Notable Group of Scottish Theologians of the First Episcopal Period, 1610 to 1638*, London 1909 [= MacMillan, *The Aberdeen Doctors*].

T. M. McCoog SJ, *The Society of Jesus in Ireland, Scotland, and England, 1589-1597: Building the Faith of Saint Peter upon the King of Spain's Monarchy*, Abingdon (Oxon.) – New York 2016 [= McCoog, *The Society of Jesus*].

C. G. McCrie, *The Confessions of the Church of Scotland: Their Evolution and History. The Seventh Series of the Chalmers Lectures*, Edinburgh 1907 [= McCrie, *The Confessions of the Church of Scotland*].

J. M. McDougall, 'Popular Festive Practices in Reformation Scotland', in W. I. P. Hazlett (ed.), *A Companion to the Reformation in Scotland, ca. 1525-1638, Frameworks of Change and Development*, Leiden – Boston 2022, p. 468-486 [= McDougall, 'Popular Festive Practices'].

T. McInally, *The Sixth Scottish University. The Scots Colleges Abroad: 1575 to 1799*, Leiden – Boston 2011 [= McInally, *Sixth Scottish University*].

W. McMillan, *The Worship of the Scottish Reformed Church, 1550-1638. The Hastie Lectures in the University of Glasgow, 1930*, Dunfermline – Edinburgh – London 1931 [= McMillan, *The Worship*].

T. Maruyama, *The Ecclesiology of Theodore Beza: The Reform of the True Church* (*Travaux d'Humanisme et Renaissance* 166), Genève 1976 [= Maruyama, *The Ecclesiology of Theodore Beza*].

W. D. Maxwell, *A History of Worship in the Church of Scotland*, London – Glasgow 1955 [= Maxwell, *A History of Worship*].

S. Mechie, 'Episcopacy in Post-Reformation Scotland', *Scottish Journal of Theology* 8 (1955), p. 20-35. [= Mechie, 'Episcopacy'].

D. G. Mullan, *Scottish Puritanism 1590-1638*, Oxford 2000 [= Mullan, *Scottish Puritanism*].

—, *Episcopacy in Scotland: The History of an Idea, 1560-1638*, Edinburgh 1986 [= Mullan, *Episcopacy in Scotland*].

—, 'Revolution, Consensus, and Controversy in Reformation Scotland', in W. I. P. Hazlett (ed.), *A Companion to the Reformation in Scotland, ca. 1525-1638, Frameworks of Change and Development*, Leiden – Boston 2022, p. 149-176 [= 'Revolution, Consensus, and Controversy'].

Oxford Dictionary of National Biography, Oxford 2004-, online edition [= *ODNB*].

W. B. Patterson, *King James VI and I and the Reunion of Christendom*, Cambridge 1997 [= Patterson, *King James*].

S. J. Reid, *Humanism and Calvinism: Andrew Melville and the Universities of Scotland, 1560-1625*, Aldershot 2011 [= Reid, *Humanism and Calvinism*].

G. M. Richard, '*Clavis Cantici*: A Key to the Reformation in Early Modern Scotland', in A. C. Denlinger (ed.), *Reformed Orthodoxy in Scotland: Essays on Scottish Theology 1560-1775*, London – New York 2015, p. 157-173 [= Richard, '*Clavis Cantici*'].

A. Roberts, 'Jesuit Missions in the Highlands: Three Phases', *Journal of Jesuit Studies* 7 (2020), p. 103-116 [= Roberts, 'Jesuit Missions in the Highlands'].

A. Rosie, *Scottish Handwriting 1500-1700*, [Edinburgh] 1994.

G. J. Schochet, *Patriarchalism in Political Thought: The Authoritarian Family and Political Speculation and Attitudes especially in Seventeenth-Century England*, Oxford 1975 [= Schochet, *Patriarchalism in Political Thought*].

Selections from Wodrow's Biographical Collections: Divines of the North-East of Scotland, ed. R. Lippe, Aberdeen 1890 [= Lippe, *Selections*].

D. G. Selwyn, 'The First Scottish Episcopacy', *Church Quarterly Review* 180 (1920), p. 193-218 [= Selwyn, 'The First Scottish Episcopacy'].

D. Shaw, *The General Assemblies of the Church of Scotland, 1560-1600: Their Origins and Development*, Edinburgh 1964 [= Shaw, *General Assemblies*].

G. G. Simpson, *Scottish Handwriting, 1150-1650: An Introduction to the Reading of Documents*, East Linton 1998.

K. Spierling, *Infant Baptism in Reformation Geneva: The Shaping of a Community, 1536-1564*, Aldershot 2005 [= Spierling, *Infant Baptism*].

B. D. Spinks, 'The Emergence of a Reformed Worship Tradition', in W. I. P. Hazlett (ed.), *A Companion to the Reformation in Scotland, ca. 1525-1638*, Leiden – Boston 2022, p. 258-285 [= Spinks, 'Emergence of a Reformed Worship Tradition'].

R. S. Spurlock, 'Catholicism in Scotland to 1603', in J. Kelly – J. McCafferty (eds), *The Oxford History of British and Irish Catholicism, Volume I: 1530-*

1640, Oxford 2023, p. 68-88 [= Spurlock, 'Catholicism in Scotland to 1603'].

—, 'Post-Reformation Scottish Catholic Survival', in W. I. P. Hazlett (ed.), *A Companion to the Reformation in Scotland, ca. 1525-1638*, Leiden – Boston 2022, p. 578-604 [= Spurlock, 'Post-Reformation Scottish Catholic Survival'].

—, 'The Laity and the Structure of the Catholic Church in Early Modern Scotland', in R. Armstrong – T. Ó hAnnracháin (eds.), *Insular Christianity. Alternative Models of the Church in Britain and Ireland, c.1570–c.1700*, Manchester 2012. p. 231-251 [= Spurlock, 'Laity and the Structure of the Catholic Church in Early Modern Scotland'].

M. Todd, 'Bishops in the Kirk: William Cowper of Galloway and the Puritan Episcopacy of Scotland', *Scottish Journal of Theology* 57/53 (2004), p. 300-312 [= Todd, 'Bishops in the Kirk'].

—, *The Culture of Protestantism in Early Modern Scotland*, London - New Haven (CT) 2002 [= Todd, *Culture of Protestantism*].

J. C. Whytock, *«An Educated Clergy»: Scottish Theological Education and Training in the Kirk and Secession, 1560-1850*, Milton Keynes 2007 [= Whytock, *Scottish Theological Education*].

R. Wodrow, *Early Letters of Robert Wodrow, 1698-1709* (*Publications of the Scottish History Society* 3/24), ed. D. W. Sharp, Edinburgh 1937.

—, *The Correspondence of Robert Wodrow edited from Manuscripts in the Library of the Faculty of Advocates, Edinburgh*, ed. T. McCrie, 6 vols, Edinburgh 1843 [Wodrow, *Correspondence*].

J. Wormald, 'The Headaches of Monarchy: Kingship and the Kirk in the Early Seventeenth Century', in J. Goodare – A. A. MacDonald (eds), *Sixteenth-Century Scotland: Essays in Honour of Michael Lynch*, Leiden 2008, p. 367-393 [= Wormald, 'The Headaches of Monarchy'].

—, '«No bishop, no king»: The Scottish Jacobean Episcopate, 1600-1635', in B. Vogler (éd.), *Miscellanea Historiae Ecclesiasticae VIII. Colloque de Strasbourg (Septembre 1983) sur l'institution et les pouvoirs dans les églises de l'antiquité à nos jours* (*Bibliothèque de la Revue d'Histoire Ecclésiastique* 68), Bruxelles 1987, p. 259-297 [= Wormald, 'The Scottish Jacobean Episcopate'].

M. Yellowlees, *«So strange a monster as a Jesuite»: The Society of Jesus in Sixteenth-Century Scotland*, Colonsay 2003.

CONCILIUM ABERDONIENSE ECCLESIAE SCOTICANAE
1616

CONSPECTUS MANUSCRIPTORUM ET EDITIONUM

( ) = not extant or missing
——— = directly from
- - - = partly from

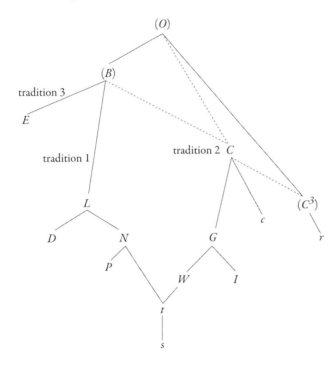

Manuscripts

(O) Register and original records, not extant
(B) A pre-1638 Book of the Universal Kirk (up to 1616), not extant

Tradition 1

L Glasgow University Library, Special Collections, MS Gen 1122
D Glasgow University Library, Special Collections, MS Gen 1132
N National Library of Scotland, Edinburgh, Adv. 17.1.8 [or MS 1766]

Tradition 2

C   British Library, London, Archives and Manuscripts, Add MS 4739
(C³) Missing or not extant

1048   CONSPECTUS MANUSCRIPTORUM ET EDITIONUM

G   Glasgow University Library, Special Collections, MS Gen 1195
W   New College Library, Edinburgh, MS CALD
I   National Library of Scotland, Edinburgh, Adv. 33. 6. 1

Tradition 3

E   Centre for Research Collections, Edinburgh University Library, Dc. 3. 54

Editions

r   Calderwood, *True History* (1678/1679)
p   *BUK* - ed. Peterkin (1839)
t   *BUK* - ed. Thomson (1845)
c   Calderwood, *History*, ed. Thomson (1849)
s   *Acts and Proceedings*, ed. Shaw (2004)
Spott   Spottiswoode, *History,* ed. Napier – Russell (1847/1851)

GENERALL ASSEMBLIE OF THE KIRK OF SCOTLAND, HALDEN AT ABERDEIN THE 13 DAY OF AUGUST 1616: WHERE WAS PRESENT THE ERLE OF MONTROIS, COMMISSIONER FOR HIS MAJESTIE, LORDS AND BARONES, TOGETHER WITH THE ARCHBISHOPS, BISHOPS, AND COMMISSIONERS FROM PRES-BITRIES.

PROCLAMATION BE THE KING FOR HOLDING THE GENERAL ASSEMBLY AT ABERDEEN, IN AUGUST 1616.

James, be the grace of God, King of Great Britane, France, and Ireland,

---

2 13 day] Saturday   **3** Erle of Montrois] John Graham (1573-1626), fourth earl of Montrose, and a member of the King's Privy Council. He was also on the unified ecclesiastical Court of High Commission established by James in 1610 along with episcopal jurisdiction. See *ODNB, ad vocem*   Commissioner] representative of the Scottish monarch in either Parliament or the Church's General Assembly   **5** Archbishops] the two historic archdioceses in Scotland were St Andrews and Glasgow   Bishops] including Glasgow and St Andrews, there were thirteen bishoprics, revived with functioning ecclesiastical jurisdiction in 1610; they had continued to exist nominally and with some titular bishops after the Reformation of 1560, but with their revenue mostly retained by lay patrons including the Crown   Commissioners from Presbitries] presbyteries incorporated parishes in districts or regions generally smaller than dioceses, and commissioners were a selection of appointed presbytery ministers and elders at a General Assembly. The elders are to be distinguished from 'lay commissioners', delegates of the Crown, nobility, shires, and towns (even if in fact they might also be elders) and who represented the secular authority   **7/8** Proclamation – 1616] this text is the second draft (19 July) and published royal proclamation of the act passed by the Privy Council ('the Lords of Secret Council') on the previous day (18 July); for the latter see *RPCS*, vol. 10 (1891), p. 580-581. The main differences are a switch from third to first person plural when the King is the subject, and the addition of legal formulae in the last two sentences. Text also in *BUK* (Thomson), vol. 3 (1845), p. 1114-1115 (the text reproduced above); Calderwood, *History*, vol. 7 (1845), p. 220-221; Shaw, *Acts and Proceedings*, p. 1509-1510   **9** King of Great Britane] not an official title, but preferred by James who saw himself as monarch of a united kingdom rather than as monarch of two kingdoms (as in a double monarchy)

---

1 halden] *intellege* held   **7/43** Proclamation – Consilii] *inserui*   **9** be] *intellege* by

1050 CONCILIUM ABERDONIENSE ECCLESIAE SCOTICANAE – 1616

10 Defender of the Faith: To our Lovits, etc. Messingers, our Shireffs in that part, conjunctly and severally, specially constitute, greeting.

For as much as the Prelats and reverend Fathers of the Kirk, forseeing that there is a great decay in religion, and a grouth and increase of Poprie within this our kingdome – and that the samen is like to produce many dangerous
15 effects against the Estates, both in Kirk and Policie – and the saids Prelats having gravely advised upon the best and readiest means both for preventing and suppressing of this grouth of Popery, and for reforming of the disorders and abuses flowing therfra, they have found that nothing is more expedient for effectuating their good works than a National Assembly and meeting of the
20 whole Kirk. And by their petitions presented unto us they have humbly craved our license for the holding of the said Assembly; lykas we allowing of their goode advice and opinion in this point, and being willing to hold hand to them in all and every thing which may procure the good of the Kirk – we have most willingly and freely given and granted our consent, license, permission
25 and allowance for holding of the said Assembly, and ordaining the same to hold at our Burgh of Aberdeen, and to begin, God willing, upon the 13 day of August next approaching, in this instant year of God, 1616 yeers.

Our will is heirfor, and we charge you straitly, and command that incontinent these letters seen, ye pass and in our name and authority make publica-
30 tion thereof, be open proclamation at the Mercat Cross of the head burrowes of this our kingdom and other places needful, wherethrough none pretend ignorance of the same. And that ye warn all and sundry Archbishops, Bishops, Commissioners from the Kirks, and others having vote in the said Assembly, that they repair in due and lawfull tyme to our Burgh of Aberdeen against the
35 said 13ᵗʰ day of August nixt, and assist the said Assembly and meeting with

---

10 Defender of the Faith] a title appertaining to the English Crown only, originally granted by the Pope to Henry VIII **16/17** preventing – Popery] the King's short missive from England (12 July) authorising this act of Privy Council had not only highlighted this, but also 'to procure an uniformity in religion amongst our subjects', a statement omitted from both the Privy Council act and the royal proclamation. See *RPCS*, vol. 10 (1891), p. 581

---

10 Lovits] *intellege* dear subjects   **11** constitute] *intellege* appointed   **15** Policie] *intellege* civil government   **16** gravely advised upon] *intellege* consulted on   **18** therfra] *intellege* from that   **21** lykas] *intellege* similarly   allowing of] *intellege* accepting   **22** hold hand to] *intellege* endorse   **26** hold] *intellege* convene   **27** instant] *intellege* current   **28** heirfor] *intellege* for that   charge] *intellege* order straitly] *intellege* firmly   incontinent] *intellege* immediately   **29** pass] *intellege* implement   **30** Mercat] *intellege* Market   head burrowes] *intellege* chief burghs (towns)   **31** wherethrough] *intellege* whereby   **32** warn] *intellege* summon **34** against] *intellege* by

CONCILIUM ABERDONIENSE ECCLESIAE SCOTICANAE – 1616   1051

their presence and votes, and doe and performe that which to their charges in
such cases appertaines, and they will answer upon the contrair at their perill.
The which to doe we committ to you, conjunctly and severally, our full pouer
by these our Letters, delivering them, by you duely execute and indorsit, again
40 to the beirer.

Given under our Signet, at Edinburgh, the 19 day of July, and of our
reignes the 49 and 14 yeirs, 1616.

Per Actum Secreti Consilii.

Sessio 1ᴬ· 13. Augusti.

45   A Fast was indicted, be Proclamation and sound of trumpet, to be keeped
this day: Patrick Forbes, Laird of Corse, taught in the morning; the Bishop of
Sanct Andrews before noon; Mr William Forbes after noon.

---

42 49] as King of Scotland since 1566   14] as King of England and Ireland (and Great
Britain) since 1603   **44** Sessio – Augusti] this record of the first or opening session is
a paraphrased reconstruction by Calderwood interspersed with some polemical glosses
45 A Fast] although it abolished fast days and fasting by individuals as a vain work of
merit, the reformed Church of Scotland instituted solemn, public, collective fasting for
Eucharistic and special national occasions or crises, according to the Old Testament
and the Genevan model. The Scottish Kirk was the only Reformation Church to have a
prescribed order for public fasting in its service book, the *Book of Common Order*. See
McMillan, *The Worship*, p. 330-333 and Hazlett, 'Playing God's Card'   **46** Patrick
Forbes] (1564-1635), minister of Keith, Banffshire. Sharply anti-Catholic writer from
the gentry class, in polity he gradually moved from presbyterian to episcopal
sympathies, becoming bishop of Aberdeen in 1618 and patron of the six 'Aberdeen
Doctors'. See *ODNB* and *DSCHT, ad vocem*   Corse] estate with a castle, north of
Aberdeen   **46/47** Bishop of Sanct Andrews] i.e. John Spottiswoode   **47** Mr] not
abbreviation for 'Minister' or 'Mister', but for Master of Arts (*Magister*)   William
Forbes] (1585-1634). Minister of Moneymusk, Aberdeenshire, he was a scholar-
theologian of alleged but unsubstantiated Arminian tendencies who had travelled and
studied in northern and eastern Europe. Soon after the Assembly he was appointed
minister of St Nicholas Kirk, Aberdeen, and later the first bishop of the new diocese of
Edinburgh. His appeal to James VI lay in his irenical theology of conceivable
reconciliation of Protestant and Roman Churches based on alignment to the norms of

---

36 votes] *intellege* opinions   **37** answer upon the contrair] *intellege* disobey
41 Signet] *intellege* little seal   **42** 49] 44 *C c*   **44** Sessio – Augusti] *inserui, sed om.
omnes Mss et editiones.* Cfr 62/63 et al., *forma eiusmodi iam in omnibus Mss*   1a]
intellege prima   **45/64** A – Papists] *C G W I r t c s – L D N P hab. solummodo*
Exhortatione being made be [Patrick Forbes] Mr Johne Spottiswoode archbishope of
St Androis was chosen moderator   **45** indicted] *intellege* announced   **46** taught]
intellege preached

1052   CONCILIUM ABERDONIENSE ECCLESIAE SCOTICANAE – 1616

The King ordained by his Letter: the Primat to rule the Clergie, and his Commissioner, the Earle of Montrose, to order the Laitie; and desired the Assembly to advise upon certain overtures for the rooting out of Popery, which he promised to authorize be his lawes. So Mr John Spotswood, Archbishop of Sanct Androis, stepped into the Moderators place without election. Secretar Hamiltoun and the Lord Carnegie were appointed by the King to assist the Earle of Montrose. The Catalogue of the Presbytries was not called,

50

Scripture and Christian antiquity. See *ODNB* and *DSCHT, ad vocem*   **48** Primat] a courtesy title only sometimes applied to the archbishop of St Andrews   **49** Laitie] i.e. the non-ecclesiastical commissioners and other attendees from the gentry and town councils, not to be confused with elders who as presbyters were ordained in Reformed thought   **50** the rooting out of Popery] the chief pretext for convening the Assembly   **51** John Spotswood] John Spottiswoode (1565-1639). Formerly a presbyterian, he came to favour both pragmatic episcopacy and Erastian concepts of Church-state relations and was a royal privy councillor. See Goodare, 'How Archbishop Spottiswoode became an episcopalian'. Previously archbishop of Glasgow (consecrated in England by some English bishops) and becoming archbishop of St Andrews in 1615, he was the churchman most identified with King James's religious policies (if more diplomatic), also sharing the latter's doctrinal Calvinism. His *History* (posthumously published 1847-1851) was an apology for royal and episcopal strategies in the Church. He corresponded with Isaac Casaubon in Paris whose via media notions in religion influenced James. See *ODNB* and *DSCHT, ad vocem*   **52** Moderators] Moderator is the chairman of presbyteries, synods, and general assemblies, but with no inherent authority beyond the Reformed and presbyterian concept of *primus inter pares*, and elected by an Assembly for one year only. Under James's Church policy, there was a tendency to re-elect bishops as 'constant moderators' as a controversial compromise; Spottiswoode became a constant moderator of the General Assembly   **53** Secretar Hamiltoun] Thomas Hamilton (1563-1637), earl of Melrose and of Haddington, and Lord Binning, at this time Secretary of State and Lord President of the Court of Session (the Scottish supreme court), and a moderate enforcer of the royal episcopalian policy. Educated in Paris, his commitment to Protestantism has been viewed as formal and prudent. See *ODNB, ad vocem*   Lord Carnegie] David Carnegie (1574/1575-1658), Lord Carnegie of Kinnaird. An important government functionary, he was frequently a royal commissioner on civil and ecclesiastical bodies; he was also a member of the Court of Session. See *ODNB, ad vocem*   **54/55** The – limited] A properly presbyterian Assembly would have recorded which presbytery commissioners – be they ministers or elders – had been nominated to attend the Assembly by patrons, i.e. landowners or gentry who paid ministers' salaries and paid for the maintenance of the church building – hence 'limited' – and those who were freely or autonomously nominated by the presbytery. The subtext here is that the Assembly was structurally and procedurally dominated by bishops and other King's men, and so biassed against presbyteries. Cfr notes for lines 5/6 and 59/63

---

50 overtures] *intellege* proposals   **54** Catalogue] *intellege* register; roll-call

CONCILIUM ABERDONIENSE ECCLESIAE SCOTICANAE – 1616   1053

55 nor Commissioners considered, whether free or limited. A number of Lords and Barones decored the Assembly with silks and sattins, but without lawfull Commission to vote. Bishops had no Commissions from Presbytries. The Moderators of the Presbytries came according to the Bishops Missives.

The whole Bishops, and Lords of Councel that were present, together 60 with the Kings Commissioner, and his Assisters, the Secretary, and the Lord Carnegy, and fifteen other Lords and Barones, with twenty Ministers, or thereby, were appointed to sit upon the Privie Conference. The first four dayes were spent in preaching, renewing old acts, and making some new acts against Papists.

65   SESSIO 2ᴬ· 14 AUGUSTI.

In the second session, efter Bishope Bannatyne had taught upon the Epistle of Jude, 20, 21, 22, were read certain conclusions, agreed upon by the privie conference for order taking with papists:

Forsameikle as the most urgent causes of the convocation of this present 70 Assemblie is to obviat the great increase of Papistrie within this realme, and to

---

66/67 Epistle – Jude 20 21 22] cfr Iudae 20-23

55/58 A – Missives] the point of these sentences (part of the interpolation from a disapproving presbyterian editor Calderwood) was to emphasise that the Assembly's usual procedures and conventions were being flouted in the episcopal and royal interests   **59** Lords of Councel] the general aristocratic body of active government or royal servants who sat in the unicameral Parliament as members of the first and second Estates, or were members of the royal privy council, or headed government administration, finance, and justice systems   **62** Privie Conference] a select committee which met separately and privately to discuss the agenda in advance of the plenary sessions   The first four dayes] i.e. 13-16 August   **66** Bishope Bannatyne] Adam Bannatyne or Ballantyne or Bellenden (c. 1572-1648), recently appointed bishop of Dunblane; previously an opponent of episcopacy. See *ODNB, ad vocem*

---

56 decored] *intellege* adorned   **58** Missives] *intellege* letters of credentials   **59** The whole] *intellege* all the   **64** Papists] *C r add.* The first four dayes wer spent in preaching, renewing old acts, and making some new acts against papists, as if no acts had beene made against papists before at assemblies or parliaments. But thus would they protract the tyme, that ministers being wearied might withdraw themselfes, speciallie these that came from the farre south, and then they might treat of the maters cheeflie aimed at – *r* (p. 657) *add.* I have here subjoined the Proceedings and Acts of this Assembly, as they are extant in the Clerk's scrolles   **65** 2ª] *intellege* secunda   **66/68** In – papists] *C G W I C, sed om. r t s*   **68** order taking with] *intellege* measures concerning   **69** Forsameikle] *intellege* forasmuch   **70** is] *intellege* are (as Scots singular form can have plural sense)

1054　CONCILIUM ABERDONIENSE ECCLESIAE SCOTICANAE – 1616

try out the just causes heirof, to the effect that sufficient remedies may be
provided for redressing of the same in all tyme coming; and that it is found be
the whole Assemblie, that ane great part of the causes of the said increase
relyes partlie upon the slackness of the Ministrie in thair holie professioun,
and partlie upon the not executing of the laws, alsweill civil as ecclesiasticall,
against such persons as either were excommunicat themselves, and oppinly
contemnit the said censure – or quho intertaines, receipts, and maintaines
quho were excommunicat – or quho were traffiquers against the true religioun
presentlie profest within this realme. For remeid quherof, the whole Assemblie in ane voyce hes statute and ordaint in maner after following:

[1] In the first, For the better tryall and discovering of Apostates, it is
statute and ordainit, that quhosoever hes confessit the true religioun
presentlie professit within this realme, and hes subscryvit the samein, and hes
received the holy sacrament of the Supper of the Lord, and communicat conforme to the ordour observit within this realme; if at any tyme heirafter he or
sche be found any tyme, either to reason against the said true religioun
presentlie profest within this realme, or any article or heid therof, or to raile
against the same, or els directlie or indirectlie to be a seducer or perverter of
uthers from the said trueth presentlie profest, as said is; or if he or sche be
found to receipt or intertaine any traffiqueing Papists, Jesuites, or Seminarie
Priests: Any of the said facts or deids salbe a sufficient cause of apostasie, and
these doers salbe reput, haldin and punishit as apostates.

[2] And because the probatioun in the saids causes is difficile and almost
impossible, in respect that the saids deids are committit covertlie, and quherin

---

75 the not executing of the laws] severe penal laws were already on the statute book of
parliamentary legislation, but only rarely applied with full force　**78** true religioun]
the Reformation faith as embodied in the parliamentary *Scots Confession of Faith*
(1560), legalised by royal assent (1567), and supplemented by the *King's Confession* (or
Negative Confession) of 1581. See also *Synod of Fife*, p. 52-54　**81** Apostates] in this
context, crypto-Catholics or 'Church Papists' externally conforming to the Reformed
Church　**85** the ordour] order of service as provided in the *Book of Common Order*
(sometimes known as *Knox's Liturgy*) and derived from the Genevan *Forme des prières*
90 Jesuites] see Yellowlees, '*So strange a monster as a Jesuiste*', p. 119-158; Roberts,
'Jesuit Missions in the Highlands', p. 113-116

---

71 try out] *intellege* investigate　**74** relyes] *intellege* depends　**75** alsweill civil as
ecclesiasticall] *intellege* both civil and ecclesiastical　**77** contemnit] *intellege* showed
contempt for　quho] *intellege* who　receipts] *intellege* resets; harbours; gives refuge
78 traffiquers] *intellege* conspirators　**79** remeid] *intellege* remedy　quherof]
intellege whereof; of which　**81** tryall] *intellege* investigation　**87** heid] *intellege*
chapter　**92** salbe] *intellege* shall be　haldin] *intellege* considered　**93** probatioun]
intellege prosecution　saids] plural adjective form of 'said'

CONCILIUM ABERDONIENSE ECCLESIAE SCOTICANAE – 1616

95 probatioun can hardly be deducit: Therefor it is statute, that in case uther
probatioun cannot be had, that it sall be lawfull to prove the samein be the
aith of the partie alledgit committer of the saids facts and deids; and that it
sall not be leisum to him to refuse to give his oath in the saids matters, upon
quhatsoevir colour or pretence of criminall actioun, or uthers following ther-
100 upon: and to this effect that ane supplicatioun be directit to his Majestie, that
it might please his Hienes to sett downe ane ordinance for ratificatioun of the
former statute, to the effect it may be receivit in all Judicatories.

[3] Item, It is statute, if any person or persons quho hes conformit himselfe to the true religioun presentlie profest within this realme, and hes
105 subscryvit the Confessioun of the Faith, and receivit the Communioun, if at
any tyme heirafter he or they doe not haunt the ordinar exercises of religioun,
being admonischit be thair ordinar Pastour *trina admonitione directed from
the Sessioun of the Church,* the same being proven salbe ane sufficient cause to
punish them as hald and repute apostates.

110 [4] Item, It is statute and ordainit, that quhatsumevir person, known of
before tyme to have bein a Papist, and after his reconcileing to the Kirk, he
salbe tryed and found to weare and beare under person Agnus Dei, beids,

---

107 trina admonitione] cfr Matth. 18, 15-18

97/99 it – actioun] and thus no right of silence that could have been exercised due to
risk of self-incrimination **101/102** the former statute] i.e. resolution [1] above
107 trina admonitione] triple warning. Cfr 'De sententia excommunicationis', in
Decretales Gregorii P. IX, lib. 5, tit. 39, cap. 48, hrsg. A. Friedberg (*Corpus iuris canonici
2: Decretalium collectiones*), Leipzig 1881, col. 909-910. Calderwood's interpolation was
intended to recall that, in the presbyterian order, the exercise of discipline at the
parochial level was vested in the Kirk Session of elders and minister or pastor, and that
such individual office-bearers could only act by delegation, not by virtue of any
individual or sacerdotal right **110/116** 4 – apostates] Calderwood recorded the
emendation of this section made by Spottiswoode in the margin of the not extant
original Register. See Calderwood, *True History*, p. 658; *History*, vol. 8 (1849),
'Appendix', p. 97 **112** Agnus Dei] any form of image of the Lamb of God was
disapproved of in view of its association with the adoration of the sacrament and the
sacrifice of the Mass

95 deducit] *intellege* conducted **96** prove] *intellege* try; test **97** aith] *intellege* oath
partie] *intellege* involved; concerned **98** leisum] *intellege* permissible **99** actioun]
intellege charge **101** Hienes] *intellege* Highness **102** Judicatories] *intellege* civil and
ecclesiastical courts **106** haunt] *intellege* attend, frequent ordinar exercises of
religioun] *intellege* regular worship **109** hald and repute apostates] *intellege* apostates
by habit and repute **110** quhatsumevir] *intellege* whatsoever **112** tryed] *intellege*
examined under person] *in (O) eras. Spott. secundum r* under] *intellege* on their
beids] *intellege* Rosary beads

1056 CONCILIUM ABERDONIENSE ECCLESIAE SCOTICANAE – 1616

croces, crucifixes, or to have in their houses idols and images, or in thair books
sick things as befor they have superstitiouslie used, the samein sall inferre just
suspitioun of apostasie, and falling back in the saids errours and they being
convict thereof, salbe haldin and repute as apostates.

[5] Item, It is statute and ordainit in all tyme heirafter, quhensoever any
Minister sall receive any Papist returning from his errours to the besome of the
Kirk, that at the tyme of his receiving, the Minister sall first take his aith
solemnlie sworne, that he sall declare the veritie of his faith and beliefe in
every particular point and article, contained in the Confessioun of the Faith,
quhilk salbe speirit at him; and that immediatlie therafter the said Minister
sall examine him particularlie upon everie heid conteinit in the Confession of
Faith, and receive his particular answer therupon affirmativé, conforme to the
samein; utherwayes that he sall not be receivit.

[6] Item, It is statute anent the wyves of Noblemen, Gentlemen and
others professing Papistry quho recepte traffiqueing Papists, Jesuites, and Seminarie Preists, as if the same were done against the will and knowledge of thair
husbands, that all such wemin salbe callit and conveinit for the said recept and
intertainment; and thair being convict therfor, that they salbe wardit ay and
quhill they find sufficient cautioun to abstaine from the lyke receipt or intertainment, in any tyme comeing, under a certaine paine – but prejudice of any
actioun that may be competent against thair husbands, conforme to the laws
of this realme.

---

113 idols] statuettes or figures of Jesus, Mary, the saints and so on   **118/119** besome
of the Kirk] the 'bosom of the Church' is a concept closely associated with that of
'Mother Church' in patristic and Catholic traditions, and inherited by the Reformers,
e.g. Calv., *Instit.* (1559), 4, 1, 1 (vol. 2, p. 187)

113 croces] *intellege* crosses   crucifixes] *in (O) ins. Spott. secundum r* on their persons
114 sick] *intellege* such   samein] *intellege* same   inferre] *intellege* lead to   **115/**
116 and¹ – apostates] *eras. Spott.*   **122** quhilk salbe speirit at him] *intellege* on which
he shall be interrogated   **125** utherwayes] *intellege* otherwise   **126** anent] *intellege*
regarding   **129** wemin] *intellege* women   callit] *C c add.* (befor the High
commission, copeis beare)   conveinit] *intellege* summoned   **130** therfor] *intellege* for
that   wardit] *intellege* kept in custody   **130/131** ay and quhill] *intellege* until
132 under] *intellege* subject to   paine] *intellege* punishment   but prejudice of]
intellege without detracting from the right of

CONCILIUM ABERDONIENSE ECCLESIAE SCOTICANAE – 1616   1057

[7] Item, Because the speciall cause of increase of Papistrie proceids upon the not putting to execution of the statutes and acts of Parliament made against traffiqueing Papists, Jesuites, and Seminarie Priests: that therfor a supplication be direcit to his Majestie, that it will please his Hienes to take such ordour that the loveable lawis and acts of Parliament, made be his Majestie in tymes bypast against traffiqueing Papists, Jesuites, and Seminarie Priests, may be put to executioun, in all tymes comeing with all severitie.

[8] Item, It is ordainit, that the haill names of Papists recusants within this realme be givin in be the Commissioners of this present Assemblie to the Clerk, to be delyverit be him to the Archbishops of Sanct Androes and Glasgow, conforme to thair severall Provinces, to the effect they may be callit and conveinit before them in the Hie Commissioun, and punished as accords; but prejudice alwayes of uther ecclesiasticall censure and discipline of the Kirk statute agains them of befor.

[9] Item, It is ordainit that every ane of the Ministrie give up the names of such of thair paroch as hes past furth of the countrey, and not found catioun for thair behaviour and sincere professioun of the religioun foorth of the samein conforme to the act of Parliament, to the effect they may be callit, conveinit, and punischit conforme to the said act.

[10] Item, It is ordainit that the whole names of the persons excommunicat within this realme, quhilk salbe givin up be the Commissioners, be delyverit to the Bischop of every Dyocie, quho fall delyver a catalogue of the names to every Minister within his Dyocie, ordaining every Minister to make publick intimatioun thereof, at every ane of thair paroch kirks, upon Sonday, in tyme of divyne service, that no man pretend ignorance of the same; chargeing and inhibiteing every ane of thair paroch, that they neither receipt the said

---

135/137 Because – Priests] See *Act. Scot. Parl.*, 1587: 'Concerning the trial and punishment of the offences of the adversaries of the true religious presently professed within this realm', where the target is 'Jesuits or seminary priests'. In 1592, a further act was passed: 'Against Jesuits, seminary priests and their resetters [i.e. hosts or protectors]', and which also refers to 'trafficking papists'. There were further similar acts in 1600, 1607, and 1609   **142** Papists recusants] i.e. Roman Catholics refusing to attend Reformed worship   **146** Hie Commissioun] the supreme ecclesiastical court for the Church of Scotland when bishops are in place, established in 1610, superseding the authority of the General Assembly   **150** catioun] i.e. one who stands surety or takes responsibility for another's behaviour. In mind are Scots abroad who attend Mass

---

139 loveable] *intellege* laudable (*gallica lingua* louable)   **142** the haill] *intellege* all the
146 Hie] *intellege* High   **148** statute] *intellege* decreed   **149** ane] *intellege* one
150 hes past furth of] *intellege* have left   **151/152** foorth of the samein] *intellege* abroad   **155** quhilk] *intellege* which   givin up] *intellege* submitted

1058   CONCILIUM ABERDONIENSE ECCLESIAE SCOTICANAE – 1616

excommunicants, nor intercommune with them: certifieing them and they doe in the contrair, they salbe callit and conveinit as receipters of traffiqueing Papists and excommunicat persons, and be punischit for the same.

165 [11] Item, The Assemblie recommends to the care of Bischops within thair Dyocies, and Ministers within thair congregatiouns to travell with noblemen, gentlemen, and burgesses that ther be ordinar exercise of reiding and prayer within thair houses, as also ane prayer for the Kings Majestie and his children, after every meale. And that the Minister of every parish haunt the houses to see the same observed.

170   SESSIO 3^{A.} 15 AUGUSTI 1616.

[1] Item, Because ther are some pamphletts and bookes full of calumnies quyetlie sett foorth, and spred within this countrey be the Papists and enemies of the true religioun: therfor the Assemblie hes ordainit that Mr William Scott, Minister at Couper, and Mr William Struthers, Minister at Edinburgh, 175 the Laird of Corse, and the Bishop of Galloway sall make answers to the saids bookes and pamphletts, to the effect that therby the peiple may be instructit how to beware of the samein, and the said errours and calumnies may be refutit.

[2] Item, Because it is certainely informed that certaine wemen taks upon 180 them to bring up the youth in reiding, sewing, and uther exercises in schooles; under pretext and colour quherof, traffiqueing Papists, Jesuites, and Seminarie Preists hes thair appointit tymes of meeting; at quhilk tymes they catechise

---

166 ordinar exercise of reiding] i.e. regular Bible reading   **173/174** William Scott] or Scot (c. 1558-1642); strongly presbyterian and opponent of royal religious polices; author of *An Apologetical Narration* (see Bibliography). See *ODNB* and *DSCHT, ad vocem*   **174** Couper] Cupar, Fife   William Struthers] (c. 1576-1633). While supportive of the King's liturgical and episcopalian policies, he was opposed to royal supremacy in the Church. See *ODNB, ad vocem*   **175** Laird of Corse] i.e. Patrick Forbes (see above, l. 46)   Bishop of Galloway] William Couper or Cowper (1568-1619), bishop since 1612; a prolific writer of anti-Catholic and anti-presbyterian tracts as well as a keen patristician; a notable liturgist who drafted the proposed new liturgy for the Perth General Assembly in 1618. He advocated a mixed system of bishops and subordinate presbyterian courts. Cfr *ODNB* and *DSCHT, ad vocem*; see Todd, 'Bishops in the Kirk'

---

161 certifieing] *intellege* warning and] *intellege* that if **162** receipters] *intellege* hosts **168/169** And – observed] *t inser. ex C* **170** 3^a] *intellege* tertia **172** quyetlie sett foorth] *intellege* secretly published **175** the¹ – Galloway] *t inser. ex C* **181** colour quherof] *intellege* guise of which

CONCILIUM ABERDONIENSE ECCLESIAE SCOTICANAE – 1616   1059

and pervert the youth in their young and tender age in such sort that hardlie
therafter, by great paines and travells, can they be brocht fra their errours to
the acknowledging of the trueth presentlie professit within this realme: It is
therfor statute and ordainit that it sall not be leisum to quhatsumevir person
or persons to hold any schooles for teaching of the youth, or to teach them
therin except they first have the approbation of the Bishop of the Diocie, and
be first tryit be the Ministers of the Presbytrie quher they dwell and have thair
approbation to the effect forsaid.

[3] Item, Because ther is a great abuse in peiple passing to pilgrimages to
wells, to trees and auld chappels – as likewayes in putting up of banefyres:
Therfor it is ordainit, that the brethren of the Ministrie be diligent in teaching
of the peiple, and preaching against such abuses and superstitioun, to the
effect they may be recallit from the saids errours: as lykewayes that the Ministrie take diligent tryall of the names of those quho haunts these pilgrimages,
and to delate the same to the Archbischops of Sanct Androes and Glasgow,
every ane within thair awin provinces, to the effect they may be callit befor the
Hie Commissioun and punischit for the same. It is lykwayes ordainit that thair
names be delyverit to the Justices of Peace, with the places of thair pilgrimages,
and dayes of thair meetings; and that they may be requistit and desyrit to
attend upon the saids dayes of thair meetings, and to disturb and divert them
therfrom, be apprehending and punishing of them.

[4] Item, It is ordainit that every Minister give up the names of ydle song-
sters within thair parishes to the Justices of Peace, that they may be callit and
conveinit befor them and punischit as ydle vagabounds, conform to the Acts
of Parliament, and power given to the saids Justices of Peace theranent.

[5] Item, Because it is found that diverse of the said Jesuites, traffiqueing
Papists, and Seminarie Preists goes about, under the colour and pretext of
Doctours of Physick and Apothecaries, deceiving and perverting the peiple

---

191/192 pilgrimages to wells] most notably, the nationally popular Christ's Well near
Stirling. See McDougall, 'Popular Festive Practices', p. 476-477   **192** auld chappels
See *Act. Scot. Parl.*, 1581: 'Against passing in pilgrimage to chapels, wells and crosses,
and the superstitious observing of diverse other popish rights'. Cfr Burns, 'Enforcing
Uniformity', p. 120-121   **204** ydle songsters] wandering folk singers or minstrels who
were otherwise unemployed, seen as frivolous

---

183 hardlie] *intellege* only with difficulty   **184** travells] *intellege* exertions   fra]
intellege from   **186** quhatsumevir person] *intellege* any person whatsoever   **189** tryit]
intellege examined   **192** auld] *intellege* old   banefyres] *intellege* bonfires   **196** take
diligent tryall of] *L* properly inquire into   quho haunts] *intellege* who frequent
197 delate] *intellege* report   **201** requistit and desyrit] *intellege* requested and wanted
204 give up] *intellege* hand in   **207** theranent] *intellege* in that respect

1060 CONCILIUM ABERDONIENSE ECCLESIAE SCOTICANAE – 1616

from the true religioun profest within this countrie: Therfor ane supplicatioun wald be direct to his Majestie, that it wald please his Hienes to statute
and ordaine that none heirafter be sufferit to use and exercise the office of ane
Doctour of Physick or Apothecar, quhill first he have ane approbatioun from
the Bishop of the Dyocies, quher he makes his residence, of his conformitie in
religioun; as lykewayes from the Universities quher he learnit and studied, of
his qualification and sufficiencie in the said art.

[6] In the Assembly it was ordained: That forasmuch as His Majesty had
by proclamation recalled such as were gone forth of the country to be educated in the colleges of the Jesuits or other popish universities, within the space
of a year, upon pain to be declared incapable of succession either to goods or
lands, a trial and exact search should be made of all those that were sent or
gone into foreign parts within these last ten years; and that every minister
should send a particular note unto his ordinary of those within his parish that
were gone to follow his studies in places abroad, with their age, profession,
and families whereunto they appertained, to the end they may be known, and
the dangers prevented wherewith their corrupt education did threaten the
Church.

The quhilk day compeirit in presence of the haill Assemblie John Gordoun of Buckie, in name and at the direction of ane noble and potent Lord,
George Marqueis of Huntlie, and presentit a petitioun, direct be the said

---

218/228 In – Church] uniquely testified in Spottiswoode, *History*, vol. 3 (1851),
p. 235-236, and was presumably a resolution made by the Assembly in the fifth session
and that may have gone missing from the Clerk's papers   **220** the colleges of the
Jesuits] in mind would have been Scots Colleges at this time in Douai and Rome
staffed or directed by Jesuits. See *DSCHT*, entry 'Scots Colleges'; McInally, *Sixth
Scottish University*   **224** ordinary] i.e. bishop   **229/230** John Gordoun of Buckie]
presumably a kinsman of George Gordon, marquis of Huntly   **231** George Marqueis
of Huntlie] George Gordon (1561/1562-1636). Promoted from (sixth) earl to (first)
marquis in 1599, he was the leading Catholic magnate and sometime rebel in Scotland
who had a good personal – but often troubled – political relationship with King James.
He nominally and prudentially converted to the Reformed faith in 1588, and several
times thereafter, although intermittently excommunicated or exiled due to his private
involvement in religious and political Catholic causes. He also became a privy
councillor in 1599, but was sometimes suspended. The Kirk oscillated between
prosecuting and reconciling him. Cfr *ODNB, ad vocem*; *Synod of Fife*, p. 54, 57, 70, 74,
76; Spottiswoode, *History*, vol. 2 (1851), p. 23 and 26; vol. 3 (1851), p. 13-14, 62, 192, 208,
230, 232, and 235   Marqueis] marquis was the second most senior rank in the Scottish

---

214 quhill] *intellege* until   **215** quher] *intellege* where   **217** sufficiencie] *intellege*
competence   **218/228** In – Church] *deest in omn. Mss et editionibus*   **229** compeirit]
intellege appeared

CONCILIUM ABERDONIENSE ECCLESIAE SCOTICANAE – 1616

George, Marqueis of Huntlie, to the said Assemblie, subscrivit with his hand, craving to be absolved orderly from the sentence of excommunication, and desyring ane answer of the same to be given be the Assemblie; quherof the tenour followes, as is to be found in the end of this Assembly.

The Bishop of Sanct Androes presented ane letter direct from the Archbishop of Canterburie, together with ane uther letter from the Kings Majestie, concerning the absolutioun of the said Lord Marqueis from the sentence of excommunication made be the said Archbischop of Canterburie, quhilk were both red in presence of the said Assemblie, and ordainit to be registrat in the Acts of the Generall Assembly ad perpetuam rei memoriam, quherof the tenour followis:

[*1. The archbishop of Canterbury's letter to the archbishop of St Andrews*]
Salutem in Christo.

Because I understand that a General Assembly is shortly to be held at Aberdeen, I cannot but esteem it an office of brotherly love

---

peerage after duke   **233** craving – excommunication] subject to various excommunication proceedings by courts of the Kirk (presbyteries and synods) since 1605, the one by the General Assembly at Linlithgow in 1608 against Huntly secured royal sanction, although punishments were lenient. See Calderwood, *History*, vol. 6 (1845), p. 751-758. A similar petition had been made by Huntly to the Glasgow General Assembly of 1610, the outcome of which was not decisive. See Spottiswoode, *History*, vol. 3 (1851), p. 208   **234/235** quherof – Assembly] no such petition of Huntly is extant; but since this sentence is somewhat ambiguous, it may refer to the Assembly's 'answer' found in the *Acta Sessione ultima* below   **238/239** the³ – Canterburie] see below   **239** Archbischop of Canterburie] George Abbott, archbishop from 1611 to 1633, firm Calvinist and on good terms with James, to whom he owed his appointment. He had Scottish connections, partly in his role as privy councillor and English chaplain to the Scottish pro-episcopalian earl of Dunbar (George Hume) in the King's London court, and partly through his visit to the Scottish General Assembly at Linlithgow in 1608. There he spoke on episcopacy, which along with 'ceremonies' he characterized as 'indifferent' (adiaphora). As bishop of London (1609-1610) he presided at the consecration of the Scottish bishops of Glasgow, Galloway, and Brechin. Cfr *ODNB*, *ad vocem*; Calderwood, *History*, vol. 6 (1845), p. 735; *Original Letters*, vol. 2, p. 146   **241** ad perpetuam rei memoriam] as requested by the King. See below   **243** The – St Andrews] copies of both letters are absent from all Ms copies of the Assembly records, but are accessible in *Original Letters*, vol. 2, p. 476-468, and Spottiswoode, *History*, vol. 3 (1851), p. 233-235. Note that the language of each is southern English

---

233 orderly] *intellege* formally   **242** followis] *L D N p C G W I ins.* Heir to insert the two letters quhilk is to be found afterward   **244/340** Salutem – come] *deest in omn. Mss*

to yield you an account of that great action which lately befell us here with the marquis of Huntly. So it was then, that upon the coming up of the said marquis, his majesty sharply entreating him for not giving satisfaction to the Church of Scotland, and for a time restraining him from the royal presence, the marquis resolving to give his majesty contentment, did voluntarily proffer to communicate when and wheresoever his highness should be pleased; whereupon his majesty being pleased to make known that offer to me, it was held fit to strike the iron whilst it was hot, and that this great work should be accomplished before his majesty's going to progress; whereunto a good opportunity was offered by the consecration of the bishop of Chester, which was to be in the chapel at Lambeth the seventh of this month, at which time a solemn communion was there to be celebrated.

The only pause was, that the marquis being excommunicated by the Church of Scotland, there was in appearance some difficulty how he might be absolved in the Church of England; wherewith his majesty being made acquainted, who wished that it be not deferred, we grew to this peaceable resolution, which I doubt not your lordship and the rest of our brethren there will interpret to the best.

For, first, what was to be performed might be adventured upon, as we esteemed, out of a brotherly correspondency and unity of affection, and not only of any authority; for we well know, that as the kingdom of Scotland is a free and absolute monarchy, so the Church of Scotland is entire in itself, and independent upon any other Church.

Secondly, we find by the advice of divers doctors of the civil law, and men best experienced in things of this nature, that the course of ecclesiastical proceedings would fairly permit that we might receive to our communion a man excommunicated in another church – if the said person did declare that he had a purpose hereafter for some time to reside among us, which the lord marquis did openly profess that he intended, and I know his majesty doth desire it; and for my part, I rest satisfied that it can bring no prejudice, but rather contentment, unto you and to that kingdom.

---

252 proffer to communicate] i.e. offer to participate in the Lord's Supper **256** before – progress] a reference to the monarch's traditional, stately journey away from London in mid-summer **259** this month] July

---

268 correspondency] *intellege* relationship

CONCILIUM ABERDONIENSE ECCLESIAE SCOTICANAE – 1616   1063

Thirdly, it pleased God the night before the celebration of the sacrament, to send in our brother, the bishop of Caithness, with whom I taking counsel, his lordship resolved me, that it was the best way to absolve the lord marquis, and assured me that it would be well taken by the bishops and pastors of the Church of Scotland. I leave the report of this to my Lord Caithness himself, who was an eye-witness with what reverence the marquis did participate of that holy sacrament. For all other circumstances, I doubt not but you will be certified of them from his majesty, whose gracious and princely desire is, that this *bruised reed* should not be broken, but that so great a personage (whose example may do much good) should be cherished and comforted in his coming forward to God; which I for my part do hope and firmly believe that you will endeavour, according to the wisdom and prudence which Almighty God hath given you.

And thus, as your lordship hath ever been desirous that I should give you the best assistance I could with his majesty for the reducing or restraining this nobleman, so you see I have done it with the best discretion I could; which I doubt not but all our brethren with you will take as proceeding from my desire to serve God and his majesty, and the whole Church of Scotland. I send you herewith the form which I used in absolving the lord marquis in the presence of the lord primate of Ireland, the lord bishop of London, and divers others. And so beseeching the blessing of God upon you all, that in your Assembly with unity if spirit you may proceed, to the honour of Christ and to the beating down of Antichrist and popery, I leave you to the Almighty,

From my house of Croydon, July 23, 1616.

---

291 Is. 42, 3; Matth. 12, 20

283 bishop of Caithness] Alexander Forbes (1564-1617). Erastian, high-profile careerist bishop, constant moderator of the Caithness presbytery since 1606, and member of the High Commission. His role in the matter of Huntly's absolution, claiming to speak on behalf of the Scottish clergy, was seen by some as dubious, but it helped him become bishop of Aberdeen – Huntly's territory – in 1617. He died later that year. Cfr *ODNB, ad vocem*   **301** the form] text in *Original Letters*, vol. 2, p. 474, and Spottiswoode, *History*, vol. 3 (1851), p. 232   **303** lord primate of Ireland] Christopher Hampton, archbishop of Armagh. He had attended and spoken at the Glasgow General Assembly in 1610, which restored episcopacy in the Scottish Church. See *ODNB, ad vocem*   lord bishop of London] i.e. John King

1064 CONCILIUM ABERDONIENSE ECCLESIAE SCOTICANAE – 1616

[2. Letter from the King to the archbishop of St Andrews]

First, That in absolving the marquis, nothing was intended to the prejudice of the Church of Scotland, but what was done was out of a christian necessity, it being needful that the marquis should be absolved before he was admitted to the participation of the holy sacrament.

Secondly, he willed the Church to consider that his absolution at home was only deferred upon the scruple he made of the presence of our Saviour in the sacrament, and that upon his confession, swearing and subscribing the other points of religion, they themselves had suspended his excommunication, the lawfulness whereof he would not dispute, but remit the same to the canonists, yet the suspension standing, it was not much from an absolution.

Thirdly, that the absolution given him in England did necessarily imply an acknowledgment of the authority of the Church of Scotland; whereas, if the archbishop of Canterbury had received him to the holy communion, and not first absolved him (being excommunicated by the Church of Scotland), the contempt and neglect had been a great deal greater.

Fourthly, that the marquis being come into England, and making offer to perform whatsoever should be required of him, it was more fitting to take him in that disposition, than to have delayed it unto his return into Scotland.

For these reasons, he said, and especially because all that was done was with a due acknowledgment and reservation of the power and independent authority of the Church of Scotland, which the archbishop of Canterbury had by his own hand testified, it was his pleasure, that upon the marquis return, a full form of absolution should be given, or a ratification made of that which was done in England; so as neither the archbishop of Canterbury his doing should be disapproved as unlawful, nor the same so approved as it might seem that the Church of Scotland was inferior in any sort to that effect should be put in record, and kept as a perpetual monument for ages to come.

---

309 Letter – St Andrews] the original 'long letter', from Nottingham, referred to by Spottiswoode is paraphrased here in the third person by him, see l. 310/331; see Spottiswoode, *History*, vol. 3 (1851), p. 232-233, and *Original Letters*, vol. 2, p. 475   **315/ 321** Secondly – absolution] allusion to the understanding of the outcome of a similar petition by Huntly at the Glasgow General Assembly of 1610; see Spottiswoode, *History*, vol. 3 (1851), p. 208; *BUK* (Thomson), p. 1098-1099

CONCILIUM ABERDONIENSE ECCLESIAE SCOTICANAE – 1616   1065

With the quhilk the Assemblie being rypelie advisit, hes thoght it most expedient that the said Marquese compeer in the presence of the haill Assemblie, ther to testifie his conformitie in the points of religioun, and resolution to abide therat; and swa to be absolvit from the sentence of excommunica-
345 tioun pronuncit against him: And, therfor, ordains the said John Gordoun of Buckie to advertise the said Lord Marqueis, that he compeir befor the Assemblie, on Wednesday nixt to come, the xxj day of August instant, to the effect forsaid: And for the better furtherance heirof the Assemblie hes desyrit the Lord Commissioner and Lord Archbischop Moderator to wryte thir letters to
350 the said Lord Marqueis for the causes forsaids: and the whole Assembly was charged to stay while that time.

The Bishope of Canterburie excuses Huntlie's absolution in England. The reasons moving the Bishope of Canterburie. 1. His Majestie's sute, assuring him that he was fullie resolved. 2. The Bishope of Sanct Androes had requeist-
355 ed him diverse times to further that man's conversion, whensoever occasion was offered. 3. He was resolved by the best learned in England, that he might absolve him. 4. That he did it of brotherlie affection, and not as claiming anie superiority over the Kirk of Scotland. 5. He was informed be the Bishope of Caithnes then present at court, that it wold be acceptable service to the Kirk
360 of Scotland.

SESSIO 4ᴬ· DECIMO SEXTO AUGUSTI, 1616.

The said day, the Lord Commissioner for his Majestie produceit certaine instructiouns direct by his Majestie to the said Lord Commissioner to be proponit to this present Assemblie, anent the provisioun of the remedie for
365 the defectioun and falling away of many from the trueth: quherof the tenour followeth:

---

349 Lord Archbischop Moderator] i.e. Spottiswoode   **352/360** The¹ – Scotland] this paragraph is Calderwood's summary of the two letters and is retained here

341 rypelie] *intellege* amply   **344** therat] *intellege* in it   swa] *intellege* so
346 advertise] *intellege* advise   **349** thir] *intellege* these   **351** while] *intellege* until
352 excuses] *a.c.* excus, *intellege* explains   **353** sute] *intellege* exhortation
354 resolved] *intellege* persuaded   **361** Sessio 4ᵃ] *addidi*   4ᵃ] *intellege* quarta
364 proponit] *intellege* proposed

1066 CONCILIUM ABERDONIENSE ECCLESIAE SCOTICANAE – 1616

Instructions to our right trustie and welbelovit Cusigne and Counsellour the Erle of Montrois.

1. That order be taken with the delapidation of benefices, and the progress
370 thereof stayed, and some means devysed to recover that which is lost.

2. That the chief burrow touns be planted with sufficient, wise, learned, and peaceable men; especially such places as are now vacant, as Aberdeen, Perth, Edinburgh and Bamfe etc.

3. That the most learned, discreet Ministers be appointed and transported
375 to places where Noblemen has their residence, specialy suspect of Papistry; and if the means of the provision be small where they are transported, to take the rents and stipend which they had before with them, till better order be taken: and to this effect the Assembly ordaines that ilk Bishop within his Diocy, with advice of the Synod, shall transport Ministers as they shall think expe-
380 dient.

4. That a special canon be made that all Archbishops and Bishops in their visitation, either be themselves, or if they may not overtake the samen, the Ministers of the parish make all young children of six years old be presented to them to give confession of their faith, that they may appear in what religion
385 they are brought up. After which every two or three years they shall be examined, till they come to 14 years of age. After sufficient growth of knowledge they may be admitted to the Communion: and that punishment be appointed for them that presents them not, or are negligent in their instruction.

5. That a true and simple Confession of Faith be set doun, to the which all
390 shall sweare before they be admitted to any office in Kirk or Commonweale; and all students in Colledges.

---

367 Instructions] the text of the *Instructions* is also in *Original Letters*, vol. 2, p. 481-484, and Calderwood, *History*, vol. 7 (1845), p. 227-230   Cusigne] i.e. cousin. Montrose's great-great grandfather was an illegitimate son of James IV   Counsellour] he was a member of the Privy Council   **369** order – benefices] cfr *Act. Scot. Parl.*, 1605: 'Regarding the dilapidation of bishoprics'   **391** students in Colledges] probably on graduation rather than matriculation

---

367/368 Instructions – Montrois] *L D N p* Heir to be insert – *r* Here are to be insert the Instructions   **369/436** 1. – free] *L D N p r deest*   **369** 1.] *C G W I in marg.* Anent the delapidatione of benefices   **371** 2.] *C G W I in marg.* Planting of Burrow townes   planted] *intellege* provided   **374** 3.] *C G W I in marg.* Planting of Noblemens dwellings   discreet] *intellege* judicious   transported] *intellege* translated **378** ilk] *intellege* each   **381** 4.] *C G W I in marg.* Tryel of children   canon] *intellege* regulation   **382** overtake] *intellege* accomplish   **389** 5.] *C G W I in marg.* Confession of faith   simple] *intellege* easily understood *uel* straightforward   set doun] *intellege* composed   **390** Commonweale] *intellege* secular realm

CONCILIUM ABERDONIENSE ECCLESIAE SCOTICANAE – 1616   1067

6. That a short and compendious Catechism be made, which every kirk and familie shall have for the instruction of their children and servants, whereof they shall give account before the Communion, and every one be examined conforme thereto.

7. That all children and schools shall have and learn be heart the Catechism, intituled God and the King; which already be Act of Consell is ordained to be read and taught in all schooles.

8. That a Liturgie be made, and form of divine service, which shall be read in every church, in common prayer, and before preaching every Sabbath, be the Reader, where there is one, and where there is none, be the Minister befor he conceive his oun prayer, that the common people may learn it and by custom serve God rightly.

---

392 a short and compendious Catechism] to supersede *Craig's Catechism* (1581) which was widely used till then   **397** intituled God and the King] this was based on a tract of the same name published in England in 1616, namely, *God and the King: or, A dialogue shewing that our Soueraigne Lord King Iames, being immediate under God within his dominions, doth rightfully claime whatsoeuer is required by the Oath of allegiance*, London 1616, and also published in Scotland in 1616. Authored apparently by Dr Richard Mocket of All Souls College, Oxford, who had close links with Archbishop Abbot. See *Scottish Liturgies*, p. 104-106. It reflects James patriarchial theory of government embodied in his *True Law of Free Monarchies*. Cfr Schochet, *Patriarchalism in Political Thought*, p. 88-90   be Act of Consell] 14 April 1616, *RPCS*, vol. 10 (1891), p. 534-538. See also the report on the matter of a committee chaired by the archbishop of Glasgow (James Law), 6 June 1616, in *Original Letters*, vol. 2, p. 804-805. As the government had already made such provision, this particular item was omitted from the Assembly's decrees the following day   **399** Liturgie] the matter had been raised by the King in 1584 and by the Burntisland General Assembly in 1601. See the Introduction   **400** in common prayer] that is, daily as well as Sunday worship   **401** the Reader] where a reader was available, Sunday service consisted of two phases: first, the reader's service of Bible readings, Psalms and prayers of adoration; secondly, the minister's part, including a Psalm, a self-composed prayer, and especially the sermon. Readers had performed an important function in the early decades of the Reformation when there was a shortage of ministers. In 1581, the General Assembly decided to make no more appointments, but existing readers continued. See especially *DSCHT*, entry 'Readers (Reformation)'

---

392 6.] *C G W I in marg.* A catechisme for kirks & famileis   **396** 7.] *C G W I in marg.* A catechisme for schooles   **399** 8.] *C G W I in marg.* Anent a Liturgie

1068   CONCILIUM ABERDONIENSE ECCLESIAE SCOTICANAE – 1616

9. That the Communion be celebrat four times ilk year in the burrow
405 touns, and twice in landwart; and one of the times to be at Easter yearly. And
if any communicat not once in the year, the act of Parliament is to strike upon
them with all severity.

10. That there be an uniformity of discipline; and to that effect the
Canons of the former Councils and Assemblies to be extracted; and where the
410 same are defective, to be supplied be former Canons and Ecclesiastical meetings. For setting doun whereof the Commissioners following are ordained to
conveen with the Bishops, in Edinburgh, the first day of December next to
come, viz. the Laird of Corse, Mr John Reid, Mr George Hay, Doctor Hendrie
Philip, Mr David Lindsay in Dundie, Mr William Scott, Doctor Robert

---

405 landwart] rural areas. The existing *Book of Common Order* recommended
monthly communion, but quarterly urban communion or biannually in rural areas
became the norm for practical reasons. In fact, the sacrament seems to have been
celebrated even less frequently. See Maxwell, *A History of Worship*, p. 51-52; Burnet, *The
Holy Communion*, p. 16-17   at Easter yearly] inconsistency prevailed before, largely
due to the early Scottish reformers' critique of the liturgical 'Christian year' and its
frequent parallels with superstitious folk festivals. See McDougall, 'Popular Festive
Practices', p. 473-476. In 1614 and 1615, the King had urged Easter communion by royal
proclamation or act of privy council. See *RPCS*, vol. 10 (1891), p. 215-217 and 316-317;
Act. Scot. Parl., 1615; *Original Letters*, vol. 2, p. 450. See also *Scottish Liturgies*, p. xv;
McMillan, *The Worship*, p. 102 and 195-196; Maxwell, *A History of Worship*, p. 51-52;
Foster, *The Church*, p. 181-182; Burnet, *The Holy Communion*, p. 67-69   **405/
406** And – year] as in Catholic tradition and the Church of England's canons of 1603
408 discipline] in this context, 'discipline' refers chiefly to procedures for appointing
bishops and ministers, to the forms of the sacraments and marriage, and to the
desideratum of confirmation. Until then, Church practice and procedure were not
codified. See Spottiswoode's memorandum in *Scottish Liturgies*, p. xvi; *Original
Letters*, vol. 2, p. 445-456. Cfr *Synod of Fife*, p. 5 (meeting in 1611)   **413** Laird of
Corse] i.e. Patrick Forbes   Mr John Reid] minister of Logie Buchan, Aberdeenshire
Mr George Hay] minister of Turriff, Aberdeenshire   **413/414** Doctor Hendrie
Philip] minister of Arbroath   **414** Mr David Lindsay] (1575-1639/1640). Member of
the Court of High Commission, advocate of royal supremacy in the Church, resolute
defender of the *Five Articles of Perth* (1618), later bishop of Brechin and then
Edinburgh; father-in-law of Archbishop Spottiswoode. See *ODNB*, *ad vocem*   Mr
William Scott] see above   **414/415** Doctor – Howie] see the Introduction

---

404 9.] *C G W I in marg.* Celebration of the communion   **405** landwart] *intellege*
rural areas   **408** 10.] *C G W I in marg.* Uniformitie of Discipline   **413** Hendrie]
addidi   **414** Robert] *addidi*

CONCILIUM ABERDONIENSE ECCLESIAE SCOTICANAE – 1616   1069

415 Howie, Mr John Mitchelson, Mr Patrick Galloway, Mr John Hall, Mr Edward Hepburn, Doctor Robert Abernethy, Mr Robert Scott, Mr William Birnie, Mr William Areskine, or the mostpart of them.

11. For the help of the posterity, and furtherance of religion, that a special care be taken of the Divinity Colledge in Sanct Andrews, and to that effect 420 that every Diocie shall furnish two Students, or so many as may make the number to extend to twenty six; and the half thereof to be children of poor Ministers, to be preferred be the Bishop of the Diocie: provyding always, that these who are furnished within the Province of Glafgow, that is to say, the Diocies of Glasgow, Galloway, Argile, and the Isles, shall be brought up in the 425 College of Glasgow, and not be astricted to Sanct Andrews, but when they pass Doctours only.

12. That none teach in pulpit publictly before the people, but these that have received imposition of hands; and whosoever does otherways be incapable of the Ministry.

---

415 Mr John Mitchelson] minister of Burntisland, Fife   Mr Patrick Galloway] see the Introduction   Mr John Hall] (c. 1559-1627) minister at this time of Edinburgh New or Little Kirk and constant moderator of the Edinburgh presbytery; co-author of the *New Confession*; critical of liturgical changes, he was banished from Edinburgh by the King in 1619. See *Scottish Liturgies*, p. xxi   **415/416** Mr Edward Hepburn] minister of Preston, Berwickshire   **416** Doctor Robert Abernethy] minister of Jedburgh, Roxburghshire   Mr Robert Scott] († 1629). Minister of Glasgow Cathedral (High Kirk)   Mr William Birnie] (1563-1619). Minister of Ayr, pro-episcopal, and a member of the High Commission   **417** Mr William Areskine] (or Erskine), minister of Dunino, Fife   **419** the Divinity Colledge in Sanct Andrews] i.e. St Mary's College, St Andrews University (founded 1413)   **424** Argile] i.e. Argyll   **425** College of Glasgow] Glasgow College, or Glasgow University (founded 1451)   **426** Doctours] the doctorate in theology was traditionally unique to St Andrews among the three ancient universities of St Andrews, Glasgow, and Aberdeen, but cfr Denlinger, 'The Aberdeen Doctors', p. 280   **427** 12.] in mind here is ordination in order to remove the abuse of preaching by teenage university graduates, as alluded to in the royal policy statement accompanying the establishment of the Ecclesiastical High Commission in 1610. Cfr Spottiswoode, *History*, vol. 3 (1851), p. 211-212, items 9 and 13. In the Reformed Kirk, attitudes to 'imposition by hands' differed widely; it was disapproved of by the *First Book of Discipline* (1560), but authorized by the *Second Book of Discipline* (1578). The 1597 Assembly ordered it for the sake of uniform ministerial ordination. See *BUK* (Thomson), vol. 3 (1845), p. 925. Cfr Donaldson, *Scottish Reformation*, p. 116-118; Mechie, 'Episcopacy', p. 30-35; Foster, *The Church*, p. 141-142

---

415 Howie] *a.c.* Howi   **416** Robert¹] *addidi*   **418** 11.] *C G W I in marg.* Anent students, Of Discipline   **425** astricted] *intellege* restricted   but] *intellege* except **427** 12.] *C G W I in marg.* Publict teachers

1070   CONCILIUM ABERDONIENSE ECCLESIAE SCOTICANAE – 1616

430   13. That every Minister shall minister the Sacrament of Baptism quhensoever it shall be required, under the pain of deposition – the godfather promising to instruct the infant in the faith.

14. That every Minister have a Register of baptisms, mariages, and defuncts, within the parish, to be presented to ilk Synod. For doing whereof it is
435   statute, the Ministers, their wives, and executors shall have the quotts, and confirmation of their testaments free.

Quhilk being red in audience of the haill Assemblie, they give most humble thanks to his Majestie for the great care and solicitude his Majestie always tooke for the advancement of the glorie of God, and professioun of the true
440   religioun within this realme, and holding downe and suppressing of Papistrie and superstitioun within the same: And as to the saids instructioun, the brethren was ordainit to advyse therwith quhill the morne.

SESSIO 5ᴬ· DECIMO SEPTIMO AUGUSTI, ANTE MERIDIEM.

Anent the saids instructioun directit from the Kings Majestie to this
445   Assemblie, the said Assemblie being rypelie advysit therwith, hes statute and ordainit as followeth:

430/431 That – required] since this formulation is arguably permissive of private or domestic baptism, which was banned by the early Reformers except in emergency, it may be seen as anticipating its explicit introduction in the *Five Articles of Perth* (1619). On the disparity of practice in Scotland in regard to the venue, day, and liturgical context of baptism, see especially McMillan, *The Worship*, p. 254-260   **431/432** under – faith] godfathers (rather than godparents including godmothers) were foreseen in the *Book of Common Order*. They had been much discussed at the Council of Trent: see Jedin, *Geschichte*, vol. 3, p. 176. See also Coster, *Baptism and Spiritual Kinship*, p. 85-87; Spierling, *Infant Baptism*; Todd, *Culture of Protestantism*. This statute seems to be directed against both the presence of too many godparents and those who wished to abolish godparents altogether: see McMillan, *The Worship*, p. 248-249   **433/434** That – Synod] every (diocesan) Synod when it meets biannually. The standard of such roll-keeping was poor   **434/436** For – free] A 'quot' was a fee, traditionally a share (one twentieth) of the moveable estate of a deceased person due to the diocesan bishop; now it was presumably used to help supplement modestly the income of a ministerial family in return for such a registration service

---

430 13.] *C G W I in marg.* Anent Baptisme   **433** 14.] *C G W I in marg.* Anent the Register   defuncts] *intellege* deaths   **436** confirmation of their testaments] *intellege* probate of last wills   **442** ordainit to advyse therwith quhill the morne] *intellege* directed to consult on them until the following day   **443** Sessio 5ᵃ] *addidi*   5ᵃ] *intellege* quinta

CONCILIUM ABERDONIENSE ECCLESIAE SCOTICANAE – 1616   1071

[1] In the first, concerning the causes of the defectioun and falling away of many from the true religioun in this kingdome, and the remedies therof, the Assemblie hes sett them downe in the articles made befor in this present Con-ventioun: And therfor most humblie desyres his Majestie to confirm and allow them, and make them receive execution.

[2] Item, Because the laik of competent maintainance to Ministers is the cheefe cause of the evill, quhilk lay upon this Kirk, quhilk for the most part proceids from dilapidation of benefices: to the effect therfor, that the pro-gresse of that mischeife may be stayit, and some meanes devysit to recover that quhilk by iniquitie of tyme hes bein losit, the Assemblie remitts the tryall, cognitioun, and whole dispositioun of this matter to the Commissioners appointit from this Assemblie, for the causes underwrytin: And in the mean-tyme inhibites and discharges all Ministers quho are beneficit persons, and uthers quho are members of any Chapter, to sett in tack or assedatioun any part of thair benefices, either in long or short tackis, to quhatsumevir person or persons; or as members of Chapter to give thair consents to any tack or assedatioun sett be uthers, quhill the saids Commissioners have conveinit and takin ordour anent delapidatioun of benefices, and forme and maner of setting of tacks, under the paine of excommunicatioun of the persons setters of the saids tacks and consenters therto; and deprivatioun of them from thair bene-fices.

[3] Item, Because the provisioun of learnit, wise and peaceable men to be Ministers at cheife Burrowstounes in vacant places, sick as Edinburgh, Perth, Aberdein, Banffe, and uther places vacant, is ane most effectuall meane to roote out Poperie, and perpetuat the professioun of the true religioun: It is therfor ordainit, that the Burrowtounes be provydit with the most learnit, wife and peaceable men that may be had. And because the Commissioners for the Towne of Edinburgh hes no commissioun from the said towne, anent the provisioun of Ministers to the vacant places in the said Kirk: Therfor the care thereof is remittit to the saids Commissioners, to quhom it salbe injoynit in thair commissioun, that they sie the same performit. And as to Perth, the

---

447/451 In – execution] namely the decrees of the second and third session of 14 and 15 August (see above)   **460** Chapter] i.e. cathedral chapter. With the restoration of episcopal temporalities in 1606, the virtually-defunct chapters became active again. See Foster, *The Church*, p. 40-41

455 mischeife] *intellege* misfortune   stayit] *intellege* stopped   **457** cognitioun] *intellege* investigation   **460** to sett in tack or assedatioun] *intellege* lease out   **469** Burrowstounes] *intellege* towns; cities   **476** injoynit] *intellege* enjoined; directed

1072   CONCILIUM ABERDONIENSE ECCLESIAE SCOTICANAE – 1616

Assemblie ordaines my Lord Bishop of Galloway to deale with the Commissioners of the Towne of Perth, for provisioun of that vacant place. And sick-
480 lyke ordaines the Provest of Aberdein to advyse with the Counsell, anent the planting of the said Kirk; to the effect sufficient and qualified men may be nominat and provided to the said places, befor the dissolving of this Assemblie.

[4] Item, Because a special care should be had of noblemen thair resi-
485 dence, cheiflie of such as were thoght to inclyne towards Poperie: Therfor the Assemblie statutes and ordaines, that the Lords Archbischops and Bischops, with the advyce of thair Synods, take care that most learnit and discreit persons of the Ministrie be appointit to attend the saids places, and be transportit therto, sick as to the Kirks of Dumbenen, Bellie, North Berwick, Cock-
490 burnespath, Peislay, and such uther places quher Noblemen makes residence, cheifly those quho are thought to inclyne towards Poperie; and that they have a care of thair manteinance and sufficient provisioun: And if the same be small, that these that are appointit to attend at the saids Kirks, carrie thair livings and rents with them, quhill farder order be taken.

495   [5] Item: Forsameikle as one of the most speciall meanes for staying of the increase of Poperie, and settling of the true religioun in the hearts of the peiple, is that a speciall care may be takin in the tryall of young children, thair educatioun, and how they are catechisit; quhilk, in the tyme of the primitive Church was most carefullie attendit as one of the most effectuall meanes to
500 cause young childrein in thair verie tender yeirs drink in the true knowledge of God and his religioun; bot is now altogether neglectit, in respect of the great abuse and errours quhilk creip in in the Popish Church, upon the said good ground, be bigging therupon ane Sacrament of Confirmatioun: Therfore

---

478 Lord Bishop of Galloway] William Cowper (see above)   **480** Provest of Aberdein] Sir Thomas Menzies, Laird of Durn. The provost is the Scottish equivalent of mayor   Counsell] i.e. the town council   **489** Dumbenen] Dunbennan, Aberdeenshire   Bellie] in Aberdeenshire. Both Dunbennan and Bellie were parishes in the territory of the Catholic marquis of Huntly   Cockburnespath] a township between North Berwick and Edinburgh, in East Lothian   **490** Peislay] Paisley, Renfrewshire. Notable suspected recusants in this area had been – among others – John Maxwell of Stanely, the Maxwells of Newark, the Maxwells of Kilmacolm, James, seventh earl of Glencairn, Margaret, countess of Glencairn, the Dowager Lady Duchal, the second marquis of Hamilton, the countess of Abercorn. See Lees, *The Abbey of Paisley*, p. 248-281   **498/499** in – meanes] in mind may be the *Didache* ('Teaching of the Twelve Apostles'), known about, but still undiscovered, in the early-modern era

---

479 place] *intellege* position; post   sicklyke] *intellege* similarly   **494** quhill farder order be taken] *intellege* until further arrangements be made   **499** attendit] *intellege* attained   **503** bigging] *intellege* building

CONCILIUM ABERDONIENSE ECCLESIAE SCOTICANAE – 1616 1073

to the intent that all errours and superstitioun quhilk hes bein biggit upon the
505 said ground may be rescindit and takin away, and that the matter itselfe, being
most necessar for educatioun of youth, may be reduceit to its awin integritie, it
is statute and ordainit that the Archbischops and Bischops, in the visitatioun
of the Kirks, either be themselves, or quher they cannot overtake the bussines,
the Minister of the paroch, make all young childrein of six yeirs of age be
510 presentit befor them, and to give confession of their faith, that so it may
appeare in quhat religioun they have bein brocht up; and that they be com-
mendit to God by solemne prayer at the tyme, for the increase of thair knowledge and continuance of his grace with them. After that tryall, that the Minister of the paroch, every two or thrie yeir, ance at the least, reexamine them,
515 that after sufficient growth in knowledge they may be admittit to the holie
Communioun. And it is desyrit, that ane supplicatioun be directit to the
Kings Majestie, humblie craveing that it wald please his Hienes to injoyne ane
punischment upon such parties, as either doe not present thair childrein, or
salbe found negligent in thair right instructioun; and that they be callit and
520 conveint therfor befor the High Commissioun.
[6] Item, It is statute that the simple confessioun of faith underwrytin be
vniversallie receivit throughout this whole kingdome, to the quhilk all
heirafter salbe bound to sweare and sett thair hands; and in speciall all persons
that beare office in the Church at thair acceptatioun of any of the saids offices;
525 and lykewayes students and schollers in colledges.
Of the quhilk Confession the tenour followes:

509/510 make – faith] referring probably to traditional rudiments as in the Lord's
Prayer, the *Apostles' Creed*, and the Ten Commandments. See Burnet, *The Holy
Communion*, p. 45-50 **513/516** After – Communioun] if Catholic infants could
receive confirmation and first communion at the age of seven, children in Reformed
churches were only admitted to communion at about the age of fourteen after
examination of their religious knowledge and understanding **521** 6] existing
confessional subscription had related to the *Scots Confession* of 1560 and the *King's
Confession* of 1581 (both merged into one) the simple confessioun of faith
underwrytin] i.e. the *New Confession* below, on which see the Introduction

506 reduceit] *intellege* restored **510** confession of their faith] *C t hab.* The
Confession of Faith **514** ance] *intellege* once **523** sett thair hands] *intellege*
subscribe **526** followes] *L D N* Heir to insert the confessione off the faith

1074 CONCILIUM ABERDONIENSE ECCLESIAE SCOTICANAE – 1616

The New Confession of Faith

Wee beleeve with our hearts and confesse with our mouthes these articles of religion following:

530 [1] That God is a spirit immutable, aeternall, infinite in power, in wisdome, in goodness and glorie; from whom, be whom, to whom are all things; in whom we live, in whom we have our being; who is one onlie God and three persons, which are co-essential, co-aeternal, and co-equal. The first is the father, who is of none. The second is the sonne, who from all aeternitie is

535 begotten of the father. The thrid is the holy ghost, who from all aeternitie proceedeth from the father and the sonne. This glorious God from all aeternitie out of his wisdome and infinit knowledge decreed all things that were after to be done. This God, before the foundation of the world wes layed, according to the good pleasure of his will, for the praise of the glorie of his grace, did

540 predestinat and elect in Christ some men and angels unto aeternall felicitie – and others he did appoint for aeternall condemnation, according to the counsell of his most free, most just and holie will, and that to the praise and glorie of his justice.

[2] In the beginning of tyme, when God created out of nothing all things

545 that are in heaven and are in earth, visible and invisible, he made them verie good. And above all things he made men and angells conform to his owne image, in righteousness and true holines. But some of the angells of their owne free motive sinned against God, left their original righteousness, forsooke their habitation and abode not in the truthe, and therby became damned

550 devills.

[3] Then Sathan abused the craftie serpent for his instrument, seducing our mother, Eva. She tempted her husband Adam. So both disobeyed the commandement of God, and therby made themselves and their whole posteritie the bondmen of Satan, slaves of sinne and heires of aeternall condemna-

555 tion.

[4] By this fall of Adam all his posteritie are so corrupted from their conception and nativitie that not ane of them can doe or will anything truelie

---

536/540 This – felicitie] cfr Eph. 1, 4-5 **544/554** In – condemnation] cfr Gen. 1, 3

527 The New Confession of Faith] for two independent, orthographically modernised, English renderings, see Shaw, *Acts and Proceedings*, vol. 3, p. 523-531, and Dennison, 'Scottish Confession (1616)'

527/790 The – judgement] *L D N omnino deest, sed C G W I r t c s posuerunt ad fin.*
527 The – Faith] *titulum apud C* **548** motive] *intellege* will righteousness] *inserui, C c t deest*

CONCILIUM ABERDONIENSE ECCLESIAE SCOTICANAE – 1616   1075

acceptable to God, till they be renewed by the will and Spirit of God and by faith ingrafted in Jesus Christ.

560   [5] This, our originall and native corruption, by regeneration in part is weakened and mortified; yitt it is sinne indeid remaining in ws, alwayes lusting against the Spirit, and tempting ws to sinne actuallie as long as we live.

    [6] Albeit all mankinde be fallen in Adam, yitt onlie these who are elected before all tyme are in tyme redeemed, restored, raised and quickened 565 againe, not of themselfes or of their works, lest anie man sould glorie, but onlie of the mercie of God through faith in Jesus Christ, who of God is made unto us wisdome and righteousnes, sanctification and redemption – that according as it is writtin, *He that glorieth, lett him glorie in the Lord.*

    [7] This, then, is life eternall – to know the true God and whom he has 570 sent, Jesus Christ; wheras vengance sall be taiken on them that know not God, and doeth not subject themselfs to the Gospell of the Lord Jesus Christ by the obedience of faith.

    [8] We beleeve that the rule of this knowledge, faith and obedience, yea, and of the whole worship of God, and of all christian conversation, is not the 575 witt or will of man, nor unwritten traditions whatsoever, but the wysdome and will of God, which is sufficientlie revealed in the canonicall scriptures of the old and new Testament, which are Genesis, Exodus, etc., exclusis apocryphis.

    [9] We beleeve that the authoritie of the holie Scriptures is divine; for 580 they are all of divine inspiration, and hes God for their author. Their authoritie depends upon God and not upon man. They have power over all fleshe, and no creature hes power over them. We are absolutelie bound to beleeve them for their owne testimonie, which is the testimonie of God himself speaking in them. And our faith dependeth not upon any externall testimonie of 585 the kirk witnessing of them. All things necessarie to salvation are conteaned therin. All the doctrines of the kirk must be warranted be them. All controverseis of the kirk must be decydit be them as the livelie and plaine voice of God, who is supream judge in maters of faith and worship.

---

568 II Cor. 10, 17   **569/570** This – Christ] cfr Ioh. 17, 3

---

575 unwritten traditions] as in Catholic dogma. See Council of Trent, Sess. IV (April 1546) 'Decretum primum: precipiuntur libri sacri et traditiones apostolorum', in *COGD* III, p. 15-16   **579/588** against the Council of Trent's reaffirmation of the Church's magisterium, Sess. IV (April 1546) 'Decretum secundum: recipitur vulgata editio Bibliae praescribiturque modus interpretandi s. Scripturam', in *COGD* III, p. 16-17

1076   CONCILIUM ABERDONIENSE ECCLESIAE SCOTICANAE – 1616

[10] Wee beleeve that all points of faith and worship are so sett doun in
590 the word of God, that what is obscourelie proponnit in one place is most
cleerlie expoundit in other places. Neither receeve we anie interpretation of
anie scriptures in these maters which is not warranted be other scriptures.

[11] These holie writts are delivered be God to his kirk, to make us wise to
salvation by faith in Jesus Christ, whose persone, office and benefits they most
595 cleerlie and fullie sett furthe unto ws.

[12] The lord Jesus Christ is declared in Scripture to be the eternall sonne
of God, begotten from all eternitie of the father, by whom he created the
world, by whom also he does governe and susteane all things that he hes made.
And this eternall sone of God, when the fulnes of tyme came, was made man
600 of the woman of the tribe of Juda, and of the seede of David and Abraham,
even of the blessed virgin Marie by the holie Ghost comming upon her, and
the power of the most high overshadowing her, by whose mervalous and
divine operation the sone of God was made man of a humane bodie and soul,
and in all things like unto ws, sinne onlie excepted. And yett so he wes made
605 man, that he ceased not to be God. And so is God that he is also man, having
both the natures, divyne and humane, united together in a personall union, so
that in ane admirable persone the two natures ar distinct and not confoundit
in respect of their essence, their essential properties, and proper operations.

[13] And becaus of the union of the nature of man in one persone with
610 the sone of God, Christ, God and man, is to be adored and worshiped of us.
For to Christ, God and man, all power in heaven and earth is given, and *He
hath gotten a name above everie name, that at the name of Jesus everie knie sould
bow.*

[14] The puritie of the humane nature of Christ is to be ascribed to the
615 supernaturall operation of the holie ghost, who separated the seed of the
woman from the naturall corruption – and not to the purity of the Virgine
Mary his mother. For she dowbtless was conceaved and borne in sinne, and
had need of her sonne to be her saviour, als well as other weamen.

[15] The Lord Jesus Christ as God and man is the Saviour of his kirk,
620 which is his bodie. And the fulnes of him filleth all things. Neither is there
salvation in anie other thing.

593/594 to² – Christ] cfr II Tim. 3, 15   **596/597** The – father] cfr Ioh. 1, 14-18   **599/
603** was – soul] cfr Matth. 1, 18-25   **611/613** Phil. 2, 9-10   **619/621** kirk – thing] cfr
I Cor. 12, 12-13 et 27; Eph. 1, 22-23

593 writts] *intellege* writings   **596/613** 12 – bow] D [12] *et* [13] *non separuntur*

CONCILIUM ABERDONIENSE ECCLESIAE SCOTICANAE – 1616

[16] This blessed lord hes fulfilled the whole law for us, to our behove and in our place, both doing all that the law requireth of ws and suffering the punishment due to our disobedience, even the curse of the law and death of the crosse – wherby the fullfiling of the law our redemption wes sealed and consummatted.

[17] We beleeve that as he died for our sinne and rose for our righteousnesse, so he ascendit to heavin to prepare a place for ws, and sitteth at the right hand of God to make intercession for ws, and is able perfytlie to save them that come to God by him, who albeit in his manhood he be so in the heaven, that he is no more in the earth. For the heavens must conteane him, till he come to *judge the quick and the dead*. Yitt in his godhead he is so present evriewhair, be his power sustaining all things, and be his gracious spirit directing and governing his Kirk militant upun earth.

[18] We beleive that the lord Jesus Christ wes appointed and anoynted of the father to be the King and hie preist, and supreame teacher of his Kirk.

[19] We beleeve – concerning the propheticall office – that he is the onlie master and teacher of his kirk, whom God be his owne voice from heavin commandit ws to heare, who hes revealed the whole will of the father touching our salvation. And what he hes heard of the father he hath made knowne to ws, speaking nothing to his Kirk which he did not before heare of his father, that his Kirk might learne to receave nothing in faith and worship which she hes not heard of him.

[20] As concerning his preistly office: we believe that he is our *onlie mediator* both of redemption and intercession. And that by the sacrifice of himself once offered on the cross he hes made a full satisfaction for all our sinnes, and doth continnually make intercession for ws to God. And, therefor, we abhorre that supposed reiterating of the sacrifice of Christ in the messe, and we renounce all kind of intercession of Saints and Angels.

[21] As concerning the kingdome of Christ: beside his absolute impire, wherby he ruleth all things, we beleeve him to be our eternall King and onlie

---

622 This – us] cfr Matth. 5, 17   **624/625** curse – consummatted] cfr Gal. 3, 13
628 ascendit to heavin] cfr Act. 1, 9-11   **628/629** sitteth – God] cfr Act. 2, 33
632 Act. 10, 42; II Tim. 4, 1   **636** King and hie preist] cfr Hebr. 7   **637** propheticall office] cfr Ioh. 6, 14   **644** I Tim. 2, 5   **645/647** And – God] cfr I Ioh. 1, 1-2

622 behove] *intellege* advantage   **622/623** and – place] *W om.*   **648** reiterating] *intellege* repetition

1078   CONCILIUM ABERDONIENSE ECCLESIAE SCOTICANAE – 1616

head of his Kirk universall. Neither he nor his kirk hath anie neid of a lieutenant depute in his place, seing he is present in his Kirk alwayes be his spirit,
powerfullie working therin, calling, collecting, quickening and graciouslie
655 ruling her be the ministrie of the word and sacraments to the consummation
of the world.

[22] We beleeve that our communnion with Christ our head is spirituall
by the holie Spirit, which dwelleth powerfullie both in the bodie and in the
head, making the members conforme to the head. And it is no wayes corpor-
660 all, or by anie fleshlie receaving of his bodie.

[23] We beleeve that be vertue of this communion Christ is ours, and we
are Christs; and his suffering is our satisfaction. And by it we have right, title
and interest in all the benefits which he did promerite and purchase to ws be
his suffering.

665 [24] We beleeve that God justifies sinners by remitting of their sinnes,
and by imputing to them the righteousnes and obedience of Christ, wherby he
fulfilled the whole law in our place, both in doing the commandements therof
and in suffering the curse therof, which was due to ws becaus of our disobedience.

670 [25] We beleeve that that righteousnes wherby we are justified befor God
is not inherent in us, but in Jesus Christ; and that it is freelie given to ws of
Gods free grace, through our faith in Jesus Christ.

[26] We beleeve that we ar justified by faith, as it is ane instrument apprehending and applying the righteousnes of Christ to us, and not as it is a quali-
675 tie and vertue inherent in us – so that the meritorious caus of our justification
is not in the faith which apprehendeth, but in the righteousness of Christ be
faith apprehendit.

[27] We beleeve that albeit we be not justified by good works before God,
and can merit nothing at Gods hand, yett they ar the way to the Kingdome of
680 God, and ar of necessity to be done for obedience to God, for gloryfieing of
his name, for confirming ourselves anent our election, and for good example
to uthers. And constantlie we affirme that faith which bringeth not furth
good works is deid, and availeth nothing to justification or salvation.

---

652 head – Kirk] cfr Col. 1, 18; Eph. 5, 23   **665/668** We – disobedience] cfr Rom.
4-6   **673** justified by faith] cfr Rom. 1, 17   **682/683** And – salvation] cfr Iac. 2, 14-26

652/653 lieutenant depute] polemical allusion to the concept of the Pope as vicar of
Christ

---

663 promerite] *intellege* procure

CONCILIUM ABERDONIENSE ECCLESIAE SCOTICANAE – 1616   1079

[28] We beleeve that the elect – being renewed – ar sealed with the holie
Spirit of promise, in suche sort that albeit they bear about in their fleshe the
remnants of that originall corruption, and albeit they offend through infirm-
itie, and through the entisements therof sinne greivouslie to the great offence
of God, yit they cannot altogether fall from grace, but ar raised againe
through the mercie of God, and keiped to salvation.

[29] Concerning the certaintie of our salvation: we beleeve that everie ane
of ws in particular ought to be fullie perswadit therof, giving credit both to
the external promise of the word, and internall witnesse of the spirit. And as
for the dowbtings therof, which we oftin find in ourselves, we doe not allow –
but contrarie way damne them as the fruits of the fleshe fighting against our
faith.

[30] We beleeve that God hes appointed his word and sacraments as
instruments of the holie ghost to work and confirame faith in man.

[31] We beleeve that the word of God ought to be preached and the sacraments administred, and all divine service, as praying and praising, in all
languages knowne and understood be the people.

[32] We beleeve that the sacraments ar certane visible seales of Gods eternall covenant, ordained be God to represent unto ws Christ crucified, and to
seal up our spirituall communion with him.

[33] We beleeve that the sacraments ar to be ministred onlie be them who
ar lawfullie called therto be the kirk of God.

[34] We beleeve that the sacraments have power to confirme faith and
conferre grace, not of themselfis, or ex opere operato, or force of the externall
action – but onlie by the powerfull operation of the holie ghost.

[35] We beleeve that there be onlie two sacraments appointed by Christ
under the new testament: Baptisme and the Lords supper.

[36] We believe that Baptisme is necessary to salvation, if it can be orderlie had; and, therefor, that not the want of it, but the contempt of it doeth
damne.

---

692 internall witnesse of the spirit] cfr Rom. 8, 16   **701/703** We – him] cfr I Cor.
11, 25

---

688 yit they cannot altogether fall from grace] since in Reformed orthodoxy the elect
are in possession of irresistible grace and are thus indefectible, despite continuing
manifestations of sinfulness   **706/707** We – operato] against Concilium
Tridentinum, Sess. VII 'Canones de sacramentis in genere', in *COGD* III, p. 40-41

---

699 praising] *intellege* singing   **711/712** if it can be orderlie had] *intellege* if it is
formally available

1080   CONCILIUM ABERDONIENSE ECCLESIAE SCOTICANAE – 1616

[37] We beleeve that Baptisme sealeth up unto ws the remission of all our
715 sinns wherof we are guiltie, either before or efter our Baptisme.

[38] We beleeve that Baptisme is to be administred simplie in the element
of water, with the rite of dipping, washing, or sprinkling *in the name of the
father, sone, and holie Ghost*, according to Christs institution, without other
elements or sacramental rites devised be men.

720 [39] We beleeve that the Lords supper is to be given to all communicants
under the elements of bread and wyne, according to Christs institution.

[40] We beleeve that the elements of bread and wine in the Lords supper
are not transsubstantiat or changed in the substance of the bodie and bloode
of Christ – but that they ar sacraments of his bodie and bloode, thus changing
725 their use and not their substance.

[41] We beleeve that the bodie and blood of Jesus Christ ar truelie present
in the holie supper, that they ar truelie exhibit unto ws; and that we in verie
truthe doe participat of them, albeit onlie spirituallie and by faith, not carnal-
lie or corporallie.

730 [42] We beleeve that the Lords supper is a commemoratione of the sacrifice of Christ, which once offered did fullie expiat our sinnes. With his one
sacrifice once offered, we ar all fullie content; neither doe we seeke anie other
expiatorie or propitiatorie sacrifice. But as for sacrifices of praise and thanks-
givings, the sacrifice of a contreat heart, almes and charitable deeds, these we
735 ought daylie to offer as acceptable to God in Jesus Christ.

[43] We beleeve that the sacrifice and merites of Christ is not applyed to
ws by the work of a sacrificing messe preist, but that faith, which is wrought in
our soules by the holie Ghost, is the meane wherby the sacrifice and merit of
Christ is applyed to ws; and being applyed to ws, becomes our satisfaction,
740 atonement and merit.

[44] We beleeve that soules of Gods children which depart out of this
present life in the faith of Jesus Christ, after the separating from their bodies
immediatelie passe into heaven, and ther rest from their labours untill the day
of judgement – at which tyme they sall be reunited with their bodeis and
745 injuy life everlasting with Christ. Lykeas the soules of the wicked immediatlie
pass to hell, ther to remaine untill the day of judgment, which day, being con-

---

714/715 We – sinns] cfr Act. 2, 38   **717/718** Matth. 28, 19   **720/721** We –
institution] cfr Matth. 26, 26-29; I Cor. 11, 23-29   **730/731** sacrifice – sinnes] cfr
Rom. 3, 25; I Ioh. 2, 2   **733/735** sacrifices – Christ] cfr Hebr. 13, 15-16   **741/
747** We – fire] cfr Matth. 25, 32-46; Apoc. 20, 4-15

---

734 contreat] *intellege* contrite   **745** injuy] *intellege* enjoy

CONCILIUM ABERDONIENSE ECCLESIAE SCOTICANAE – 1616   1081

joined with their bodies, they sall susteane the judgement of everlasting fire. And besides these two, a thrid place for soules we doe not acknowledge.

[45] We believe that there is ane holie Catholick or universall Kirk, which is the holie companie of all these who, according to the purpose of Gods eternall election, since the beginning of the world wer called – and to the end of the world sall be called – to the kingdome of Christ and to the communion of eternall life in him.

[46] We beleeve, that the true members of his Kirk ar onlie the faithfull, who ar chosen to life everlasting.

[47] THIS Kirk we beleeve to be but one, and that out of it ther is no remission of sinnes to salvation.

[48] We beleeve that this kirk is partlie triumphant in heaven, partlie militant on earth. The whole militant kirk on earth is dividit in manie and divers and particular kirks, which ar visible and conspicuous to the eyes of men.

[49] We beleeve not that all these particular kirks on earth ar pure, but these onlie which continue in the doctrine of the prophets and apostles, according to the holie canonicall scripture, worshiping God purelie, and ministring the Sacraments according to the same. And these be the true marks wherby a true visible kirk on earth may be discerned and known.

[50] As concerning the worship of God: we confesse and affirme that all religious worship and service is onlie to be given to God as his proper due and glorie, which he will communicat to no other; beleeving firmly, that God is to be worshiped onlie according to his owne will revealed in his word.

[51] And, therfor, we abhorre all *will-worship*, all invocation of Saints or Angels, all worshiping of images, crucifixes, relicts, and all other things which are beside the true God.

[52] We beleeve and confesse that God hath ordeaned kings, princes and magistrats for the good of commonwealth, for the better governing the kirk, and to be nurse fathers of the same: And, therfor, that all their subjects ar bound in duty to obey them in all things they command lawfullie, not repug-

---

771 Col. 2, 23 (Septuaginta)   **776/777** And – lawfullie] cfr Rom. 13, 1-5

748 And – acknowledge] i.e. purgatory   **749** 45] this embraced all categories of the elect distinguished in Reformed orthodoxy: the (as yet) uncalled elect, the externally called elect, and the effectually called elect. Cfr Hazlett, 'Church and Church/State Relations', in U. L. Lehner – R. A. Muller – A. G. Roeber (eds), *The Oxford Handbook of Early Modern Theology, 1600-1800*, New York 2016, p. 244   **765** true marks] in contrast to the *Scots Confession*, discipline is not understood as a third *nota ecclesiae*; cfr 'Confessio Scotica', p. 273 l. 6-12

1082 CONCILIUM ABERDONIENSE ECCLESIAE SCOTICANAE – 1616

nant to the will of God; and that they ar oblidged to pray for them daylie, that under them we may lead a godlie and peaceabill life.

780   [53] We beleeve and constantlie affirme that the kirk of Scotland, through the aboundant grace of our Lord, is one of the most pure kirks under heaven this day, both in respect of truthe in doctrine, and puritie in worship: and, therfor, with all our hearts we adjoyne ourselves therto, and to the religion publictlie professed therin by the Kings majestie and all his true subjects, and

785 authorized by his majesties lawes; promising be the grace of God to continue therin to the end of our life, according to all the articles which are heere sett doun: Which as we beleeve with our hearts, so we confesse with our mouthes, and subscribe with our hands; understanding them plainlie as they are heare conceaved, without aequivocation or mentall reservation whatsomever.

790   Swa may God help us in the great day of judgement.

    [7] Item, It is statute and ordainit that a Catechisme be made, easie, short, and compendious, for instructing the commoun sort in the articles of religioun, quhilk all families salbe subject to have, for the better informatioun of thair childrein and servants, quho salbe holdin to give accompt therof in thair

795 examinatiouns befor the Communioun. And for the better effectuating heirof, the Assemblie hes ordainit Mr Patrick Galloway and Mr John Hall, Ministers at Edinburgh, and Mr John Adamsone, Minister at Libbertoun, to forme the said Catechisme, and to have the same in readines, befor the first day of October nixt to come, to the effect the same may be allowit, and printit with the

800 Kings Majesties licence: The quhilk Catechisme being so printed, it is statute and ordainit, that no uther heirafter be printed within this realme, nor used in families for instructioun and examinatioun of thair bairnes, servants, nor the peiple in all tyme coming.

    [8] Item, It is statute and ordainit, that ane vniforme ordour of Liturgie or

805 Divyne Service be sett down to be red in all kirks, on the ordinarie dayes of prayer, and every Sabbath day befor the sermoun, to the end the commoun peiple may be acquaintit therwith, and by custome may learn to serve God rightlie. And to this intent, the Assemblie hes appointit the saids Mr Patrick

---

789 without – reservation] dissimulation by crypto-Catholic subscribers is in mind. See also below, *Acta Sessione ultima 21 Augusti*   **796/798** the – Catechisme] see the Introduction   **799/800** and – licence] see the Introduction   **804/805** Liturgie or Divyne Service] 'Liturgy' was the term favoured by most episcopalians, 'divine service' by presbyterians

784 majestie] *a.c.* ma   **785** majesties] *a.c.* ma   **790** Swa] *intellege* so   **793** subject] *intellege* obliged   **802** bairnes] *intellege* children

CONCILIUM ABERDONIENSE ECCLESIAE SCOTICANAE – 1616   1083

Galloway, Mr Peter Ewat, Mr John Adamsone, and Mr William Erskine, Minister at Dunino, Fife to revise the Booke of Commoun Prayers containit in the Psalme Booke, and to sett downe ane commoun forme of ordinarie service, to be used in all tyme heirafter; quhilk salbe used in all kirks quher there is exercise of commoun prayers; as lykewayes be the Minister before the sermoun, quher ther is no Reidar.

[9] Item, It is statute and ordainit that in all tyme heirafter the holie Communioun be celebrate in all kirks within this realme, at the tymes following, viz. in Burrowstounes, the Communioun salbe celebrate foure tymes in the yeir, and twyse in the yeir in landwart Kirks; swa that ane of the tymes, as weill to Burgh as to Landwart, salbe at the terme of Easter yeirlie: and if any person sall not communicat yeirlie ance in the yeir at one of the forsaid tymes, that it be humblie requyrit of his Majestie that the penaltie of the act of Parliament may be exactit of such persons with all rigour.

[10] Item, It is thoght most necessar and expedient that ther be ane uniforme ordour of Church Discipline throughout all the Kirks of this kingdome; and to that effect it is statute and ordainit, that a Booke of Canons be made, publised in wryte, drawin foorth of the bookis of former Assemblies; and quher the same is defective, that it be supplied be the Canons of Counsells and Ecclesiasticall Conventiouns in former tyme: The care quherof the

---

809 Mr Peter Ewat] Peter Hewat (or Howat), an Edinburgh minister, also titular abbot of Crossraguel in Ayrshire giving him a seat in Parliament. He was deprived and confined after 1617 for his concern about encroachment on the liberties of the Church, which angered the King. See *Scottish Liturgies*, p. xxii; Spottiswoode, *History*, vol. 3 (1851), p. 244-245   **810/811** Booke of Commoun Prayers containit in the Psalme Booke] i.e. the *Book of Common Order* (1562), to which the *Book of Psalms* was appended, also known as *Knox's Liturgy*   **811** commoun forme] see the Introduction ordinarie service] Hewat was the conservative editor of the committee's first draft, soon superseded with revised versions by Bishop Willam Cowper, the third of which was authorized by the Perth Assembly (1618), but whose publication was aborted. See *Scottish Liturgies*, p. xxiii-xxiv and xxxii-xxxiii; Donaldson, *The Making of the Scottish Prayer Book*, p. 33-34 and 35-38; 'A Scottish Liturgy', p. 89-91; Spinks, 'Emergence of a Reformed Worship Tradition', p. 270-272. For the text of Hewat's first draft, titled *A Forme of Service*, see *Scottish Liturgies*, 'Appendix', p. 117-139   **817/818** foure – yeir¹] quarterly communion   **821** penaltie] fines, the amounts varying according to social class. Cfr *Act. Scot. Parl.*, 1600, 'Act regarding non-communicants', in which absence is seen as a pretext to conceal 'Papistrie'   **825** Booke of Canons] as in the Church of England since 1603   **827/828** Counsells – tyme] pre-Reformation synods and councils in Scotland

---

810 Dunino, Fife] *inserui*   **812/813** in² – prayers] *t inser. ex* C   **818** twyse] *intellege* twice   **818/819** as weill to ... as] *intellege* both ... and   **819** terme] *intellege* period

1084 CONCILIUM ABERDONIENSE ECCLESIAE SCOTICANAE – 1616

Assemblie be thir presents committs to the Right Reverend James Arch-
830 bischop of Glasgow, and Mr William Struthers, Minister at Edinburgh, quho
sall put in forme the said Ecclesiasticall Canons, and present them in wryte to
the Commissioners appointit be this Assemblie, to quhom power is givin to
try, examine, and allow the samine, and after thair allowance and approbatioun thereof, to supplicat to his Majestie, that the same may be ratified and
835 approved by his Royal authoritie, with priviledge to put the same in print.

[11] Item, It is statute and ordainit that for the help of posteritie, and to
continue the light of the Gospell with ages to come, the Divinitie Colledge
foundit at Sanct Androes, quhilk sould be the seminarie of the Kirk within
this realme, be maintainit and upholdin, and ane speciall care takin therof.
840 And because the rent therof is meane for the present, it is ordainit that for the
provisioun of some students in Divinitie, every Dyocie sall intertaine two – or
according to the quantitie of the Dyocie, so many as the number may arise to
twentie sixe in haill, respect being had to the meannes of some Dyocies, and
greatness and power of uthers; so that the least Dyocies in thair contributioun
845 salbe helped and easit be the greater: In the quhilk number it is ordainit that
the halfe at leist be the sonnes of pure Ministers, and be presentit be the Bishops of the Dyocies to the place.

[12] Item, The Assemblie ratifies and approves the former Act made in the
Assemblie haldin at Halierudehous, the tent day of November 1602, anent the
850 sacrament of baptisme, that the same be not refuseit if the parent crave the

---

829/830 Right Reverend James Archbischop of Glasgow] James Law († 1632), a
leading member of the King's party in the Church, archbishop of Glasgow since 1615.
See *ODNB*, *ad vocem*   834/835 that – print] see the Introduction   837 Divinitie
Colledge] usually known as St Mary's College, founded originally as a trilingual college
in 1538 and reconstituted as a counter-Reformation college in 1554, but adapted to
Reformation concepts after 1560. Its complete religious reformation and general
restructuring under Andrew Melville as the New College was legitimised by a 1579
parliamentary act   838/839 the seminarie of the Kirk within this realme] this
exclusiveness is at variance with the royal *Instructions* (no. 11), which anticipated the
retention at least of Glasgow University's provision of theology. Not mentioned are the
claims of two other Aberdeen universities (King's College and Marischal College) and
the emerging Town College in Edinburgh, all of which also educated ministers   848/
849 Act – 1602] see *BUK* (Thomson), p. 1002   849 Halierudehous] Holyroodhouse
(Edinburgh), royal residence and venue of the 1602 General Assembly

---

829 be thir presents] *intellege* with this document   840 rent therof is meane]
intellege funds for that are low   841 intertaine] *intellege* provide maintenance;
support   842 quantitie] *intellege* size   843 in haill] *intellege* in toto   846 pure]
intellege poor

CONCILIUM ABERDONIENSE ECCLESIAE SCOTICANAE – 1616   1085

same, he giving a Christian confessioun of his faith, upon any uther particular pretence of delay to tyme of preaching; with this extension and additioun, that baptisme sall no wayes be denyed to any infant, quhen either the parents of the infant, or any faithfull Christian in place of the parents, sall requyre the
855 same to the infant; and that the same be granted any time of day, but any respect or delay till the houre of preaching.

[13] Item, It is ordainit that every Minister have a perfyte and formall Register, quherin he sall have registrat the particular of the baptisme of every infant within his paroch, and quho wer witnesses therto; the tyme of the
860 mariages of all persons within the same; and the special tyme of the buriall of every ane deceisand within thair parochin; and that they have the same to be in readines to be presentit be every ane at thair nixt Synod or Assemblie, under the paine of suspensioun of the Minister, not fulfilling the same, from his Ministrie. And it is desyrit that the saids Commissioners, in thair supplica-
865 tiouns direct to his Majestie, wold crave humblie that his Majestie wald ordaine the extract foorth of the saids Registers to make faith in all tyme comeing: and quho so observes this Act, the Archbischops and Bischops sall let them have thair quots of thair testaments gratis.

ACTA SESSIONE ULTIMA 21 AUGUSTI

870   The quhilk day, in presence of the whole Assemblie, compeirit ane noble and potent Lord, George Marqueis of Huntlie, and declarit that he had direc-tit of befor John Gordoun of Buckie to present his supplicatioun to this present Assemblie, quherof the tenour is insert before; lykeas of new he reiter-

---

857/858 every – Register] presumably pre-Reformation Church priests did not keep registers of baptisms, marriages and burials; rather, it had been a matter for canon lawyers, now extinct   **862** or Assemblie] most likely added by Calderwood, who as a convinced presbyterian would have preferred 'Assemblie' to 'Synod' in view of the latter's episcopal connotations   **869** Acta – Augusti] a letter from Alexander Forbes, bishop of Caithness, on 17 August at the conclusion of the Assembly's main business, confirms that Huntly's appearance before the Assembly would take place on 21 August. Cfr *Original Letters*, vol. 2, p. 484-485. This is corroborated by a letter of 22 August from Lord Binning (Hamilton) to the King, reporting that Huntly's public absolution at the Assembly occurred 'yesterday'. Cfr *Original Letters*, vol. 2, p. 486-487

851/852 upon any uther particular pretence] *intellege* with the particular excuse   **855** but] *intellege* except   **857** perfyte] *intellege* complete   **861** deceisand] *intellege* dying   parochin] *intellege* parishes   **866** foorth of] *intellege* from   make faith] *intellege* to be valid; to be authoritative (*ex latino sermone* fidem facere)   **869** 21 Augusti] *addidi*   **872** of befor] *intellege* previously   **873** of new] *intellege* again

1086 CONCILIUM ABERDONIENSE ECCLESIAE SCOTICANAE – 1616

at the said supplicatioun, declaring the sorrow and greife he had conceivit, in
875 that he had lyin so long under the fearefull sentence of excommunicatioun;
and, therfor, most humblie desyrit to be absolvit from the same; lykeas he
faithfullie promised, in face of the haill Assemblie, to perform and fulfill the
heids and conditiouns under specifeit, viz.:

1. The said noble Lord faithfullie promised befor God, his hand holdin
880 up, to professe and abyde be the true religioun presentlie professit within this
realme, and allowit be the laws and acts of Parliament of the same.

2. He faithfullie promised to communicat at the first occasioun he should
be requyrit, and so to continue conforme to the ordour of the Kirk.

3. He sould cause his childrein, servants, and haill domesticks be obedient
885 to the Kirk and discipline therof; and sould cause them haunt the kirk at ordinar tymes of preaching.

4. He sall not receive Papists, Jesuites, nor Seminarie Preists in his house,
nor nane of his lands, but put them out of his bounds with all diligence.

5. He allows the Confessioun of the Faith presentlie sett downe be the
890 said Assemblie; and in tokin of his constant confessioun and professioun
therof, he hes subscryvit the same in presence of the haill Assemblie.

Quhilk haill promises above specifiet the said noble Lord protests and
declares that he hes made and subscryvit truelie and with ane honest heart,
but any equivocatioun, mentall reservatioun, or subterfuge quhatsumevir
895 devysit be the Romisch Kirk and thair supposts.

---

882 communicat] i.e. participate in communion   **889** Confessioun of the Faith] i.e.
the *New Confession* (as above)   **894** mentall reservatioun] mental reservation and
equivocation were a controversial area of casuistry associated with some Jesuits and
others (e.g. Martin de Azpilcueta), used in British Isles contexts to assist Catholic
survival by means of dissimulation and external conformity in Protestant
environments. In late-sixteenth-century England, Jesuit tracts in support of the practice
were written by Robert Southwell and Henry Garnet   **894/895** subterfuge
quhatsumevir devysit be the Romisch Kirk] many Protestants believed – without firm
evidence – that the Roman Catholic Church issued dispensations enabling the
practice; however, canon law did not justify such actions. They were ultimately
condemned in 1679

875 lyin] *intellege* remained   **878** heids] *intellege* terms   under] *intellege* below
879 1.] *L D N*[in marg.]   **882** 2.] *L D N*[in marg.]   **884** 3.] *L D N*[in marg.]   **887** 4.] *L D*
N[in marg.]   **888** nane] *intellege* in any   **889** 5.] *L D N*[in marg.]   **892** Quhilk haill]
intellege all of which   **894** but] *intellege* without   **895** supposts] *intellege* supporters

CONCILIUM ABERDONIENSE ECCLESIAE SCOTICANAE – 1616

Attour, the said noble Lord faithfullie promises to plant his whole kirks, quherof his Lordship hes the teinds in tack, possessioun, or utherwayes, at the sight and conclusioun of my Lord Archbischop of Sanct Androes, the Bishop of Murray, and the Laird of Corse, unto whose modificatioun the said noble Lord submitts himselfe, be the tenour of thir presents, giveand them power to modifie compleit stipends to the saids kirks; and as they salbe modified be them, he oblisches him to make payment of the same to the Ministers provydit or to be provydit to the said kirks.

And in respect of the premisses, the Assemblie ordainit the said noble Lord to be absolvit from the sentence of excommunicatioun led and deduceit aganis him befor.

Conforme quherto, the Right Reverend Father John Archbischop of Sanct Androes, Moderatour, in face of the haill Assemblie, absolvit the said noble Lord, George Marqueis of Huntlie, from the said sentence of excommunicatioun led and deducit against him and receivit him againe into the bosome of the Kirk.

The quhilk day, the Generall Assemblie of the Kirk of Scotland presentlie conveinit, having entrit in consideratioun of the causes of the defectioun and falling away of many from the true religioun, and having found the lack of the competent manteinance to Ministers not to be the least cause of the evills, quhilk lyes upon the Kirk presentlie; the ground and fundament quherof, for the most part, hes proceidit from the dilapidatioun of benefices, with the quhilk if some solid ordour be not takin in tyme, the same is apparent to bring foorth greater evill and desolatioun in this Kirk. And seeing that the Kings Majestie hes requirit that ordour may be takin with the saids delapidatiouns, Therfor, in respect the same cannot be suddenly done, but will requyre ane lang tyme and mature deliberatioun, the Assemblie hes givin, grantit and committit, lykeas they, be the tenour heirof, gives, grants, and committs thair full power and commissioun to the brethren underwrytin; they are to say:

898/899 Bishop of Murray] Alexander Douglas, bishop of Moray   **899** Laird of Corse] Patrick Forbes

---

896 Attour] *intellege* in addition   plant] *intellege* provide (ministers) for   his whole] *intellege* all his   **897** teinds] *intellege* tithes   in tack] *intellege* on lease   **897/898** at – sight] *intellege* under supervision   **898** conclusioun] *intellege* report   **899** modificatioun] *intellege* assessment of a salary   **900** be the tenour of] *intellege* according to the intent of   giveand] *intellege* giving   **902** oblisches him] *intellege* promises   **904** premisses] *intellege* aforesaid   **905** led and deduceit] *intellege* pronounced   **907** Conforme quherto] *intellege* accordingly   **918** solid ordour be not takin in tyme] *intellege* remedial action be not taken soon   **921** in respect] *intellege* considering

1088 CONCILIUM ABERDONIENSE ECCLESIAE SCOTICANAE – 1616

925
the Reverend Fathers in God,
John Spottiswoode, Archbischop of Sanct Androes
James Law, Archischop of Glasgow
Alexander Lindsay, Bischop of Dunkeld
......
930
Alexander Douglas, Bischop of Murray
Patrick Lindsay, Bischop of Ross
William Cowper, Bischop of Galloway
Andro Lamb, Bischop of Brechin
George Graham, Bischop of Orknay
935
Alexander Forbes, Bischop of Cathness
Adame Bellenden, Bischop of Dumblaine
Andro Boyd, Bischop of Argyle
Andro Knox, Bischop of the Isles
Patrick Forbes of Corse, Minister at Keith
940
George Douglas, Minister at Cullen
Mr John Reid, Minister at Logie Buchan
Mr George Hay, Minister at Turreff
Doctour Hendrie Philip, Minister at Arbroth
Mr David Lindsay, Minister at Dundie
945
Mr William Scott, Minister at Couper
Doctour Robert Howie, Rector of Sanct Androes University
Mr John Mitchelsone, Minister at Bruntiland
Mr Patrick Galloway, Minister at Edinburgh
Mr John Hall, Minister at Edinburgh
950
Mr William Struthers, Minister at Edinburgh
Mr Robert Scott, Minister at Glasgow
Mr Edwart Hepburne, Minister at Haughe

---

929 ......] the bishop of Aberdeen is missing from the list; the see seems to have been vacant at this point   **936** Dumblaine] Dunblane   **938** Andro Knox Bischop of the Isles] he was simultaneously bishop of Raphoe in north-western Ireland   **944** Dundie] Dundee   **952** Haughe] Prestonkirk

926 Spottiswoode] *addidi*   **927** Law] *addidi*   **928** Lindsay] *addidi*   **929** ......] *(O) C c t hab.*   **930** Douglas] *addidi*   **931** Lindsay] *addidi*   **932** Cowper] *addidi* **933** Lamb] *addidi*   **934** George – Orknay] *deest L D N p*   George] *t* Andro *(dittographia)* Graham] *addidi*   **935** Alexander – Cathness] *deest L D N p*   Forbes] *addidi*   **936** Bellenden] *addidi*   **937** Boyd] *addidi*   **938** Knox] *addidi* **939** Minister at Keith] *addidi*   **946** University] *addidi*   **948** Minister at Edinburgh] *addidi*   **949** Minister at Edinburgh] *addidi*   **951** Minister – Glasgow] *addidi*

CONCILIUM ABERDONIENSE ECCLESIAE SCOTICANAE – 1616   1089

Doctour John Abernethie, Minister at Jedburt
Mr William Birnie, Minister at Air
Mr William Erskine, Minister at Dunino.

Giveand, grantand, and committand to them, or the most part of them, their full power and commissioun to coveine at Edinburgh, the first day of December nixt to come, in this instant yeir of God 1616, and ther to take ordour with the dilapidatioun of benefices, and to sett downe solid grounds how the progresse of that mischeife might be stayed, and to devyse upon some meanes to recover and restore the estate of these benefices, quhilk be iniquitie of tyme hes bein losit; and if neid beis, to call and persew befor them these quho hes made the saids dilapidatiouns, and punisch them therfor; and as they sall conclude, the same to be inactit and have the force of this present Assemblie.

With power lykewayes to the saids Commissioners, or the most part of them, as said is, to take ordour anent the planting of sufficient and qualified Persons in burrowtounes presentlie vacand, and are not plantit at this present Assemblie.

With power lykewayes to receive from the right Reverend Father, James Law, Archbischop of Glasgow, and Mr William Struthers, Minister at Edinburgh, the Canons of Church Discipline committit to thair charge, and to revise the samein, allow and dissallow therof; and to direct a supplicatioun to his Majestie desyreing that it wold please his Hienes to ratifie and approve the samein, and to warrant the printing therof be his authoritie Royall.

These words following were added by the Archbishop:

Item, power to receive the books of Liturgie or Divine Service, allow and disallow therof, as they shall think expedient; and the same being allowed, to cause publish the samine in print for the service within the Kirks of all the kingdom: As also to revise the Confession of Faith presented to this Assemblie, and after mature deliberation to take order that the same may be pub-

---

953 Jedburt] Jedburgh   **954** Air] Ayr   **976** These – Archbishop] the last ten lines, from Calderwood, are not actually in any surviving Calderwood manuscript, although it was most likely in the lost or missing MS (*C³*), whence it was published in *r* (i.e. Calderwood, *True History*, p. 666-667), copied in *BUK* (Thomson), p. 1132, and by D. Laing in Calderwood, *History*, vol. 8 (1849), 'Appendix', p. 111

955 Dunino] *addidi*   **959** sett downe solid grounds] *intellege* draft firm proposals on   **960** devyse upon] *intellege* consider   **962** neid beis] *intellege* necessary   persew befor them] *intellege* prosecute directly   **963/964** as they sall conclude] *intellege* what they recommend   **964** force] *intellege* authority   **968** vacand] *intellege* vacant   **971** Law] *addidi*

lished; and in all these things to do as they will be answerable to God, and the Kings Majesty, and the Church.

Thus far out of the Scrolles, together with the Bishops additions and alterations.

---

984 the Bishops] possessive singular, i.e. Archbishop Spottiswoode

984/985 Thus – alterations] *om. t*

CONSPECTUS MATERIAE

Conciliorum Oecumenicorum
Generaliumque Decreta, VI/1

GENERAL INTRODUCTION
(A. Melloni) .... V-XIV

EDITOR'S NOTE
(G. Braghi) XV

LIST OF ABBREVIATIONS .... XVII-XVIII

EDITIONS 1-563

CONCILIUM HOMBERGENSE – 1526
(ed. J. Schilling) 1-57

CONCILIUM IULIOMAGENSE – 1527
(ed. C. Scheidegger) 59-87

DISPUTATIO ET DECEM THESES BERNENSES – 1528
(ed. P. Hildebrand) 89-103

CONCILIUM AUGUSTANUM – 1530
(ed. K. I. Stjerna) 105-213

CONCILIUM BERNENSE – 1532
(ed. P. Hildebrand) 215-277

CONCILIUM CAMPI FORANEI (iuxta Hengroniam)
– 1532 (ed. G. Braghi) 279-311

SYNODUS TIGURINA – 1532
(ed. E. Campi) 313-345

CONCILIUM ARGENTORATENSE – 1533/1534
(ed. G. Braghi & G. Murdock) 347-379

CONCILIUM GENEVENSE – 1541
(ed. G. Braghi & G. Murdock) 381-414

1092 CONSPECTUS MATERIAE

CONCILIA HUNGARICA ET TRANSSYLVANICA
– 1545, 1567, 1570 (ed. Z. Csepregi) 415-492
CONCILIUM VENETIANUM-FERRARIENSE – 1550
(ed. D. Dainese) 493-529
CONCILIA LUTETIANUM ET RUPELLENSE – 1559/1571
(ed. I. Dingel) 531-563

CONSPECTUS MATERIAE TOMI PRIMI 565-566

LIST OF ABBREVIATIONS .... V-VI

EDITIONS 567-1090
CONCILIUM LONDINENSE – 1563/1571
(ed. T. Kirby) 567-631
CONCILIUM ANTVERPIANUM – 1564
(ed. G. Braghi & G. Murdock) 633-655
CONVENTUS VESALIENSIS ET SYNODUS EMBDANA
– 1568–1571 (ed. H. P. Jürgens) 657-733
CONCILIUM SANDOMIRIENSE – 1570
(ed. M. Ptaszyński) 735-791
CONCILIUM SAXONICUM – 1577
(ed. I. Dingel & J. Hund) 793-893
CONCILIUM UPSALIENSE – 1593
(ed. O. Bexell) 895-927
ARTICULI LAMBETHANI – 1595
(ed. T. Kirby) 929-944
CONCILIUM TUISCOBURGENSE – 1610
(ed. A. Mühling) 945-965
CONCILIUM HIBERNICUM – 1614/1615
(ed. T. Kirby) 967-998
CONCILIUM ABERDONIENSE ECCLESIAE
SCOTICANAE – 1616 (ed. I. Hazlett) 999-1090